MW01635689

Cover: Victoria's Inner Harbour at sunset. The elegant Empress Hotel stands guard over the Causeway Floats. Neil Rabinowitz photo.

Waterways, Bays and Marinas

Visit Our Web Site

★

http://www.waggonerguide.com

e-mail waggtalk@waggonerguide.com

EXCLUSIVE DISCOUNT CRUISING COUPONS™ SAVE $$ ★ SEE OUR SPECIAL SECTION

We want to hear from you

Your comments, suggestions, and corrections are invited. Please let us know if you find any significant errors in this publication. Also let us know what you would like to find in future editions of the Waggoner Cruising Guide. We want to expand our dining and activities information, and we seek your experiences.
You can contact us by telephone, mail, or e-mail. Don't hold back. We'd love to hear from you.

Caution

This book was designed to provide experienced skippers with cruising information about the waters covered. While great effort was taken to make the Waggoner Cruising Guide complete and accurate, it is possible that oversights, differences of interpretation, and factual errors will be found. Thus none of the information contained in the book is warranted to be accurate or appropriate for any specific need. Furthermore, variations in weather and sea conditons, a mariner's skills and experience, and the presence of luck (good or bad) can dictate a mariner's proper course of action. The Waggoner Cruising Guide should be viewed as a guide only, and not a substitute for offical government charts, tide and current tables, coast pilots, sailing directions, and local notices to mariners. The Waggoner Cruising Guide assumes the user to be law-abiding and of good will. The suggestions offered are not all-inclusive, but are meant to help avoid unpleasantness or needless delay.

The publisher, editors, and authors assume no liability for errors or omissions, or for any loss or damages incurred from using this publication.

Printed in the United States of America

Published by Weatherly Press Division
Robert Hale & Co. Inc.
1803 132nd Ave. NE, Suite 4
Bellevue, WA 98005-2261
USA

ISSN 1076-1578
ISBN 0-935727-12-4

1997 WAGGONER CRUISING GUIDE

Editor/Publisher Robert Hale
Managing Editor
Stacia A.M. Green
Contributing Editor
Tom Kincaid, Nor'westing, Inc.
Contributors Don Douglass & Norm Culver
Production Editor
Sheri Heckard
Production Assistant
Debbie Biebel

Cover photo by Neil Rabinowitz
Cover design by Elizabeth Watson
Reference maps by Daniel Hale & Sheri Heckard
Photos by Robert Hale & Stacia A.M. Green

Advertising
Advertising inquires should be directed to:

Waggoner Cruising Guide
Robert Hale & Co. Inc.
1803 132nd Ave. NE, Suite 4
Bellevue, WA 98005-2261
USA

Telephone (206)881-5212
Fax (206)881-0731
Toll-Free (800)733-5330

Web Site
http://waggonerguide.com
e-mail:
waggtalk@waggonerguide.com

PUBLISHER'S COLUMN

http://www.waggonerguide.com

BEGINNING IN JANUARY 1997, the Waggoner Cruising Guide launched its own world wide web site, http://www.waggonerguide.com. The e-mail address is waggtalk@waggonerguide.com. At this point I'm a novice at e-mail and the Internet. In a year I'll be good, I know I will. For now, I'm glad an expert is helping us.

The expert is our son Dan Hale. Dan has been developing web sites for the past couple of years, and he helped produce the first two editions of the Waggoner. He understands what we want to do, and how to go about doing it.

We believe we can make waggonerguide.com easier to navigate and more useful than many commercial web sites we've seen. Too often, when you take away their glitz and glamour, many web sites are little more than a listing of products. The viewer who wants real information doesn't get much.

With waggonerguide.com, we intend to go the other way. It will be light on elaborate graphics, and heavy on local cruising information and ease of use. We are determined to keep the content timely and relevant.

One of the important functions will be to update and correct our 1997 listings. In addition to updates, waggonerguide.com will have links to weather and tides information, and carry news about our cruising area. Did the big storm take out any docks? Have customs requirements changed? What about licensing requirements? Fuel availabilities? New facilities or facilities no longer in business? We plan to have the answers.

I fully expect that the most popular page will be the forum for our readers' input and response. It's a big coast between Olympia and Alaska. We're eager to hear what our readers know about this coast. We're also eager to post readers' questions and responses to the questions. This page can be a clearing house for cruising information.

Send us your e-mail or even old-fashioned cards and letters, and share your experiences with other boaters.

Waggonerguide.com will start small, but we will expand it relentlessly. One at a time, good ideas will be incorporated. Cyberspace, here comes the Waggoner.

Bob Hale

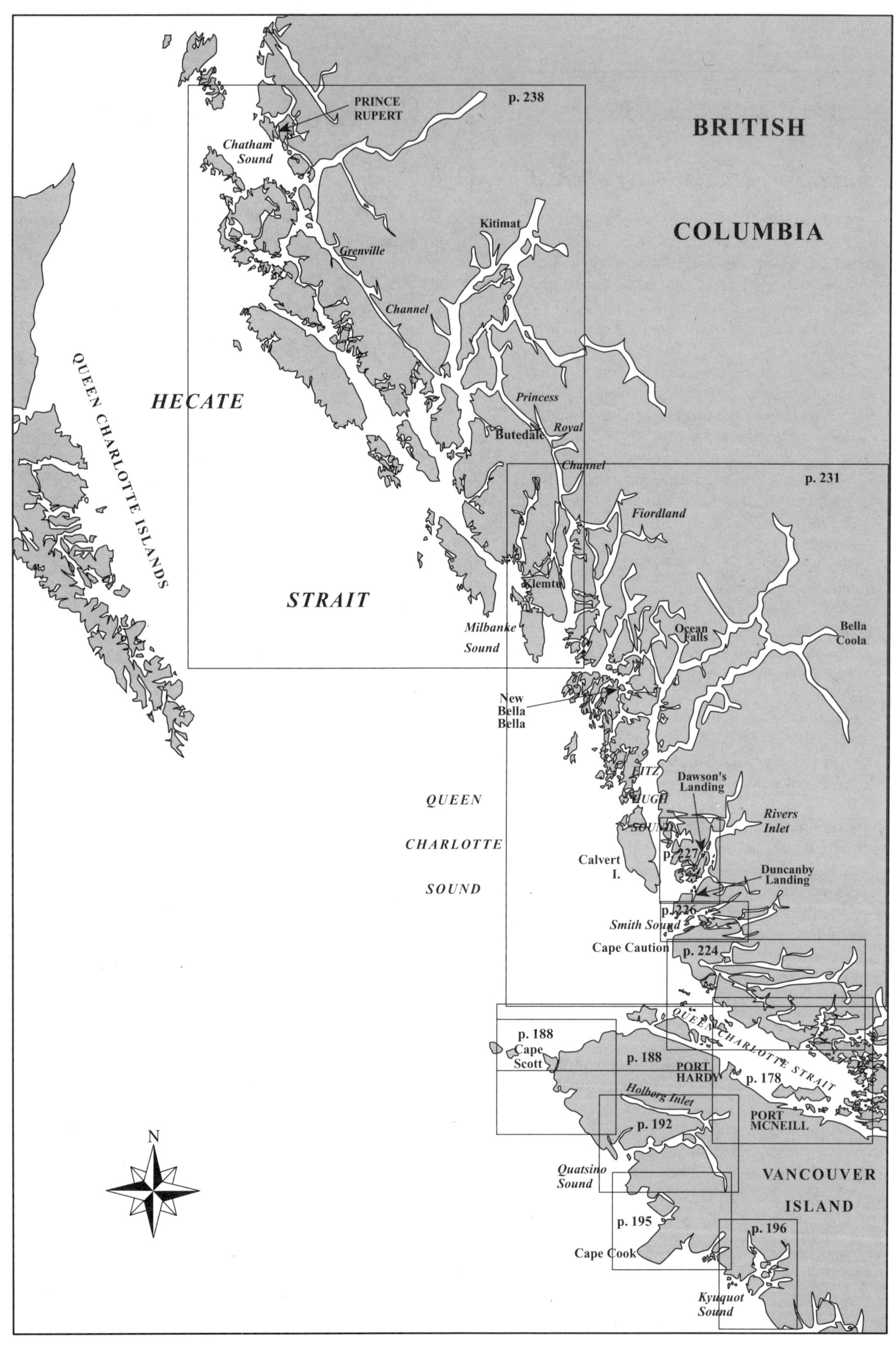

BRITISH
COLUMBIA
p. 238
PRINCE
RUPERT
Chatham
Sound
Kitimat
Grenville
Channel
QUEEN CHARLOTTE ISLANDS
HECATE
STRAIT
Princess
Royal
Channel
Butedale
p. 231
Fiordland
Klemtu
Milbanke
Sound
Ocean
Falls
Bella
Coola
New
Bella
Bella
FITZ
HUGH
SOUND
QUEEN
CHARLOTTE
SOUND
Dawson's
Landing
Rivers
Inlet
Calvert
I.
p. 227
Duncanby
Landing
p. 226
Smith Sound
Cape Caution
p. 224
QUEEN CHARLOTTE STRAIT
p. 188
Cape
Scott
p. 188
PORT
HARDY
p. 178
Holberg Inlet
PORT
MCNEILL
p. 192
N
Quatsino
Sound
VANCOUVER
ISLAND
p. 195
p. 196
Cape Cook
Kyuquot
Sound

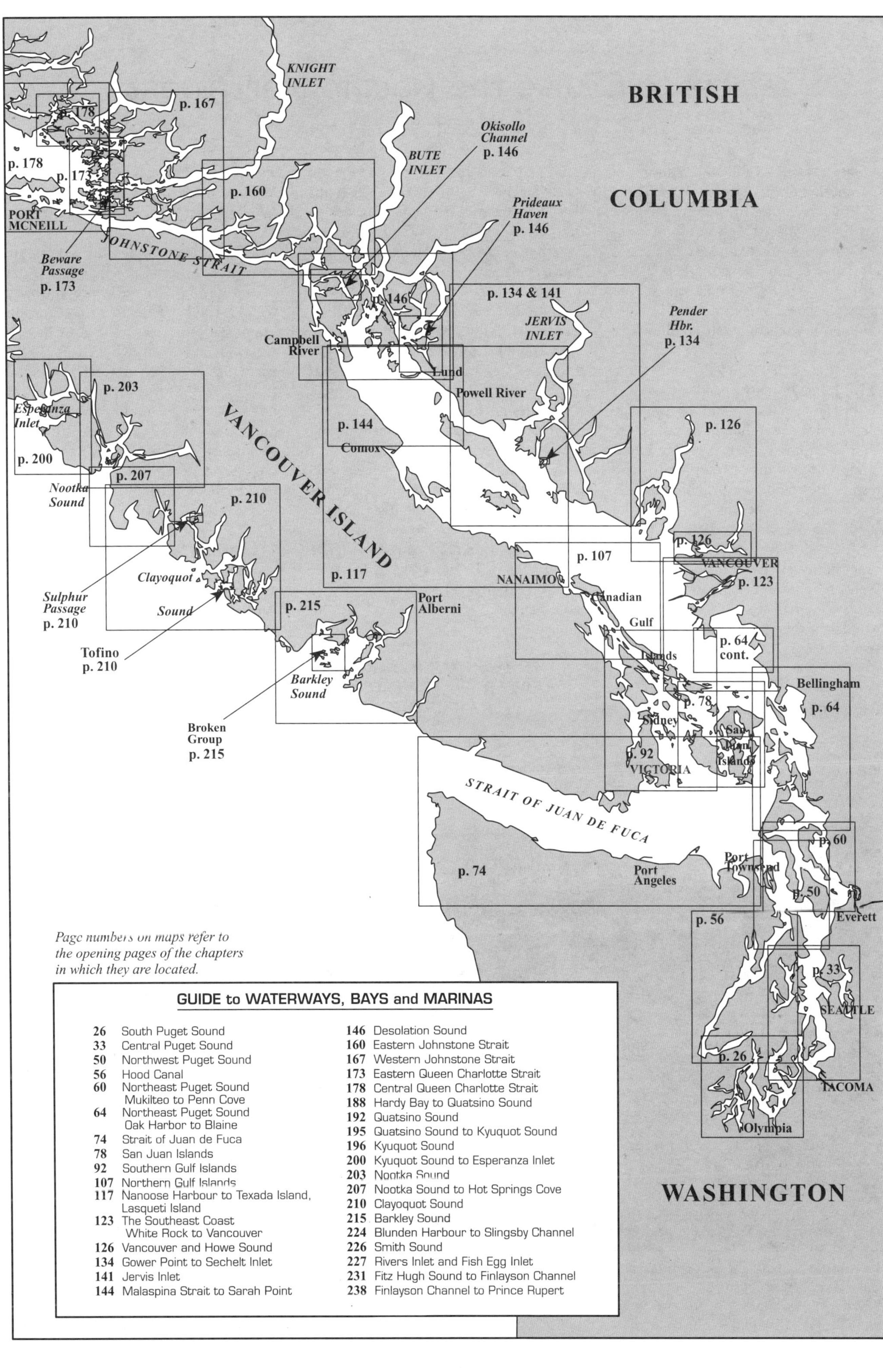
KNIGHT INLET
BRITISH
COLUMBIA
p. 167
p. 178
p. 178
p. 173
Okisollo Channel p. 146
BUTE INLET
p. 160
PORT MCNEILL
JOHNSTONE STRAIT
Prideaux Haven p. 146
Beware Passage p. 173
p. 146
p. 134 & 141
JERVIS INLET
Pender Hbr. p. 134
Campbell River
Lund
Powell River
p. 203
Esperanza Inlet
p. 144
Comox
p. 126
p. 200
VANCOUVER ISLAND
Nootka Sound
p. 207
p. 210
p. 126
p. 107
VANCOUVER
p. 117
NANAIMO
p. 123
Clayoquot Sound
Sulphur Passage p. 210
p. 215
Port Alberni
Canadian Gulf Islands
p. 64 cont.
Tofino p. 210
Barkley Sound
Bellingham
p. 78
p. 64
Broken Group p. 215
Sidney
San Juan Islands
p. 92
VICTORIA
STRAIT OF JUAN DE FUCA
p. 60
p. 74
Port Angeles
Port Townsend
p. 50
Everett
p. 56
p. 33
SEATTLE
p. 26
TACOMA
Olympia
WASHINGTON
Page numbers on maps refer to the opening pages of the chapters in which they are located.
GUIDE to WATERWAYS, BAYS and MARINAS
26 South Puget Sound
33 Central Puget Sound
50 Northwest Puget Sound
56 Hood Canal
60 Northeast Puget Sound Mukilteo to Penn Cove
64 Northeast Puget Sound Oak Harbor to Blaine
74 Strait of Juan de Fuca
78 San Juan Islands
92 Southern Gulf Islands
107 Northern Gulf Islands
117 Nanoose Harbour to Texada Island, Lasqueti Island
123 The Southeast Coast White Rock to Vancouver
126 Vancouver and Howe Sound
134 Gower Point to Sechelt Inlet
141 Jervis Inlet
144 Malaspina Strait to Sarah Point
146 Desolation Sound
160 Eastern Johnstone Strait
167 Western Johnstone Strait
173 Eastern Queen Charlotte Strait
178 Central Queen Charlotte Strait
188 Hardy Bay to Quatsino Sound
192 Quatsino Sound
195 Quatsino Sound to Kyuquot Sound
196 Kyuquot Sound
200 Kyuquot Sound to Esperanza Inlet
203 Nootka Sound
207 Nootka Sound to Hot Springs Cove
210 Clayoquot Sound
215 Barkley Sound
224 Blunden Harbour to Slingsby Channel
226 Smith Sound
227 Rivers Inlet and Fish Egg Inlet
231 Fitz Hugh Sound to Finlayson Channel
238 Finlayson Channel to Prince Rupert

How to Cruise the Pacific Northwest

by Robert Hale

LAST SUMMER, I talked a man out of cruising from Anacortes, Washington to Princess Louisa Inlet. It's a fabulous trip, but he was trying to do it in a six-day charter. He would have to make two crossings of the Strait of Georgia, and time at least one set of tidal rapids, both ways. He would have to run all day, every day, and the schedule left no allowance for bad luck or bad weather.

Instead of the trip to Princess Louisa Inlet, I urged him to spend the six days in the San Juan Islands and the Canadian Gulf Islands. He and his family could anchor out, catch some fish and go swimming, and visit interesting marinas and resorts. He could treat his wife to excellent dining, and perhaps spend an entire sunny day doing . . . nothing.

The man surprised me by taking my suggestions. He cut short his plans and spent six relaxing days in spectacular islands closer to home base. He had a wonderful time. He's coming back this year for more.

FROM OLYMPIA NORTH, you needn't go far to have an outstanding cruise. Don't try to pack too much into a limited holiday afloat. Cruising takes time. On any given morning you can be up and out at first light, but over the course of a week most people are lucky to be out by noon (well, maybe 10:30). Two or three hours later, it's time to stop. If you've met some interesting people, or it's foggy or the weather socks in, perhaps you won't move at all.

The farther north you go, the more spectacular the scenery gets. Puget Sound is perfect, except that the San Juan Islands are better. As good as the San Juans are, the Canadian Gulf Islands have a special appeal. Desolation Sound, 200 miles north of Seattle, is outstanding. And so on, around Vancouver Island and all the way to Alaska.

Wherever you are in these waters, you can have a memorable cruise. Speed is not important, nor is the distance you cover. The farther you go, the more time it takes, and the more it costs. If you have the time and the money (and the boat and the experience), go the distance. If you don't have the time and/or the money, enjoy the waters close aboard.

THREE EXCEPTIONS: CHARTERING, FLYING AND TRAILERING

Chartering. While most charter agencies are located in Puget Sound and the southern part of B.C., charter boats are available in Desolation Sound and north. You may not have as wide a choice in the more distant areas, but boats are there.

Flying. Many people cruise the more distant waters via the magic of float planes. It is not uncommon for one party to take the boat north to Desolation Sound (about a week for most boats), and enjoy a week or two there. A second party flies in to Refuge Cove in Desolation Sound, and the first party flies home. Successive parties swap by float plane until it's time to move the boat back south. The final party delivers the boat home. Everybody has a fabulous time in the northland, but nobody takes the boat both ways. It works.

Trailering. A significant number of people trailer a boat to popular cruising grounds as far north as the top of Vancouver Island. It's faster than going by boat, it's affordable, and it avoids difficult passages across rough waters. Trailer boats can launch to see Puget Sound, the San Juan Islands, the Gulf Islands, Princess Louisa Inlet, Desolation Sound, Blackfish Sound, and even the sounds on the west coast of Vancouver Island. Some people have launched at Port Hardy, and—watching the weather *very* carefully—gone north around Cape Caution to Rivers Inlet and beyond.

This group of five trailerable sailboats cruised the San Juan Islands and Gulf Islands, then trailered home to California.

HERE IS A BRIEF LOOK at what to expect in what we call "Waggoner waters."

South Puget Sound. For beauty, cruising in South Puget Sound is similar to cruising the San Juan Islands, except the crowds aren't there. Neither are the restaurants. South Sound has a number of excellent marine parks, and several marinas, such as Jarrell's Cove, Longbranch and Boston Harbor. Plan to enjoy the scenery, swing on the anchor, catch some fish, and swim a little. But except for Olympia and Gig Harbor, don't plan to go to town.

Central and North Puget Sound. Anchor out, dine out, enjoy the scenery, and have a jolly old time in these waters. The towns and cities of Gig Harbor, Tacoma, Des Moines, Winslow, Bremerton, Port Orchard, Poulsbo, Seattle, Edmonds,

Kingston, Port Ludlow, Everett, Langley, Coupeville, Oak Harbor, LaConner, Anacortes, and Port Townsend offer a world of interesting stops. Anchorages abound in this area. Wintertime cruising is mother's milk for the locals. In the summer they all go north for vacation.

One new marina must be singled out—the Bell Harbor Marina on the Seattle waterfront. Close to shopping, dining, and the excitement of downtown Seattle, the Bell Harbor Marina is destined to be a legend. For a cosmopolitan experience, it can't be beat.

San Juan Islands. Who needs better cruising than the San Juan Islands offer? With their mountainous terrain, protected waterways, quiet anchorages and busy marinas, the San Juans are a paradise. We have spent weeks enjoying the San Juans, and each spring we go back for more.

Gulf Islands. Read the San Juan Islands paragraph above and make it Canadian, only with more dining, more anchorages, and more marinas to spend time at. Each September we like to spend a week in the Gulf Islands. In fact, we think September is the best cruising month of all.

Vancouver. Vancouver is the most worldly city on the west coast of North America. Not the biggest or the most glittery, but the best. See it from False Creek or the new Coal Harbour Marina, or by bus from the elegant Union Steamship Marina on Bowen Island in Howe Sound.

Princess Louisa Inlet. It takes effort to get there, but the reputation is earned. Princess Louisa Inlet is majestic.

Desolation Sound. Books have been written about Desolation Sound. It's beautiful, rugged, and remote, yet with pockets of civilization. A week is good, but not enough. Two or three weeks are more like it. You'll bore your friends with your tales when you get back home, and you won't care.

North to Sullivan Bay. To expand your cruising grounds north from Desolation Sound to Sullivan Bay we're talking about four-week cruises on well-equipped boats. Amazingly, the scenery only gets better. High mountains, anchorages in bowls carved into the rock, dangerous tidal rapids (except at slack water), and a small number of gourmet dining spots that will please you. Best for the more experienced boaters.

West Coast of Vancouver Island. Rugged and dangerous. Likelihood of high winds and steep seas. Rocks. Little contact with the outside world. Fog. Two to four weeks required. No finer cruising anywhere. When you've circumnavigated Vancouver Island, you've accomplished something.

Sullivan Bay to Prince Rupert. How good can the cruising life be? It's hard to believe that anything could improve on all that's listed above, but somehow the central and northern B.C. coast manages to do it.

We're talking about time, now. Four weeks for part way, six weeks to hurry through and back again, eight weeks to do it right. Thousands of miles of shoreline, deserted anchorages, abandoned camps and villages, even an abandoned city. Abundant fishing. High mountains, eagles, raven, mink, cougar, wolves, bear, deer—all kinds of wildlife. Few people. You're on your own.

Carry ample fuel, water and food. Mostly protected waters, but a few areas where the seas can sink a boat. Typical anchorages 10-15 fathoms deep. Paradise for those lucky enough and skilled enough to make the trip.

Best months. The prime cruising months begin in April and end by October, with July-August being the most popular. People use their boats year-round in Puget Sound. On winter weekends the popular ports can be surprisingly busy. Cabin heat is a must.

North of Puget Sound, pleasure boating is best done between early May and late September. Really dependable weather normally doesn't arrive until July. We usually take our long summer cruise beginning in early June and ending mid-July. As we work north we see fewer and fewer boats. On the return trip in July the situation is different. Boats everywhere.

Be careful with winter cruising north of Puget Sound. (Be careful in Puget Sound, too.) In the winter, storms lash the British Columbia coast. When you see what winter storms do to trees on exposed parts of the B.C. coast, you'll be happy to wait for summer.

About charts and other publications. To keep this book informative and up-to-date, we have stuck our nose into nearly every port, bay, cove, and notch along the coast. In the process, we have become staunch advocates of nautical charts and navigation publications. We now own more than 200 charts, and use them constantly. A good selection of charts not only will keep a boat out of trouble, but will let you enter places you wouldn't want to try without the chart.

Annual tide and current tables are essential. The U.S. *Coast Pilot* and the Canadian *Sailing Directions* should be considered essential. U.S. and Canadian light lists will be useful. We subscribe to the U.S. *Notices to Mariners* and the Canadian

Continued next page

Notice to Shipping and *Notices to Mariners*, and find them extremely helpful. No charge for either one. Contact the respective Coast Guard offices.

An astonishing amount of information exists about this coast and safe navigation around it. I have trouble understanding the mentality that will invest great sums on the boat and its fuel, then scrimp on charts and other navigation publications. Actually, the money has nothing to do with it. The rocks, tides and weather are indifferent to the amount spent on any boat. They treat all boats equally.

Necessary equipment. The marine supply industry can provide useful boat equipment for as long as you care to pay for it. I happen to be a boat equipment junkie. Each year, our sturdy little research boat *Surprise* settles deeper on her marks as yet more gear is brought aboard.

I feel that the *minimum* navigation equipment for safe cruising could be reduced to just five items: a high-quality compass, adjusted by a professional compass adjuster; a quality hand bearing compass; a depth sounder or fish finder; a VHF radio with a good antenna; and a radar reflector. Of course, complete Coast Guard safety equipment is a must.

But I know a couple who cruised around Vancouver Island on their 26-foot Folkboat equipped only with a bulkhead compass, a hand bearing compass, complete charts, a radar reflector and a large Bruce anchor. Nothing else, not even a depth sounder. For depths they use a leadline.

Surprise has a few extra pieces of equipment: GPS, loran, radar, autopilot, two VHF radios, handheld VHF radio, Steiner binoculars, two cabin heaters, inverter, microwave oven, survival suits . . . the list is longer, embarrassingly so.

Clothing. Except for Desolation Sound in the summer, the waters in this area are cold. Even during warm weather you may welcome a sweatshirt or jacket. Layering works well. While rain gear is essential on sailboats, it can be useful on an enclosed powerboat. Shoreside attire can be as nice as you want to go, but most people do fine with comfortable sports clothes. I carry a necktie, just in case. I've never put it on.

Crossing the Border

U.S. and Canadian Customs Information

Customs must be cleared whenever the U.S.-Canadian border is crossed, either direction. Generally the process is quick and straightforward, but if the skipper isn't prepared with the proper information, it can be time-consuming. It is extremely important to follow all the rules, and be polite. While Customs officers are trained in courtesy and usually are cordial, they have at their disposal regulations that can ruin your day.

U.S. CUSTOMS

U.S. residents out of the U.S. less than 48 hours can import merchandise up to $25 in value per person without duty. If more than 48 hours the limit is $400 per person. For ease and simplicity, try to restrict what you bring back home to products made or grown in Canada.

Canadian citizens and U.S. citizens do not need passports but do require identification. The skipper should know the nationality of all persons on board.

Processing fee. Pleasure vessels 30 feet in length or more must pay an annual processing (user) fee of $25 to to enter or re-enter the United States. Vessels less than 30 feet are not subject to the fee, provided they have nothing to declare. Payment is required at or before the vessel's first arrival each calendar year. If you report by telephone, a fee application will be mailed. A non-transferable decal will be issued upon payment. To get a decal early, call the Customs office at Blaine, (360)332-6318.

Reporting to U.S. Customs. Customs *must* be cleared at a designated point of entry or by telephone (800)562-5943. We clear customs by cellular telephone while underway, with excellent results. To avoid delays, have the following information available at the time you report your arrival:

- Vessel registration number. Be sure to use the same number that you use when you report to Canada Customs.
- Vessel name and length.
- User fee decal number if applicable.
- Canadian clearance number. *Required* for U.S. moored boats.
- Estimated date of departure. *Required* for Canadian moored vessels.

Release Number. You will receive a release number when you complete your arrival report to customs. Log this number with the date, time and place where the vessel reported. Keep the number for at least one year.

PIN Small Boat Clearance. Most pleasure vessel operators who have entered the U.S. in the Puget Sound area have already been assigned Personal Identification Numbers (PINs). With the PIN, the vessel operator can call (800)562-5943 to clear U.S. Customs easily. Vessel operators who do not have a PIN will be assigned one at their first customs clearance. With a PIN, you can report your arrival any time from one hour before departing Canada to the time when you land in the U.S., or while underway.

I-68 Program. The U.S. Immigration and Naturalization Service's I-68 "Canadian Border Boat Landing Permit" program has caused a great deal of confusion, uncertainty, and ill-will in B.C. and Washington State.

I-68 allows qualified Canadian and U.S. residents to pre-clear with the U.S. Immigration and Naturalization Service for an entire season's arrival in the U.S. by small pleasure craft. Except for a short time in the spring of 1993, in-person clearance with the INS (or an I-68 pre-clearance) has not been necessary in the Pacific Northwest.

We have spoken at some length with officials from the U.S. Immigration and Naturalization Service and from the Border Patrol about I-68 and border crossing. We have been told that *until further notice, in the Pacific Northwest, entry to the U.S. can be made by small pleasure craft either in person or by telephone, without regard to the I-68 program. No Form I-68 need be carried; none will be asked for.* In other words, you don't have to worry about I-68. Telephone clearance will continue to be sufficient. This applies to U.S. and Canadian citizens only. Persons who normally must

present passports when they cross between the two countries still must appear in person to a Customs officer or an INS officer at a Port of Entry. *Disclaimer:* The government agencies can change their minds at any time. We don't think they will, but they can.

Designated U.S. Ports of Entry

To report your entry weekdays 0800-1700, call these telephone numbers:

Aberdeen	(360)532-2030
Anacortes	(360)293-2331
Bellingham	(360)734-5463
Blaine	(360)332-6318
Everett	(206)259-0246
Friday/Roche Hbr.	(360)378-2080
Neah Bay/ Port Angeles	(360)457-4311
Port Townsend	(360)385-3777
Seattle	(206)553-4678
Tacoma/Olympia	(206)593-6338

Above numbers for weekdays only. Nights, weekends, holidays call toll-free (800)562-5943.

CANADA CUSTOMS

Except for vessels clearing by CANPASS-Private Boats (see below), all vessels arriving in Canada from a foreign country must clear customs immediately after the vessel comes to rest. The master or the master's designated representative must report to customs in person or by telephone from a designated port of entry. No one else may leave the vessel, and no baggage or merchandise may be removed from the vessel.

U.S. citizens do not need passports, but do need to carry identification. Citizens of other countries need passports, and some need visas. *Carry birth certificates for all minors aboard*—you may be asked for them. If you are bringing a child other than your own into Canada, have a notorized statement authorizing you to take the child into Canada, and proof that the person signing the statement does have custody of the child.

You *must* report at a designated port of entry. At some locations customs officers will be present; at many others you will report by telephone. Even if you report by telephone, your boat may be subject to inspection.

To avoid delays, have the following:

- Vessel registration number.
- Vessel name and length.
- Names, addresses, citizenship and birthdates of all passengers.
- U.S. Customs clearance number for a returning Canadian boat.
- Estimated departure date (for U.S. boats).

Canada Customs will give you a clearance number and instructions for where to post it on your boat (usually a side window). Log this number, with the date, time, and place of clearance. Vessels are subject to reinspection while in Canadian waters, usually by RCMP officers when their patrol boat reaches a marina. The officers are well trained and very polite, but be sure you don't have anything aboard you shouldn't have.

CANPASS-Private Boats. In August 1995 Revenue Canada introduced CANPASS-Private Boats, a pre-clearance program for Canadian and U.S. residents entering Canada from the U.S. by boat. With CANPASS, a vessel clears Canadian Customs and Immigration by calling, toll-free, (888)226-7277 not less than one hour before departing U.S. waters, and not more than two hours.

The CANPASS application comes with four pages of instructions. Briefly, however, the program is limited to citizens or permanent residents of Canada or the U.S. with no criminal activities, no customs or immigration violations. The approval process takes several weeks. Each person aboard must be approved for CANPASS or the vessel must clear customs at a designated reporting station. One application can cover the applicant, spouse, and any dependent children residing with the applicant. The cost is $25 (Cdn.), and they can charge your Visa or Mastercard account. Renewal forms are sent yearly.

To get more information and an application, call (888)226-7277, or write: CANPASS-Private Boats, #28-176th St., Surrey, B.C. V4P 1M7, Canada.

Firearms restrictions. You may not bring handguns, automatic weapons, or mace into Canada. If you are carrying a shotgun or long rifle, be sure it is registered with U.S. Customs *before* you enter Canada. Contact Canada Customs for specific instructions, (604)666-0545.

Food restrictions. Other than restricted foods, you can carry quantities of food appropriate to your anticipated stay. However, no apples, no pitted fruit (such as apricots, plums, quince, peaches, nectarines). Cherries are okay. No potatoes, no fresh corn. House plants are okay if carried aboard.

Pets. Owners of dogs and cats must bring a certificate issued by a licensed American or Canadian veterinarian clearly identifying the pet and certifying that it has been vaccinated against rabies sometime during the previous 36 months.

Liquor restrictions. Not more than 40 ounces of liquor or wine, or 24 12-ounce bottles of beer or ale per person of legal drinking age. Legal drinking age in B.C. is 19 years old.

Designated B.C. Points of Entry for Pleasure Craft Reporting
All locations contact Canada Customs toll-free (888)226-7277

All locations, year-round 24 hours except Bedwell Harbour

Location	Points of Entry
Bamfield:	Fisherman's Dock West Kingfisher Marina
Bedwell Hrbr.:	May 1 - Sept. 30 only 0800-2000 daily Standby: 2000-2400 2400-0800 ($54.00 fee)
Campbell River:	Discovery Chevron Dock Discovery Marina Dock
Nanaimo:	Nanaimo Harbour Commission Basin Brechin Point Marina
Port Alberni:	Government Dock
Powell River:	Government Dock
Prince Rupert:	Fairview Government Dock Yacht Club Cow Bay Govt. Dock Rushbrook Govt. Dock
Sidney:	Angler's Anchorage Marina Canoe Cove Marina Port Sidney Van Isle Marina
Vancouver:	Crescent Beach Marina False Creek Government Dock Steveston Government Dock Coal Harbour All marinas until further notice
Victoria:	Oak Bay Marina, Royal Victoria YC (Cadboro Bay & Tsehum Harbour) Victoria Customs Dock
White Rock:	White Rock Government Dock

How to Cross the Strait of Juan de Fuca

To the San Juan Islands, Haro Strait, Victoria

Important: Courselines suggested below are approximate and for reference only. They assume good conditions and the absence of current. Since current always is present, appropriate course adjustments will be called for.

THE STRAIT OF JUAN DE FUCA has a well-earned reputation for being rough at times. It's true that a boat crossing the strait can take a beating its crew will not want to repeat, but often the crossing can be almost flat. And if conditions truly are foul, alternate routes exist. The secret to an easy crossing lies in picking your times and not being foolhardy.

Summer weather pattern

During the high summer cruising season, the "typical" weather pattern calls for near-calm conditions in the early morning, when the air over the entire region is cool. As the summer sun heats the land, the air over the land rises. Colder ocean air funnels down the Strait of Juan de Fuca to replace the rising land air. This is called a sea breeze, and usually it develops in the late morning or early afternoon. By late afternoon the sea breeze can be quite strong, creating short, high seas that can really work you over. After sundown, as the interior air cools and drops, the wind dies away.

The general plan, therefore, calls for an early morning departure. Listen care fully to the VHF marine radio's official weather reports and forecast. If the report says the wind already is blowing 15-20 knots, with more wind expected, don't cross. Wait until the wind subsides, or take an alternate route.

The most popular alternate route is around the south end of Whidbey Island, north through Saratoga Passage, and through LaConner. Continue out Guemes Channel and across Rosario Strait to Thatcher Pass. Thatcher Pass will take you into the San Juan Islands, where you can work your way to your destination in protected waters. Rosario Strait can be rough, too, but usually not as rough as the eastern Strait of Juan de Fuca. And Rosario Strait is only four miles wide between the Guemes Channel and Thatcher Pass, so even if the water is rough you won't be in it for long.

Point Wilson to Middle Channel (Friday Harbor)

Let's say you want to cross from Point Wilson, at the mouth of Puget Sound, to Middle Channel, known locally as Cattle Pass, at the southern tip of San Juan Island. That's the direct route to Friday Harbor. Crossing the Strait of Juan de Fuca to Cattle Pass, the ideal plan is to time your arrival at Cattle Pass for shortly after the current turns to a flood. Use the San Juan Channel current predictions.

If you do it right, you'll carry the last of a dying ebb out Admiralty Inlet, past Point Wilson, and well across the strait.

Just before reaching Cattle Pass, the current will turn to flood, flushing you nicely through the pass and into San Juan Channel. Since you can have 2-4 knots of current in Admiralty Inlet, and a couple knots of current in the strait, riding the ebb can save considerable time, even in a fast boat. The less time you're exposed, the less time you have to meet trouble.

The current can run hard through Cattle Pass, so it's best not to fight it. In a slow boat, you can just sit there making little headway.

If you draw a straight line between Point Wilson and Cattle Pass (hard to do: it takes two charts), the line would go approximately through Smith Island. Smith Island lies about half-way across the strait. It is a low, lonely pile of brown sand with a big lighthouse on it. Shoals, covered with dense kelp, extend westward from the island for nearly two miles.

So you can't go straight to Cattle Pass; you have to run west of Smith Island, then make a turn to starboard. At Point Wilson you'll set a course of 301 degrees Magnetic until you're abeam the Smith Island light, where you'll turn to a course of 330 degrees Magnetic to fetch Cattle Pass. (From Cattle Pass to Point Wilson, reverse the process: run 150 degrees Magnetic until the Smith Island light bears abeam to port, then turn to 121 Magnetic to fetch Point Wilson.)

You may find that once you've raised it, Smith Island won't let you go. It takes forever to put Smith Island astern.

Partridge Bank, between Point Wilson and Smith Island, should be avoided. Heavy kelp is an obstacle, and if the wind is up the seas will be worse in the shallow water over the bank.

To Rosario Strait or Deception Pass

From the mouth of Admiralty Inlet, plot a course that leaves the Point Partridge bell buoy off Whidbey Island to starboard. From the Point Partridge bell buoy, plot a course to take you *east* of Lawson Reef, which lies about 1¾ miles off the entrance to Deception Pass. A bell buoy marks the reef. Once past Lawson Reef, turn to port to run into Rosario Strait. (The straightest course from the Point Partridge bell buoy to Rosario Strait would take you inside and parallel to the commercial traffic lane. Pleasure craft are restricted from running in the commercial lanes in that way.)

To Haro Strait (Roche Harbor)

Leaving Point Wilson, run 301 degrees Magnetic until the Smith Island light is abeam to starboard. Then turn to starboard just enough to run toward the west side of San Juan Island, but east of the commercial traffic lane. The course should be about 310 degrees Magnetic. Once near San Juan Island, turn to port and follow the island coastline north.

If you're returning from Roche Harbor, follow the San Juan Island coastline until you're off False Bay, then turn to 130 degrees Magnetic until the Smith Island light is abeam to port. Turn to 121 degrees Magnetic to fetch Point Wilson.

Both the flood and ebb currents run strongly along the west side of San Juan Island. Even in a fast boat it is best to make this passage with favorable current. The Canadian Hydrographic Service's book *Current Atlas: Juan de Fuca Strait to Georgia Strait* illustrates these current flows in convincing diagram form, and is highly recommended. Our Weatherly Press publication *Washburne's Tables* makes using the *Current Atlas* much easier.

To Victoria

From Point Wilson, a course of approximately 275 degrees Magnetic will get you to Victoria. Settle down for a 30-

mile trip, and watch for floating kelp and other drift. Returning from Victoria, a course of about 95 degrees Magnetic should raise Point Wilson in time to make late-run corrections for the effects of current. In slow boats, the trip between Victoria and Point Wilson usually can be made on a single favorable tide. In all boats, significant time will be saved by using the current.

Even the best plan can go awry. While over the years the editors have made many easy crossings of the strait (only a few have been "memorable"), it's important to understand that conditions can change with little warning. When you're several miles offshore and the wind decides to make up, you can't pull over until things improve. You have no business in the strait unless you're in a seaworthy, well-equipped boat.

Fog

Fog can develop unexpectedly on the strait. Sometimes it is only a thin mist, other times it can be pea-soup thick. While you're in good visibility, keep regular plots of your progress. *Always know exactly where you are.* This way, when fog hits you'll be able to plot courses that will keep you safe. In fog, put up a radar reflector so large vessels can see you on their radar in time to steer clear of you. Slow to 5 or 6 knots to dodge drift and avoid other boats that appear close aboard. Speeds of 5 or 6 knots are easy to use for time-speed-distance calculations. At 5 knots, a mile takes 12 minutes. At 6 knots, a mile takes 10 minutes.

Regardless of the size of your boat, it is in fog that you and your crew will be grateful for your relatively modest investment in a large, high-quality compass, and the compass adjuster's time to adapt the compass to your boat. *Trust that compass.* Fog disorients even the most experienced mariners. If you run a compass course you know to be good, at a speed you can depend on, for a time you calculate based on speed and distance, you should arrive surprisingly close to your destination.

The Strait of Juan de Fuca is not to be feared, but it is to be respected. The strait will punish lack of respect. Be sure your boat is seaworthy, well-equipped, and in excellent condition. Carry plenty of fuel. Let the weather set your plans. Don't be afraid to wait. Know where you are always, and watch for changes. Chances are it'll be a piece of cake.

The Point Wilson Rip

One of the most frustrating pieces of water we face in the Northwest is the infamous Point Wilson tide rip just off Port Townsend. The rip usually (but not always) forms on a fairly strong ebb tide, and may or may not be accompanied by westerly wind. The patch of rough water can extend for several miles north and west of Point Wilson.

I have learned three ways to avoid being bounced around by the Point Wilson rip.

The first is to round Point Wilson at or near slack water. Usually, the rip doesn't form until well into a strong ebb cycle, so timing your arrival to coincide with slack water should get the job done.

If, however, you must go that way while the rip is tearing the Strait of Juan de Fuca to shreds, you can pick one of two routes around it.

The first is to hug the Point Wilson shore as closely as you dare, keeping close to shore until you pass Middle Point, before heading across to the San Juan Islands or heading west to Victoria. The fact that the current runs more slowly close to shore prevents the rip tide from having the same wild effect as farther out.

The other route is to stay close to the Whidbey Island shore (avoiding the shoal water off Partridge Point and staying east of Partridge Bank) until past Smith Island before turning toward your destination.

We were making a night crossing of the Strait one year, on our way to Victoria for the Swiftsure sailboat race. It had been a warm, calm evening, so the forward hatch was propped open. One of the forward vee-berths was occupied by our friend Ned Brown, and the other was Ole Hansen's. Ole was at the helm when we pumped head-on into the Point Wilson rip. We buried the bow, hurling water over the deck and back into the cockpit, where Ole struggled to keep the boat on course.

Ned woke up when he was slammed against the overhead, but noted sleepily that all the water cascading down through the open hatch was landing on Ole's bunk, not his, so he rolled over and went back to sleep.

Ole hasn't entirely forgiven Ned to this day, and I started to develop my theories about how to avoid that nasty rip, which hasn't caught me since.

—*Tom Kincaid*

About Anchoring

In addition to being the editor of the Waggoner, for the past 13 years I have been the Pacific Northwest sales representative for Bruce anchors. I have specified anchors, compared anchors, argued anchors, studied anchors, taught anchors, and written about anchors. Most importantly, I have gone out and used anchors. Gathering information for the Waggoner has meant that more time is spent at docks, but given the choice, the little ship *Surprise* prefers to anchor.

Many people do not share this enthusiasm for anchoring. Watching how some of them go about it, their fears are understandable. But there are a few general principles that will help even a novice anchor successfully.

Use good gear. Big, strong anchors work; small, cheap anchors don't. The most experienced cruisers seem to carry the biggest anchors. For obvious reasons I like Bruce anchors. But the other popular designs are good, too. Well-equipped, wide-ranging boats are found carrying all of the common designs: Bruce, CQR (plow), Danforth, and Northill.

Make sure your anchor is made of high-quality steel. If it's wedged in a rock, you don't want it to bend. While Danforth style anchors are easiest to bend, within the limits of their design they can be made strong and expensive, or weak and cheap. There are no strong, cheap Danforth style anchors.

Read the sizing charts carefully, and *size your anchor for storm conditions.* Some sizing charts are written for 20-knot winds. Others are written for 30 knots. The Bruce chart is written for 42 knots. When the wind comes on to blow *hard* at 3:00 A.M., you don't want a 20-knot anchor out there.

Carry ample rode. For an anchor to bury and hold properly, you should pay out anchor rode at least *five times* the water depth. In 20 feet of water you would want 100 feet of rode out. In 60 feet of water you would want 300 feet out. Often, especially in crowded anchorages during high summer season, it will not be possible to anchor on 5:1 scope (five times the depth of the water). That is understood. But I've watched people put out 30 feet of rode in 20 feet of water, and wonder why the anchor wouldn't bite. For the deep waters of the Pacific Northwest, carry at least 300 feet of anchor rode, whether all-chain or combination chain and rope. Opinions vary about how much chain a combination rode should include, but no one would criticize you for having about a foot of chain for every foot of boat length.

Read the tide tables. If the overnight low tide isn't very low, a shallow anchorage can be just right. On the other hand, if the moon is either new or full (the two times during the month when the tidal range is the greatest) the shallow anchorage might go dry at low tide. You also want to know the maximum height of the tide during your stay. Set your scope for five times the water depth at high tide, or if you can't get five times, as much as you can get away with.

Set the anchor well. To get the best bury in the bottom, you want the angle between the anchor and the boat to be as flat as possible. After lowering the anchor, back down, down, before you snub the rode on a cleat and set the hook. After the anchor is set, you can shorten up to avoid swinging into other boats or onto a sand bar.

You'll know, by the way, when the anchor is set. The anchor rode pulls straight, and it makes a sound as it comes tight on the cleat. The boat *stops.* If you have any doubt as to whether the anchor is set, then probably it isn't. Weed can foul an anchor, especially a Danforth style anchor, and many bottoms have weed. I've heard of anchors grabbing a sunken tire and dragging it across the bottom. Contributing Editor Tom Kincaid recalls an anchor caught in a mess of old electrical wire.

Once the anchor is set, you don't have to pour on all 600 horsepower to prove your point. Anchors gain holding power through pulling and relaxing over time, a process called *soaking.* An anchor put down for lunch might be recovered with little effort. Left overnight it might feel as if it had headed for China.

Look at your chart. For happy anchoring you want a good holding bottom, appropriate depths, and protection. The nautical chart can help you with all these needs. If the chart says *Foul,* don't anchor there. If the chart shows submerged pilings at the head of the bay, avoid the head of the bay. If the chart shows 200-foot depths right up to the shoreline, that's a bad spot. If the chart shows the bay open to the full sweep of the prevailing wind and seas, find another bay or you'll be in for a rough night.

I find the easiest anchorages to be in 20-50 feet of water, with a decided preference for the 20-30 foot depths. Approach slowly, take a turn around the entire area to check the depths, and decide where you want the boat to lie after the anchor is set. Then go out to a spot that will give you a 5:1 scope, and lower the anchor. Back way down, set the hook, and shorten up to the desired location.

Carry a shore-tie. In many locations you will set the anchor offshore, back in toward shore to set, and take the dinghy in with a rope from a stern cleat to tie around a rock or tree. Boats line Tod Inlet tied this way. In many deep bays it's the only way you can anchor. And sometimes you'll find a little niche that will hold just your boat, if the stern is tied to shore. Carry at least 600 feet of inexpensive polypropylene rope for shore ties. Often you will be able to pass the line around a tree and bring it back to the boat. When you depart, you can recover the shore tie without leaving the boat.

Secure the anchor rode to the boat. I remember talking with a man with a 32-foot boat, a brand-new Bruce anchor, and several hundred feet of expensive anchor rode, which he had not made fast to the boat. He laid the anchor down in deep water and backed away. The anchor rode snaked out faster and faster, until to his horror the man saw the rope's end shoot across the foredeck and vanish overboard.

Cruising from dock to dock is a lot of fun, and no one can fault the conveniences. But a whole world of possibilities opens to those who have good anchoring gear and know how to use it. These guidelines cover most anchoring situations. Practice in good anchorages, where it's safe. Watch how other boats anchor. The skills are easy to learn.

Buoys, Beacons and Ranges

Red, Right, Returning means leave ***Red*** navigation aids off your ***Right*** hand when you're ***Returning*** from seaward. If the navigation mark is *not* red, leave it off your *left* hand when you're returning from seaward.

This is the general rule in U.S. and Canadian waters, with two subtle refinements:

- A red and white aid marks mid-channel. Both inward bound and outward bound, leave the red and white buoy off your left hand.
- A red and green aid marks an obstruction, or marks the meeting of two or more channels, but the aid can be passed on either side safely.

Nuns

All red buoys marking channels are shaped as cones, and are called NUNS. Most nun buoys are painted solid red. If the nun buoy has a green horizontal band painted on it, the buoy marks the meeting of two channels, with the left channel being the preferred, or main, channel. (If you leave the buoy off your right hand, you will be in the left channel.) Nuns can be lighted or unlighted. If lighted, the light will be red.

Cans

All green buoys marking channels are called CANS. They are shaped like, well, *cans.* Most can buoys are painted solid green. If the can buoy has a horizontal red band painted on it, the buoy marks the meeting of two channels, with the right channel the preferred, or main, channel. Cans may be lighted or unlighted. If lighted, the light will be green.

Buoys float, and are held in place by heavy anchoring systems. The chain between the buoy and the anchor must be long enough to let the buoy float in the highest tides and largest seas possible. As a result, at low tide the buoy can swing in a large circle. Winds and tidal currents move the buoys. They don't stay in exactly the same place.

Beacons

BEACONS are permanent navigation aids attached to the earth. They can be located on land, installed on docks or breakwaters, or mounted on pilings. A lighthouse is a beacon. A beacon not on land will be placed in shallow water *outside* a channel. Leave a beacon considerable room. Do not pass a beacon close aboard, especially at low tide.

An unlighted beacon is called a DAYBEACON. A lighted beacon is called a MINOR LIGHT. A minor light marking the right side of a channel will carry a red light (red, right, returning). A minor light marking the left side of a channel will carry a green light. If a minor light marks the meeting of two channels, the light will be red if the left channel is preferred (red, right, returning); green if the right channel is preferred.

DAYMARKS are the colored panels mounted on beacons. Red panels are triangle shaped; green panels are square. A triangle shaped red panel with a green horizontal stripe indicates the meeting of two channels, with the left channel the preferred, or main channel. A square panel painted green with a red horizontal stripe indicates the meeting of two channels, with the right channel the preferred, or main channel.

Whenever a navigation aid is marked with a horizontal stripe of contrasting color, the color at the top of the aid indicates the preferred, or main, channel.

Approaching a channel from seaward, buoys and beacons are numbered, beginning with the marks to seaward. Red buoys, beacons, and minor lights carry even numbers, such as 2, 4, 6, and so on. Green buoys, beacons, and minor lights carry odd numbers, such as 1, 3, 5, and so on. Depending on the channel, it might be appropriate to skip some numbers, so that buoy 6 is roughly opposite buoy 5, even if no buoy 4 exists.

For a vessel returning from the sea, the green painted can buoy marks the left side of the channel, and the red painted nun buoy marks the right side. The left-side mark has an odd number, and the right side mark has an even number. Either or both buoys could be lighted or unlighted.

Ranges

RANGES are used to help a boat stay in the middle of a narrow channel.

Ranges are rectangular panels, stood vertically, each with a wide stripe running from top to bottom down the middle of the panel. Ranges don't float. They are attached to the earth, and are arranged in pairs, one behind the other. The rearmost range board stands taller than the front board. To use a range, steer until the rear range board appears to be on top of the front board. You can steer toward a range, looking ahead, or away from a range, sighting astern.

Buoys and beacons are not selected and placed at random. They follow a plan, although to a newcomer the plan may at times seem obscure. In the San Juan Islands, for instance, the navigation aids in Lopez Sound and Harney Channel assume that entry from the sea is from

The Shilshole Bay Entrance Range. To use a range, align the boards one above the other, as these boards are, and follow that course. The boards have lights for night approaches. The first (lower) board's light is shown on the chart as Qk Fl R 20ft.*—Quick Flashing Red, 20 feet above Mean High Water. The upper board's light is shown on the chart as* E Int R 6sec 81ft. E Int *means Isophase. With an Isophase light, the duration of light and darkness are equal. The red light shows for three seconds and is dark for three seconds.*

the east, from Rosario Strait. Coming from the east, such as from Lopez Pass or Thatcher Pass, you would leave the red navigation aids off your right hand.

However, the situation changes at the ferry dock located at Upright Head, at the north tip of Lopez Island. There, the assumption is that one is returning from the sea via Upright Channel, and the light on the dock is red. If you were coming from Lopez Sound or Thatcher Pass, this light would be on your left hand—the opposite of what you might expect.

Despite the complexity of the buoyage and light system, you will find that as you understand it better your enjoyment afloat will increase. At some point you will want a thorough explanation of the entire system. For U.S. waters it will be found in the introduction to the Coast Guard *Light List.* For Canadian waters it will be found partly in the introduction to the Canadian Coast Guard *List of Lights, Buoys and Fog Signals,* and completely in the Canadian Coast Guard publication, *The Canadian Aids to Navigation System.* Latest editions of these publications should be aboard every boat. Available at chart agencies.

Inner Light 8, a minor light marking the Shilshole Bay entrance channel, illustrates many facts about navigation aids. First, it is a beacon, attached to the earth. Second, it is attached to the earth outside the navigable channel. This is why it is good practice to give beacons a generous berth, even when they are surrounded by water — the tide might be in. Third, the red-painted triangular dayboard shows that this beacon marks the right side of the channel, and should be off the right hand when returning from the sea (red, right, returning). Because all right-side channel markers carry even numbers, the number 8 in the middle of the dayboard confirms that the beacon is on the right. Last, the white board with the red circle means "restricted operations." In this case the restriction is the 7-knot speed limit.

Differences Between U.S. and Canadian Charts

CANADA AND THE UNITED STATES are two separate nations, and their charts, while similar in many ways, have a number of important differences.

U.S. charts are in fathoms and feet; most Canadian charts are metric. *With all charts, read the chart title and margin information to see if the chart is metric, fathoms and feet, or feet.* The U.S. has announced its intention to convert its charts to metric, but at the moment only one U.S. chart in the Pacific Northwest has metric measurement. That chart is *18460, Strait of Juan de Fuca Entrance.* One side of the sheet is in fathoms and feet; the other side is metric. A few Canadian charts haven't been updated to metric and remain in fathoms and feet.

Metric charts show soundings and heights in meters. A meter (spelled *metre* in Canada) equals 39.37 inches, or just over 3 feet (3.28 feet, to be exact). Two meters equals 6 ft.7 inches, or just over one fathom. The difference is significant. Don't confuse fathoms with meters.

Waters appear to be deeper on U.S. charts. This difference is important wherever the water is shallow, and is the result of the two countries using different CHART DATUMS.

Depths on a chart are measured from the chart datum, also called the REFERENCE PLANE or TIDAL DATUM. On Canadian charts, the chart datum is either Lowest Normal Tides, or Lower Low Water, Large Tide. For that reason, you don't find many "minus tides" in Canadian tide tables.

On U.S. charts, however, the chart datum is Mean Lower Low Water. Mean Lower Low Water is the mean level of the lower of the two low tides each day. Since the U.S. chart datum has half the lower waters above it and half below it, U.S. tide books show minus tides.

It's not a question of whether the tide drops lower in Canada or the U.S. It's a question of where the depth is measured from. U.S. charts start their measurements from a point higher than Canadian charts. The difference can be as much as 1.5 meters, or almost 5 feet.

Example: Assume that you are in the U.S., skippering a sailboat. The sailboat's keel draws 5 feet, and you want to anchor overnight in a bay with a charted depth of one fathom (6 feet). According to the tide table, low tide will be minus 1.5 feet at 0700. Knowing that your boat, with its 5 feet of draft, would be aground in 4.5 feet of water, you would look for a more suitable anchorage.

If this bay were in Canada, the Canadian chart would show a depth of perhaps just 1 metre (assuming a Lowest Normal Tide lower than the tide at 0700). The tide table would show a low tide at 0700 of perhaps .4 meters. You would add the 1 metre depth from the chart to the .4 metre low tide from the tide table, and get 1.4 metres of water at 0700. Since you draw more than 1.4 metres (55 inches), you would not anchor in the bay that night.

Important exception: Both Canadian and U.S. charts show soundings in the other country's system when the charts cover both sides of the border. The U.S. chart would convert Canadian metres to U.S. fathoms, but would adopt the Canadian chart datum in Canadian waters. The Canadian metric chart would convert U.S. fathoms to meters, but would adopt the U.S. chart datum in U.S. waters. This is explained in the chart legends.

Clearances appear to be greater on U.S. charts. U.S. charts measure clearances from Mean High Water. One-half the high waters are above the mean. Canadian charts measure clearances from Higher High Water, Large Tides. The same bridge, over the same waterway, would show less vertical clearance on a Canadian chart than on a U.S. chart. Metric Canadian charts show heights and depths in metres, while charts in fathoms and feet show heights in feet, and depths in fathoms. A Canadian metric chart might show a bridge clearance as "3", meaning 3 metres above Higher High Water, Large Tides. A U.S. chart would show a similar bridge clearance as "12" or more, meaning 12 feet or more above Mean High Water.

Canadian charts use more symbols to show buoys and tide rips. Canadian charts use symbols that approximate the shapes of buoys, with descriptive letters to indicate the buoy's characteristics. U.S. charts use a single diamond-shaped symbol for nearly all navigation buoys, with descriptive letters to indicate the buoy's characteristics. On U.S. chart 18421, Strait of Juan de Fuca to Strait of Georgia (1:80,000), for example, the bell buoy marking Buckeye Shoal, north of Cypress Island, is shown as

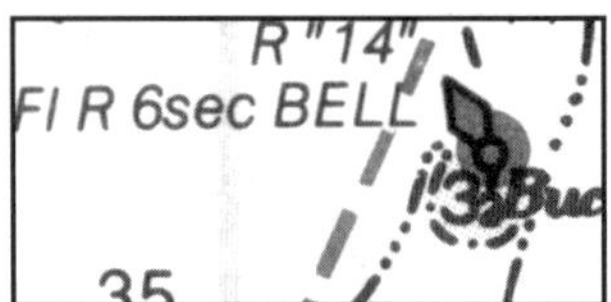

But on Canadian chart 3462, Juan de Fuca Strait to Strait of Georgia (1:80,000), the buoy is shown as

Canadian charts may use arrows to show the location of the buoy or beacon. If other detail on the chart makes precise location difficult, the Canadian chart will offset the symbol slightly, in the direction of the preferred navigable water. The offset is indicated by an arrow pointing to the actual location of the buoy or beacon. Sometimes the arrow is not easily noticed at a quick glance, so be aware.

Chart No. 1 cracks the code. Nautical charts are filled to overflowing with important navigation information. Unfortunately, so much of the information is in the form of symbols, abbreviations, and undefined terms that it can be offputting to the inexperienced. Each country publishes a book that shows each symbol, explains each abbreviation, and defines each term used on its charts. The U.S. book is titled *Chart No. 1,* and the Canadian book is titled *Chart 1.* They are available at their respective chart agencies, and the prices are modest.

The Canadian Coast Guard publication *The Canadian Aids to Navigation System* explains the Canadian buoyage and light system, and is highly recommended. The cost is $7.50 (Canadian) from Canadian Hydrographic chart agents.

Don't overlook the introductions to these books. The introductions are full of essential information.

VHF Radio Procedures

THE VHF RADIO IS AN IMPORTANT PIECE of safety equipment, and should be monitored when the boat is underway. While monitoring, you will hear weather and safety warnings, and be aware of much that is happening around you. A boat close by, for example, may be having problems and call for help. By monitoring your radio you can respond.

Station licenses

U.S. vessels. Until 1996, U.S. pleasure craft were required to have station licenses for their VHF radios. In 1996, however, the requirement was dropped *for use inside the U.S. only.* A U.S. vessel operating *outside* the U.S. still must carry a station license. If you plan to cruise in Canada, your boat will need a U.S. station license. The cost is $75 for 10 years, and covers VHF radios, radar, EPIRBs, and a number of other radio products. Applications are available wherever VHF radios or other electronic equipment are sold, or from the Federal Communications Commission at (888)225-5322.

One station license serves the entire boat, regardless of the number of radios the boat has. The station license also covers the use of a tender's VHF radio (such as a handheld model) as long as it is used in tender service, and as long as it is not used on land. While in the tender, use the main vessel's call sign. It's all right for two or more radios from the same ship with the same call sign to talk to each other.

Canadian vessels. The station license must be renewed each year. The first year's license costs $47; yearly renewals, $36.

In both Canada and the U.S., the station license must be displayed near the primary radio. Penalties may be assessed for operating a radio without a station license, or an expired license, or for misuse of the radio. Radio traffic is listened to, expiration dates are verified, and fines assessed for infractions.

Operator's Permit

Canada requires each person operating a VHF radio to have a Restricted Operator's Certificate. For Canadian residents a test must be passed, but the certificate is free and issued for life.

The U.S. does not require operator's permits for VHF radio use within the U.S. For foreign travel, however, a Restricted Radio Operator's permit is required. The U.S. individual permit is issued for life. The cost is $45.

Cellular telephones

No license is required for marine use of a cellular telephone. Cellular telephone coverage is excellent throughout Puget Sound, the San Juan Islands, and the entire Strait of Georgia area. For AT&T Wireless and CanTel subscribers, coverage ceases at the north end of the Strait of Georgia. For U.S. West and B.C. Cellular subscribers, coverage extends, with a few "holes," to Port Hardy. For a fee, AT&T Wireless and CanTel subscribers can arrange for temporary service from B.C. Cellular by calling (800)661-2355. Short term and monthly programs are available.

For emergency, distress, and rescue operations, *cellular telephones are not substitutes for VHF radios.* If you have a problem and need help, get on Channel 16 and start calling. The Coast Guard and neighboring vessels will hear you. You will be impressed with the Coast Guard's efficiency and professionalism.

How to use the VHF radio

The easiest way to get a general sense of radio use is to monitor channel 16, channel 22A, and the working channels. You'll hear experienced, and inexperienced, people in action. The difference will be clear. To use the radio, call on the *calling channel,* channel 16. Pleasure craft in the U.S. are encouraged to use the alternative calling channel 09. When communication is established, switch to a *working channel* for your conversation. Except for distress, you may not have a conversation on channel 16. Channel 09 may be used for conversations, but because it is an alternate calling channel in the U.S., conversations should be brief.

Recommended reading

We can recommend two good books on radio. The first is *Chapman's Communications Afloat,* by Elbert Maloney, $14.95 U.S. The book is short, readable, and complete. The second book is *A guide for the maritime VHF radiotelephone operator,* published by Communications Canada, a branch of the Canadian Government. It is available without charge from Industry Canada.

The low power switch

VHF radios can transmit at 25 watts, their highest power rating, or at 1 watt, the low power mode. Handheld VHF radios usually have a maximum power of 4.5 to 5 watts, and low power of 1 watt. Whenever practical, use the low-power mode. Other vessels a few miles away then can use the same channel without interference from you. The difference between high power and low power affects transmission distance only. Reception ability is unaffected.

Handheld radios should use low power whenever possible. The battery lasts longer.

MAREP weather reporting

MAREP stands for Mariner Reporting Program. MAREP was set up by the Canadian Atmospheric Environment Service with the cooperation of the Canadian Coast Guard. With MAREP, individual vessels can report, in plain language, actual weather conditions around them. The weather patterns throughout the region surrounding Vancouver Island are extremely difficult to predict. Often, large differences in weather can be found across an area of just 20 miles.

MAREP stations are established around the north end of Vancouver Island at Bonilla Island, Cape Scott, and Kyuquot. While no MAREP stations are located in southern waters, the Canadian Coast Guard actively solicits reports from all vessels. If you find significant differences between the forecasted weather and your local weather, the Coast Guard wants to know. Call the Canadian Coast Guard on channels 26, 84, or 22A. Your information will be relayed to the Atmospheric Environment Service, and quite possibly will influence the next forecast. The Coast Guard has told us that it receives very few MAREP reports, and wants more.

Marine operator telephone communication

Boats that do not have cellular telephones, or boats outside the cellular telephone coverage area, will use their VHF radio and marine operators for telephone calls. The complete list of marine operators is included in this section. Calls can be made collect or billed to a calling card or credit card.

In 1996, Mari*TEL*, based in Gulfport, Mississippi, purchased the U.S. West marine operator operations in the Pacific Northwest. The marine operator channels were retained, but all services and billing now are through Mari*TEL*. Vessel owners can establish a Mari*TEL* account, which simplifies billing and provides extra security. Mari*TEL* offers a subscriber plan that limits costs to $1.49 per minute with an annual subscriber fee. Non-subscribers will pay $7.00 for the first 3 minutes, and $1.49 per minute thereafter. Non-subscribers can call collect, bill to a calling card or credit card, or use third-party billing. Marine Identification Numbers (MINs) issued by U.S. West no longer are valid. For more information, contact Mari*TEL* at (888)627-4835.

Canadian vessels can establish a marine account and Marine Identification Number (MIN) for easier billing. For more information, contact B.C. Tel at (800)663-0640 (inside B.C.), or (604)432-2574 (outside B.C.). Telephone calls also can be made through the Candian Coast Guard.

Ship to Shore Public Correspondence. *Do not call the marine operator on channel 16.* Marine operators do not monitor 16.

Washington waters: To place a call in Washington waters, select the telephone channel with the transmitter closest to your vessel location. If the channel is clear of traffic, press the transmit button for six seconds. If connection is made, you will hear recorded message with instructions from Mari*TEL*. If not, change to another nearby marine operator channel or wait until your vessel is in another location.

B.C. waters: In Canada, call the B.C. Tel marine operator on the channel closest to your vessel location. To place a call through the Canadian Coast Guard, contact the Coast Guard on channel 16. They will direct you to an appropriate working channel.

Shore to Ship Public Correspondence.

Washington waters: To place a call to any vessel cruising in U.S. waters, contact Mari*TEL* at (800)955-9025 or (888)627-4632. The Mari*TEL* operator will call the vessel on channel 16.

B.C. waters: To place a call to a vessel cruising in British Columbia waters, contact the marine operator in Vancouver, B.C. and ask the operator to call the vessel via the appropriate Canadian Coast Guard station. The Coast Guard station will call the vessel on channel 16. If the vessel does not promptly respond, the call may be put on a wait list and the vessel will be notified at each Coast Guard information broadcast.

Weather Broadcasts

WX1 CONTINUOUS BROADCAST, Seattle, Neah Bay, Cape Lazo, Alert Bay, Eliza Dome, Klemtu

WX2 CONTINUOUS BROADCAST, Saltspring Island, Nootka, Calvert Island, Mt. Gil, Dundas Island

WX3 CONTINUOUS BROADCAST, Olympia, Mt. Helmcken, Bowen Island

21B/161.65 MHz CONTINUOUS BROADCAST, Mt. Park, Discovery Mtn., Holberg, Mt. Ozzard, Mt. Hays, Kitimat

Marine Operator Channels Washington Waters

Bellingham	26/85
Everett	24
Olympia	85
Port Angeles	25
Seattle	25/26
Tacoma	28
Whidbey Is.	87

Marine Operator Channels B.C. Waters

Alert Bay	26/86
Bamfield	27
Bella Bella	25
Big Bay	25
Brooks Peninsula	87
Campbell River	27
Campbell River (Elk Falls)	64
Cape Caution	02
Courtenay	23
East Thurlow	24
Estevan Point	23
Ganges	27/64
Grenville Channel	24
Holberg	60
Jordan River	23
Kyuquot	01
Madeira Park	25
Nanaimo Harbour	87
Pachena Point	87
Parksville (Qualicum)	28
Patrick Point	24
Pender Harbour	25
Port Hardy	24
Powell River	85
Prince Rupert	25/26
Prince Rupert (Mt. Hays)	27
Rivers Inlet	03
Sarah Point	60
Sayward (Newcastle Ridge)	28
Sechelt	86
Stuart Island	25
Tofino	24
Vancouver	23/25/26
Vancouver (Bowen Island)	24
Vancouver (Fraser River)	86
Victoria.	26/86
W. Vancouver (Hood Pt.)	85
Winter Harbour	27

For a complete list of VHF channels and their use, see the last page of the special ***Cruising Coupon*** section.

The Northwest Cruiser's Bookshelf

Nautical charts. Long-time cruisers and professional mariners understand the value of nautical charts, and they have extensive libraries of charts on board. We like charts and recommend charts. If you were to navigate by the written warnings in this book and others, you could be scared off from many places. A study of the chart, however, usually shows exactly how to proceed, and in you go.

Government publications
U.S. and Canadian government publications are extremely useful. The introductions contain astonishing amounts of information, usually well-presented.

U.S. publications
- Chart No. 1 (explains chart symbols)
- Chart Catalog 2, Pacific Coast (free)
- Coast Pilot, Volume 7
- Light List, Volume 6
- Tide Tables, Current Tables (2-volume set, now privately produced. We suggest locally produced tables by Island Canoe. For Puget Sound/San Juan Islands/Strait of Juan de Fuca we *strongly recommend* Captn. Jack's Tide & Current Almanac.)

Canadian Publications
- Chart 1 (explains chart symbols)
- Canadian Aids to Navigation System
- Pacific Coast Catalog 2 of Nautical Charts and Related Publications
- Sailing Directions, British Columbia Coast (South Portion)
- Small Craft Guide, 7th Edition
- Small Craft Guide, 8th Edition
- Tide and Current Tables, vols. 5 & 6
- Current Atlas, Juan de Fuca Strait to Strait of Georgia (Use with privately-published Washburne's Tables)
- Pacific Coast List of Lights, Buoys and Fog Signals

Chart Books
Compare these different products and choose the one(s) that suit you best.
- Chart Kit
- Evergreen Pacific Cruising Atlas
- Evergreen Pacific Cruising Guide: Washington Waters
- Evergreen Pacific San Juan Cruising Atlas
- Marine Atlas, vols. 1 & 2
- Waterproof Charts (Not chart books, but privately-produced completely waterproof charts that cover all of Puget Sound, San Juan Islands, Strait of Juan de Fuca, and Gulf Islands. Excellent for small boat and cockpit use.)

Waypoint Guides
Pre-plotted waypoints for GPS or Loran.
- Weatherly Waypoint Guide, Vol. 1: Puget Sound, San Juan Islands, Strait of Juan de Fuca
- Weatherly Waypoint Guide, Vol. 2: Gulf of Georgia

Cruising Guides
Much overlap here, but all are useful, some are treasures. The Wolferstan cruising guides to B.C. are exceptional, as are those by Don Douglass.
- Captains' Handbook (Shrock & Schott)
- Coastal Companion (Upton)
- Crow's Nest Views of South Puget Sound (Vinton)
- Cruising Beyond Desolation Sound (Chappell)
- Cruising Guide to British Columbia: Desolation Sound (Wolferstan)
- Cruising Guide to British Columbia: Gulf Islands (Wolferstan)
- Cruising Guide to British Columbia: Sunshine Coast (Wolferstan)
- Cruising Guide to the West Coast of Vancouver Island (Watmough)
- Cruising Guide to Puget Sound (Scherer). Essential.
- Cruising the San Juan Islands, 2nd Edition (Calhoun)
- Docks and Destinations (Vassilopoulos)
- Explorer's Guide to Marine Parks of B.C. (Chettleburgh)
- Exploring Puget Sound & B.C. (Hinson)
- Exploring the Inside Passage to Alaska (Douglass)
- Exploring the North Coast of B.C. (Douglass)
- Exploring the South Coast of B.C. (Douglass)
- Exploring Vancouver Island's West Coast (Douglass)
- Far-Away Places (Lawrence)
- Gulf Islands Explorer (Obee)
- Gunkholing in South Puget Sound (Bailey & Nyberg)
- Gunkholing San Juan Islands; Gulf Islands; Desolation Sound (Bailey & Cummings). These books are out of print and hard to find, but worth the search.
- Henning's Guide to Boat Ramps of Washington (Helstrom)
- Marina Handbook SW B.C. (Fox)
- Marina Handbook NW Wash. (Fox)
- Middle Puget Sound Afoot & Afloat (Mueller)
- North Puget Sound Afoot & Afloat (Mueller)
- Northern Gulf Islands Explorer (Jones)
- Pacific Rim Explorer (Obee)
- San Juan Islands Afoot & Afloat (Mueller)
- South Puget Sound Afoot & Afloat (Mueller)

Boat Handling, Navigation Books
- Chapman Piloting, Seamanship, and Small Boat Handling (The bible)
- Dockmanship (How to handle a boat around a dock—wonderful)
- Marine Weather Hazards Manual (B.C. weather—excellent)
- Navigation Rules: Rules of the Road
- Northwest Marine Weather
- Southeast Alaska Current Atlas (use with the yearly Washburne's Tables for SE Alaska)

Kids
- Let's Discover the San Juan Islands
- Adventuring in Greater Puget Sound

Things to Do and Travel Guides
- Essential San Juan Islands Guide, 2nd ed.
- Walks and Hikes on the Beaches Around Puget Sound

Great Reads
- Curve of Time (The classic)
- Homesteads & Snug Harbours
- Row to Alaska by Wind and Oar
- Seven-Knot Summers
- Three's a Crew
- Upcoast Summers

Binoculars for the Boat

FINE BINOCULARS ARE A JOY to own and use, and the boat provides a perfect excuse to get some at last. Binoculars, after all, are safety equipment. They must pick out navigation aids in the gloom of mist and failing light. In those conditions only the best will do.

Long experience has shown that 7×50 binoculars work best on a boat. The 7 indicates 7× magnification; the 50 indicates the 50 mm diameter of the objective, or outside, lens. The exit pupil of a 7×50 binocular is 7 mm in diameter, which matches the typical person's eye pupil in very dim light. When the binocular exit pupil is the same size as the pupil of your eye, you get the most from the instrument's light grasp. Thus, the 7×50 binocular is called a "night glass."

Higher magnification 10×50 binoculars transmit less light. This takes them out of the night glass catagory. Also, they are much more difficult to hold steady.

You also can buy lower power binoculars, such as 6×30. On small boats especially, this can be a good way to go. With lower magnification the image is steadier, and light gathering is sufficient for all but the dimmest conditions.

On most binoculars, the outer barrels are offset, so they are wider than your eyes. This offset makes objects seem more 3D in appearance, and helps separate one object from another.

You will find 7×50 binoculars priced from under $100 (U.S.) to four figures. The better glasses have better optics, are better built, and are waterproof.

Better optics. The saying is old but true: "You can get good optics and cheap optics, but you can't get good, cheap optics." With high-quality optics the image is sharp from the centers to the edges. With low-quality optics the image may or may not be sharp at the centers, and almost certainly will not be sharp at the edges. High-quality optics have a series of costly coatings that reduce glare and improve the transmission of light. Low-quality optics will be coated, but not as well as high-quality optics. With good optics, a red buoy in the distance will appear as red, even at last light; with poor optics the buoy could be gray.

Better built. If the two barrels of the binocular are not perfectly aligned, the binocular will not be sharp. You may see the buoy but be unable to read its number. High-quality binoculars are built more strongly, so the barrels will be more apt to stay in alignment. Inside, all the optics themselves are mounted more solidly. With high-quality binoculars, alignment can be restored if dropping or a blow knocks them out of alignment.

Rubber armor coating keeps a binocular from sliding around on a hard surface, helps it absorb shock, and will protect against minor bumps. The armor does not, however, make a fragile instrument rugged, and binoculars are fragile instruments.

As Bill Cook, the manager of the optical shop at Captain's Nautical Supplies, in Seattle, points out, "You can rubber coat an egg, but it's still an egg. Armored or not, if you drop your $800 binocular on something harder than a soft grassy lawn, chances are good that you'll be in for a costly surprise."

Waterproof. Binoculars are dry nitrogen charged and made waterproof so they won't draw air (and humidity) inside. Once inside the binocular, moisture can fog the glass and corrode internal parts. In the moist marine environment, a waterproof binocular will work without fogging.

While the built-in compass has nothing to do with the quality of optics, construction, or waterproofing, many of the better marine binoculars are equipped with compasses. You can buy a binocular with a compass or without, however. Bill Cook, from Captain's, points out that as a repairman he finds a binocular's compass to be the part most often damaged. The compass "sticks out" from the binocular, and is vulnerable.

You can compare such things as sharpness, color transmission and ease of handling during the day, but the only way to compare low-light ability is in low light. Only in dim light can you compare night glasses for their image brightness.

About cost. High quality marine binoculars, with compass, cost $600-$1000 (U.S.). Without the compass deduct $50-$100. For a couple hundred dollars less you give up only a small amount of brightness. It's wise to try before you buy. See how different glasses feel in your hands, up to your eyes, and around your neck. Whether you buy the best binoculars or the cheapest, you probably intend to keep them for many years. The question comes down to how well they will work when you need them most, and how proud you will be of them.

State and Provincial Parks and Public Wharves

The waters from Puget Sound north into B.C. are dotted with more than 200 state and provincial parks, and in B.C., more than 220 public wharves. The properties range from primitive, with no amenities, to fully developed, with well-tended trails, ample parking, docks and mooring buoys, running water and hot showers, campsites, interpretive centers and park rangers.

Washington Parks

At the state level, parks are administered by the Washington State Parks Department and by the Department of Natural Resources (DNR). Usually, DNR sites are on the primitive side. State Parks, which tend to be more developed, often charge for overnight moorage at buoys and docks. For docks and floats, expect to pay $8 per night for boats under 26 feet, $11 per night for boats 26 feet and over. For mooring buoys expect to pay $5 per night. No fee is charged for anchoring. Day use is free.

Most state parks charge moorage fees from May 1 through September 30, except year-round at Blake Island, Jarrell Cove, Fort Worden, Cornet Bay (Deception Pass), and Mystery Bay.

Annual moorage permits are valid from January 1 through December 31. Permits cost $50 for boats under 26 feet, and $80 for boats 26 feet and over. You can get a permit through any park that charges moorage fees, or through the Washington State Parks Moorage Permit Program, (360)902-8608.

Campsite fees must be paid in addition to dock or mooring buoy fees. The annual moorage permit does not apply to campsite fees.

Self-register ashore for moorage or campsites. If a ranger must come out to your boat, you may be charged an additional $5 (even if you have an annual permit displayed). Moorage is limited to 72 hours at any park.

Watercraft launch sites

State parks with watercraft launches charge fees of $3 or $4, depending on the park. Watercraft launching is without charge if a campsite fee has been paid. An additional $1 launch fee is charged at "Popular Destination" parks: Birch Bay, Deception Pass, Fort Canby, Fort Casey, Fort Ebey, Fort Worden, and Larrabee.

Annual launch permits cost $40. If you buy before April 30, the cost is $30. Contact Washington State Parks HQ, (360)902-8608.

Reservations

Washington state parks moorage is unreserved. Leaving a dinghy or other personal property at a buoy or dock does not reserve moorage. Rafting is permitted but not mandatory. Rafting is allowed on buoys, within safe limits.

Reservations (for campsites only) in all state parks are now accepted. For more information, call toll-free at (800)452-5687.

Department of Natural Resources parks generally are primitive or have few facilities, and most do not charge fees.

B.C. Parks

British Columbia has an extensive marine parks system. Most parks have floats or mooring buoys, and most have safe, all-weather anchorages. Marine parks are open year-round. Some have no on-shore facilities, others have day-use facilities, picnic areas, and developed campsites. Parks with developed campsites will have toilet facilities. Most parks have drinking water, although you might see signs at the taps instructing that water be boiled before drinking. Some parks turn the water off in the winter.

Moorage fees are charged at only three B.C. Provincial marine parks: Sidney Spit, Newcastle Island, and Montague Harbour. Tent sites at these parks are extra.

No rafting is permitted on mooring buoys. One boat per buoy. For more information and maps of B.C. Parks, contact B.C. Parks General Information, (250)387-5002.

Government Wharves

In British Columbia, government wharves provide moorage for commercial vessels (primarily the fishing fleet) and pleasure craft. Commercial fishing boats have priority at many government wharves. Especially in the off-season, government wharves are filled with fishing boats, leaving little or no moorage for pleasure boats. Facilities vary, from a dock only to fully-serviced marinas. Most of the fully-serviced marinas now are operated by local harbor authorities or their equivalents (see below). Government wharves are easily identified by their red-painted railings.

The Canadian government is in the process of divesting control of its wharves to local authorities. Locally run public wharves charge market rates, and may reserve space for pleasure craft. Moorage fees vary.

For more information on government wharves in B.C., call (604)666-6271.

A mother and daughter feed a tame deer at Jones Island Marine State Park in the San Juan Islands.

Waterways, Bays, and Marinas

Olympia to Prince Rupert

Marinas • Fuel Docks • State Parks • Provincial Parks • Piloting • Anchoring

A beautiful sunset silhouettes the marina and moored boats at Duncanby Landing, Rivers Inlet, B.C.

In the chapters that follow, THE WAGGONER CRUISING GUIDE presents complete and up-to-date information about the waterways and facilities between Olympia and Prince Rupert, including the West Coast of Vancouver Island.

The data on marinas, fuel docks, and state and provincial parks was compiled by direct interview right up to press time. The descriptions of waterways and anchorages are from our own experience, and the experience of people we trust.

South Puget Sound

Olympia • Case Inlet • Carr Inlet • Tacoma Narrows

Charts	
18448	Puget Sound, Southern Part (1:80,000)
18445sc	FOLIO SMALL-CRAFT Puget Sound—Possession Sound to Olympia including Hood Canal (1:80,000) [excellent]
18456	Olympia Harbor and Budd Inlet (1:20,000)
18457	Puget Sound—Hammersly Inlet to Shelton (1:20,000)

BUDD, ELD, TOTTEN INLETS

Budd Inlet (Olympia) Use chart 18456 (recommended); 18448. The entrance to Budd Inlet is a mile wide between Dofflemeyer Point and Cooper Point, and deep enough for all recreational boats. Approaching from the north, simply round Dofflemeyer Point, where a minor light blinks every 10 seconds, and head for the Capitol dome (unless the fog from a convening Legislature obscures it). Continue past Olympia Shoal, which is marked by lights on piling structures on the shoal's east and west sides. From Olympia Shoal pick up the 28-foot-deep dredged and buoyed channel that leads into the harbor. A spoils bank, from channel dredging, lies east of the channel. The spoils area is quite shoal. Parts of it dry. Stay in the channel.

South of the privately-owned West Bay Marina the channel branches at a piling intersection marker. The eastern leg leads to the Port of Olympia's East Bay Marina; the western, or main, channel leads past the Port docks to moorages at the head of the inlet. On both sides of the channel, the water shoals rapidly to drying flats. Stay well within the channel.

Moorages in Olympia include the privately-owned West Bay Marina on the west side of Budd Inlet; the Port of Olympia's East Bay Marina; Percival Landing; and the Olympia Yacht Club. The Olympia Yacht Club has guest moorage for members of reciprocal yacht clubs only. A timbered walkway surrounds the Percival Landing area. It's a pleasant place for a stroll, with an excellent view of harbor activities.

All the moorages give access to Olympia, including the Capitol itself, which is just a few blocks uptown. Deschutes Basin, the southernmost tip of Puget Sound, and Capitol Lake are blocked by a dam and crossed by city streets. They are used by small boats launched from the city park just across the street from Percival Landing and the yacht club.

Anchorage in Budd Inlet is in 10 to 20 feet, mud bottom, along both shores, with Butler Cove and Tykle Cove preferred. Many waterfront homeowners have mooring buoys along the shores, so consider your swinging room when choosing an anchoring site. A launch ramp is located at the Thurston County park just south of Boston Harbor near Dofflemeyer Point, and the City of Olympia's Priest Point Park has one of the finest sand beaches in southern Puget Sound.

Dining: Budd Bay Cafe

① **Percival Landing Park,** 217 Thurston Ave., Olympia, WA 98501. (360)753-8382. Located at the southern tip of Budd Inlet, adjacent to downtown Olympia, near shopping, restaurants, other facilities. Guest moorage accommodates 50-70 boats in two sections: one (50 boats) with 30 amp power; one with no power. Both sections share restrooms, showers, pumpout, portapotty dump. Nearby doctor, post office, groceries, liquor store. Limited guest moorage during Wooden Boat Show, May 9-11, 1997; Olympia Lakefair, July 15-20, 1997; Harbor Days, with its tugboat races, August 29-Sept. 1, 1997. Percival Landing has a lovely promenade, and is the center of Olympia's boating activity.

② **West Bay Marina,** 2100 West Bay Drive, Olympia, WA 98502. (360)943-2022. Located on west side of Budd Inlet, a short distance from town. Open all year. Diesel and gasoline at the fuel dock. Guest moorage in unoccupied slips as available. Haulout, restrooms, showers, laundry, pumpout, 20 & 30 amp power, marine supply store, restraurant. *(Marina map page 32)*

③ **Port of Olympia/East Bay Marina,** 1022 Marine Drive NE, Olympia, WA 98501. (360)786-1400. Monitors VHF channel 65A. Open all year, guest moorage available, no fuel. Restrooms, showers, laundry, pumpout, portapotty dump, 20 & 30 amp power. Two-lane launch ramp, dry boat storage. Nearby fuel, groceries, restaurants, post office, doctor, liquor store. Downtown Olympia is within walking distance.

Percival Landing, Olympia, at the south end of Budd Inlet. Puget Sound begins here.

Reference only — not for navigation

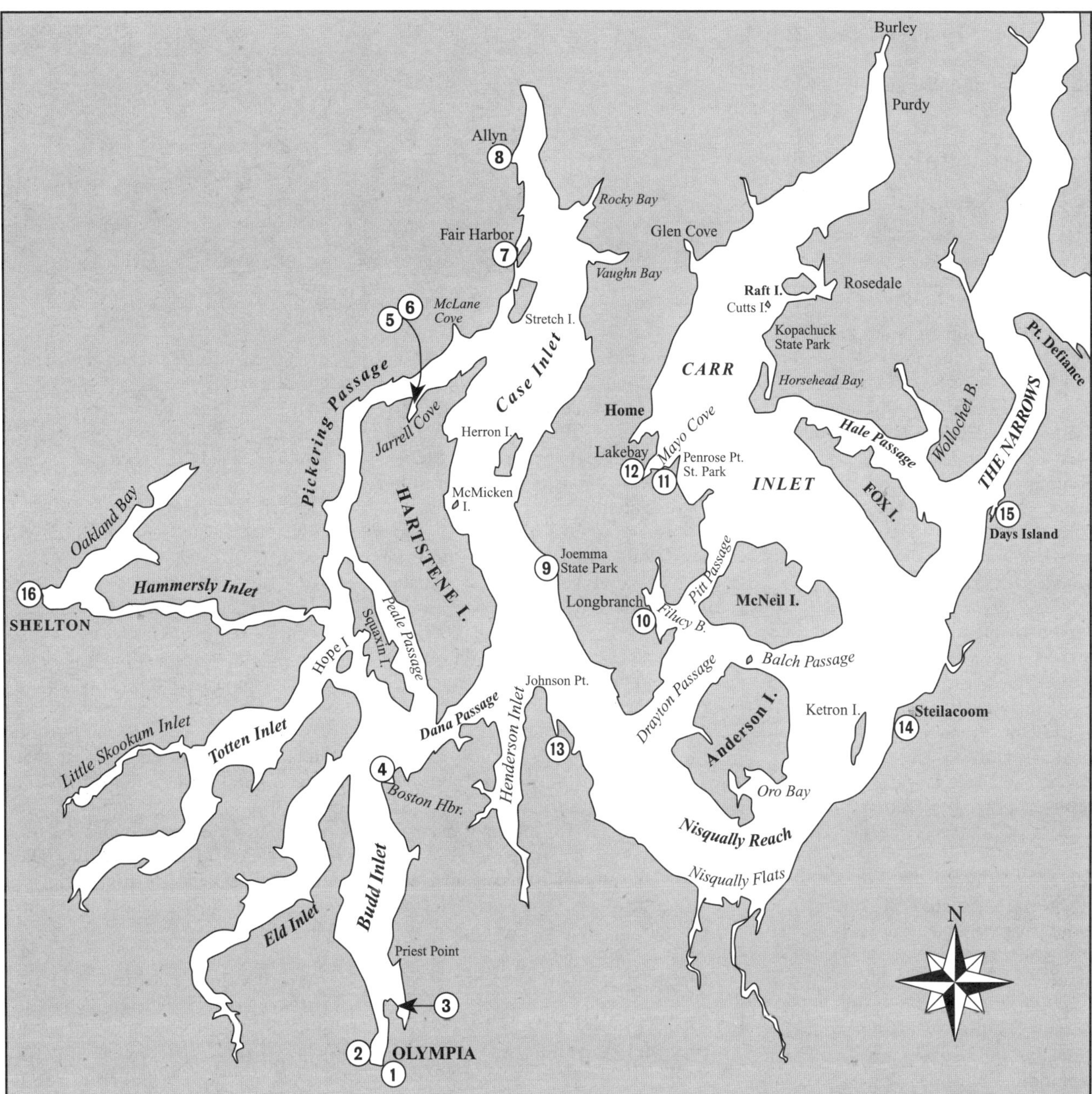

Priest Point Park, at Priest Point, east side of Budd Inlet. Open summer and winter, day use only. Restrooms, no showers, no power. Anchor out only, well offshore due to shoaling. Park is 250 acres. Stretch of sandy beach, picnic tables and shelters, children's play equipment, trails.

Burfoot County Park, ½ mile south of Dofflemeyer Point. This is a 60-acre county park, open all year, day use only. Restrooms, no showers, no power. Has picnic tables and shelters, trails, play area. Anchoring or beaching only. Buoys mark an artificial reef for scuba diving.

Boston Harbor. Use chart 18448. Boston Harbor is a halfmoon-shaped bay between Dofflemeyer Point and Dover Point. Anchorage is possible, but this bay is the site of Boston Harbor Marina.

④ **Boston Harbor Marina,** 312 73rd Ave. NE, Olympia, WA 98506, (360)357-5670. Open all year, six guest slips, gasoline and diesel, CNG, 20 amp power, picnic area, restrooms, no showers. Easily seen from the mouth of Boston Harbor. The store has groceries and ice, some marine supplies, rentals. *(Marina map page 32)*

Eld Inlet. Use chart 18448. Eld Inlet lies immediately west of Budd Inlet, and extends about five miles south from Cooper Point before it becomes Mud Bay (aptly named). Hold to a mid-channel course past Cooper Point, which has an extensive drying shoal northward from the point.

Eld Inlet has no marinas, but anchorage is good, mud bottom, along both shores. A shallow bay about a mile south of Flapjack Point includes Sam Devlin's boat building shop and an unused marine railway, as well as a launch ramp. Directly across the inlet is the waterfront activities center for The Evergreen State College. The center has a float, and buildings to store the canoes and other

See area map page 27

small craft used by the students. Despite considerable research [Kincaid], we are unable to confirm that nude bathing occurs at the site.

Frye Cove County Park, just north of Flapjack Point in Eld Inlet. Open all year for day use only, toilets, no other services. Anchoring or beaching only. The park has picnic shelters, barbecues, hiking trails.

Hope Island Marine State Park, junction of Totten Inlet and Pickering Passage. Use chart 18448. This is one of the newest parks in the state system, and is essentially undeveloped. A resident caretaker lives on the island. The park has a mooring buoy, and decent anchorage can be had in 30 feet or less on the east side. Other than trails through primeval woods, no facilities ashore. No fires permitted, pack out all garbage.

Totten Inlet. Use chart 18448. Enter Totten Inlet past Steamboat Island. Steamboat Island is connected to the mainland by a causeway from Carlyon Beach. Homes and a private marina are located on the island and mainland beach. The beach is marked by a quick flashing light. All of Totten Inlet is less than 10 fathoms deep. The inlet shoals to drying mud flats toward its south end, called Oyster Bay.

On the west side of Totten Inlet, about three miles southwest of Steamboat Island, is the entrance to **Skookum Inlet**, called by the locals "Little Skookum," to differentiate it from Hammersley Inlet, which they call "Big Skookum." Little Skookum is a pleasant exploration, but not navigable beyond Wildcat Harbor except by dinghy. Little Skookum contains one of Southern Puget Sound's major oyster growing areas.

HAMMERSLY INLET AND SHELTON

Hammersley Inlet. Use chart 18457 (recommended); 18448. Hammersley Inlet extends westward about 6 miles to Oakland Bay and the city of **Shelton**. A marked shoal blocks the entrance to Hammersley Inlet, with the preferred channel to the north of the buoy marking the shoal. The shoal has geoducks—Contributing Editor Tom Kincaid admits that he dug some there one day while he was aground. As chart 18457 shows, depths in Hammersley Inlet range from 10-30 feet. Currents flood into Hammersley Inlet and ebb out. The strongest currents occur around Cape Horn, a sharp, constricted bend just inside the entrance.

Jarrell's Cove Marina has complete facilitites. The Marine State Park is directly across the cove.

Moorage is available at the Shelton Yacht Club, and is about a mile from town. Shelton is the site of major lumber and pulp mills, with acres of rafted logs in storage in front of the town. **Oakland Bay** becomes increasingly shallow north of Shelton, but is navigable at other than extreme low tide, and could offer anchorage in mud bottom.

⑯ **Port of Shelton,** West 410 Business Park Rd., Shelton, WA, 98584, (360)426-1151. The marina is managed by the Shelton Yacht Club, (360)426-9476. Generally 15-20 slips available for visiting boats of average size. No fuel. Least depth 10 feet, 30 amp power, pumpout, but no restrooms, no showers. Groceries, restaurants, services 1 mile.

PEALE AND PICKERING PASSAGES AND CASE INLET

Pickering Passage. Use chart 18448. Pickering Passage extends northward from Totten Inlet past the west sides of Squaxin Island and Hartstene Island. Mid-channel courses encounter no obstructions. **Peale Passage** extends along the east side of Squaxin Island, through shallow but passable depths. The **Squaxin Island State Park** is closed. Too bad. It was lovely.

Hartstene Island. Use chart 18448. Hartstene Island is connected to the mainland at Graham Point by a bridge with a Mean High Water vertical clearance of 31 feet. Along the northwest shore of the island is **Jarrell Cove**, which contains both a 43-acre Jarrell's Cove State Marine Park and the Jarrell's Cove Marina.

The small marina between Jarrell Cove and Dougall Point is private, and serves Hartstene Island residents.

⑤ **Jarrell's Cove Marina,** E. 220 Wilson Rd., Hartstene Island, Shelton, WA 98584, (800)362-8823, (360)426-8823. Use chart 18448. The fuel dock has diesel and gasoline. Facilities include 30 amp power, restrooms, showers, laundry, pumpout, portapotty dump, 200 feet of guest moorage. Get a slip assignment from the fuel dock before landing, even for a short stay. This is a large, well-maintained marina with many facilities, and a popular destination for boating groups. The store has groceries, ice, some marine hardware, books. Open 7 days a week Memorial Day to Labor Day, closed Mondays and Tuesdays during the winter. Owners: Gary and Lorna Hink. *(Marina map page 29)*

⑥ **Jarrell's Cove Marine State Park,** northwest end of Hartstene Island, (360)426-9266. Open all year. This is a large, attractive park with 682 feet of dock space, 14 mooring buoys, restrooms, showers, pumpout, portapotty dump, picnic shelters, standard campsites. Mooring buoys have minimum 10 feet of water at all times, but the dock can rest on mud bottom on minus tides. Fishing, clamming, hiking, birdwatching.

McLane Cove, located across Pickering Passage from Jarrell Cove, is protected, quiet, and lined with forest. Anchorage is in 10 to 20 feet. It is a peaceful alternative to the more popular Jarrell Cove.

Stretch Island. Use chart 18448. Stretch Island has good anchorage in the bay that lies south of the bridge to the mainland. The bridge has a 14-foot vertical clearance. The channel under the

See area map page 27

bridge goes dry at low tide. The 4-acre Stretch Point State Park has mooring buoys but no other facilities.

Stretch Point Marine State Park, Stretch Island. Open all year, accessible only by boat. No power, water, restrooms or showers. Day use only, with 5 buoys for overnight mooring. Buoys are close to shore because of a steep dropoff. Swimming and diving, oysters and mussels, smooth sand beach. Rustic shelters have been built on shore, but no camping is allowed. Pack out all garbage.

Reach Island. Use chart 18448. The southern end of Reach Island is **Fair Harbor**, home of Fair Harbor Marina. The bay provides limited anchorage only. The channel north of the marina, under a bridge with a vertical clearance of 16 feet, goes dry on a minus tide.

⑦ **Fair Harbor Marina,** P.O. Box 160, E. 5050 Grapeview Loop Rd., Grapeview, WA 98546, (360)426-4028. Open 7 days in the summer, call for hours in the winter. Gasoline only at the fuel dock, 350 feet of guest moorage, 30 amp power. Showers and washrooms are planned for the 1997 season. A comfortable marina in a lovely setting, owned and operated by Susan and Vern Nelson. Best to call ahead for moorage space. Has facilities for minor repairs and haulout. Kerosene, alcohol, propane, charts, hardware, tackle & bait, groceries, picnic areas. If you wish to golf at Lakeland golf course or visit the Maritime Museum of Puget Sound, both nearby, you must call well ahead to arrange for transportation.

Allyn. The town of Allyn, located near the head of Case Inlet, has a launch ramp and limited moorage on a float at the end of a long pier. Allyn is surrounded by shoal water, but can be approached by holding a midchannel course until opposite the pier, then turning in.

⑧ **Port of Allyn,** P.O. Box 1, Foot of Drum St., Allyn, WA, 98524, (360)275-2192. Open all year, launch ramp, 10 slips, 20 & 30 amp power, restrooms, no showers, no fuel. Shallow; no sailboats or large boats on low tides. Services and restaurants nearby.

Rocky Bay. Rocky Bay offers some protection for anchoring, particularly behind a small sandspit extending from Windy Bluff. Enter with caution, and round the little rocky islet off the end of the spit before circling in to anchor.

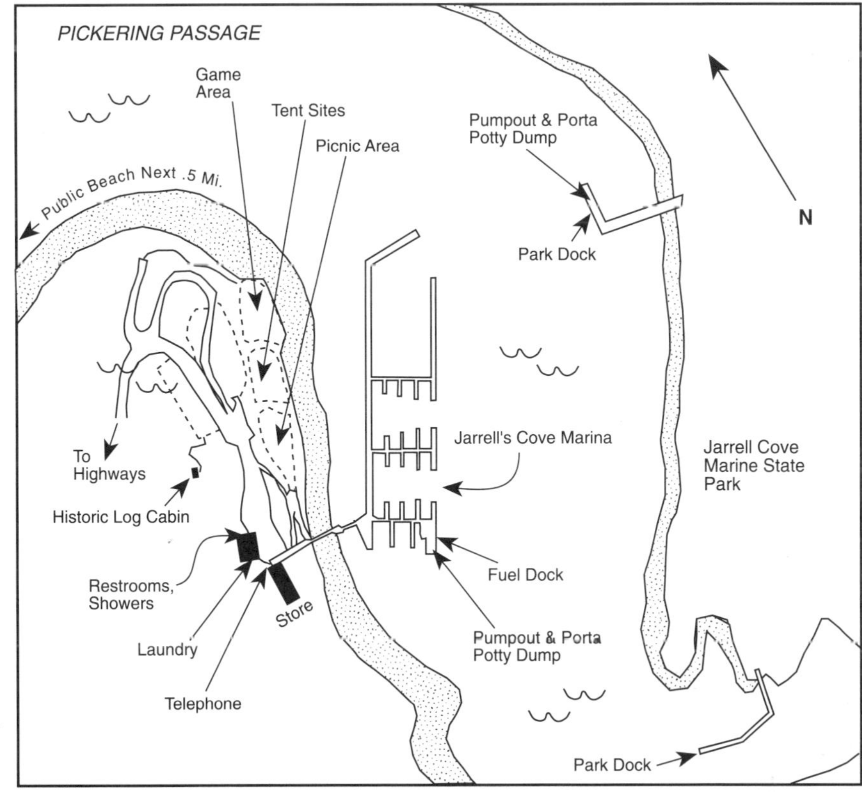

Jarrell Cove

Vaughn Bay. Use chart 18448. Vaughn Bay can be entered at half-tide or better. Take a mid-channel course past the end of the spit, then turn to parallel the spit until safe anchoring depths are found near the head of the bay. Water skiers and jet-ski enthusiasts can be disruptive during the day, but they quit at sundown and leave the bay peaceful during the night. The small town of Vaughn on the north shore has a launch ramp and some supplies.

Herron Island. Herron Island is all privately owned, with a ferry to the mainland.

McMicken Island Marine State Park, on Case Inlet, off the east side of Hartstene Island, (360)426-9226. Use chart 18448. Open all year, 5 mooring buoys, toilets, but no power, water or showers. Mooring buoys lie on the north and south sides of McMicken Island. There's plenty of room to anchor on either side, good bottom. McMicken Island is accessible by boat only, except on low tides, when you can cross to Hartstene Island by foot. You'll find primitive trails, but watch for poison oak. No overnight camping. An artificial reef is north of the island. Fishing, good clamming, camping, swimming. Do not pass east of McMicken Island because of a drying spit and an uncharted rock (we touched there once, in a boat that draws less than 3 feet).

Hartstene Island State Park, east shore of Hartstene Island. This park lies across the bay from McMicken Island, and was acquired by the state park system in 1990. Open all year, day use only, no power, water or toilets. Hiking trail. At low tide you can cross to McMicken Island State Park. Anchoring only. Clamming and beachcombing.

⑨ **Joemma State Park,** formerly Robert F. Kennedy State Park, southeast Case Inlet, just north of Whitman Cove. Summer only, closed October through April. The park has 500 feet of dock space, 4 mooring buoys, boat launch, new restrooms, picnic areas, primitive campsites, no power, no showers. This is the most recent addition to the state marine parks system, and includes a Cascadia Marine Trail campsite. The park is not highly developed, but it's close to a number of public beaches, some of them

See area map page 27

marked by white square posts. Most of the beach is privately owned.

DRAYTON PASSAGE, PITT PASSAGE, BALCH PASSAGE

Anderson Island. Use chart 18448. Taylor Bay offers limited anchorage near the entrance, but is exposed to southerlies. **Oro Bay** has a shallow entrance, but limited good anchorage is available once inside. Tacoma Yacht Club and Bremerton Yacht Club have outstations in Oro Bay. **Amsterdam Bay** is very shallow. Safe anchoring depths are right in the middle, when that spot is not already occupied by local residents' boats. Amsterdam Bay's shores are rural and picturesque. If low tide isn't too low, it's a good place to spend the night. **Eagle Island Marine State Park,** off the north shore of Anderson Island, has mooring buoys.

Eagle Island Marine State Park, Balch Passage, between Anderson Island and McNeil Island. Use chart 18448. Open all year, day use only, 3 mooring buoys, no toilets, power or water. Boat access only. Avoid the reef, marked by a buoy, off the west side of the island. Fishing and clamming. Watch for poison oak on the island. No camping or fires, no garbage collection.

Filucy Bay. Use chart 18448. Filucy Bay is a popular destination and a fine anchorage. You can anchor inside the spit to the south of the entrance. The north section of Filucy Bay is wooded, quiet, and protected, with good bottom. The Longbranch Marina welcomes visiting boaters. A store is across the road from the docks.

⑩ **Longbranch Improvement Club Marina,** P.O. Box 111, Longbranch, WA, 98349, (206)884-5137. Monitors VHF channel 16, switch to 68. A popular south sound stopover. Open all year, but hours vary in winter. Has 45 slips plus 800 feet of dock space for guest moorage. The marina has 30 amp power, portable toilets, no showers.

Glen Miller is the dockmaster. He makes life on the Longbranch docks extremely pleasant, with docking assistance, gentle banter, introductions, and a close eye on everything. Expansion of the docks was completed in 1996. Usually, there is no charge for 2-hour day moorage, but if day moorage boats are taking space from incoming overnight boats, they may be asked to pay a fee or move along. Anchorage is available in the sheltered bay.

Glen Miller is the longtime dockmaster at Longbranch Improvement Club Marina.

The new covered area (left side of photo) and excellent docks make Longbranch a popular stop.

Nearby groceries, tackle and bait. Mechanic and divers on call. Dances are held Memorial Day, Fourth of July, and Labor Day at the Longbranch Improvement Club; though they are usually sold out. Great views of Mt. Rainier.

Pitt Passage. Use chart 18445sc (highly recommended), or 18448. Pitt Passage is a winding, shallow passage between McNeil Island and the mainland. Because the passage is shoal, many skippers avoid it. Safe passages can be made, however, between tiny Pitt Island and McNeil Island. The water west of Pitt Island is shoal.

If you are coming from the south (such as from Longbranch), set a course to pass the red buoy 6 and the red daymark 4 off your port side by about 50 yards. Continue toward McNeil Island until you can turn north and pass the red daybeacon 2, off the north tip of Pitt Island, by about 50 yards. Once abeam daybeacon 2, bear left to pass Wyckoff Shoal buoy 3 by about 50 yards on your starboard side. From there, bear toward Wyckoff Shoal buoy 1, to clear it to starboard by 50 yards.

Buoy 6, at the south end of Pitt Island, and the Wycoff Shoal Buoy 3 have

See area map page 27

been added since the most recent chart reprinting, and do not appear on charts. McNeil Island is the site of a major state prison, and boaters are asked to maintain a 100-yard clearance from its shores.

CARR INLET

Mayo Cove. Use chart 18448. Mayo Cove has Penrose Point State Park on its eastern shore, and the town of Lakebay, complete with a marina, at the head of the bay. The bay is shallow, and drying shoals on either side require a mid-channel approach, but Mayo Cove is very pretty and worth the visit. For exploring, take the dinghy up the inlet that leads to Bay Lake.

Penrose Point State Park has a good dock and excellent facilities ashore.

⑪ **Penrose Point Marine State Park,** west shore of Carr Inlet at Mayo Cove, (206)884-2514. Summers, open for mooring and camping 7 days; winters day use only, except overnight mooring weekends and holidays. Dock has 304 feet of tie-up space, 8 mooring buoys and a mooring float. The float will ground on lower tides. This is a large and popular park, and an excellent destination in South Sound. Facilities include picnic sites, restrooms, showers, pumpout, portapotty dump, showers. No power. Standard and primitive campsites, hiking trails, nature trail, clamming, swimming, fishing. At low tide enter the cove with care.

⑫ **Lakebay Marina,** 15 Lorenz Road K.P.S., Lakebay, WA 98349, (206)884-3350. Open all year, gasoline at fuel dock, propane available, 10 slips guest moorage, launch ramp, fishing supplies, restrooms, no showers. You may have to call ahead for services in the winter. Maximum boat length 50 feet, draft 6 feet. Groceries, ice, beer and wine.

Von Geldern Cove. Use chart 18448. Von Geldern Cove is a shallow bay, but anchorage is possible near the entrance, although exposed to northerly winds. Most of the shoreline is residential. The town of Home, with a launch ramp, has some supplies. Take the dinghy under the bridge at the head of the bay and explore the creek until it gets too shallow.

Maple Hollow State Park, Carr Inlet, across from Kopachuck State Park. Use chart 18448. Open all year, day use only, with overnight moorage. Has 2 mooring buoys, toilets, no power or showers. Enjoy hiking trails, picnic areas with pit toilets. No overnight camping.

Glen Cove is protected by a spit, but is very shallow and not recommended for overnight anchorage.

Rosedale is a small community tucked in behind **Raft Island**. Use chart 18448. Good anchorage. Enter the bay to the north of Raft Island, since a causeway connects the island to the mainland across the very shoal south side.

Cutts Island Marine State Park, Carr Inlet. Open all year, day use only and overnight moorage, 9 mooring buoys. Accessible by boat only. Toilets, but no power or water. No camping or fires on island. Underwater marine park. Easy row to Kopachuck Marine State Park. Cutts Island is connected to Raft Island by a drying shoal.

Kopachuck Marine State Park, 2 miles north of Fox Island, just north of Horsehead Bay, (206)265-3606. Open all year for day use, overnight camping and mooring. Two mooring buoys, restrooms, showers. Good bottom for anchoring if buoys are occupied, but unprotected. Underwater park with artificial reef for scuba diving. Kitchen shelters, picnic sites. Standard and primitive campisites, including a Cascadia Marine Trail campsite. Playground, short trail. Clamming, fishing. Swimming in shallow water off the beach area.

Horsehead Bay. Use chart 18448. Horsehead Bay is an excellent anchorage, surrounded by fine homes. A launch ramp is near the harbor entrance. On one visit we tried several times to anchor just inside the gravel spit that separates Horsehead Bay from Carr Inlet, but couldn't get the anchor to bite. A short distance inside the bay brought excellent holding ground.

Fox Island. Use chart 18448. Fox Island is connected to the mainland by a bridge across Hale Passage. The bridge has a 31-foot vertical clearance at high water. Good anchorage can be found behind **Tanglewood Island**, which has a pavilion frequently used by yacht clubs and other groups for special occasions. Residents of Fox Island are very protective of their privacy, so it would be a good idea to stay aboard until invited ashore.

Wollochet Bay. Use chart 18448. Wollochet Bay winds a couple of miles into the mainland off Hale Passage. The shores of the bay are lined with homes, many with mooring buoys out front, but good anchorage can be found. The mouth of the bay is open to southerly winds. Inside, the waters are protected. Tacoma Yacht Club has an outstation near the head of the bay.

Ketron Island is privately owned, and has a ferry service to Steilacoom.

See area map page 27

HENDERSON INLET, NISQUALLY, STEILACOOM, TACOMA NARROWS

Henderson Inlet. Use chart 18448. Henderson Inlet extends about 5 miles south from Itsami Ledge. The inlet has been the site of major logging operations over the years, and log rafts are still stored along the west side. Anchorage is good along about half of the inlet before it becomes too shallow, near the entrance to Woodward Creek.

⑬ **Zittel's Marina, Inc.,** 9144 Gallea St. NE, Olympia, WA 98506, (360)459-1950. Open all year, hours may vary in the winter. Gasoline and diesel at fuel dock. Guest moorage in unoccupied slips when available (don't count on availability), 20 & 30 amp power, restrooms, no showers. Haulout and repairs available, store with limited marine supplies, groceries, stove alcohol, bait and tackle.

Johnson Point is a popular salmon fishing area. Two launch ramps are located at Johnson Point, but no facilities for visiting boaters.

Tolmie Marine State Park, 8 miles northeast of Olympia. Open all year for day use and overnight moorage, except closed Mondays and Tuesdays for day use in winter. Five mooring buoys, restrooms, showers, but no power. Buoys lie well offshore; beach and shallows extend out some distance. The underwater park for scuba diving includes sunken wooden barges. Hiking trails, picnic sites with kitchens. Nice sandy beach. The park includes a small saltwater lagoon marsh area with interesting wildlife. No camping.

Nisqually Reach. Use chart 18448. Nisqually Reach is the body of water south of Anderson Island to the mainland. It is a navigable channel marked by buoys and the extensive mudflats of the Nisqually River delta. The delta area is a wildlife refuge. It is accessible by boat only at half-tide or better, by way of the Luhrs Beach launch ramp near Nisqually Head. Contributing Editor Tom Kincaid has entered the river itself by dinghy, but from the water side the entrance is hard to spot.

Steilacoom. Use chart 18448. There is very limited moorage at Steilacoom Marina. A picnic area is on a small pebble beach nearby. Steilacoom has a launch ramp, float and fishing pier.

⑭ **Steilacoom Marina,** P.O. Box 88876, 402 First Street, Steilacoom, WA 98388, (206)582-2600. Open all year, 100 feet of guest moorage, 20 amp power, restrooms, showers, laundry, portapotty dump. Convenience store has a little bit of everything. Steilacoom, incorporated in 1854, is the oldest incorporated town in Washington. If you'd like to see a real, old-style soda fountain, Bair Drug, a short distance away, is the place. Restaurant and other services nearby.

Tacoma Narrows. Use chart 18474; 18448. All of the water in southern Puget Sound flows through Tacoma Narrows, with 3-4 knot currents common. At the south end of the Narrows on the east side is Day Island, home to the Day Island Yacht Club, Narrows Marina, and Day Island Marina. The yacht club, which recently dredged its moorage, welcomes members of reciprocal yacht clubs. The Tacoma Narrows Bridge is one of the world's longest suspension bridges. It is more than a mile long in its entirety, has a 180-foot vertical clearance in the center, and is nearly ½ mile wide between the massive piers that support the cables.

If you go through the Tacoma Narrows against the current, you can find opposite-flowing current along the sides.

⑮ **Narrows Marina Bait & Tackle,** 9007 S 19th St., Tacoma, WA 98466, (206)564-4222. Open all year, gasoline and diesel fuel. Has restrooms, no showers. Launch ramp, nautical charts, electronics, hardware, tackle and bait. This is a large, fishing and marine oriented stop.

Titlow Park, Tacoma Narrows Waterway. Located on the Tacoma side, about 1 mile south of the Tacoma Narrows Bridge. Open all year, mooring buoys, park with swimming pool, volleyball, and tennis courts. Titlow Park is a state-designated marine preserve, with excellent diving.

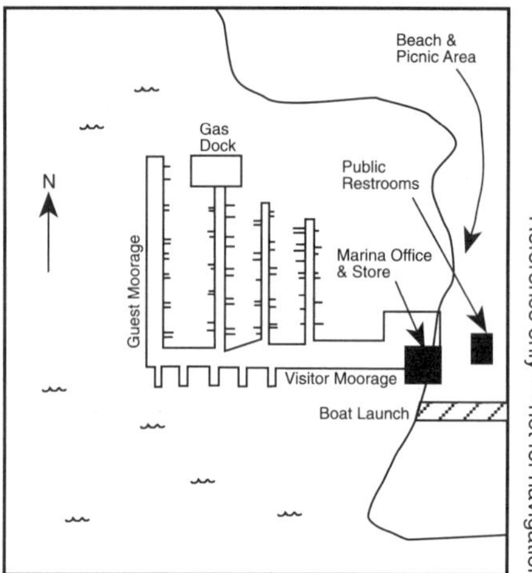

Boston Harbor Marina

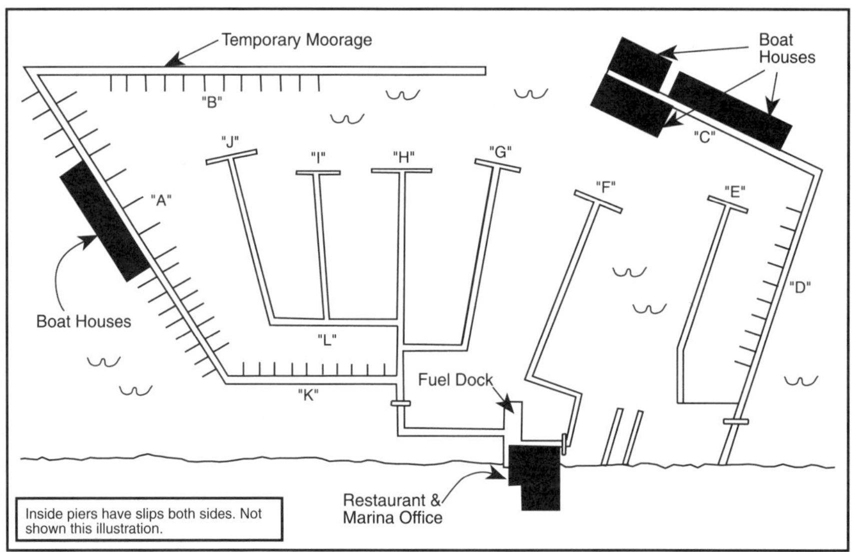

West Bay Marina

Reference only — not for navigation

Central Puget Sound

Gig Harbor • Tacoma • Vashon Island • Bremerton • Poulsbo Bainbridge Island • Seattle

Charts

18441	Puget Sound—Northern Part (1:80,000)
18474	Puget Sound—Shilshole Bay to Commencement Bay (1:40,000)
18449	Puget Sound—Seattle to Bremerton (1:25,000)
18446	Puget Sound-Apple Cove Pt. to Keyport (1:25,000) & Agate Passage (1:10,000)
18445SC	FOLIO SMALL-CRAFT Puget Sound-Possession Sound to Olympia including Hood Canal (1:80,000)
18447SC	FOLIO SMALL-CRAFT Lake Washington Ship Canal (1:10,000) & Lk. Washington (1:25,000)

GIG HARBOR

Gig Harbor. Use chart 18474; 18448. Gig Harbor is one of the most perfectly protected harbors in all of Puget Sound. The south shore is lined with moorages that serve large commercial fishing and pleasure boat fleets. The entrance to Gig Harbor is narrow, especially at low tide. Maintain a mid-channel course around the end of the spit.

Gig Harbor offers all services to boaters, from overnight moorage to major repairs and haulouts. Anchorage is available throughout most of the bay, although it shoals close to both shores and toward the head of the bay. Weed on the bottom can foul some anchors.

The City of Gig Harbor maintains Jerisich Park with its long moorage float.

In Gig Harbor, fuel is available only at Stutz Fuel Oil Service, located next to the Tides Tavern. Gasoline, diesel, lubricants, kerosene by the pail.

Book lovers owe themselves a visit to Mostly Books in Gig Harbor. Harry and Shirley Dearth, the owners, are genuine book people, and their marine shelf is unusually complete.

Dining: Try the Tides Tavern for pizza. We have had an excellent dinner at Marco's Ristorante, and a tasty, informal supper at LeBistro Coffee House.

The Jerisich Park dock will hold several boats. Watch depths at the inner end.

① **Arabella's Landing,** 3323 Harbor View Dr., Gig Harbor, WA 98332, (206) 851-1793. Open all year, ample guest moorage along 1500 feet of dock, 30 & 50 amp power, restrooms, showers, laundry, and pumpout available. Stan and Judy Stearns developed this classy new marina, located a short distance past the city dock on the south (city) side of Gig Harbor. They have a well-trained crew of dockhands to help with landings and make life pleasant.

The marina can accommodate boats larger than 100 feet. It has excellent concrete docks, impeccable lawns, lush flower gardens, winding brick walkways, complete wheelchair access, and a comfortable clubhouse. The moorage fee includes power and showers. Reservations recommended. The Bayview Marina, just east of Arabella's Landing, is under the same ownership.

① **Peninsula Yacht Basin,** 8913 N Harborview Drive, Gig Harbor 98335, (206)858-2250. Open all year, several guest slips plus unoccupied slips as available. Maximum boat length 80 feet, 10 foot depth at zero tide, 30 amp power, restrooms, showers. Located on the north shore of Gig Harbor, next to Shoreline Marina. Reciprocal priviliges with Gig Harbor Yacht Club. Park nearby.

① **Jerisich Park,** P.O. Box 145, Harbor View Drive, Gig Harbor, WA (206)851-8136. Open all year, 352 feet of dock space. This is a popular and attractive public dock and park, located just west of the Tides Tavern on the downtown side of Gig Harbor. Restaurants, services, book store, restrooms, portapotty dump all within walking distance. Expansion of the dock is slated for 1997 with the possible addition of a pumpout station. Check your tide table; close to shore you could be left dry at low tide.

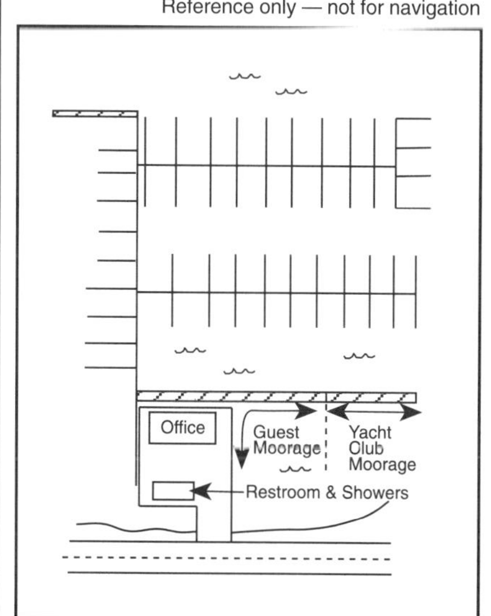

Peninsula Yacht Basin

See area map page 35

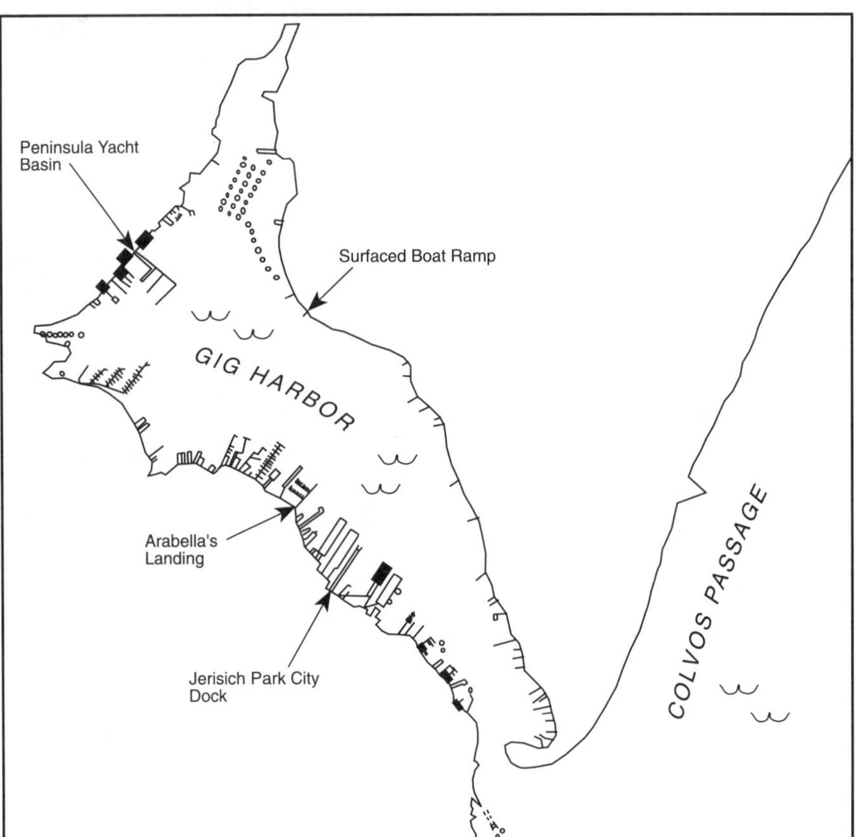

Gig Harbor

Pleasurecraft Marina. Pleasurecraft Marina no longer sells fuel or marine supplies.

TACOMA AREA

Point Defiance. Use chart 18453; 18474; 18448. Point Defiance marks the northern end of Tacoma Narrows, and is noted for swirling currents and excellent salmon fishing. The entire point is a major Tacoma park, complete with trails, a zoo, aquarium, gardens, sports facilities and picnic areas. A number of mooring buoys are placed along the shore between the point and Ruston.

Ruston is about 2 miles east of Point Defiance. This is the Tacoma terminus of the ferry to Vashon Island. The smelter slag breakwater protects the Tacoma Yacht Club's moorage. Members of reciprocal yacht clubs are welcome. This harbor is also the site of Breakwater Marina, where moorage, fuel and other amenities are available. Just inside the ferry dock is moorage at the Point Defiance Boathouse Marina and a 2-lane launch ramp operated by the Park Department. Gas and pre-mix are available at a dock just west of the ferry dock, where there are also restaurants and other businesses for visitors to the area.

② **Breakwater Marina**, 5603 N. Waterfront Drive, Tacoma, WA 98407, (253)752-6663, fax (206)752-8210. Open all year, gasoline, diesel fuel, stove alcohol, propane, 15 & 30 amp power, guest moorage in unoccupied slips, repairs, pumpout station nearby. They have a tidal grid that accommodates boats to 50 feet in length.

② **Point Defiance Boathouse Marina,** 5912 N. Waterfront Drive, Tacoma, WA 98407, (206)591-5325. Open 7 days a week all year except Thanksgiving and Christmas. Gasoline and pre-mix available, 300 feet of dock space, mooring buoys. Restrooms, pumpout, no power or showers. Nearby 3-lane launch ramp; bait, tackle, some groceries, snacks, souvenirs and gift items at Point Defiance Boathouse Tackle Shop. Pumpout located at transient float. Check in at the tackle shop. The Boathouse Grill at the marina offers views

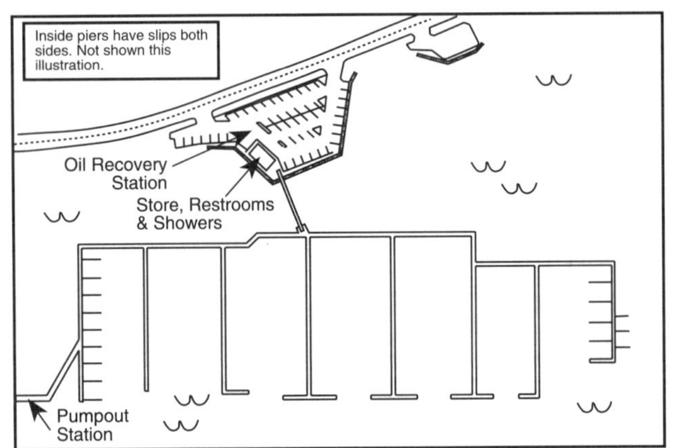

Chinook Landing Marina

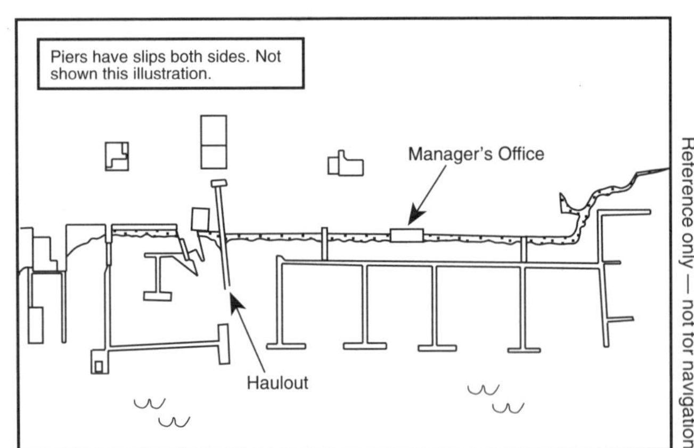

Ole & Charlie's, Hylebos Waterway, Tacoma.

Reference only — not for navigation

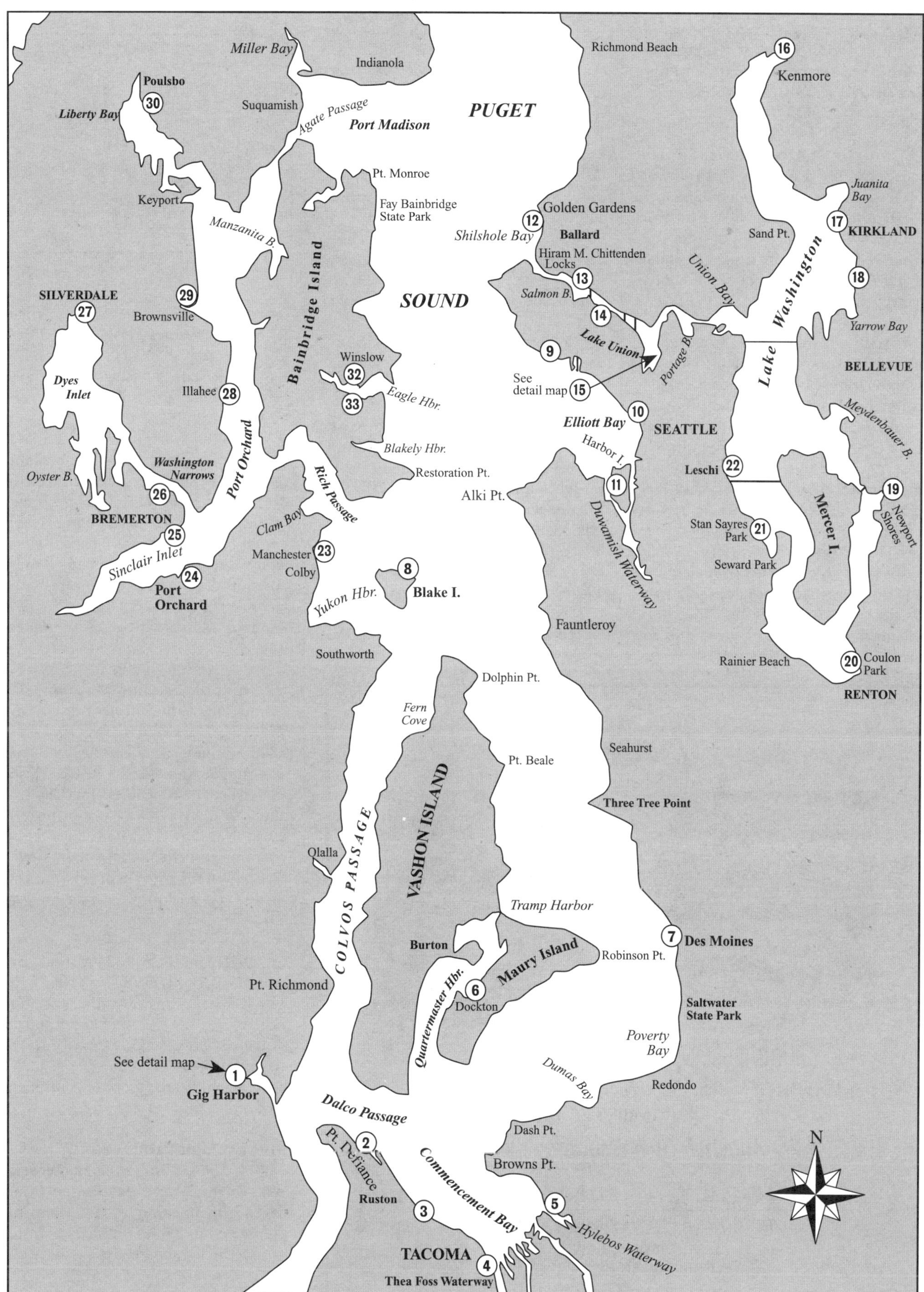

See area map page 35

across Puget Sound—open for breakfast, lunch and dinner. Public fishing pier. Within walking distance to the Point Defiance Zoo and Aquarium. Bus service to greater Tacoma.

③ **Old Town Dock,** next to Commencement Park, Tacoma. Open all year, 50 feet of dock space, 4 mooring buoys. Restroom (primitive), no power, no showers. The history of old Tacoma is displayed on panels. A large old sundial marks the time and can be seen from the water.

The southern shoreline of Commencement Bay is mostly parks, interspersed with buildings, housing, restaurants and other facilities. Numerous mooring buoys, maintained by the Metropolitan Park District, are available for overnight stays. At least two restaurants provide moorage for their patrons, and moorage is available at Old Town dock. Following this shoreline southeastward leads into the **Thea Foss Waterway** (formerly City Waterway) which is lined with moorages and boating related businesses. The public dock at 15th Street has 200 feet of visitor moorage, part of it reserved for seaplanes, and is just a short walk from the heart of downtown Tacoma.

The Port of Tacoma occupies much of the delta land at the mouth of the Puyallup River, which is navigable by skiff as far as Sumner

④ **15th Street Dock,** City of Tacoma Public Works, 15th and Dock Street, Thea Foss Waterway, Tacoma, WA 98409, (253)591-5014. Open all year, 200 feet of dock space, no power, water or restrooms. The dock is a designated float plane port, and boats can use it only as room is available. You must give way to float planes. Tie up on the shorter part of float located south of gangway. Watch the depth at zero tide or lower.

④ **Totem Marina,** 821 Dock St., Tacoma, WA 98402, (253)272-4404. Unoccupied slips used for guest moorage when available. Restrooms, showers, laundry, pumpout, 20 & 30 amp power. Haulout and dry storage. Nearby groceries, bait and tackle, restaurant, picnicking, post office. Walk to downtown Tacoma and the Tacoma Dome.

Hylebos Waterway. The Hylebos Waterway is the other waterway of particular interest to recreational boaters. It follows the north shore of Commencement Bay, and includes a number of moorages, boat builders, and boat service businesses. Along the north shore, a mile or so in from Browns Point, the Tyee Marina (no facilities for visiting boats) is tucked in behind a breakwater made of derelict boats and concrete barges. Entry to the marina is at the east end between two of the derelicts, one named *Talitiga,* which is tied to a round red buoy, and a concrete barge tied to a white buoy. Guest moorage is available at the new Chinook Marina farther up the waterway.

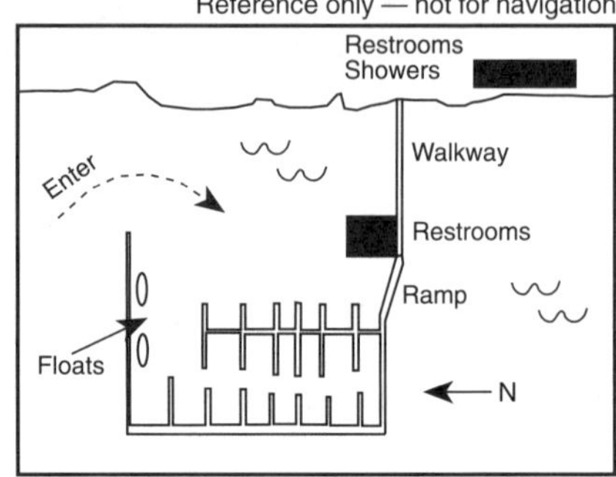

Dockton Park

⑤ **Chinook Landing Marina**, 3702 Marine View Drive #100, Tacoma, WA 98422, (206)627-7676, fax (206) 383-2823. Monitors VHF channel 79. Open all year, guest moorage available. This is an excellent new facility, 8-foot depth at zero tide, 30 & 50 amp power, restrooms, showers, laundry, pumpout, 24-hour security, and a small convenience store. Larger boats should call ahead for availability. *(Marina map page 34)*

⑤ **Ole & Charlie's,** 4224 Marine View Drive, Tacoma, WA 98422, (206) 272-1173. Two to 3 guest moorage slips available during the week; unoccupied slips used on weekends. Depth 10 feet at zero tide. Engine and outdrive repair and boat launch. Nearby groceries, restaurant, post office. *(Marina map page 34)*

Browns Point Park, Use chart 18453; 18474; 18448. Browns Point, Tacoma, WA. Open all year, day use only and overnight mooring. Has 3 mooring buoys, picnic tables and a swimming beach. The lighthouse is the focal point.

See area map page 35

VASHON ISLAND, COLVOS PASSAGE, EAST PASSAGE, DES MOINES, BLAKE ISLAND

Colvos Passage. Use chart 18474; 18448. The current always flows north in Colvos Passage, so when heading north in an flood tide it is a good choice. Colvos Passage offers little to entice a boater to stop, although Contributing Editor Tom Kincaid has anchored off Olalla and dinghied in to the little store for a snack.

Harper State Park, 1.5 miles west of the ferry landing at Southworth. Open all year, day use only. Anchoring only. The gravel launch ramp is usable at high tide only, but is the closest launch to Blake Island, 1 mile away.

Quartermaster Harbor. Use chart 18474; 18448. Quartermaster Harbor indents the south end of Vashon Island for about 4 miles. It is protected on the east by Maury Island, which connects to Vashon Island by a narrow spit of land. Dockton Park is a major destination point for boaters from all over Puget Sound.

Anchorage is good throughout most of Quartermaster Harbor, including Burton, beyond the Burton Peninsula. Burton includes the moorage of the Quartermaster Yacht Club (members of reciprocal clubs welcomed). The village of Burton has groceries and several other small shops. The private marina no longer has a fuel dock. Anchorage is well-protected with excellent holding, in a bottom made of unusually sticky mud. Be prepared to spend extra time cleaning the anchor and chain.

⑥ **Dockton Park,** P.O. Box 11, Vashon, WA 98070, (206)463-2947. Open all year, launch ramp, 58 guest slips, rafting OK, restrooms, showers, pumpout and portapotty dump (March through October only), no power, no services within walking distance. Dockton is a popular 23-acre park on the west side of Maury Island, in Quartermaster Harbor. The park has a launch ramp, play equipment, trails, bandstand, firepits, picnic tables, and a picnic shelter with barbecues inside. The picnic shelter can be reserved. Excellent destination.

East Passage. Use chart 18474; 18448. East Passage lies between Vashon Island and the mainland. Most seagoing ships bound to or from Tacoma or Olympia use this route. Tidal currents normally are a little stronger in East Passage than in Colvos Passage on the west side of Vashon Island, so boaters frequently use East Passage when running with the current, and Colvos Passage when bucking the current.

Blake Island. The longhouse and excellent grounds make this an outstanding marine park.

Dash Point State Park, 5 miles northeast of Tacoma, (206) 593-2206. Use chart 18474; 18448. Open all year, mooring buoys, restrooms, showers, no power. Sandy beach, standard, utility and primitive campsites and swimming. Fishing from the public fishing pier.

Redondo has an excellent launch ramp, complete with a float.

Saltwater Marine State Park, 2 miles south of Des Moines, (206)764-4128. Open all year, 2 mooring buoys, overnight camping. Restrooms, showers, no power. This park emphasizes scuba diving, and has an outside shower for scuba rinse-off. Great sand bottom swimming beach. The mooring buoys are exposed to southerly winds. Vault toilets. Primitive campsites. Picnic tables and shelters, kitchen shelter, children's play equipment. Seasonal concession stand.

Point Robinson. Use chart 18474; 18448. Point Robinson is surrounded by a county park that can be approached by dinghy. The lighthouse is beautiful, and the park has a nice beach, but no other facilities for boaters.

Tramp Harbor, where Vashon Island joins with Maury Island, offers convenient anchoring depths, but only minimal protection from winds, particularly from the north. It is seldom used for overnight anchorage.

Des Moines Marina

⑦ **City of Des Moines Marina,** 22307 Dock St. S., Des Moines, WA 98188, (206)824-5700. Use chart 18474; 18448. Open all year. Gasoline, diesel fuel, propane. This 840-slip marina and public pier has 65 guest slips. Maximum boat length is 55 feet, channel depth 10 feet. Stop at the fuel dock for directions to an empty berth. The docks have 20, 30 & 50 amp power. You'll find restrooms, showers, pumpout, and a portapotty dump. At the south end of the harbor the Des Moines Yacht Club has

See area map page 35

The protected marina at Blake Island has room for several boats, but always seems full. This photo was taken in April.

guest moorage for visiting members of reciprocal clubs. Several marine supply stores are nearby. All services, including laundry, groceries, and several restaurants, are within walking distance. The 670-foot public fishing pier runs east-west. To enter the marina, pass by south side of the fishing pier.

Yukon Harbor. Use chart 18449; 18474; 18448; 18441. Yukon Harbor offers good anchorage, well protected from the south but open to the northeast.

⑧ **Blake Island Marine State Park.** Use chart 18449; 18474; 18448; 18441.Open all year, with mooring buoys around the island and 1744 feet of dock space in the breakwater-protected marina. Blake Island is located just a short hop from Elliott Bay or Shilshole. The park is accessible only by boat, and is one of the most popular stops on Puget Sound. Trails criss-cross the island, and wildlife is abundant.

Blake Island has primitive campsites, including a Cascadia Marine Trail campsite. Water is available, but no garbage drop. There is an underwater reef for scuba diving. The park has picnic shelters, volleyball courts, nature trail, and approximately 12 miles of hiking trails through dense forest. The restaurant is a replica of an Indian longhouse and is open June through Labor Day.

The marina is on the northeast shore of the island. To enter, follow the dredged channel marked by red and green marked beacons. Stay in the marked channel. The water is shoal on both sides of the beacons. Immediately inside the breakwater, one float is for the boat that brings guests to the Indian longhouse restaurant, and another is for the State Parks boat. The rest are available on a first-come, first-served basis.

A gem of a park.

SEATTLE

Elliott Bay. Use chart 18449; 18474; 18448; 18441. Elliott Bay, the center of Seattle's shipping industry, is one of the busiest ocean ports in the world. Keep a sharp watch for ferries coming and going from Coleman Dock, for tugs with tows, and for commercial vessels of all kinds. These large vessels are very slow to maneuver, and should always be given a wide berth. When there's any doubt, cross *behind* commercial vessels, not in front of them.

Piers 89, 90 and 91 in Smith Cove are heavily used by commercial ships. The Port of Seattle's grain terminal occupies part of the shoreline north of the regular commercial piers, and Myrtle Edwards Park, including a fishing pier, stretches along about a mile of the Elliott Bay waterfront. The piers on the central waterfront, now considered too small for modern maritime commerce, have been converted to a number of other uses, including a hotel, shops, museums, a wonderful aquarium, and places to sit and watch the harbor activity.

South of the ferry dock, at Pier 36, the U.S. Coast Guard has its Seattle headquarters, including the Coast Guard Museum, the Vessel Traffic System, and such services as licensing and documentation.

Downtown Seattle now is served by two excellent marinas: the Elliott Bay Marina under Magnolia Bluff, and the Port of Seattle's new Bell Harbor Marina at Pier 66 on the Seattle waterfront. These two marinas make downtown Seattle easy and safe to visit. We like them both, and strongly recommend them to our readers.

⑨ **Elliott Bay Marina,** 2601 W. Marina Place, Seattle, WA 98199, (206)285-4817; fax (206)282-0626. Monitors VHF channel 78A. This is a beautiful new marina, open all year. The fuel dock has gasoline and diesel (see Yacht Care, below). Guest boats use unoccupied slips when available. Make reservations by phone (preferred) or radio. The marina has 30 & 50 amp power, restrooms, showers, laundry, pumpout, portapotty dump. Excellent 24-hour security.

Enter through either end of the breakwater. The marina office is on the ground level of the main building, between Maggie Bluffs cafe and Elliott Bay Yacht Sales. A concierge service can book reservations at other marinas, get float plane tickets, help with routes, set up repairs, and more. Dockside service. Free cable TV hook-up. Elegant and casual dining at three restaurants on the property. Mini-mart at fuel dock. Five minutes by car to downtown Seattle.

A bike and walking path runs from the marina along a scenic waterfront park to the downtown waterfront. We took about an hour each way to walk between the marina and Pier 70. Seattle Yacht Club has an outstation at the ma-

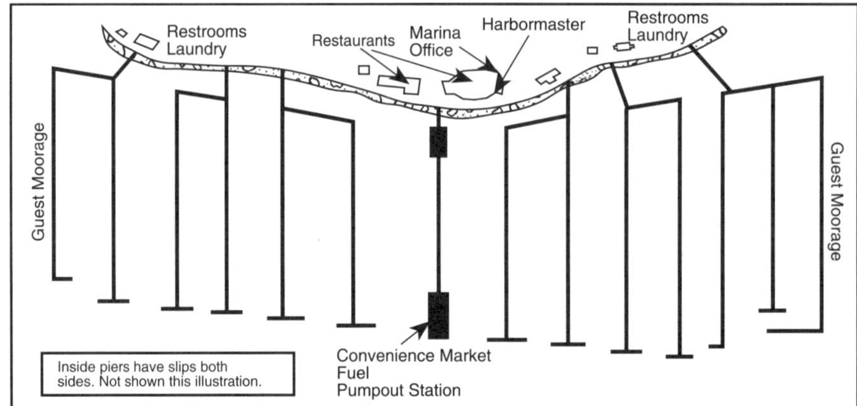

Elliott Bay Marina

Downtown Seattle makes a dramatic backdrop for the new Bell Harbor Marina.

rina. Great views of downtown, Mt. Rainier, Olympics.

Yacht Care, 2601 W. Marina Place, Seattle, WA 98199, (206)285-2600. Open 7 days, summer and winter. Gasoline and diesel fuel. Restrooms, pumpout, no power, no showers. Customs clearance is available. Located in the Elliott Bay Marina at the end of "G" dock. Service department open weekdays for mechanical repairs. Mini-mart carries beer and wine, snacks, bait, fishing licenses.

⑩ **Bell Harbor Marina,** Pier 66, 2203 Alaskan Way, Seattle, WA 98121, (206)615-3952, fax (206)615-3965. Monitors VHF channel 66A. Open year-round. This new marina has 30 & 50 amp power, water, restrooms and showers, garbage/recycling pickup, pumpout, and 24-hour security.

The Port of Seattle's Bell Harbor Marina is part of Seattle's new Central Waterfront Development. The marina opened in 1996, and has made downtown Seattle an easy cruising destination. Depending on the mix, the docks will hold as many as 100 visitor boats. The waterfront, with its aquarium and variety of shops and eateries, is available. It's a safe, 2-block walk to the excitement of the Pike Place Market. A quaint trolly runs the length of the waterfront, all the way to Pioneer Square. Visitors can leave the boat at Bell Harbor and take in a Kingdome event. Anthony's has a good restaurant at the marina. A maritime museum is in the works. Marine supplies and groceries are planned, but at press time have not opened.

We think this marina will become extremely popular. With its views of Seattle's skyscrapers and the commercial bustle all around, the cosmopolitan atmosphere is the opposite of a snug little anchorage hidden up the coast. It's a chance to use the boat as a base for a holiday in the city, and heavy emphasis is placed on security. We spent a night at Bell Harbor in late summer, walked the waterfront, had an excellent supper and a perfect night's sleep. Next morning we shopped for hours at the Pike Place Market.

Bell Harbor's facilities are top-notch, with the best wheelchair access we've seen. The staff is professional and alert. Except for boating groups, however, no reservations are taken.

Because of rough water in Elliott Bay, the breakwater entry is narrow. Boats larger than 70 feet will find the entry and turning basin a little tight. Approximately 1900 feet of outside pier apron will be devoted to major cruise line ships. This will be a busy place. The Seattle waterfront has taken a major turn for the better.

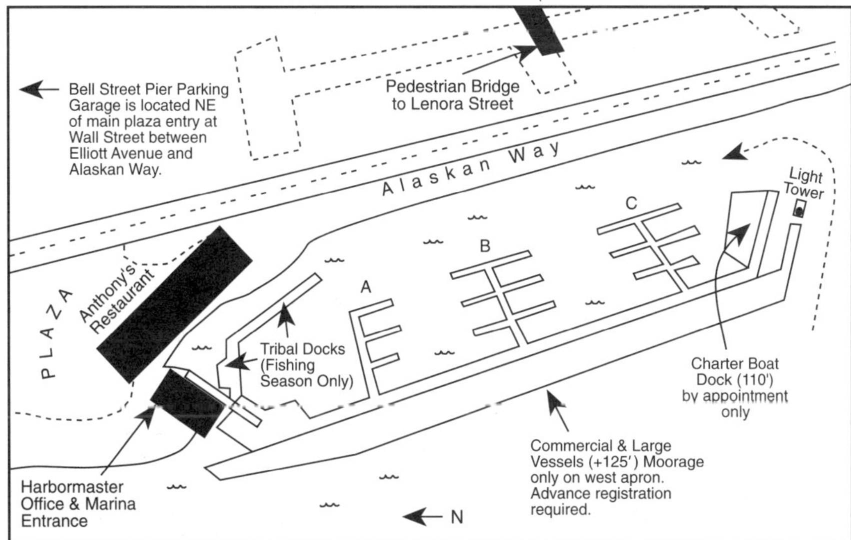

Bell Harbor Marina

Washington Street Moorage. The Washington Street Moorage, alongside the city's fire department, provides moorage for only a few boats. There is no protection from the wakes of passing ferries, and security can be a problem. The moorage is close to the Kingdome, and is sometimes used by people attending events there.

East Waterway. Both sides of East Waterway are lined with docks for commercial vessels, most of them loading or unloading containers. The waterway is navigable to Spokane Street, where a fixed bridge and foul ground block further navigation.

West Waterway. West Waterway leads past major shipbuilding yards and other commercial facilities to Harbor Reach, the dredged and straightened mouth of the Duwamish River. Two marinas offer

See area map page 35

full services to boaters in the area, and ship building and repair facilities line the west side. Duwamish Waterway continues past the "back door" of the Boeing Company's Plant 2 to the First Avenue Bridge, vertical clearance 41 feet. The bridge will open on signal except during rush hour traffic. The waterway changes character above this point, and becomes navigable only for small boats. Contributing Editor Tom Kincaid has followed the river upstream as far as Kent in an outboard powered dinghy.

Basic locks technique. Fenders on both sides of the boat, prepare to help the next boat, and be patient. Mrs. Hale makes "Surprise's" bow line fast, while the publisher tends the stern line.

Don Armeni Park and Seacrest Park are located between Harbor Island and Duwamish Head. Don Armeni Park has a 4-lane launch ramp with floats. Seacrest Park has a day use-only moorage float, a fishing pier and concessions.

⑪ **Harbor Island Marina,** 1001 SW Klickitat Way #101, Seattle, WA 98134, (206)467-9400. Open 7 days in summer, Wed.-Sun. in winter, gasoline and diesel at the fuel dock, 150 feet of dock space, restrooms, showers, pumpout. The store carries snacks and coffee, ice, bait, film, tackle.

Seacrest Boathouse, on Harbor Ave. SW, southwest of Duwamish Head, (206)932-1050. Open all year, day moorage only, restrooms, no power, no showers. Two fishing piers, one at south end of park, one at boathouse. Transient moorage floats are inside the fishing pier at the breakwater. Benches, picnic tables, boathouse. Tackle bait, deli, concession stand (summer only). Boat rentals, mechanical ramp for rental boats only. Viewpoint. Good spot for scuba diving.

Shilshole Bay. Use charts 18441, 18446, 18447, 18473 (18446 & 18447 show the best detail). Shilshole Bay indents the shoreline of Puget Sound north of West Point, and leads via a dredged channel to the Hiram A. Chittenden Locks and the Lake Washington Ship Canal. The Shilshole Bay Marina lies to the north of the dredged channel, with entrances from both the north and the south behind a long rock breakwater.

Lacking local knowledge, boats bound for the locks should pick up the Shilshole Bay Lighted Approach Buoy (locally called the Ballard Blinker) and follow the marked channel to the locks. *Caution:* The water between the channel and Magnolia Bluff shoals rapidly. Each year a number of boats go aground there.

⑫ **Shilshole Bay Marina,** 7001 Seaview Ave. NW, Seattle, WA 98117 (206)728-3385. Monitors VHF channel 17, 24 hrs. Open all year, office hours 0800-1630 Monday-Friday; 0800-1300 on Saturday. This is a large, popular, well-equipped marina operated by Port of Seattle. Gasoline, diesel, kerosene and pre-mix are available at the Shilshole Texaco Marine fuel dock. The marina has 40 guest slips and 1900 feet of dock space for visiting boats. Unoccupied slips are used when available. Minimum 15 foot depth at zero tide. Has 30, 50, 100 amp power, restrooms, showers, laundry, pumpout, portapotty dump. Customs clearance is available. Guest moorage is on a first-come, first-served basis, or by reservation 72 hours in advance. The reservation fee is $25, and the daily rate is doubled. Waste oil disposal stations, recycling and trash recepticles are available.

A complete boatyard (Seaview West) with haulout is at the south end of the marina. The boatyard has propane. A 4-lane launch ramp is at the north end of the marina. Walking distance to several restaurants with lounges, two hamburger stands, two nearby marine hardware stores (West Marine and Crow's Nest), and a used equipment store (Admiralty Marine). Regular bus service to all of Seattle. Golden Gardens Park, with beach and picnic areas, is located a short walk north of the marina.

⑫ **Shilshole Texaco Marine,** 7029 Seaview Ave. NW, Seattle, WA 98117,

The Center for Wooden Boats is an excellent place to visit at the south end of Lake Union.

See area map page 35

The WAGGONER *research boat "Surprise" at visitor moorage outside Chinook's restaurant, Fishermen's Terminal.*

(206)783-7555. Open 7 days a week all year. Texaco fuel dock with gasoline, diesel, kerosene. The Port of Seattle operates a pumpout at the outer end of the dock. Small store carries ice, beverages, snacks, local guidebooks. Friendly people, clean, efficient operation.

Hiram A. Chittenden Locks. Use chart 18447. The dredged channel leading to the Hiram Chittenden Locks is well marked, and passes under the Burlington Northern bascule bridge with a 43-foot vertical clearance. The bridge is kept open unless a train is due, at which time it will close until the train is past. The opening signal is one long and one short blast, the same signal as for the Ballard, Fremont and Montlake bridges. The University bridge responds to one long and three short blasts.

Wing walls on both sides of the channel are available for boats to tie up while they wait to enter the locks. Red and green lights on the large and small locks indicate when it is proper to enter. Entry is on a first-come, first-served basis, except that government vessels always have first priority and commercial boats have second priority, and may be called to enter ahead of private pleasure craft. All others should stay in line and enter in the order they arrived. The signal to open the locks is two long blasts followed by two short blasts.

Lock attendants do not respond to most radio calls from pleasure craft, but if you must communicate with them, call on VHF channel 13, using the 1-watt low-power mode.

There are two locks, one large and one small. The large lock is 825 feet long and 80 feet wide; the small lock is 150 feet long and 30 feet wide. Lock attendants will direct entering vessels to one lock or the other by light signals or loud hailer. Each vessel should have available bow and stern mooring lines at least 50 feet long with a 12-inch eye spliced in one end. Fenders should be deployed on both sides of the boat.

The lock attendants are conscientious, experienced and helpful. They are polite, but they give orders. If you are at all uncertain, do exactly what they tell you to do. They have seen everything, and know how to deal with problems.

If directed into the large lock, prepare to hand the eyes of your mooring lines to the lock attendant, and make the other ends fast to bow and stern cleats. There is usually some current in the locks. The current always flows from the lakes toward the sound. Enter as slowly as you can and still maintain steerage way. Once your lines are made fast, prepare to assist other boats that may be directed to lie alongside. When the lock is closed and the water begins to rise or fall, it is best to keep a half-turn on the cleat and continuously take in or pay out slack. When the water has stopped rising or falling, make all lines fast until told to leave.

If directed into the small lock, you will lie alongside a floating bollard equipped with yellow painted "buttons." The floating bollards rise or fall with the water level, so you can secure to them without the need to tend your lines during the transit. The approved technique is to make one end of each line fast to the boat, pass a loop around the "button," and return the other end of the line to the cleat. *Caution:* It is always possible that a floating bollard could jam in its tracks. Stand by to slack your lines quickly if that should happen.

When directed to do so, move out of the locks slowly but with steerage way. Except for a marked course in the middle of Lake Union, a 7-knot speed limit is in force all the way to Webster Point, where the Lake Washington Ship Canal enters Lake Washington.

Just inside the locks, the north shore of the Lake Washington Ship Canal has major fuel depots, ship repair yards, and moorages. Also on the north shore, at the foot of 24th Ave. NW, is a 300-foot dock, available for visits to Ballard's business district, a short distance away.

⑬ **24th Avenue Landing,** foot of 24th Ave. NW on the north side of the Ship Canal, east of locks. Open 0700-0200. all year, no overnights. Dock has 300 feet of space, 40-foot maximum boat length. No power, water or showers. Restrooms are next door at the Yankee Diner restaurant/lounge. Other restaurants, QFC grocery store, liquor store, Ballard business district all within walking distance.

Salmon Bay. Use chart 18447. The Port of Seattle's Fishermen's Terminal is located on the south side of the Lake Washington Ship Canal at Salmon Bay, a half-mile east of the locks. Fishermen's Terminal caters primarily to the large Seattle based fishing fleet, although a guest float is located along the inner bulkhead. Fuel is available, as well as access to major repair facilities, and stores offering a great variety of marine services and supplies. There are also two restaurants.

Dining: Chinook's, with a short-term moorage float adjacent, is good.

⑬ **Ballard Oil Co.,** 5300 26th Ave. NW, Seattle, WA 98107, (206)783-0241. Open 7 days in the summer. Just east of the locks, on the north side of the Ship Canal. Diesel only. Set up to handle larger and commercial vessels.

See area map page 35

Covich & Williams Chevron, 5219 Shilshole Ave. NW, Seattle, WA 98107, (206)784-0171. On the north side of the Ship Canal. Open all year, gasoline, diesel, kerosene. No power, restrooms or showers. Carries filters, absorbent products, anti-freeze, environmental products, fuel additives. Will honor permits.

Delta Western Fuel Dock, Pier 4, Fishermen's Terminal, Seattle, WA 98119, (206)282-1567. Open all year, with 24-hour service by appointment. Diesel only. Lube oil, filters, some parts and supplies are available.

⑬ **Ballard Mill Marina,** 4733 Shilshole Ave. NW, Seattle, WA 98107, (206)789-4777. Open all year, guest moorage limited to unoccupied slips as available. Restrooms, pumpout, 20 & 30 amp power, showers. Directly across the canal from the Marco shipyard, halfway between the Ballard Bridge and the locks. Free pumpout on the east dock. Stores, restaurants, haulout and repairs nearby.

Just east of the Salmon Bay terminal, you will pass under the **Ballard Bridge**, vertical clearance 45 feet at the center. A launch ramp is located on the north side of the canal, east of the bridge. Working east, you will pass large ship building and ship repair facilities. Then you will pass park areas on both sides of the waterway as you approach the **Fremont Bridge**, vertical clearance 30 feet. The Fremont Bridge is the lowest of the bridges that cross this waterway. Both the Ballard Bridge and the Fremont Bridge open to one long and one short blast. During weekdays, all the bridges that cross the Lake Washington Ship Canal remain closed from 0700-0900 and from 1600-1800, *except* the Montlake Bridge, whose afternoon closures are from 1530-1800.

The bridges are unattended at night between 2300 and 0700. One crew, based at the Fremont Bridge shops, is available to open bridges for vessel traffic. During these nighttime hours you must call one hour ahead on VHF channel 13, or by telephone (206)386-4251 to arrange openings.

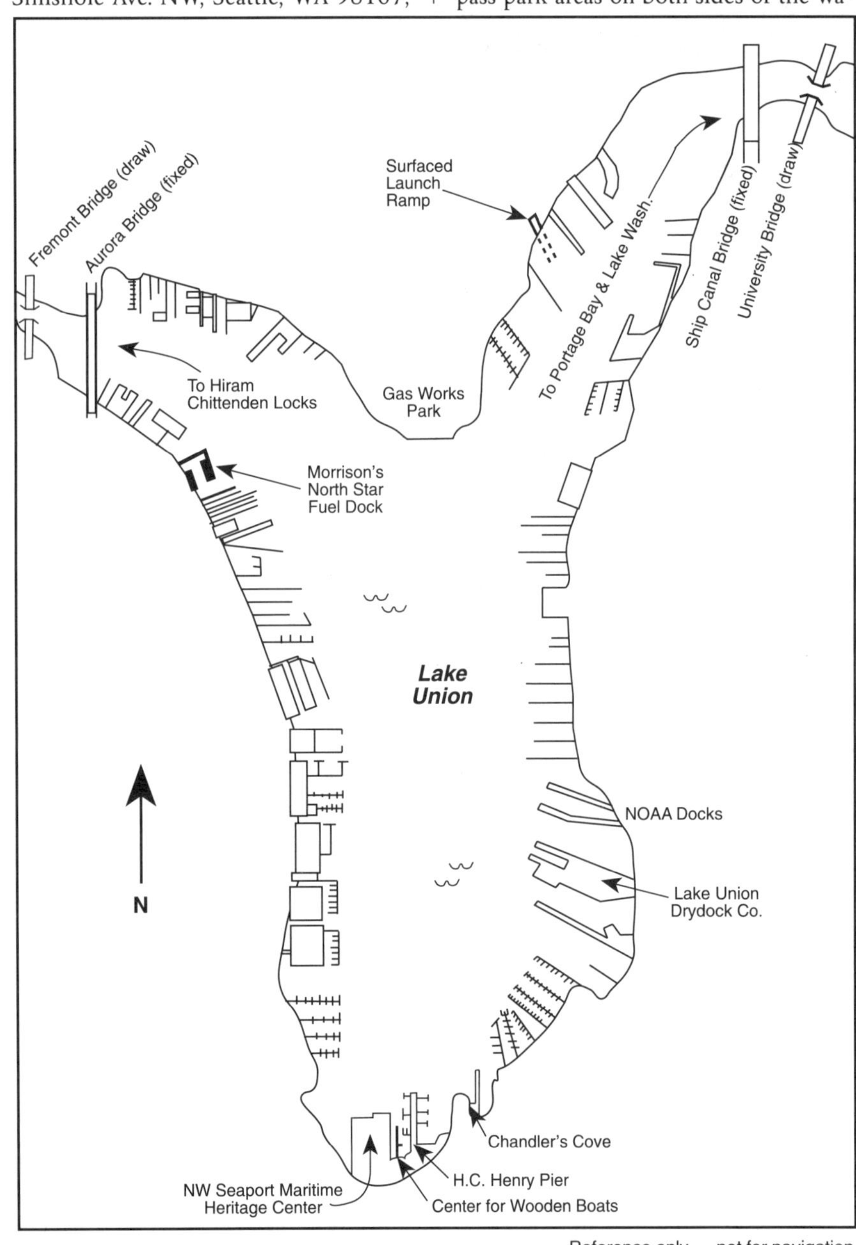

Lake Union

⑭ **Ewing Street Moorings,** 624 W. Ewing St., Seattle, WA 98119, (206)283-1075. Open all year, 2 transient slips, call for availability. Has 20 & 30 amp power, restroom, no showers. This is a small, cozy and somewhat rustic moorage, almost hidden from the canal.

Lake Union. Use chart 18447. Lake Union is surrounded by ship and boat moorages, houseboat moorages, and boating related businesses. In the middle of the lake a speed range, marked by four buoys, allows boats to be given sea trials. Other than the speed range, a 7-knot speed limit is enforced. Lake Union is the center of Seattle's boat sales industry. A launch ramp is on the north shore, east of Gas Works Park. Gas Works Park is easily identifiable by the painted remants of an industrial coal gas plant. Tyee Yacht Club and Puget Sound Yacht Club have moorages on Lake Union.

The south end of Lake Union is the home of Northwest Seaport, whose 4-masted schooner *Wawona* is open for tours. Next door is the Center for Wooden Boats and the Naval Reserve Center. Two chandleries are within walking distance. A major ship repair yard and the National Oceans and Atmospheric Administration (NOAA) fleet of survey vessels are along the eastern shore.

⑮ **Chandler's Cove,** 901 Fairview Ave. N. #C170, Seattle, WA 98109, (206)628-0838. Open all year, 480 feet of dock space, reservations preferred. Has 30 & 50 amp power, restrooms and pumpout, but no showers. A beautiful fa-

See area map page 35

cility at the south end of Lake Union. Three-hour courtesy moorage when dining. A 60-foot dock is in front of the restaurant. No power at this dock. Three restaurants, snacks, ice. Walking distance to Center for Wooden Boats and Northwest Seaport.

⑮ **H.C. Henry Marina,** 809 Fairview Place N., Seattle, WA 98109, (206)624-6534. Open all year, 24 hours, 7 days a week, with 100 feet of guest space. Located at the south end of Lake Union. Has 220 volt power only and pumpout, but no restrooms or showers. Four full-service restaurants with lounges are within walking distance. Several small shops nearby. Close to downtown Seattle. A West Marine store and a BOAT/US store are nearby.

⑮ **Marina Mart,** 1500 Westlake Ave. N., Seattle, WA 98109, (206)682-7733. No guest moorage, free pumpout only.

⑮ **Morrison's North Star Marina,** 2732 Westlake Ave. N., Seattle, WA 98109, (206)284-6600. Open all year, 7 days a week. Union Oil fuel dock with gasoline and diesel, no guest moorage. Restrooms, no showers. Handles oil changes; call for appointment. Carries kerosene, limited marine hardware, local charts, bait, groceries, ice. Pumpout available. Friendly and well-run.

Portage Bay. East of the University Bridge, vertical clearance 44 feet, Portage Bay is the home of Seattle Yacht Club and Queen City Yacht Club, as well as houseboat and other moorages. The University of Washington has several facilities along the north shore.

Lake Union is the center for boat sales and repair in Seattle. Several waterfront restaurants are located along its shores.

Montlake Cut. East of Portage Bay, the Montlake Cut connects Lake Washington with Lake Union. The cut is narrow, and during periods of heavy boat traffic wakes can be turbulent as they bounce off the concrete side walls. Slow, steady speeds are called for. The **Montlake Bridge,** which crosses the Cut, has a vertical clearance of 46 feet in the center. The bridge opens to 1 long blast and 2 shorts.

Union Bay. Use chart 18447. Union Bay lies just east of the Montlake Cut, and connects with Lake Washington. The dredged channel is well marked. The University of Washington's waterfront activities center is on the north shore, and the arboretum is on the south shore. Except for the dredged channel, the bay is shoal.

LAKE WASHINGTON

Lake Washington. Use chart 18447. Lake Washington, 16 miles long, forms the eastern border of Seattle, and washes the edges of Kenmore, Bothell, Kirkland, Medina, Bellevue, Mercer Island and Renton. The SR-520 floating bridge has a vertical clearance of 45 feet at its west end and 54 feet at its east end. The I-90 floating bridge has a vertical clearance of 35 feet in the center of each end.

Sand Point. North from Webster Point, the first notable place for visiting boats is Sand Point. This former Naval Aviation base now includes Magnuson Park, which has a 2-lane launch ramp with floats. Sand Point is also the Northwest District headquarters for the National Oceans and Atmospheric Administration (NOAA), which has a long piling pier along its north shore. The small marina west of the NOAA pier belongs to the Navy.

Kenmore. The Harbor Village Marina at Kenmore provides access to a restaurant, and anchorage is possible anywhere in the area. Kenmore is home to a major seaplane operation. Stay well clear of seaplane operating areas. Kenmore is also the mouth of the Sammamish River. Shoal water abounds. Find the buoys and stay in the dredged channel. The river is navigable by small, shallow-draft boats all the way to Lake Sammamish.

⑯ **Harbor Village Marina,** 6155 NE 175th St., Seattle, WA 98155, (206)485-7557. Open all year, limited guest moorage. Unoccupied slips used when available. Power, restrooms, showers, laundry, pumpout. Also a 300-foot breakwall for guests to tie to during daylight hours; no fee, tie up at your own risk. Restaurant nearby. Marina has one of the few pumpout stations on Lake Washington.

See area map page 35

Making Sense of Navigation Aids

This is the Bainbridge Reef Buoy Lighted Bell Buoy 4. Since it is painted solid red, it carries a number. Leave this buoy off your right hand when returning from the sea (headed west through Rich Passage). The light is red, and flashes every 4 seconds.

(16) **Davidson's Marina,** 6201 NE 175th St., Seattle, WA 98155, (206)486-7141. Open all year, except closed Sundays during the winter. Gasoline at the fuel dock. Restrooms, no power, no showers. Store carries life jackets, parts, accessories, ice. Repairs available.

Logboom Park, north shore of Lake Washington, Kenmore. Open all year, day use only, moorage available. Restrooms, no power, no showers. Trails, fishing pier, children's play equipment, picnic areas, outdoor cooking facilities. The park is on the Burke-Gilman Trail, a walking and cycling trail running from from Lake Union to the Sammamish River Trail.

Saint Edward State Park, northeast shore of Lake Washington. Open all year, day use only. Restrooms, showers, no power. Anchoring or beaching only. Picnicking, trails, fishing, indoor swimming pool. Tennis and handball courts, gymnasium. The 300+ acre park is at the top of a bluff; trails lead down to a sandy beach.

Juanita. Anchorage is possible in Juanita Bay, which shoals gradually toward all shores.

Kirkland. The City of Kirkland, in Moss Bay, operates the Marina Park docks for the use of visitors, and has a good launch ramp. It's a popular destination for Lake Washington cruising. Kirkland's downtown area, with excellent restaurants and a wide variety of shops and galleries, is just a few steps from the docks. A mile south of Marina Park is the privately owned Carillon Point Marina, with guest moorage and access to restaurants and other businesses. Several restaurants in the area have their own docks for patrons.

(17) **Marina Park,** 123 Fifth Ave., Kirkland, WA 98032, (206)828-1218; fax (206)828-1290. Launch ramp adjacent; fee required. Open all year, 66 guest slips, restrooms, no power or showers. This is a large and popular Lake Washington destination. Excellent access to all the shops and restaurants of downtown Kirkland. Nearby groceries, ice, doctor, post office, liquor store.

(18) **Carillon Point Marina,** 3240 Carillon Point, Kirkland, WA 98033, (206)822-1700; fax (206)828-3094. Open all year, guest moorage in unoccupied slips used when available, 30 & 50 amp power, restrooms, showers, pumpout, portapotty dump. This is a nice marina adjacent to a high-quality hotel, with restaurants and shopping. They give 2-hour free moorage while dining or shopping. Lunchtime concert series in the summer. Downtown Kirkland is 1.5 miles away by road.

(18) **Wilcox's Yarrow Bay Marina,** 5207 Lake Washington Blvd., Kirkland, WA 98033, (206)822-6066. Fuel dock with gasoline and diesel open all year. No guest moorage. Has restrooms, pumpout, no showers.

Cozy Cove is entirely residential, but anchorage is possible. The same is true of **Fairweather Bay**.

Meydenbauer Bay. Meydenbauer Bay is the home of a private marina that does not normally offer overnight moorage, and the Meydenbauer Bay Yacht Club, which can accommodate members of reciprocal clubs. Downtown Bellevue, with excellent shopping, is nearby. Anchorage is possible in Meydenbauer Bay, al-

See area map page 35

though the water is deeper than most pleasure craft prefer. The marina off Beaux Arts Village, a short distance south of Meydenbauer Bay, is reserved for Beaux Arts residents.

Luther Burbank Park, Northeast end of Mercer Island, (206)296-2976. Open all year, day use only, dock space for 30 or more boats. Restrooms, no power, no showers. Park has picnic areas, swimming areas, tennis courts, amphitheater, art displays.

Newport Shores. Newport Shores has a large marina and launch ramp. The East Channel Bridge has a vertical clearance of 65 feet.

⑲ **Mercer Marine,** 3911 Lake Washington Blvd SE, Bellevue, WA 98006, (206)641-2090. Open all year, except closed on Sundays during the winter. The fuel dock has gasoline. Restrooms are available, but no showers. No guest moorage. Located at the Newport Yacht Basin. Complete repairs available. Also stove alcohol, propane, marine supplies and parts. Adjacent to a public launch ramp.

⑳ **Gene Coulon Memorial Beach Park,** 1201 Lake Washington Blvd., Renton, WA 98055, (206)235-2560; fax (206)277-5541. Open all year, day use and overnight moorage. The park has 13 guest slips available, restrooms, showers, no power. Pay at drop box. Showers in summer only, at the swim center. Ivar's restaurant in the park. Eight lanes for boat launching, very well organized. This is a big, attractive, and much-used park, with picnic shelters, playground equipment, tennis courts, horseshoe pits, volleyball courts, grassy areas and beaches. It has a fishing pier and a paved walkway along the water. Located on the southeast shore of Lake Washington, next to the Boeing complex.

Rainier Beach has a launch ramp and a private marina. It is the home of the Rainier Yacht Club, which can offer limited guest moorage to visiting members of reciprocal clubs.

Seward Park occupies the Bailey Peninsula. Andrews Bay is a popular anchoring spot. The park includes a fish hatchery, hiking trails. A small private marina, with a small guest dock, is at Lakewood.

㉑ **Lakewood Moorage,** P.O. Box 18403, 4500 Lake Washington Blvd. S., Seattle, WA 98118, (206)722-3887. Open all year; closed Mondays in summer and closed Sundays in winter. Has 3 slips for guest moorage, unoccupied slips used when available, call ahead. Power, restrooms, no showers. Security gate. Store carries ice, marine supplies, gift items, apparel, snacks.

Stan Sayers Memorial Park, southwest edge of Lake Washington. Open all year. Temporary, day-use moorage only, not enough depth for larger boats. Restrooms, no power, no showers. Launch ramp with boarding floats. Tie up to the floats. Pit area for hydroplanes during Seafair.

㉒ **Leschi Yacht Basin**, 120 Lakeside, at Leschi Marina, Seattle, WA 98122, (206)328-4456. Open summer 7 days a week, rest of the year depending on weather. Fuel dock has gasoline. No power, no showers. Look for the banner from water. Oil, ice, snacks, and T-shirts for sale. Restrooms are in the restaurant. Adjacent restaurants have their own guest docks.

The Bremerton Marina is a popular place, even on a cloudy day.

RICH PASSAGE, PORT ORCHARD, BREMERTON, SILVERDALE

Rich Passage. Use chart 18449; 18474; 18448. Rich Passage, winding but well buoyed, is the ferry route between Seattle and Bremerton. Keep a sharp lookout ahead and astern and give the ferries room to maneuver. Naval vessels of all kinds also use Rich Passage to and from the Bremerton Naval Shipyard. From the west entrance the city of Bremerton and the Naval Shipyard are clearly visible. The Navy asks that boats cruising past the shipyard maintain a 100-yard clearance from the ends of its piers.

Manchester State Park, Middle Point, Rich Passage. Open summers 7 days, day use and overnight camping; weekends and holidays only in the winter for day use and overnight camping. Restrooms, showers, no power. Anchoring only; a bit rough because of boat traffic in Rich Passage. Park is located in a shallow cove; good for wading in summer; scuba diving offshore. Picnic tables and shelters with fireplaces. Standard and primitive campsites. Nature and hiking trails, volleyball court and horseshoe pits. Old gun battery and emplacements to explore.

㉓ **Port of Manchester**, P.O. Box 304, Manchester, WA 98353, (360)871-2510. Open all year, 200 feet of guest dock space, day use only. Dock can be dry on low or minus tide. A launch ramp is adjacent to the dock. No power or other facilities at the dock, but restaurants, groceries, restrooms, and drinking water are nearby.

Fort Ward Marine State Park, southwest of Winslow on Bainbridge Island. Open all year, overnight moorage at 2 buoys. The buoys are exposed to wind and wakes from passing boat traffic. Toilets, launch ramp, picnic tables, and hiking trails. Underwater park is for expert scuba divers only, because of strong currents in Rich Passage. Clamming, crabbing, fishing. Birdwatching from two bird blinds. Remains of historic fort emplacements to explore. No camping.

Port Orchard. Use chart 18449; 18448. The city of Port Orchard has long been a popular destination for Puget Sound boaters. It has a number of

See area map page 35

marinas that welcome visiting boats, including one, the Port Orchard Marina, that is operated by the Port of Bremerton. The Port Orchard Yacht Club, which welcomes visiting reciprocal yachts, is west of the Port Orchard Marina. Several other marinas offering permanent moorage. Anchorage is in 5-10 fathoms, mud bottom.

Dining: Friends suggest The Lighthouse.

㉔ **Port Orchard Marina,** 8850 SW State Hwy 3, Port Orchard, WA 98366, (360) 876-5535. Monitors VHF channel 16. Open all year, 7 days, except closed Thanksgiving and Christmas. Guest moorage in 44 slips (40-foot maximum), and 1500 feet of dock space. The marina has 30 & 50 amp power, restrooms, showers, laundry, pumpout and portapotty dump. This is one of Puget Sound's most popular destinations. No charge for day use. It's one block to downtown Port Orchard. You can walk to the shopping area, library, liquor store, post office, doctor. Marine supplies and repairs are nearby. Close to Waterfront Park, boat launch. Seasonal farmers' market. Enter the marina around the west end of the breakwater. The entrance is marked with navigation lights.

㉕ **Bremerton Marina,** 8850 SW State Hwy 3, Port Orchard, WA 98633 (mailing address), (360)373-1035. Monitors VHF channel 16. Open all year, except closed Thanksgiving and Christmas. All guest moorage, 45 slips, 500 feet of dock space. The marina has 30 amp power, restrooms, showers, laundry, pumpout and portapotty dump. This is an excellent new marina, located in downtown Bremerton, next to ferry dock. It is operated by the Port of Bremerton. Restaurants and services are within walking distance. Points of interest include the Naval Museum and the historic ship U.S.S. *Turner Joy*, the adjacent waterfront park, city boardwalk, and seasonal farmers' market. Fuel is available across the waterway at the Port Orchard Marina. The Bremerton Marina is secured by a locked gate, as are the restrooms and laundry area. The lock combination is displayed on the inside of the gate, where visiting boaters can see it. The Kitsap County transit buses can take you anywhere you wish to go.

Washington Narrows. Use chart 18449. Washington Narrows connects Port Orchard with Dyes Inlet. The Narrows is crossed by two bridges with a minimum vertical clearance of 80 feet. Tidal currents, averaging over 2 knots, flood west and ebb east. Signs ask boaters to maintain minimum speed to reduce wake damage to the shorelines and to boats moored at the marina in Anderson Cove. A launch ramp with float and fishing pier are on the north side of the Narrows about halfway along, part of the Lebo Street Recreation Area.

㉖ **Port Washington Marina**, 1805 Thompson Drive, Bremerton, WA 98337, (360)479-3037. Open all year, 7 days. Guest moorage includes 6 slips, 100 feet of dock space, 6-foot least depth. The marina has 30 and limited 50 amp power, restrooms, showers, laundry, pumpout. Groceries and restaurants are within walking distance.

Phinney Bay. Phinney Bay is the home of the Bremerton Yacht Club, with guest moorage for visiting reciprocal yachts. Anchorage is good throughout the bay, which shoals toward each shore.

Ostrich Bay. Use chart 18449. Ostrich Bay offers good anchorage, mud bottom. The most popular anchorage is along the west side of the bay, facing the dense forest of Washington Park. We have spent a number of pleasant nights at this spot. For some reason this entire area is over-

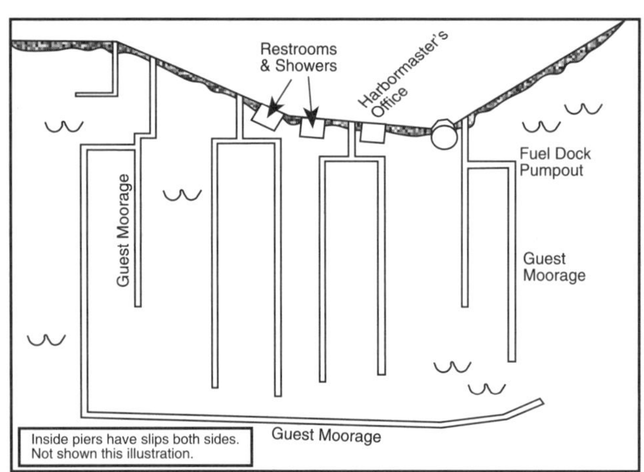

Port Orchard Marina

Reference only — not for navigation

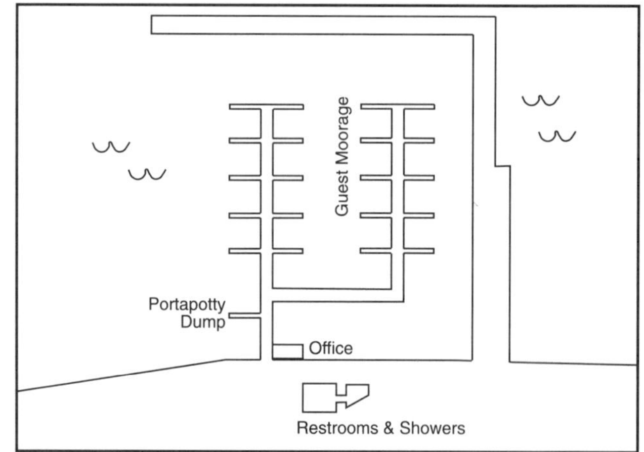

Bremerton Marina

Reference only — not for navigation

looked. Even when the docks at Port Orchard and Bremerton are full on summer 3-day weekends, Ostrich Bay has been almost empty.

Oyster Bay. A narrow but easily-run channel leads off Ostrich Bay into Oyster Bay, where perfectly protected anchorage is available toward the center of the bay. To enter, keep between the lines of mooring buoys and mooring floats on both sides of the channel. The channel shoals to about 1 fathom at zero tide. Deep draft vessels should use it only when there is enough water. Oyster Bay is surrounded by homes.

(27) **Silverdale Marina (Port of Silverdale),** P.O. Box 310, Silverdale, WA 98383, (360)698-4918. Use chart 18449. Open all year. Guest moorage has 60 slips with a least depth of 10 feet at low tide. Restrooms, no power, no showers, 2-lane launch ramp. The marina is adjacent to county-run Silverdale Waterfront Park. This park has picnic tables, fire pits, children's play area, and a pavilion. Restrooms are at the park. Services are available close by, including groceries.

BROWNSVILLE, POULSBO, NORTHERN PORT ORCHARD

(28) **Illahee Marine State Park.** Use chart 18449. Located on Port Orchard Bay, 3 miles northeast of Bremerton, (360)478-6460. Open all year, mooring and overnight camping. Guest moorage has 350 feet of dock space, 5 mooring buoys. Restrooms, portapotty dump, no power or showers. The dock is protected by a floating concrete breakwater. Park has 3 kitchen shelters, picnic tables, campsites, horseshoe pits, ball field, hiking trails. Popular for fishing and sunbathing. Most services are in the upland area, reached by a steep trail.

(29) **Port of Brownsville**, 9790 Ogle Rd. NE, Bremerton, WA 98311, (360)692-5498. Monitors VHF channel 16, switch to 68. Use chart 18446 or 18449. Open all year, 7 days. Fuel dock has gasoline, diesel, propane. Guest moorage has 30 24-foot slips and along 500 feet of dock, 20 & 30 amp power, restrooms, showers, laundry, free pumpout, portapotty dump. Paved 2-lane launch ramp and parking. A breakwater marks the entrance to the marina. The area around the fuel dock has been dredged, so you don't have to hug the south side of the dock, as in prior years. The Brownsville Marine and Deli has groceries and deli items, limited marine supplies. There is an adjacent park with picnic tables and barbecue. The Keyport Naval Museum of Undersea Warfare (excellent, worth the visit) is nearby. This is a pleasant, friendly marina. *(Marina map page 49)*

Fletcher Bay. Use chart 18449. Fletcher Bay is very shallow, with a shallow entry, drying shoals in the middle, and a narrow dredged channel that serves homes along the shore. It is not a good anchorage.

Manzanita Bay. Use chart 18446. Manzanita Bay is a popular overnight sheltered anchorage for Seattle-area boats. The bay is all residential and has no public facilities ashore, but the holding ground is excellent. Although the bay is lined with lovely homes, the surrounding hills and forests give a feeling of seclusion. We like Manzanita Bay.

See area map page 35

Poulsbo. Use chart 18446. Poulsbo, on **Liberty Bay**, is one of the most popular destinations on Puget Sound, partly because it is close to the major population centers, and partly because it is such a delightful place to visit. Settled originally by Scandinavians, the downtown business district still loudly (to say the least) maintains its Norwegian heritage. Everything most boaters need is available either near the water or at the malls located on the highway about a mile away.

The waterfront portions of Poulsbo make for a lovely walk. Victorian homes and gardens have been restored and preserved to perfection. The highway above may have the malls, but the town below has the charm.

The entrance to Liberty Bay is past the Keyport Naval torpedo research and testing facility, and around Lemolo Point. The Navy asks a no-wake speed past its facility. A sign on the beacon off Lemolo Point asks boaters to slow down in all of Liberty Bay. Buoys posting the speed limit are in the bay. Three major marinas are located along the north shore of Liberty Bay: a private marina; the Poulsbo Yacht Club; and the marina owned by the Port of Poulsbo.

The private marina has no guest moorage. At the Poulsbo Yacht Club, guest moorage, available to visiting members of reciprocal clubs, is along the northwest perimeter of the floating breakwater. Some guest moorage is still available on the inside of the older breakwater.

(30) **Poulsbo Marina/Port of Poulsbo**, P.O. Box 732, 18721 Front St., Poulsbo, WA 98370, (360)779-3505. Open all year, 7 days. Register (no credit cards) by 2000 hours to get the combination for the showers and restrooms. The fuel dock has gasoline & diesel. The marina has 130 guest slips, 12-foot depths at low tide, 20 amp power, good restrooms and showers, laundry, pumpout, portapotty dump, launch ramp, and picnic area. Groceries, tackle and bait are nearby. Manny Xenos's Viking Marine Center has just about everything you might need for the boat, including charts and books.

Restaurants and many shops that specialize in gifts, collectibles, and home accessories, are nearby in downtown Poulsbo. Dining and shopping are popular. The marina is close to doctors, a post office, and a liquor store. The Marine Science Center is worth a visit. Shopping centers, with supermarkets and the usual stores, are a few blocks away.

Poulsbo in early April. The docks are full.

Dining: That's A Some Italian Ristorante is excellent.

Agate Passage. Use chart 18446. Agate Passage connects Port Orchard with Port Madison, and is crossed by a highway bridge with a vertical clearance of 75 feet. Currents in the pass can run as high as 6 knots at spring tides, flooding south and ebbing north. The channel through the pass is well marked, but in general, a mid-channel course will serve.

For some reason, many craft go through Agate Passage too fast, creating havoc for slower craft. Agate Pass isn't very long. Keep the speed down, look astern to judge the wake, and give fellow boats a break.

PORT MADISON AND BAINBRIDGE ISLAND

Miller Bay. Use chart 18446. Miller Bay indents the Northwest corner of Port Madison, and is very shallow, including the entrance. It should be entered only at half tide or better, or with local knowledge. Like many such bays on Puget Sound, Miller Bay has a drying shoal in the middle, so navigable water can be found only around the perimeter.

Bay Marine, Inc., P.O. Box 396, 20622 Miller Bay Road, Suquamish, WA 98392, (360)598-4900. Open Tuesday-Sunday, all year, 3 guest slips, 35-foot maximum length. No other facilities. Haulout to 34 feet, parts and complete repairs are available. Launch ramp. Most services are available in nearby Suquamish.

Suquamish. Suquamish has a dock but no float. Ashore is largely an Indian village, one highlight of which is Chief Seattle's grave on a hillside a block from the waterfront. The Suquamish Tribe also maintains an Indian museum along Agate Passage, south of Suquamish.

Indianola. Indianola is distinguished by the long dock that used to serve passengers and freight during Mosquito Fleet days. Now a log float is installed during the summer to give access to the town, which has some supplies. Overnight moorage is not allowed.

Inner Port Madison. Use chart 18446. The inner bay extends for about 1.5 miles into the north end of Bainbridge Island. It is residential, but with a loading and unloading dock on publicly owned beachfront on the east side. Inner Port Madison is the home of the Port Madison Yacht Club and an outstation of the Seattle Yacht Club. Anchorage is good throughout the bay, with a wide bight about ¾-mile inside the entrance. Farther in, **Hidden Cove** is preferred. For Seattle area boats, this is an often-overlooked area to have a picnic lunch or a quiet night at anchor. The shores are private, but the setting is idyllic.

See area map page 35

Fay Bainbridge State Park, south of Point Monroe on Bainbridge Island. Open all year, 3 mooring buoys, exposed. Restrooms, showers, no power. The park has three kitchen shelters, fireplaces, fire rings, a beach area, launch ramp, and utility and primitive campsites. Also children's play equipment, horseshoe pits, fishing and clamming, concession stand in summer.

Murden Cove. Murden Cove has convenient anchoring depths, but little protection from winds. It's a long row to shore, partially over drying flats. The residential community of Rolling Bay is at the head of the bay.

Eagle Harbor. Use chart 18449. Eagle Harbor is the site of the city of Winslow, and is the western terminus of a ferry to downtown Seattle. The city has a lighted visitors' float off a fine waterfront park. Several of the marinas can provide guest moorage if a permanent tenant is away. Queen City Yacht Club, Meydenbauer Bay Yacht Club and Seattle Yacht Club have outstations in Eagle Harbor. The grocery store has *everything*. We enjoy walking the streets of Winslow. Its shops offer art, crafts, books, and antiques.

Enter Eagle Harbor by way of a marked channel past foul ground that extends south from Wing Point. Nun buoy 2 is at the end of this foul ground. The Tyee Shoal Beacon is a short distance south of buoy 2. The ferries round Tyee Shoal Beacon, but other craft can use buoy 2 safely, following the rule of Red, Right, Returning. Follow the markers all the way in. Shoal water extends out to the channel on both sides.

㉜ **Eagle Harbor Waterfront Park,** downtown Winslow. Open all year, day use and overnight moorage at 100 feet of dock, use both sides. Watch your depth at low tide. Restrooms, but no power, water or showers. Good anchorage is in the harbor, and a dinghy dock is provided. A good spot, popular year-round. Playground, tennis courts, picnic sites. Winslow's retail shops and restaurants are within walking distance.

㉜ **Harbour Marina,** P.O. Box 11434, Eagle Harbor, at Harbour Pub, Bainbridge Island, WA 98110, (206)842-6502. Open all year, call ahead. Unoccupied slips used for guest boats when available. Has 30 amp power, restrooms, showers, laundry, pumpout. Located directly below Harbour Public House, an English-style pub with beer, wine, and food. The pub is bright, clean, and pleasant, and the food is good. No kids allowed in pub. There is day moorage allowed (if available) for visiting the pub. It's a 5-10-minute walk to downtown or Waterfront Park.

The Port of Brownsville Marina has ample room for visiting boats and good facilities ashore.

㉜ **Winslow Wharf Marina,** P.O. Box 10297, Winslow, WA 98110, (206)842-4202. Monitors VHF channel 09. Open all year, 7 days in summer, 5 days in winter. Guest moorage in unoccupied slips when available. Maximum boat length 50 feet, 20 & 30 amp power, restrooms, showers, laundry, pumpout, portapotty dump. Look for the sign at the end of the registration dock. A deposit is required for a security gate and restroom card, and the gate is locked at 1700. The Chandlery, a well-stocked marine supply store, carries a little bit of everything. Two blocks to downtown; restaurants, many galleries, farmers' market. Seattle Yacht Club and Meydenbauer Bay Yacht Club each have some dock space reserved for their members. The spaces are clearly marked, and non-member boats may not use them.

㉝ **Eagle Harbor Marina,** 5834 Ward Ave. NE, Bainbridge Island, WA 98110, (206)842-4003. Open all year, but limited guest moorage, call ahead for availability. Marina has 20, 30 & 50 amp power, restrooms, showers, laundry, pumpout. Located on the south side of Eagle Harbor. A sauna and exercise room are available, and a B&B is adjacent to the marina. No restaurants or stores in the immediate area.

Blakely Harbor. Use chart 18449. In the early days Blakely Harbor was the site of major lumbering and shipbuilding activities, but now it is a quiet residential neighborhood. Some stub pilings remain from old docks. Anchorage should be chosen well away from the head of the bay. Good anchorage in 6-8 fathoms can be found far enough into the bay to be well protected, yet still have a view of the Seattle skyline. Sunset on a clear evening is beautiful. The entrance is unobstructed except by Blakely Rock, ½ mile off. Give Blakely Rock a good offing.

Reference only — not for navigation

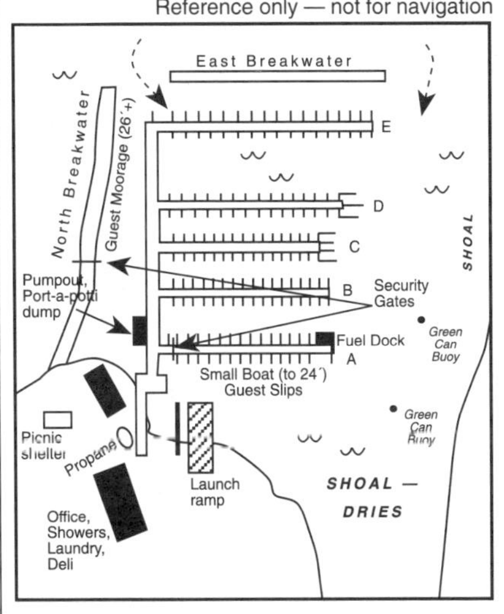

Port of Brownsville

Northwest Puget Sound

Edmonds • Kingston • Admiralty Inlet • Port Townsend

Charts	
18441	Puget Sound—Northern Part (1:80,000)
18445SC	FOLIO SMALL-CRAFT Puget Sound—Possession Sound to Olympia including Hood Canal
18464	Port Townsend (1:20,000)

Edmonds. Use chart 18473; 18446; 18441. Edmonds, a prosperous community with a small-town feel to it, is about 8 miles north of Shilshole Bay on the east side of Puget Sound. It has a major rock breakwater-protected marina (the Port of Edmonds Marina) with excellent facilities for visiting boats. Marine repair shops are located near the harbor. In the town, a short distance away, one finds excellent restaurants, and interesting shops and galleries.

① **Port of Edmonds,** 336 Admiral Way, Edmonds, WA 98020, (206)774-0549. Monitors VHF channels 16 & 69. Open 7 days a week all year. The fuel dock has gasoline & diesel. The marina has 1100 feet of guest dock space, plus unoccupied slips when available. They can accommodate boats to 70 feet. The docks are served by 20 & 30 amp power, restrooms, showers, pumpout.

Enter through middle of the breakwater. Guest moorage and the fuel dock are immediately to the south. The marina has a large do-it-yourself boatyard, haulout and towing. Limited groceries, tackle, and bait are available, with complete shopping in town. Two excellent public beaches are nearby, and a 950-foot-long public fishing pier. An artificial reef for scuba diving is located next to the ferry dock. Fishing charters available. It's a short walk to several nearby restaurants. Liquor store, post office, doctor, laundry, groceries and shops are in town, about 9 blocks away. The marina provides a van service for guests. The personnel are friendly and helpful. A good stop. *(Marina map page 55)*

The Edmonds Marina entrance is through an opening in the middle of the breakwater. Turn right immediately after entering. The guest dock and fuel dock will be just ahead.

Kingston. Use chart 18446; 18473; 18441. Kingston, in Appletree Cove on the west side of Puget Sound, is the western terminus of the ferry run to Edmonds. A Port-owned marina lies behind a breakwater in Appletree Cove. A marine supply store is nearby, and shopping is a short distance up the road. A farmers' market is held each Saturday during the summer in a park next to the marina.

Dining: Friends recommend the Kingston Hotel Cafe.

② **Port of Kingston,** P.O. Box 559, Kingston, WA 98346, (360)-297-3545.

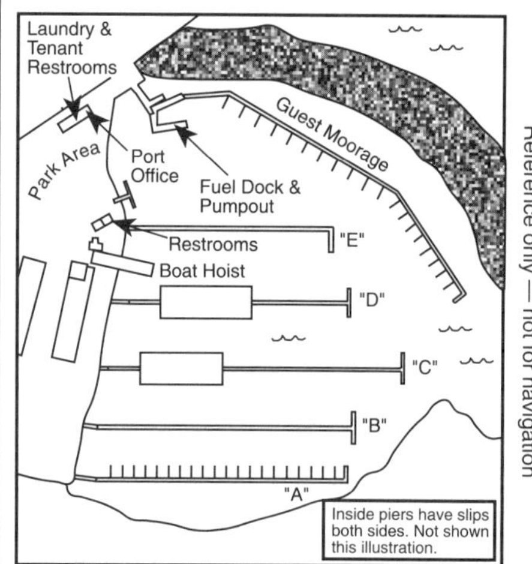

Port of Kingston

Reference only — not for navigation

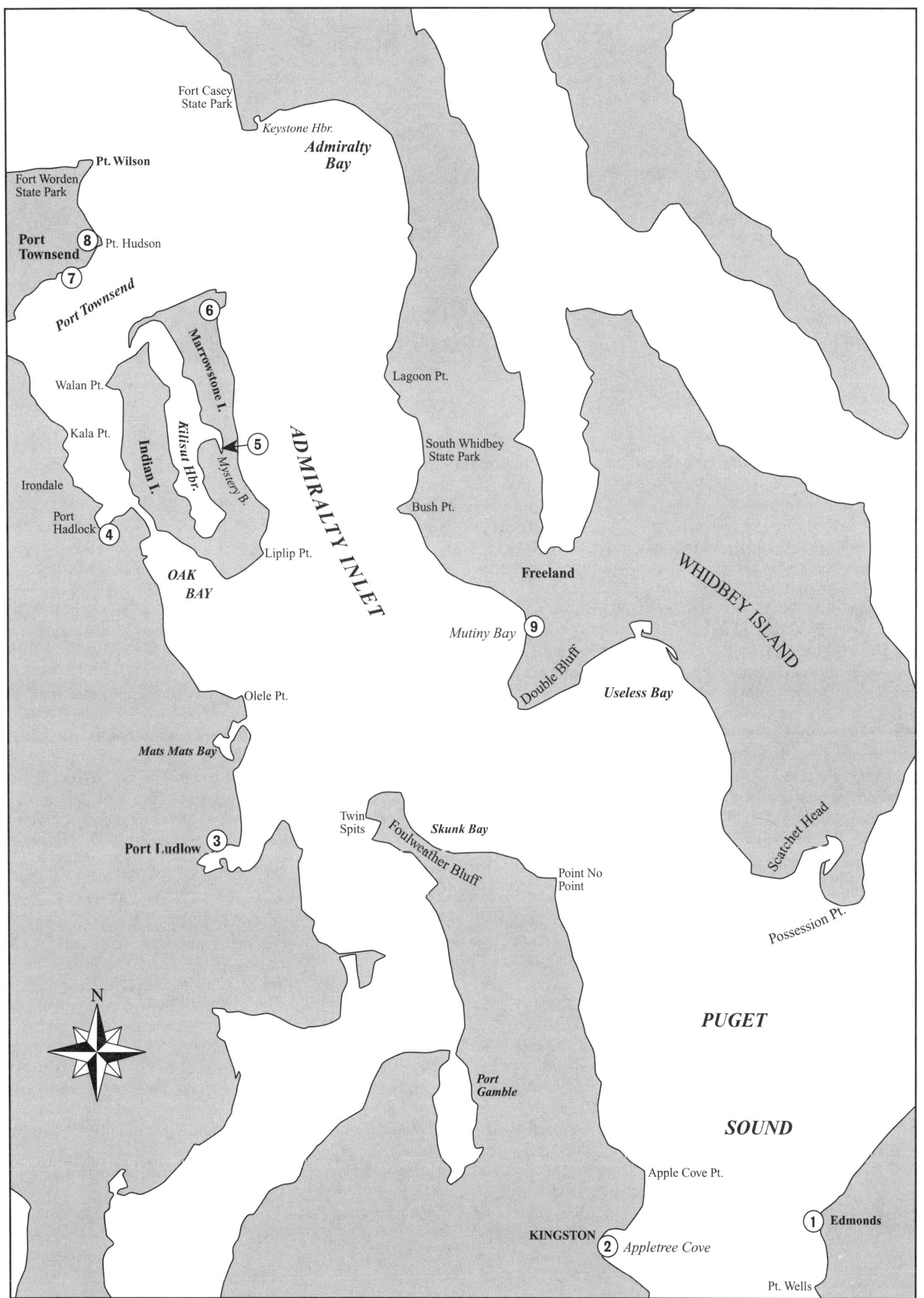

See area map page 51

Monitors VHF channel 65. Open all year, 39 guest slips, 30 amp power, restrooms, showers, laundry, pumpout, portapotty dump. The fuel dock has gasoline, diesel, propane.

Enter the marina around the end of the rock breakwater, leaving two pilings that mark the edge of the dredged channel to port. Guest moorage is along a dock that runs parallel to the breakwater, with the fuel float at the shore end of the channel. Moorage is first-come, first-served. Moor in any unreserved space and walk to the Port office to register. Kingston has an overhead crane launching system, and a chandlery. *(Marina map page 50)*

Private homes have replaced the dense forest that once surrounded the Port Ludlow inner harbor. Still, the bay remains popular.

ADMIRALTY INLET

Port Ludlow. Use chart 18477; 18473; 18441. Port Ludlow indents the western shore of the Olympic Peninsula. It was once the site of a major Pope & Talbot sawmill, and has now been turned into a fine residential area and destination resort. Anchorage is good south of the marina, and in the inner harbor.

The landlocked Port Ludlow inner harbor is reached by passing between two little islands near the head of the bay. Good anchorage, mud bottom, can be found in about 15 feet. Check your chart before entering the inner harbor, to assure that you are passing *between the two islets.* We know of one skipper who inadvertently passed between the westernmost islet and the mainland, and went aground. Deeper draft boats should watch the depth sounder closely when entering the inner harbor at low tide. The passage is more shallow than the bays it connects.

The inner harbor is a favorite destination in Puget Sound, protected from all winds. Until a few years ago it was surrounded by dense forest. Development has removed much of the forest and replaced it with private homes, but the bay retains at least some of its old charm. Meydenbauer Bay Yacht Club has an outstation on the peninsula that forms the inner harbor.

③ **Port Ludlow Marina,** 1 Gull Drive, Port Ludlow, WA 98365, (360)437-0513; (800)308-7991. Monitors VHF channel 16, switch to channel 68, CB channel 09. Open all year, 7 days. Gasoline, diesel, propane, CNG, stove alcohol. Guest moorage is in 100 slips and along 460 feet of dock, plus unoccupied slips when available, with 30 & 50 amp power, restrooms, showers, laundry, pumpout, portapotty dump. Reservations best by telephone, but OK by radio.

Two restaurants, both with comfortable lounges, are within walking distance, one in the original upland building, the other in the new hotel. Free shuttle to 27 hole golf course for marina guests. The marina store carries groceries, beer, wine, ice, sundries, fishing tackle and bait, limited marine hardware and supplies. Nearby doctor, camping, post office. Marine mechanics are on call from Port Townsend. This is a well-protected harbor, but when entering, watch charts and depth sounder.

Mats Mats Bay. Use chart 18477; 18473; 18441. A course between Port Ludlow and Mats Mats Bay should be drawn to avoid Snake Rock, close to shore, and Colvos Rocks and Klas Rocks, farther offshore. Colvos Rocks are marked by a buoy at each end, and Klas Rock is marked. Snake Rock is not.

Mats Mats Bay has a dogleg entrance with a least depth of 5 feet. A lighted range shows the center of the narrow channel. Once in the bay, you'll find anchorage in 15 to 20 feet in the middle. Mats Mats Bay is well protected from almost any wind, and is a favored hideyhole. A launch ramp is at the south end of the bay. A large rock used to almost block the entrance to the bay, but it was blasted out several years ago, and buoys now mark the channel. Pay attention to all buoys, and do not stray from the marked channel, especially at low water.

Oak Bay. Use chart 18477; 18473; 18441. Oak Bay is a residential area, with convenient anchoring depths approaching the Port Townsend Canal. Oak Bay County Park is on the west side of the channel, a mile or so south of the entrance to the canal.

Oak Bay County Park, northwest shore of Oak Bay. Open all year, restrooms, no power, water or showers. Anchoring or beaching only. Marked by a rock jetty. Boat launch ramp, campsites, picnic tables, swimming, scuba diving, clamming, crabbing.

Port Townsend Canal. Use chart 18464; 18441. The Port Townsend Canal (also known as the Hadlock Canal)

See area map page 51

runs from Oak Bay to Port Townsend Bay through a relatively narrow dredged channel. The canal is spanned by a bridge with a 58-foot vertical clearance. Currents run 2.5-3 knots. Port Townsend Canal is a secondary station under the Deception Pass reference station in the current tables.

Irondale and Port Hadlock. Use chart 18464; 18441. The towns of Irondale and Port Hadlock are west of the northern entrance to the Port Townsend Canal. An old alcohol plant has been converted into a resort at Hadlock, complete with a breakwater-protected marina. Anchorage in the area is good, sand bottom, but be careful to stay north of the little island between Irondale and Port Hadlock.

④ **Port Hadlock Bay Marina,** P.O. Box 1369, Port Hadlock, WA 98339, (360)385-6368; (800)785-7030, fax (360)385-6955, e-mail: PTHADMAR@OLYMPUS.NET. Open all year, 30 amp power with 50 amp being added for 1997, reservations recommended. Restrooms and showers, pumpout installed for 1997. The marina has mostly permanent moorage. The adjacent Old Alcohol Plant Lodge has a restaurant and lounge. No groceries, repairs, or marine supplies at marina, but a general store and laundromat are close.

Kilisut Harbor. Use chart 18464. Kilisut Harbor is entered through a channel between Walan Point and the spit that protects the harbor. The channel is well marked, though shallow, averaging about 11 feet. The channel swings past Fort Flagler State Park on the north shore, where there is a launch ramp. Picnicking and camping facilities ashore.

Reference only — not for navigation

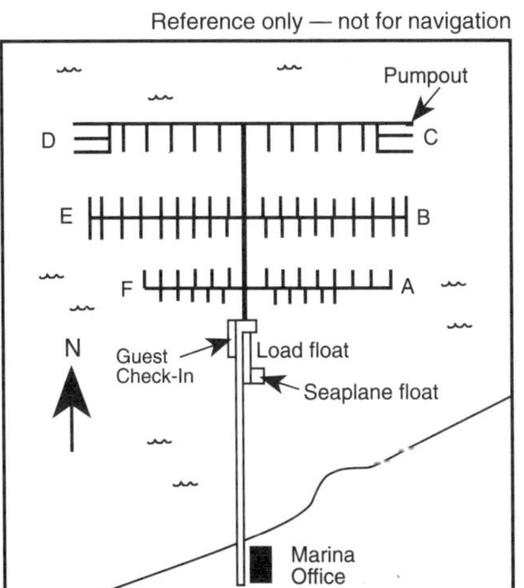

Port Hadlock Bay Marina

Following the channel into Kilisut Harbor leads to Mystery Bay, where the little town of Nordland has a float and a store. Mystery Bay State Park has a long mooring float parallel to the shore. Small boats can be launched over the beach. Anchorage is good, mud bottom, throughout the bay.

⑤ **Mystery Bay Marine State Park,** in Kilisut Harbor on Marrowstone Island. Use chart 18464. Open all year, 683 feet dock space with 4.5-foot depth at zero tide, 7 mooring buoys. Pumpout, portapotty dump, no power, no restrooms, no showers. The park is open for day use only, but overnight mooring is okay at the dock. The dock lies parallel to shore. Vault toilet on shore. One-lane launch ramp.

⑥ **Fort Flagler Marine State Park,** on Marrowstone Island. Use chart 18464 (preferred); 18441. Open all year, day use, overnight mooring and camping. Has 244 feet of dock space with 6-foot depth at zero tide, 7 mooring buoys (buoys removed in winter). Restrooms, showers, laundry, portapotty dump, no power. A popular park. Boat launch, underwater park for divers. Snack and grocery concession. Boat rentals, fishing supplies. Standard, utility and primitive campsites. Campsite reservations are a good idea in summer. Call (800)452-5687 for reservations application.

Port Townsend. Use chart 18464; 18441. Port Townsend has two marinas, the privately-operated Point Hudson Marina and the Port of Port Townsend's Boat Haven marina. Point Hudson is closer to downtown, but Boat Haven is closer to a supermarket.

Port Townsend is a major marine center, with craftsmen skilled in every nautical discipline available to service boats. It is the home of the annual Wooden Boat Festival, held each year the weekend after Labor Day.

This is one of our favorite towns. The commercial district is lined with imposing stone and brick buildings from before 1900, when the residents hoped that Port Townsend would become the principal city on Puget Sound. Victorian homes, most of them beautifully restored and cared for, are on the hill above the business district. Port Townsend's upper business district is located at the top of a long flight of stairs from the lower district. Port Townsend is a haven for writers, craftspeople and artists of all kinds. Tourists overwhelm the town during the summer, but that shouldn't keep anybody away.

Dining: We've had excellent suppers at Lanza's and the Fountain Cafe.

⑦ **Port of Port Townsend,** P.O. Box 1180, 2601 Washington Street, Port Townsend, WA 98368, (360)385-2355. Monitors VHF channel 9. Open all year, 7 days. Gasoline and diesel fuel at The Fish'n' Hole (see below). Guest moorage includes 900 feet of dock space and unoccupied slips as available, with 20 & 30 amp power, restrooms, showers, laundry, pumpout, portapotty dump, moderate-risk waste facility. Customs clearance is available.

The marina is west of the ferry dock, and is entered between a rock breakwater and a piling wavebreak. The first section is reserved for Coast Guard vessels and commercial fish boats. The fuel dock is to starboard after passing the Coast

See area map page 51

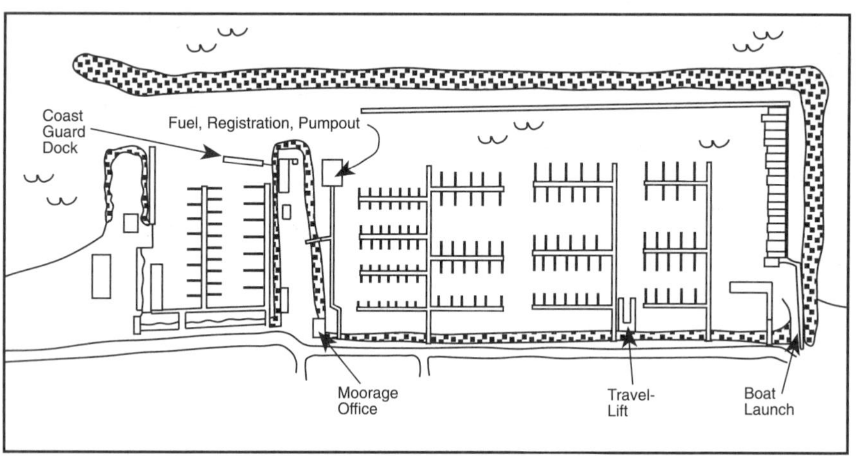

Port of Port Townsend

Reference only — not for navigation

Guard pier. Arrangements for moorage should be made at the fuel dock.

You can call ahead to check availability of slips. After hours, see a map outside the marina office, with empty slips marked. Do not moor at the fuel dock—temporary tie-up only while getting a slip. Haulout and a boatyard are adjacent to the marina. Repairs for everything are available nearby. A large Safeway supermarket is across the highway.

Major boat building and repair facilities and a chandlery (Admiral Ship Supply) are adjacent to this marina. Admiral Marine Works, which recently launched a 163-foot yacht, the largest fiberglass yacht yet built in the U.S., is nearby.

The Fish'n' Hole, Port of Port Townsend, Port Townsend, WA 98368, (360)385-7031. Gasoline and diesel fuel, open all year. Fuel dock only. Located inside the breakwater of the Port of Port Townsend Marina. Floating store carries snacks, bait, tackle.

⑧ Point Hudson Resort & Marina, Point Hudson, Port Townsend, WA 98368, (360)385-2828; (800)826-3854. Open 7 days a week all year, 60 slips and 800 feet of dock space, maximum boat length approximately 85 feet. Has launch ramp, 20 & 30 amp power, restrooms, showers, laundry. Reservations recommended. Customs clearance is available. Limited groceries, charts, motel, two restaurants, RV parking, motel and guest house. Walking distance to downtown. Haulout, repairs and marine supplies available at Fleet Marine, at the head of the harbor.

Enter Point Hudson between two piling breakwaters that force the channel into a distinct bend, directly into the prevailing northwesterly summer winds. This discourages sailing into the Point Hudson marina in anything larger than a dinghy. Inside are a number of finger floats on the east shore, and a long float along the west shore. The marina office is in a white building on the east side. Haulout facilities (Fleet Marine) are located at the end of the dredged basin, with a work yard for maintenance. Other marine businesses in the area include Hasse & Company sailmaker, Brion Toss's Center Harbor Rigging shop, and several wooden boat shops.

Old Fort Townsend Marine State Park, between Glen Cove & Kala Point, Port Townsend, WA, (360)385-3595. Use chart 18464; 18441. Open summers only, 4 mooring buoys, restrooms, showers, no power. The park has swimming, playgrounds, hiking trails, picnic tables, fire rings, kitchen shelters, playground equipment. Self-guided nature trail, clamming, fishing, scuba diving. Standard and primitive campsites.

Fort Worden Marine State Park, north of Port Townsend, (360)385-4730. Use chart 18464; 18441. Open all year, 128 feet of dock space, 8 mooring buoys. Restrooms, showers and laundry, no power. The dock is protected by a wharf. Use the dock or buoys; this is not a good anchorage. Underwater park for scuba diving. Boat launch with two ramps. Tennis courts, picnic areas, snack bar concession near moorage area. Hiking trails, swimming, fishing. Utility and primitive campsites. Campsite reservations taken year-round. Call (800)452-5687.

Upland, the old officers' quarters can be rented overnight. Fort buildings house the Centrum Foundation, which conducts a series of workshops and semi-

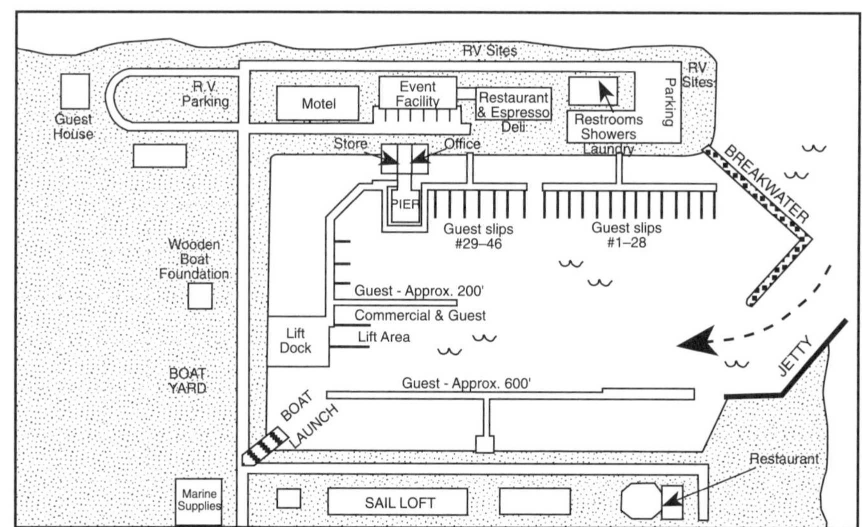

Point Hudson Resort & Marina

Reference only — not for navigation

See area map page 51

Kayakers at the Point Hudson Marina enjoy a water-level view of classic wooden boats during the annual Wooden Boat Festival. The festival is held the weekend after Labor Day at Point Hudson in Port Townsend.

nars on the arts each summer, and the Marine Science Center, where visitors can view a variety of marine life exhibits.

ADMIRALTY INLET—WHIDBEY ISLAND

⑨ **Mutiny Bay Resort,** P.O. Box 249, 5856 S. Mutiny Bay Rd., Freeland, WA 98249, (360)331-4500. Use chart 18477; 18473; 18441. Open all year, reservations recommended for guest moorage. The mooring buoys are available only for resort guests. Restrooms, showers, no power. Resort sells charts, tackle, bait. Nearby doctor, post office, liquor store.

South Whidbey State Park, on Admiralty Inlet, 3 miles south of Greenbank, Whidbey Island, (360)331-4559. Use chart 18441. Open all year, day use and overnight camping, except overnight camping is restricted to weekends and holidays between November 15 and February 14. Restrooms, showers, no power. Anchoring in calm conditions or beaching only, underwater park for scuba diving. Picnic sites. Several-mile-long hiking trail. Standard and primitive campsites.

Fort Casey State Park, 3 miles south of Coupeville on Admiralty Inlet. Use chart 18441. Open all year, day use and overnight camping, restrooms, no power or showers. Anchoring or beaching only, 2-lane launch ramp with boarding floats. Underwater park with artificial reef for scuba divers. Picnic areas, standard and primitive campsites. Lighthouse and interpretive center. Historic displays, remains of old fort.

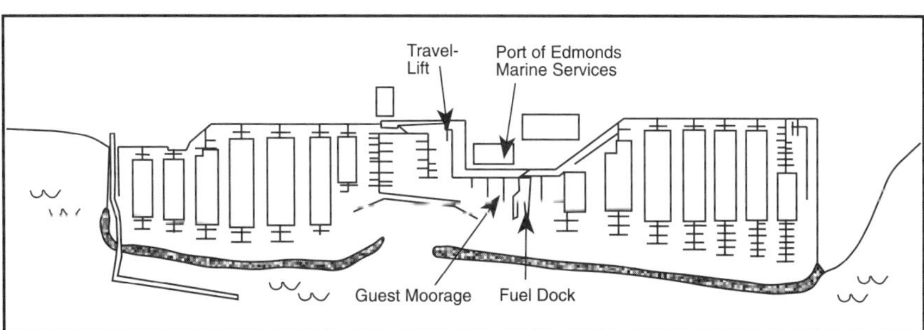

Port of Edmonds

Reference only — not for navigation

Navigation Tip

Tom and Barbara Wilson, on their boat *Toba,* have a good system to keep them out of trouble. "We agree where we are, or we stop the boat until we do," they told us one day. Mrs. Hale and I have followed that practice somewhat over the years, but since meeting the Wilsons we have tried to follow it religiously.

In the summer of 1996 the Wilson's system paid off handsomely. At high tide, we were entering Montague Harbour from the northwest, off Trincomali Channel. We would leave Wise Island to port and Sphinx Island to starboard. As the chart shows, it's important to favor the Sphinx Island side of the passage, because a reef lies off the south end of Wise Island. A dot islet is on the reef, approximately in the middle of the passage.

At high tide I mistook the dot islet for Sphinx Island, and prepared to pass between the islet and Wise Island. Mrs. Hale, bless her, was not so sure. She didn't like the look of the water where I intended to go, and insisted that we confirm our location. Grudgingly I complied, remembering the Wilson's requirement that they stopped the boat until they agreed where they were.

Careful observation confirmed that Marilynn was correct. Chagrined, I went through the proper passage instead of over the top of the reef.

Thank you Tom and Barbara Wilson.

—*Robert Hale*

Hood Canal

Charts	
18445SC	FOLIO-SMALL CRAFT Puget Sound—Possession Sound to Olympia including Hood Canal
18477	Puget Sound—Entrance to Hood Canal (1:25,000)
18458	Hood Canal—South Point to Quatsop Point including Dabob Bay (1:25,000)
18476	Hood Canal to Dabob Bay (1:40,000)

Use charts 18476; 18445sc; 18477; 18458; 18441; 18448. Hood Canal is a 65-mile-long fjord, carved by glaciers. Because the shorelines are fairly straight, with few protected anchorages, it is less used by pleasure craft than many other waterways. Fishing is reported to be good, however, and in clear weather the views of the Olympic Mountains are spectacular.

The best chart for Hood Canal is 18476, which shows the entire canal except for the very mouth. That area is shown well on charts 18473 and 18477. Small Craft chart 18445 shows the entire canal, but in less convenient format.

Several rivers flow from the Olympic Mountains into Hood Canal, and each has formed a mudflat off its mouth. Although the shoal off the Dosewallips River, a couple of miles south of Pulali Point, is marked, the shoals off the Duckabush, Fulton Creek, Hama Hama and Lilliwaup Rivers are not marked, nor is the extensive shoal off the Skokomish River at the Great Bend. Care must be taken to avoid running aground.

Pleasant Harbor and the Alderbrook Inn Resort can take larger boats, but many of the other marinas and parks on Hood Canal are aimed at trailerable boats. This has disappointed some people in larger boats, who had hoped for more facilities for boats their size.

Hood Head. Anchorage can be found behind Hood Head on the western shore of Hood Canal, but the water shoals rapidly to drying flats near the head of the bay.

Bywater Bay State Park, 1 mile north of Hood Canal Bridge on the west shore of Hood Canal. Day use only, toilets, no power, water or showers. Anchoring only, well offshore. Launch ramp, crabbing and clamming, hiking trails.

Port Gamble. Use chart 184473; 18477; 18476. Port Gamble is a fine anchorage, protected from wave action by a sandspit at the entrance. Anchorage in 3 to 5 fathoms is possible everywhere. Many people prefer the area just inside the spit. A range outside Port Gamble will keep you to a mid-channel course as you enter or depart. Sight astern to keep the range lined up while entering. Your course will lead you close to the ends of the Pope & Talbott sawmill docks. A section of the old I-90 floating bridge from Lake Washington is moored in the bay, with some Indian-owned fishboats tied to it. Mooring to this bridge is discouraged.

Hood Canal Floating Bridge. Use chart 184473; 18477; 18476. The east end of the Hood Canal Floating Bridge has a vertical clearance of 55 feet. Clearance on the west end is 35 feet. The bridge can be opened for larger vessels.

Salsbury Point County Park, just off the northeast end of the Hood Canal Bridge. Day use only, restrooms, no power or showers. Anchoring only, 2 boat launch ramps. Picnic tables, fireplaces, children's play area. Nature trail. Sandy beach for experienced scuba divers, because of strong currents.

Squamish Harbor. Squamish Harbor has convenient anchoring depths, but the harbor is quite open, and has numerous rocks and reefs that must be avoided. It is seldom used for overnight anchorage.

Thorndyke Bay. Thorndyke Bay is too open to provide a snug anchorage.

Restricted Area. Use chart 18476. For about 4 miles south from Vinland, the eastern shore of Hood Canal is a Naval restricted area, and is patrolled constantly to keep passing vessels well offshore. This is the location of the Bangor Naval Station, home port for a fleet of nuclear submarines. Several of these awesome machines usually are visible to passing craft.

Seabeck Bay. Use chart 18476. Anchorage is possible behind Misery Point, with good protection from the south and west.

① **Seabeck Marina,** PO Box 310, 15376 Seabeck Hwy NW, Seabeck, WA 98380, (360)830-5179. Monitors CB channel 13. Open all year. Gasoline only. Guest moorage available, 2-fathom depth at zero tide, reservations needed May-August. Restrooms, portapotty dump, no power or showers. Groceries, water and ice. Take-out pizza, espresso, deli, store. Sling for haulout, repairs available. Some marine supplies. Fishing tackle and bait. Camping at Scenic Beach State Park ½ mile away. Seabeck conference grounds nearby.

Kitsap Memorial Marine State Park, 4 miles south of Hood Canal Bridge, (360)779-3205. Use chart 18476. Open all year, day use and overnight camping, 2 mooring buoys. Restrooms, showers, no power. Picnic sites, kitchen shelters, fireplaces. Standard campsites. Swimming beach. Playground, horseshoe pits, volleyball courts, baseball field. Buoys are exposed to wind and tidal currents.

Scenic Beach State Park, south of Seabeck, (360)830-5079. Use chart 18476. Open for day use all year and overnight camping summer only. Restrooms, showers, no power. Anchoring only. Kitchen shelter, fireplaces, fire rings, horseshoe pits, volleyball areas. Standard and primitive campsites. Scuba diving, swimming, hiking, shellfishing.

Fisherman Harbor. Use chart 18476. Fisherman Harbor can be entered only on top of high water, but once inside offers protected anchorage in 5 to 15 feet. Follow the natural channel into the bay, then turn south and follow the spit until anchoring depths are found. All the land around the bay is privately owned. Years ago, we tiptoed into Fisherman Harbor in a sailboat at something less than high tide. It was slow going, with a close watch from the bow and a bit of

Reference only — not for navigation

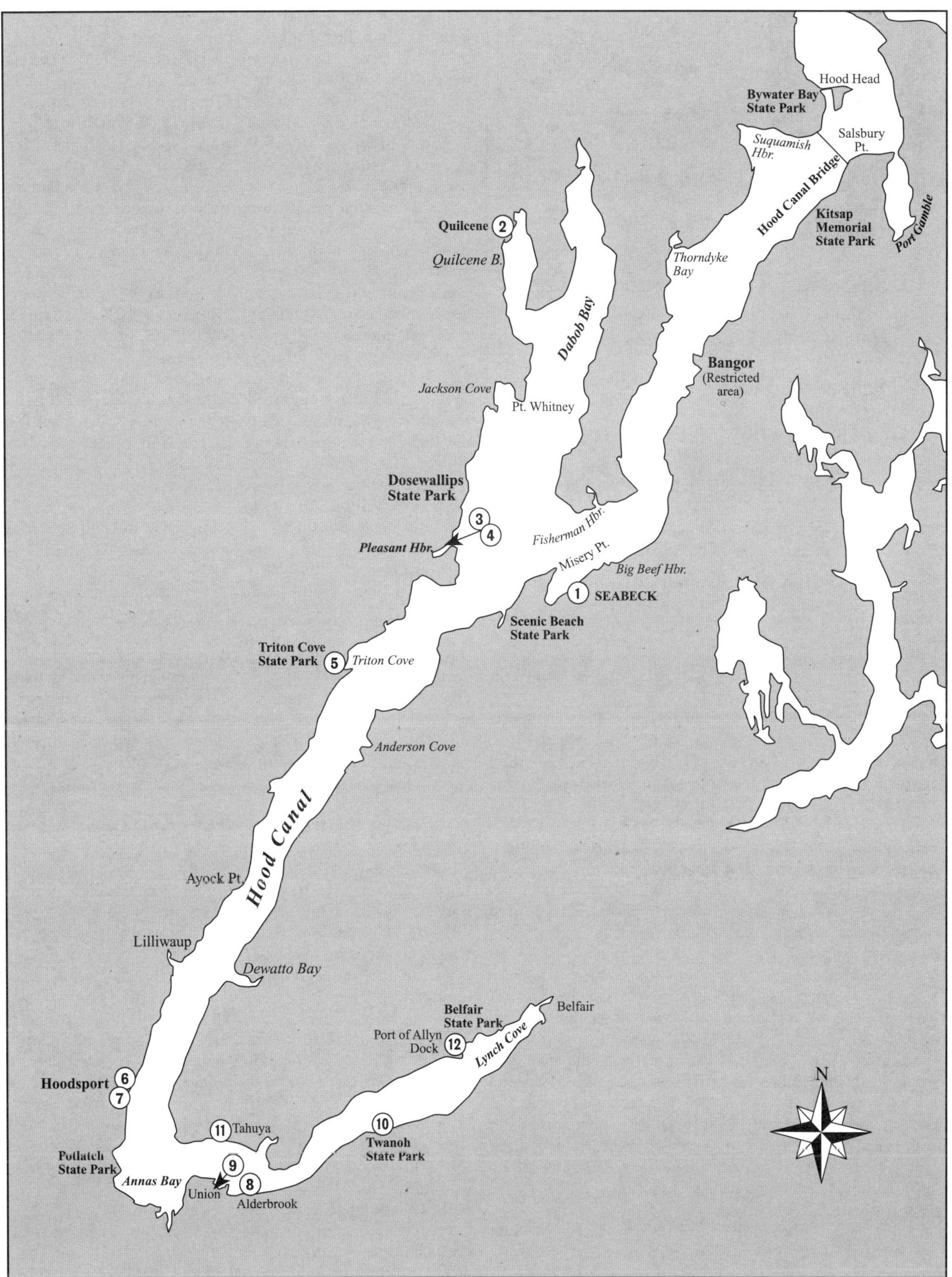

See area map page 57

luck, but the boat got in without touching. Less foolish souls should wait for higher water.

Dabob Bay. Use chart 18476. Most of Dabob Bay is a Naval restricted area, with lights on Point Syloplash, Point Whitney, and Point Zelatched that warn when caution must be used (flashing green) or when the area is closed (flashing red). South of Pulali Point, the western shore of Dabob Bay is not within this restricted area, and includes **Jackson Cove**, where good anchorage can be found.

A State Fisheries Department oyster research laboratory is at Whitney Point, with a good launch ramp alongside. A breakwater-protected marina is at the village of **Quilcene**. Caution should be exercised when transiting Dabob Bay and Quilcene Bay to avoid the large number of shrimp pots throughout the bays in season.

② Quilcene Boathaven, 1731 Linger Longer Rd, Quilcene, WA 98376, (360)765-3131. Open 7 days in summer, as needed in winter. Gasoline and diesel at fuel dock. Some guest moorage available. Has 20 & 30 amp power, restrooms, showers, pumpout, portpotty dump. This is a small, rustic marina away from the more heavily-used destination marinas nearby.

Pleasant Harbor. Use chart 18476. Pleasant Harbor is a major stopping point on Hood Canal, with a fine destination resort marina and a State Park float. Anchorage is possible in 3-7 fathoms, mud bottom. The Pleasant Harbor Marina has excellent facilities for visiting boats. The "Old" Marina has no guest moorage.

③ Pleasant Harbor Marina, 308913 Hwy 101, Brinnon, WA 98320, (360)796-4611. Monitors VHF channels 09 & 16. Open all year 0800-1900, except closed Thanksgiving and Christmas. Gasoline and diesel at the fuel dock. The marina has 30 guest slips plus unoccupied slips as available, with 30 amp power, restrooms, showers, laundry, pumpout, portapotty dump.

It is a popular destination marina, with groceries, ice, bait, tackle, marine hardware and charts, beer and wine, pizza parlor, gift shop, barbecue and picnic area, swimming pool, and hot tub.

Betty and Chuck Finnila, who bought the marina in 1994, already have upgraded the grounds, begun replacing the docks, and improved the facilities. The gift shop is very nice, and the pizza is superb. Near Dosewallips State Park and Olympic National Park.

Pleasant Harbor "Old" Marina. No guest moorage is available.

④ Pleasant Harbor Marine State Park, (360)796-4415. Open all year for day use and overnight mooring. No camping. Dock has 218 feet of space. Vault toilet, portapotty dump, pumpout, no power.

Dosewallips State Park, 1 mile south of Brinnon. Open all year for day use and overnight camping. Restrooms, showers, no power. Anchorage only, outside the delta flats. Hiking trails, picnic areas, standard, utility, and primitive campsites.

Triton Head. Use chart 18476. A State Park launch ramp is at Triton Head, and anchorage is possible off this little bight.

⑤ Triton Cove State Park, west side of Hood Canal, south of the Dosewallips River. Open all year, day use only, small dock with float. Restrooms, no power, no showers. Improved concrete launch ramp, picnic area.

⑥ Hoodsport Marina & Cafe, 24080 Hwy 101, Hoodsport, WA 98548, (360)877-9657. Open all year, guest moorage, call ahead for availability. Restrooms, no power or showers. Restaurant (free moorage while dining). Water, gasoline nearby. Groceries 1 block away.

⑦ Sunrise Motel & Resort, North Hwy 101, Hoodsport, WA 98548, (360)877-5301. Open all year, no power. Restrooms and showers in motel rooms. Stay on your boat or rent rooms. Popular spot for divers. Underwater park and scuba air station. A dive shop is nearby.

Potlatch Marine State Park, south of Hoodsport, (360)877-5361. Use chart 18476. Open all year, day use and overnight camping and mooring. Restrooms, showers, no power. Five mooring buoys are offshore in deep water. The park has a picnic area, an underwater park for scuba diving, short hiking trails, and standard, utility and primitive campsites. Good wildlife-watching.

⑧ Alderbrook Inn Resort, E. 7101 Hwy 106, Union, WA 98592, (360)898-2200; (800)622-9370. Open all year, 2400 feet of dock space, 30 amp power, restrooms, showers, pumpout, portapotty dump. Reservations taken for large vessels. A fine resort, with an 18 hole golf course, tennis courts, indoor pool and Jacuzzi. Boat rentals and crab pot rentals are available. Swimming dock, playground, volleyball court, horseshoe pit, outdoor barbeques. Full service restaurant and lounge. Fuel, groceries, laundry nearby.

⑨ Hood Canal Marina, P.O. Box 86, E 5101 Hwy 106, Union, WA 98592, (360)898-

The pocket-sized Quilcene Boat Haven has limited moorage and a fuel dock.

2252. Open all year. Gasoline and diesel fuel. Guest moorage available, call ahead. Full-time mechanic on-call. Grocery store nearby.

⑩ **Twanoh State Marine Park,** 8 miles west of Belfair, (360)275-2222. Use chart 18476. Open all year, day use and overnight camping & mooring, except no camping in winter. Has 192 feet of dock space, 7 mooring buoys. Restrooms, showers, pumpout, porta-potty dump, no power. This is a large and popular park, with launch ramp, wading pool and playground, picnic areas, kitchen shelters, and fireplaces. Standard, utility and primitive campsites, tennis courts, hiking trails, seasonal concession stand.

⑪ **Summertide Resort & Marina,** NE 15781 Northshore Rd, Tahuya, WA 98588, (360)275-9313, (206)925-9277. Moorage available from May-September, 560 feet of dock space, 21-foot maximum boat length. Restrooms, showers, laundry, no power. Launch ramp and RV spaces. Small boat marina, most people rent cottages or camp. Small store carries ice, propane, groceries, bait, tackle, fishing licenses.

Hood Canal becomes shallow toward its end near Belfair, with extensive drying flats in Lynch Cove, where the Union River enters Hood Canal. Convenient anchoring depths, mud bottom, can be found throughout this end of the Canal.

Belfair State Park, 3 miles west of Belfair on the north shore of Hood Canal. Open all year for day use and overnight camping. Restrooms, showers, no power. Anchor far offshore if at all. Drying mudflats restrict approach to small, shallow-draft boats only. Popular, well-equipped park, camping reservations required in summer. Call (800)452-5687.

⑫ **Port of Allyn**, North shore of Hood Canal, 3 miles south of Belfair, (360)275-2192. Open all year, 4 slips, watch depth at low tide. Has 20 & 30 amp power, restrooms, no water or showers. Launch ramp. Very limited space for visiting boats. Call ahead if you want to hook up to power.

The Essex County Country Club New Year's Anchor Drag

I LEARNED A VALUABLE LESSON one winter night a number of years ago. The lesson is that few pleasure boats carry anchor gear sufficient to hold more boats than itself.

We were attending what was then called a meeting of the "Essex County Country Club" (the derivation of the name is another story)—a New Year's Eve get-together of cruising sailors in the inner harbor at Port Ludlow. This event, which became one of the most boisterous on-the-water parties extant, was started by a group of sailors from the Port Madison Yacht Club who thought they would be excused from paying King County property taxes on their boats if the boats were out of the county on January 1.

Besides myself, two other boats from Edmonds attended: Ole Hansen and his family aboard the 38-ft. ketch *Tangaroa*, and Ned Brown and his family aboard the 36-ft. Hanna ketch *Four B's*. Since Ned arrived in the harbor first, he put down his anchor and Ole and I rafted on either side. Ned's anchor was, if I recall correctly, a 75-lb. Danforth with an all chain rode. We felt perfectly safe in that tight little harbor swinging on so much anchor gear.

After partying until after midnight, we all turned in and were sound asleep in the wee small hours when I awoke to the sound of tree branches scraping against the side of my cabin. I jumped out of the sack and ran on deck. Sure enough, an easterly wind had sprung up and we were slowly dragging, three boats abreast, through the narrow entrance to the harbor.

Within minutes all the skippers were on deck in their skivvies, unlashing the three boats and powering back into the harbor—this time each to his own anchor.

By daylight we discovered that Ned's anchor had fouled in a big mass of old electrical wire that had been dumped there years earlier. When the wind came up, *Four B's* and her attendant boats dragged the whole thing. How we managed to drag without hitting anything remains a mystery. The Lord obviously looks after fools and New Year's Eve revelers!

Although since that time I have happily rafted to other boats for an evening of socializing, I almost always move off and set my own anchor before turning in for the night. Nobody carries enough anchor gear to hold more than his own boat if it comes up to blow during the night.

—*Tom Kincaid*

Northeast Puget Sound—Mukilteo to Penn Cove

Everett • Langley • Port Susan • Saratoga Passage • Coupeville

Charts	
18445sc	FOLIO SMALL-CRAFT Puget Sound—Possession Sound to Olympia including Hood Canal
18423sc	FOLIO SMALL-CRAFT Bel-lingham to Everett including San Juan Islands (1:80,000) Blaine (1:30,000)
18441	Puget Sound—northern part (1:80,000)
18443	Approaches to Everett (1:40,000)
18444	Everett Harbor (1:10,000)

Mukilteo. Use chart 18443. The Mukilteo State Park has a large launch ramp with floats in season. It is exposed to ferry wakes and waves generated by winds on Possession Sound and Port Gardner. Adjacent to the ferry dock a small float, part of the state park, gives access to restaurants and other businesses ashore.

Mukilteo State Park, south of the Mukilteo ferry dock. Open all year for day use and overnight moorage, floats removed in the winter. Restrooms, no power or showers. A small float is north of the ferry dock for day and overnight stays, plus park area south of the ferry dock. The park area (south) has a 4-lane boat launch ramp with boarding floats. This is the only launch ramp in the area. The park has picnic tables, fireplaces, and stoves. Visit the Mukilteo Lighthouse.

Everett. Use large-scale chart 18444 (preferred) or chart 18443. The Port of Everett Marina is the largest marina north of Marina del Rey, and is home to a substantial fishing fleet as well as private pleasure craft. Entry is about a mile upstream from the marked mouth of the Snohomish River. Information about moorage can be obtained from the fuel dock just inside the piling breakwater. *Caution:* River currents can be quite strong, particularly on an ebb tide. Allow for the current as you maneuver.

While you are in the river and approaching the marina entrance, watch for debris in the water and pay close attention to your navigation. Several buoys, including one buoy marking a sunken ship, can be confusing. While the channel can be entered between buoy 3 and buoy 5 off the south end of Jetty Island, for complete safety we recommend that you enter by leaving buoy 5 to port. The channel leads past the newly-constructed U.S. Navy homeport facilities. Large-scale chart 18444 is very helpful. We urge you to use it.

Caution: At night, lights ashore in the new navy facilities make the entrance channel buoys very difficult to see and identify. Any vessel approaching at night should be extremely careful.

Everett has all services, including fuel, water, electricity, pumpout, haulout and repair. Chandleries and a wide range of supply and repair shops are on port property or line Marine Drive. The marina is a good long hike from the central business district, but bus and taxi service are available.

Across the river from the marina is a Port-owned float at Jetty Island, which has what is probably the largest pure sand beach on Puget Sound. The Langus Waterfront Park, with a fine launching facility, is on the north shore of the main river channel, a short distance upstream from the Port of Everett Marina.

Farther up the Snohomish River, Dagmar's Landing is a large dry-land storage facility with a huge fork lift truck and a long float. A detailed chart or local knowledge are required before attempting to go up the river beyond Dagmar's.

① **Port of Everett Marina,** P.O. Box 538, 1720 W. Marine View Drive, Everett, WA 98206, (206)259-6001. Monitors VHF channel 16, switch to 69. Open all year, gasoline and diesel at fuel dock. Guest moorage along 1500 feet of dock with depths 11-20 feet, unoccupied slips used when available, 20 amp power, restrooms, showers, laundry, pumpout, portapotty dump. Customs clearance is available. Watch for strong currents when landing at the guest dock. Haulout and yard storage are available for repairs and maintenance. The portapotty dump and pumpout are free of charge. The Everett Marine Park, a 13-lane boat launch run by Port, is just north of marina. The Port of Everett is a large, complete marina, with shops, full repairs and services nearby, served by Harbor Marine, Crow's Nest, and West Marine, all of them well-stocked marine chandleries. *(See marina map page 63)*

Run and jump among the logs on Jetty Park's beach. The docks have room for several boats.

Reference only — not for navigation

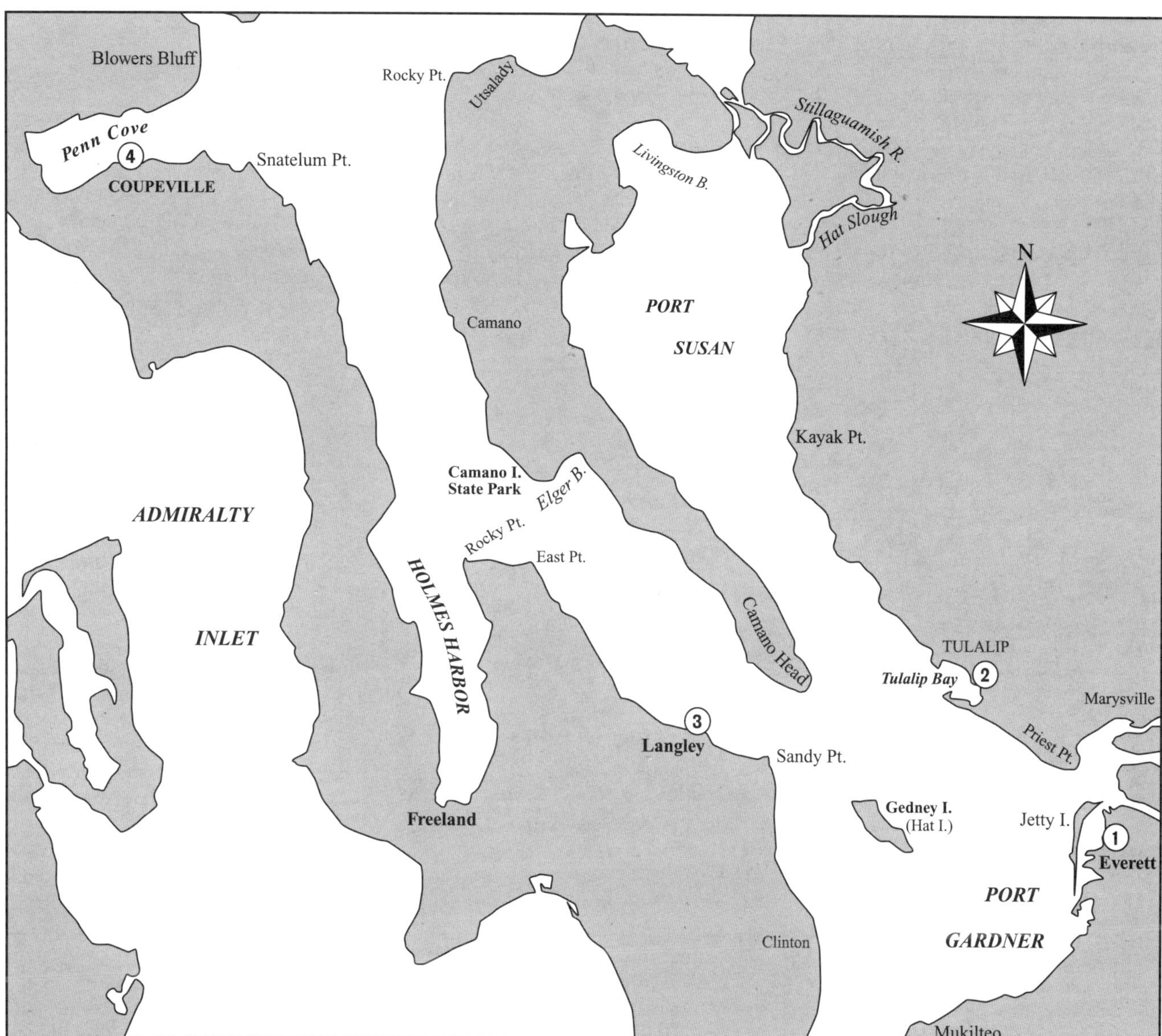

Jetty Island. Jetty Island is a delightful low sand island located across the river from the Everett Marina and Everett Marine Park. It is open all year for day use, with dock space for several boats. Boats can overnight at the dock. Jetty Island has toilets, but no showers, no power, and no water for boats. The toilet is closed in the winter.

River currents can make landing at the docks interesting. Before approaching the dock, be sure your boat is well fendered, with dock lines ready and contigency plans agreed upon. Jetty Island is a wildlife preserve, with great birdwatching. The Parks Department offers nature programs during the summer, and runs boats from the Port of Everett to the island. For information call (206)259-6001.

① **Everett Marine Park** is on the the Snohomish River, north of the Port of Everett Marina. The park is open all year, with 700 feet of guest moorage, restrooms and pumpout, but no power, no showers. The park has a 13-lane launch ramp with boarding floats. An attendant is on duty summer and fall.

Snohomish River Delta. The Snohomish River Delta has three main mouths—Steamboat Slough, Ebey Slough, and the main river—each of which is navigable for all or part of its length. Cautious boaters can cruise the delta country.

Contributing Editor Tom Kincaid has cruised all of this area, some of it several times, in a 30-foot sailboat, a 36-foot powerboat, and an outboard-powered dinghy. The waters are subject to tidal action. Drying flats are off the river mouths. Enter only during the hours of highest tides. The Snohomish River Delta is a fascinating place, with wildlife, calm anchorages, and quiet.

Langus Waterfront Park, north shore of the Snohomish River. The park is open all year and has restrooms, but no guest moorage, power or showers. This is a City of Everett park, with a 2-lane concrete launch ramp and boarding floats. It has a wide concrete float for fishing and launching rowing shells.

Gedney Island. Gedney Island, known locally as Hat Island, is privately owned. The marina on the north shore if Gedney Island property owners, who are served by a private ferry from the Everett Marina.

See area map page 61

Tulalip Bay. Anchorage is possible, but Tulalip Bay is very shallow, with a reef guarding the entrance and drying shoals inside. There are several private floats and mooring buoys owned by members of the Tulalip Indian tribe, which owns the surrounding land.

② **Tulalip Marina,** 7411 Tulalip Drive, Marysville, WA 98270, (360)651-4999. Open all year, gasoline and diesel at fuel dock. Guest moorage at 15 slips; unoccupied slips used when available, reservations recommended, 50 amp power, restrooms, pumpout, no showers. The marina has a cafe and store. Kerosene and propane are available. The launch ramp is usable at high tide only. A casino is about 6 miles away.

The long dock at Coupeville has a store and deli at the end. Showers are on the back side of the building. Fuel dock is beyond. Mooring floats are on the right.

Port Susan. Use chart 18441. Kayak Point in Port Susan is a Snohomish County Park, with a launch ramp and load- and unload-only floats. Anchorage is good close to the beach. North of Kayak Point, Port Susan shoals to drying flats, through which meander the two mouths of the Stillaguamish River. At high tide it is possible to cross over these flats and enter South Pass to Stanwood, although the bridge just beyond Stanwood is very low. Contributing Editor Tom Kincaid has seen local fishboats using this channel, but has not done so himself.

Kayak Point County Park. This park is open all year, has restrooms but no showers. Anchoring only, close to shore. The anchorage is exposed to southerly winds. The launch ramp has boarding floats and the park has a fishing pier. No overnight moorage at the pier.

Saratoga Passage. Use chart 18441. Saratoga Passage separates Camano Island from Whidbey Island. The waters are better protected, and often smoother than Admiralty Inlet. Certainly the current is less. Boats running between Seattle and the San Juan Islands often choose this inside route via Deception Pass or LaConner when the wind and seas are up in Admiralty Inlet.

This not to say the waters are always smooth. In July 1996 we encountered uncomfortable seas while southbound in Saratoga Passage during a 25-knot southerly storm, and were forced to run back to Oak Harbor for shelter. Several other boats joined us.

Saratoga Passage is relatively free of all dangers, but it does have two tricks: Rocky Point(s) and Holmes Harbor. A study of the chart shows two Rocky Points in Saratoga Passage. One is on Whidbey Island at the entrance to Holmes Harbor; the other is at the north end of Camano Island.

Southbound boats may be tempted to go straight into Holmes Harbor instead of turning southeast past the Whidbey Island Rocky Point. If you're not watching your chart, the appeal is quite strong. Follow the Camano Island shoreline.

Camano Island State Park, 14 miles southwest of Stanwood, (360)387-3031. Open all year for day use and overnight camping. Restrooms, showers, no power. Anchoring only. Boat launch. Underwater park for scuba diving. Standard and primitive campsites.

Langley. Use chart 18441. The Langley Small Boat Harbor serves the charming village of Langley. If the small boat harbor is full, as it usually is during the summer, anchorage is good south of the harbor, unless strong northerly winds make the area uncomfortable. Before giving up, however, you should know that the dockmaster is quite creative when it comes to fitting boats in. *Be sure you are well-fendered.* The Langley Marina has fuel. Langley itself certainly is worth a visit. The streets are lined with old buildings that house interesting shops, excellent galleries, and fine restaurants.

③ **Langley Small Boat Harbor/Port of Langley,** P.O. Box 366, Langley, WA 98260, (360)221-4246. Guest moorage at 35 slips in the summer, 15 in the winter, follow harbormaster's directions. They try to fit everyone in. The docks have 20 & 30 amp power, restrooms, showers, boat launch. Nearby Langley has groceries, liquor store, post office, doctor. Watch early morning minus tides if anchoring.

③ **Langley Marina,** P.O. Box 681, 202 Wharf Street, Langley, WA 98260, (360)221-1771. Open all year. Gasoline at the fuel dock. Under new ownership. Restrooms, showers, portapotty dump, no power. Kerosene, alcohol, marine hardware, charts, fishing tackle and bait are available. Complete dive shop. Also haulouts and repairs. Next to small boat harbor, walk to shopping.

Elger Bay. Elger Bay is a good anchorage, mud bottom, with surprisingly good protection from northerly winds. Watch your depths close to the head of the bay.

Holmes Harbor. Use chart 18441. Holmes Harbor indents the eastern shore of Whidbey Island for about 5 miles in a southerly direction. It is deep and relatively unprotected from strong northerlies, but offers anchorage along either shore. Honeymoon Bay is a good spot. Holmes Harbor is subject to williwaws, the unusually strong gusts of wind that spill across the low portion of Whidbey Island. A friend in a heavy 36-foot sailboat was knocked flat and all the battens torn out of his mainsail by one such williwaw while he was maneuvering to anchor with the main still set.

Honeymoon Bay. Honeymoon Bay is a favored anchorage on the west shore of Holmes Harbor. Private mooring buoys take up most of the good spots, but with a little dilligence satisfactory anchoring depths with adequate swinging room can be found. Honeymoon Bay is exposed to northerly winds.

Penn Cove. Use chart 18441. Penn Cove lies about 10 miles north of Holmes Harbor. The cove extends about 3 miles west from Long Point, and is the site of the town of Coupeville. Anchorage is good along both shores and toward the head of the bay. This is where the famous Penn Cove mussels come from. Watch for the mussel-growing pens, and give them ample room.

Coupeville. Use chart 18441. The town of Coupeville has a long piling wharf that extends over the beach to deep water. During the summer season a float is installed for visitors. The town caters to tourists, with displays of Indian canoes and a variety of shops, galleries, and restaurants. Penn Cove is also subject to williwaws, although we have never experienced one there.

④ **Coupeville Wharf, operated by Port of Coupeville,** P.O. Box 577, Coupeville, WA 98239-0577, (360)678-5020. Open all year, 350 feet of dock space, watch depths at low and minus tides. Gasoline and diesel at the fuel dock. Restrooms and showers are available, but no power. There is also room to anchor. The dock store has a deli and some groceries, books, snacks (great noodles!), and ice. Marine repairs are nearby. More groceries, restaurants, and antique shopping are within 4 blocks.

Captain Coupe Park, 9th Street near Wastewater Plant, Coupeville, WA, (360)678-4461. Open all year with restrooms and nearby portapotty dump, no power, no showers. Anchoring only. Boat launch. The dump station is a short distance upland from beach; designed for RV use but portapotties are okay. The park is about ¼-mile by water from Port of Coupeville. It's better to anchor closer the Port. There are mud flats around the boat launch area at low tide.

Three Men in a Rowboat Trying to Get Ashore

My first visit to Oak Harbor was years before the marina was built, and before any of the channel markers had been placed. Three of us were aboard my sailboat returning from a cruise in the San Juan Islands, and one of our number, whose turn it was to prepare dinner, offered to take all of us out to a restaurant. We anchored approximately in the middle of the bay and piled into my 8-foot pram, which thus loaded drew about a foot, and rowed toward shore. The dinghy grounded in soft mud while still a quarter-mile from shore, so we backed off and tried another spot. Before long we got to giggling as we tried all the shorelines with the same result. Eventually we gave up and returned to a late dinner aboard.

— Tom Kincaid

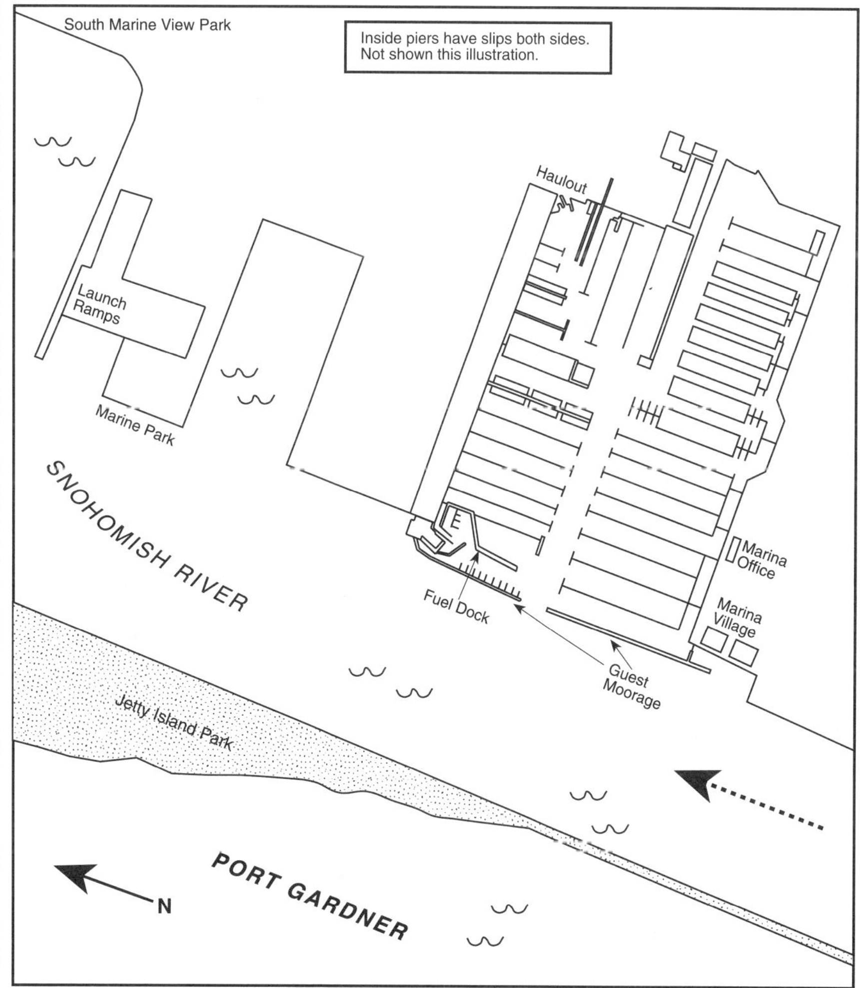

Port of Everett Marina

Reference only — not for navigation

Northeast Puget Sound—Oak Harbor to Blaine

Oak Harbor • LaConner • Deception Pass • Anacortes • Bellingham
Semiahmoo Bay • Point Roberts

Charts

18445SC	FOLIO SMALL-CRAFT Puget Sound—Possession Sound to Olympia including Hood Canal
18423SC	FOLIO SMALL-CRAFT Bellingham to Everett including San Juan Islands (1:80,000) Blaine (1:30,000)
18441	Puget Sound—Northern part (1:80,000)
18443	Approaches to Everett (1:40,000)
18428	Oak and Crescent Harbors (1:10,000)
18427	Anacortes to Skagit Bay (1:25,000)

No shortage of guest moorage at Oak Harbor. Picnic tables are part of the guest dock.

OAK HARBOR TO ANACORTES

Oak Harbor. Use chart 18428 *(large-scale, recommended)*; 18441. Oak Harbor is a shallow and well protected port with a major, city-owned marina. We strongly suggest that you use large-scale chart 18428. The entrance channel is marked by red and green markers, beginning with buoy 2, offshore about 1 mile south of Maylor Point. A shoal north of buoy 2 is littered with large boulders. The channel takes a 90-degree turn to the east for the final mile that leads to the marina. Shoals line each side of the channel all the way in. At low tide especially, you will go aground if you stray.

The Oak Harbor Marina is protected by a floating concrete breakwater. Guest moorage is along the inside of this breakwater, or along the long float that leads to shore. The marina has complete facilities, and park grounds ashore for dog-walking, games, or strolling. It's a bit of a walk to town, however, and the nearest grocery store is 1¾ miles away. You may want to call a cab.

Good anchorage can be found just outside the marina, close to the entry channel. A small float for dinghies is in front of the business district, about a 1-mile walk from the marina. The float goes dry at low tide. Use it with caution.

① **Oak Harbor Marina,** 865 SE Barrington Dr., Oak Harbor, WA 98277, (360)679-2628; fax (360)240-0603. Monitors VHF channel 16, CB channel 35. Open all year, 100 slips of guest moorage, unoccupied slips used when available. Fuel dock has gasoline & diesel. Depth at zero tide is 8 feet, call ahead if your boat is over 50 feet. The marina has 20 & 30 amp power, restrooms, showers, pumpout. Restrooms and showers are on the lower level of the administration building, at the head of the docks. Additional showers, (newly rebuilt and excellent) are in buildings a short distance away. Propane is available. Haulout is available. Catalina Marine Service has repairs and a chandlery. One mile to restaurants. Nearby doctor, post office, liquor store. Entering Oak Harbor, keep red buoys close to starboard. Guest moorage is not available during Crow's Nest Race Week, July 19-26, 1997. Dave Williams is the harbormaster. *(See marina map page 66)*

Crescent Harbor, just east of Oak Harbor, is controlled by the Navy. Use chart 18441; 18428 *(large-scale, recommended)*. The Navy facility along the western shore near the head of the bay has large old hangars that once housed

Reference only — not for navigation

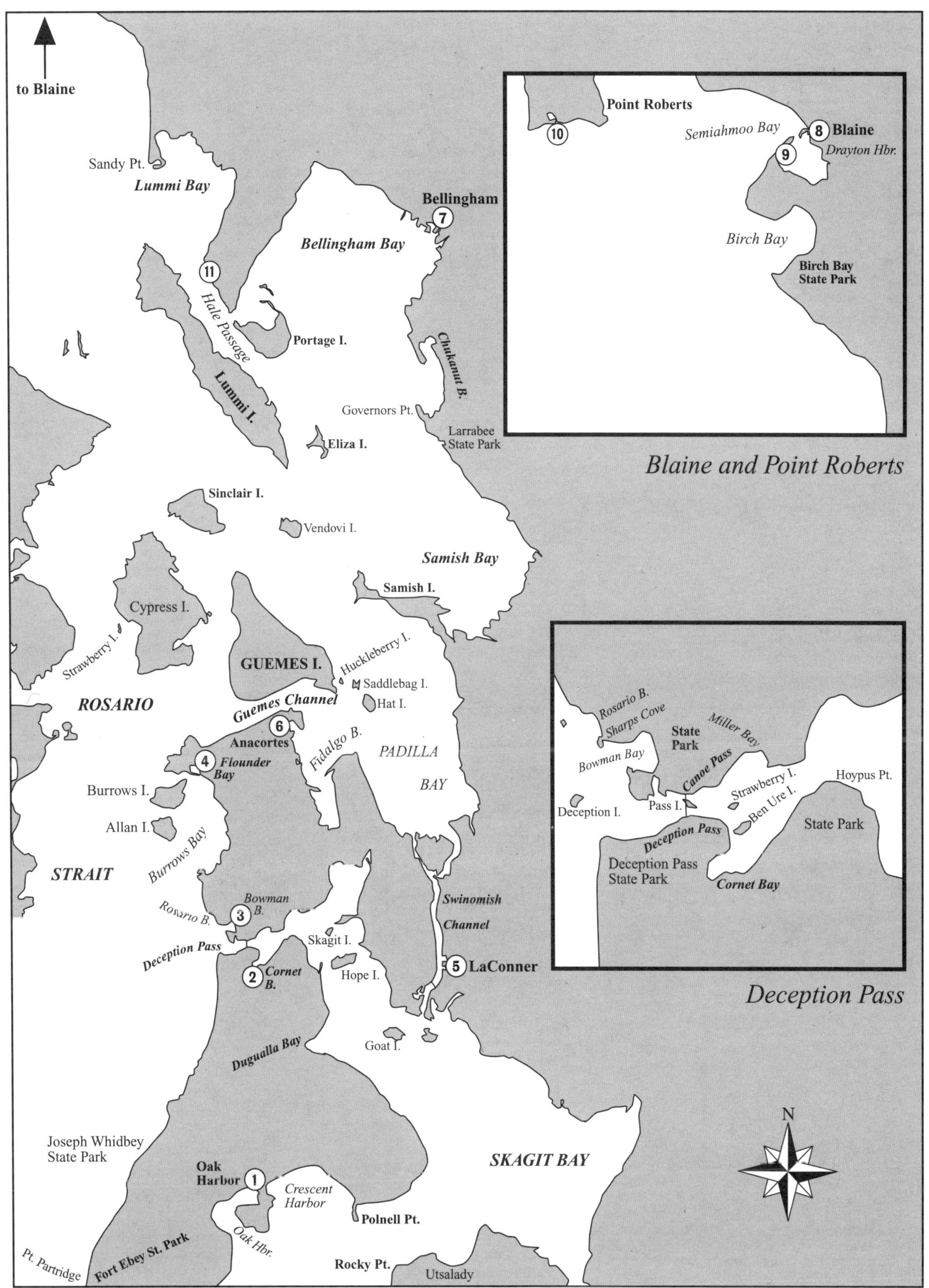

See area map page 65

Catalina flying boat aircraft. The docks are for Navy use.

Rocky Point. Use chart 18441. Tidal currents meet off Rocky Point. North of the point they flood from north to south out of Deception Pass and the Swinomish Channel. South of Rocky Point they flood from south to north out of Saratoga Passage.

Skagit Bay. Use chart 18427. Skagit Bay extends from Polnell Point and Rocky Point to Deception Pass. The bay becomes increasingly shoal toward the east. The navigable channel parallels the Whidbey Island shore, and is well marked by buoys. Use caution in this channel, since buoys can be dragged out of position by tugs with tows. The village of Utsalady, with a launch ramp, is on the Camano Island side of the channel. Anchorage is possible, mud bottom, although not protected from northerly winds and waves.

Hope Island. Use chart 18427. Hope Island is a State Marine Park, with mooring buoys on the north side and good anchorage, particularly along the south shore. **Skagit Island** just to the north also has mooring buoys. **Similk Bay** is shoal, but navigable over most of its area for shallow draft boats. Anchorage is possible anywhere.

Deception Pass Marine State Park, Skagit Island and Hope Island area. Use charts 18427; 18423SC. Open all year for day use and overnight camping and mooring. The park has 6 mooring buoys, 2 of them located off the north shore of Skagit Island, 4 of them off the north shore of Hope Island. No power, water, restrooms or showers. Boats can also anchor.

Cornet Bay. Cornet Bay, tucked in behind Ben Ure Island, indents the north shore of Whidbey Island just east of Deception Pass. A dredged channel marked by pilings leads to the Deception Pass Marina and a state park, both of which offer visitors' moorage. The passage west of Ben Ure Island should not be attempted except at high tide, and then only by shallow draft craft.

② **Deception Pass Marina,** 5191 N. Cornet Bay Road, Oak Harbor, WA 98277, (360)675-5411. Monitors VHF channel 16, switch to 68, CB channel 10. Formerly the Cornet Bay Marina. Open all year. The marina has several slips reserved for visiting boats, and uses unoccupied slips as available. The docks have 30 amp power, but only limited room for larger boats. Gasoline and diesel at fuel dock, stove alcohol, kerosene and propane available. The store carries groceries, bait, tackle, fishing licenses, charts, books, beer and wine. Restrooms, no showers. Call ahead for availability of guest moorage. Laundry, haulout, towing and emergency rescue. Barbecue, picnic areas, launch ramp, hiking at nearby Deception Pass State Park. Stay in the marked channel. *(Marina map page 67)*

② **Deception Pass Marine State Park, Cornet Bay area.** Open all year for day use and overnight moorage. The park has 1140 feet of dock space, restrooms, showers and pumpout, but no power. Moorage is at a T-dock with slips and floats. There are also floats that are not connected to land. A 4-lane boat launch has boarding floats. Nearby are hiking trails and picnic areas. Groceries, laundromat and services are at nearby Deception Pass Marina. Park has campsites, but not near this area.

Deception Pass. Use chart 18427; 18421. Deception Pass narrows to 200 yards at Pass Island, which is one of the anchors for a spectacular 144-foot-high bridge that connects Whidbey Island to Fidalgo Island. Currents at maximum can hit 8 knots, with strong eddies and overfalls. Dangerous waves can form when a big ebb tide meets strong westerly winds. It is best to time your approach to enter the pass at or near slack tide. Tidal current predictions are shown under "Deception Pass" in the tide and current books. An even narrower pass, Canoe Pass, lies north of Pass Island.

From the west, the preferred route to Deception Pass lies just to the south of Lighthouse Point and north of Deception Island.

North of Lighthouse Point, **Bowman Bay**, also known as Reservation Bay, is part of Deception Pass State Park. Bowman Bay offers good anchorage, a mooring float and buoys in season, and a launch ramp.

③ **Deception Pass Marine State Park, Bowman Bay (Reservation Bay).** Use chart 18427 (preferred) or 18421. Open all year for day use and overnight camping & mooring. Five mooring buoys. Restrooms, no power, no

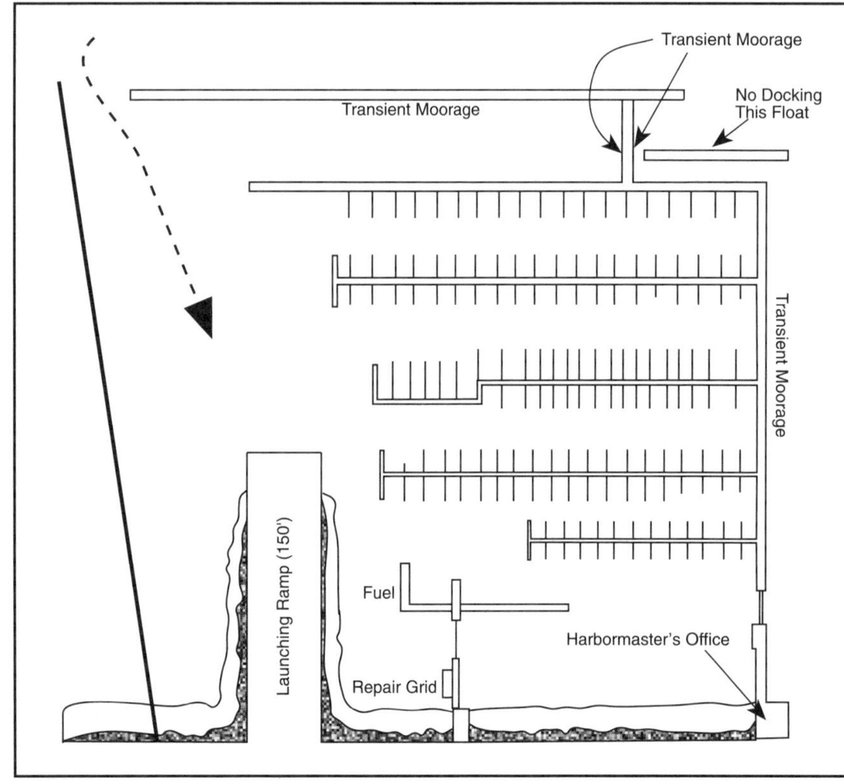

Oak Harbor Marina

See area map page 65

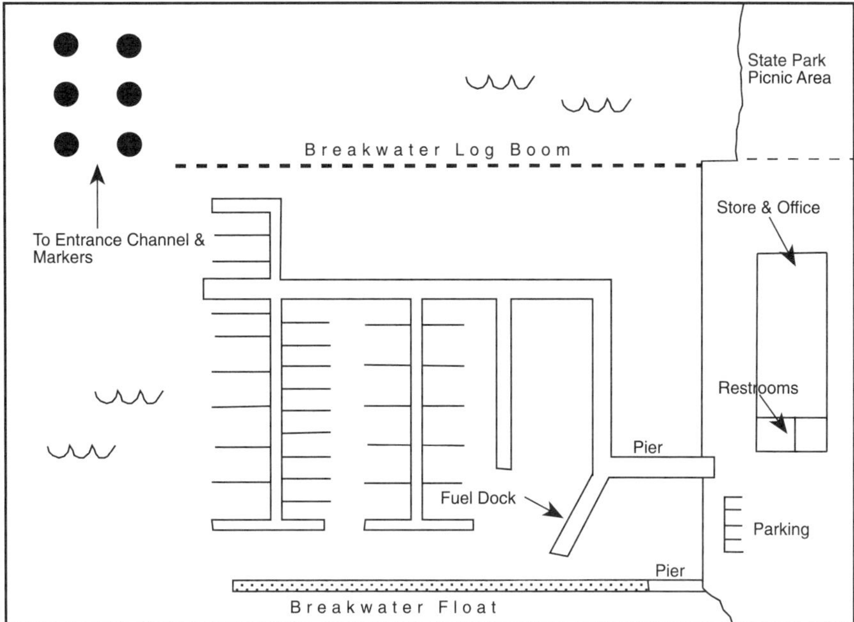

Deception Pass Marina

Reference only — not for navigation

showers. Bowman Bay has a gravel 1-lane boat launch ramp. Standard campsites are on the north shore. The park has picnic sites and kitchens. An underwater park for diving is near the mouth of Bowman Bay, near Rosario Head. When entering Bowman Bay take care to avoid Coffin Rocks and Gull Rocks, which cover at high tide. Safe entry can be made by staying fairly close to the Reservation Head side of the entrance. Anchorage is also available in the bay north of Rosario Head, but it is exposed to wave action from Rosario Strait.

③ **Deception Pass Marine State Park, Rosario Bay/Sharpes Cove.** Open all year for day use and overnight camping & mooring. The park has 128 feet of dock space, restrooms, showers, portapotty dump, but no power. Picnic sites, kitchen, standard campsites are located east of Sharpes Cove on the north shore of Bowman Bay.

Fort Ebey State Park, west side Whidbey Island, (360)678-4636. Open all year for day use and overnight camping. The park has restrooms and showers, but no power. Anchoring only, or small boats can be beached. Standard campsites, picnic sites. Interesting bunkers and gun batteries are in the old fort.

Joseph Whidbey State Park, northwest shore of Whidbey Island on Admiralty Inlet, (360)678-4636. Open summers only, March 31 through Sept. 29, day use only. Toilets, no power, water or showers. Anchor or beach only. One mile of sandy beach on Puget Sound. Picnic sites.

Alan Island. Alan Island is privately owned, but anchorage can be had in the little bight on the east shore.

Burrows Island State Park, open all year, no facilities. Use chart 18427. This is an undeveloped 330-acre state park. Anchor in Alice Bight, on the northeast shore, or beach. No camping or fires. Pack out all garbage. Do not disturb wildlife or surroundings. Most of the shoreline is steep cliffs. A lighthouse is on the west tip of the island.

Flounder Bay. Use chart 18427. Flounder Bay has been dredged to provide moorage for the Skyline real estate development. The Skyline Marina and ABC Yacht Charters are inside the spit. There are chandleries, a restaurant, overhead launching system and other facilities, including a large building that is used for the dry storage of boats. Entry is from Burrows Bay, along a dredged channel marked by pilings.

④ **Skyline Marina,** 2011 Skyline Way/Flounder Bay, Anacortes, WA 98221, (360)293-5134. Monitors VHF channel 16, switch to channel 68. Open all year, gasoline and diesel at two fuel docks. Guest moorage has 20 & 30 amp power, restrooms, showers, laundry,

See area map page 65

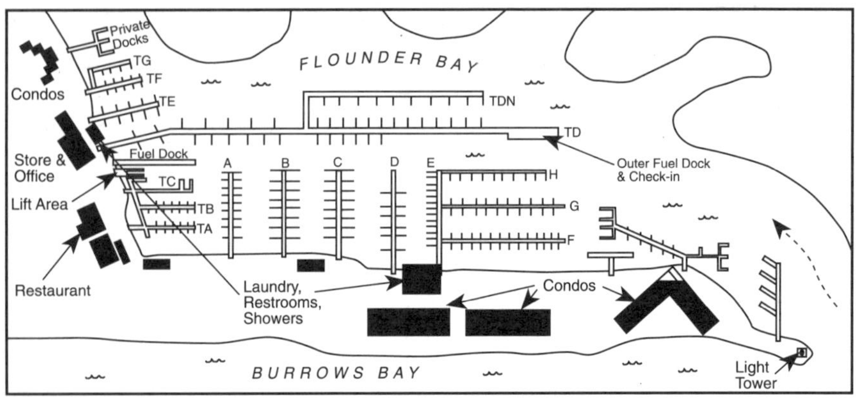

Skyline Marina

Reference only — not for navigation

pumpout and new vacuum pumpout system. Customs clearance is available 0800-1700. The marina also has haulout and repairs, propane, CNG, marine charts, books, supplies, bait and tackle. Groceries and restaurant nearby. Water taxi available to San Juan Islands. The marina is 4 miles from downtown Anacortes. *(Marina map this page)*

Swinomish Channel. Use chart 18427. The southern entrance to Swinomish Channel lies just north of Goat Island. Do not to turn into the channel until the range markers in Dugualla Bay are in line. Check that range as you go; tidal currents flow across the channel and can sweep a boat off course. The channel is well marked but narrow, particularly if you meet a tug with a tow of logs. The channel bends sharply at Hole in the Wall, around a high rock outcropping. Swirling currents in this area can call for close attention.

North of Hole in the Wall, the entrance to Shelter Bay indents the western shore of Swinomish Channel, with numerous private moorages. The town of LaConner stretches along the eastern shore of the channel. Before arriving at LaConner, you pass under the Rainbow Bridge, a lovely structure with a vertical clearance of 75 feet in the center. The Swinomish Indian Reservation occupies most of the west side of the channel. There is a long float that was used by visitors to an Indian-owned restaurant ashore. The restaurant may not be open. Across the channel, several privately-owned floats lead to restaurants and other businesses along LaConner's waterfront, as well as a fuel station.

Just north of LaConner is another point where the flood and ebb currents meet, ebbing south past LaConner, and north toward Anacortes. The channel is marked by buoys and ranges, but follows a generally northerly direction until it passes under a swinging railroad bridge and fixed highway bridges to enter Padilla Bay. The railroad bridge is seldom used, and normally is open. The highway bridges are high enough that they don't impede pleasure craft traffic.

LaConner. Use chart 18427. The Port of Skagit County maintains two large marinas just north of downtown LaConner. Both marinas have guest moorage and full facilities for visitors, including fuel, propane, laundry, showers, haulout and repair, and nearby chandleries. Currents in Swinomish Channel can be quite strong. Make allowances for the current before landing anywhere along the channel.

The town of LaConner is completely charming. It has good restaurants, many galleries, museums, and shops (including a bookstore with an excellent nautical selection), and antique dealers that are worth visiting. Public floats line the business district. During the summer, hordes of visitors arrive by auto and tour bus, so the town is crowded, but still enjoyable.

⑤ **LaConner Marina,** 613 N. 2nd St., LaConner, WA 98257, (360)466-3118. Open all year, 2300 feet of dock space for visiting boats, unoccupied slips used when available. The marina has 30 amp power, restrooms, showers, laundry,

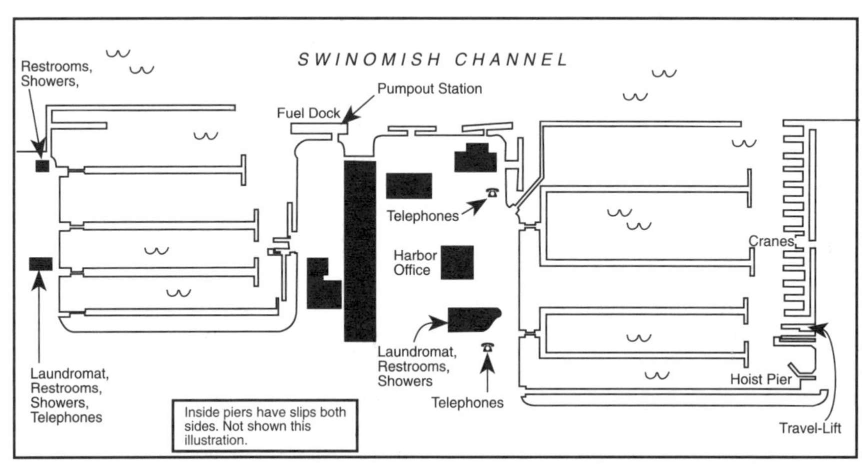

LaConner Marina

Reference only — not for navigation

See area map page 65

LaConner, on the Swinomish Channel, is a popular stop. Public marinas are located at the north end of town, to the left of the photo.

pumpout. A fuel dock is adjacent. All shopping and services within walking distance.

⑤ **LaConner Landing Marine Services,** P.O. Box 1020, LaConner, WA 98257, (360)466-4478. Open all year. Fuel dock with gasoline and diesel. Has a restroom and pumpout, but no power or showers. The store has fishing tackle, bait, ice, beer and wine, marine items, and some groceries.

Padilla Bay. Use chart 18427. The well-marked channel through Padilla Bay is about 3 miles long, between drying flats. Don't take any shortcuts until past beacon 2, which marks the edge of Guemes Channel. Deeper draft boats, such as sailboats, should hold to a mid-channel course, especially at low tide. We once put a sailboat gently aground while toward the edge of the marked channel. To the west of the channel are long docks serving tankers calling at the two major oil refineries in Anacortes. Often, one or more tankers lie at anchor awaiting room at the docks.

ANACORTES TO BLAINE

Anacortes. Use chart 18427; 18421. Anacortes is a major boating center, with fishing and pleasure craft facilities both in Fidalgo Bay and along Guemes Channel. The city's marine businesses can provide for boaters' every need, from food and fuel to complete overhaul.

Three marinas are located on the Fidalgo Bay side of town. The privately-owned Marine Servicenter has fuel, haulouts, and repairs. The marina is protected by a piling breakwater, and is entered through a dredged channel marked by pilings that extend from deep water near Cap Sante.

The new Fidalgo Marina was completed in 1993, and primarily offers permanent covered moorage.

The Cap Sante Marina is owned by the Port of Anacortes, and offers guest moorage, fuel, water, electricity, and haulout facilities. The marina is entered between the arms of a piling breakwater due west of Cap Sante. Guest moorage is along "C" float, the first long float to the north of the entrance. The harbormaster's office is at the head of this float.

⑥ **Cap Sante Boat Haven/ Port of Anacortes,** P.O. Box 297, 1019 Q Ave., Anacortes, WA 98221, (360)293-0694, fax (360)293-0998. Monitors VHF channel 66A; CB channel 05. Open all year. Visiting boats use the guest dock and unoccupied slips when available. Phone ahead or call by radio for slip assignment. The fuel dock (Cap Sante Marine, see below) has gasoline, diesel and propane. Docks have 20 & 30 amp power, with some 50

See area map page 65

Charts—Anacortes to Blaine

18421	Strait of Juan de Fuca to Starit of Georgia (1:80,000)
18423sc	FOLIO SMALL-CRAFT Bellingham to Everett including San Juan Islands and Blaine
18424	Bellingham Bay (1:40,000) Bellingham Harbor (1:20,000)
18430	Rosario Strait—Northern Part (1:25,000)
18429	Rosario Strait—Southern Part (1:25:000)

amp power available. The marina has excellent restrooms, showers and laundry, a pumpout and a portapotty dump. In the summer, 12 mooring buoys south of the breakwater. Customs clearance is available. This is a clean and popular stop, located in the heart of downtown Anacortes. Complete facilities, with marine stores (Cap Sante Marine; West Marine; Marine Supply & Hardware) are nearby. *(Marina map this page)*

⑥ **Cap Sante Marine,** Cap Sante Marina, P.O. Box 607, Anacortes, WA 98221, (360)293-3145, (800)422-5794, fax (360)293-2804. Monitors VHF channel 16, switch to 09. Open all year. Fuel dock with gasoline, diesel and propane, well-stocked marine supply store with charts, parts, sundries, gifts, boat launch, haulout to 55 tons and rescue service for stranded boaters. Look for the Shell sign.

⑥ **Marine Servicenter,** P.O. Box 1506, 2417 T Avenue, Anacortes, WA 98221, (360)293-8200; fax (360)293-9648. Open all year. Fuel dock with gasoline, diesel and propane. Restrooms, pumpout, no power, no showers. Complete repair facilities. Located a short distance south of Cap Sante Marina.

⑥ **Wyman's Marina,** 202 U Avenue, Anacortes, WA 98221, (360)293-2410. South shore of Guemes Channel, east end. Open all year, but little or no guest moorage. Fuel dock with gasoline & diesel. They have a 24 hour card lock system for after hours use. Restrooms, showers, no power. Customs clearance available. Has haulout and marine supplies, propane.

Guemes Channel. Use chart 18427; 18421. The Port of Anacortes owns docks along the Guemes Channel side of Anacortes, where fish boats and other large vessels often are moored. Farther west, Lovric's Sea Craft marina has two large marine ways and facilities for repairing any kind of vessel.

Ship Harbor is the eastern terminus for ferry boats serving the San Juan Islands. Washington Park at Sunset Beach has a fine launch ramp, and camping and picnicking sites ashore.

Washington Park, west shore of Fidalgo Island. Open all year for day use and overnight camping. Restrooms, showers, no power. Anchoring or beaching only at this 220-acre city-owned park at Sunset Beach on the Guemes Channel. Boat launch ramp, picnic tables, picnic shelters, fireplaces, campsites. Playground equipment. The loop road is 3.5 miles in length, and is good for walking or jogging. It has forested areas and viewpoints along the beaches.

GUEMES ISLAND TO POINT ROBERTS

Guemes Island. Use chart 18429; 18424; 18421. Guemes Island has no facilities specifically for boaters, although anchorage can be found along the north shore. Anchorage also can be found on the eastern shore, in a tiny notch called Boat Harbor. A ferry connects Guemes Island to Anacortes.

Saddlebag Island Marine State Park. Open all year for day use and overnight mooring and camping. Use chart 18429 (preferred), or 18421. Boat access only. Anchorage is good off the north or south shore, mud bottom, but there is no float. Water depths are inconveniently deep on the west side, and inconveniently shallow on the east. The better anchorage is on the north side; not much protection on the south side. Vault toilets, primitive campsites. Cascadia Marine Trail campsite. One mile hiking trail. "Hot spot" for crabbing.

Huckleberry Island State Park, north end of Padilla Bay. Open all year, day use only. No services. This is an undeveloped 10-acre island, with anchoring or beaching only. No fires or camping. Pack out all garbage. Attractive to kayakers and scuba divers. Gravel beach on the southwest side of the island.

Cypress Island. Use chart 18430; 18424; 18421. A park ranger once told

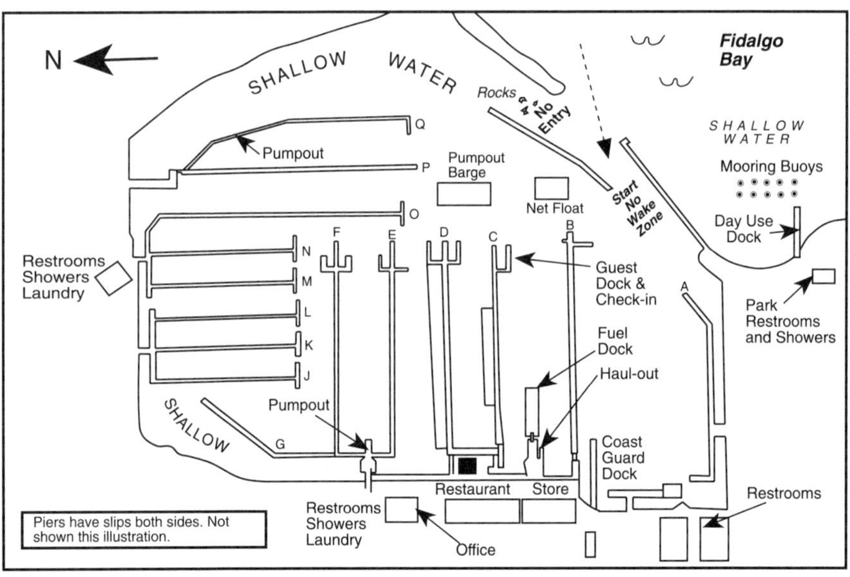

Cap Sante Boat Haven

Reference only — not for navigation

See area map page 65

us he considers Cypress Island to be the "crown jewel of the San Juans." We wouldn't want to argue with him. Cypress Island, now largely in public ownership, is beautiful, and is an excellent place to stretch the legs. Access is hindered by a shortage of good anchorages, though, so you won't be bothered by large crowds. Several trails lead off from Pelican Beach at the northeast corner of the island. They can provide leisurely walks or vigorous hikes.

About a half-mile south of Pelican Beach, just past a small headland, two little coves are quite pretty, and have room for one or two boats each.

Eagle Harbor is shallow, especially at low tide. Watch out for a shoal in the middle. If you have sufficient depth, Eagle Harbor is quite protected. Deepwater Bay, with its fish farms, is unattractive. If you get downwind from the fish farms you'll be in for a sensory experience.

Pelican Beach Park, a DNR park on the northeast side of Cypress Island. Open all year for day use and overnight camping and mooring. The park has 6 mooring buoys, a gravel beach, 4 campsites, clean vault toilets, picnic shelter, fire pit, information board. Many kinds of wildlife and birds can be observed. Public DNR beaches extend from the park around the north end of Cypress Island for 1.5 miles until just south of Foss Cove, and south of the park for 0.5 mile to Bridge Rock. The moorage is unprotected to the north. If anchored or moored to a buoy and the northerly wind comes in, you'll not want to stay.

Cypress Head, east side of Cypress Island. Open all year for day use and overnight camping and mooring. The park has 5 mooring buoys and 5 campsites, picnic sites, vault toilets, no other facilities. Three miles of public tidelands extend from the moorage/recreation area. Many types of birds and wildlife, good fishing. Tidal rips at the south end of the island cause high wave action.

Strawberry Island State Park, west of Cypress Island in Rosario Strait. Open all year. Anchoring or beaching only, Anchorage in settled weather only. Strong currents and submerged rocks make landing difficult; skiffs or kayaks are best for landing. Park has 3 Cascadia Marine Trail campsites, vault toilet.

Visitor docks in the older Squalicum Harbor Marina are tight. When full, visitor boats occupy slips across the waterway. Not much room to maneuver.

Visitor docks in the newer Squalicum Harbor Marina have much more room. Boats 36 feet and longer should use these docks.

Sinclair Island. A piling breakwater protects a loading and unloading dock on the south shore of Sinclair Island, but there are no facilities specifically for pleasure boaters. **Vendovi Island** is privately owned, with no public facilities. **Eliza Island** is also privately owned, with a private dock and float on the north side. Anchorage is possible several places around the island.

Chuckanut Bay. Use chart 18424. Chuckanut Bay is a good anchorage, with protection from prevailing winds in the north or south arms. Enter close to Governors Point to avoid extensive rocky shoals that partially block the entrance. The land around the bay is privately owned.

Larrabee State Park, 7 miles south of Bellingham on Samish Bay, (360)676-2093. Open all year for day use and overnight camping. The park has restrooms and showers. This was Washington's first official state park, dedicated in 1923. It covers 2000 acres and is heavily used. Facilities include a boat launch ramp, kitchen shelters, picnic tables, standard, utility and primitive campsites. Fishing, clamming, crabbing, scuba diving. Trails allow access to two freshwater lakes within the park. A 5.5 mile walking/bicycling trail connects with Bellingham.

Bellingham. Use chart 18424. Bellingham is the largest city north of Everett, with extensive marine facilities for both commercial and pleasure craft.

See area map page 65

Bellingham is the southern terminus of the Alaska Marine Highway Ferry System, and has an international airport. Moorage and all other needed supplies and services are available at the Port of Bellingham's Squalicum Harbor, which holds commercial and recreational boats. The harbor is divided into two sections, each with its own entrance. The older section's guest dock is tight, and boats larger than about 36 feet should use the newer section, whose guest docks are much more accessible. The harbor master's office is located in the Squalicum Mall, in the older section of the harbor development. The homes of the Bellingham and Squalicum Yacht Clubs are nearby. Taxi and bus service connect the harbor with downtown.

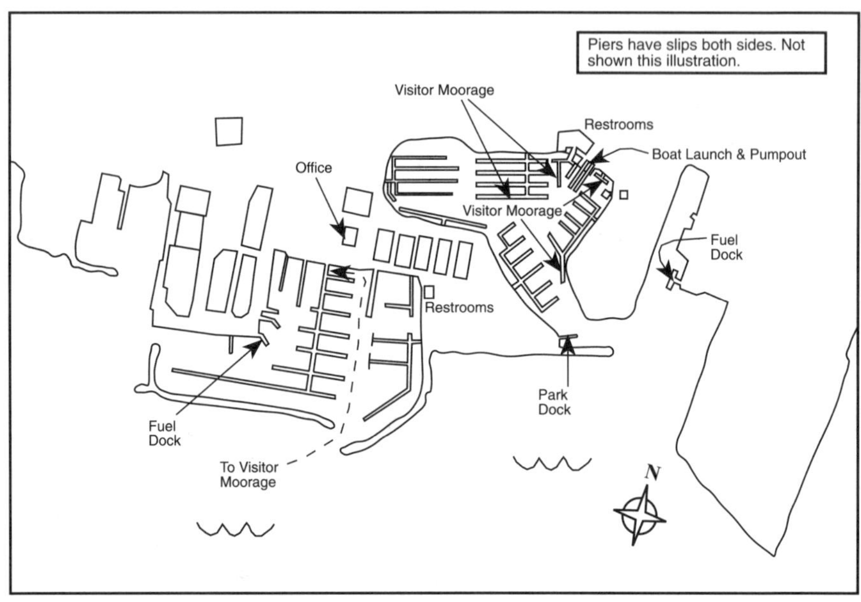

Squalicum Harbor

Reference only — not for navigation

⑦ **Squalicum Harbor/Port of Bellingham,** #22 Squalicum Mall, Bellingham, WA 98227, (360)676-2542; fax (360)671-6149. Monitors VHF channel 16. Open all year, guest moorage along 1500 feet of dock space, unoccupied slips used when available. Two fuel docks in the harbor. The marina has 20, 30 & 50 amp power, restrooms, showers, laundry, pumpout, portapotty dump. Customs clearance is available. Call ahead for availability of guest moorage. A full service shipyard is in the harbor. They also have a marine life tank. Groceries, restaurant, and snack bar are nearby. Also chandleries, engine repair shops.

⑦ **Hawley's Hilton Harbor,** 1000 Hilton Ave., Bellingham, WA 98225, (360)733-1110. Fuel dock with gasoline only. Located at the south entance to Squalicum Harbor at the foot of Hilton Avenue. Look for the Texaco sign. Travelift, repairs. Oil disposal available.

⑦ **Harbor Marine Fuel,** 21 Squalicum Fill, Bellingham, WA 98225, (360)734-1710. Open all year. Fuel dock with gasoline and diesel. Store carries motor oils, snacks and ice. Located in northern Squalicum Harbor, behind the breakwater. Look for the big Shell sign.

Lummi Island. Use chart 18424; 18421. Lummi Island is very high (1480 feet), and has no facilities specifically for visiting boaters, although anchorage is good in several places. The Bellingham Yacht Club has an outstation in Inati Bay on the east side, and anchorage is possible along either shore of Hale Passage. A ferry connects Lummi Island to the mainland, and a mooring float is located alongside the mainland ferry dock. Restaurants and other businesses are near this dock. The Lummi Indians haul their boats, including reef net boats, on the beach south of the ferry dock.

⑪ **Fisherman's Cove Marina,** 2557 Lummi View Dr., Bellingham, WA 98226. Open all year, fuel dock with gasoline only, propane, haulout to 34 feet, repairs. Adjacent to the ferry dock on Gooseberry Point.

Inati Bay. Use chart 18424; 18421. Inati Bay is located on the east side of Lummi Island, approximately 2 miles north of Carter Point. It is the best anchorage on Lummi Island, protected from all but northeasterly winds (rare in the summer), with good holding. Great views, picnic facilities ashore. The Bellingham Yacht Club has an outstation at Inati Bay.

Lummi Island Recreation Site, southeast shore of Lummi Island. Open all year, 1buoy, vault toilets, campsites.

Sandy Point. No public facilities are available at Sandy Point, at the north entrance to Lummi Bay. It is a private real-estate development consisting of several canals with homes on them. Long docks serving a refinery and an aluminum plant extend from shore north of Sandy Point.

Birch Bay. Use chart 18421. Birch Bay is very shoal, but could provide anchorage in calm weather. Watch the tides. The

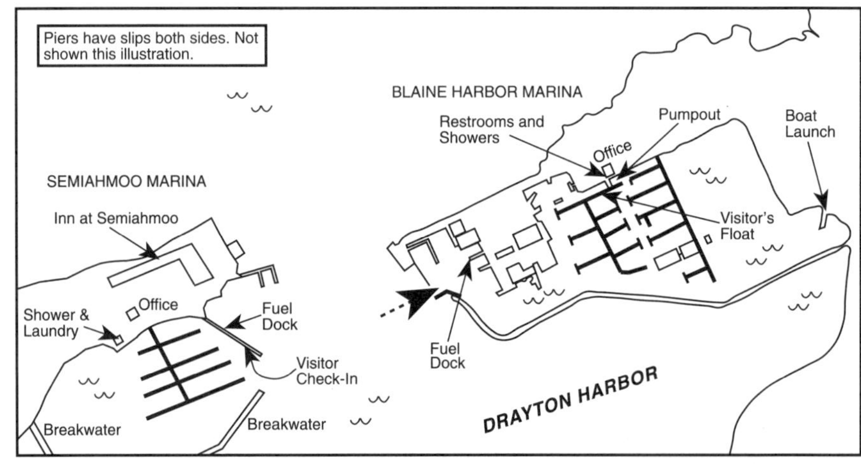

Blaine Harbor

Reference only — not for navigation

See area map page 65

Birch Bay State Park ashore has campsites, picnic and playground equipment, but no facilities for boaters. For campsite reservations, call (800)452-5687.

Blaine. Use chart 18421. Blaine has two moorages in Drayton Harbor. One of them is owned by the Port of Bellingham; the other, Semiahmoo, is privately owned. The approach through Semiahmoo Bay is shoal at all stages but high tide. Pay close attention to the buoys along the drying bank on the south side of the bay, and turn into the entrance channel before getting too close to the eastern shore.

The Port of Bellingham's marina is on the east (port) side as you enter. Entry to that marina is through an opening in the piling breakwater, with a fuel dock on the land side. Once through the breakwater, turn to starboard and follow the signs to the guest moorage, located about in the middle of the harbor.

The Semiahmoo Marina is on the west side of the entrance channel. Both marinas have fuel, water, electricity, small chandleries, and other facilities ashore. The Port's marina gives access to the town of Blaine and a number of boating-related businesses. The privately owned and operated Semiahmoo Marina has a hotel and a fine golf course, but is a considerable distance by road from town. Blaine is a U.S. Customs port.

⑧ **Blaine Harbor/Port of Bellingham,** 275 Marine Drive, Blaine, WA 98230, (360)332-8037; fax (360)332-1043. Monitors VHF channels 16 & 66A. Guest moorage along 170 feet of dock, unoccupied slips used when available. Services include 20 amp power, restrooms, showers, pumpout, portapotty dump. Phone-in customs clearance. Watch depths as you approach. Repairs, haulout, supplies available. Two blocks to town. Boat launch, fishing charters, restaurants nearby. *(Marina map page 72)*

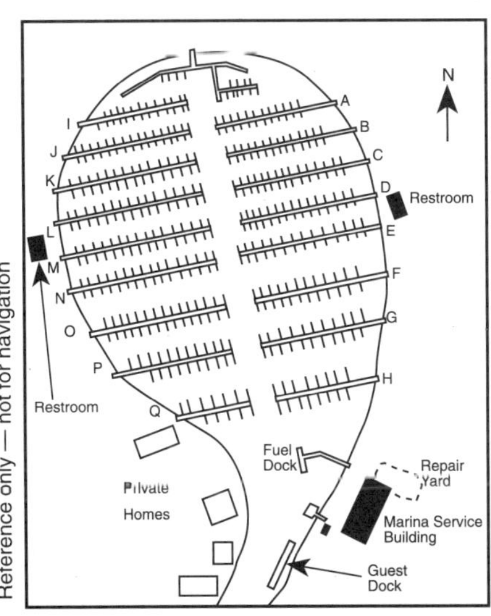

Point Roberts Marina

⑧ **Blaine Marina,** PO Box 1849, Blaine, WA 98231, (360)332-8425. Open all year. This is the fuel dock at the Blaine Harbor Marina. It has *high sulphur* diesel fuel (usually for commercial vessels) only. As of press time in Jan. 1997, they did not have gasoline available. They hope to have it available for the 1997 season. Waste oil disposal is available at Blaine Harbor.

⑨ **Semiahmoo Marina,** 9540 Semiahmoo Parkway, Blaine, WA 98230, (360)371-5700, fax (360)371-2420. Monitors VHF channel 68. Open all year. Gasoline and diesel at fuel dock. Propane and kerosene available. Guest moorage at 500 feet of dock space, unoccupied slips used when available. Call for availability. Services include 30 amp power, restrooms, showers, laundry, pumpout, portapotty dump, chandlery with marine supplies, haulout. Mechanics on duty. Access to Inn at Semiahmoo Resort health club for additional $8 per person. Resort has an Arnold Palmer 18 hole golf course, restaurant, snack bar.

White Rock, in Canada, is almost due north of Blaine, in Boundary Bay. White Rock is a Canadian Customs port of entry. Call (888)226-7277. A long pier crosses tide flats, with floats at the outer end. The village of White Rock has interesting shops and galleries.

Point Roberts. Use chart 18421; 3463 (Cdn.). Point Roberts is a low spit of land extending south from Canada into U.S. waters. Although physically separated from the U.S., Point Roberts is U.S. territory and part of the state of Washington. The Point Roberts Marina is on the south shore. Enter via a dredged channel through drying flats. Ice, groceries, liquor, and doctor are available at Point Roberts.

⑩ **Point Roberts Marina,** 713 Simundson Drive, Point Roberts, WA 98281, (360)945-2255; fax (360)945-0927. Open all year, gasoline and diesel at fuel dock. Propane available. Guest moorage at unoccupied slips, call ahead. Services include 30 & 50 amp power, restrooms, showers, laundry, pumpout. Customs clearance is available. The Dockside Pub and The Grotto restaurant are open all year, shorter hours in the winter. Other restaurants and groceries are nearby. Westwind Marine Services, a well-stocked chandlery, is in the main building.

Lighthouse Marine County Park, Point Roberts, WA. Open for day use and overnight camping in summer, day use only in winter. The park is located on the southwest corner of Point Roberts. Anchor north of the park and row in, or moor at Point Roberts Marina. The park has a launch ramp. Boarding floats are installed in May and removed in October. Facilities include campsites, picnic shelters, fire pits, stoves, restrooms but no showers, sand and gravel beach. Also a whale exhibit. A viewing platform allows you to watch the three local whale pods that follow the salmon.

Strait of Juan de Fuca

Sequim • Port Angeles • Clallam Bay • Neah Bay
Port San Juan • Sooke Inlet

U.S. Charts	
18460	Strait of Juan de Fuca Entrance (1:100,000)
18465	Strait of Juan de Fuca—Eastern Part (1:80,000)
18423SC	FOLIO SMALL-CRAFT Bellingham to Everett including San Juan Islands
18471	Approaches to Admiralty Inlet—Dungeness to Oak Bay (1:40,000)
18468	Port Angeles (1:10,000)
18484	Neah Bay (1:10,000)
18485	Cape Flattery (1:40,000)

Canadian Charts	
3606	Juan de Fuca Strait (1:110,000)
3461	Juan de Fuca Strait, eastern part (1:80,000)
3647	Port San Juan and Nitinat Narrows Port San Juan (1:18,000) Nitinat Narrows (1:12,000) Nitinat Narrows (1:2,000)
3410	Sook Inlet to Parry Bay (1:20,000)
3411	Sooke (1:12,000)

Discovery Bay. Use chart 18471. Discovery Bay lies west of Point Wilson on the Washington side. It is somewhat protected from the Strait of Juan de Fuca by Protection Island, a wildlife refuge. Discovery Bay is open and unobstructed, but is seldom used as an overnight anchorage by pleasure craft. There is a launching ramp at Gardiner, halfway down the bay.

Sequim Bay. Use chart 18471. Sequim Bay is tucked in behind Dungeness Spit. It is a beautiful, quiet anchorage with a public marina (the John Wayne Marina) and a state park with floats. Sequim Bay is protected by a spit that extends from the eastern shore. To enter, steer for the middle of this spit, then turn sharply west and cruise parallel to the spit. Like many Northwest bays, Sequim Bay has a large shoal in the middle, with passage around the eastern and western sides. The marked channel, which leads to the Port of Port Angeles John Wayne Marina, is around the west side. This route is best when approaching Sequim Bay State Park.

The actor John Wayne, who visited Sequim Bay often aboard his *Wild Goose*, donated 22 waterfront acres to the Port of Port Angeles, on condition that the Port build a marina on the site.

① **John Wayne Marina,** 2577 W. Sequim Bay Road, Sequim, WA 98382, (360)417-3440, fax (360)417-3442. Open all year, gasoline and diesel at the fuel dock, guest moorage at 30 slips and 200 feet of dock. Services include 20 & 30 amp power, restrooms, showers, laundry, pumpout, portapotty dump, and launch ramps. A restaurant, and a store with some marine supplies, sundries & books are ashore. Groceries are nearby, also a picnic area and beach access. Use the latest edition of chart 18471. Land at the first float inside the breakwater to check in.

① **Sequim Bay Marine State Park.** Sequim Bay Marine State Park occupies 92 acres along the western shore of Sequim Bay. The park has floats, campsites, a launch ramp and trailer parking area, as well as other state park facilities. Open all year, day use and overnight mooring & camping, 424 feet of dock space and 6 buoys. Facilities include restrooms, showers, portapotty dump, but no power. The mooring buoys are in deep water. The water around the dock and mooring float is shallower. Watch your depths at low tide. Boarding floats at the launch ramp are removed in the winter. Beachfront, scuba diving. The park has picnic sites, kitchen shelters, standard, utility and primitive campsites.

Dungeness Spit. Use chart 18471. Dungeness Spit, 9 miles long, provides protection from westerly weather, and convenient anchoring depths along its inner edge before an attached cross-spit forces the channel south. Shallow draft boats can continue into the inner harbor, where there is a launch ramp and protected anchorage. Dungeness Spit is a wildlife refuge, open to hikers, but has no public facilities.

Port Angeles. Use harbor chart 18468; small-scale chart 18465. Port Angeles is a substantial small city on a bay protected by Ediz Hook. The Port Angeles City Pier, with guest moorage available, is near the south end of the business district. The Port of Port Angeles Boat Haven is a breakwater-protected marina at the southwest corner of the bay.

Port Angeles is a customs port, and is the terminus for a ferry to Victoria. The northern side of the bay is taken up by log storage serving the several mills around the bay. The outer end of Ediz Hook is a Coast Guard station. Just west of the Coast Guard station is the Port Angeles Pilot Station, where ships bound to or from Puget Sound ports board and disembark pilots. Contributing Editor Tom Kincaid recalls that when he was much younger, he spent a couple of enjoyable years skippering the pilot boat at the station.

② **Port Angeles Boat Haven,** Port of Port Angeles, 832 Boat Haven Drive, Port Angeles, WA 98362, (360)457-4505. Open all year, gasoline and diesel at the fuel dock. Guest moorage along 700 feet of dock space, rafting allowed; unoccupied slips used when available. Maximum boat length 120 feet. Services include 15 amp power, restrooms, showers, pumpout, portapotty dump. Customs clearance is available. Kerosene, stove alcohol, marine supplies, charts, snacks are available. The cafe is open 6 days. Marine repairs and haulout: boat lift and marine railway handle up to 200 tons. Boat Haven is located in the southwest corner of the harbor. Groceries, doctor, post office, laundry, liquor store are nearby.

② **Port Angeles City Pier,** 321 E. 5th, Port Angeles, WA 98362, (360)457-0411. Open Memorial Day through Labor Day only, with guest moorage in 1 60-foot slip and 4 40-foot slips. Restrooms, but no showers, no power. These are new floats, right downtown.

Reference only — not for navigation

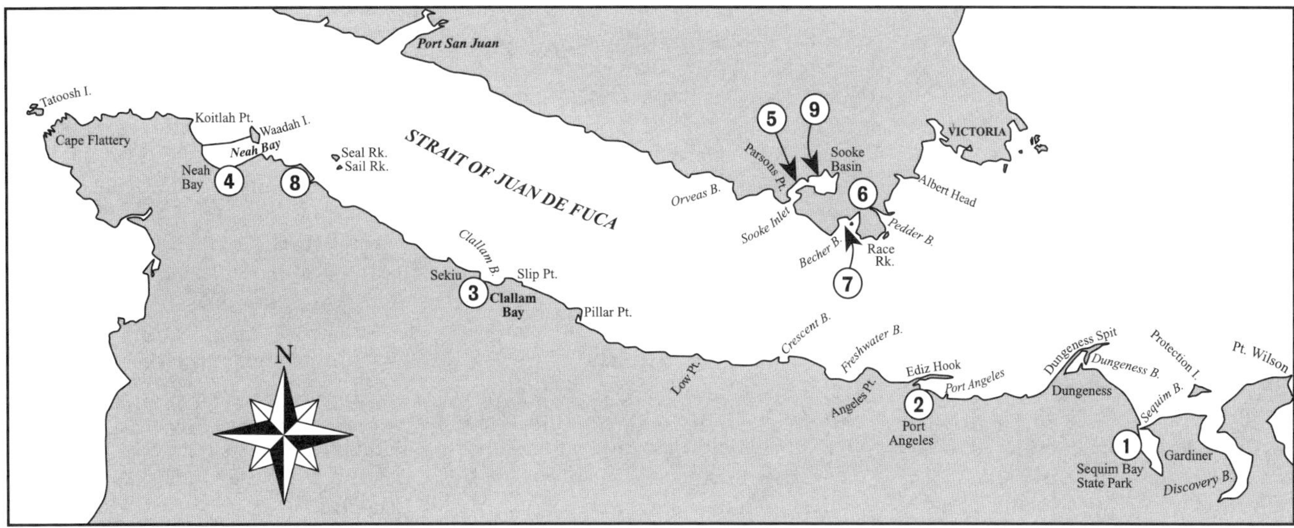

Watch depths at head of floats. Nearby groceries, restaurants, laundry. Showers are available at City pool. Adjacent to City park. Look for the viewing tower in front of the Red Lion Hotel.

② **Thunderbird Boat House & Gift,** 826 Boat Haven Drive, Port Angeles, WA 98362, (360)457-4274. Open summers only, beginning in April. Gasoline only at fuel dock. Guest moorage along 400 feet of dock, 30-foot maximum boat length. Services include restrooms and pumpout, but no power, no showers.

Crescent Bay. Use chart 18465. Crescent Bay is a possible anchorage if conditions on the Strait of Juan de Fuca become untenable. Close to the western shore it offers a little protection from westerlies, but swells can still work into the bay and make for an uneasy stay.

Pillar Point. Pillar Point has a fishing resort with launch ramp and float, but is not available for transient moorage. In a westerly, the area close to and a little east of the point is a notorious windless spot—a "hole" in sailboaters' language.

CLALLAM BAY

Clallam Bay. Use chart 18460. Clallam Bay is somewhat protected from westerlies, and has convenient anchoring depths along the shore. A reef, marked by a buoy at its outer end, extends from the eastern point. Leave the buoy to port when entering the bay. A breakwater-protected marina will cater to transient boats unless the slips are taken by trailerable boats there for the fishing.

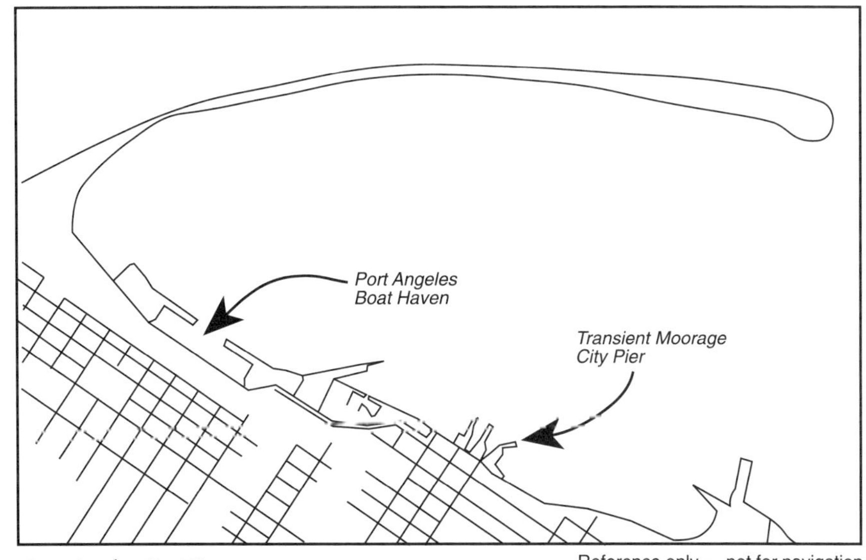

Port Angeles City Pier

Reference only — not for navigation

Sekiu has several fishing resorts, as well as restaurants and stores catering to fishermen.

③ **Van Riper's Resort,** Front & Rice Street, Sekiu, WA 98381, (360) 963-2334. Open summers, closed winters. Guest moorage along 2800 feet of dock space. Services include restrooms, showers, portapotty dump, no power. Includes campground, concrete launch ramp. Boat and motor rentals, charter service, ice, groceries, charts and books. Nearby post office, restaurant and bar, liquor store, marine supplies.

③ **Olson's Resort,** PO Box 216, Sekiu, 444 Front St., WA 98381, (360)963-2311. Monitors CB channels 14 & 21. Open February 1 - October 15. Gasoline and diesel at the fuel dock. Guest moorage at 300 slips, 40-foot maximum boat length. Services include restrooms, showers, laundry, portapotty dump, pumpout, launch ramp, no power. Motel units available. Busy during salmon season. Charter fishing trips, boat and motor rentals.

③ **Curley's Resort,** P.O. Box 265, Sekiu, WA 98381, (360)963-2281. Open April 1 - October 15, guest moorage along 750 feet of dock space, 30-foot maximum boat length. This is a resort with moorage, motel units and cabins for rent.

③ **Coho Resort,** HCR 61, Box 15, Sekiu, WA 98381, (360)963-2333. Open all year, some guest moorage, 25-foot maximum boat length, call ahead. Services include restrooms, showers,

See area map page 75

laundry, launch ramp. No power or water. Carries bait, tackle, licenses.

NEAH BAY

Neah Bay Use chart 18485; large-scale chart 18484. Neah Bay has several resorts with moorage for transient boats. Fish company floats can sometimes accommodate transient pleasure craft. Anchorage is good, sand bottom, throughout the bay. The Coast Guard station at the entrance to the bay serves the west end of the Strait of Juan de Fuca and the northern Pacific Ocean coast. Neah Bay is a customs port and has a full array of stores and services to serve the needs of boaters.

④ **Big Salmon Resort,** P.O. Box 204, Front Street, Neah Bay, WA 98357, (360)645-2374. Monitors VHF channel 68; CB channel 16. Open April 1 - September 20. Gasoline and diesel at fuel dock. Services include 20 amp power, restrooms, launch ramp, no showers. Maximum boat length 60 feet. Waiting list during salmon season, so call ahead for availability. Small store carries tackle, some groceries, local charts. Motels, doctor, post office nearby.

④ **Farwest Resort,** P.O. Box 131, Front Street, Neah Bay, WA 98357, (360)645-2270. Monitors VHF channel 16. Open April 1 - September 25. Gasoline only at fuel dock. Services include restrooms, showers, laundry, launch ramp, no power. This is a fishing resort with moorage as space is available. Call ahead. Also has fishing charters, boat rentals, local charts, tackle & bait, aqua lung refills. Nearby groceries, post office, two restaurants.

⑧ **Snow Creek Resort,** P.O. Box 248, Neah Bay, WA 98357, (360)645-2284. Monitors VHF channel 16. Open May 1 - September 30. Guest moorage along 400 feet of dock and at 35 buoys, maximum boat length 28 feet. Services include restrooms, showers, boat launch, campsites and RV parking, limited groceries, diving air, haulout.

PORT SAN JUAN

Those needing a place to get off the Strait can consider **Port San Juan**, about halfway between Victoria and Barkley Sound. Port San Juan is a rectangular notch in Vancouver Island, with Port Renfrew on the eastern shore near the head of the bay. There is a float at Port Renfrew, but if heavy swells are running in the Strait, that float becomes an uncomfortable place to lie.

Better protection can be had anchoring close to shore along the west side, or rafting to one of the log rafts boomed in the mouth of the Gordon River, at the northwest corner of the bay.

SOOKE

Sooke Harbour. Sooke Harbour is entered between Company Point and Parsons Point. The harbor is protected by Whiffen Spit, which nearly blocks the passage. Enter by keeping Whiffen Spit (with its small lighthouse) close to port, and follow the marked channel to town. An area just inside Whiffen Spit has good anchorage. The Sooke Harbour Marina, with guest moorage and other facilities, is south of the Sooke government wharf. The city floats usually are taken by commercial fishboats, but pleasure craft will find room when the fleet is out.

Sooke has a wide variety of services close to the city floats, including a marine railway and machine shop, groceries, fuel, and restaurants. Currents run quite strongly along the city waterfront. Be careful when landing.

The inner harbor at Sooke is seldom visited by pleasure craft. The channel—very shallow—follows the curve of the shoreline on the east side of the bay until the inner harbor opens up, where there is ample water. Contributing Editor Tom Kincaid has anchored in a little, almost landlocked, bay behind Pim Head.

Sooke is the only completely protected harbor between Victoria and Barkley Sound. It is 15 miles closer to Barkley Sound than downtown Victoria, and often used as a departure point for boats heading up the west coast of Vancouver Island.

Cruising that coast, you will occasionally see a local fishboat anchored along the shore. With local knowledge, it is possible to anchor in several places, including the mouth of the Jordan River.

Note: No customs clearance is available in Sooke. The nearest Canadian Port of Entry is Victoria.

⑤ **Sooke Harbour Marina,** RR 4, 6971 West Coast Road, Sooke, BC V0S 1N0, (250)642-3236. Open all year. Guest moorage along 200 feet of dock space, and unoccupied slips are used when available. Call ahead for availability. Services include washrooms, showers, laundry, and launch ramp. This is the first marina as you come into the harbor.

Sooke Harbour Authority, open all year, guest moorage along 797 feet of dock. No washrooms, showers or power.

⑨ **Sunny Shores Resort & Marina,** 5621 Sooke Rd., Sooke, BC V0S 1N0, (250)642-5731; fax (250)642-5737. Monitors VHF channel 16; CB channel 13. Open all year. Gasoline and diesel at fuel dock. Guest moorage for 6-10 average size boats, call ahead for availability. Services include 15 amp power, washrooms, showers, laundry. Motel accommodations and campground. Swimming pool, mini-golf, playground. Convenience store carries ice, fishing tackle, limited groceries, local charts. Boat maintenance, haulout and repair available. Taxi to town 3 miles away; bus to Victoria, 28 miles away.

Pedder Bay. Pedder Bay is a mile-long inlet, shallow and narrow, just south of Williams Head. A launch ramp with floats is at the head, and moorage might be available for larger boats.

Reference only — not for navigation

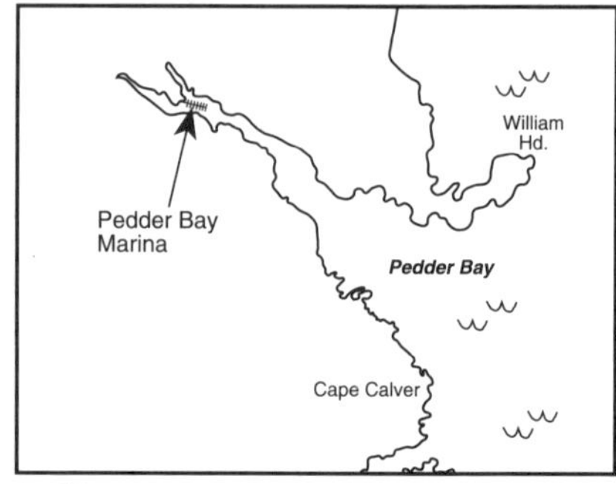

Pedder Bay Marina

⑥ **Pedder Bay Marina,** 925 Pedder Bay Drive, Victoria, BC V9B 5B4, (250)478-1771; fax (250)478-2695. Monitors VHF channel 68. Open all year, gasoline and diesel at fuel dock. Most guest moorage maximum 26-foot boat length. Call ahead for larger boats. Services include 15 amp power, washrooms, showers, laundry. Full grocery, with dairy and fresh foods during summer. The Galloping Goose Trail and diverse sea life are attractions. Approach-

See area map page 75

ing, use chart 3641; watch the breeze. Located between Pearson College and Dept. of National Defence (you can't stop there; it has a prison facility).

Becher Bay. Becher Bay is a pleasant anchorage. There is a bay on the west side with excellent anchorage, being careful of a drying rock near the south end. Contributing Editor Tom Kincaid has anchored behind the island in the middle of the bay. The water is a bit deep for convenience, but protection is good and the holding ground is excellent.

⑦ **Pacific Lions Marina Ltd.,** RR 6, 241 Becher Bay Rd., Sooke, BC V0S 1N0, (250)642-3816. Open May 1 - September 30. Gasoline only at fuel dock. Limited guest moorage, maximum boat length 30 feet, call ahead. Services include washrooms, launch ramp, no showers or power. Camping available.

⑦ **Cheanuh Marina,** Box 1, RR 1, 4901 E. Sooke Rd., Sooke, BC V0S 1N0, (250)478-4880; fax (250)478-3585. Monitors VHF channel 16, CB channel 13. Open all year. Gasoline only at fuel dock. Guest moorage in 310 slips, unoccupied slips used when available, call ahead. Services include 3-lane launch ramp, washrooms, no showers or power. Popular fishing marina. Around 300 boats are launched per day in summer; someone on staff usually stays until all have returned. Owned by the Becher Bay Indians.

The Learning Never Stops

Every boat owner goes through a learning curve that never stops. A person can, of course, start a little farther along the curve by spending time with others aboard their boats, or have the smarts to be born into a boating family, or, at the very least, take a Power Squadron or Coast Guard Auxiliary course. It may also be possible to take a few practical lessons from the person who sold you the boat.

But the curve remains, stretching endlessly into the future. After more than 60 years of boating, I'm still struggling to learn more, and seldom leave the harbor without some new problem presenting itself, calling on me to find a solution resulting in another little inch of travel along that curve.

Stretching out along the learning curve usually means doing something you haven't done before, whether it's adjusting the valves on your diesel engine or crossing the Strait of Juan de Fuca. Once you've done these things, they seem to be pretty simple. But until you try, they appear to be the product of some occult art.

Most people, when they first buy a boat, spend enough time close to the dock to get used to the "feel" of the boat: how quickly it turns, how it steers in reverse, how long it takes to stop, and where the sides of the boat are in relation to the dock. Before long, however, it will be time to head out for larger waters. If those first experiments were in Seattle's Lake Union, as many are, the skipper is going to have to deal with the Ballard Locks before those larger waters can be experienced. Approaching the locks for the very first time takes a leap of courage. You sure don't want to make a fool of yourself in front of all those "expert" skippers and the usual crowd of gawkers lining the lock walls.

But having screwed up the courage to try, you will soon find that running the locks doesn't take the skill of a brain surgeon. A little common sense and patience, and you're free of the confining lakes and out into the broad reaches of Puget Sound, where a boating family can easily spend a cruising lifetime.

On the other hand, you will have heard about the glorious San Juan Islands, invitingly situated only 20 miles or so across the Strait of Juan de Fuca. If you're like most of us, eventually you'll take a deep breath and brave the Strait for a chance to vacation in our own world famous islands. Once again, you'll discover that making that crossing is not beyond your ability, and that trip can become almost routine. Almost, I say, because the Strait can kick up a fuss, and part of your learning curve will will be discovering how to handle rough water, how to pick a time to avoid the rough water, or some combination of both.

In any event, you will have made another major step up the learning curve. You can handle yourself and your boat under another set of conditions. And the steps stretch out as far as you can imagine. There's the Strait of Georgia in order to reach Desolation Sound; a series of rapids and Johnstone Strait in order to reach the Fife Sound cruising area; Queen Charlotte Strait, Dixon Entrance, the West Coast of Vancouver Island. All are milestones on the learning curve. All can be (and have been) negotiated by thousands of people in all sorts of boats.

And they aren't all brain surgeons or old salts either. Most are just ordinary folks, screwing up the courage to take that next step up the learning curve.

—Tom Kincaid

San Juan Islands

Lopez Sound • Lopez Island • San Juan Island • Orcas Island • Sucia Island

Charts

18421	Strait of Juan de Fuca to Strait of Georgia (1:80,000)
18423SC	FOLIO SMALL-CRAFT Bellingham to Everett including San Juan Islands
3462	Juan de Fuca Strait to Strait of Georgia (Cdn) (1:80,000)
18429	Rosario Strait, Southern Part (1:25,000)
18430	Rosario Strait, Northern Part (1:25,000)
18432	Boundary Pass (1:25,000)
18433	Haro Strait—Middle Bank to Stuart Island (1:25,000)
18434	San Juan Channel (1:25,000)

With protected coves, interesting towns, fine resorts, beautiful marine parks and an ideal climate, the San Juan Islands are the destination of choice for thousands of boaters every year. Fishing for salmon and various bottom fish is often very good. The islands contain the U.S.'s largest flocks of bald eagles south of Alaska. Sailing in the company of porpoises and whales is almost commonplace.

Approaching from the east, the heart of the San Juans archipelago can be entered through four passes: Lopez Pass, between Lopez Island and Decatur Island; Thatcher Pass, between Decatur Island and Blakely Island; Peavine Pass, between Blakely Island and Obstruction Island; and Obstruction Pass, between Obstruction Island and Orcas Island. At times, these waters can be turbulent (see sidebar on page 87).

① **James Island Marine State Park.** Use chart 18429; 18421. Open all year, day use, overnight mooring & camping. James Island is one of our favorite spots. We enjoy hiking its trails and watching its wildlife. Visiting boats can use both sides of a 65-foot-long float, and mooring buoys. Toilets are ashore, but no power or water. Anchoring can be difficult in the west cove. Use the float (removed in winter).

The east cove is exposed to wakes from passing traffic in Rosario Strait, but has mooring buoys. The park has a picnic shelter and 13 primitive campsites. A Cascadia Marine Trail campsite is at Pocket Cove (high bank gravel beach). Excellent hiking, picnicking, scuba diving. Pack out all garbage. Raccoons will go aboard unattended boats at the dock if food is left in the open. Best to stow food well, and close the boat tight.

James Island, looking northeast. A rugged but inviting park in the San Juans.

Unnamed Island #3. This island, an undeveloped state park, is in the little bay at the south tip of Decatur Island, and joins Decatur Island at low tide. Open all year, day use only. Anchor out. No fires or overnight camping. Pack out all garbage. Do not disturb wildlife or alter the surroundings. This is one of Contributing Editor Tom Kincaid's favorite anchorages. When the Kincaid children were small, they would use the concrete structure on the island as a fort.

LOPEZ SOUND

Lopez Sound, the body of water between Decatur Island and Lopez Island, has several favorite anchorages. Among them, **Mud Bay** and **Hunter Bay** are good. Use chart 18424 (larger scale, preferred) or 18421.

Mud Bay Tidelands, south end of Lopez Sound. Open all year, day use only. No facilities. Includes all of the southwest end of Mud Bay and the southeast shore of Mud Bay up to Shoal Bight, except some private tidelands on the southeast side of the bay. Anchor out at this undeveloped state park property. No fires or overnight camping. Pack out all garbage. Do not disturb the wildlife or alter the surroundings.

Hunter Bay, southwest corner of Lopez Sound. Hunter Bay is a good place to anchor, surrounded by forest, protected from all but northeast winds, with good bottom. The small float is for loading and unloading only. No facilities are ashore, and the land is privately owned. Nice spot to put the hook down, though.

Center Island. Good anchorage can be found by simply cruising around Center Island into **Reads Bay** until you find an area out of the prevailing wind.

Brigantine Bay, between Trump Island and Decatur Island, is pretty, with anchorage in 4-7 fathoms, but the dock and all the land ashore are private.

Sylvan Cove is in the northwest corner

Reference only — not for navigation

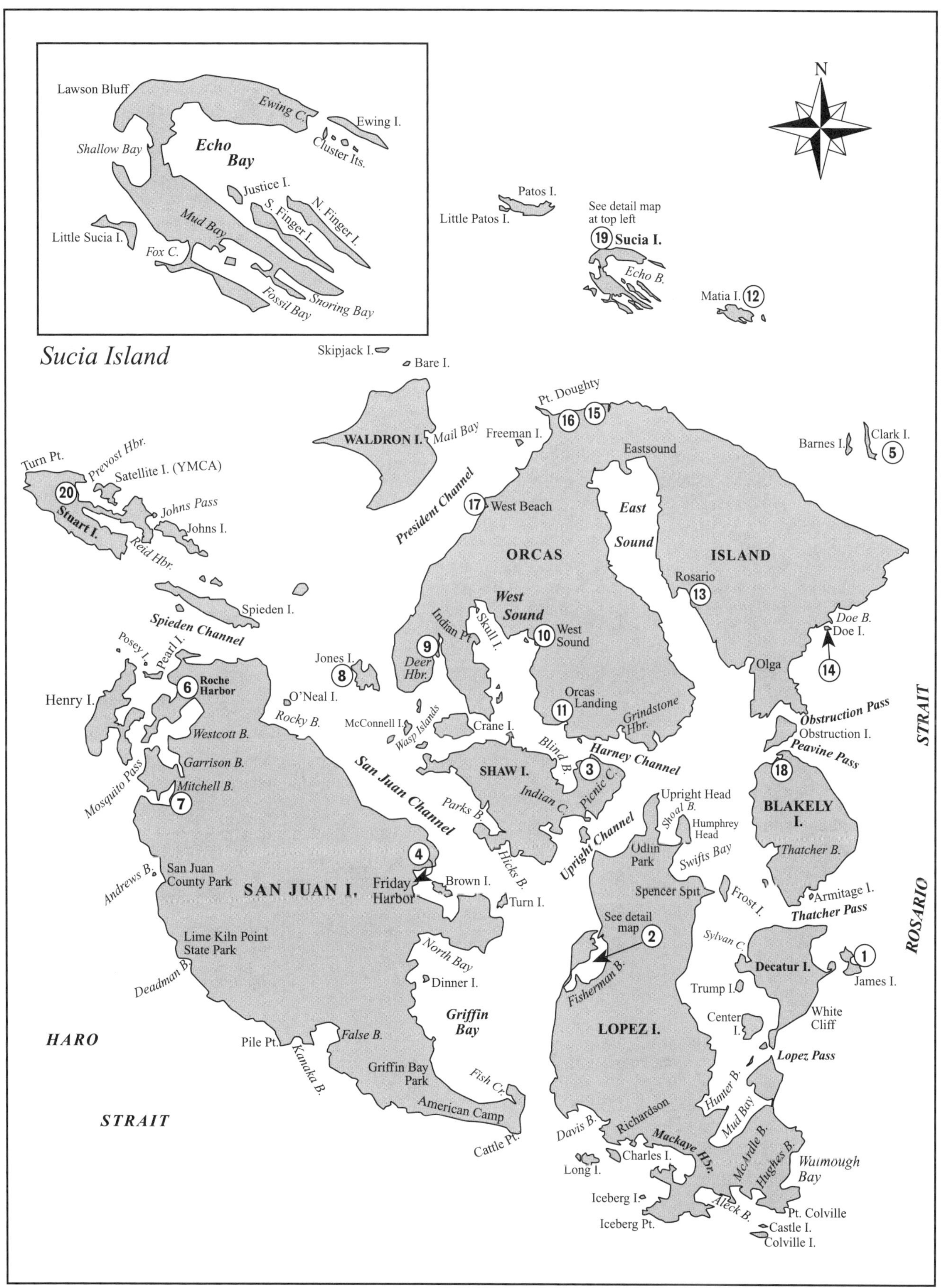

See area map page 79

This log cabin and interpretive sign are at the end of Spencer Spit.

of Decatur Island, and offers good holding bottom in convenient depths. The bay is truly beautiful, with New England-style buildings ashore. All the land ashore is private, as are the mooring buoys, the dock, and float that serve homeowners in the area.

Spencer Spit Marine State Park, east shore of Lopez Island, (360)468-2251. Open all year, day use and overnight mooring and camping. The park has 16 buoys. Services include restrooms upland but because of limited water supply, no showers. Spencer Spit is a popular park. Mooring buoys usually fill up quickly. Anchoring is good, however, as long as your anchor is properly set. A saltwater lagoon, fed from the north side, is in the middle of the spit. If you are on the north side, you must walk around the tip of the spit and back down the south side to get to the upland part of the park. The park has standard and primitive campsites. Bunny rabbits abound. Interpretive signs help exploration. Spencer Spit is a Cascadia Marine Trail campsite. Close to the ferry dock. Although the pass between Spencer Spit and Frost Island is narrow, it is deep and safe.

Swifts Bay. Use chart 18429; 18421. Swifts Bay, lying behind Flower Island and Leo Reef, is shallow, and strewn with several rocks and reefs. An anchored boat is subject to northerly winds and the wakes from passing craft. Not a good choice.

Shoal Bay. Use chart 18430; 18421. Shoal Bay indents the northern tip of Lopez Island between Humphrey Head and Upright Head, and offers good, fairly protected anchorage. We think the best spot is behind the breakwater and off the marina along the east shore. Numerous crab pot buoys must be avoided in picking an anchorage.

Fisherman Bay. Use chart 18434 (strongly recommended); 18421. Fisherman Bay extends southward about 1.5 miles into the western shore of Lopez Island. The entrance is winding and shallow, and should not be attempted by deep draft boats at less than half tide. Use U.S. chart 18434, which provides a comfortable, large-scale view of the waters. About 200 yards off the entrance, a beacon marks the tip of a drying shoal. Leave this beacon to starboard, then follow the well-marked channel into the bay. Anchorage can be found in 1-5 fathoms, mud bottom. Resist the temptation to cut inside any navigation marks (remember: Red, Right, Returning).

The northernmost marina in Fisherman Bay belongs to Islands Marine Center. The middle marina belongs to the Islander Lopez Restaurant, and was extensively rebuilt and enlarged during 1993. The Galley Restaurant and Lounge has moorage (free to diners), and is the third float from the bay's entrance.

② **Islands Marine Center,** P.O. Box 88, Fisherman Bay Road, Lopez, WA

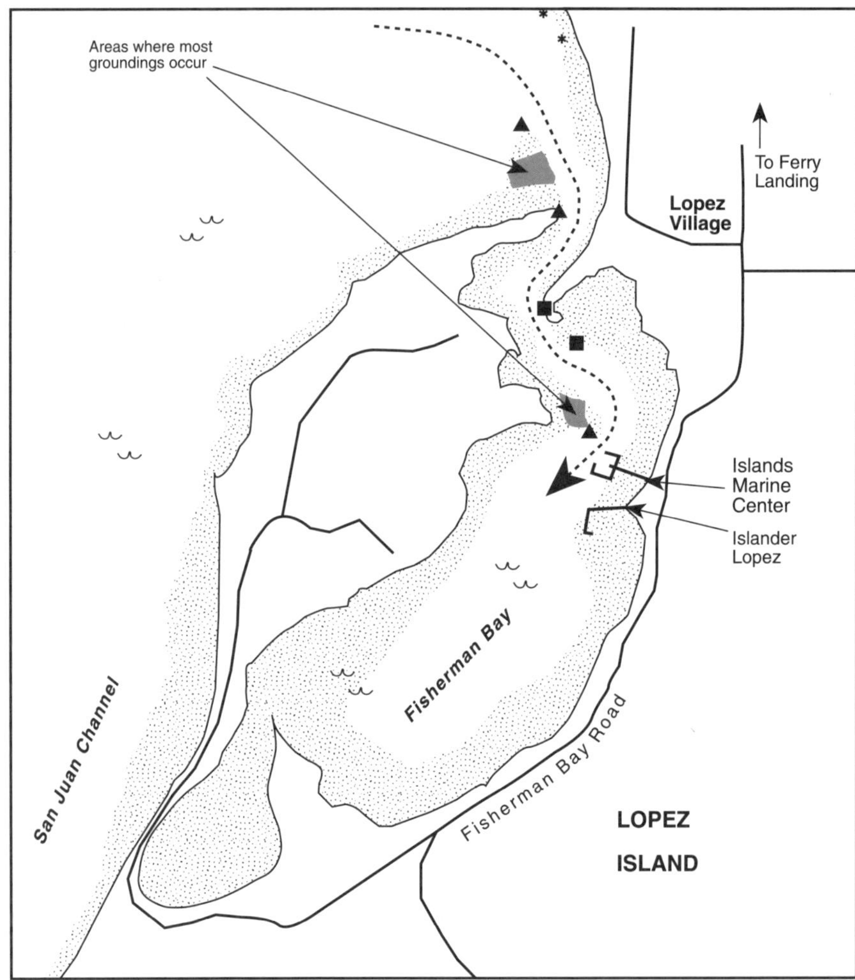

Fisherman Bay, Lopez Island

Reference only — not for navigation

See area map page 79

98261, (360)468-3377; fax (360)468-2283. Monitors VHF channels 16 & 69, CB channel 09. Open all year, except closed Sundays during the winter. Guest moorage along 1000 feet of dock space. Call ahead. Services include 20 & 30 amp power, restrooms and showers, pumpout and portapotty dump. This is a large, well-run, full-service marina, with haulout, repair, and complete marine supplies. Good depth at all docks. Ron Meng is the longtime owner. Lopez Village shopping is nearby.

② **Islander Lopez Marina Resort,** P.O. Box 549, Fisherman Bay Rd., Lopez, WA 98261, (800)736-3434, (360)468-2233. Open all year. Gasoline & diesel at fuel dock. Guest moorage at 35 slips, unoccupied slips used when available. Services include 30 & 50 amp power, restrooms, showers, laundry, swimming pool. The Dock Store has ice and bait. Restaurant and lounge are open seasonally (free moorage while dining).

Odlin Park, west side of Lopez Island. Open all year. Located between Flat Point and Upright Head. Good bottom for anchoring, but exposed to northwest winds. Small float for dinghies, or they can be beached. Campsites, restrooms. Beach area and sea wall, picnic sites and tables, cooking shelter and fire pits. Baseball diamond, open areas and trees. Use chart 18434; 18421.

Upright Channel State Park, northwest side of Lopez Island. Day moorage only at 3 mooring buoys. Services include restrooms, but no other facilities. Day use only, 4 picnic sites.

SOUTH LOPEZ ISLAND

Use charts 18429 and 18434 (larger scale, preferred), or 18421. The southern end of Lopez Island is heavily indented by several bays, and guarded by numerous rocks and reefs. The geography is rugged and windblown, the result of the prevailing westely winds from the Strait of Juan de Fuca. It is a fascinating shore to explore when the wind is down. The village of **Richardson** used to be famous for its quaint general store (which stocked everything anybody might need, ever), but the store burned to the ground a few years ago, and has not been rebuilt. The Richardson fuel dock, with gasoline and diesel, is still operating, but you must lie next to a high pier while fueling. Most of its customers are fish boats and larger vessels. Anchorage at Richardson is marginal.

Mackaye Harbor. Use chart 18429 or 18434 (larger scale, preferred), or 18421. Mackaye Harbor and **Barlow Bay** are a favorite overnight for boats planning an early morning crossing of the Strait of Juan de Fuca, before the summer westerly fills in. The harbor has excellent anchorage, although swells from an afternoon westerly in the strait cause a certain amount of motion at anchor. MacKaye Harbor is the site of a fishboat marina. During the summer months a large fishboat fleet can be found in the harbor.

Iceberg Island, an undeveloped state park in outer Mackaye Harbor. Open all year, day use only. Anchor out. No facilities. No fires or overnight camping. Pack out all garbage. Do not disturb wildlife or alter the surroundings.

Aleck Bay. Use chart 18429 (larger scale, preferred) or 18421. Aleck Bay is

See area map page 79

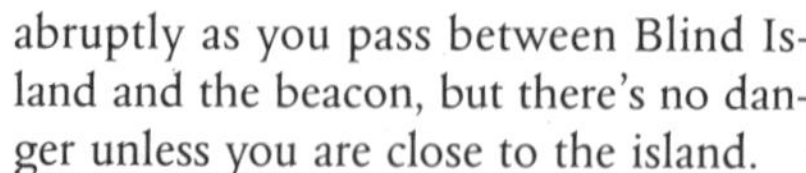

not particularly scenic, but it is big and easy to get into. Anchor close to the head of the bay in 5-6 fathoms. The bay is open to the east.

Hughes Bay. Use chart 18429 (larger scale, preferred) or 18421. Hughes Bay is somewhat exposed, but Contributing Editor Tom Kincaid has anchored overnight as far into the bay as he could get and still have swinging room.

Blind Island, at the mouth of Blind Bay in the San Juan Islands, is a primitive state park. Anchor or moor at a buoy.

McArdle Bay. Use chart 18429 (larger scale, preferred) or 18421. McArdle Bay provides good anchorage in 4-5 fathoms, but is completely exposed to southerly winds coming off the Strait of Juan de Fuca. Lovely homes are on the hills above the bay. Just outside, the chart shows a rock in the passage between Blind Island and Lopez Island. The rock is actually a reef.

Castle Island, an undeveloped state park off the southeast end of Lopez Island. Use chart 18429 (larger scale, preferred) or 18421. Anchor out. No facilities, day use only. No fires or overnight camping. Pack out all garbage. Do not disturb wildlife or alter the surroundings.

Watmough Bay. Use chart 18429 (larger scale, preferred) or 18421. Watmough Bay has been one of Contributing Editor Tom Kincaid's favorites for 50 years. While a northerly could be a problem, Watmough Bay is protected from weather on the Strait of Juan de Fuca, and is the first such bay to offer refuge after a stormy crossing from Port Townsend. A beautiful high sheer rock wall is on the north side. The chart shows the bottom as rocky, but we have found excellent holding in blue mud in 2-3 fathoms, about halfway in.

SHAW ISLAND

Blind Bay. Use chart 18434 (larger scale, preferred) or 18421. Blind Bay, on the north side of Shaw Island, has good anchorage throughout the center portion. Blind Island is a minimally developed state park, with several mooring buoys on its south side. A notable collection of rocks obstruct the waters west of Blind Island. Do not pass west of Blind Island. East of Blind Island, a white, privately maintained beacon marks a rock that lies midway between Blind Island and the Shaw Island shore. Enter Blind Bay midway between Blind Island and that beacon. The water will shoal abruptly as you pass between Blind Island and the beacon, but there's no danger unless you are close to the island.

Blind Island Marine State Park, Blind Bay. Open all year, day use and overnight mooring & camping. Facilities include 4 mooring buoys, toilets. Accessible by boat only. Four primitive camping & picnic sites. Cascadia Marine Trail campsite. Pack out all garbage. Must enter bay on east side. Watch channel and rock markers carefully.

③ **Little Portion Store,** P.O. Box 455, at Shaw Island Ferry Terminal, Shaw Island, WA 98268, (360)468-2288. Open all year, but shorter hours in winter. Closed Sundays. Limited guest moorage, call ahead. Groceries, ice, gift items, restrooms. The store is run by Franciscan nuns, who greet the ferries wearing their distinctive brown habits. The marina is small, adjacent to the ferry dock.

Parks Bay. Use chart 18434; 18421. Parks Bay is a fine anchorage. The land ashore is owned by the University of Washington as a biological preserve, and is generally off limits to visitors. There are stub pilings at the closed end of Parks Bay, but there is plenty of anchoring room, mud bottom, throughout the bay.

Parks Bay Island Park, north entrance to Parks Bay. Day use only, no facilities. Anchor out at this undeveloped state park property. No fires or overnight camping. Pack out all garbage. Do not disturb wildlife or alter the surroundings.

Hicks Bay. Hicks Bay has good anchorage, although exposed to southerlies. When entering, take care to avoid a reef that extends from the southern shore.

Indian Cove. Use chart 18434; 18421. Indian Cove, a popular anchorage area, is big and open feeling, somewhat protected from southerlies by nearby Lopez Island and Canoe Island. Watch for drying rocks between Canoe Island and Shaw Island, and a shoal 200 yards west of the southern point of Canoe Island. The Shaw Island County Park, with launch ramp, has an excellent beach.

Picnic Cove. Use chart 18434; 18421. Picnic Cove is immediately east of Indian Cove. It's a pretty little nook, with room for a couple of boats. A mid-channel en-

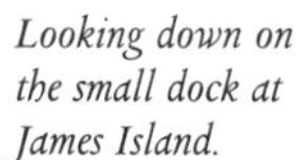

Looking down on the small dock at James Island.

See area map page 79

Friday Harbor on a quiet morning. Large marina, lots of room.

trance is best, to avoid reefs on each side of the cove. The head of the cove shoals to drying flats. Anchor in 3-4 fathoms.

SAN JUAN ISLAND

San Juan Island is the second largest of the San Juan Islands, and the most heavily populated. Friday Harbor, the only incorporated town, is the seat of county government.

Fish Creek. Fish Creek is a tiny indentation near the southern tip of San Juan Island. It is lined with the docks and mooring buoys of the private homes along its shores. Fish Creek has no public facilities, and swinging room is very restricted between the homeowners' floats.

Middle Channel (Cattle Pass). Use chart 18434 (larger scale, preferred) or 18421. Middle Channel, locally known as Cattle Pass, runs between the south end of San Juan Island and Lopez Island. It is the only southern entrance to the San Juan Islands, and connects with San Juan Channel. Whale Rocks lie just out side the southern entrance to the pass. It's easy to get close to them if you're not careful. When we enter Cattle Pass from the south, we try to leave Buoy 3, the gong buoy marking Salmon Bank, to port, and make a course for the middle of the entrance. This avoids Whale Rocks.

Tidal currents run strongly through Cattle Pass, and the waters can be turbulent with rips and eddies. A big ebb against a westerly wind can be unpleasant. Current predictions are shown under San Juan Channel in the current books.

It's possible to pass behind Goose Island and avoid foul current, but local knowledge is called for.

Griffin Bay. Use chart 18434 (larger scale, preferred) or 18421. You can anchor in several places in Griffin Bay. A stretch of beach inshore from Halftide Rocks is Griffin Bay Park, a public campground. From the campground it is a short walk to American Camp, maintained by the U.S. Park Service as a historical monument to the 1860 "Pig War." The Pig War resulted in setting the boundary between the U.S. and Canada in Haro Strait, and so kept the San Juan Islands in the U.S.

Griffin Bay Park, next to American Camp. Open all year, 2 mooring buoys. Toilets, no other facilities. Four campsites and picnic area. Watch for shallow water and pilings.

Unnamed Island #119, in Griffin Bay,

See area map page 79

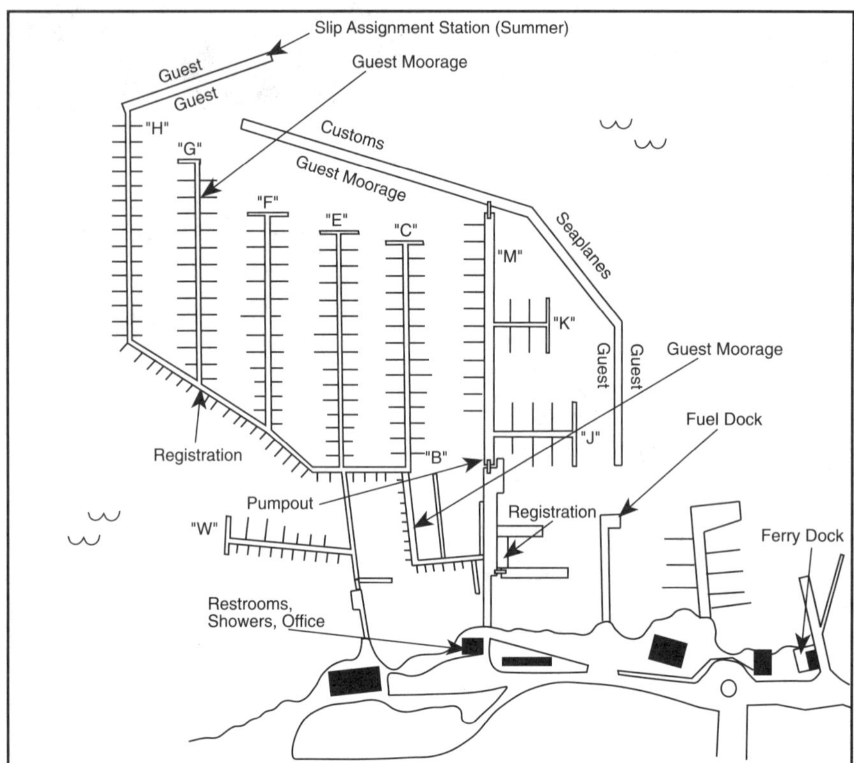

Port of Friday Harbor

south of Dinner Island. Open all year, day use only, no facilities. Anchor out at this undeveloped state park property. No fires or overnight camping. Pack out all garbage. Do not disturb wildlife or alter the surroundings.

Turn Island Marine State Park, off northeast tip of San Juan Island. Use chart 18434 (larger scale, preferred) or 18421. Open all year, day use and overnight mooring & camping. Currents can be quite strong in the pass between Turn Island and San Juan Island, but the mooring buoys are placed safely out of the current. Anchorage is also possible. Toilets, no other facilities. Boat access only. Camping in designated primitive campsites in treed area south of the moorage. Pack out all garbage. Hiking, fishing, crabbing, birdwatching. Most of this park is a designated wildlife refuge. Do not disturb animals in their natural habitat.

Friday Harbor. Use chart 18434 (larger scale, preferred) or 18421. Friday Harbor is the government and commercial center of the San Juan Islands. It is a customs port, and the terminus for ferries from Anacortes that also serve Sidney, B.C. Friday Harbor swells with tourists during the summer months, and has many boutiques, shops, galleries, restaurants and lounges to serve them. Two well-stocked grocery stores are on the main street. You can moor at the Port of Friday Harbor marina or anchor out. Anchorage is good in the cove north of the marina, and throughout the area behind Brown (Friday) Island.

Enter Friday Harbor around either end of Brown Island. A buoy marks a 3-fathom shoal off the northwest corner of the island. Another buoy marks the end of a drying reef off the southwest corner. Take care to avoid interfering with the ferries and the large number of float planes taking off and landing in the harbor. Friday Island is privately owned, and has its own dock and floats.

A fuel dock is located between the Port marina and the ferry dock. The floats just south of the ferry dock are owned by the condominium apartments ashore. Jensen's Marina, at the south end of the harbor, is a complete boat yard where repairs of any kind can be done.

④ **Port of Friday Harbor,** P.O. Box 889, 204 Front Street, Friday Harbor, WA 98250, (360)378-2688, fax (360)378-6114. Monitors VHF channel 66A. Open all year. Gasoline and diesel available nearby. Ample guest moorage along 1500 feet of dock, plus slips in guest docks and unoccupied slips as available. Slips handle maximum length of 40 feet. Call ahead for reservations. Services include 30 amp power, restrooms, showers, garbage, pumpout. Customs clearance is available. Call for slip assignment if you do not have reservations, but wait until you are in sight of the marina. In the summer, a slip assignment station is staffed at the end of the customs dock. Boats larger than 40 feet must tie up to the floating breakwater/ guest dock. A dinghy float and day moorage are available. Kerosene, stove alcohol and propane are available. Nearby haulout, repairs. Mobile and stationary pumpouts. The town of Friday Harbor has marine supplies, charts, books, groceries, many shops and restaurants, all within easy walk. Laundry, doctor, post office, groceries, liquor store are nearby.

④ **Port of Friday Harbor Fuel Pier,** 1 Front Street, Port of Friday Harbor, Friday Harbor, WA 98250, (360)378-3114, fax (360)378-4699. Open all year, 7 days a week. Fuel dock with gasoline and diesel. Carries oil, lubricants, propane, ice, and bait.

Rocky Bay. Use chart 18434 (larger scale, preferred) or 18421. Rocky Bay, close inshore from O'Neal Island, is a good anchorage and fairly well protected. Take care to avoid a drying shoal and a covered rock.

Lonesome Cove Resort, 5810 Lonesome Cove Rd., Friday Harbor, WA 98250, (360)378-4477. Open all year, moorage available only for resort guests. Docks not available in winter. Log cabins with fireplaces. A "hideaway" resort with no TV or phones in the cabins.

Roche Harbor. Use chart 18433 (larger scale, preferred) or 18421. Roche Harbor has a number of interesting anchorages and moorages. From the north (Speiden Channel), enter Roche Harbor past Pearl Island. Most boats favor the west side of Pearl Island, although shallow draft boats can use the passage on the east side. From the south (Haro Strait), entry is through **Mosquito Pass**. The flood current sets north in Mosquito Pass. The ebb current sets south, out of Roche Harbor. Currents can be strong at times. The channel is narrow but well-marked. *Stay in the channel.*

The mooring buoys off the Roche Harbor Resort belong to the resort, and they charge for mooring. They may be removed in 1997. Contact the resort. Anchorage is excellent throughout the bay. Roche Harbor is a customs port. The customs dock is clearly identified.

⑥ **Roche Harbor Resort and Boatel,** P.O. Box 4001, Roche Harbor, WA 98250, (360)378-2155, (800)451-8910. Monitors VHF channel 78A. Open all year, 200 feet of dock space, 110 guest slips, unocccupied slips used when available. New docks have been added, but the mooring buoys may be removed in 1997. Call ahead. Gasoline and diesel at the fuel dock. Services include 20, 30, 50 & 100 amp power, restrooms, showers, laundry. Cable and telephone hookup available with an extra charge. Customs clearance is available at the customs dock. This is one of the most popular spots in the islands. Roche Harbor has a historic hotel, Olympic-size swimming pool, tennis courts, golf course, well-stocked grocery store, restaurant and bar. Snack bar serves breakfast. The moorage fee includes water, power, trash disposal, and use of resort facilities.

Posey Island Marine State Park, north of Roche Harbor. Use chart 18433 (larger scale, preferred) or 18421. Day use and overnight mooring & camping. Services include pit toilet, no other facilities. Cascadia Marine Trail campsite (primitive). The island is less than 1 acre in size. Water surrounding the island is shallow. Anchor out and row in by dinghy. Great sunset views on the west side.

Henry Island. Use chart 18433 (larger scale, preferred) or 18421. Anchorage is possible in Open Bay on Henry Island, although it is exposed to southerly winds. Nelson Bay is the site of a Seattle Yacht Club outstation. Nelson Bay is shallow, so use your depth sounder and tide tables before anchoring.

Wescott Bay. Use chart 18433 (larger scale, preferred) or 18421. Wescott Bay has good anchorage, but is partly taken up with a major shellfish culture business. Although the bay is shallow, adequate anchoring depths can be found throughout.

⑦ **Snug Harbor Resort,** 2371 Mitchell Bay Road, Friday Harbor, WA 98250, (360)378-4762. Use chart 18433 (larger scale, preferred) or 18421. Open all year. Permanent and guest moorage, maximum boat length 70 feet, minimum depth at minus tide 4 feet. Gasoline only at the fuel dock. Propane available. Services include 20 amp power, restrooms, showers, laundy, portapotty dump. Popular fishing resort with lodging and camping, launch ramp, haulout and repairs to 30 feet, general store.

These eroded sandstone cliffs are at the mouth of Fox Cove, Sucia Island.

Garrison Bay. Use chart 18433 (larger scale, preferred) or 18421. Garrison Bay, the location of British Camp, is a popular and excellent anchorage, with room for a large number of boats. It's a good stop for families with children. British troops were garrisoned here during the 1860 Pig War. The buildings and grounds have been restored as a historical site by the U.S. Park Service. You can tour the grounds and several of the buildings. The grounds include a cemetery where several people from that era are buried. A steep trail leads to the top of Young Hill, the highest point on San Juan Island, for a marvelous view.

British Camp Historical Park, San Juan Island, (360)586-2165. Open all year. Excellent park, described above. Restrooms, no other facilities.

Mitchell Bay. Use chart 18433; 18421. Snug Harbor Marina offers moorage, a launch ramp, a small store, and cabins ashore. Past the marina there is shallow anchorage.

Haro Strait is a favorite hunting ground for orcas, the so-called "killer whales," that often cruise within a few yards of shore. Washington State Parks has acquired a site at Lime Kiln Point, where people can watch and photograph the whales. Anchorage offshore from this park would be very difficult, and is not recommended.

San Juan County Park, 380 West Side Road N., Friday Harbor, WA 98250, (360)378-2992. Use chart 18433 (larger scale, preferred) or 18421. Open all year. Facilities include launch ramp, restrooms, no power, no showers. A popular park for kayak campers who can pull up on the beach.

Unnamed Island #40, on the southwest side of San Juan Island, approximately 1 mile northwest of Pile Point. Open all year, day use only, no facilities. Anchor out at this undeveloped state park property. No fires or overnight

See area map page 79

Pastoral Olga, in East Sound, is served by a float in the summer.

camping. Pack out all garbage. Do not disturb wildlife or alter the surroundings. Use chart 18433 or 18434 (larger scale, preferred), or 18421.

Unnamed Island #38, southwest side of San Juan Island, near the center of Kanaka Bay. Open all year, day use only, no facilities. Anchor out at this undeveloped state park property. No fires or overnight camping. Pack out garbage. Do not disturb wildlife or alter the surroundings. Use chart 18433 or 18434 (larger scale, preferred), or 18421.

Wasp Islands. Use chart 18434 (strongly recommended) or 18421. The Wasp Islands are a rock and reef strewn area where navigation should be done very carefully. Not all the underwater hazards are marked, and the unwary can come to grief. Wasp Passage, however, is free of dangers, and the skipper who pays attention to stay in the channel will have no problems.

All the Wasp Islands are privately owned except **Yellow Island**, which is owned by The Nature Conservancy.

Northwest McConnell Rock, northwest of McConnell Island. Use chart 18434 (strongly recommended) or 18421. Open all year, day use only, no facilities. Anchor out only at this undeveloped state park property. No fires or overnight camping. Pack out all garbage. Do not disturb wildlife or alter the surroundings. At low tide McConnell Rock is connected to McConnell Island by a sandspit.

Unnamed Island #112, east of McConnell Island. Open all year, day use only, no facilities. Undeveloped state park property; anchoring only. No fires or overnight camping. Pack out garbage. Do not disturb wildlife or alter the surroundings.

⑧ Jones Island Marine State Park. Use chart 18434 (larger scale, preferred) or 18421. Open all year, day use and overnight mooring and camping. The bay at the north end of Jones Island is an excellent anchorage, with a 264-foot-long mooring float and 7 mooring buoys. A few mooring buoys are in a small bay on the south side of the island. The well often runs dry late in the season. Use water sparingly. Jones Island is a Cascadia Marine Trail site, with 19 primitive campsites.

The dock at Jones Island Marine Park has room for several boats.

Jones Island suffered a severe blowdown of mature trees during a severe storm in 1990. For environmental reasons, most of the downed trees were left to rot on the ground, although campsites and trails were cleared and the logs bucked up for firewood. Evidence of the blow-down can be seen everywhere.

Jones Island is excellent for families with children. They will enjoy the hikes and probably will meet tame deer. During the summer, mooring buoys and float space can be hard to get. In the north cove, many boats anchor and run a sterntie to shore. *Caution:* Raccoons will go aboard unattended boats at the dock if food is left in the open. Stow food well, and close the boat tight.

ORCAS ISLAND

Orcas Island is the largest of the San Juans, and is deeply indented by Deer Harbor, West Sound, and East Sound. Deer Harbor is the most westerly, and the smallest, of these inlets. It is the location of the Deer Harbor Marina, at the village of Deer Harbor on the eastern shore. The resort is a popular destination, and anchorage is excellent throughout the bay. One of our favorite anchoring spots is behind little Fawn Island, close to the western shore.

⑨ Deer Harbor Marina, 200 Deer Harbor Road, Deer Harbor, WA 98243, (360)376-3037; fax (360)376-6091. Use chart 18434 (larger scale, recommended) or 18421. Monitors VHF channels 78 & 16. Open all year. Facilities include gasoline and diesel at the fuel dock, ample guest moorage, 30 amp power, new restrooms and showers. The Deer Harbor moorage and fuel dock came under new ownership in 1996, and a major rebuilding, with new docks, should be complete by 1997. The new restrooms and showers are outstanding. A popular spot, with restaurant, pool, spas, gift shop, market, shuttle to Orcas ferry dock and Eastsound, and more. The shoreside services are under separate ownership, but marina guests have full access. Best to call ahead for mooring reservations.

West Sound. For all of West Sound, use chart 18434 (larger scale, recommended) or 18421. West Sound is the middle inlet of Orcas Island, where the Wareham family's West Sound Marina offers some overnight moorage and complete service facilities. Next to the marina is the home of the Orcas Island Yacht Club, which has moorage for visiting members of re-

See area map page 79

ciprocal clubs. A San Juan County public dock lies next to the Orcas Island Yacht Club dock. The county dock is for day use only. Good anchorage is available at the head of the bay (watch out for covered Harbor Rock). Anchorage is also good off the village of West Sound, and behind Double Island. We have anchored behind Double Island several times over the years, and enjoyed it each time.

⑩ **West Sound Marina,** P.O. Box 19, Orcas Island, WA 98280, (360)376-2314; fax (360)376-4634. Monitors VHF channel 16, switch to 09. Open all year, except closed Sundays in the winter. Facilities include gasoline and diesel at the fuel dock, propane, 6 guest slips, 300 feet of guest dock, 20 & 30 amp power, restrooms, pumpout, showers. Full service haulout and repairs, including enclosed area for major work. Chandlery has most boating supplies. Grocery and deli nearby. Stay close to the docks when approaching. The water shoals toward Picnic Island.

Victim Island, west side of West Sound. Open all year, day use only, no facilities. Anchor out at this undeveloped state park property. No fires or overnight camping. Pack out all garbage. Do not disturb wildlife or alter the surroundings.

Unnamed Island #80, west of Indian Point in West Sound. Open all year, day use only, no facilities. Anchor out at this undeveloped state park property. No fires or overnight camping. Pack out all garbage. Do not disturb wildlife or alter the surroundings.

Skull Island, north end of Massacre Bay. Open all year, day use only, no facilities. Anchor out at this undeveloped state park property. No fires or overnight camping. Pack out all garbage. Do not disturb wildlife or alter the surroundings.

Unnamed Island #81, near the West Sound Marina. Open all year, day use only, no facilities. Anchor out at this undeveloped state park property. No fires or overnight camping. Pack out all garbage. Do not disturb wildlife or alter the surroundings.

⑪ **Orcas Landing.** Use chart 18434 (larger scale, recommended) or 18421. Orcas Landing has a float alongside the ferry dock, and a good store at the head of the dock. Other shops are at hand. It's a good place to browse. Great ice cream cones, too. Fuel service is available. Be well-fendered and securely tied to the dock at Orcas Landing. Passing boat and ferry traffic in Harney Channel can make for a rough ride.

Dining: The Orcas Hotel has excellent sandwiches, and friends say the dinners are good.

⑪ **Island Petroleum Services,** Orcas Village, (360)376-3883. Open all year, fuel dock with gasoline and diesel. Limited hours in the winter. Other services, shopping at Orcas Village.

Grindstone Harbor. Use charts 18434 or 18430 (larger scale, recommended), or 18421. Grindstone Harbor is a small, shallow anchorage, with two major rocks in its entrance. One of these rocks became famous a few years ago when the Washington State ferry *Elwha* ran aground on it while doing a little sightseeing. Favor the east shore all the way in. Private mooring buoys take up much of the inner part of the bay, but there's room to anchor if you need to.

Guthrie Bay. Use charts 18434, 18430 (larger scale, recommended) or 18421. Guthrie Bay indents Orcas Island between Grindstone Harbor and East Sound. It's a pleasant little spot with private mooring buoys around the perimeter and homes on the hillsides. Anchor in 4-7 fathoms.

East Sound. Use chart 18430 (larger scale, recommended) or 18421. East Sound, the largest of Orcas Island's indentations, extends about 6 miles north from Foster Point. The shores on both sides are steep-to, and offer few anchorage possibilities. The Rosario Resort is on the east side, a short distance up the sound. The village of Eastsound is at the head. Fresh winds sometimes will blow in East Sound, while outside the air will be calm.

Eastsound. Use chart 18430 (larger scale, recommended) or 18421. The town of Eastsound, located at the head of East Sound, is the largest settlement on Orcas Island. A small public mooring float is on the eastern shore. A 10-minute walk leads from the float to town. Anchorage, in 5 to 10 fathoms, is possible off the town. Eastsound has several good restaurants, a large grocery, a liquor store, many interesting shops, and on Saturdays during the summer, a farmers' market.

Caution in Rosario Strait

Lopez Pass, Thatcher Pass, Peavine Pass and Obstruction Pass all connect with Rosario Strait. Especially during an ebb, when current in the passes sets east into Rosario Strait, expect rougher water at the mouths of the passes. If a big southflowing ebb in Rosario Strait is opposed by a strong southerly wind, expect severe turbulence. The tide rips and heavy seas can persist completely across the strait.

We have seen some vicious rips at the south end of Rosario Strait. Walt Woodward (*How to Cruise to Alaska without Rocking the Boat Too Much*) recalls that a rip outside Lopez Pass was the worst he had ever encountered.

The waters between Guemes Channel and Thatcher Pass can be rough or even dangerous in these conditions (southflowing ebb in Rosario Strait opposed by fresh southerly wind). Guemes Channel enters Rosario Strait from the east, and Thatcher Pass enters from the west. The conflict of the three currents, combined with the opposing wind, creates confused, high and steep beam seas as you cross. It seems that all experienced local yachting families (ourselves included) have their own horror stories of crossings in such conditions. Those who have not had the experience take note.

—*Robert Hale*

See area map page 79

⑬ **Rosario Resort,** One Rosario Way, Eastsound, WA 98245, (360)376-2222; (800)562-8820. Monitors VHF channel 78. Open all year, gasoline and diesel at the fuel dock (in winter, fuel dock operation varies according to weather), 22 slips and 400 feet of dock, 20 & 30 amp power, 38 mooring buoys, restrooms, showers, laundry. Rosario is a world-renowned, deluxe resort. The more notice the better to assure reservations. Rental cars are available.

The center of the resort is the Moran Mansion, listed on the National Register of Historic Places. The Mansion houses restaurants, a lounge, gift shop, indoor pool, two outdoor pools, spa facilities and exercise equipment, all available to marina guests. The second floor of the mansion is becoming a fascinating museum—well worth the visit. Moran State Park is 1½ miles away. Restrooms and showers at the marina were upgraded in 1996.

Olga. Use chart 18430 (larger scale, recommended) or 18421. Olga, a pastoral, tiny village, is on the east shore of East Sound, near the entrance. While Olga has a dock and 105-foot-long mooring float, it has no power, no restrooms, no showers. The float is removed in winter. A box for overnight moorage payment is at the bottom of the ramp. A sign above the dock lists local stores and locations. Olga Village has a post office and (summer only) a store. Orcas Island Art Works, about ¼-mile up the road, sells interesting arts and crafts, and has an *excellent* cafe. Good anchoring offshore, but exposed to southeasterly winds.

Twin Rocks, west of Olga. Open all year, day use only, no facilities. Anchor out at this undeveloped state park property. No fires or overnight camping. Pack out all garbage. Do not disturb wildlife or alter the surroundings.

The marina at Blakely Island has excellent concrete floats and is perfectly protected.

Lieber Haven Resort, P.O. Box 127, Olga, WA 98279, (360)376-2472. In the middle of Obstruction Pass. Marina open April 1 – October 1, resort open all year. Not your usual place. Day moorage only. Store carries charts, groceries, beer and wine, and some marine supplies. Cabins for rent. Kayaks and Poulsbo boats for rent. Sailboat and fishing charters. See Kitty and Dave Baxter, daughter Nora and their parrots.

Obstruction Pass Campground, southeast tip of Orcas Island. Open all year, moorage at 2 buoys, toilets, no power or showers. Good anchoring on a gravel bottom. Campground has campsites, fireplaces, picnic tables, hiking trails.

⑭ **Doe Island Marine State Park,** southeast side of Orcas Island. Open all year for day use and camping, overnight mooring in summer only. A beautiful tiny island with a rocky shoreline dotted with tidepools. Dense forest, lush undergrowth. A trail leads all around the island. The mooring float is 30 feet long. Tie to both sides and raft out if necessary. The park has toilets, but no power, water or showers. Primitive campsites. Pack out all garbage. Adjacent buoys are privately owned. Don't use them. Currents run strongly between Doe Island and Orcas Island. If anchored, be sure of your set and your swing. Use chart 18430 (larger scale, recommended) or 18421.

⑮ **Smuggler's Resort,** P.O. Box 79, Eastsound, WA 98245, (360)376-2297; fax (360)376-5597, e-mail: smuggler @pacificrim.net. Located on the north coast of Orcas Island. Open all year, launch ramp and 400-foot dock available to guests of the resort only. Use chart

See area map page 79

18430 or 18431(larger scale, preferred), or 18421.

⑯ **Bartwood Lodge,** Rt. 1, Box 1040, Orcas Island, WA 98245, (360)376-2242. Located on the north coast of Orcas Island. Open all year, guest moorage available, 12 mooring buoys (summer only). Gasoline only at the fuel dock. Launch ramp. Accommodations, restaurant.

Freeman Island, on President Channel. Use chart 18432 (larger scale, preferred) or 18421. Open all year, day use only, no facilities. Anchor out at this undeveloped state park property. No fires or overnight camping. Pack out all garbage. Do not disturb wildlife or alter the surroundings.

⑰ **West Beach Resort,** Rt. 1, Box 510, Orcas Island, WA 98245, (360)376-2240; fax (360)376-4746. Use chart 18432 (larger scale, preferred) or 18421. Open all year, gasoline only at the fuel dock, 26-foot maximum boat length in the slips. Keel sailboats tie to mooring buoys. The dock and mooring buoys can take between 35 and 38 boats. The store has a little bit of everything, including some groceries, ice, propane, kerosene, stove alcohol, scuba air, beer and wine. West Beach is a popular fishing resort, with cabins for rent, launch ramp and parking. Be careful anchoring out. The eelgrass bottom is not good in many places and you can drag.

Blakely Island. Use chart 18430 (larger scale, preferred) or 18421. Blakely Island lies east of Lopez Island and Shaw Island. It and tiny Armitage Island, off the southeast corner, are privately owned, with no shore access. Anchorage is possible in Thatcher Bay, and, with care, behind Armitage Island. The Blakely Island General Store & Marina, at the north end of Blakely Island, is a popular destination. Since Blakely Island, including the roads, is private, confine your stays to the marina property.

⑱ **Blakely Island General Store & Marina,** #1 Marina Drive, Blakely Island, WA 98222, (360)375-6121. Open all year, except closed in January. Fuel dock has gasoline and diesel. Facilities include excellent concrete docks with 70 slips, 20 & 30 amp power, ample water, large, clean restrooms and showers, and laundry. The resort has a large covered picnic area, with sinks. The general store serves island residents, as well as marina guests. The store is well stocked with food, clothes, gifts.

Barnes Island and **Clark Island.** Use chart 18430 (larger scale, preferred) or 18421. These two beautiful islands lie parallel to each other in Rosario Strait, between Orcas Island and Lummi Island. Barnes Island is privately owned. Clark Island is a state park, with mooring buoys installed during the summer. Camping and picnicking sites are ashore, and trails along the island.

⑤ **Clark Island Marine State Park.** Open all year, day use and overnight mooring & camping. Clark Island is exposed to Rosario Strait and Georgia Strait, and best for settled weather only. Mooring buoys are deployed between Clark Island and Barnes Island, and in the bay on the east side. Note the nasty rock that lies in the entrance to the bay. Park has 9 mooring buoys. Toilets, no power, no water. Picnic sites, fire rings, primitive campsites. Pack out all garbage.

⑫ **Matia Island Marine State Park.** Use charts 18430 or 18431 (larger scale, preferred), or 18421. Open all year, day use and overnight mooring and camping. Facilities include a float in Rolfe Cove, 2 buoys, toilet, no power, water or showers. The mooring float is removed in winter. The favored anchorage is in Rolfe Cove, which opens from the west. Strong currents can run through Rolfe Cove. The bottom is rocky. Be sure the anchor is well set, and swinging room is adequate. Anchorage is also good in the bay that indents the southeast corner. The remains of an old homestead are located at the head of that bay.

Matia (pronounced "Mah-TEE-ah") Island is a popular destination, beautiful and interesting. The island is part of the San Juan Island National Wildlife Refuge (run by the U.S. Fish and Wildlife Service). All access is restricted except the loop trail and the designated 5-acre moorage and camping area. The rest of the island is off-limits to protect nesting wildlife.

⑲ **Sucia Island Marine State Park.** Use chart 18431 (larger scale, preferred)

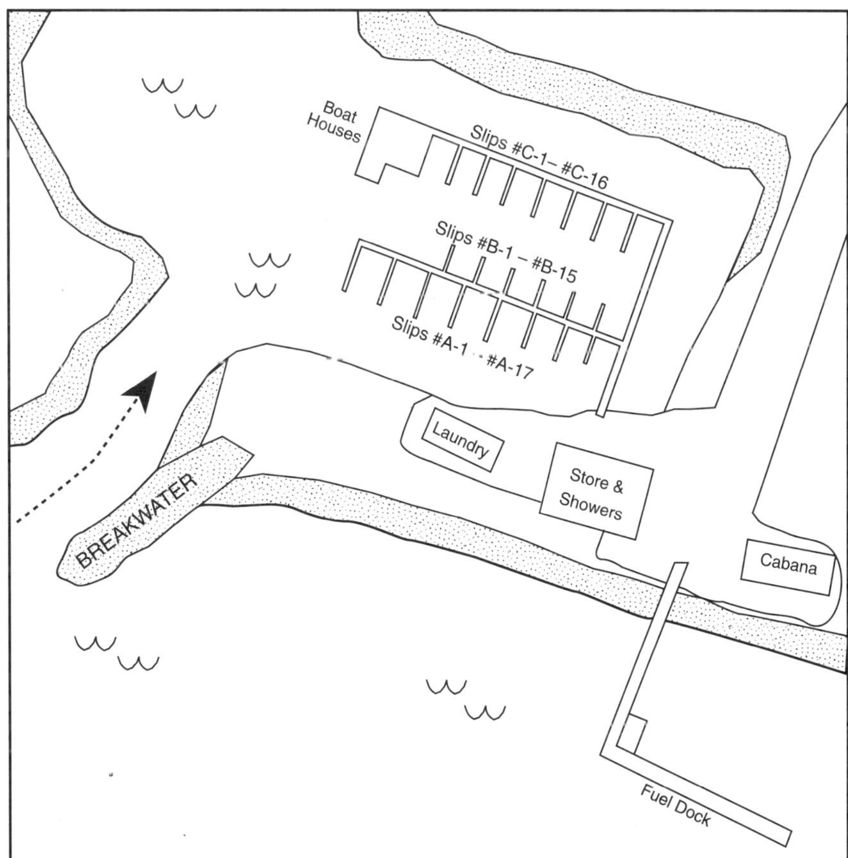

Blakely Island General Store & Marina

Reference only — not for navigation

See area map page 79

or 18421. Open all year, day use and overnight mooring & camping. For information call (800)233-0321. Facilities include dock space, mooring buoys, toilets, portapotty dump. Water, but no power, no showers. This probably is the most heavily used marine park in the system. As many as 700 boats can visit on one weekend in the high summer season. Like Matia and Patos Islands, Sucia Island is made of sandstone carved by water and wind into dramatic shapes. Many fossils can be found in Sucia Island's sandstone. It is illegal to disturb them or remove them.

Fossil Bay, Sucia Island, has the best facilities for visiting pleasure craft.

The park has 55 primitive campsites, and 2 group campsites which can be reserved. Camping is permitted in designated areas only. The day use/picnic area, with picnic shelters, is on the neck of land separating Echo Bay and Shallow Bay, and can be reserved. The park has several miles of hiking trails and service roads. The most developed facilities are at Fossil Bay. Fresh water is available April through September at Fossil Bay and near Shallow Bay.

Sucia Island has several fingers that separate small bays. Facilities in these bays are as follows: Fox Cove: 4 mooring buoys; Fossil Bay: dock, 16 mooring buoys; Snoring Bay: 2 mooring buoys; Echo Bay: 14 mooring buoys. Ewing Cove: 4 mooring buoys; Shallow Bay: 8 mooring buoys;

Fox Cove. Enter Fox Cove from either side. Waters off the southern entry can be turbulent. At the west entry the foul ground extends west farther than you expect. Tie to mooring buoys or anchor behind Little Sucia Island. A pretty spot with deeply carved sandstone cliffs.

Fossil Bay. Fossil Bay is easy to enter, nicely protected, and beautiful. Anchor out, tie to one of the mooring buoys, or moor at the dock. At the head of the dock a plaque commemorates the yacht clubs that were members of the Interclub Boating Association of Washington, when Interclub bought the island and gave it to the state as a state park forever. One of the points of land overlooking Fossil Bay is named for Ev. Henry, the first president of Interclub, who conceived the idea and carried out the project.

Snoring Bay. Snoring Bay is easy to enter, and has 2 mooring buoys. A good spot. As we understand the story, a park ranger was caught sleeping on duty in this bay, hence the name.

Echo Bay. Echo Bay is the largest of Sucia's bays. While it is the most exposed, it is the most popular. When the wind blows expect some anchor dragging. Mooring buoys line the western shore. Picnic facilities are on the narrow neck of land that separates Echo Bay from Shallow Bay.

The two long islands in Echo Bay (North Finger Island and South Finger Island) are privately owned. The south half of Justice Island (the small island off South Finger Island) is park-owned but closed to the public as a nature preserve.

Ewing Cove. In our opinion, cozy little Ewing Cove, tucked in behind Ewing Island on the north side of Echo Bay, is the most charming of Sucia Island's bays. The cove has 4 mooring buoys and a lovely beach at the northeast end. The narrow pass at the northeast end is deep and easily run. Danger Reef lies just outside.

Shallow Bay. Shallow Bay is an excellent, popular anchorage. Lots of room. Tie to a mooring buoy or anchor. Easy entry as long as you pass *between* the 2 beacons that mark the entrance. Beautiful sunsets.

Patos Island Marine State Park. Use chart 18432 (larger scale, preferred) or 18421. Open all year, day use and overnight mooring and camping. Facilities include 2 mooring buoys in Active Cove, toilets, primitive campsites. The only possible anchorage is in Active Cove, on the west tip of the island. Strong currents make anchoring difficult, however. The remains of the dock that served the lighthouse on Alden Point are still there, but the dock is not usable for moorage. Use the mooring buoys when possible. Pack out all garbage. The island is a breeding area for birds.

Waldron Island. Use chart 18432 (larger scale, preferred) or 18421. Waldron Island has no public facilities. In settled weather anchorage is good in Cowlitz Bay and North Bay. Mail Bay, on the east shore, is rocky but usable. The mail boat from Bellingham used to call here, leaving the mail in a barrel hung over the water.

Stuart Island. Use chart 18432 (larger scale, preferred) or 18421. The center portion of Stuart Island, including Reid Harbor and Prevost Harbor, is a state park. A trail and dirt road from Reid Harbor and Prevost Harbor lead out to the automated Turn Point lighthouse. It's an excellent walk.

⑳ Stuart Island Marine State Park, Prevost Harbor. Open all year, day use and overnight mooring and camping. Facilities include 256 feet of dock space, 7 mooring buoys, toilets, 18 primitive campsites. The favored entrance to Prevost Harbor is around the west end of Satellite Island. The passage to the east of Satellite Island is foul, and many people recommend against it. Contributing Editor Tom Kincaid reports, however, that with care these waters are passable at half-tide or better, or by shallow draft boats. Use caution. Prevost Harbor is a popular destination, with good anchoring and miles of trails and roads on Stuart Island. Shoreside facilities are shared with Reid Harbor, on the narrow but steep neck of land that separates them.

Stuart Island Marine State Park, Reid Harbor. Open all year, day use and overnight mooring & camping. The entrance is straightforward. A mooring float is located on the north shore, mooring buoys dot the bay, and mooring floats are placed within easy dinghy distance of the landing pier. Facilities include toilets, pumpout, portapotty dump. Reid Harbor is long and narrow, and protected by high hills. The bottom is excellent for anchoring, and the harbor holds a great number of boats. The setting is beautiful. It is a popular destination. Shoreside facilities are shared with Prevost Harbor, on the narrow but steep neck of land that separates them.

Johns Pass. Use chart 18432 (larger scale, preferred) or 18421. Johns Pass separates Stuart Island and Johns Island, and is used regularly. At the south end of the pass foul ground, marked by kelp, extends about 0.6 miles southeast from Stuart Island. Boats heading southeast through Johns Pass should head for Gull Reef, then turn when well clear of the kelp. Anchorage is possible in Johns Pass and along the south side of Johns Island.

Drift

Throughout these coastal waters, from Olympia north, skippers must watch for debris in the water. While some of the debris is in the form of cushions, fenders, and other equipment lost from boats, most of it is wood. Lumber, tree branches, entire trees, logs, and chunks of wood of all sizes are floating around out there, ready to bend a propeller or damage a bottom.

Collectively, this debris is called drift, and whoever's on the helm must watch for it constantly. It's a good idea, in fact, to have two pairs of eyes watching ahead whenever the boat is underway — especially if the boat is traveling faster than 10 knots.

Drift can be anywhere, but usually it collects along the shear line where two currents meet. If you see one piece of drift, look sharp for more. Usually it'll be there. On calm days shear lines will seem to meander across an entire waterway. In many areas the currents eddy, forming shear lines that appear, one after another, for what seem like miles. When approaching a shear line, the wise skipper of a faster boat slows from cruise speed to 6-8 knots, and picks a relatively safe way through the rubble. Often a shift to neutral is called for, to protect the propeller.

Much drift is easy to see, but sometimes it is not. I have seen 60-foot-long logs floating barely awash, almost invisible until the boat is right upon them. At sunrise or sunset, while running toward the sun, reflections off the water can hide a lot of drift. Occasionally a log will hang vertically in the water, the upper end hardly visible. These are called deadheads. When such a log buries its lower end in the bottom, a boat hitting the upper end can suffer catastrophic damage.

—Robert Hale

This heavy plank took out both props, but impaled itself on a blade in the process. Outside Boston Harbor, near Olympia. Jim and Peggy Townsend, "Peggy T."

Southern Gulf Islands

Victoria • Sidney • Saanich Inlet • Ganges • Active Pass
Montague Harbour • Saturna Island

Charts

3440	Race Rocks to D'Arcy Island (1:40,000)
3313	SMALL CRAFT CHARTS (chart book) – Gulf Islands and adjacent Waterways (new, 1995)
3419	Esquimalt Harbour (1:5,000)
3415	Victoria Harbour (1:6,000)
3424	Approaches to Oak Bay (1:10,000)
3441	Haro Strait, Boundary Pass and Satellite Channel (1:40,000)
3476	Approaches to Tsehum Harbour (1:10,000)
3477	Plans – Gulf Islands Bedwell Harbour to Georgeson Passage (1:15,000)
	Telegraph Harbour and Preedy Harbour (1:15,000)
	Pender Canal (1:4,000)
3442	North Pender Island to Thetis Island (1:40,000)
3478	Plans – Saltspring Island Cowichan Bay to Maple Bay (1:20,000)
	Birds Eye Cove (1:10,000)
	Genoa Bay (1:10,000)
	Ganges Harbour and Long Harbour (1:20,000)
	Fulford Harbour (1:15,000)

VICTORIA AREA

About customs
Vessels entering Canada are required either to have a CANPASS customs preclearance or to clear Canadian Customs at their first stop in Canada. The customs ports most convenient to the Gulf Islands are Victoria (includes Oak Bay and Cadboro Bay), Sidney, and Bedwell Harbour. Bedwell Harbour is on South Pender Island, just 4 miles north of Stuart Island in the San Juans, but its customs station is open only from May 1 through September 30. For more information about clearing customs, see the chapter titled "Crossing the Border."

Esquimalt Harbour. Use chart 3419; 3440. Esquimalt Harbour has some anchorage toward the head of the bay. The Canadian Navy moors some of its ships just inside Duntze Head, and a drydock there handles Navy as well as other large ships. The head of the bay is used to boom logs, but Contributing Editor Tom Kincaid reports that he has always found plenty of room to swing at anchor without interfering with the tugs.

Fleming Beach, west of Victoria Harbour, in Esquimalt. Use chart 3419; 3440. Open all year. Facilities include launch ramp (fee charged), and washrooms. This is a charming little cove, protected by a rock breakwater, overlooked by most boating people. It is the home of Esquimalt Anglers' Association, a private sportfishing and fish enhancement group. The launch ramp boarding floats have room for temporary moorage while shopping nearby, or you can anchor out. Walkways and picnic areas have been built. Fleming Beach is adjacent to old coastal gun emplacements, which are interesting to explore.

Victoria. Use chart 3415; 3440. Victoria is the provincial capital, and the largest city on Vancouver Island. There is regular ferry service from Port Angeles, Vancouver, and Seattle. Scheduled float planes also connect with Vancouver and Seattle.

Because of the volume of traffic, including regular float plane arrivals and departures, no sailing is allowed past the breakwater.

Inside Ogden Point, the Erie Street Wharf is reserved primarily for commercial fishboats, but often has room for pleasure craft when the fleet is out. A large chandlery is across the street from this marina. The Broughton Street Wharf customs dock is at the head of the inlet, across the street from the buildings of downtown. A seaplane float and moorage for government fisheries patrol vessels are at the same location. To the left of the customs dock is Wharf Street Wharf and Floats. It is a public marina with transient moorage, power and water available. To the right of the customs dock is the Ship Point wharf, usually

See area map page 94

Photo courtesy of Tourism Victoria

The Victoria Causeway floats are next to the Parliament buildings and the Empress Hotel (not shown).

used by larger commercial fishing boats, but available to pleasure craft willing to tend their lines as the tide rises and falls.

The City of Victoria Causeway Floats are to the right of Ship Point and across the street from the Empress Hotel. These are the docks that fill up first. Another small moorage, the Johnson Street Wharf, is near the Johnson Street Bridge (the Blue Bridge, locally), and sometimes has room for one or two visiting boats.

A few years ago the Port of Victoria instituted a "meet and greet" program for visiting boats. When entering Inner Harbour, hail them on VHF channel 73 and they will direct you to available guest moorage.

For an interesting side trip, take the dinghy through Gorge Waters to Portage Inlet. You'll travel first through the industrial part of the city, then through park and residential areas. It's about a 3-mile trip; currents are a factor if you intend to row.

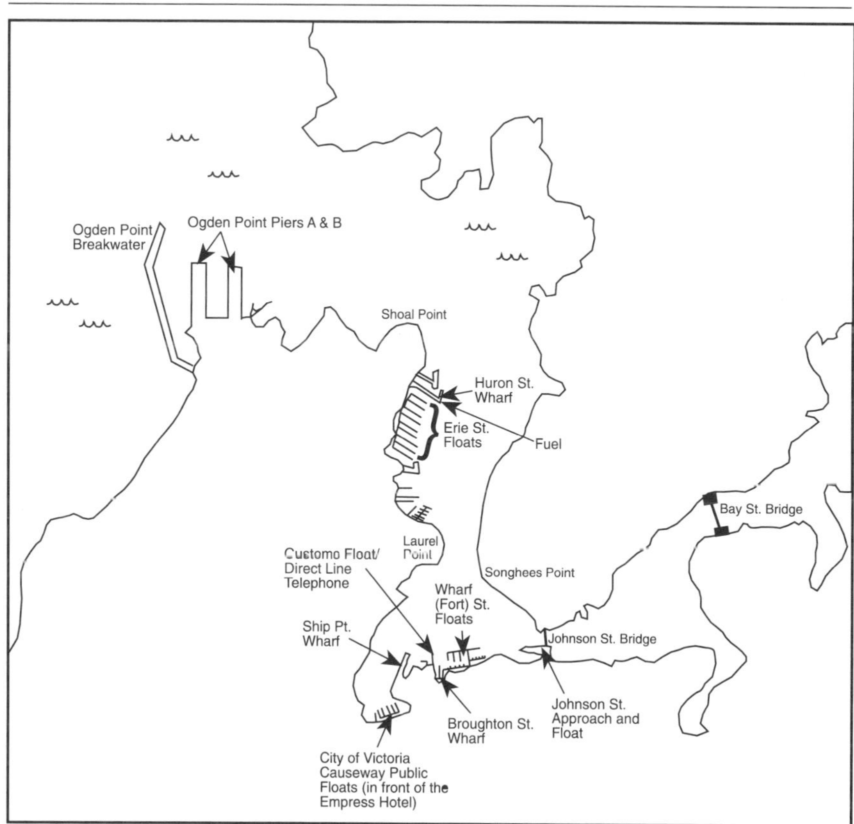

Victoria Harbour

Reference only — not for navigation

① **City of Victoria Causeway (James Bay),** (250)363-3273. Monitors VHF channel 73. Open all year. Facilities include 1300+ feet of dock space, washrooms, showers, laundry, limited power. No reservations taken, and a 2-day limit if full. Rafting is mandatory. These are the picturesque and popular floats located directly in front of the Empress Hotel. Downtown Victoria surrounds. Fabulous restaurants, shopping, hotels, museums, sightseeing. Marine supplies are nearby at two well-stocked chandleries (Bosun's Locker and Trotac Marine). In the winter the washroom hours are reduced, showers and laundry are closed.

① **Victoria (Ogden Point) Govt. Wharf,** (250)363-3273. Monitors VHF channel 73. Open all year, no power, no washrooms, no showers. This wharf is for larger commerical vessels only. No guest moorage for pleasure craft.

① **Victoria (Erie Street) Govt. Wharf,** (250)363-3273. Monitors VHF channel

Reference only — not for navigation

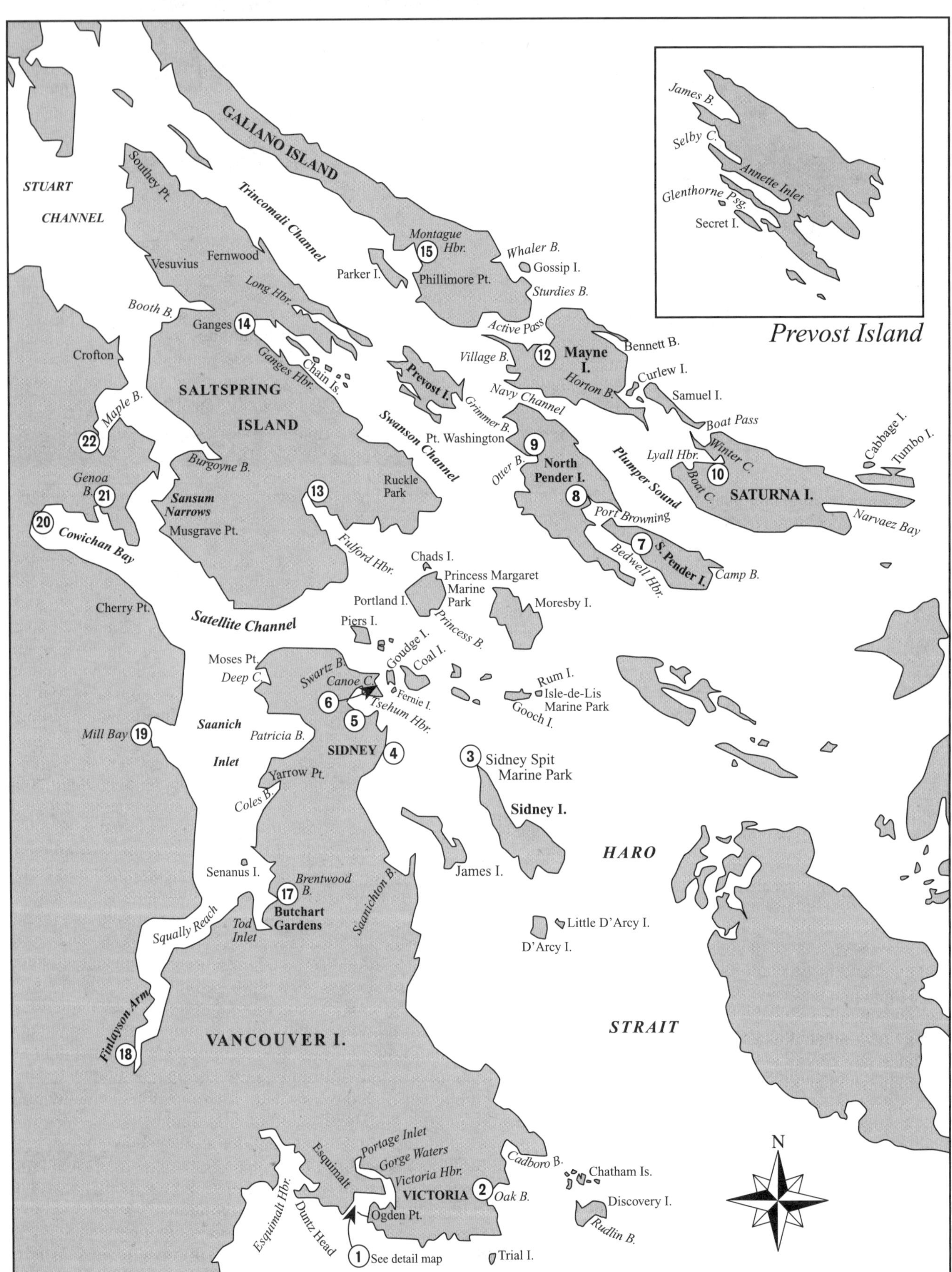

See area map page 94

73. Open all year, 3180 feet of dock space, 20 amp power, washrooms, showers. Also known as Fishermen's Wharf. When fish boats are out, usually you'll find lots of dock space. Rafting is mandatory. Fuel is next door.

① **Ocean West Marine Fuels,** 327 Maitland St., Victoria, B.C. V9A 7G7, (250)388-7224. Open all year, but with shorter hours in winter. Fuel dock with gasoline and diesel. Carries kerosene and stove alcohol, fishing licenses, snacks, food items. Chart agent. This is the only fuel dock in the Inner Harbour.

① **Victoria (Broughton Street) Govt. Wharf,** Open all year, 24-hour customs clearance. Monitors VHF channel 73. Located on your starboard side as you enter the harbor. If you are visiting Canada and have not yet cleared customs, stop here before going ahead.

① **Victoria (Wharf Street) Govt. Wharf,** (250)363-3273. Monitors VHF channel 73. Open all year, 1780 feet of visitor dock space, 20, 30 & 50 amp power, washrooms, showers, garbage collection. Right downtown, to the left of the Causeway docks as you come in. Washrooms and showers are a 5-minute walk down the causeway. In the winter the washroom hours are reduced and the showers and laundry are closed. Power availability varies, depending on location.

① **Victoria (Johnson Street) Govt. Wharf,** (250)363-3760. Monitors VHF channel 73. Open all year, 220 feet of dock space, no power, washrooms or showers. Rafting mandatory.

Oak Bay. Use chart 3424 (larger scale, preferred) or 3440. Oak Bay is on the east side of the south tip of Vancouver Island, west of the Chatham Islands. The channels between the various rocks and reefs are well marked. This is the route taken by many tugs with tows, and commercial fishing boats of all sizes. The Oak Bay Marina and a separate small repair yard, with marine railway, are located behind the breakwater.

② **Oak Bay Marina,** 1327 Beach Drive, Victoria, BC V8S 2N4, (250)598-3369, (250)598-3366; fax (250)598-1361. Monitors VHF channel 68. Open all year. Gasoline and diesel at the fuel dock, customs clearance telephone at the fuel dock. Ample guest moorage for boats to 110 feet, call ahead for availability. Facilities include 15 & 30 amp power, washrooms, showers, laundry. Marina has undergone a major upgrade, with new docks, a good restaurant, deli and gift shop added. A small chandlery carries essential marine hardware. Repairs are available at a small boatyard in the next building. Complete shopping at charming Oak Bay Village, a short distance away. Regular bus service to downtown Victoria, with extra shuttle bus service in the summer.

Discovery Island Marine Park. Open all year. An undeveloped park suitable for beachable boats only. The island was once the home of Capt. E.G. Beaumont, who donated the land as a park. The northern part of Discovery Island, adjacent Chatham Island, and some of the smaller islands nearby are Indian Reserve lands; no landing.

Cadboro Bay. Use chart 3424; 3440. Cadboro Bay is entirely residential except for the Royal Victoria Yacht Club, which has a breakwater-protected marina on the western shore. Anchorage in Cadboro Bay is excellent, mud and sand bottom, beyond the yacht club moorage. Moorage at RVYC is available for members of clubs with reciprocal agreements with Royal Vic. Customs clearance available.

SOUTHERN GULF ISLANDS

D'Arcy Island Marine Park. Use chart 3441. Open all year, 2 mooring buoys. This is an undeveloped island park with no facilities other than some primitive campsites. Numerous reefs and shoals are in the area, so approach with caution. Enter from the west, south of the lighthouse. D'Arcy Island was B.C.'s first leper colony; from 1891 until 1926 it housed Chinese lepers. The colony was closed in 1926 and the island reverted to provin-

Port Sidney Marina has new docks and excellent facilities adjacent to downtown Sidney.

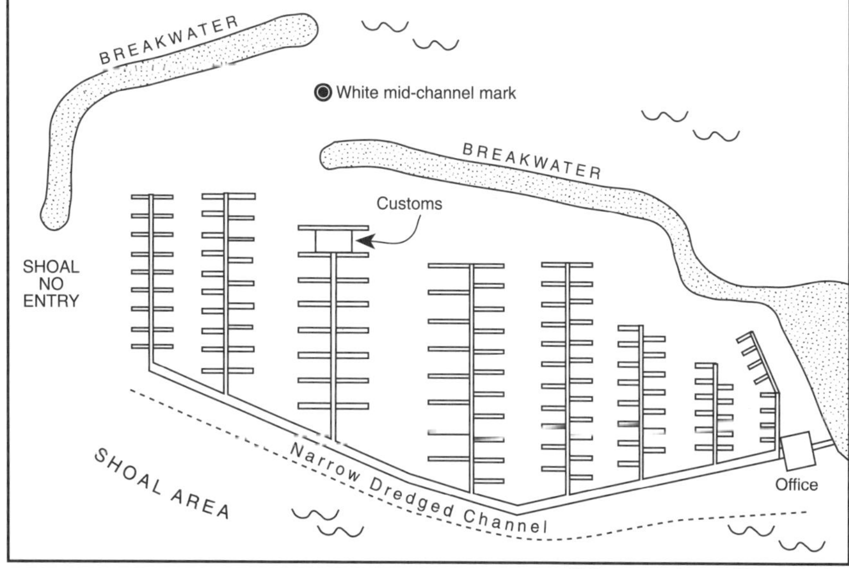

Port Sidney Marina

See area map page 94

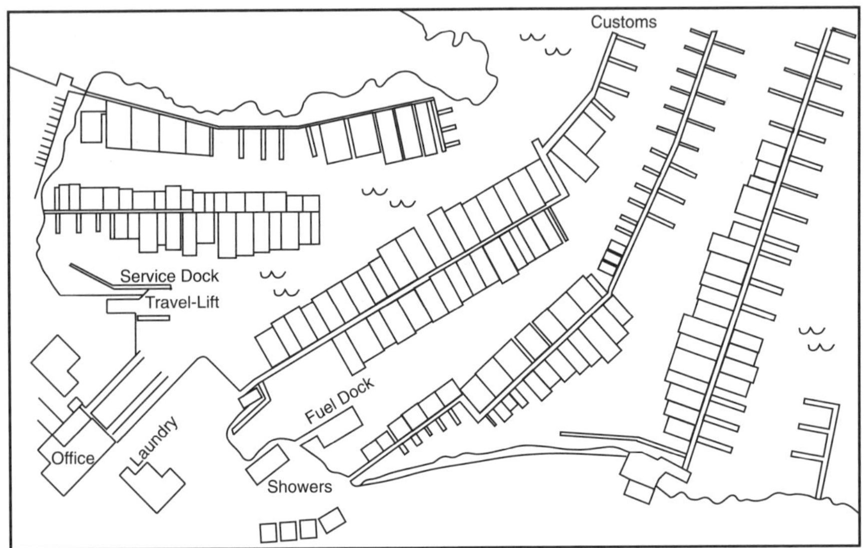

Canoe Cove Marina

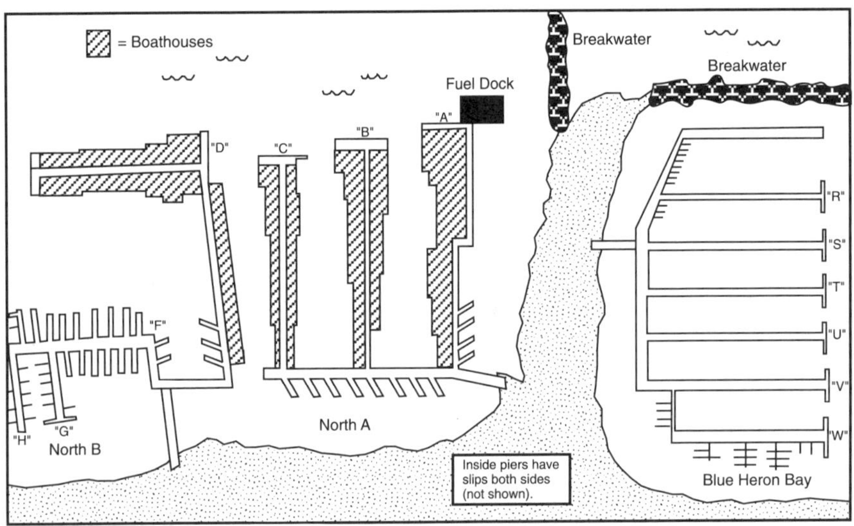

North Saanich Marina

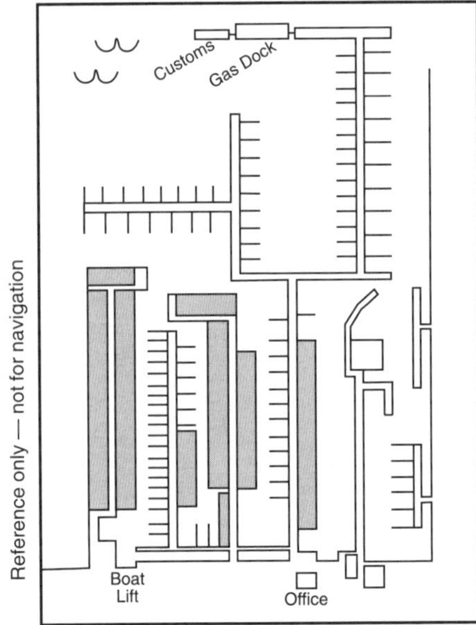

Van Isle Marina

cial jurisdiction. Plans for the island as a federal penitentiary were never realized. D'Arcy Island remained undeveloped, and was established as a marine park in 1961. To the east, Little D'Arcy Island is private property.

③ **Sidney Spit Marine Park.** Use chart 3441. Sidney Spit Marine Park is on a mile-long sandspit that extends from the north end of Sidney Island. It is one of the most popular of the Gulf Islands provincial parks. The park is open all year, has 35 mooring buoys, landing floats for small craft in summer, toilets and campsites. The anchoring is good, and there's much to do ashore. In the summer a passenger ferry runs to Sidney.

Isle-de-Lis (Rum Island). Use chart 3441. Open all year, anchoring only, no facilities. This is a small, undeveloped and very pretty natural park area with a walking trail and beaches. Rum Island is located at the east end of Gooch Island, where Prevost Passage meets Haro Strait. Anchorage is either to the north or the south of the gravel spit that connects Rum Island to Gooch Island. The northern anchorage is preferred. Rum Island is said to have come by its name honestly during Prohibition. In 1995 the warship *HMCS Mackenzie* was sunk in 17 fathoms off Rum Island to create an artificial reef for divers.

Princess Margaret Marine Park, Portland Island, (250)387-4363. Use chart 3476; 3441. Open all year, picnic and camp sites, toilets, no other facilities. In honor of her last visit to Victoria, Portland Island was donated to Her Royal Highness Princess Margaret, who later deeded the island to British Columbia. Portland Island is now Princess Margaret Marine Park.

Portland Island is hilly and heavily wooded, with hiking trails that provide excellent exercise. Anchor in Royal Cove (behind Chads Island) on the north side of the island, or in Princess Bay, behind Tortoise Island on the south side. Royal Cove is often used as an anchorage, but suffers mightily from the wash of passing B.C. ferries. If you can get well inside the cove you can have a quiet night. Princess Bay is more roomy, but somewhat exposed to southerly winds. In summer it usually is fine. Watch your depths as you approach the head of Princess Bay. The bottom shoals rapidly, farther from shore than you might expect.

The *G.B. Church*, a sunken freighter off the southwest shore of the island, provides an artificial reef for divers. The freighter lies in 30 fathoms of water and is marked with bow and stern buoys.

Sidney. Use chart 3476 (larger scale, preferred) or 3441. Sidney and nearby Tsehum Harbour have much to attract boaters, including excellent bakeries just up Beacon Avenue (Sidney's main street). The town also offers good dining, several art galleries, many interesting shops, marine supplies, a large bookstore (Tanner's), nautical chart agencies, a liquor store, and groceries. The museum at the foot of Beacon Avenue has an excellent exhibit of early history in Sidney, and a superb whale exhibit. Admission by donation. Highly recommended, especially for families.

For boats crossing from Roche Harbor or the northern San Juan Islands, Sidney is a natural first stop to clear customs, stroll around, and re-stock with fresh produce, meat, spirits, and other consumables. The new Port Sidney Marina is delightful, with efficient staff, large, clean washrooms and showers, and wide concrete docks.

Sidney is the western terminus of the Washington State ferry run from Anacortes and Friday Harbor, and is a Canadian Customs port. The customs dock used to be located at the public pier at the end of Beacon Street. Now it is part of the Port Sidney Marina, just north of the public pier. During summer months Customs officers may be stationed at the check-in dock (with its unique canopy) just inside the breakwater entrance. When officers are not present, customs check-in can be accomplished by a telephone at the dock.

Dining: For excellent Chinese food, try the Maple Palace. Friends suggest Theo's, Cafe Mozart, Odyssia, Squid Roe Pub. In Tsehum Harbour, the Latch Restaurant and the Blue Peter Inn are good bets.

④ **Port Sidney Marina,** 9835 Seaport Place, Sidney, B.C. V8L 4X3, (250)655-3711; fax (250)655-3771. Monitors VHF channel 68. Open all year, 325 slips plus guest dock. Facilities include 30 & 50 amp power, water, washrooms, showers, laundry, pumpout, customs clearance. Call on VHF channel 68 for slip assignment. The customs dock is located just inside the entrance. If officers are not present, use the telephone to arrange clearance.

When entering, pass between the two buoys just off the breakwater. The northernmost of these buoys marks a reef. Do not try to enter between the north end breakwater and the shore. If you are directed to the shore side of the long, main pier, do not stray outside the marked channel. The bottom has been dredged alongside the dock, but shoal water lies just a few feet inshore. This is an popular marina, new and well-maintained, adjacent to downtown. They have hanging flower pots in the summer, shuttle service to Victoria and Butchart Gardens, and other activities. *(Marina map page 95)*

④ **Sidney Beacon Ave. Public Wharf,** Open all year, 738 feet of dock space, no power, water, washrooms or showers. Garbage collection at dock.

Tsehum Harbor. Use chart 3476 (larger scale, preferred) or 3441. About 1.5 miles north of Sidney is Tsehum Harbour, a shallow but navigable inlet that contains a number of public, private, and yacht club moorages. Enter favoring the Armstrong Point (south) side to avoid a marked rock. A number of excellent boat yards are located in Tsehum Harbour. Van Isle Marina, the first marina on the south side, has a customs check-in telephone, fuel, and guest moorage. Philbrooks Shipyard is next door to Van Isle Marina. Other moorages in Tsehum Harbour belong to Capitol City, Royal Victoria, and other yacht clubs, and private marinas.

⑤ **Tsehum Harbour Govt. Wharf,** located in Shoal Harbour. Open all year, 1043 feet of dock space, power, washrooms, no showers. Commercial fishing vessels have priority. Launch ramp. Breakwater. Garbage collection. Lights, telephone.

See area map page 94

⑤ **Van Isle Marina,** 2320 Harbour Road, Sidney, B.C. V8L 2P6, (250)656-1138. Monitors VHF channel 68. Open all year, 7 days, gasoline and diesel at fuel dock, customs clearance, 15, 30 & 50 amp power, oil pumpout, washrooms, laundry, holding tank pumpout, portapotty dump, showers. Best to call ahead for availability. This is a large and busy marina, about a mile from downtown. Much new dock space has been added in recent years. Haulout and repair services are available. Yacht brokerage. Launch ramp. Taxi and car rentals. The coffee shop burned in 1996, but is scheduled to reopen in 1997. The Latch Restaurant is a short walk away, and the Blue Peter Pub is next door. We had an excellent informal supper at the Blue Peter Pub in 1996. *(Marina map page 96)*

⑤ **Westport Marina,** 2075 Tryon Road, Sidney, B.C. V8L 3X9, (250)656-2832; fax (250)655-1981. Open all year, 20 amp power, washrooms, showers. Uses unoccupied slips as available for guest moorage. Call ahead for availabity. Has marine parts, ice, some charts and books, limited groceries. Marine ways and repair facilities.

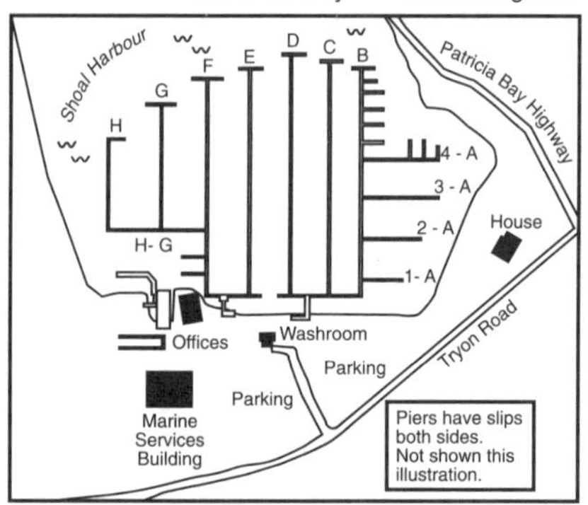

Westport Marina

⑤ **North Saanich Marina,** P.O. Box 2001, 1949 Marina Way, Sidney, B.C. V8L 3S3, (250)656-5558; fax (250) 656-1574. Open all year, gasoline and diesel at fuel dock. Primarily a fuel dock and permanent moorage marina. Store carries bait, tackle, ice. They might have some transient moorage if you are desperate. Call ahead. *(Marina map page 96)*

Canoe Bay. Use chart 3476 (larger scale, preferred) or 3441. Canoe Bay, commonly called Canoe Cove, is tucked in behind a group of islands, only some of which have navigable passages between them. The clearest passage is **John Passage**, along the west side of Coal Island. From John Passage turn west into **Iroquois Passage**, and follow Iroquois Passage between Fernie Island and Goudge Island into Canoe Bay. From the south, **Page Passage**, west of Fernie Island, will lead to Canoe Bay, and many boats use Page Passage. *Caution*: Page Passage should be run only with local knowledge or close study of large-scale chart 3476. Tidal currents can run strongly, especially on spring tides. Canoe Bay has moorage with all the amenities.

⑥ **Canoe Cove Marina,** P.O. Box 2099, 2300 Canoe Cove Road, Sidney, B.C. V8L 3S6, (250)656-5566; fax (250) 655-7197. Monitors VHF channel 68. Open all year, gasoline, diesel, propane at fuel dock, 15 & 30 amp power, washrooms, showers, laundry, 24-hour customs clearance. This is a 400-berth marina with mostly permanent moorage. Visiting boats are assigned unoccupied slips as available. They rarely turn anybody away. They have a full repair facility with marine railway, and a well-stocked chandlery. Coffee shop on premises, nearby pub. A short trail leads to the Swartz Bay ferry terminal. Harbor taxi connects the marina with Sidney. Watch your navigation as you approach the marina. Rocks are marked, often by sticks, and must be avoided. Easy to do if you pay attention. The staff and management are friendly and competent. *(Marina map page 96)*

Swartz Bay Govt. Wharf. Use chart 3476 (larger scale, preferred) or 3441. Open all year, adjacent to the ferry terminal. Has 85 feet of dock space with no facilities available.

Piers Island Govt. Wharf. Use chart 3476 (larger scale, preferred) or 3441. Open all year. Has 200 feet of dock space, no facilities.

Bedwell Harbour. Use chart 3477 (larger scale, preferred) or 3441. Bedwell Harbour has a resort with mooring floats that give access to a pub and restaurant, fuel, and a store. Anchorage is good at Beaumont Provincial Park, north of the resort, and in Peter Cove, on the west side of the harbor. The Pender Canal, a man-made channel between North Pender Island and South Pender Island, connects Bedwell Harbour with Port Browning. The canal is crossed by a bridge with a 27-foot vertical clearance.

Peter Cove. Use chart 3477 (larger scale, preferred) or 3441. Peter Cove is located at the southern tip of South Pender Island. It is a well protected little anchorage, but permanently moored

See area map page 94

boats make anchoring a bit tight. A significant reef guards the mouth of the cove. Enter and depart north of the reef.

⑦ **Bedwell Harbour Resort,** 9801 Spalding Road, RR #3, South Pender Island, B.C. V0N 2M3, (250)629-3212, (800)663-2899; fax (250)629-6777. Monitors VHF channel 68. Open April through Sept., closed all winter. Gasoline, pre-mix, diesel and ice at the fuel dock. Facilities include 100 slips for guest moorage, 15 & 30 amp power, washrooms, showers, laundry. Customs clearance available 0800-2000 May-Sept., extra charge for after-hours clearance. This is a popular resort, with groceries, fresh meat and produce, some marine supplies, swimming pool, restaurant, bar and bistro, live entertainment weekends and some weekday evenings, and kids' activities. Hotel accommodations are available. Moored guests have access to selected services. Lots to do, and a golf course is 20 minutes away by resort shuttle.

Bedwell Harbour Govt. Wharf, South Pender Island. Open all year, 312 feet of dock space. No facilities, but customs clearance is available. Lights and telephone at dock. Fishing vessels have priority.

Beaumont Marine Park, west side of South Pender Island, in Bedwell Harbour. Open all year. Facilities include 15 mooring buoys, toilets, no power, no showers. Walk-in campsites, picnicking, walking and hiking trails. A beautiful and popular park. Enter from Swanson Channel from the south, or from Plumper Sound and Port Browning through the Pender Canal.

Port Browning. Use chart 3477 (larger scale, preferred) or 3441. Port Browning has a resort (Port Browning Marina) with moorage and other facilities. Anchorage is good throughout the harbor. The Driftwood Center shopping area is located about a ½-mile walk from the marina. The center has groceries, a bank, gift shop, bakery, liquor store, pharmacy, post office, hair care, and a laundromat.

⑧ **Port Browning Marina,** North Pender Island, B.C., (250)629-3493. Monitors VHF channel 68. Open all year, 100 slips, 15 amp power, washrooms, laundry. Facilities include launch ramp, groceries, beer & wine store, marine hardware, charts, tackle, bait. Coffee shop and pub. Pool and tennis courts. Shopping center nearby. Port Browning is a popular marina in the Gulf Islands. The atmosphere is very relaxed, and the pub serves decent meals.

Browning Harbour Govt. Wharf, Open all year, 89 feet of dock space, no facilities. Commercial fishing vessels have priority.

⑨ **Otter Bay Marina,** RR 1, North Pender Island, B.C. V0N 2M0, (250)629-3579 phone and fax. Monitors VHF channel 68. Use chart 3442. Open all year, 15 & 30 amp power, washrooms, showers, laundry, launch ramp, new docks, gazebo and heated pool. Kayak, bike, and boat rentals. Nearby restaurant. Five-minute walk to a golf course and the ferry. Reservations recommended. The word is getting out on the Otter Bay Marina. We think it is one of the nicest you'll find. It is maintained in spotless order, the grounds are beautiful, the gift shop well stocked, and the management efficient. The pool has adult hours in the afternoons. The showers are some of the best on the coast. The marina is located on on the west side of North Pender Island, facing Swanson Channel. Kay and Chuck Spence are the managers. At Kay's suggestion we took the pleasant walk past the ferry dock to the Poplars Restaurant, and were rewarded with an excellent supper.

Port Washington Govt. Wharf, North Pender Island. Use chart 3442. Open all year, 147 feet of dock space, unoccupied slips used when available. No facilities. Watch for a rock located off the southeast dock. Aircraft float.

Hope Bay Govt. Wharf, east side of North Pender Island, facing Navy Channel. Use chart 3442. Open all year, 226 feet of dock space, lights and telephone but no other facilities. Commercial fishing vessels have priority.

Irish Bay. Use chart 3477; 3442. Irish Bay, on the east side of Samuel Island, is a good anchorage, but the island is privately owned. If you venture above the foreshore the caretaker will shoo you off.

Winter Cove. Use chart 3477 (larger scale, preferred) or 3442. Winter Cove,

See area map page 94

between Samuel Island and Saturna Island, has an attractive park (Winter Cove Provincial Park), on the Saturna Island side, and shallow anchorage between numerous rocks and reefs. The best anchorage is behind Winter Point, or just off the provincial park. Deep draft boats generally favor the Winter Point site, which is deeper. Boat Pass runs between Winter Cove and the Strait of Georgia, and can run at 7 knots past several nasty rocks and reefs. Deep draft boats should take this pass only at or near high water slack.

Winter Cove Marine Park, north tip of Saturna Island. Open all year, toilets, no other facilities. A spacious, attractive park looking out on Georgia Strait. Anchorage only, 1-fathom depth at zero tide. Exposed to northwest winds. Broad sand and mud beaches and forested uplands. Open areas, picnic areas. Hiking and walking trails. Launch ramp for small boats only. Minx Reef can pose a hazard when approaching from Plumper Sound, but watch your chart and you'll avoid it. The park is accessible by car ferry from Swartz Bay.

Lyall Harbour. Use chart 3477 (larger scale, preferred) or 3442. Lyle Harbour, on Saturna Island, is a large but well protected anchorage, with a ferry landing and store near the entrance. Nearby Boot Cove looks perfect, but is subject to willawaws blowing over a low swale on Saturna Island. Contributing Editor Tom Kincaid anchored there one afternoon. Before night his anchor line was stretched tight by 40-knot winds, and remained that way the next morning. "I dinghied to the nearest beach that afternoon," he reports, "and walked to the store for a loaf of bread. I asked the proprietor if he'd heard when the wind was supposed to die down. 'Oh, you must be in Boot Cove,' he said. 'It always blows in Boot Cove.' So we weighed anchor, set sail, flew out the entrance—and coasted to a stop, windless, just outside."

Lyall Harbour Govt. Wharf, located next to the ferry dock. Open all year, 200 feet of dock space, gasoline, diesel at nearby fuel dock, no power, no water, no washrooms, no showers. Commercial fishing vessels have priority. Garbage collection at dock.

⑩ **Saturna Point Store,** 102 E. Point Rd., Saturna Island, B.C. V0N 2Y0, (250)539-5725. Open all year. Gasoline and diesel at fuel dock. Grocery store. Nearby restaurant with take-out area, and the Lighthouse Pub. Liquor store 1.5 miles away.

Cabbage Island Marine Park. Use chart 3441 or chart book 3313. Open all year, 10 mooring buoys, toilets, no water, no showers. This is a pretty anchorage between Cabbage Island and Tumbo Island, right out on Georgia Strait. The chart shows the entrance from the north, between two long reefs. A friend told us we could cross the reef on the Tumbo Channel side if we went between two patches of kelp, a short distance from the north tip of Tumbo Island. We followed his suggestion, and showed 30 feet under the keel all the way across. Chart Book 3313, pg. 24, shows good depths at that location, confirming our experience. We picked up one of several mooring buoys, and enjoyed a quiet lunch. The park has picnic sites, campsites, and a wonderful sandy beach. Crabbing is reported to be excellent.

ACTIVE PASS AREA

Active Pass. Use chart 3473 (larger scale, recommended) or 3442. Active Pass, which separates Mayne Island and Galiano Island, has long been one of the most popular fishing areas in the Gulf Islands. It is also the route taken by most commercial traffic, including ferries that run between Tsawwassen and Swartz Bay. Currents in Active Pass run to 7 knots at springs. They flood eastward toward the Gulf of Georgia. See the Tide and Current Tables, Vol. 5. Unless your boat is quite fast, a slack water passage is recommended. If you are in the current, you can minimize turbulence by sagging into Miner Bay.

Dinner Bay. Dinner Bay, between Crane Point and Dinner Point, looks to be a good anchorage, but is exposed to ferry

These flags on the breakwater at Otter Bay Marina are easy to see from the water.

Gracious and relaxing. The marina building houses the gift shop at Otter Bay Marina. Covered picnic area to the left; fenced swimming pool to the right.

See area map page 94

wash and northwest winds.

Oceanwood Country Inn, 630 Dinner Bay Road, Mayne Island, B.C. V0N 2J0, (250)539-5074. Buoy available May-Nov. for guest moorage, cozy rooms, excellent dinners.

Village Bay. Use chart 3473 (larger scale, recommended) or 3442. Village Bay is wide and deep, but with convenient anchoring depths near the head. The bay is open to northwest winds and waves, but well protected from everything else. Village Bay has a ferry terminal.

Miners Bay. Use chart 3473 (larger scale, recommended) or 3442. A government wharf is in Miners Bay on the south side of Active Pass, but it is subject to swirling tidal currents and the wash from passing ferries. Fuel is available at a float alongside the government wharf. Convenient anchoring depths are close to shore—most of the bay is quite deep.

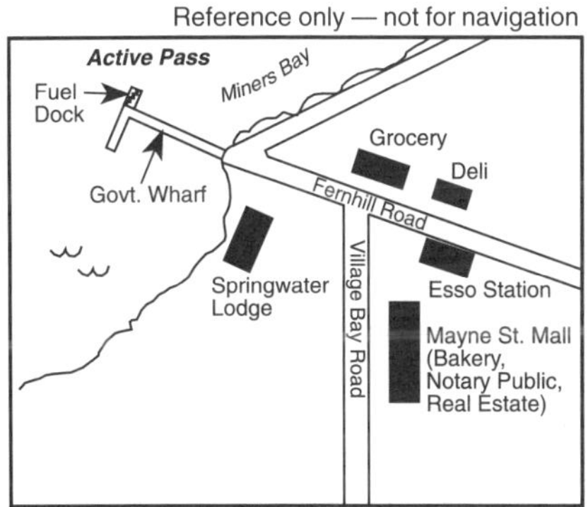

Active Pass Auto and Marine

⑫ **Active Pass Auto & Marine,** Mayne Island, B.C. (250)539-5411. Open all year, gasoline and diesel at fuel barge. Mechanic on duty for repairs. Propane, stove alcohol, tackle, bait, fishing licenses. Affiliated service station 200 yards away has snack bar, video rentals.

Sturdies Bay. Use chart 3473 (larger scale, recommended) or 3442. Sturdies Bay, on Galiano Island toward the eastern end of Active Pass, is another ferry stop for boats coming to and from Tsawwassen. A public float is alongside the ferry dock. The community of Sturdies Bay, just up the road, has a number of stores and a post office.

Rocks and water near sundown. Scenes like this are part of the pleasure of cruising the Gulf Islands.

Whaler Bay. Use chart 3473 (larger scale, recommended) or 3442. Whaler Bay is on the east side of Galiano Island, just north of Active Pass. It is full of rocks and shoal water. Enter (very carefully) through a rock-strewn passage from the south, or through a more open passage around the north end of Gossip Island. Whaler Bay has a government wharf. There is good protection near the wharf, but very little swinging room for those choosing to anchor.

Whaler Bay Govt. Wharf. Open all year, 350 feet of dock space, no facilities except garbage collection. Commercial fishing vessels have priority.

MAYNE ISLAND, CAMPELL BAY TO HORTON BAY

Campbell Bay. Use chart 3442. Campbell Bay, on the northwest side of Mayne island, is entered between Edith Point and Campbell Point, on the northeast corner of Mayne Island. It is open to southeasterly winds, but has anchoring depths near the head, mud bottom.

Bennett Bay. Use chart 3477 (larger scale, preferred) or 3442. Bennett Bay, south of Campbell Point, has good anchorage, but is exposed to southeast winds. Curlew Island and Samuel Island are privately owned.

Georgeson Passage. Use chart 3477 (larger scale, recommended) or 3442. Georgeson Passage, between Mayne Island and Samuel Island, is short and pretty. Currents, based on Active Pass, are about one-half as strong as those in Active Pass, both flooding and ebbing. Still, they run vigorously. See the Georgeson Passage secondary station under Active Pass in the Tide & Current Tables, Vol. 5.

Horton Bay. Use chart 3477 (larger scale, recommended) or 3442. Horton Bay is a perfect landlocked bay, with lots of room to anchor, mud bottom. The government wharf has room for 10–12 30-foot boats, plus rafting. Entering the area between Mayne and Samuel Islands requires some care, but is completely navigable. From the Gulf Islands side the best route is through Georgeson Passage, east of Lizard Island. Be careful of a kelp-covered rock in less than 1 fathom of water.

SALTSPRING ISLAND, FULFORD HARBOUR TO LONG HARBOUR

Fulford Harbour. Use chart 3478 (larger scale, preferred) or 3441. Fulford Harbour is wide and open. Fulford Village, a public wharf, and the Fulford Marina are near the head, all adjacent to the ferry landing. The village has a good grocery store (Patterson's), and a wide assortment of interesting art galleries, crafts, collectibles, and country clothing. We are charmed by the village.

⑬**Fulford Marina,** 2810 Fulford-Ganges Rd., Saltspring Island, B.C. V8K 1Z2, (250)653-9600; fax (250)653-9800. Monitors VHF channel 68. Open all year, gasoline and diesel at the fuel dock. Guest moorage is available, 20 & 30 amp power, washrooms, showers. The marina building has a store on its top floor, and has groceries, souvenirs, books, a deli counter and ready-made snacks.

See area map page 94

Plants for any purpose, with collectibles in the tiny store. All at Stuff and Nonsense, one of the delightful shops at Fulford Village.

Kerosene and alcohol. Tennis courts. Walking distance to a pub with dining, and the village of Fulford. Next door to the ferry to Swartz Bay. Owned by Eric Manchester and Mona Ferguson. Jason Ferguson is the manager.

Harbour Authority of Salt Spring Island Fulford Harbour Wharf. Open all year, 52 feet of dock space, no facilities. Exposed to winds, wash. Near ferry terminal.

Ruckle Park, Beaver Point on Saltspring Island. Use chart 3441. Open all year, day use and overnight camping. Exposed anchorage, no mooring facilities. This is an extensive park that encloses 8 small coves and bays. Miles of shoreline, rocky headlands. Walk-in campsites. Great views of southern Gulf Islands.

Reference only — not for navigation

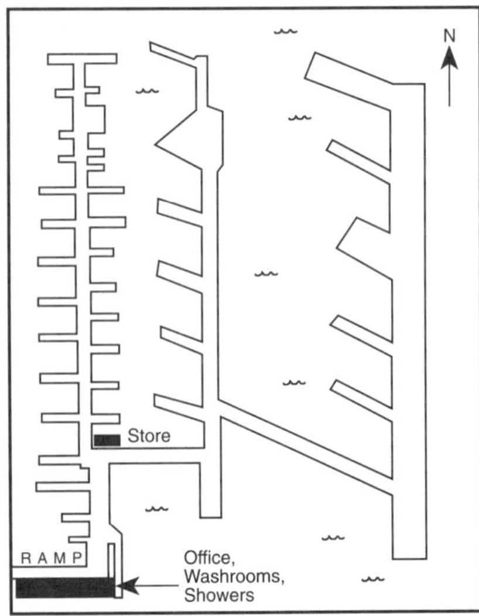

Ganges Marina

Ganges. Use chart 3478 (larger scale, preferred) or 3442. Ganges is a recommended stop. The town of Ganges is the district capital for the Gulf Islands, although it is not incorporated as a town. Ganges Harbour indents the southeast side of Saltspring Island for about 2 miles. The entrance channel is flanked on the east by the Chain Islands, several of which have homes or other buildings. There are two harbour authority moorages, a small one in the outer harbor with no facilities, and the boat harbor wharf, with marina facilities. The privately-owned Ganges Marina offers all normal amenities. Ganges is busy and thriving. It has stores and services to handle any need, all within a block or two of the marinas.

⑭ **Harbour Authority of Salt Spring Island Ganges Wharf Boat Harbour.** Open all year. Has 1070 feet of breakwater-protected dock space, power, washrooms, showers. Also has a launch ramp, garbage collection, waste-oil disposal. Telephone at dock.

⑭ **Ganges Marina,** Box 299, 161 Lower Ganges Road, Ganges, B.C. V8K 2V9, (250)537-5242, fax (250)537-4322. Monitors VHF channel 68. Open all year, gasoline and diesel at fuel dock. Guest moorage in 125 slips, 3000 feet of dock space. Located in the North Harbour. Facilities include 15, 30 & 50 amp power, washrooms, showers, laundry. Shuttle to golf course and tennis courts. Propane available. Groceries, restaurants, all services within walking distance. E-mail: guinness@saltspring.com.

⑭ **Salt Spring Marina,** Box 349, 120 Upper Ganges Rd., Ganges, B.C. V8K 2S2, (250)537-5810, (800)334-6629. Monitors VHF channel 68. Guest moorage for all sizes of boats. 15 & 30 amp power, washrooms, showers, laundry. Facilities include chandlery, gift shop, scuba shop, fishing tackle and bait, restaurant and pub with full dining and takeout. Kayak, boat, and scooter rentals.

Long Harbour. Long Harbour lies parallel to Ganges Harbour, but is much narrower. It is the site of the ferry that serves Saltspring Island from Vancouver. Good anchorage can be found beyond the ferry dock, taking care not to anchor over a posted cable crossing. Royal Vancouver Yacht Club has an outstation in Long Harbour.

PREVOST ISLAND

Prevost Island. Use chart 3442. Prevost Island has been a favorite of ours for many years, particularly the four bays that indent its northwest end. The bays indenting from the southeast also look inviting, but with ferry traffic flying by in Swanson Channel, it might get a little lumpy. We've never spent the night in one of these bays. But the northwest bays are excellent. **Glenthorne Passage** is the westernmost of these bays. The bottom is good, the water quiet, and the surroundings agreeable. In summer months the sun sets in the narrow passage between Glenthorne Point and Secret Island. **Annette Inlet** is narrow and flanked by homes, but we've always been able to find room to swing on short scope. **Selby Cove** is a little wider, and has a good sandy beach at its head. There is a farmhouse ashore, but we haven't seen any no trespassing signs. **James Bay** is even wider, with room for perhaps 30 boats in a pinch (such as on a beautiful summer weekend). There is no ferry service to Prevost Island, and thus less population than the larger islands.

MONTAGUE HARBOUR

Use chart 3473 (larger scale, preferred) or 3442. Montague Harbour is a popular stopping spot in the central Gulf Islands. It is well protected, and has an excellent marine park. Depending on wind direction, you can find good anchorages around the bay—except in the southwest corner, behind the narrow peninsula that ends at Winstanley Point. Holding can be iffy in that area.

A new bus service called Go Galiano now connects the golf course, the marina, the ferry dock at Sturdies Bay, and the interesting restaurants and guest lodgings on Galiano Island. Montague Harbour Marina is a pick-up point. The Montague Harbour Marina has a fuel dock. A small government float is between the marina and the Montague Harbour ferry dock. Entrance to the harbor is unobstructed, either from the southeast past Phillimore Point, or from the northwest, east of Parker Island.

Dining: Everybody recommends the Hummingbird Inn Pub. In summer, the Pub Bus ride is memorable.

⑮ **Montague Harbour Marine Park.** Montague Harbour Marine Park, at the north end of Montague Harbour, is much used. The park is open all year, has excellent beaches, a dinghy dock and 300-foot-long mooring float, 25 mooring buoys, walk-in campsites and toilets. The park has anchorage for many boats on both sides of Gray Peninsula, depending on wind direction.

⑮ **Montague Harbour Marina,** RR 1, Site 21-C17, Galiano, B.C. V0N 1P0, (250)539-5733; fax (250)539-2010. Monitors VHF channel 68. Open Easter to Canadian Thanksgiving (mid-Oct.). Gasoline and diesel at the fuel dock, also stove alcohol. Facilities include guest moorage, 15 & 30 amp power, store, books and charts. Bob Walker and his family bought the marina in late 1994, and have revitalized it already. They expanded the small store, added an espresso bar, a licensed cafe, and stocked the gift shop with local Galiano Island arts and crafts, along with the usual T-shirt and sweatshirt fare. The docks are being rebuilt, and service is vastly improved. In season they serve thousands of hand-dipped ice cream cones.

⑮ **Montague Harbour Govt. Wharf.** Open all year, 160 feet of dock space, no facilities.

Montague Harbour Marina, under new ownership, has ample room for visitors. This is where the bus to the Hummingbird Inn Pub picks up customers.

SAANICH INLET

Use chart 3441. The Saanich Inlet extends south into Vancouver Island for about 12 miles. The northern part of the inlet is fairly civilized, especially along the Saanich Peninsula shore to Brentwood Bay, the location of Butchart Gardens. For a beautiful and often-overlooked trip, continue your run south through Squally Reach and Finlayson Arm. Boat traffic usually is minimal, and the high mountains rising from the shorelines make for a remote feeling only a short distance from the more popular spots.

Deep Cove. Use chart 3441. Wain Rock, with good water on both sides, lies about 0.2 miles off Moses Point. The remains of a public wharf are in the south part of the cove. The float was removed in 1978 and only the pier, unused but still robust, remains. The Deep Cove Marina (formerly named Chart House Marina) is adjacent to this pier.

Deep Cove Marina, 10990 Madrona Dr., Deep Cove, B.C. V8L 5R7, (250)656-0060. Open all year, guest moorage available, power, washrooms, showers.

Patricia Bay. Patricia Bay, locally called Pat Bay, is open, but all the facilities are reserved for use by the Canadian Government's Institute of

See area map page 94

Reference only — not for navigation

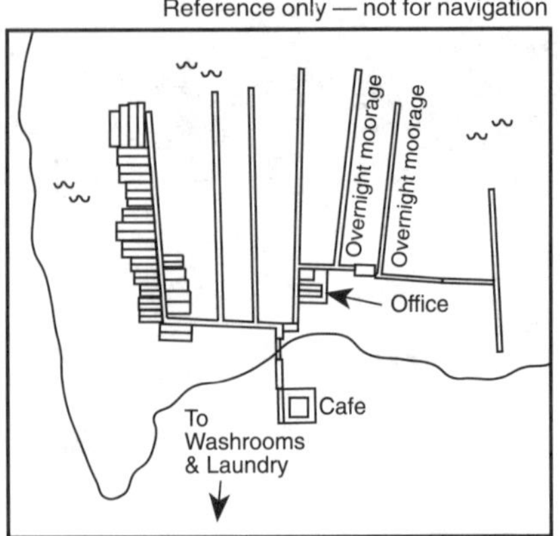

Genoa Bay Marina

Ocean Sciences. It is here that the Canadian Hydrographic Service develops and maintains charts and related publications for western Canada.

Coles Bay. Coles Bay lies east of Yarrow Point. It is good for temporary anchorage, but open to southerly winds. If approaching from the north, the Canadian *Small Craft Guide* recommends that you give Dyer Rocks, off Yarrow Point, a 0.5-mile berth to avoid shoals extending south from the rocks.

Brentwood Bay. Use chart 3441. Brentwood Bay can be entered on either side of Senanus Island. Telephone customs clearance can be made from Angler's Anchorage Marina. The Mill Bay ferry departs from Sluggett Point. A rock, marked by Buoy U22, lies close to the ferry dock. Do not pass between the buoy and the daybeacon, or you risk going aground on rocks. The town of Brentwood Bay is worth a visit. In addition to Angler's Anchorage Marina and the new Brentwood Inn Resort, there is a public dock and floats. The town has the look of an English seaside resort, complete with afternoon tea.

⑰ **Butchart Gardens.** Brentwood Bay is the back door to the celebrated and astonishing Butchart Gardens. The Gardens are a must-see attraction. At night the Gardens are lighted, creating an entirely different effect from the day. On Saturday evenings during the summer a fireworks display is held on a large field in the gardens. Many people arrive early and have a picnic supper while waiting for darkness. Bring blankets, cushions, and folding chairs or camp stools. Even for jaded viewers, it's worth the trip. The most interesting fireworks are done at ground level—you have to be on the scene to see it.

The Gardens' dinghy dock is in a small cove, with buoys for two or three overnighting yachts. Most visitors put the anchor down in adjacent Tod Inlet and go by dinghy to the dinghy dock.

⑰ **Angler's Anchorage Marina,** 933 Marchant Road, Brentwood Bay, B.C. V8M 1B5, (250)652-3531. Open all year with 1000 feet of guest moorage, 15 & 30 amp power, washrooms, showers, laundry, restaurant, customs clearance. The marina has locked gates for security, and is close to Butchart Gardens.

⑰ **Brentwood Inn Resort,** 7172 Brentwood Drive, Brentwood Bay, B.C. V8M 1B7, (250)652-3151; fax (250)652-2402. Monitors VHF channel 68. Open all year, guest moorage available, 15 & 30 amp power, washrooms, showers, laundry. Ample guest moorage, plus a large pub with outside dining in the summer, live music on weekends, two restaurants, motel units. They sell fishing tackle and bait. Close to doctor, post office, liquor store. Close to Butchart Gardens. When entering, keep between the ferry dock and the red spar at the end of the dock.

Brentwood Bay Govt. Wharf. Open all year, dock is 72 feet, no facilities.

Tod Inlet. Use chart 3441. Tod Inlet reaches back behind the Butchart Gardens, and has ample anchoring room. The inlet is narrow when seen from Brentwood Bay, but opens somewhat after a bend. In the narrow sections you should plan to run a stern-tie ashore. Boats in the more open sections around the bend can swing without a stern-tie.

⑱ **Goldstream Boathouse.** RR 6, 3540 Trans-Canada Hwy, Victoria, B.C. V9B 5T9, (250)478-4407. Use chart 3441. Open all year, gasoline only at fuel dock. Guest moorage available, best to call ahead. Marina has complete repair facility and haulout, launch ramp. Friendly, relaxed atmosphere. The Goldstream Boathouse is located at the head of Finlayson Arm, at the edge of drying flats off the mouth of the Goldstream River. The shoal water seems to be extending farther north, so come in close to the docks. If the approach is made from mid-channel, the unsuspecting skipper could find himself aground.

Mill Bay. Use chart 3441. Mill Bay is a good anchorage. The west shore provides a lee from the usual summer west or northwest winds. The bay is, however, open to southeast winds. In addition to the public dock, the Mill Bay Marina is friendly and equipped with all the amenities.

⑲ **Mill Bay Marina,** P.O. Box 231, 740 Handy Road, Mill Bay, B.C. V0R 2P0, (250)743-4112, (800)253-4112. Monitor VHF channel 68, CB channel 10. Gasoline and diesel at fuel dock, guest moorage available, 15 amp power, washrooms, showers, laundry. They carry marine supplies and charts; tackle and bait. Close to good shopping, hospital, liquor store. This is an easy-going and informal marina, owned and cared for by Fred and Marilyn Laba. Nice people.

⑲ **Mill Bay Govt. Wharf.** Open all year, 50 feet of dock space, no facilities, commercial fishing vessels have priority.

⑲ **Cherry Point Marina,** RR#3, 1241 Sutherland Road, Cobble Hill, B.C. V0R 1L0, (250)748-0453. Open all year, limited guest moorage, call ahead. Washrooms, 15 & 20 amp power.

The Genoa Bay Marina is a popular stop, with store, gift shop, and excellent restaurant.

COWICHAN BAY

Use chart 3478. The town of Cowichan Bay, located near the southwest corner of Cowichan Bay, is picturesque and worth a stroll. The public docks are behind a log and plank breakwater, with the entrance near shore. The privately owned marinas are located west of the public wharf. At low tide the entrance can seem rather narrow, but it is navigable.

Cowichan Bay Harbour Authority Wharf. Open all year, 941 feet of dock space, power, washrooms, no showers. Breakwater protected, tidal grid, garbage collection, waste oil disposal available.

⑳ **Masthead Restaurant & Marina,** 1505 Cowichan Bay Rd., Cowichan Bay, B.C. V0R 1N0, (250)748-3714. Open all year, 2 guest slips, 30 amp power, washrooms. This is a dinner restaurant and small marina located next to the public dock. Moorage availability varies, so call ahead.

⑳ **Kilpahlas Beach Resort,** 1681 Botwood, P.O. Box 39. Cowichan Bay, B.C. V0R 1N0, (250)748-6222; fax (250)748-7122. Formerly Inn at the Water Resort. Open all year, washrooms, showers, swimming pool. Beer and wine store. Located behind the breakwater. The dock is small, so call ahead.

⑳ **Bluenose Marina,** P.O. Box 38, 1765 Cowichan Bay Road, Cowichan Bay, B.C. V0R 1N0, (250)748-2222; fax (250)748-8982. Guest moorage available, 30-foot maximum boat length, 15 amp power, washrooms, showers, laundry, 4 mooring buoys. Nearby launch ramp. Public playground. Groceries, restaurant within walking distance.

⑳ **Coastal Shipyard & Marine Services,** 1759 Cowichan Bay Rd., Duncan, B.C. V9R 1N0, (250)746-4705. Open all year, but full of commercial boats in the winter. Call ahead always. Facilities include 30 amp power, washrooms, no showers. Haulout and repairs available. Five minutes to downtown Duncan, maritime museum next door.

⑳ **Pier 66 Marina Ltd.,** 1745 Cowichan Bay Rd., Cowichan Bay, B.C. V0R 1N0, (250)748-8444. Open all year, gasoline, diesel, pre-mix at fuel dock. Washrooms, no showers, 15 amp power, haulout. Limited moorage for boats to 50 feet. Marine hardware, supplies, charts, kerosene, alcohol, tackle. Walking distance to services, maritime museum, and marine biology lab open to the public.

Genoa Bay. Use chart 3478 (larger scale, preferred) or 3441. Genoa Bay indents the north shore of Cowichan Bay. You can anchor off the resort docks, or use one of the transient spaces at the dock. The Genoa Bay Marina has a moorage with all the amenities.

㉑ **Genoa Bay Marina,** 5100 Genoa Bay Rd., Duncan, B.C. V9L 1M3, (250)746-7621. Monitors VHF channel 68 approximately mid-May through Labour Day. Open all year, guest moorage in 30 slips, 1200 feet of dock space, call ahead. Washrooms, showers, laundry, 15 amp power and launch ramp. This is a popular summer stop for pleasure craft. The Grapevine Cafe (formerly Genoa Bay Cafe) is known for its excellent meals. The cafe is closed Dec. 15 through March. Most marina facilities are closed from September through re-opening sometime in May, but dock space is available with payment on an honor system. Electricity is limited. During the summer season the store is well stocked with convenience items. Fresh baked goods are available in the mornings at the store. Good fishing. *(Marina map page 104)*

Musgrave Landing. Use chart 3478 (larger scale, preferred) or 3441. Musgrave Landing is located on the southwest corner of Saltspring Island, at the mouth of Sansum Narrows. Although it has only a small public float, no facilities, and very restricted anchorage nearby, it is a popular stopover. The setting is secluded feeling, and upland you'll find good hiking along miles of logging roads. A housing development, with private dock, is on Musgrave Point.

SANSUM NARROWS TO DUCK BAY

Use chart 3478 (larger scale, preferred) or 3442. Sansum Narrows connects Satellite Channel to the south with Stuart Channel to the north, and leads between high hills on Saltspring Island and Vancouver Island. The wind funnels down the axis of the narrows, turning at the bends. It also funnels down the valleys leading to the channel, so wind directions can be erratic. Currents seldom exceed 3 knots; usually they are less.

Burgoyne Bay. Use chart 3478 (larger scale, preferred) or 3442. Burgoyne Bay has some anchorage at its inner end, but is subject to willawaws that blow across a low swale on Saltspring Island. Most of the bay is too deep for convenient anchoring. A 32-foot public wharf is in Burgoyne Bay.

Maple Bay. Use chart 3478 (larger scale, preferred) or 3442. Maple Bay is a major

See area map page 94

pleasure boat center, with public moorages and all needed facilities and services. Birds Eye Cove, off the southwest corner of Maple Bay, is home to the Maple Bay Marina and Birds Eye Cove Marina, both with fuel docks, and the Maple Bay Yacht Club, which welcomes visitors from reciprocal clubs. Anchoring is good in Birds Eye Cove, but *avoid the area just off the dock located on the east side of the cove, opposite the marina docks.* We spoke with a couple who fouled their anchor on the wreck of a sunken fish boat about 100 feet off the end of that dock, and it took a diver to get the anchor free.

Maple Bay Marina has gasoline and diesel fuel, and ample guest moorage. Restaurant/pub, groceries, and marine supplies are available.

Dining: The Quamichan Inn is renowned, and the Shipyard Restaurant & Pub serves meals.

㉒ **Maple Bay Marina,** 6145 Genoa Bay Rd., Duncan, B.C. V9L 1M3, (250)746-8482; fax (250)746-8490. Monitors VHF channel 68. Open all year. Gasoline and diesel at the fuel dock, power, washrooms, showers, laundry, propane, CNG. This is a popular stop, scenic and well protected from winds and seas. The Maple Bay Marina advertises the "cleanest washrooms on the coast." Our experience confirms that the washrooms are spacious, warm, and indeed clean, with good showers. The shopping complex includes a store with groceries, marine supplies, books and charts; a gift shop; hairdresser; and coin-op laundry. The Shipyard Restaurant & Pub is a lively spot. A mechanic and a shipwright are available, and a shuttle bus serves Cowichan Bay and Chemainus. Coal Harbour Air provides scheduled float plane service to Vancouver.

㉒ **Maple Bay Govt. Wharf.** Open all year. Has 150 feet of dock space, no other facilities. Commercial fishing vessels have priority.

㉒ **Norseman Marine at Birds Eye Cove Marina,** 6271 Genoa Bay Rd., Duncan, B.C. V9L 1M3, (250)748-3142. Monitors VHF channel 16, switch to 69. Open all year, gasoline and diesel at fuel dock, 15 & 30 amp power, no washrooms or showers. Limited guest moorage. Look for the new mural on the side of the building as a landmark.

Crofton Govt. Wharf, Box 128 (Infocentre), Crofton, B.C. V0R 1R0. Use chart 3475 (larger scale, preferred) or 3442. Open all year, 518 feet of dock space, 20 & 30 amp power, washrooms, showers, laundry, garbage collection. Breakwater protected. Located next to the Saltspring Island ferry terminal. The adjacent Infocentre houses the washrooms with showers (sunrise to sunset, summer only). The Infocentre has visitors' information for all of B.C. Walking distance to all services, including groceries, restaurants, fishing supplies and licenses. Playground 2 blocks away. Nearby outdoor swimming pool and tennis courts, hiking trails.

Vesuvius. Use chart 3442. North of Sansum Narrows along the Saltspring Island shore, Vesuvius has a public wharf, and is the terminus for the ferry to Crofton. The Vesuvius Inn, an informal pub, is located at the head of the dock.

Duck Bay, just north of Vesuvius Bay, has good anchorage, with steep, wooded cliffs rising on its east side.

Northern Gulf Islands

Chemainus • Wallace Island • Pirates Cove • Gabriola Passage Silva Bay • Dodd Narrows • Nanaimo

Charts

3313	SMALL CRAFT CHARTS (chart book) – Gulf Islands and adjacent waterways
3442	North Pender Island to Thetis Island (1:40,000)
3443	Active Pass, Porlier Pass, and Montague Harbour Active Pass, Porlier Pass (1:12,000) Montague Harbour (1:18,000)
3475	Plans – Stuart Channel Chemainus Bay (1:12,000) Ladysmith Harbour (1:12,000) Dodd Narrows to Flat Top Islands (1:18,000) Dodd Narrows (1:9,000) Osborn Bay (1:15,000)
3458	Approaches to Nanaimo Harbour (1:20,000)

Chemainus. Use chart 3475 (larger scale, preferred) or 3442. Chemainus, on the Vancouver Island side of Stuart Channel, has a small government wharf and floats for visitors. Anchorage is possible toward the head of the bay, but much of the available anchorage is taken up by rafted logs. Chemainus is a wonderful town, filled with shops, galleries, and antique shops. Thirty-two of the building owners have had large murals painted on their buildings, most of them depicting the town's past as an Indian campground and its heritage as a mining, logging and mill town. A well-stocked grocery store is at the head of the government wharf. A ferry crosses to Chemainus from Telegraph Harbour.

Ladysmith. Use chart 3475 (larger scale, preferred) or 3442. Ladysmith Harbour is approximately 6 miles north of Chemainus, on Vancouver Island. The town of Ladysmith is located about ½ mile from the public boat basin, up a long flight of stairs and across the highway. In the town you'll find a large supermarket with liquor store nearby, and all the other services, but little for the boat itself. The public boat basin is the first major set of docks you come to on the south side of the harbor, behind Slag Point. The Ivy Green Marina, farther into the harbor, has no guest moorage. The Mañana Lodge & Marina is at Page Point, on the north shore. Seattle Yacht Club has an outstation along the north side of the Dunsmuir Islands, in Sibell Bay.

② **Ladysmith Fisherman's Wharf**. Open all year, 700 feet of dock space, power, garbage collection, telephone, but no other facilities. Breakwater and tidal grid. Launch ramp. Commercial fishing vessels have priority. Stairs lead up the hill toward the town of Ladysmith, about ½ mile away.

② **Mañana Lodge & Marina**, 4760 Brenton-Page Rd., Ladysmith, B.C. V0R 2E0, (250)245-2312. Open summer 7 days a week for guest moorage and restaurant. Winter has limited transient moorage, restaurant open Fri.-Sun. only. Fuel dock has gasoline and diesel. Facilities include 15 amp power, washrooms, showers, laundry. A popular stop in the summer. The restaurant has an excellent reputation, and the people are friendly. They have bed & breakfast rooms, gift shop, car rentals. A golf course is 10-15 minutes away. Owners: Don and Gail Kanelakos, Jim and Ruth Bangay.

② **Ivy Green Marina, Ltd.**, Box 88, 1335 Rocky Creek Rd., Ladysmith, B.C. V0R 2E0, (250)245-4521. Open all year, washrooms, showers, no power. This marina is mostly permanant moorage. Haulout and complete repairs available from Oyster Harbour Marine Services.

① **Inn of the Sea**, 3600 Yellow Point Rd., RR #3, Ladysmith, B.C. V0R 2E0, (250)245-2211; fax (250)245-3442. Open mid-April to mid-October, 200 feet of dock space, 6 mooring buoys, washrooms, showers, laundry. This is a family-oriented hotel and marina, with pool and tennis courts, and a restaurant with full-service dining. Courtesy moorage for guests. Approach from the southeast. The shoal (well marked on charts) extends southward from the north shore of the bay. The shoal is covered at high tide.

Telegraph Harbour. Use chart 3477 (larger scale, preferred) or 3442 or 3443. Telegraph Harbour is one of the Gulf Is-

The delightful town of Chemainus has 32 different murals painted on buildings. Chemainus is a favorite stop for antiques enthusiasts.

Reference only — not for navigation

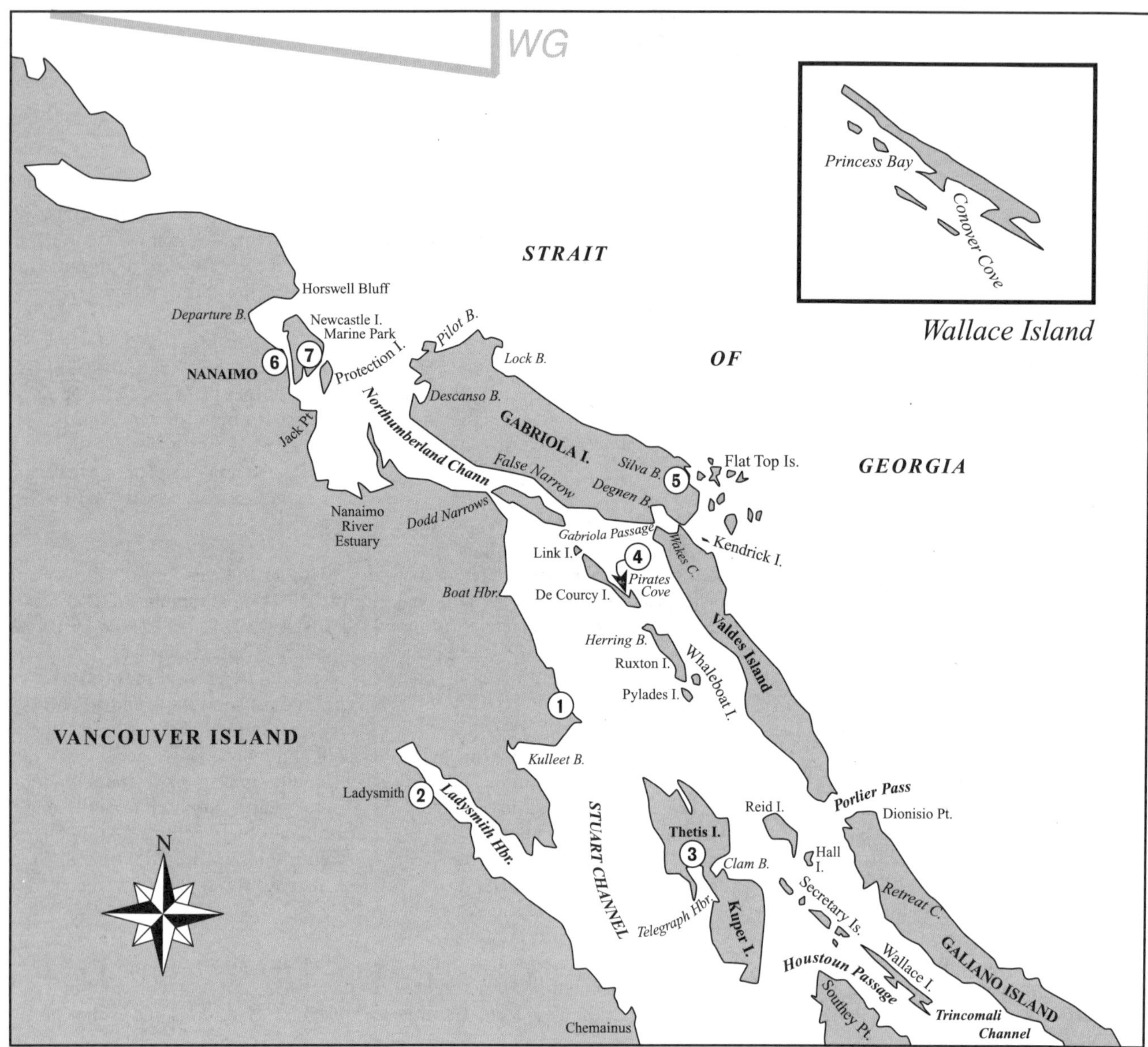

lands' most popular stops. It is located across Stuart Channel from Ladysmith, between Thetis Island and Kuper Island. Telegraph Harbour has two marinas, the Thetis Island Marina, and the Telegraph Harbour Marina. Both marinas are served by an inter-island ferry to Chemainus.

③ **Thetis Island Marina**, Thetis Island, B.C. V0R 2Y0, (250)246-3464. Monitors VHF channel 68. Open all year, gasoline and diesel at the fuel dock, 2200 feet of dock space, 15 & 30 amp power, propane, washrooms, showers, laundry. This is a full-service marina, with good docks, groceries, kerosene, snacks, ice, and post office. It has a fully licensed restaurant and pub, (good pub food, too) with patio dining. Mechanic available. Large playground for the kids. It's a 10-minute walk to the ferry to Chemainus.

Paul and Dawn Deacon have made substantial improvements to the Thetis Island Marina, including what is perhaps the first commercial water desalination system in the islands. Water is still precious because the system is expensive to maintain and operate, but they never run out of water. If you're interested in how such a system works, Paul would be glad to walk you through.

③ **Telegraph Harbour Marina**, Box 7-10, Thetis Island, B.C. V0R 2Y0, (250)246-9511; fax (250)246-2668. Open summers 7 days a week; winter call for fuel and store hours. Gasoline & diesel at the fuel dock. The marina has 3000 feet of dock space, and reservations are recommended in July and August. Facilities include 15 & 30 amp power, washrooms, showers, laundry. The general store carries groceries, charts, fishing tackle, bait, licenses, gifts. The coffee shop serves sandwich and ice cream specialties. They have a large building for group meetings and barbecues, and a picnic area with tables and barbecues. Playgound for kids. It's a 10-minute walk to the Chemainus ferry.

John and Jan Ohman, the owners, know how to make people welcome and comfortable. Locals often gather in the coffee shop in the morning, and visiting boaters are treated with courtesy. Several boating groups have annual get-togethers at the marina.

North Cove. Use chart 3443 or 3442. North Cove, which indents the north end of Thetis Island, is a good anchorage, although open to the usual summer northwesterly winds.

Clam Bay. Use chart 3442 or 3443. Clam Bay is a large, relatively open bay with good anchoring in convenient depths. The mouth of the bay is partly blocked by Centre Reef, and Rocket Shoal is in the middle of the bay. Lacking familiarity, the safest entry is south of Centre Reef, between buoy U42 and Penalakut Spit, which extends from Kuper Island. The chart shows everything. Clam Bay is one end of The Cut, a drying channel that separates Thetis Island from Kuper Island. The Cut leads to Telegraph Harbour, but should be tried only in a small boat or with local knowledge, and at half-tide or higher.

Southey Bay. Use chart 3442. At the north tip of Saltspring Island, tucked in beside Southey Point, is a little notch that Contributing Editor Tom Kincaid has used as an anchorage in past years. An increasing number of private mooring buoys have restricted the swinging room, but it's still a possible anchorage.

Fernwood Govt. Wharf, Use chart 3442. Walker Hook, Saltspring Island. Open all year, 40 feet of dock space, no facilities.

Secretary Islands. Use chart 3442. The Secretary Islands have several nice little anchorages, with the emphasis on *little*. The most popular is Conover Cove on the west side of Wallace Island. Wallace Island is now a provincial park, purchased with help from the Northwest boating community. There's also room for a few boats in the little notch on the Trincomali Channel side between the two Secretary Islands.

Wallace Island Marine Park. Use chart 3442. Open all year. Very small dock/dinghy float, toilets, campsites, picnic areas, trails. Wallace Island is a low-lying island in Trincomali Channel. Enter from Houstoun Passage. You'll find sheltered anchorages at Conover Cove and Princess Bay. The park has campsites, picnic areas, trails. Please respect the two private properties on the island.

Conover Cove. A reef lies directly offshore from the entrance to Conover Cove, but the reef can be avoided by going around either end. Anchorage, on short scope, and a float give access to the island. The bay shoals toward both ends. Before anchoring, check that the depth will be adequate for overnight. The entrance to Conover Cove is shallow at low tide.

Princess Bay. Princess Bay lies just northwest of Covover Cove, and has room for a few boats to anchor. In 1994, several mooring eyes were installed along the Princess Bay shoreline to facilitate stern-ties. We're told you have to look to find them.

Retreat Cove. Use chart 3442. Across Trincomali Channel from the Secretaries is Retreat Cove on Galiano Island, a small notch protected by Retreat Island. Entry is from either direction around the island, although the 75-foot government wharf, no facilities, is in the southern approach. The bottom dries for a distance behind the island, so circumnavigating the island is possible only at high tide.

North Galiano. Use chart 3442 or 3443. North Galiano has anchorage and a small government dock, with 40 feet of dock space, no facilities. A well-stocked store is up the road from the dock.

Dionisio Point Park. Use chart 3473 (larger scale, preferred) or 3442 or 3443. Open all year, day use and overnight camping, toilets, no power, no showers. Anchor only. The park overlooks Porlier Pass. It has sandy beaches, rocky headlands and forested uplands.

See area map page 108

Porlier Pass. Use chart 3473 (larger scale, preferred) or 3442 or 3443. Porlier Pass separates Galiano Island and Valdes Island, and is the most heavily traveled pass into the Gulf Islands. Several times a year, currents on large tides will reach 9 knots. Current predictions are shown in the Tide and Current Tables, Vol. 5. The current floods north, into Georgia Strait, and ebbs south, into the Gulf Islands. The best time for transit is at slack water. A study of the chart shows that it is safest to transit Porlier Pass on the south sides of Black Rock and Virago Rock, keeping toward the Galiano Island side of the pass.

Approaching from Georgia Strait, begin your entry near lighted bell buoy U41. South of the buoy, pick up the range on Race Point and Virago Point. Follow that range into Porlier Pass, to clear the rocks that extend from the northeast tip of Galiano Island. Once clear of the rocks, you can turn to follow a mid-channel course between Virago Rock and Galiano Island. Charts 3442 and 3443 show the range and the rocks to be avoided on both sides, but the larger scale chart 3473 really helps understanding. The new chart book 3313 (replaces strip charts 3310) also shows the pass in excellent detail. We recommend that you carry either chart 3473 or chart book 3313.

This photo was taken in September 1995, during the Canadian Tollycraft rendezvous at Telegraph Harbour Marina. Excellent docks, spacious grounds, and good management make the marina ideal for large groups.

De Courcy Group. Use chart 3443. The De Courcy Group has several interesting small anchorages. **Whaleboat Island**, just off the southeast shore of Ruxton Island, is a relatively undeveloped provincial park. The preferred anchorage is south of the island, taking care to avoid a drying rock. The north end of **Ruxton Island** has **Herring Bay**, one of the most attractive small anchorages in the northern Gulf Islands, and frequently used when the anchorage at Pirates Cove is overfull (which it often is in the summer).

Whaleboat Island Marine Park, just south of Ruxton Island. No facilities. Whaleboat Island is undeveloped, but provides limited alternate anchorage to Pirates Cove Marine park. Use chart 3443.

④ **Pirates Cove Marine Park**. Use chart 3477 (larger scale, preferred) or 3443. Open all year, toilets, no other facilities. Pirates Cove is a perfectly protected little harbor, with room for a couple dozen boats (on short scope). Iron rings are set into the sandstone cliffs for stern-ties. There are two dinghy docks. Most of the land surrounding the cove is a provincial park. The park has walk-in campsites, hiking and walking trails, and picnicking. As you enter, the dock to starboard is private.

There were no navigation marks when Contributing Editor Tom Kincaid first called at Pirates Cove over 30 years ago. The rock spit guarding the entrance was crossed by tracks of red bottom paint from boats that missed the very narrow entrance channel. Now a concrete beacon marks the end of the reef and a red buoy marks the other side, so entry is easy. Pirates Cove has a poor holding bottom. If the wind comes up during the night, you can expect a fire drill as boats drag anchor all over the bay.

On Ruxton Passage, the little notch at the south end of De Courcy Island is also part of this park, and has mooring buoys. Additional anchorage is available at Whaleboat Island Marine Park, nearby. Another "Pirates Cove overflow" notch is just north of Pirates Cove off Link Island.

See area map page 108

Boat Harbour. Use chart 3443. Boat Harbour, across Stuart Channel from the De Courcy Group, used to be home to a man named Ken Kendall, who looked and dressed like a pirate, and sometimes fired a brass cannon to herald your arrival in his lair. The actor John Wayne was a regular visitor. Alas, Kendall died years ago. Beth Hill writes engagingly of him in her book *Seven-Knot Summers.*

At **Kenary Cove** in Boat Harbour, Julian Matson runs Boat Harbour Marine Ltd., a boatbuilding and repair shop. Julian Matson worked with Kendall for a period of time before Kendall's death, and recalls that Kendall was brilliant and creative, an engineer by training, with a fondness for explosives. Kendall made cannons, but also set off some blasts just for the fun of seeing them go. Kenary Cove is a blending of Ken and Mary, Mary being one of Kendall's wives. Kenary is pronounced "Canary," like the bird. The cove offers well sheltered anchorage for small craft in 2-3 fathoms, mud bottom. The marina in the cove is private, permanent moorage only.

Shipyard Rock, between Tugboat Island and Vance Island has claimed many boats over the years.

Gabriola Passage is best run near slack. This photo was made from Dogfish Bay, behind Kendrick Island.

GABRIOLA PASSAGE TO NANAIMO

Those going north of the Gulf Islands have three choices of route: Dodd Narrows, False Narrows, or Gabriola Passage.

Gabriola Passage. Use chart 3475 (larger scale, preferred) or 3443. Gabriola Passage is the northernmost entrance to the Gulf Islands from the Strait of Georgia. From Bowen Island on the east side of the strait, it is 14 miles to Gabriola Passage, the shortest crossing between the lower mainland and the islands. The B.C. *Small Craft Guide* recommends that mariners avoid an afternoon crossing in the summertime, when winds can create rough conditions on the west side of the Strait. Instead, an early morning crossing is recommended, or a crossing in late afternoon or early evening, after the afternoon wind has died away.

Tidal currents at springs can run to 8 knots in Gabriola Passage, both flood and ebb. Typical maximum currents are around 4 knots, so transiting is best at slacks. The current in Gabriola Passage sets east on the flood and west on the ebb. Times of slacks and maximum currents are given in the Tide and Current Tables, Vol. 5.

Degnen Bay. Use chart 3475 (larger scale, preferred) or 3443. If you take Gabriola Passage you will pass Degnen Bay, one of the best anchorages in the islands. Favor the east side, close to Josef Point, as you arrive or depart, to avoid rocks in the middle of the entrance. An Indian petroglyph of a killer whale is on a slab of rock near the head of the bay. A government dock provides access to Gabriola Island.

Degnen Bay Govt. Wharf. Has 190 feet of dock space, power, garbage collection, telephone, but no other facilities. Commercial fishing vessels have priority.

Wakes Cove. Use chart 3475 (larger scale, preferred) or 3443. Wakes Cove, on Gabriola Passage at the north end of Valdes Island, is a safe anchorage, but open to northwest winds and to the wash of boats in the pass.

Kendrick Island. Use chart 3475 (larger scale, preferred) or 3443. Kendrick Island, on the south side of Gabriola Passage at the east entrance, creates a narrow and shallow bay, known locally as **Dogfish Bay**. Dogfish Bay is well protected and the holding ground is good. West Vancouver Yacht Club has an outstation on Kendrick Island.

Flat Top Islands. Use chart 3475 (larger scale, preferred) or 3443. The Flat Top Islands are appropriately named, and from the north or east they're a little hard to tell apart. If approaching from the Strait of Georgia, pass on the north side of **Thrasher Rock Light**. The light marks the northern end of Gabriola Reefs. All the Flat Top Islands are privately owned.

Silva Bay. Use chart 3475 (larger scale, preferred) or 3443. Silva Bay is a popular destination in the Flat Top Islands, well protected, with good holding bottom. From the north, entry can be made behind Vance Island; from the south, between Gabriola Island and Sear Island. Many boats, however, go through Commodore Passage, between Acorn Island and Tugboat Island. They turn to enter Silva Bay between Tugboat Island and Vance Island. In this passage you will

See area map page 108

meet the notorious *Shipyard Rock*, on the south side of the channel.

When entering, give the beacon that marks the rock a wide berth to port, and *do not turn at once for the Silva Bay floats or other facilities.* Shipyard Rock is larger than it appears on the charts. Continue instead until about halfway to Law Point before making your turn. A buoy now marks the inner end of Shipyard Rock, but give the rock plenty of room anyway. Royal Vancouver Yacht Club has an outstation on Tugboat Island.

Silva Bay has gone through some rough times in the past, with the boatyard and Silva Bay Resort closed for a couple of years. In 1995, however, Sterling Resorts bought the Silva Bay Marina & Resort and is in the process of making it a first-class marine destination.

⑤ **Silva Bay Boatel & Store**, RR#2, Site 33-C2, Gabriola, B.C. V0R 1X0, (250)247-9351. Open all year, 600 feet of dock space, 4 feet of depth, no big sailboats. Facilities include 15 amp power, washrooms, laundromat, no showers. Under the same ownership for 25 years. The store has groceries, fishing tackle and licenses, but no wine or beer.

⑤ **Silva Bay Marina & Resort (Sterling Resorts),** RR #2, Site 31, Comp. 2, Gabriola, B.C. V0R 1X0, (250)247-8662, fax (250)247-8663. Monitors VHF channel 68. Open all year with guest moorage. Facilities include 15 & 30 amp power, washrooms, showers, laundry, swimming pool, tennis courts, mountain bikes, marine ways and Travelift. The resort offers childcare while you eat at Latitudes, their upscale restaurant. Reservations recommended. There is also the Bitter End Pub (good food) and a general store.

⑤ **Page's Resort & Marina**, RR#2, Coast Road, Site 30, Gabriola Island, B.C. V0R 1X0, (250)247-8931, www.island.net/~.preeve/index.htm. Open all year, gasoline and diesel at the fuel dock, guest moorage in 10 slips and along the dock. Facilities include 15 amp power, washrooms, showers, laundry. They have cottages for rent in addition to moorage. The store has interesting books and charts; the dive shop has an air refill station. Ten-minute walk to grocery store, cab service available.

Drumberg Provincial Park, south end of Gabriola Island. Use chart 3475 (larger scale, preferred) or 3443. Open all year, day use only, toilets, no other facilities. Overlooks Gabriola Passage. Has shelving sandstone rocks and a small sandy beach.

False Narrows. Use chart 3475 (larger scale, preferred) or 3443. False Narrows lies east of Dodd Narrows, and offers an alternate but risky connection between the Gulf Islands and Northumberland Channel. If you choose to go by way of False Narrows, you will be traveling between reefs in a shallow channel that is best used at half tide or better. Maximum currents in False Narrows are about half what they are in Dodd Narrows, which is about the only reason for going this way.

Dodd Narrows. Use chart 3475 (larger scale, preferred) or 3443. Dodd Narrows has tidal currents to 9 knots as the water swirls through the narrow but deep passage between rock cliffs. The narrows are best taken at slack water, and for the

Doc Freeman's

Marine Specialty Stores

Sea Gear
Foulweather gear, Safety equipment & Sport fashion
3839 Stone Way • Seattle • (206)545-1555

Doc Freeman's
Everything from fasteners to marine engines—over 80,000 items!
999 N. Northlake Way • Seattle • (206)633-1500
In WA (800)247-2149 • USA & Canada (800)423-8541

Doc's Galley Northwest
Marine Stoves, Heaters & Galley equipment
3831 Stone Way • Seattle • (206)545-1444

Doc's Marine Warehouse
Marine surplus, closeouts, *bargains!* & General Surplus
106 N. 35th St. (Fremont) • Seattle • (206)633-3121

Doc Freeman's
999 N. Northlake Way
Seattle, WA
(206) 633-1500
In WA
(800) 247-2149
USA & Canada
(800) 423-8541

1997 WAGGONER CRUISING COUPON

Harnish Lamp
Regular Price $95.50
With Coupon, $59.00
110/12 Volt • Solid Brass Table Lamp
Danish Made • Numbered Edition

Valid 1/1/97 Through 12/31/97 • No Cash Value • Coupons Cannot Be Combined
Coupon Must Be Presented At Time Of Purchase

Port Ludlow Marina

Gateway to Hood Canal & Strait of Juan De Fuca

Fine Dining	Golf
Fuel Dock	Pumpout Station
Full Resort Facilities	Reservations

1 Gull Drive • Port Ludlow, WA • 98365
Phone (360) 437-0513/ (800) 308-7991 • Fax (360) 437-2428

Port Ludlow Marina
1 Gull Drive
Port Ludlow, WA • 98365
Phone (360) 437-0513
or (800) 308-7991
Fax (360) 437-2428

1997 WAGGONER CRUISING COUPON

50% Off Second Night's Moorage

Valid 1/1/97 Through 12/31/97 • No Cash Value • Coupons Cannot Be Combined
Coupon Must Be Presented At Time Of Purchase

Armchair Sailor

Books • Charts • Marine Art • Gifts

2110 Westlake Avenue N. • Seattle, WA • 98109
Phone (206) 283-0858/ (800) 875-0852 • Fax (206) 285-1935

Armchair Sailor
Books • Charts • Marine Art • Gifts
2110 Westlake Avenue N.
Seattle, WA • 98109
Phone (206) 283-0858
Toll-free (800) 875-0852
Fax (206) 285-1935

1997 WAGGONER CRUISING COUPON

Two Black & White Chart Copies For The Price Of One
(Up to 10 Charts)

Valid 1/1/97 Through 12/31/97 • No Cash Value • Coupons Cannot Be Combined
Coupon Must Be Presented At Time Of Purchase

West Marine

We make boating more fun!™

Nine Northwest Locations To Serve You:

Anacortes • (360) 293-4262	Portland • (503) 289-9822
Bellevue • (206) 641-4065	Seattle • Mercer Street • (206) 292-8663
Bellingham • (360) 650-1100	Seattle • Seaview Ave. NW • (206) 789-4640
Bremerton • (360) 479-2200	Tacoma • (206) 926-2533

NEW! Everett • Port Gardner Landing • (206) 303-1880

West Marine
We make boating more fun!™

Good At These Northwest Locations:
Anacortes
Bellevue
Bellingham
Bremerton
Everett • Port Gardner Landing
Portland
Seattle • Two Locations
Tacoma

1997 WAGGONER CRUISING COUPON

Five Dollars Off Any Purchase Over $25

Valid 1/1/97 Through 12/31/97 • No Cash Value • Coupons Cannot Be Combined
Coupon Must Be Presented At Time Of Purchase

West Marine

We make boating more fun!™

Nine Northwest Locations To Serve You:

Anacortes • (360) 293-4262	Portland • (503) 289-9822
Bellevue • (206) 641-4065	Seattle • Mercer Street • (206) 292-8663
Bellingham • (360) 650-1100	Seattle • Seaview Ave. NW • (206) 789-4640
Bremerton • (360) 479-2200	Tacoma • (206) 926-2533

NEW! Everett • Port Gardner Landing • (206) 303-1880

West Marine
We make boating more fun!™

Good At These Northwest Locations:
Anacortes
Bellevue
Bellingham
Bremerton
Everett • Port Gardner Landing
Portland
Seattle • Two Locations
Tacoma

1997 WAGGONER CRUISING COUPON

Buy One, Get One Free
1 Qt. West Marine Boat Soap
(Model #245050)

Valid 1/1/97 Through 12/31/97 • No Cash Value • Coupons Cannot Be Combined
Coupon Must Be Presented At Time Of Purchase

CONVERSION TABLES

TEMPERATURE

Fahrenheit to Celsius

To convert temperature from Fahrenheit to Celsius:

(F° - 32) x .555 = C°

Example: Convert 40° F to C:
(40 - 32) = 8; 8 x .555 = 4;
thus 40° F = 4° C

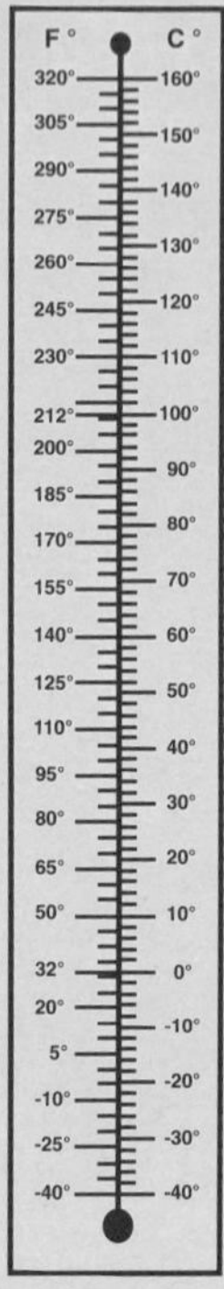

Celsius to Fahrenheit

To convert temperature from Celsius to Fahrenheit:

(C° x 1.8)+32 = F°

Example: Convert 4° C to F:
(4 x 1.8) = 7.992;
7.992 + 32 = 39.992 (round to 40);
thus 4° C = 40° F

32° Fahrenheit =
0° Celsius

0° Fahrenheit =
-17.8° Celsius

VOLUME

U.S. Gallons to Liters

1 U.S gallon = 3.7854 liters

To convert U.S. gallons to liters, multiply U.S. gallons times 3.785.
Example: 40 U.S. gallons x 3.785 = 151 liters

To convert liters to U.S. gallons, divide by 3.785.
Example: 151 liters ÷ 3.785 = 39.89 U.S. gallons (round to 40)

Imperial Gallons to Liters

1 Imperial gallon = 4.546 liters

To convert Imperial gallons to liters, multiply Imperial gallons times 4.546.
Example: 40 Imperial gallons x 4.546 = 182 liters

To convert liters to Imperial gallons, divide by 4.546.
Example: 182 liters ÷ 4.546 = 40.035 (round to 40)

U.S. Gallons to Imperial Gallons

1 U.S. gallon = .833 Imperial gallons

To convert U.S. gallons to Imperial gallons, multiply U.S. gallons x .833.
Example: 40 U.S. gallons x .833 = 33.32 Imperial gallons

To convert Imperial gallons to U.S. gallons, multiply Imperial gallons x 1.20.
Example: 33 Imperial gallons x 1.20 = 39.6 U.S. gallons

Liters and Quarts

1 liter = 1.0567 quarts, or 33.8 ounces
1 quart = .9467 liters, or 947 ml

CONVERSION TABLES

WEIGHT

1 kilogram (kg) = 2.2 pounds (lbs.)

1 pound = .4545 kilograms

1 U.S. gallon of fresh water weighs 8.333 lbs., or 3.787 kg

1 Imperial gallon of fresh water weighs 10 lbs., or 4.545 kg

1 liter of fresh water weighs 2.2 pounds, or 1 kg

1 U. S. gallon of gasoline weighs 6.2 lbs., or 2.82 kg

1 Imperial gallon of gasoline weighs 7.44 lbs., or 3.38 kg

1 liter of gasoline weighs 1.64 lbs., or 0.744 kg

1 U.S. gallon of No. 2 diesel fuel weighs 6.7 pounds, or 3.05 kg

1 Imperial gallon of No. 2 diesel fuel weighs 8.04 pounds, or 3.66 kg

1 liter of No. 2 diesel fuel weighs 1.77 pounds, or 0.8 kg

Note on Fuel Volume: Most fuels are stored in underground tanks at approximately 54° F (12° C), and will expand when they warm.

DISTANCE

1 foot = .3048 meter

1 meter = 3.28 feet

1 fathom = 6 feet

1 fathom = 1.83 meters

1 cable = 120 fathoms

1 statute mile = 5280 feet; 7.4 cables; 1.609 kilometers

1 nautical mile = 6076 feet; 8.5 cables; 1.852 kilometers

1 statute mile = 0.868 nautical mile

1 nautical mile = 1.15 statute mile

SPEED

Convert knots to miles per hour: Knots x 1.15

Convert miles per hour to knots: MPH x .868

INTERNATIONAL MORSE CODE & PHONETIC ALPHABET

A ALPHA • —
B BRAVO — • • •
C CHARLIE — • — •
D DELTA — • •
E ECHO •
F FOXTROT • • — •
G GOLF — — •
H HOTEL • • • •
I INDIA • •
J JULIET • — — —
K KILO — • —
L LIMO • — • •
M MIKE — —

N NOVEMBER — •
O OSCAR — — —
P PAPA • — — •
Q QUEBEC — — • —
R ROMEO • — •
S SIERRA • • •
T TANGO —
U UNIFORM • • —
V VICTOR • • • —
W WHISKEY • — —
X X-RAY — • • —
Y YANKEE — • — —
Z ZULU — — • •

1 ONE • — — — —
2 TWO • • — — —
3 THREE • • • — —
4 FOUR • • • • —
5 FIVE • • • • •
6 SIX — • • • •
7 SEVEN — — • • •
8 EIGHT — — — • •
9 NINE — — — — •
0 ZERO — — — — —

DISTRESS - SOS
• • • — — — • • •

ISLANDS MARINE CENTER

YOUR HOME PORT IN THE SAN JUANS

100 SLIP MODERN MARINA WITH WATER, POWER, ICE, PUMPOUT
HAULOUT TO 15 TONS EMERGENCY REPAIRS
RESTAURANTS AND SHOPPING NEARBY

P.O. Box 88 • Fisherman Bay • Lopez Island, WA • 98261
Phone (360) 468-3377 • Fax (360) 468-2283 • VHF 16

P.O. Box 88
Fisherman Bay
Lopez Island, WA • 98261
Phone (360) 468-3377
Fax (360) 468-2283
VHF 16

1997 WAGGONER CRUISING COUPON

25% Discount on Any Store Purchase
(Not including electronics and outboards)

Valid 1/1/97 Through 12/31/97 • No Cash Value • Coupons Cannot Be Combined
Coupon Must Be Presented At Time Of Purchase

49° 23' N.-123° 19'W. V H F CHANNEL 68

HOWE SOUND'S
Union SteamShip Marine Resort

Offering Boutiques, Shops & Restaurants On The Boardwalk, Walking & Cycling In 600-Acre Crippen Park

Box 250 • Snug Cove • Bowen Island, B.C. Canada • V0N 1G0
Phone (604) 947-0707 • Fax (604) 947-0708

Union SteamShip Marine Resort
Box 250 • Snug Cove
Bowen Island, B.C.
Canada • V0N 1G0
Phone (604) 947-0707
Fax (604) 947-0708

1997 WAGGONER CRUISING COUPON

25% Off On Overnight Moorage

Valid 1/1/97 Through 12/31/97 • No Cash Value • Coupons Cannot Be Combined
Coupon Must Be Presented At Time Of Purchase

BOSUN'S LOCKER LTD

ESTABLISHED 1959

Quality Gear for Every Yachting Enthusiast . . .

Equipment and Supplies	National Charts and Publications for the Whole World	Foul Weather Gear Footwear	Power and Sail Rigging Specialists

Diesel Mechanic & Welder Available

580 Johnson Street • Victoria, B.C. Canada • V8W 1M3
Phone (250) 386-1308 • Fax (250) 383-7774
email: bosuns@islandnet.com

BOSUN'S LOCKER LTD
ESTABLISHED 1959

580 Johnson Street
Victoria, B.C.
Canada • V8W 1M3
Phone (250) 386-1308
Fax (250) 383-7774

1997 WAGGONER CRUISING COUPON

10% Discount On Any Purchase
(Not including charts)

Valid 1/1/97 Through 12/31/97 • No Cash Value • Coupons Cannot Be Combined
Coupon Must Be Presented At Time Of Purchase

Come and Visit Our 3,300 Square Foot Store!

The Boathouse Marine Centre

HUGE INVENTORY!

FRIENDLY, KNOWLEDGEABLE STAFF!

The Area's Largest & Best Marine Supplies Centre for Sail & Power

2-2379 Bevan Avenue • Sidney, B.C. Canada • V8L 4M9
Phone (250) 655-3682 • Fax (250) 655-3676

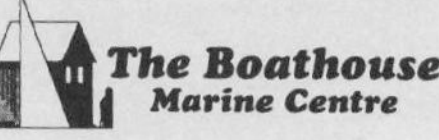

2-2379 Bevan Avenue
Sidney, B.C.
Canada • V8L 4M9
Phone (250) 655-3682
Fax (250) 655-3676

1997 WAGGONER CRUISING COUPON

10% Discount On Any Purchase
(Not including electronics, charts or sale items)

Valid 1/1/97 Through 12/31/97 • No Cash Value • Coupons Cannot Be Combined
Coupon Must Be Presented At Time Of Purchase

GOLF
KAYAKING
BIKE RENTALS
SHOWERS & LAUNDRY
STORE

POOL
BOAT RENTALS
CLOSE TO THE FERRY TERMINAL ON NORTH PENDER ISLAND

A Beautiful Quiet Paradise in the Heart of the Gulf Islands
Easy Access ✦ Well Protected

RR 1 • North Pender Island, B.C. Canada • V0N 2M0
Phone & Fax (250) 629-3579

RR 1
North Pender Island, B.C.
Canada • V0N 2M0
Phone & Fax
(250) 629-3579

1997 WAGGONER CRUISING COUPON

One Free Cappuccino
No purchase necessary

Valid 1/1/97 Through 12/31/97 • No Cash Value • Coupons Cannot Be Combined
Coupon Must Be Presented At Time Of Purchase

CURRENCY CONVERSION

Generally, the most favorable exchange rates are on credit card transactions. Banks give slightly less favorable rates, and merchants tend to be the least favorable. Expect to pay more than the official exchange rate when you buy currency, and receive less when you sell.

Examples:

Assume an official exchange rate of $.75 U.S./$1.3333 Cdn. (Exchange rates change constantly.)

To convert $100 Canadian to U.S. $, multiply Canadian $ by 0.75 or divide by 1.33
$100 Cdn × 0.75 = $75.00 U.S.
$100 Cdn ÷ 1.3333 = $75.00 U.S.

To convert $75 U.S. to Canadian $, multiply U.S. $ by 1.33 or divide by 0.75
$75 U.S. × 1.3333 = $100 Cdn.
$75 U.S. ÷ 0.75 = $100 Cdn.

BEAUFORT WIND SCALE

Scale Number	Wind Speed		Effects
	Knots	MPH	
0	under 1	under 1	Calm
1	1-3	1-3	Ripples
2	4-6	4-7	Small wavelets
3	7-10	8-12	Large wavelets; small crests
4	11-16	13-18	Small waves; some whitecaps
5	17-21	19-24	Moderate waves; some spray; many whitecaps
6	22-27	25-31	Larger waves; whitecaps everywhere
7	28-33	32-38	Sea heaps up; white foam from breaking waves
8	34-40	39-46	Moderately high waves of greater length; foam blown in well-marked streaks
9	41-47	47-54	High waves; sea begins to roll; dense streaks of foam; spray reduces visibility
10	48-55	55-63	Very high waves with overhanging crests; sea takes on a white appearance; rolling is heavy
11	56-63	64-72	Exceptionally high waves; sea covered with white foam patches; visibility still more reduced
12	64 & over	73 & over	Air filled with foam; sea completely white with driving spray; visibility greatly reduced.

VHF CHANNELS FOR PLEASURE CRAFT

Washington Waters

05A	Vessel Traffic Service Seattle—Strait of Juan de Fuca west of Victoria.
06	Ship-to-ship safety communications. For Search and Rescue (SAR) liason with Coast Guard vessels and aircraft.
09	Intership and ship-to-shore, all vessels. Working channel. Alternate calling channel (Strait of Juan de Fuca, San Juan Islands, Puget Sound waters of U.S. only).
11	
13	Vessel bridge to vessel bridge, large vessels. Low power only. May also be used to contact locks and bridges. For pleasure vessels in Seattle for nighttime bridge opening contact on Lake Washington Ship Canal.
14	Vessel Traffic System Seattle—Puget Sound.
16	International distress and calling. Calling channel. Used only for distress and urgency traffic, for safety calls and short calls to other stations. Listen first to make sure no distress traffic is in progress. Do not transmit if a *SEELONCE MAYDAY* is declared. Keep all communications to a minimum. Do not repeat a call to the same station more than once every two minutes. After three attempts, wait 15 minutes before calling the same station.
22A	Coast Guard liason. For safety and liason communications with the Coast Guard (both U.S. and Canada). The U.S. Coast Guard may not be monitoring Channel 22A.
68	Intership & ship to shore, pleasure vessels. Working channel.
69	Intership & ship to shore, pleasure vessels. Working channel.
70	Digital Selective Calling (DSC) only. No voice. For distress and calling.
71	Intership & ship to shore, pleasure vessels. Working channel.
72	Intership & ship to shore, all vessels. Working channel.
73	Intership & ship to shore, all vessels. Working channel.
74	
78A	Intership & ship to shore, pleasure vessels. Working channel. Marinas in Puget Sound are encouraged to use this as a secondary working channel.

British Columbia Waters

05A	Vessel Traffic Service Seattle—Strait of Juan de Fuca west of Victoria.
06	Ship-to-ship safety communications. For Search & Rescue (SAR) liason with Coast Guard vessels and aircraft.
09	Intership & ship to shore, all vessels. Working channel.
11	Vessel Traffic Service Vancouver—Strait of Juan de Fuca east of Victoria; Haro Strait; Boundary Passage; Gulf Islands; Strait of Georgia.
13	
14	
16	International distress and calling. Calling channel. Used only for distress and urgency traffic, for safety calls and short calls to other stations. Listen first to make sure no distress traffic is in progress. Do not transmit if a *SEELONCE MAYDAY* is declared. Keep all communications to a minimum. Do not repeat a call to the same station more than once every two minutes. After three attempts, wait 15 minutes before calling the same station.
22A	Coast Guard liason. For safety and liason communications with the Coast Guard (both U.S. and Canada). The Canadian Coast Guard does monitor Channel 22A.
68	Intership & ship to shore, pleasure vessels. Working channel. Also for marinas south of Courtenay. Do not call marinas in Canada on Channel 16.
69	Intership & ship to shore, pleasure vessels. Working channel.
70	Digital Selective Calling (DSC) only. No voice. For distress and calling.
71	Vessel Traffic Service Vancouver—East of Vancouver Island and North of Strait of Georgia.
72	Intership, all vessels. Working channel.
73	Intership & ship to shore, all vessels. Working channel. Also for marinas Campbell River and north.
74	Vessel Traffic Service Vancouver—Fraser River.
78A	

hour or so before the predicted turn, boats collect at each end waiting for the right time. These boats include commercial craft, even tugboats with tows of logs, so the period around slack water can get pretty exciting. Generally, the boats on the upstream side will go first, as they catch the last of the dying fair current. When they are through, the boats on the other end will go through, picking up the beginnings of the new (for them) fair current. It all works well as long as no one gets pushy.

Northumberland Channel. Use chart 3458 (larger scale, preferred) or 3443. The Northumberland Channel is the road from the Gulf Islands to Nanaimo. It starts at False Narrows and runs northwest between Gabriola Island and Vancouver Island. The Northumberland Channel exits in the Gulf of Georgia, or, at Jack Point, makes the turn to Nanaimo. Because of considerable log boom towing in the area, watch for floating debris. If you are not yet ready for civilization, you might lie over at **Pilot Bay,** on the north end of Gabriola Island. It's a dandy anchorage.

The setting sun turns Nanaimo aglow. Scene from anchor, Newcastle Island.

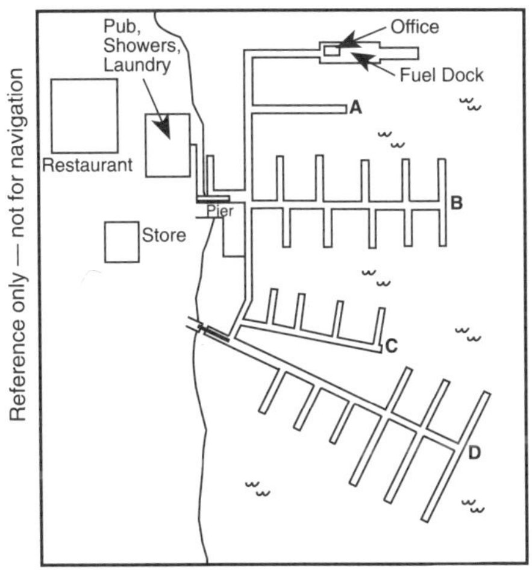

Silva Bay Resort and Marina

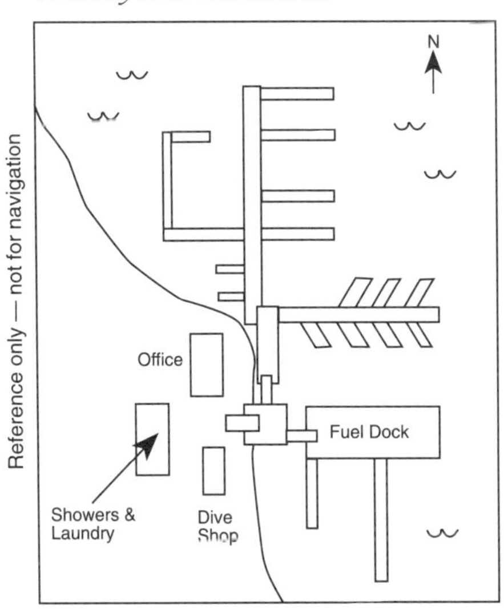

Page's Resort and Marina

Gabriola Sands Park, north end of Gabriola Island. Use chart 3458 (larger scale, preferred) or 3443. Open all year, day use only, toilets, no other facilities. This park fronts on Taylor Bay and Pilot Bay. It has a sandy swimming area and a playfield. Good for kids.

Sandwell Park, northeast side of Gabriola Island. Use chart 3458 (larger scale, preferred) or 3443. Open all year, day use only, toilets but no other facilities. This is a small sea-front park with a sandy beach and forested uplands.

Nanaimo. Use chart 3457 & 3458 (both larger scale, preferred) or 3443. As you pass Jack Point the city of Nanaimo opens up. The harbor is wide, and protected from the Strait of Georgia by Protection Island and Newcastle Island. The Port of Nanaimo public marina is located at the south end of the business district near Nanaimo's famous bastion, with access to downtown Nanaimo.

Canada Customs and moorages for float planes are just north of the public marina. Other moorages, including the Nanaimo Yacht Club, are in Newcastle Island Passage, the channel that leads behind Newcastle Island to Departure Bay. The Nanaimo Yacht Club maintains guest moorage for visiting reciprocal members.

Newcastle Island Passage is posted for

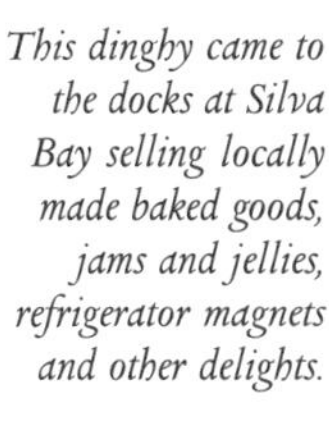

This dinghy came to the docks at Silva Bay selling locally made baked goods, jams and jellies, refrigerator magnets and other delights.

See area map page 108

"No-Wake" speeds, and the harbor patrol enforces the speed limit. Oregon Rock, marked by a beacon, lies in the channel. Pass between the rock and Newcastle Island. Fuel docks and repair facilities capable of handling any needed job are located along the channel.

Nanaimo is the natural point of departure for boats headed across the Strait of Georgia or north to Campbell River or Desolation Sound and beyond. It is the second largest city (behind Victoria) on Vancouver Island, and filled with surprises. Shops of all kinds line the narrow, winding streets. Just about any needed supplies and repairs are readily available. The small but beautifully-done Centennial Museum features a lifelike reproduction of a coal mine. A winding promenade takes walkers along the waterfront. The dinners at Katerina's Place, a Mediterrean restaurant, are among the most enjoyable we have ever had.

Dining: We've had good dinners at Katerina's Place, Beefeater's, and the Wesley Street Cafe.

⑥ **Port of Nanaimo**, P.O. Box 131, 104 Front Street, Nanaimo, B.C. V9R 5K4, (250)754-5053; fax (250)753-4899. Monitors VHF channel 67. Open year-round for visiting pleasure craft. In winter many commercial fishing vessels are in the basin, but pleasure craft moorage is available. No water on the docks in the winter, however. Gasoline and diesel at the fuel dock.

A new floating breakwater dock has been installed in the center of the marina entrance, and the Eco Barge for pumpout and portapotty dump is located adjacent to this dock. Arriving and departing vessels must pass south of the floating breakwater dock. The northern entrance is reserved for aircraft. *(Marina map page 115)*

Marina facilities include 9000 feet of dock space, 15, 30, 50 & 100 amp power, washrooms, showers, laundry, waste oil disposal, 1000 pound hydraulic crane. Customs clearance available. Three hours of moorage no charge; charges assessed thereafter.

The public boat basin has room for most summer crowds, although it is wise to arrive early rather than late. During the summer, all the docks except B dock are open on a non-reserved basis for pleasure craft. Reservations are taken for the new 600-foot breakwater pier and the Cameron Island floats, which give good inside protection for larger boats. During July and August call (250)755-1216.

The basin can hold 250-300 boats at a time. Summertime turnover averages about 100 boats a day. Rafting is permitted. In summer, dock assistants can help you tie up. Most days, fresh fish is for sale right at the dock. Theaters, walkway, tennis courts, golf nearby. Adjacent seaplane terminal. All of the Nanaimo commercial district is at hand.

⑥ **Nanaimo Yacht Club**, 400 Newcastle Ave, Nanaimo, B.C. V9S 4J1, (250)754-7011. Open all year, 15 amp power, washrooms, showers, laundry, customs clearance available. Moorage is for members of reciprocal yacht clubs only.

⑥ **Moby Dick Boatel**, 1000 Stewart Ave., Nanaimo, B.C. V9S 4C9, (250)753-7111. Open all year, power, no washrooms, no showers. The marina can hold about 60 boats, but the slips fill up April through October, so there's not much left for transients. Phone ahead for availability.

See area map page 108

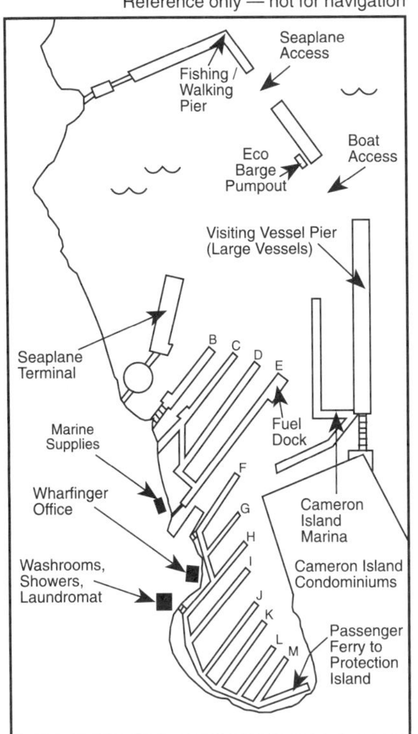

Port of Nanaimo

⑥ **Stone's Marina and RV Park**, 1690 Stewart Ave., Nanaimo, B.C. V9S 4E6, (250)753-4232; fax (250)753-4204; e-mail: stones@island.net. Open all year, 15, 20 & 30 amp power, washrooms, showers, laundry, customs clearance available. This is an RV park and campground with a 220-berth marina. Call ahead for availability. The complex has two marine pubs that serve food, with 500 feet of guest moorage.

⑥ **Brechin Point Marina**, 2000 Zorkin, Nanaimo, B.C. V9R 5K9, (250)753-6122; fax (250)753-9378. Open all year, gasoline and diesel at fuel dock, washrooms, no power, no showers. Customs clearance available. They have a 200-foot dock for temporary moorage. Also carry aviation fuel and jet-B fuel, 50:1 mix, kerosene, propane, stove alcohol. Customs clearance point for commercial float planes also; you can pick up a flight here. Located at the north end of Newcastle Channel, close to Departure Bay and ferries to Vancouver and Tsawwassen.

⑥ **Newcastle Marina**, 1300 Stewart Ave., Nanaimo, B.C. V9S 4E1, (250)753-1431. Open all year, guest moorage in unoccupied slips when available, 42-foot maximum boat length. Facilities include

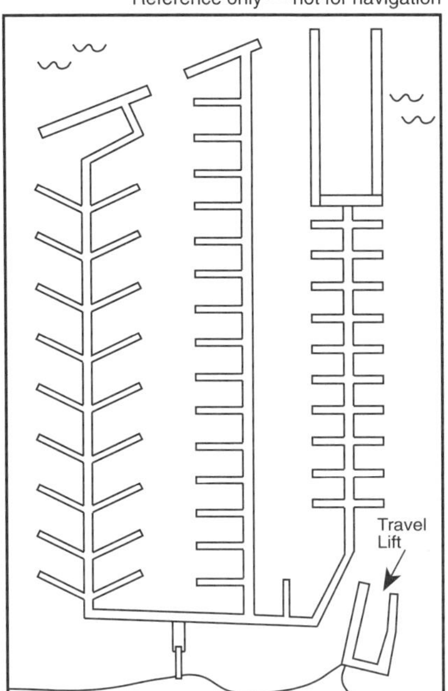

Newcastle Marina

15 amp power, washrooms, showers, laundry, 50 ton Travelift, drydock.

⑥ **Anchorage Marina**, 1520 Stewart Ave., Nanaimo, B.C. V9S 4E1, (250)754-5585. Open all year, guest moorage in approximately 10 slips, 20 & 30 amp power, washrooms. The store carries marine hardware, accessories, boats and motors, charts, books, fishing tackle and licenses. Restaurants, pub within walking distance. Located ½ mile from Nanaimo, halfway along Newcastle Channel.

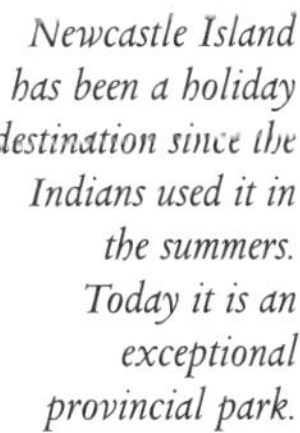

Newcastle Island has been a holiday destination since the Indians used it in the summers. Today it is an exceptional provincial park.

⑥ **Nanaimo Harbour City Marina**, 1250 Stewart Ave. Nanaimo, B.C. V9S 4C9, (250)754-2732; fax (250)754-7140. Open all year, limited moorage available, 30 amp power, washrooms, showers, customs clearance available. Call ahead by phone to check availability. They have a full-service boatyard and brokerage.

⑥ **Nanaimo Shipyard**, 1040 Stewart Ave., Nanaimo, B.C. V9S 4C9, (250)753-1151, 753-1244; fax (250)753-2235. Open all year, guest moorage in unoccupied slips when available, 20 & 30 amp power, washrooms, customs clearance available. Full service shipyard. Moorage usually no problem in summer, but larger boats should call ahead. Right on the channel, look for red and yellow striped shed at the end of the dock.

Dinghy Dock Pub, Nanaimo, B.C. V9R 5M2, (250)753-2373. Monitors VHF channel 18. Temporary moorage only, no charge while dining. If you are anchored out nearby, call on VHF channel 18, ask for "Dinghy Dock." A shuttle will pick you up and bring you to the pub. They serve lunch and dinner, and have showers and a laundry facility at the pub. Located across from Nanaimo Harbour, at Protection Island.

⑦ **Newcastle Island Marine Park.** Open all year, visitor moorage at 1500 feet of dock space, washrooms, no power, no showers. Several small bays. Beaches and playing fields. Many hiking trails. Walk-in campsites and picnic areas. In summer a passenger ferry connects the island with Nanaimo. The Pavilion houses a dance floor, a restaurant & snack bar, a visitor's center, and interpretive displays on the natural and human history of the area. Perfect for families.

See area map page 108

Marilynn Hale peers into the hole left by pulpstone quarry work on Newcastle Island.

This is an extraordinary park. Before the white men came, Newcastle Island was a summer campsite for Indians. Since the white men came it has supported a shipyard. It has been mined for coal. In the early1870s it was quarried for sandstone that built the San Francisco Mint. Between 1923 and 1932 its sandstone was quarried for pulpstones, giant cylinders that ground wood into pulp for paper making. Before WWII, Japanese fishermen ran herring salteries here. And always, Newcastle Island has been a popular holiday spot.

On its 750 acres Newcastle Island has a small lake, miles of trails, campsites for individual campers and fields for group camping, play areas, and relics of its rich history. The 1931 pavilion charms. The pulpstone quarry astonishes. The bays and beaches intrigue. We enjoy this park.

You'll probably see rare albino raccoons, and of course dozens of bunny rabbits. Arrive early enough to get literature from the visitor center. Try to spend the night. We anchored between Newcastle Island and Protection Island. The lights of Nanaimo were beautiful.

Petroglyph Park, a few miles south of Naniamo on the Island Highway—take a taxi or bus. The park contains ancient rock carvings created hundreds and thousands of years ago. Both original petroglyphs and castings can be seen. You may take rubbings of the castings.

Searching for the Bar

Several years ago my then-teenage daughter and I were coming south along the Vancouver Island side from Desolation Sound. A southeast gale was blowing, with flying haze that obscured the shoreline. I had just about given up trying to find the outer buoy to the channel across Comox Bar and was prepared to jog offshore all night, when a small Canadian troller passed me close aboard, and almost immediately turned west onto the heading (222 degrees true) of the channel. Feeling lucky to have local knowledge so close at hand, I immediately followed him, and eventually wound up in Comox safe and sound, although thoroughly wet.

After getting secured, I walked up the dock where the troller was tied to thank its skipper for leading me in. "Hell," he said, "I bought this boat yesterday and have never been here before. I was totally lost, and just guessing where that damn bar was. But when I saw you turn right behind me, I figured I must be in the right place!"

The halt leading the blind.

—Tom Kincaid

Margaret Harvey has been selling fresh fish at the Nanaimo dock for more than a decade.

Nanoose Harbour to Texada Island Lasqueti Island

Schooner Cove • French Creek • Denman Island • Hornby Island • Comox • Oyster River • False Bay • Squitty Bay

Charts

3443 Thetis Island to Nanaimo (1:40:000)
3457 Nanaimo Harbour and Departure Bay (1:8,000)
3458 Approaches to Nanaimo Harbour (1:20,000)
3512 Strait of Georgia, Central Portion (1:80,000)
3513 Strait of Georgia, Northern Portion (1:80,000)
3459 Approaches to Nanoose Harbour (1:15,000)
3527 Baynes Sound (1:40,000); Comox Harbour (1:15,000)
3311 SMALL CRAFT CHARTS (strip charts) Sunshine Coast to Desolation Sound
3312 SMALL CRAFT CHART (chart book) Jervis Inlet & Desolation Sound

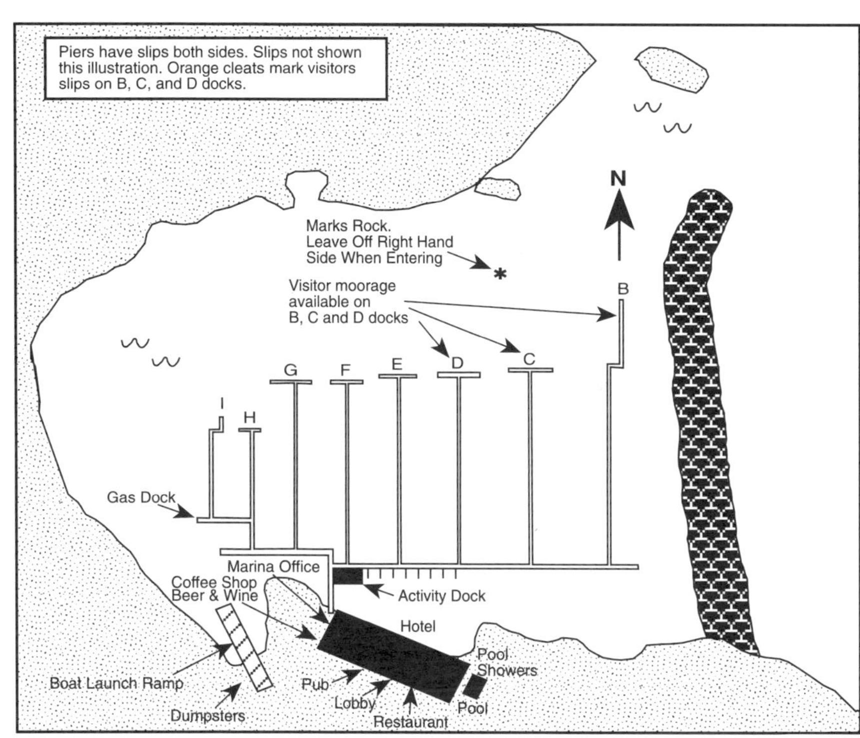

Schooner Cove Marina

Whiskey Golf. Use chart 3512. Boats headed north from Nanaimo are at once faced by the notorious "Whiskey Golf" (WG) restricted area. Whiskey Golf is a deepwater range operated by the Canadian and U.S. Navies, and is used to test torpedoes (always unarmed) and various ships' systems. The area consists of a network of underwater sensing devices joined by cables to a control site on Winchelsea Island. Torpedoes are fired from range vessels along a predetermined course, and are tracked from the Winchelsea control center. After the run the torpedoes are recovered, either by a large helicopter or by range vessels. For obvious reasons, unauthorized craft are not permitted in the area while the range is in operation.

When the range operates, normally it will be Mondays through Fridays, sometimes Saturdays, from 0700 to 1730. Winchelsea Range Control monitors VHF channels 16 and 10, and should be contacted before attempting to enter the area. In addition, Comox Coast Guard radio, Vancouver traffic, and CB Channel 09 carry notices as to the operational state of the range. These notices are broadcast only when the range is operating or scheduled to be operating. In the absence of any notices, you can cross the range safely.

The Whiskey Golf restricted area lies on the direct course across Georgia Strait from Nanaimo to Secret Cove, Smugglers Cove, Pender Harbour, and other destinations along the Sunshine Coast.

The Canadian Navy has established a safe transit route along the edges of the restricted area while the range is in use. After clearing Nanaimo Harbour or Departure Bay (being careful to avoid Hudson Rocks and Five Finger Island), head directly for the Winchelsea Islands, passing to the east of the islands within 1000 yards. Turn to pass east of the Ballenas Islands within 1000 yards. Once well past the Ballenas Islands, steer a course for your destination on the mainland side of the Strait, or northwest along the Vancouver Island side of the Strait.

If your boat is equipped with loran-C or GPS, you can use waypoints shown in our Weatherly Press sister publication, *Weatherly Waypoint Guide, Vol. 2: Gulf of Georgia,* to run a safe route past Whiskey Golf. Be aware that the waypoints shown in that book mark the corners of Whiskey Golf. You should steer a course to give those corners a clearance of a few hundred yards.

Nanoose Harbour. Use chart 3459 (larger scale, preferred) or 3512. Anchorage is good just inside the sandy spit on the south side of the entrance. The Snaw-Naw-As Marina, with moorage for visiting boats, is located at Fleet Point on the south shore, just inside the entrance. The 55-acre Arbutus Grove Provincial Park, on the south shore, houses a stand of old arbutus trees that is reputed to be the most spectacular on Vancouver Island. The docks and mooring buoys along the north shore are the base for Royal Canadian Navy and U.S. Navy vessels engaged

See area map page 119

National Defence | Défense nationale

NOTICE

CANADIAN FORCES MARITIME EXPERIMENTAL AND TEST RANGES

The Canadian Forces Maritime Experimental and Test Ranges tests ship and aircraft systems and torpedoes. Torpedoes may be launched by a surface vessel, submarine, or aircraft. No explosives are used; however, a hazard exists due to the possibility of the torpedo homing on vessels and then the vessel being struck by the torpedo on its way to the surface.

Testing is usually carried out from 0800–1730 Tuesday to Friday and occasionally on Monday or Saturday.

During testing Area "WG" is "Active". Any vessel within the area bounded by the following coordinates:

a. 49°21'00"N 123°48'24"W;
b. 49°14'50"N 123°48'24"W;
c. 49°16'45"N 124°00'54"W;
d. 49°19'21"N 124°07'42"W; and
e. 49°21'21"N 124°07'42"W

will be required to clear or stop on demand from the Canadian Range Officer at "Winchelsea Island Control" or any of the range vessels or range helicopter. The positions of these coordinates are clearly marked on the diagram.

A transit area 1,000 yards north of Winchelsea Island and 1,000 yards east of South Ballenas Island has been established to enable mariners to transit safely around the active area. It also facilitates unimpeded access to marina facilities in Schooner Cove and Nanoose Bay. This area is clearly depicted on charts 3512 and 3459 by means of pecked lines.

Additional information on active hours or for safe transit through the area may be obtained from:

a. Winchelsea Island Control (250)756-5080 or (250)468-5080 (next day's activity only);
b. CFMETR Range Officer (250)756-5002 or (250)468-5002 (long range planning);
c. Winchelsea Island Control VHF CH 10 or 16 (for safe transit area information when approaching area "WG");
d. VHF 21B or Weather 3 (listen only, for active times), or
e. CB channel 9.

Area "WG" constitutes a "Defence Establishment" as defined in the National Defence Act to which the Defence Controlled Access Area Regulations apply. Vessels which do not comply with direction from either Winchelsea Control or Range Patrol Vessels may be charged for trespassing.

Range vessels exhibit a flashing red light in addition to the prescribed lights and shapes. These vessels may operate outside of scheduled hours and should not be approached within 3,000 yards because they may be in a three-point moor with mooring lines extending to buoys 1,500 yards away. Additionally, lit as well as unlit mooring buoys are randomly located within the area and mariners are advised to use caution when transitting this area.

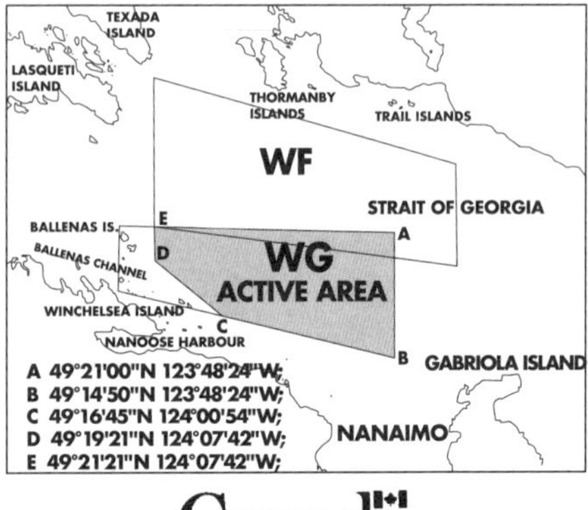

Canada

in activity on the Winchelsea (Whiskey Golf) torpedo range.

① **Snaw-Naw-As Marina Ltd.,** 209 Mallard Way, Lantzville, B.C. V0R 2H0, (250)390-2616. Open all year, gasoline & diesel at fuel dock. Guest moorage is available, best to call ahead. Moorage has 15 & 30 amp power, washrooms, showers. Marina has launch ramp, picnicking, camping. Snack bar open seasonally. Bait available. Shopping mall is 2 miles away.

② **Schooner Cove Resort & Marina,** P.O. Box 12, Schooner House, Nanoose Bay, B.C. V0R 2R0, (250)468-5364; (800)663-7060; fax (250)468-5744. Monitors VHF channel 73. Use chart 3459 (larger scale, preferred) or 3512. Schooner Cove is an outstanding marina resort, open all year, with gasoline at the fuel dock. Guest moorage is available, 30 & 50 amp power, washrooms, showers, laundry, launch ramp, some repairs. Reservations recommended. Just inside the breakwater entrance, watch for a drying rock marked by a red buoy. Keep the buoy well to starboard when entering. The moorage fee includes use of the pool, hot tub, sauna, fitness room, and tennis courts. The marina has a hotel, a good restaurant and a friendly pub. The Fairwinds golf course is part of the resort. A courtesy shuttle is available for banking, provisioning, post office.

Nuttal Bay. Use chart 3459 (larger scale, preferred) or 3512. Nuttal Bay is exposed to northwesterly winds, but protected from southeasterly winds. Lacking local knowledge, the cautious entry would be to leave the Dorcas Rock buoy to port. A fishing resort at the head of the bay has some facilities, but no floats or docks.

③ **Beachcomber Marina,** P.O. Box 21, Beachcomber RR 1, Nanoose Bay, B.C. V0R 2R0, (250)468-7222. Monitors VHF channel 16. Open all year in **Northwest Bay,** gasoline & diesel at fuel dock. Fishing supplies available, 15 & 30 amp power. Guest moorage available only if permanent tenant is away. To enter the marina, pass between the green and red buoys. Do not pass between the green buoy and the end of the breakwater—a reef runs south from the breakwater. Watch for several drying and underwater rocks along the eastern shore.

Mistaken Island. Mistaken Island is privately owned, and posted with No Trespassing signs.

Parksville. Use chart 3512. Parksville is an interesting town with a very nice beach, but shoal water extends out some distance. Except for the marina at French Creek at the north end of Parksville, no facilities are available for boaters.

④ **French Creek Boat Harbour,** 1055 Lee Rd., Parksville, B.C. V9P 2E1, (250)248-5051; fax (250)248-5123. Monitors VHF channel 68. Use chart 3512. Open all year, gasoline, diesel at fuel dock. Waste oil disposal available. Marina has washrooms, shower, laundry. Power is 15 amp with 20 amp connectors. Groceries, restaurant, pub, marine supplies, launch ramp and haulout. Two fish markets sell fresh seafood on the dock. Commercial vessels have priority, but much room for pleasure craft is available July-September when the fleet is out.

French Creek is the only breakwater-protected harbor in the 25-mile stretch between Northwest Bay and Deep Bay. Enter through a dredged channel with a least depth of 10 feet. French Creek is the western terminus of the passenger ferry to Lasqueti Island. *(Marina map page 120)*

Reference only — not for navigation

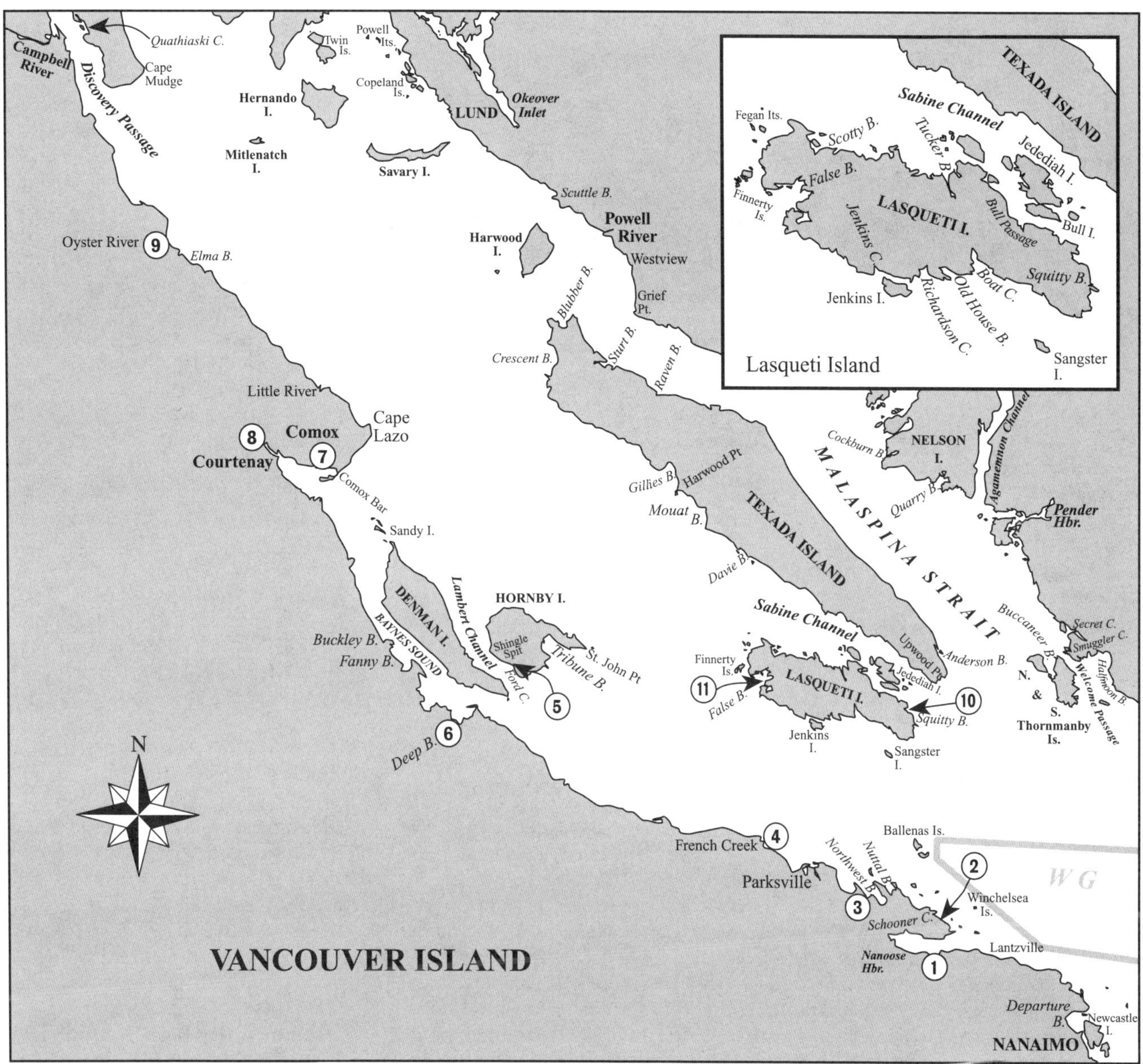

Hornby Island Use chart 3527 (larger scale, preferred) or 3513. Hornby Island has anchorages in Tribune Bay and south of Shingle Spit (where a little ferry runs to Denman Island). Both anchorages are exposed to southeast winds. In settled weather, however, **Tribune Bay** is worth a visit. Anchor offshore and dinghy in to the finest sand beach in the Gulf of Georgia. Visit Tribune Bay Provincial Park**.** Take the 3-mile hike to Helliwell Provincial Park, on St. John Point. Ford Cove, behind Maude Reef on the south corner of Lambert Channel, has breakwater-protected anchorage and moorage. The breakwater and float are shown as single inked lines on the chart, and are easily overlooked.

⑤ **Ford Cove Marina, Ltd.,** RR1, Hornby Is., B.C. V0R 1T0, (250)335-2169. Use chart 3527 (larger scale, preferred) or 3513. Open all year, gasoline, diesel, lubricants. The fuel dock is the northernmost of the three docks. Groceries, fishing tackle and bait. Art gallery, cottages. No fresh water available. Good anchorage on rocky bottom, and most larger boats anchor out.

⑤ **Ford Cove Government Wharf.** Open all year, guest moorage available, 280 feet of dock space. Tidal grid. Waste oil disposal, garbage pickup, telephone.

Baynes Sound. Use chart 3527 (larger scale, preferred) or 3513. Chart 3527 shows navigation aids not shown on chart 3513. Baynes Sound, protected from the Strait of Georgia by Denman Island, is a 12-mile refuge with generally quiet water, leading to Comox.

⑥ **Deep Bay.** Use chart 3527 (larger scale, preferred) or 3513. Anchorage is good in Deep Bay, though in deeper water than most boaters like. The public wharf and floats are open all year, with 1130 feet of dock space, guest moorage available. Commercial vessels have priority. Garbage pickup, waste oil disposal, telephone, tidal grid, launch ramp.

Fanny Bay. Use chart 3527 (larger scale, preferred) or 3513. Fanny Bay is primarily a camping area, but does have a small government mooring float. Gaso-

See area map page 119

The Chrome Island lighthouse off the south end of Denman Island is a dramatic landmark.

line is available at the float. A small freighter has been beached at Fanny Bay for many years.

Denman Island. Use chart 3527 (larger scale, preferred) or 3513. A government dock and float (78 feet of dock space) are alongside the landing for the ferry that runs to Buckley Bay, on Vancouver Island. The Denman General Store, with groceries, post office, and liquor store, is a short distance from the dock. The north end of Denman Island peters out into a long spit, littered with small islands and rocks. One of these islands, Sandy Island, is a recent addition to the provincial park system.

Sandy Island Marine Park. Use chart 3527 (larger scale, preferred) or 3513. This park includes the Seal Islets, and is accessible by boat only. Anchor on the south side, in Hornby Bay. The park has picnic areas, swimming, fishing, hiking trails, and wilderness campsites. At low tide it is possible to walk along this sandy spit all the way to its end—halfway to Comox.

Reference only — not for navigation

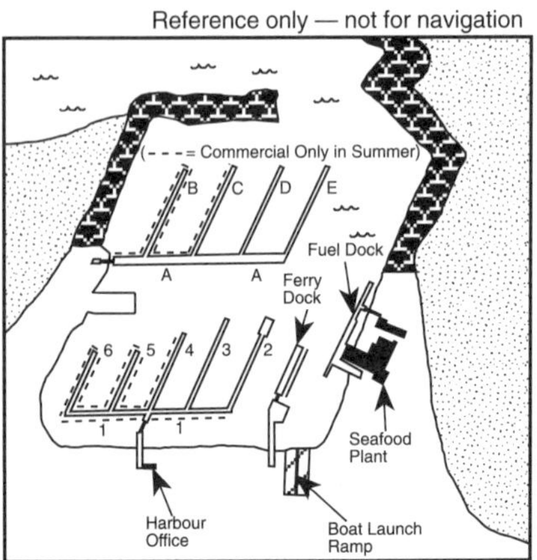

French Creek Boat Harbour

Comox. Use chart 3527 (larger scale, preferred) or 3513. If you plan to go to Comox, we strongly urge that you have Chart 3527 (1:40,000), with its inset (1:15,000) of Comox Harbour and the Courtenay River up to the Lewis Bridge. Chart 3527 shows the various ranges and other navigation aids in excellent detail, and could save you from much uncertainty. Comox is a busy little city, with a population of 8,000 and a breakwater-protected marina. The Coast Guard base that covers the northern Strait of Georgia is located at nearby Goose Point.

From Baynes Sound the entrance to Comox is well marked, but be careful of drying flats off Gartley Point and in the inner half of the bay. The Comox Harbour Authority floats (formerly the government dock) are entered around the east end of the breakwater.

The other marinas are reached by entering in the middle of the breakwater. The Comox Municipal Marina, to the far right as you enter, has guest slips for smaller boats. You can also find guest moorage in the Desolation Sound Yacht Charters slips, located immediately behind the Black Fin Fuel Dock, and at the Comox Bay Marina, just to the left as you enter. The Desolation Sound Yacht Charters slips are available Monday-Friday only. On weekends the charter boats return and use the slips.

While it's possible to enter around the west end of the breakwater, the passage between the breakwater and the docks is very narrow, especially at low tide. Other than by dinghy we don't recommend it.

You'll find showers and laundry at the Edgewater Pub, located just above the Comox Bay Marina, and in the lower level of the Black Fin Pub, located on the far side of the beautiful park that borders the marina area. Both the Edgewater and Black Fin facilities are almost new. (We have used the Black Fin facilities and found them excellent.) Comox has good shopping, a delightful bookstore, and a number of restaurants. See the Crow's Nest for marine supplies, books, and charts. A golf course is within walking distance. A hospital overlooks the bay. The town fathers have plans to make Comox into a first-class destination port, so there's a good chance future facilities will be even better.

⑦ **Black Fin Marina & Pub,** 132 Port Agusta St., Comox, B.C. V9M 3N7, (250)339-4664; fax (250)339-3022. Open all year, gasoline & diesel at fuel dock. 15 amp power. Washrooms, showers, laundry in pub building, across park from marina. Look for the Esso and Black Fin sign.

⑦ **Comox Municipal Marina,** 1809 Beaufort Avenue, Comox, B.C. V9M 1R9, (250)339-2202. Open all year, guest moorage available for boats to 27 feet. Most of the slips are for boats 20-24 feet. Call ahead if possible. Marina has power, water, launch ramp, nearby washrooms, showers, laundry.

⑦ **Comox Bay Marina**, 1805 Beaufort, Comox, B.C. V9M 1R9, (250)339-2930. Open all year, guest moorage available, please call ahead. Restrooms, showers, laundry, limited 15 amp power. Look for the Edgewater Marine Pub & Grill, above the marina.

⑦ **Comox Valley Harbour Authority,** Box 1258, Comox, B.C. V9N 7Z8, (250)339-6041. Guest moorage available on 1400 feet of docks inside the Comox breakwater. Half the dock space is reserved for pleasure craft. Garbage pickup, waste oil disposal. Rick and Heimke Webb are the wharf managers. Nice folks.

⑦ **Comox Government Wharf, Royston.** Open all year, 460 feet of dock, waste oil disposal, commercial vessels have priority.

See area map page 119

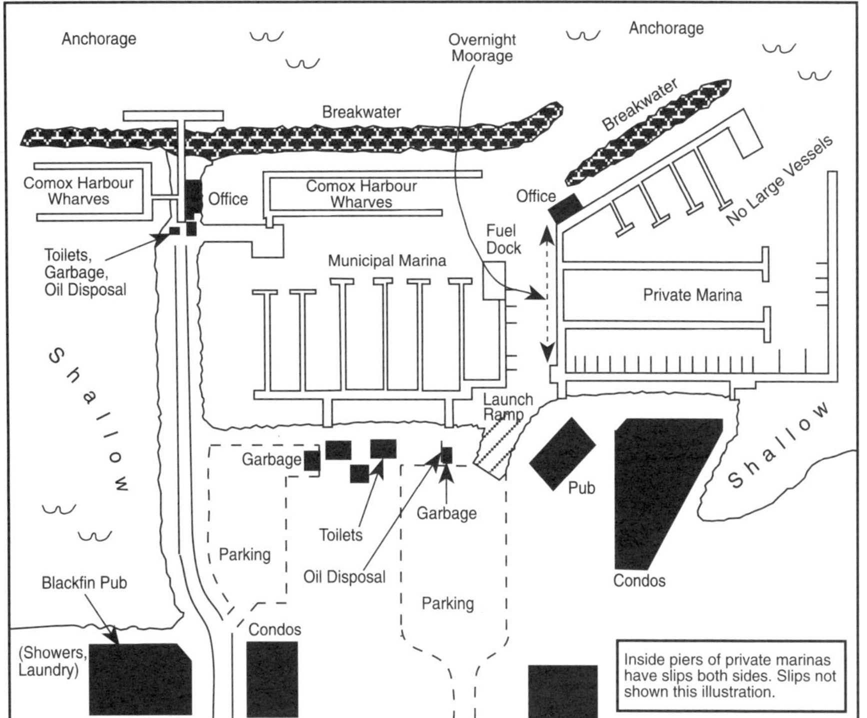

Comox Harbour

Courtenay. Use chart 3527. For a pleasant diversion, take the dinghy a short distance up the Courtenay River to the town of Courtenay. A dredged channel, marked by ranges, leads through the delta to the river mouth. The river is an interesting break from the saltwater experience out in the gulf. Just before you reach the Lewis Bridge, a slough leads off to the right, with an extensive Comox Valley Harbour Authority dock lining the shore and a French restaurant near the head. The dock is for vessels with a draft of 4 feet or less, pleasure craft welcome. The restaurant has been recommended to us by friends in Comox.

Kayakers explore the slough at Courtenay.

Comox Bar. Use chart 3527 (larger scale, preferred) or 3513. While Chart 3513 (1:80,000) seems to show the passage through the Comox Bar, the larger-scale Chart 3527 (1:40,000) shows the buoys that will guide you across safely. We urge you to use Chart 3527. The Comox Bar nearly joins Denman Island and Cape Lazo, with a shallow channel through the bar. A range, consisting of two white poles with vertical red stripes on them, is on the Vancouver Island shore. We found the range very difficult to identify on a sunny early afternoon in July. Least depth in the channel is about 15 feet. A flashing red buoy marks the Strait of Georgia end of this channel, with two additional buoys along the course. Stay close to the south of each of these buoys.

Cape Lazo. Use chart 3513. Cape Lazo is marked by a lighthouse on a high cliff. Buoys PJ and PK, offshore, mark the edge of deep water. Somewhere just north of Cape Lazo is the point at which the tidal currents change direction and begin flooding south from Cape Scott, rather than north from Victoria.

Little River. Use chart 3513. Little River, located 3 miles up-island from Cape Lazo, is the western terminus for the ferry to Westview/Powell River. Marginal moorage for a few small craft can be found behind the ferry dock.

Oyster River. Use chart 3513. A channel, dredged annually and marked by piles, leads to the protected Pacific Playgounds Marina next to the mouth of the Oyster River.

⑨ **Pacific Playgrounds Resort,** 9082 Clarkson Drive, Black Creek, B.C. V9J 1B3, (250)337-5600. Open all year, gasoline and diesel at the fuel dock, 15 amp power, tidal grid, washrooms, showers, laundry. Marina is entered via a dredged channel, least depth 2 feet at zero tide. The resort has a driving range, mini-golf, and a 9-hole golf course. The store carries marine supplies and charts, bait and tackle, limited groceries.

LASQUETI ISLAND

Use chart 3312; 3512; 3513; 3536. Chartbook 3312 has an excellent chart (1:40,000) of Lasqueti Island, with harbor charts of Squitty Bay, Scottie Bay and False Bay. Recommended. Lasqueti Island is often overlooked by pleasure craft as they hurry across the strait between Nanaimo and the Sunshine Coast, or run along the Vancouver Island shore between Nanaimo and Campbell River. Lasqueti Island is beautiful, though. It has a number of good anchorages, and a small resort and grocery store at the village of Lasqueti, in False Bay at the northwest corner.

The south and west shores of Lasqueti Island are indented by a number of bays that invite anchorage. Along the south shore are Boat Cove, Old House Bay, Richardson Cove, and Jenkins Cove, all

Jump! Swimming at Courtenay.

See area map page 119

of which are somewhat open to southerlies, but offer good protection from northerlies or in settled weather. This part of the Lasqueti shoreline is rugged and beautiful. On the southeast end is Squitty Bay—tiny, but with a public float. Several little dogholes for anchoring can be found in Bull Passage. Little Bull Passage, between Jedediah Island and Bull Island, has a number of good anchorages in both ends. Little Bull Passage is passable for most boats. Other anchorages are available in Boho Bay, Tucker Bay, and Scottie Bay. Spring Bay is only partially protected from the north by a group of small islands offshore.

False Bay. Use chart 3536; 3312; 3513. False Bay is the major settlement on Lasqueti Island, with a public float with 118 feet of dock space and a float plane tie-up. The Lasqueti Island Hotel & Resort is at the head of the dock. A passenger-only ferry runs from False Bay to French Creek on Vancouver Island. Anchorage is possible off the public float, but the preferred anchorage is on the north shore of the bay. On warm summer afternoons, strong winds, called Qualicums, can blow through False Bay and make anchoring unpleasant.

The tiny Squitty Bay harbor gets much smaller at low tide. A fascinating place to visit, however.

⑪ **Lasqueti Island Hotel & Resort,** Lasqueti Island, B.C. V0R 2J0, (250)333-8846. Open all year, gasoline and diesel at the fuel dock, store carries ice, groceries, tackle and bait. The hotel has a restaurant and lounge.

⑩ **Squitty Bay.** Use chartbook 3312 (much preferred) or 3512. Squitty Bay is a tiny, narrow and shallow notch at the southeast corner of Lasqueti Island. It would be harrowing to enter Squitty Bay in a roaring southwesterly, but at other times entry should be easy. Rocks border the north side of the entrance; favor the south side. The government dock, 150 feet long, may be largely occupied by local boats. Rafting is permitted. The trees in this area are bent and broken, obviously by strong winds. Tall trees are rare. A walk around on the roads is fascinating.

Bull Passage. Use chartbook 3312 (much preferred) or 3512. Bull Passage and the islands that lie off the south end of Jedediah Island are some of the most rugged and scenic on the coast. **Little Bull Passage**, between high rock cliffs, is narrow and beautiful. Watch for the charted rock on the Jedediah Island side. It hides at high tide. Our notes say, "The east end of Little Bull Passage is absolutely fabulous. So much variety and strength in the rock walls and islands. Worth a side trip just to see the sights."

Jedediah Island. Use chart 3312; 3512. Jedediah Island now is a marine park. We think, however, that it will not be overrun with visitors, because good anchorages are scarce. One of the best anchorages is in the little notch opposite the south end of Paul Island. Stern-ties to shore will be needed. The bay just south of the notch is usable, too. Long Bay goes dry a short distance inside the mouth.

One interesting spot is the steep-sided notch at the southeast end of Jedediah Island. The notch is narrow but protected. The sheer walls surrounding the notch will discourage much on-shore exploration, though.

TEXADA ISLAND

Use chart 3512; 3513; 3536. Texada Island has two main anchorages: Blubber Bay at the northern tip of the island, and Sturt Bay a couple of miles south along the Malaspina Strait (eastern) side. Although it has a ferry landing and public float, **Blubber Bay** is dominated by an enormous quarry, and is not inviting. Anchorage, if needed, is possible, though. **Sturt Bay,** on Malaspina Strait near the north end of Texada Island, has the best anchorage and moorage on Texada Island. The Texada Boating Club has extensive floats, well protected, with visitor moorage welcomed. Pay at the head of the dock. The floats have water, but not much power. Anchorage is available elsewhere in the bay. If Malaspina Strait is kicking up, Sturt Bay could be a delight.

Harwood Point Regional Park, in Gillies Bay, Texada Island. Use chart 3513. Anchor out only and dinghy in to a 40-acre park with grass fields, picnic tables, campsites, pit toilets.

Vananda/Sturt Bay Government Wharf, in Sturt Bay. Use chart 3513. Dock has 98 feet of mooring space. Exposed and not very interesting. Nearby Sturt Bay is preferred.

The Southeast Coast, White Rock to Vancouver

Boundary Bay • Fraser River

Charts

3463	Strait of Georgia, Southern Portion (1:80,000)
3490	Fraser River, Sand Heads to Douglas Island (1:20,000)
3491	Fraser River, North Arm (1:20,000)
3488	Fraser River, Pattullo Bridge to Crescent Island (1:20,000) (new, 1995)
3489	Fraser River, Crescent Island to Harrison Mills (1:20,000) (new, 1995)

Reference only — not for navigation

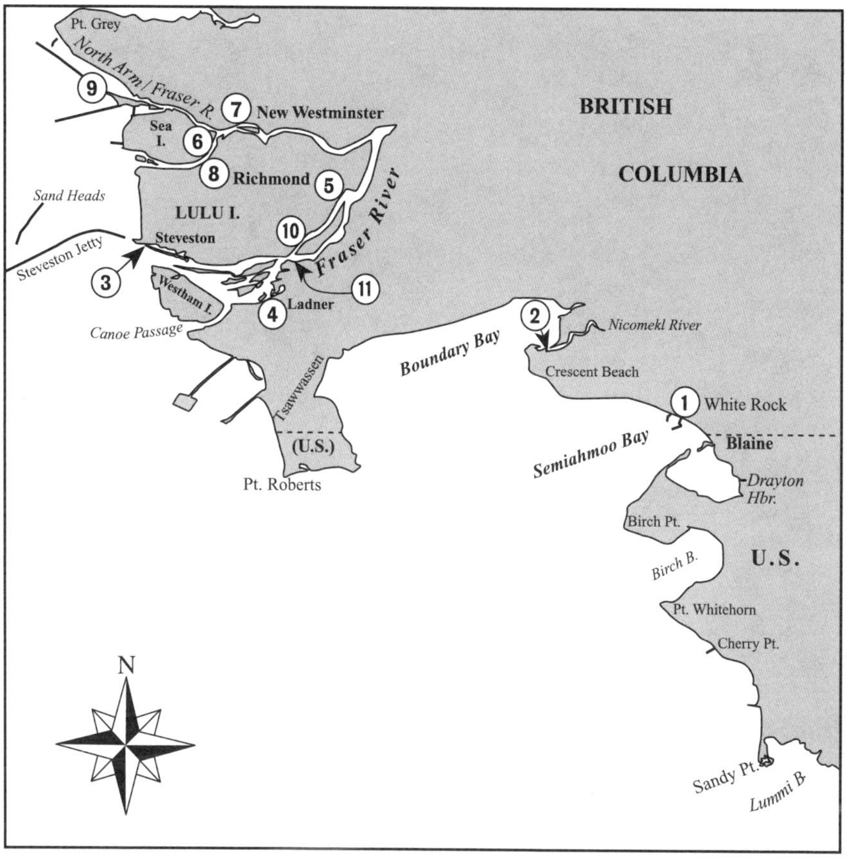

The coastline between Boundary Bay and Vancouver is uninteresting river delta, and the waters often are uncomfortable. Sediment from the Fraser River has created shoal depths for some distance offshore. The prevailing winds tend to blow against the river current in the shallow water, and steep seas can build quickly. It's usually best to stay well off in deeper water, but even there a 20-knot wind can make for a rough ride. It is for good reason that most pleasure craft choose to go north through the Gulf Islands, then pick a patch of good weather to cross the Strait of Georgia to Vancouver or Howe Sound. The shortest distance across the strait, from Gabriola Pass to Howe Sound, is 14 miles. Even slow boats can make the crossing in 2 or 3 hours; faster boats can cross in an hour or less.

① **City of White Rock Pier.** Use chart 18421 (U.S.); chart 3463 (Cdn). White Rock is a Canadian Customs port of entry. Call (888)226-7277. The south side of the eastern float is reserved for transient moorage. The village of White Rock has a number of interesting shops and galleries.

Crescent Beach. Use chart 18421 (U.S.); 3463 (Cdn). North of White Rock, the Nicomekl River empties into Boundary Bay, creating a channel that leads to the village of Crescent Beach. The channel is marked by port and starboard daymarks, and dredged every few years. While Crescent Beach is not visited by many cruising yachts, you'll find there an important luxury motoryacht manufacturing facility, and the Crescent Beach Marina. The marina is located just beyond the Burlington Northern Railway swing bridge that crosses the river to Blackie Spit. Depending on tide, bridge clearance ranges from 9 to 20 feet. The bridge is manned 7 days a week from 0630 until 2230, and will open to 3 whistle blasts. You can call the bridge at (604)538-3233. You can also call the marina at (604)538-9666, and they will contact the bridge tender.

② **Crescent Beach Marina, Ltd.** 12555 Crescent Road, Surrey, B.C. V4A 2V4, (604)538-9666. Open all year, gasoline & diesel at the fuel dock, telephone for customs clearance. Guest moorage is available for boats to 65 feet. Call first. Haulout to 40 feet, 15 amp power, repairs, chandlery, launch ramp.

Harbour Authority of Crescent Beach Wharf. Just 40 feet of dock, with temporary moorage for 2-3 boats. Customs clearance.

Tsawwassen. Use chart 3499; 3463. For members of reciprocal yacht clubs, moorage to swinging moorings is available at the Tsawwassen Yacht Club basin, on the south side of the Tsawwassen ferry dock. A dredged, narrow channel leads to the moorage.

Canoe Passage. Use chart 3463 (1:80,000). Canoe Passage is the southernmost mouth of the of the Fraser River. The seaward entrance is marked by a government buoy, but private dolphins mark its winding path through Roberts Bank. Although mainly used by commercial boats with local knowledge, Canoe Passage can be used by small craft, especially at half-tide or better on a rising

See area map page 123

The Sand Heads light marks the entrance to the South Arm of the Fraser River. Especially in springtime, onshore winds can create large seas.

tide. The swing bridge connecting Westham Island with the mainland is manned 24 hours a day, and opens to 3 whistle blasts. The bridge tender can be contacted on VHF channel 74, or by telephone (604)946-2121. In 1997 the Canadian Hydrographic Service plans to publish a chart for Canoe Passage.

Sand Heads. Use chart 3490 (1:20,000, recommended); 3463. Sand Heads marks the mouth of the South Arm (also called the Main Arm) of the Fraser River. The South Arm is the Fraser's major entry, and is protected on its north side by the Steveston Jetty. The Sand heads Light, located at the end of the jetty, is a major lighthouse, constructed on pilings topped by a wooden house. Currents in the Fraser River can run to 5 knots. depending on the volume of water in the river, which in turn depends on rain and snow melt upstream. Large flood tides will at times slow or reverse the current. *Caution:* An on-shore wind meeting an ebb current, combined with heavy outflow from the river, will create dangerously steep and high seas in the river mouth. Friends who keep their boats on the river tell of their entire boat being airborne in such conditions.

The lower part of the Fraser River is delta country, low and flat. The marshlands are havens for wildlife, and you'll see many eagles. The river itself contains much drift, and is used heavily by fish boats, tugs towing barges or log booms, Coast Guard boats, work boats of all description, and freighters. Water-oriented industrial companies are located along the shores.

Relatively few cruising boats go up the Fraser, in part because no destinations of wide interest are found there, and in part because the entire coast between Point Grey and Point Roberts is uninteresting to view and hostile in any kind of wind. Most of the marinas on the Fraser exist primarily for permanent moorage tenants, with few facilities for visitors.

The pleasure craft dock at Steveston. Best to tie to the inside of the float.

Steveston. Use chart 3490. The first stop on the Fraser River is Steveston, a long, slender harbor on the north side, protected by a sand island (Steveston Island). Although Steveston is primarily a fishing town with moorage and other services for commercial fishermen, it is becoming a tourist destination as well. Pleasure boats may use the moorage when the fishing fleet is out. Steveston has 3 fuel docks. Chandleries and all the other facilities of a small city are ashore. The streets of Steveston are quaint; the local movie industry sometimes films scenes there.

③ **Steveston Harbour Authority Wharf.** Open all year, power and water on docks. Pleasure craft may use outermost dock only. Commercial vessels have priority. Wash from passing traffic makes outside face of dock a little bumpy. We recommend that you find a spot along the inside face.

③ **Steveston Chevron,** (604)277-4712. Fuel dock with gasoline, diesel, stove oil, washrooms. Limited marine supplies available, also bait, ice, snacks.

③ **Steveston Esso Marine Station,** (604)277-5211. Fuel dock with gasoline, diesel, stove oil. Waste oil disposal available. Closed mid-November through mid-February.

③ **Steveston Petro Canada Barge,** (604)277-7744. Open all year, gasoline, diesel, stove oil. Limited marine supplies available, also ice and snacks.

Ladner. Use chart 3490. Ladner is a pretty town and an interesting visit. Leave the main branch of the Fraser River and take Sea Reach and Ladner Reach to the town, which is fronted by float homes. A fish boat moorage is on the port side. Pleasure craft are welcome when the fleet is out. Although Sea Reach and Ladner Reach are shallow, they are passable for most pleasure craft except at extreme low river levels. Beyond Ladner, a low bridge blocks passage for larger boats.

There is moorage behind Gilmour Island on the north shore of the river, used primarily by float homes. The river is lined on both sides by various industries. B.C. ferries are repaired in a basin next to the Deas Tunnel. Several large hotels near the confluence of the south and north arms of the river have mooring floats, mostly in the east end of Annacis Channel. Captain's Cove Marina, the site of another yacht club, is on the Annacis Channel, as are the Bar Port Marina and fuel docks.

⑪ **Captain's Cove Marina,** 6100 Ferry Road, Delta, B.C. V4K 3M9, (604)946-1244. Open all year, guest

See area map page 123

moorage available for boats to 50 feet, best to call ahead. The fuel dock has gasoline, diesel and lubricants. Water is available on the guest dock. You'll find washrooms, showers, laundry, waste oil disposal, pumpout and portapotty dump. Power is 30 amp. They have a cafe, haulout to 30 tons, and a yard for repairs.

④ **Ladner Yacht Club,** (604)946-4056. Depending on what's available, they may take an overnight visitor. Worth a call.

⑩ **Shelter Island Marina Inc.,** 120-6911 Graybar Rd., Richmond, B.C. V6W 1H3, (604)270-6272; fax (604)273-6282. Open all year, limited transient moorage, call ahead first. The marina has 15 & 30 amp power, washrooms, showers, laundry, haulout to 70 tons, and full service chandlery. Also beer and wine, snacks and ice. And a restaurant and pub. Shelter Island is a big, busy facility.

New Westminster. Use chart 3490. New Westminster is located at the confluence of the north and south arms of the Fraser River, and is heavily industrialized along the waterfront.

Contributing Editor Tom Kincaid has run the river past New Westminster to the Pitt River, where he spent the night at the Pitt Meadows Marina. Many friends have continued to the Harrison River, continuing up the Harrison River to Harrison Hot Springs on Harrison Lake. All suggest having a fast boat and a knowledgeable pilot aboard before attempting to run either of these rivers. The Fraser River beyond Richmond is poorly marked, with sand bars that are constantly changing. The river is navigable as far as Hope during high water stages, but mariners should rely on local knowledge before attempting this run.

Note: In 1995 the Canadian Hydrographic Service published two new strip charts of the Fraser River. Chart 3489 covers Patullo Bridge to Crescent Island; Chart 3488 covers Crescent Island to Harrison Mills.

Catherwood Towing, 8069 Coleman St., Mission, B.C. V2V 6R5, (604)462-9221. Monitors VHF channel 69. Fuel dock located on the north side of the river, just under the railroad bridge, in Mission. They have gasoline and diesel. A boat launch is adjacent.

North Arm Fraser River. Use chart 3491 (1:20,000); 3463 (1:80,000). The North Arm of the Fraser River is lined with boat building and repair yards and other businesses that serve the marine community. A jetty runs through Sturgeon Bank along the south side of the North Arm, parallel to the Point Grey shoreline. A dredged basin, known locally as "Coward's Cove" or the "Chicken Hole," is on the north side of the channel, just before the North Arm enters Strait of Georgia. The basin gives good protection to skippers while they assess conditions on the strait.

⑤ **Delta River Inn Marina,** 3500 Cessna Drive, Richmond, B.C. V7B 1C7, (604)278-1241. Open all year, guest facilities are limited, so call ahead. Limited 15 amp power. Haulout to 70 feet (operated by Delta Charters). The marina is part of the Delta Vancouver Airport Hotel. The hotel has several restaurants, a bar, and a pool. They run a bus to the local shopping mall.

⑨ **North Arm Marine,** 7831 Grauer Rd., Sea Island, Richmond, B.C. V7B 1N4, (604)276-2164. Open all year, Petro Canada fuel dock with gasoline, diesel, kerosene, washrooms, ice, bait, and fishing licenses. They also have waste oil disposal.

⑥ **Richmond Chevron,** 7891 Grauer Rd., Richmond, B.C. V7B 1N4, (604)278-2181. Open all year, gasoline, diesel, kerosene, lubricants and waste oil disposal.

⑦ **Bridgepoint Marina,** 8831 River Road, Richmond, B.C. V6X 1Y6, (604)273-8560. Open all year, guest moorage available for boats to 60 feet. The docks have 15 & 30 amp power, washrooms, showers, and laundry. Least depth is 6-7 feet. This is a big marina on south side of the river, with a restaurant and pub nearby.

⑧ **Vancouver Marina,** 8331 River Road, Richmond, B.C. V6X 1Y1, (604)278-9787. Open all year, no guest moorage, gasoline & diesel at the fuel dock. They carry fishing licenses, bait and ice. Repairs and a chandlery are located at the marina. The marina is located on the Middle Arm of the Fraser River.

Keep a sharp watch for deadheads, particularly outside the main commercial channels.

Skyline Marina, 8031 River Road, Richmond, B.C. V6X 1X8, (604) 273-3977. Open all year, guest moorage available, call ahead. The maximum boat length is 50-60 feet, power is 15 amp. The marina has haulout and repair facilities, or do your own work. Restaurants and all services are nearby. Located on the Middle Arm of the Fraser River.

Vancouver and Howe Sound

False Creek • Vancouver Harbour • Indian Arm • Horseshoe Bay
Howe Sound • Gibsons

Charts

3481	Approaches to Vancouver Harbour (1:25,000)
3493	Vancouver Harbour, Western Portion (1:10,000)
3494	Vancouver Harbour, Central Portion (1:10,000) Second Narrows (1:6,000)
3495	Vancouver Harbour, Eastern Portion (1:10,000) Indian Arm (1:6,000)
3526	Howe Sound (1:40,000)
3534	Plans – Howe Sound: Mannion Bay, Snug Cove, Fishermans Cove, Horseshoe Bay, Shoal Channel, Squamish Harbour
3311	SMALL CRAFT CHARTS (strip charts) Sunshine Coast to Desolation Sound
3512	Strait of Georgia, Central Portion (1:80,000)

Point Grey. Use chart 3481; 3463. Point Grey marks the southern entrance to Burrard Inlet. When approaching from the south, it is unwise to cut too close to Point Grey, or you risk going aground on Spanish Bank. Leave the buoys to starboard when entering.

Spanish Bank. Use chart 3481; 3463. Spanish Bank is an extensive drying bank off the north shore of Point Grey. The outer edge of the bank is marked with buoys. The daybeacons you see do *not* mark the outer edge of the bank. They mark a measured nautical mile, and are set on the bank itself. Royal Vancouver Yacht Club has its main clubhouse and sailboat moorage about 3 miles from Point Grey along the south shore of English Bay. A launch ramp is close to the Kitsilano Coast Guard station near the entrance to False Creek.

HOW TO VISIT VANCOUVER

Vancouver, the largest city in British Columbia, is the major deepwater port on the west coast of Canada. It handles cargo from all over Canada and from all maritime nations of the world. Vancouver is probably our favorite city in the Northwest. It is clean and safe, thoroughly cosmopolitan, and its architecture is exciting. Vancouver's parks, museums, hotels, and dining are wonderful. Until 1997, Vancouver was a little difficult to visit by boat. Guest moorage was not easy to find. The opening of the new Coal Harbour Marina, however, makes a stop at Vancouver much more appealing.

Approaching from the south, you could go up the North Arm of the Fraser River to a number of marinas in the Richmond area. Approaching from the north, you could tie up at Bowen Island at Snug Cove. You would take the ferry from Bowen Island to Horseshoe Bay, then board a bus for the trip into Vancouver—or as far south as White Rock if that's where you wanted to go. The Vancouver bus system is excellent and affordable. A friend who lives in Vancouver has nothing but praises for it.

For moorage in Vancouver proper, you will choose either the Vancouver Harbour area or the False Creek area. Each has its advantages, and each is good. Use large scale Chart 3493 (1:10,000) to navigate English Bay, Vancouver Harbour, or False Creek. Once you're settled, Vancouver's bus system makes it possible to get around the entire area with a minimum of delay.

FALSE CREEK

Chart 3493 shows False Creek in excellent detail, and we strongly recommend that you use it. Moorage in False Creek can be a bit of a moving target, and a stop at the Esso fuel dock at the mouth of the creek often yields the latest information. It would be polite to buy something in exchange.

You might find a slip in the Burrard Bridge Civic Marina, directly behind the fuel dock. On the north shore of False Creek, the False Creek Yacht Club usually has guest slips available. If the fishing fleet is out, a good bet for moorage is the large government marina on the south shore. If you want to be close to great shopping and excellent marine supply outlets, try the docks of Cooper Boating Center or Blue Pacific Charters, adjacent to each other on the west side of **Granville Island**. To reach these docks, you will see the prominent Bridge Restaurant on the south side as you enter False Creek. Turn just before the restaurant and work your way down to the docks. On the east side of Granville Island, the Pelican Bay Marina, next to the Granville Island Hotel, has some guest moorage.

Reference only — not for navigation

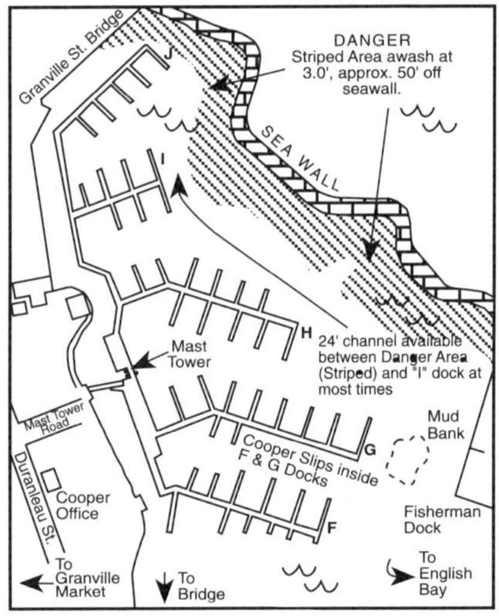

Cooper Boating Center

No anchoring is allowed in False Creek. Until the end of 1994 boats were anchored in the creek, but squatters took it over, and the City decided the only way to get them out was to ban all anchoring. You may find the 5 mooring buoys placed by the Blue Water Cruising Association. They are intended for use by travelers from foreign lands, but if unoccupied might be used for an overnight. Check things out when you arrive.

Granville Island has a lively food market, many eateries, lots of galleries

Reference only — not for navigation

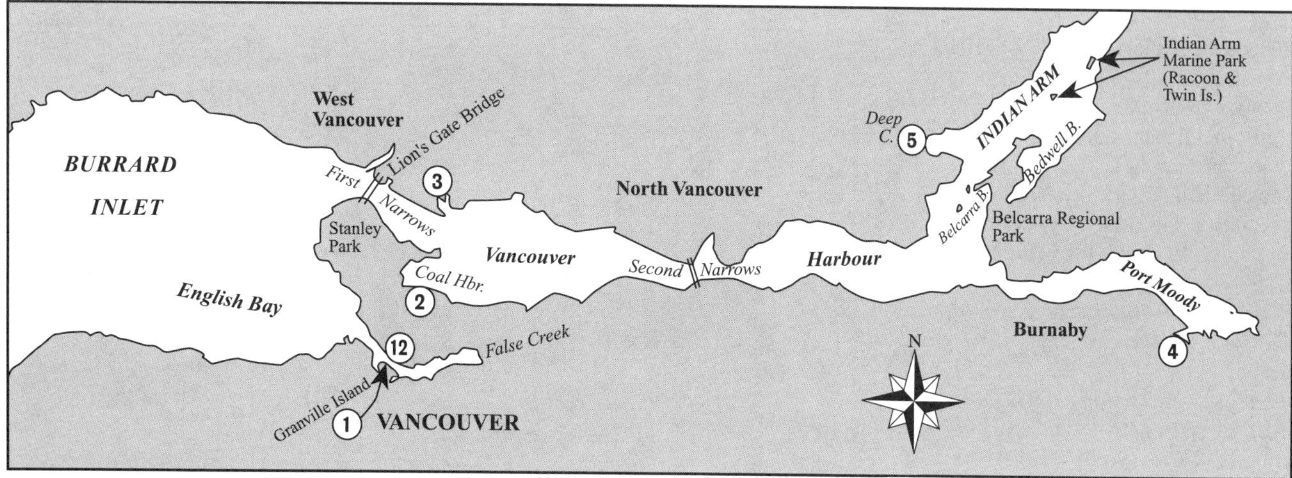

Vancouver Harbour

and shops, and a variety of marine supplies. Granville Island Marine Supply has marine hardware. Both it and The Quarterdeck have charts, books, and clothes. Two other complete marine supply stores—Kitsilano Marine Supply and Steveston Marine and Hardware—are located just off Granville Island a short walk away.

① **Burrard Bridge Civic Marina,** 1655 Whyte Ave., Vancouver, B.C., (604)733-5833. Open all year, guest moorage limited to unoccupied slips when available. This is a permanent moorage marina, and the office is open during normal office hours only.

① **False Creek Esso Marine,** P.O. Box 34125, Station D, Vancouver, B.C. V5J 4M1, (604)733-6731. Open all year. They carry gasoline & diesel, kerosene, heating oil, fishing tackle and bait, ice and snacks. They have an engine oil pumpout for oil changes, and waste oil disposal. Located at the Burrard Bridge Civic Marina, as you enter False Creek.

⑫ **False Creek Yacht Club,** 1661 Granville St., Vancouver, B.C. V6Z 1N3, (604)682-3292. Open all year, located on the north side of False Creek, directly under the Granville St. Bridge. Guest moorage in unoccupied slips. Slips usually are available. Call ahead. Facilities include 15 & 30 amp power, washrooms, showers, laundry, and pumpout. A passenger ferry runs regularly to Granville Island for shopping.

① **False Creek Government Wharf.** Open all year, a large facility located on the south shore of False Creek, west of Granville Island. Fishing vessels have priority, but space is often available in the summer.

① **Blue Pacific Yacht Charters,** 1519 Foreshore Walk, Granville Island, Vancouver, B.C. V6H 3X3, (604)682-2161, (604)682-5312. Open all year, moorage in unoccupied slips as available, haulout, towing, and repairs. Located on the west side of Granville Island.

① **Cooper Boating Center,** 1620 Duranleau St., Granville Island, Vancouver, B.C. V6H 3S4, (604)687-4110; fax (604)687-3267. Open all year, guest moorage in unoccupied slips as available. Located on the west side of Granville Island.

① **Pelican Bay Marina,** 1253 Johnson St., Vancouver, B.C. V6H 3R9, (604)682-7454; fax (604)683-3444. Open all year, adjacent to the Granville Island Hotel on the east end of Granville Island. Limited visitor moorage is available, with power and water.

Vancouver Maritime Museum. It's not possible to see and do everything worthwhile in Vancouver, but if you can, spend a few hours at the Vancouver Maritime Museum. It's located on the south shore of English Bay, at the entrance to False Creek. You should be able to find room to tie off at one of the museum's docks. The vessel *St. Roch,* which explored the Northwest Passage across the top of Canada between the Atlantic and Pacific Oceans, is on display in its own building. Guided tours are offered regularly. If you have kids aboard, they should enjoy it. So will you.

Vancouver Harbour. Vancouver Harbour is entered under the Lions Gate Bridge through **First Narrows,** in the northeast corner of Burrard Inlet. Because of heavy commercial traffic, strong currents and narrow channels, sailing craft must be under power from westward of First Narrows and throughout Vancouver Harbour. In First Narrows, a strong ebb current meeting a fresh northwesterly can create high, steep seas. A friend in a large Cheoy Lee motorsailer suffered damage while exiting First Narrows in such conditions. Current predictions are shown in Tide and Current Tables, Vol. 5. Monitor VHF channel 12 for Vancouver Vessel Traffic information.

Once into Vancouver Harbour, your best bet for moorage is along the southern shoreline in the Coal Harbour area. Be prepared to spend $1-$1.50 per foot per night. The Harbour Ferries docks are the westernmost of the marinas. They are located beside Stanley Park, near the Vancouver Rowing Club docks. Next to the Harbour Ferries docks, the Bayshore West Marina usually has guest slips available. Adjacent to the Bayshore West Marina, the Westin Bayshore Marina often has slips. The Westin Bayshore charges more, but you're a guest of the Bayshore Hotel, with full access to its facilities, even room (boat) service.

The new Coal Harbour Marina, just east of the Bayshore Hotel, makes a visit to Vancouver a real pleasure. It is first-class in every way, and is an excellent base for a few days on the town. The final choice in the Coal Harbour strip is the Barbary Coast Marina, a short distance east of the hotel. Barbary Coast is set up to cater to larger yachts. Its smallest slip is 40 feet.

These marinas are close to downtown

See area map page 130

Vancouver, a pleasant walk or short cab ride away. Wright Mariner Supply, occupying a floating structure in the Coal Harbour Marina, sells a complete range of marine supplies, clothing, charts, and books. Stanley Park is nearby.

Robson Street, with its shops, galleries and wide range of restaurants, is just a few blocks away. If you get up to Robson Street and like Greek food, give Yiannis a try. We have enjoyed excellent suppers there for 15 years. The atmosphere is warm and personal—not a bit slick or packaged. Nick and his wife Maria are the owners. Tell them Bob Hale sent you.

The north shore of Vancouver Harbour is mostly heavy commercial. The Mosquito Creek Marina, roughly across from the Bayshore Hotel, does not solicit visitor moorage, although a boat needing repairs should try to get in. Complete repairs are available from the various shops at Mosquito Creek. Farther east, you can find guest moorage at the Lynnwood Marina on the north shore, just west of Second Narrows. A number of good repair shops are located at the Lynnwood Marina.

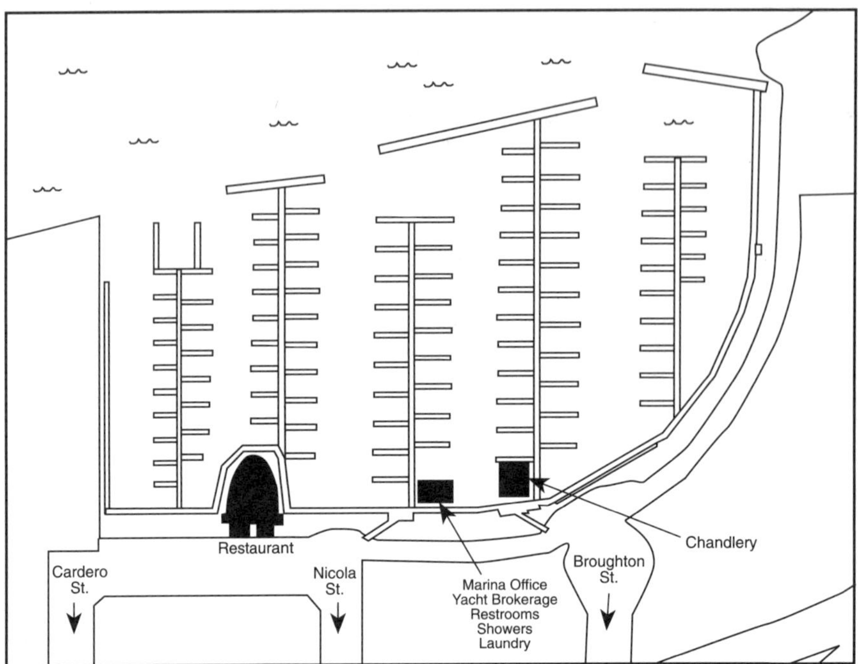

Coal Harbour Marina

② **Barbary Coast Yacht Basin,** 1601 W. Georgia St., Vancouver, B.C. V6G 2W6, (604)669-0088. Guest moorage available, call ahead for reservations. They can take the largest yacht. The smallest slip is 40 feet. Depending on the location, power includes 20, 30 & 50 amp 110-volt; 60 and 100 amp single phase 220-volt; and 100 amp 3-phase 220 volt. They have an adapter for 50 amp single phase 220 volt. They also have ample water capacity. Showers, laundry, and cable television hookup are available.

② **Bayshore West Marina,** 1755 W. Georgia St., Vancouver, B.C. V6G 3A8, (604)689-5331; fax (604)682-8298. This is a large marina, and usually has slips available for visiting boats. The marina has 30 amp power and restrooms.

② **Coal Harbour Chevron,** (604)681-7725. Fuel barge in Coal Harbour open 24 hours a day, all year. They carry gasoline, diesel, kerosene, heating oil, convenience items, rain gear. They do oil changes and have waste oil disposal. Restrooms, showers.

② **Coal Harbour Marina,** 5-466 Cardero St., Vancouver, B.C. V6G 3E7, (604)681-2628; fax (604)681-4666. Monitors VHF channel 68. Open all year, guest moorage available for boats to 170 feet, reservations recommended. They have 30, 50, & 100 amp power, concierge services, TV and telephone hook-ups, vacuum sewage system to each berth, washrooms, showers and laundry. This is a brand-new, first-class marina (scheduled opening April 1997), with wide concrete docks, complete security, a restaurant, marine supply store (Wright Mariner), and easy access to downtown Vancouver. A much-needed and welcome addition to the Vancouver waterfront.

② **Wampler Marine Services Ltd.,** Box 3888, Vancouver, B.C. V6B 3Z3, (604) 681-3841. Monitors VHF channels 12 and 16. Esso fuel barge in Coal Harbour, open 24 hours a day, all year long, with gasoline, diesel, stove oil, outboard mix, washrooms, showers, and waste oil disposal. The convenience store carries snacks, pop, fishing licenses, and some fishing tackle.

② **Harbour Ferries Marina,** No. 1 North, foot of Denman St., Vancouver, B.C. V6G 2W9, (604)687-9558; e-mail: mail@boatcruises.com. Open all year, 15 & 30 amp power, guest moorage limited to unoccupied slips when regular tenants are away. Call for availability.

② **Petro Canada Coal Harbour,** (604)681-6020. Open 24 hours a day all year long, with gasoline, diesel, stove oil, washrooms, and a small convenience store with party ice and snacks.

See area map page 130

② **Westin Bayshore Yacht Charters,** 1601 West Georgia St., Vancouver, B.C. V6G 2V4, (604)691-6936. Monitors VHF channel 68. Open all year, located in Coal Harbour, directly in front of the Westin Bayshore Hotel. Guest moorage available, 30 & limited 50 amp power, washrooms, showers, pumpout. All the services of the Westin Bayshore Hotel are available.

③ **Mosquito Creek Marina,** Foot of Forbes Ave., North Vancouver, B.C. V7L 4J5, (604)987-4113; fax (604)987-6852. The marina docks are showing their age and major replacement is in the plans. For now, the marina does not solicit visiting boats. Several repair facilities are located at Mosquito Creek, however, and a boat needing repair should see what can be arranged.

③ **Lynnwood Marina,** 1681 Columbia St., North Vancouver, B.C. V7J 1A5, (604) 985-1533. Open all year, guest moorage available, but call ahead first. The marina has 15 & 30 amp power, complete repairs including sailboat mast repair, and haulout to 60 tons. Shopping is about a 10-minute walk away.

BURNABY, PORT MOODY, INDIAN ARM

Second Narrows. Use chart 3494. To proceed eastward from Vancouver Harbour to Burnaby, Port Moody, and Indian Arm, you first must go through Second Narrows. On springs, flood currents can reach 6.5 knots and ebb currents 5.5 knots, so these narrows are not to be treated lightly. Wind and current opposing each other can create difficult seas. The best advice is to go through near times of slack, although on small tides the current should present few problems for boats with adequate power. Current predictions are shown in the Tide and Current Tables, Vol. 5. Because of extensive heavy displacement commercial traffic, monitor VHF Channel 12. No sailing is permitted in Second Narrows.

Cates Park. Cates Park is at Roche Point, near the entrance to Indian Arm. The park has a paved launch ramp, a beach, trails, playground, changing room, and picnic shelter. Temporary anchorage only.

Burnaby. Use chart 3494. A park is at Burnaby, at the site of an old sawmill. The park has no public float, but anchorage is good just east of the fishing pier.

Port Moody. Use chart 3495. Port Moody ends in drying flats, but on the south shore a dredged channel through the flats leads to Rocky Point Park. The park has a launch ramp, swimming pool and picnic areas, and is the location of the Port Moody Museum. Further development is underway. The Reed Point Marina, with moorage for about 1,000 boats, has a guest float, fuel, and the usual amenities associated with a large marina.

④ **Reed Point Marina,** 850 Barnet Highway, Port Moody, B.C. V6H 1V6, (604)931-2477, fax (604)931-2132. Open all year, gasoline and diesel, guest moorage available. Facilities include 20 amp power, washrooms, haulout to 25 tons, repairs, chandlery on site. They can handle boats to 70 feet, larger boats with advance notice.

Reference only — not for navigation

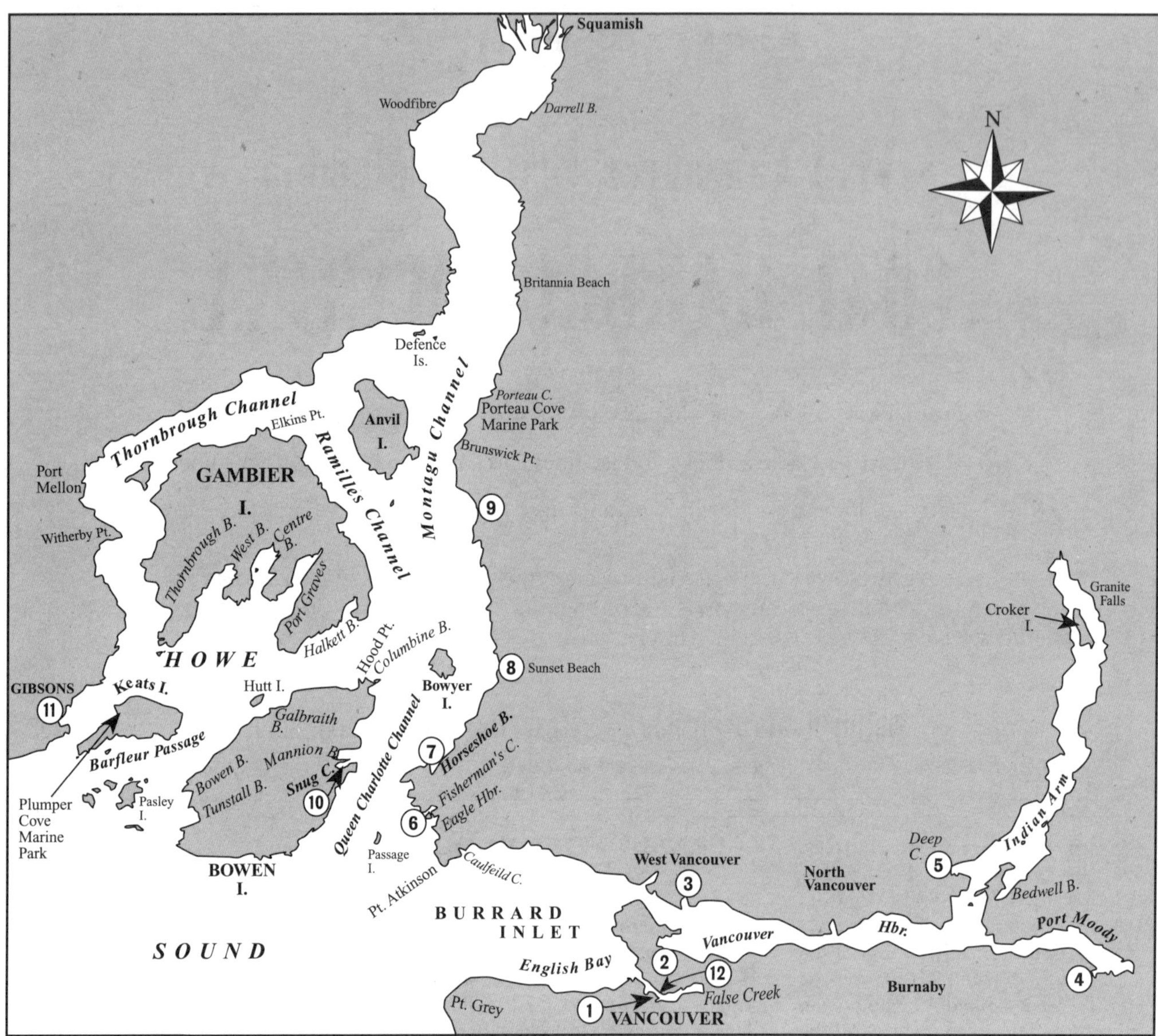

INDIAN ARM

To cruise in beautiful Indian Arm, use chart 3495 or chart 3311, sheet 1. Indian Arm extends 11 miles into mountains that soar to 5000 feet. Indian Arm is largely unpopulated beyond Deep Cove, because Deep Cove is the end of the road from North Vancouver. The waters in Indian Arm generally are calm, but can be ruffled by local downdraft winds off the mountains. Indian Arm is a little secret that Vancouver boaters have. It is remote-feeling, yet close to the city.

Indian Arm Marine Park. In 1996 the Indian Arm Marine Park was expanded from the Twin Islands and Racoon Island to include most of the fjord. Croker Island and Granite Falls are now part of the park.

Belcarra. Belcarra Regional Park is located on the east shore of Indian Arm, near the entrance. The public float is for loading and unloading only. Anchorage is good in Belcarra Bay. The park has 2 lakes, 4 miles of shoreline, and complete facilities. It's a popular stop.

Strathcona. The small Strathcona municipal float is located at the mouth of Indian Arm across from Belcarra, behind White Rock and the Grey Rocks Islands. The float dries at low tide.

Deep Cove. Deep Cove is a city of about 5,000 people. The public float provides access to shopping in the town of Deep Cove, but the float is for loading and unloading only, no overnight moorage. Deep Cove is the location of the Deep Cove Yacht Club. The Seycove Marina at the north end of Deep Cove has moorage, fuel, and other amenities.

Deep Cove Government Wharf. The dock is 145 feet long, and is within walking distance of grocery stores, restaurants, and other facilities.

⑤ **Seycove Marina,** 2890 Panorama Drive, North Vancouver, B.C. V7G 1V6, (604)929-1251. Open all year, gasoline and diesel at the fuel dock, guest moorage to 70 feet. Facilities include washrooms and marine supplies. Deep Cove Village, with restaurants and shopping, is nearby.

Bedwell Bay. Bedwell Bay has the best anchorage in Indian arm. It is sheltered from the summer fair weather winds that blow from the south up Indian Arm.

See area map page 130

Twin Islands and **Racoon Island**. The larger of the Twin Islands has a dinghy float on its east side, and picnic and sanitary facilities ashore. Unfortunately, anchorage offshore is quite deep (between 13 and 24 fathoms). Both the Twin Islands and Racoon Island are used by kayakers and canoeists who pull their craft ashore.

Granite Falls. Granite Falls, the largest of the falls that enter Indian Arm, tumbles off a cliff along the east bank. Anchorage is fair just offshore, and the climb up the cliff is good exercise for cramped muscles. Because of the questionable anchoring bottom, overnight anchoring is not recommended.

Wigwam Inn. The Wigwam Inn, at the head of Indian Arm, is a luxury resort whose rich history goes back to 1906. Today it is a Royal Vancouver Yacht Club outstation. RVYC members only.

POINT ATKINSON TO HORSESHOE BAY

Caulfeild Cove. Use chart 3481; 3526. Caulfeild Cove is a tiny bight, protected from nearly all winds and seas, tucked into the shoreline just east of Point Atkinson. A 52-foot public float lies along the east side of the cove, with 6 feet of depth alongside.

Point Atkinson. Use chart 3481; 3526. Point Atkinson is the north entrance to Burrard Inlet. The waters just off the Point Atkinson can be very rough, so a course well to seaward often is called for.

Eagle Harbour. Use chart 3481; 3526. Eagle Harbour is the site of the Eagle Harbour Yacht Club.

Fishermans Cove. Use chart 3481; 3526. Fishermans Cove, the home of West Vancouver Yacht Club, is filled with the Thunderbird Marina. Be sure to follow the markers into Fishermans Cove. There is a false entrance that could put you in trouble.

⑥ **Thunderbird Marina,** 5776 Marine Drive, West Vancouver, B.C. V7W 2S2, (604)921-7434. Open all year, limited guest moorage (call ahead), 15 amp power, washrooms, showers, waste oil disposal. They have haulout to 50 feet and complete repairs. Our good friend John Zavaglia operates Thunderbird Marine Supplies at the marina, and does an excellent job of it.

⑥ **Fishermans Cove Esso,** 5908 Marine Drive, West Vancouver, B.C. V7W 2S1, (604)921-7333. Fuel dock with gasoline, diesel, stove oil, kerosene, CNG, propane, pre-mix, waste oil system, miscellaneous supplies.

HOWE SOUND

Use charts 3526 and 3534. Howe Sound, located about 12 miles from the city, is the "backyard" for Vancouver area boaters. The sound is largely unpopulated, and creates a wilderness feeling close to home. Considerable drift is floating in Howe Sound, so watch carefully or you may be visiting your propeller repairman. Howe Sound, although beautiful, is stingy with its anchorages.

Horseshoe Bay. Use chart 3534; 3526. Horseshoe Bay is the eastern terminus of the ferries that serve the Gulf Islands, Sunshine Coast, and Vancouver Island. Sewell's Marina, a large, breakwater-protected public marina, is located to the west of the ferry docks. Boaters transiting this area are urged to use caution because of the steady procession of large ferryboats.

⑦ **Sewell's Marina Ltd.,** 6695 Nelson Ave., West Vancouver, B.C. V7W 2B2, (604)921-3474; fax (604)921-7027. Open all year, gasoline and diesel fuel, 15 & 30 amp power, launch ramp. Guest moorage for boats 40-45 feet maximum is available. They carry frozen and live bait. Restaurants, groceries, and a post office are nearby.

⑦ **Horseshoe Bay Government Wharf.** Dock is 210 feet in length, commercial vessels have priority.

⑧ **Sunset Beach Marina Ltd.,** 34 Sunset Beach, West Vancouver, B.C. V7W 2T7, (604)921-7476. Open March 1 to October 15. Gasoline, guest moorage available for boats to 30 feet, haulouts to 26 feet, repairs, launch ramp. They carry marine supplies, tackle and bait.

The Union Steamship Marina at Snug Cove is close to the ferry, modern and attractive.

⑨ **Lions Bay Marine Ltd.,** 60 Lions Bay Ave., Lions Bay, B.C. V0N 2E0, (604) 921-7510. Closed December 15 to January 15. Gasoline and propane available. They have 400 feet of dock space, and haulout to 30 feet with repairs on site. Groceries and a post office are nearby.

Bowen Island. Bowen Island, with a number of good stops, is served by ferry from Horseshoe Bay. You can stay at Snug Cove across from Horseshoe Bay; at Columbine Bay and Smugglers Cove on the northeast corner; Galbraith Bay (public float); Bowen Bay; and Tunstall Bay on the west side.

See area map page 130

Snug Cove. Use chart 3534; 3526. One of the favorite stops in Howe Sound is Snug Cove on Bowen Island. Snug Cove is served by ferry from Horseshoe Bay. A government dock and two marinas are in Snug Cove.

⑩ **Bowen Island Marina,** 19 Cardena Dr. RR 1 A 1, Bowen Island, B.C. V0N 1S0, (604)947-9710; e-mail: norma @nebulus.net. Monitors VHF channel 16, switch to 69. Open all year, guest moorage available, 15 amp power, located on right side as you enter Snug Cove. They carry fishing licenses, tackle, and bait. They also serve homemade ice cream.

⑩ **Snug Cove Government Wharf.** This dock, with 350 feet of space, is next to the ferry landing in Snug Cove, and is exposed to ferry wash.

⑩ **Union Steamship Company Marina,** P.O. Box 250, Bowen Island, B.C. V0N 1G0, (604)947-0707; fax (604)947-0708. Monitors VHF channel 68. Open all year, ample guest moorage, 30 & 50 amp power, washrooms, showers, laundry. This is one of a small number of excellent places to stop for awhile. Rondy Dike, an old friend and an architect by training, along with his wife Dorothy, has restored the Union Steamship Co. landing into a wonderful destination resort. Lots of shops, a good restaurant and pub, boardwalks, a chandlery, a 600-acre park to explore, and more. Take the ferry to Horseshoe Bay and ride the bus to enjoy Vancouver. Reservations recommended.

Mount Gardner Park Public Dock, Galbraith Bay, northwest side of Bowen Island. Has 110 feet of space.

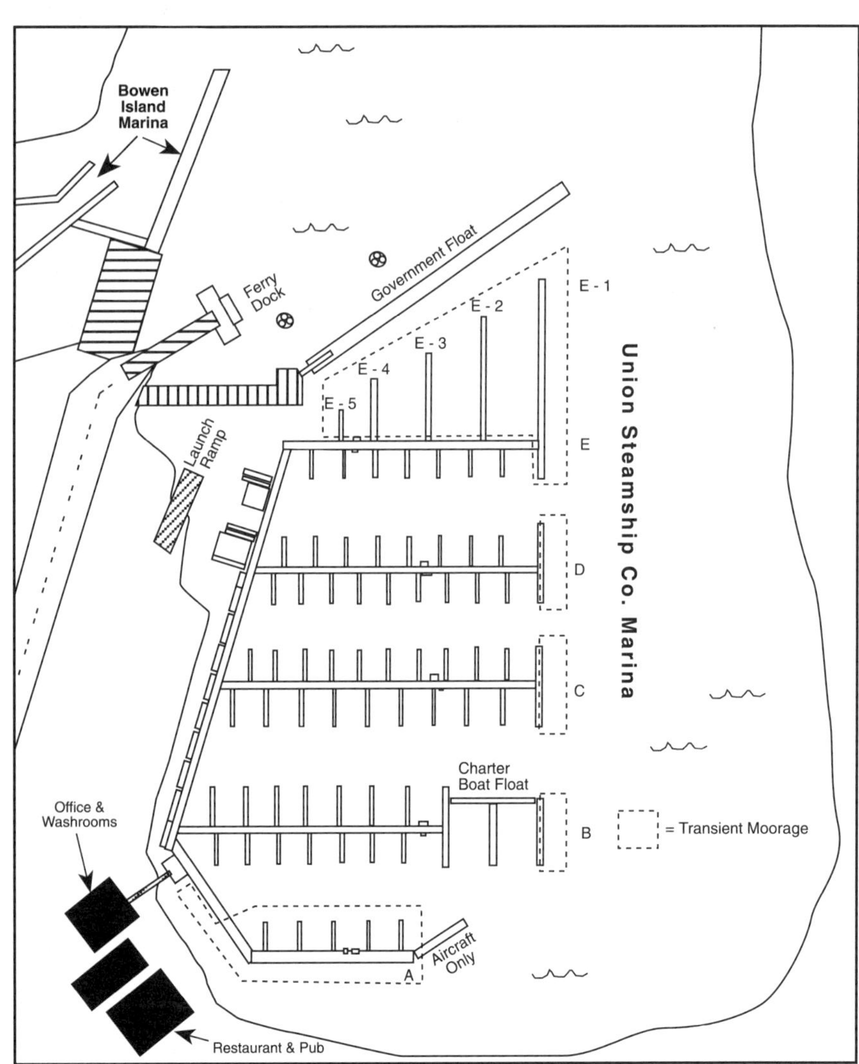

Union Steamship Company Marina

Reference only — not for navigation

Gambier Island. Use chart 3526. Gambier Island has three deep inlets, **West Bay, Centre Bay,** and **Port Graves,** all opening from the south. Port Graves has the most convenient anchoring depths, and has a small public wharf at its head. Beware of a rock that dries at about one fathom. The other two bays are quite deep, with anchorages available in 10-15 fathoms. There are public docks at **Thornbrough Bay. Halkett Bay,** on the southeast corner of Gambier Island, has room for 4 or 5 boats, but will roll a little when the south wind blows. The park ashore has primitive campsites and pit toilets. A dinghy float provides access.

Brigade Bay. Brigade Bay is on the eastern shore of Gambier Island, and is a good possibility. Anne Vipond, reporting in *Pacific Yachting,* suggests that because of deep water fairly close to shore, a stern anchor be set toward the beach with the main anchor to seaward.

Gambier Harbour Government Wharf has 100 feet of dock space.

New Brighton Government Wharf, Thornbrough Bay, has 390 feet of dock space.

Port Graves Government Wharf has 32 feet of dock space.

West Bay Government Wharf has a 164 foot wharf, no floats.

Keats Island. Use chart 3526. Keats Island features **Plumper Cove Marine Park** in a cove formed by two small nearby islands. The park has a dinghy float and several mooring buoys. A rock, marked by a buoy, lies a dozen yards off the dinghy float. There is anchorage for quite a few boats, and 78 acres of park land ashore.

Another marine park is just north of Porteau Cove. Anchorage is possible off Britannia Beach. The city of Squamish is at the head of Howe Sound. Docks at Squamish and Woodfibre serve the industry at those sites.

Porteau Cove Marine Park. Open all year, 4 mooring buoys, toilets. The park has a launch ramp, walk-in campsites, hiking trails and a picnic area. Sunken ships and manmade reefs provide excellent scuba diving. Watch your depths; some of the cove dries at low tide.

Squamish Boat Harbour, open all year, 775 feet of dock space. Located at the north end of Howe Sound, on the west bank of the east arm of the Squamish River.

Gibsons. Use chart 3534; 3526. From seaward, a sandy shoal with a least depth of 5 feet extends between Keats Island and Steep Bluff. Although waves off the Strait of Georgia tend to break on this shoal, if you know your draft and the state of the tide you should have no problems—unless it's really rough, and then you should go around Keats Island.

As you approach the marina complex at Gibsons you will see the fuel dock just ahead. Many people wrongly assume that the fuel dock is connected with the marina. It is not. The marina is just to the west of the fuel dock. Gibsons has two government docks, one with floats, the other a wharf only. The town of Gibsons has a well-stocked grocery store and most other supplies you might need. It's a good place to stretch your legs. The ferry from Horseshoe Bay arrives at Langdale, a couple of miles upsound from Gibsons.

⑪ **Gibsons Marina,** P.O. Box 1520, Gibsons, B.C. V0N 1V0, (604)886-8686. Monitors VHF channel 68. Open all year except Christmas and New Year, guest moorage available, 15 amp power, washrooms, showers, chandlery, laundry, pumpout. This is a nice size marina, friendly folks, close to shopping.

⑪ **Hyak Marine,** P.O. Box 948, Gibsons Harbour, Gibsons, B.C. V0N 1V0, (604)886-9011, fax (604)886-9011. Open all year, gasoline & diesel fuel, propane available, marine supplies, haulout to 60 feet or 100 tons, repairs, towing available.

⑪ **Gibsons Government Wharf,** (604)886-8017. This wharf has a launch ramp, 1300 feet of dock space, 15 amp power, garbage pickup and waste oil disposal. Commercial vessels have priority.

What to Do if You're Boarded by The Coast Guard

Obviously, if you're breaking the law you don't want to be boarded by the Coast Guard. But what if you're perfectly legal and not doing anything wrong and the Coast Guard comes alongside? The quick answer is that if they want to conduct a boarding, they have the full force and authority of their government behind them. Your right to freedom from unreasonable search is overridden by their right to board. So you might as well cooperate.

It is the WAGGONER's understanding that the Coast Guard boards first to look for illegal drugs, then for safety or equipment deficiencies. Therefore, don't have any illegal drugs on board, and make sure your boat complies with the equipment and safety regulations. Next, be cooperative. Be respectful, answer the officer's questions, and show the boarding team anything they ask to see. It's the best way to keep a quick check from becoming a full-blown search.

Have just one spokesperson for your vessel. Usually it's the skipper. Answer each question directly and fully, and then shut up. Don't volunteer information that's not asked for. You don't need junior saying, "What about the Uzi?" when the Uzi is a squirt-gun replica of the real thing. Worse yet if it *is* the real thing.

A boat that's dirty, in obviously poor condition, or being operated recklessly is a much higher candidate for boarding than a boat that's clean, trim, and competently-run.

If the boarding team finds a minor infraction, usually they will explain how to correct the infraction and issue a warning citation. Boarding records are kept in a database. If you're boarded again and the infraction hasn't been corrected, you'll probably get a fine.

Canadian vessels cruising in Washington. The U.S. is very sensitive about things that get into the water. So you will need a DISCHARGE OF OIL PROHIBITED placard, a MARPOL Garbage Regulation placard, and a U.S. legal head. It is possible that the curiosity of the boarding officer could be influenced by the attitude that's displayed. Be friendly, businesslike, and cooperative. Maybe they'll just ask a few questions while alongside and then depart. Maybe not, but then again, maybe.

A wonderful little booklet about boardings has been published, and it is highly recommended. The title is *Boarded! A Guide to Understanding the Coast Guard Boarding,* by Joe Meek. Joe Meek was a Coast Guard boarding officer for 13 years, and his information has the ring of truth. The cost is $6.95. Available at marine stores.

Gower Point to Sechelt Inlet

Welcome Passage • Buccaneer Bay • Smuggler Cove • Secret Cove
Pender Harbour • Egmont • Sechelt Rapids • Sechelt Inlet

Charts

3512	Strait of Georgia, Central Portion (1:80,000)
3514	Jervis Inlet (1:50,000); Malibu and Sechelt Rapids
3535	Plans – Malaspina Strait: Pender Harbour, Secret Cove/Smuggler Cove, Welcome Passage
3311	SMALL CRAFT CHARTS (strip charts) Sunshine Coast to Desolation Sound
3312	SMALL CRAFT CHART (chart book) Jervis Inlet & Desolation Sound

From Howe Sound to Pender Harbour the coast is largely a barren run. The exceptions are Buccaneer Bay, Secret Cove, and Smuggler Cove, and to a lesser extent Halfmoon Bay. When the weather gets up the going can be wet and slow. But with a weather eye, the passages can be easy.

Trail Bay. Use chart 3512. A rock breakwater protects a small Indian moorage at **Selma Park**, on the south shore of Trail Bay. One year we waited out a nasty southwesterly, riding on the hook in this hideout.

Halfmoon Bay. Use chart 3535 (larger scale, preferred) or 3512. A government dock with 170 feet of mooring space is at the head of Halfmoon Bay.

Welcome Passage. Use chart 3535 (larger scale, preferred) or 3512. Welcome Passage separates South Thormanby Island and the Sechelt Peninsula, and is used by boats of all types bound up or down the Sunshine Coast. Currents run to 3 knots at the north end of the pass and 2 knots off Merry Island at the south end. When wind and current oppose each other, the waters can be rough and uncomfortable. Watch for drift. The passage west of Merry Island is deep and easily navigated.

Buccaneer Bay. Use chart 3535; 3512. Buccaneer Bay lies between North Thormanby and South Thormanby Islands, and has a beautiful white sand beach at the south end and west side. The beach is a popular picnic and play area for people in boats of all sizes. Be careful to enter Buccaneer Bay by leaving the Tattenham Ledge Light Buoy Q51 to port. The buoy is well north of South Thormanby Island, but it marks the end of Tattenham Ledge and should be respected. Once in Buccaneer Bay, you can find anchorage behind the Surrey Islands or in Water Bay. Watching your depths, you can also snug up to the shoaling waters off Gill Beach, at the south end of the bay. In a southerly, you'll get some wind but no seas.

Irvines Landing, at the entrance to Pender Harbour, has been a trading post for more than a century. It is the first fuel dock as you enter Pender Harbour.

Smuggler Cove. Use chart 3535 or 3311. Smuggler Cove has a tricky entrance, but opens to a beautiful anchorage area that is protected from all weather. Before entering, first timers should have in hand Chart 3535, or sheet 3 from Chart 3311, Sunshine Coast strip charts. As the charts show, the channel lies very close to the Isle Capri side of the entrance, to avoid rocky shoals extending from the south shore. Inside is **Smuggler Cove Marine Park**, which has no facilities for boaters or campers, but does have trails through the park's 400 acres of woodlands. A favorite diversion is simply paddling the dinghy among all the little islets and coves. Because Smuggler Cove is such a popular area, most boaters will reduce swinging room by taking a stern-tie to rings placed in the rock ashore.

Secret Cove. Use chart 3535 or 3311. Secret Cove has three branches, each with excellent weather protection and easy anchoring depths. Unfortunately, the Secret Cove bottom is notorious for anchor dragging in strong winds, so be sure you are well and safely set if you do anchor.

Enter Secret Cove north of a light on a small rock in the middle of the entrance. Inside are the three arms. The southern arm has a very narrow entrance but adequate depths inside. This arm is surrounded by private docks that restrict the swinging room in the middle. The center arm has the moorage of the Buccaneer Marina. The north arm is occupied almost entirely by the Secret Cove Marina. There is still plenty of room for anchoring, using stern-ties to the shore. A government float is adjacent to Secret Cove Marina. Restaurants and accommodations are ashore at Lord Jim's Lodge.

① **Buccaneer Marina & Resort Ltd.,** Site C2, RR 2, Halfmoon Bay, B.C. V0N 1Y0, (604)885-7888; fax (604)885-7824. Open all year, limited guest moorage, gasoline & diesel fuel. A full service marina with 15 amp power, chandlery, washrooms, tackle and bait, boat rentals, post office, haulout to 40 feet, and repairs. Located in the center arm of Secret Cove. Primarily permanent moorage.

See area map page 140

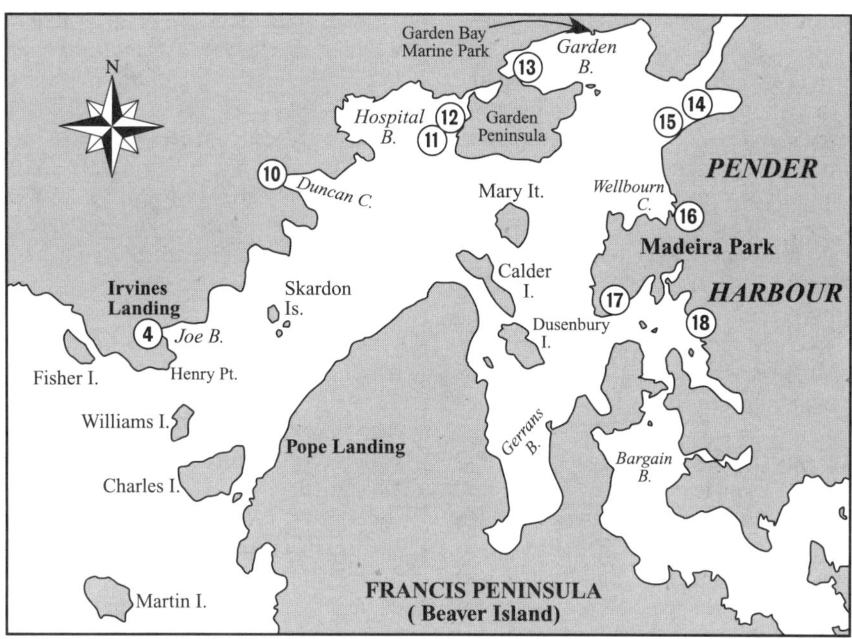

Pender Harbour

Lord Jim's Resort Hotel, Ole's Cove Road, RR 1, Halfmoon Bay, B.C. V0N 1Y0, (604)885-7038; fax (604)7036. Lord Jim's is a popular resort hotel with an excellent dining room, licensed lounge, rooms, and fishing charters. Courtesy pickup from Secret Cove Marina.

Secret Cove Government Wharf, adjacent to the Secret Cove Marina. Dock has 144 feet of moorage, commercial vessels have priority.

② **Secret Cove Marina,** P.O. Box 1118, Sechelt, B.C. V0N 3A0, (604)885-3533; fax (604)885-6037. Closed Canadian Thanksgiving (mid-October) through mid-March. This is a full service marina in the north arm of Secret Cove, with gasoline and diesel fuel, guest moorage, 15 amp and limited 30 amp power, showers, liquor agency, large store with groceries and chandlery, fishing licenses and tackle. Reservations requested.

③ **Silver Sands Resort,** RR1, Halfmoon Bay, B.C. V0N 1Y0, (604)883-2630. Located on Malaspina Strait south of Bargain Bay, behind Harness Island. Guest moorage at 300 feet of dock, 15 & 30 amp power, washrooms, showers, laundry. They have a launch ramp, RV and tent sites, and carry snacks, fishing tackle, and live herring.

Bargain Bay. Although its entrance is actually off the Strait of Georgia, Bargain Bay is properly a part of the complex of bays that make up Pender Harbour. The entrance to Bargain Bay is easy and open until well into the bay, where a drying reef and an underwater rock extend out from the west shore. A shallow, high-water-only channel, spanned by a low bridge, runs between Bargain Bay and Gerrans Bay.

PENDER HARBOUR

Use chart 3535 (recommended) or 3512. Pender Harbour is a natural stopover for boats heading north or south in Georgia Strait. For northbound boats, it's just the right day's run from Nanaimo or Howe Sound. For boats southbound from Desolation Sound, it's a good place to prepare for the long, exposed legs back to Nanaimo or Howe Sound. Boats bound to or from Princess Louisa Inlet often use Pender Harbour both coming and going.

Pender Harbour has a number of good marinas and anchorages, restaurants to enjoy, stores for shopping, and facilities for repair. A look at the chart will show that Pender Harbour is a complex of coves tucked in behind the Francis Peninsula. The entrance is by way of a marked channel north of Williams Island and the Skardon Islands.

The first marina is Irvines Landing, in Joe Bay, just inside Henny Point. Irvines Landing has moorage and fuel, a pub, and a small store ashore.

The second marina on the north shore is in Duncan Bay, where there is a resort. Hospital Bay is the third bay along the north shore, and has several marinas, including a public dock. Hospital Bay once was the site of the St. Mary's Columbia Coast Mission Hospital, built in 1929.

Garden Bay, at the northeast corner of Pender Harbour, has a substantial marina with a restaurant and pub. Seattle Yacht Club and Royal Vancouver Yacht Club have outstations in Garden Bay. The holding ground is good and the protection excellent. Many boats anchor out and dinghy either to the marinas or to Madeira Park. Garden Bay Provincial Park has about 50 feet of frontage on the north shore, but no facilities for boaters.

John Henry's fuel dock and grocery store faces Hospital Bay, on the narrow peninsula that separates Garden Bay and Hospital Bay. John Henry's store is not quite a supermarket, but it is well stocked, carries produce and meats, and has a liquor agency. Across from Garden Bay, the town of Madeira Park has a substantial public wharf. For real provisioning, Madeira Park is where you'll go. A small shopping center is located about a block from the Madeira Park public wharf, and it has whatever supplies or services you're apt to need.

Pender Harbour has several drying and underwater rocks throughout, but most of them are marked. With a detailed chart and a little care, the visitor should have no problems. Just remember to pay attention.

④ **Irvines Landing Marina & Pub,** RR 1, Garden Bay, B.C. V0N 1S0, (604)883-2296; fax (604)883-2080. Open all year, gasoline and diesel fuel at the fuel dock, 15 amp power, washrooms, showers and laundry available. Guest moorage available, pub with good food, beer and wine store, cottages available. This is the first marina to port as you enter Pender Harbour.

⑩ **Duncan Cove Resort,** 4686 Sinclair Bay Rd. RR#1, Garden Bay, B.C. V0N 1S0, (604)883-2424. Open all year, guest moorage available, 15 & 30 amp power, washrooms, showers, laundry. They have 2400 feet of dock space, a small store, cottages, motel units, and RV sites. Located on the north side

See area map page 140

of Pender Harbour, just past Irvines Landing. Judy and Albert Hull are the owners.

Hospital Bay Public Wharf, in Hospital Bay, with 520 feet of dock space.

⑪ **Fisherman's Resort & Marina,** P.O. Box 68, Garden Bay, B.C. V0N 1S0, (604)883-2336. Open all year, guest moorage available along 2300 feet of dock, 15 & 30 amp power, washrooms, showers, laundry. Located in Hospital Bay, adjacent to the John Henry's fuel dock. Wally and Susan Nowik have created a quiet, well-cared-for marina, with beautiful lawns and flower gardens, cottages and RV sites, and good docks.

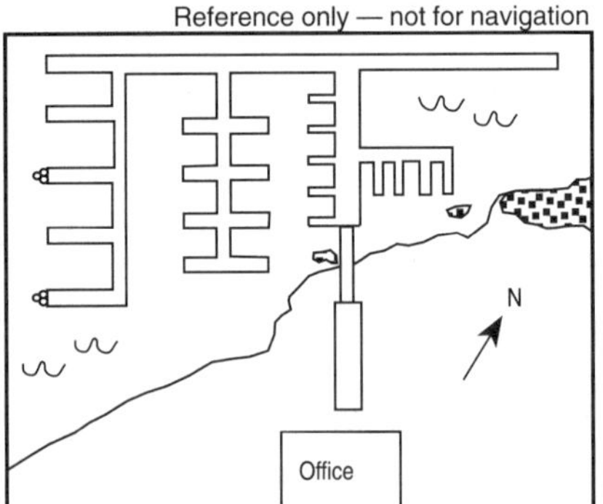

Fisherman's Resort and Marina

⑫ **John Henry's Marinas, Inc.,** P.O. Box 40, Garden Bay, B.C. V0N 1S0, (604)883-2253. Open all year. John Henry's is located in Hospital Bay. It has a fuel dock and a well-stocked store, including fresh produce and meats, charts, liquor agency, and post office. They also have fishing tackle, live bait, ice, and video rentals. Wayne and Lucy Archbold bought John Henry's in 1995.

⑬ **Garden Bay Hotel & Marina,** P.O. Box 90, Garden Bay, B.C. V0N 1S0, (604)883-2674. Open all year, guest moorage available along 1200 feet of dock, 15 & 30 amp power, washrooms available. This is a large, full-service marina with a gift shop, a popular pub, and good dining. Ted Meisinger and Heather Gratland are the owners.

Dining: The Garden Bay Hotel & Marina has been good, and friends say the Sundowner Inn, in the restored St. Mary's Columbia Mission Hospital building, is a good spot.

Gunboat Bay. Gunboat Bay is entered through a very narrow channel with a least depth of 4 feet. An underwater rock lies just to the north of the centerline. Currents in this channel are quite strong except at slack water. The bay opens up into a good anchorage before it peters out into drying flats.

⑭ **Headwater Marine,** P.O. Box 71, Madeira Park, B.C. V0N 2H0, (604)883-2406. Monitors VHF channel 68. Open all year, no guest moorage. Campsites available, washrooms, showers, marine ways for boats to 40 feet.

⑮ **Sunshine Coast Resort Ltd.,** P.O. Box 213, Madeira Park, B.C. V0N 2H0, (604)883-9177. Open all year, 300 feet of guest moorage, 15 & 30 amp power, washrooms, showers, laundry, live bait, boat rentals, accommodations. Located in the small bay to the right as you approach Gunboat Bay, about ½ mile north of Madeira Park shopping. Ralph Linnmann is the manager.

Madeira Park Public Wharf, open all year, 640 feet of moorage space, waste oil disposal, aircraft float, close to shopping. Commercial vessels have priority.

⑯ **Madeira Marina Ltd.,** P.O. Box 189, Madeira Park, B.C. V0N 2H0, (604)883-2266. Open all year. Guest moorage for their RV and motel guests only. Marine supplies available at chandlery.

Gerrans Bay. Anchorage is good in Gerrans Bay.

⑰ **Coho Marina,** P.O. Box 160, Madeira Park, B.C. V0N 2H0, (604)883-2248. Monitors VHF channel 68. Open all year, some guest moorage available, washrooms, showers, tackle, curio shop. Just off Gerrans Bay, look for the sign.

⑱ **Lowes Resort Motel,** P.O. Box 153, Madeira Park, B.C. V0N 2H0, (604)883-2456, fax (604)883-2474. Lowes is in the cove on the east side of Gerrans Bay, and is reached via a narrow entrance. They have showers and laundry, but overnight moorage is usually taken by regulars, who base their season's fishing expeditions from Lowes.

Agamemnon Channel. Agamemnon Channel runs northeastward between Nelson Island and the mainland, and is the shortest route for those heading for Princess Louisa Inlet, Egmont, or the Sechelt Inlet. The only reasonable anchorage is at Green Bay. There is a small private marina at Agamemnon Bay. The ferry to Saltery Bay leaves from Agamemnon Bay.

SECHELT INLET

Egmont. Use chart 3514 or chartbook 3312. Egmont, on the Sechelt Peninsula, is near the entrance to Skookumchuck Narrows and the Sechelt Rapids. The Sechelt Inlet lies beyond the rapids. The Egmont Marina and the Bathgate General Store and Marina both have fuel. The Egmont Marina fronts on Skookumchuck Narrows, and Bathgate lies in Secret Bay, behind a well-marked reef. The government dock is adjacent.

The reef in Secret Bay can confuse a first-time visitor, especially a visitor with limited familiarity with the navigation aids. Remember: *Red, Right, Returning.* When entering, leave the red daymark well off your right hand and you'll have

The Egmont Marina Resort has guest moorage, fuel dock, and pub.

See area map page 140

no problems. If you still aren't sure, just remember to go around the ends, *not between the two beacons.* We've been told that the Skookumchuck Burger at the Backeddy Marine Pub, at the Egmont Marina, is outstanding. Take a friend because the burger is *big.*

(5) **Bathgate General Store & Marina,** 6781 Bathgate Rd., Egmont, B.C. V0N 1N0, (604)883-2222; fax (604)883-2750. Monitors VHF channel 16, switch to 68. Open all year, gasoline and diesel at the fuel dock, some guest moorage available, 15, 20 & 30 amp power, showers, laundry. The store carries fresh vegetables, marine supplies, and has a full liquor agency. Propane is available. They have haulouts to 15 tons, with repairs available. See Doug and Vicki Martin.

(5) **Egmont Government Wharf,** in Secret Bay, 500 feet of dock space. Commercial vessels have priority. The outer end of the eastern float is reserved for float planes.

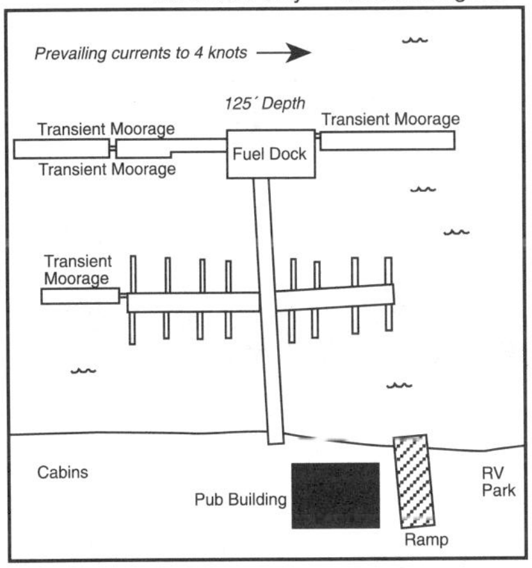

Egmont Marina Resort

(6) **Egmont Marina Resort,** General Delivery, Egmont, B.C. V0N 1N0, (604)883-2298, (800)626-0599; fax (604)883-2298. Monitors VHF channel 68. Open all year, gasoline and diesel fuel available, guest moorage available for boats to 90 feet, 15 & 30 amp power, washrooms, showers, laundry. Located opposite of Sutton Island on the south shore. Watch the current as you approach—someone is usually available to help. The Backeddy Pub serves food. They have a small store with convenience items, ice and kerosene, live bait, kayak rentals, diving air and diving charters. They also have a launch ramp, RV park, cabins, and emergency service to Princess Louisa Inlet. See John & Margaret Mills.

Sechelt Rapids. Use chart 3514 (larger scale, preferred), 3512 or chartbook 3312. The Sechelt Rapids, also known as the Skookumchuck Rapids (skookum means "big" or "strong," and chuck means "body of water"), can be extremely dangerous except at or near slack water. At full flow the rapids are a boiling cauldron, with 8-foot overfalls and 12-16 knot currents. Even an hour before slack, when many other rapids may have calmed down, the Sechelt Rapids can be menacing.

Times of turn and maximum current are shown in the Tide and Current Tables, Vol. 5. On neap tides the maximum current can be as little as 1-2 knots, and quiet. But the next exchange could have a 7.4-knot current and be very dangerous. Check the Tide and Current Tables and plan accordingly.

Lacking prior experience, do not even think about going through without chart 3514, with its 1:20,000 insert of the rapids, or chartbook 3312, with large scale insets not only of the Sechelt Rapids but of Secret Bay also. *Sailing Directions* says the best route through the rapids is west of Boom Islet (choked with kelp, but safe) and west of the Sechelt Islets Light.

We, however, have run a dogleg course without discomfort through the middle of the channel, between the Sechelt Islets and the unnamed islet directly north of the Sechelt Islets. This area is where dangerous whirlpools can develop on ebb flows, so be careful. Give Roland Point a wide berth, especially on a flood. You may meet tugs with tows in the rapids.

Either direction, the Sechelt Rapids are just fine at slack, and if you time it well (easily done) you'll slide through with no problems at all. But when the rapids are running, their roar can be heard for miles. They aren't the place to show off how brave and hairy-chested you are by going through whenever you happen to get there, without referring to the current tables.

Before making your own entrance it can be instructive to walk to the rapids from Egmont, or from a little notch just outside the rapids, to watch the channel in full boil.

See area map page 140

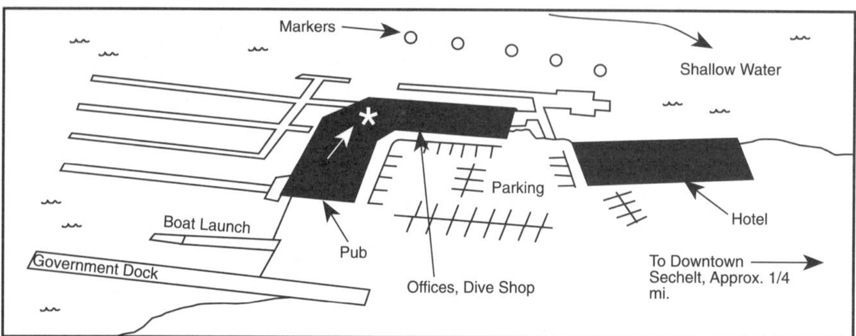

Royal Reach Marina

Reference only — not for navigation

Sechelt Inlet. Use chart 3512 or chartbook 3312. Sechelt Inlet is beautiful, but with no fuel, few anchorages, and limited facilities for pleasure craft, is often passed by—especially with Princess Louisa Inlet at the end of nearby Jervis Inlet. Sechelt Rapids also serve as a gate to keep out all but the determined.

To explore Sechelt Inlet and its arms, use chart 3512 (1:80:000) or chartbook 3312. The area is shown at 1:40,000 in chartbook 3312. Sechelt Inlet extends about 15 miles south of Sechelt Rapids. It ends at Porpoise Bay, the back door to the town of Sechelt, where there is a public float and easy anchorage. Two long arms, Salmon Inlet and Narrows Inlet, run from the eastern side of Sechelt Inlet into the heart of the Earle mountain range. There are a number of small provincial park sites in Sechelt Inlet, most of them best suited to small boats that can be pulled up on the beach.

Inflow winds can blow from south to north in Sechelt Inlet, and up Salmon Inlet and Narrows Inlet. In Sechelt Inlet, the northern parts may be near calm, but the southern part increasingly windy. In Salmon Inlet and Narrows Inlet, the inflow winds will grow stronger as the inlets deepen and narrow. Outflow winds can develop at night, but in the summer they often don't unless a strong southeasterly is blowing out on the strait.

The tidal range does not exceed 10 feet in Sechelt Inlet, and the times of high and low tide are 2-3 hours after Point Atkinson. Two secondary ports, Porpoise Bay and Storm Bay, are shown in Tide and Current Tables, Vol. 5. Current predictions for Tzoonie Narrows, in Narrows Inlet, are shown under Secondary Stations in Tide and Current Tables, Vol. 5.

⑦ **Poise Cove Marina,** RR#1, Plumridge Site, Sechelt, B.C. V0N 3A0, (604)885-2895. Monitors VHF channel 16. Open all year, limited guest moorage, limited 15 amp power, launch ramp. Located on the east side of Sechelt Inlet, about 0.3 mile from Sechelt Village, close to Porpoise Bay Marine Park, which has washrooms and showers. They have emergency towing service available.

⑧ **Royal Reach Marina & Hotel,** 5758 Wharf Rd, Sechelt, B.C. V0N 3A0, (604)885-7844. Open all year, guest moorage available on 1200 feet of dock, 15 amp power, washrooms, showers, laundry. Located at the head of Sechelt Inlet, about 0.25 mile from Sechelt Village. A restaurant and pub, and a dive shop are nearby. Watch your depths at low water.

⑧ **Chamberlain's,** 5987 Sechelt Inlet Road, Sechelt, B.C. V0N 3A0, (604)885-9358. Open all year, limited guest moorage, haulout to 30 feet, emergency tow-

The Government dock and the Bathgate fuel float in Secret Bay (upper photo) are obstructed by a nasty reef. The lower photo shows the reef and its markers.

See area map page 140

ing available. Walking distance to Sechelt Village.

Narrows Inlet. Narrows Inlet is mostly 25 to 30 fathoms deep except at the head, where the Tzoonie River makes a delta. **Tzoonie Narrows**, about a third of the way along, is a spectacular cleft in the high mountains that surround the inlet. Tidal currents run to a maximum of 4 knots through Tzoonie Narrows, but the passage is free of dangers. All but the slowest or lowest powered boats could run them at any time. Arguably the best anchorage in this area is in **Storm Bay,** at the mouth of Narrows Inlet. Storm Bay is very pretty, with a spectacular rock wall on its eastern shore. Anchor behind the little islets at the entrance or near the head of the bay.

Tzoonie Narrows Provincial Park. This park takes in both sides of the narrows, and is good for swimming, fishing, diving, picnicking. It has walk-in campsites. The 1-foot islet shown on the chart is a long, narrow reef, with large extensions under the surface. You can anchor inside the reef, or in the deep bight on the other side of Narrows Inlet.

Salmon Inlet. Salmon Inlet is very deep, although anchorage is possible in **Misery Bay**. A drying shoal almost blocks the inlet at Sechelt Creek, but can be passed safely by staying close to the north shore.

Then the engine died . . . .

When we were leaving the Sechelt Inlet after a visit, we arrived at the Sechelt Rapids an hour and 20 minutes before low water slack, and eased our way down to the Sechelt Islets to see how the rapids looked. *Surprise* has a large and powerful 454 Crusader engine that gives us the luxury of changing our minds, even in strong current. The current was carrying us faster and faster into the rapids when we decided that we were *too early.* I spun the helm and gave the engine full throttle to get back to safety. Even with the 454 wide open and gulping gasoline at 25 to 30 gallons per hour, we made just enough progress against the current to feel comfortable.

Then the engine died. In a second it caught and speeded up, *but then it died again.* Fortunately, by this time we were free of the worst of the current, and I reduced throttle. The engine had acted as if it were starved for fuel when it died. At less than full throttle it seemed to run well. Later testing showed that we had a restriction in our fuel supply, and the fuel lines were replumbed to deliver full flow.

Lesson: Even when you think you have a situation well in hand, the unexpected can occur and threaten to ruin everything. We had been imprudent in getting too close to the rapids just to save a few minutes if we found them passable. A heretofore unknown mechanical problem revealed itself at a most inopportune time, and scared us half to death. Patience, caution, and conservatism are the way to go.

–Robert Hale

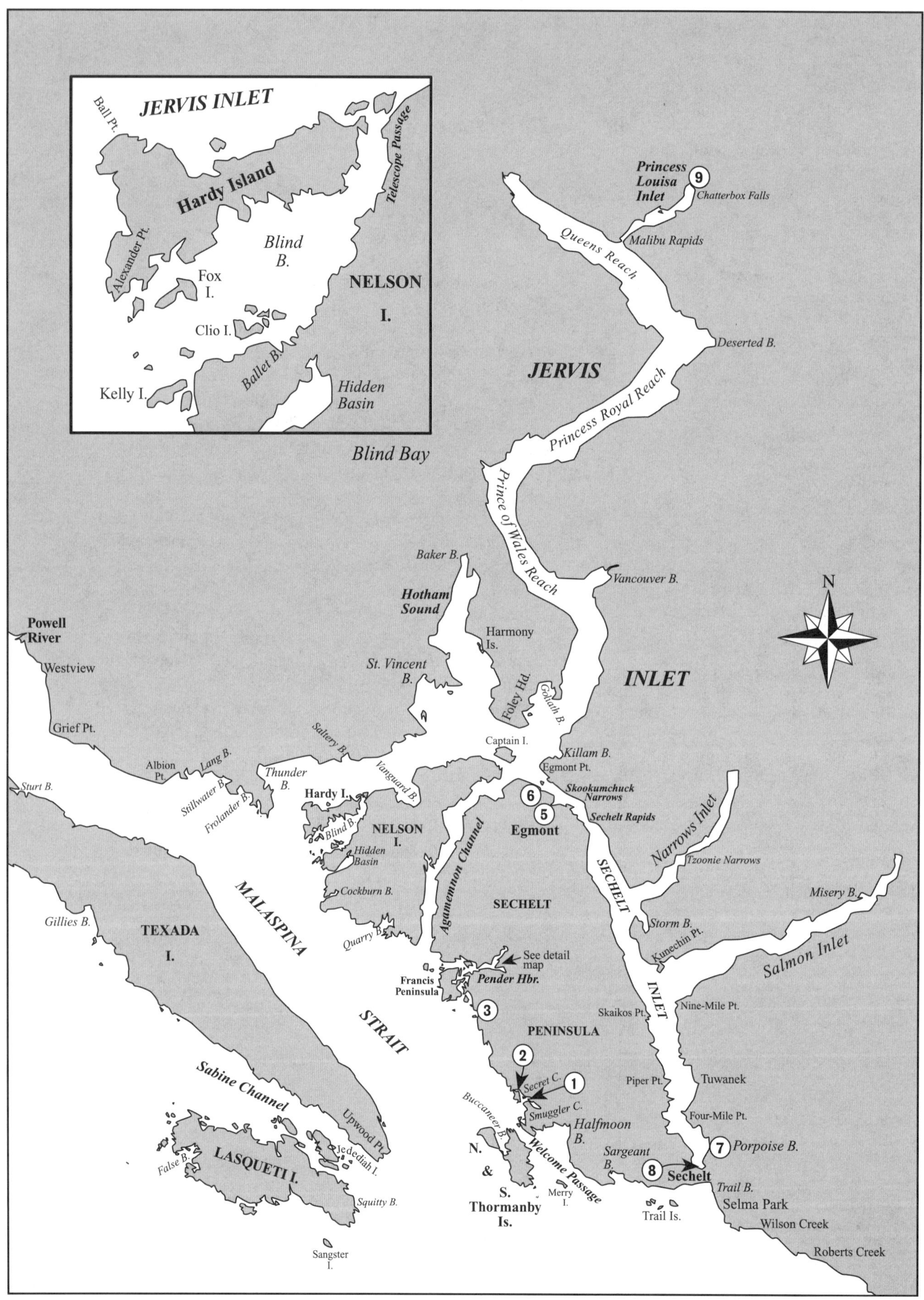
JERVIS INLET
Ball Pt.
Hardy Island
Telescope Passage
Alexander Pt.
Blind B.
Fox I.
NELSON I.
Clio I.
Ballet B.
Kelly I.
Hidden Basin
Blind Bay
Princess Louisa Inlet
9
Chatterbox Falls
Malibu Rapids
Queens Reach
Deserted B.
JERVIS
Princess Royal Reach
Prince of Wales Reach
Baker B.
Vancouver B.
Hotham Sound
Harmony Is.
N
Powell River
Westview
St. Vincent B.
Foley Hd.
Goliath B.
INLET
Grief Pt.
Saltery B.
Captain I.
Killam B.
Albion Pt.
Lang B.
Thunder B.
Vanguard B.
Egmont Pt.
Sturt B.
Stillwater B.
Frolander B.
Hardy I.
6
Skookumchuck Narrows
5
Sechelt Rapids
Blind B.
NELSON I.
Egmont
Narrows Inlet
Hidden Basin
Agamemnon Channel
SECHELT
Tzoonie Narrows
MALASPINA
Cockburn B.
SECHELT
Misery B.
Gillies B.
TEXADA I.
Quarry B.
Storm B.
Kunechin Pt.
See detail map
Salmon Inlet
Francis Peninsula
Pender Hbr.
3
STRAIT
Skaikos Pt.
INLET
Nine-Mile Pt.
PENINSULA
2
Sabine Channel
Secret C.
1
Piper Pt.
Tuwanek
Buccaneer B.
Smuggler C.
Upwood Pt.
Halfmoon B.
Four-Mile Pt.
LASQUETI I.
Jedediah I.
N. & S. Thormanby Is.
Welcome Passage
7
Porpoise B.
False B.
Sargeant B.
8
Sechelt
Trail B.
Squitty B.
Merry I.
Trail Is.
Selma Park
Wilson Creek
Roberts Creek
Sangster I.

Jervis Inlet

Blind Bay • Ballet Bay • Hotham Sound • Jervis Inlet
Princess Louisa Inlet

Charts	
3512	Strait of Georgia, Central Portion (1:80,000)
3514	Jervis Inlet (1:50,000) Malibu Rapids (1:12,000) Sechelt Rapids (1:20,000)
3311	SMALL CRAFT CHARTS (strip charts) Sunshine Coast to Desolation Sound
3312	SMALL CRAFT CHART (chart book) Jervis Inlet & Desolation Sound

Blind Bay. Hardy Island has many cozy little nooks for anchoring. Watch the depths and watch for rocks.

Quarry Bay. Use chart 3512 or chartbook 3312. Quarry Bay faces the Strait of Georgia, and is too deep and exposed to be a destination of first choice. If you must anchor there, you could work your way in among the rocks in the southeast corner of the bay. It would be a good idea to run a stern-tie to keep you from swinging onto a rock. At the north end of Quarry Bay a little cove, surrounded by homes, is well protected and has good anchoring depths. It would be a good hideout if you needed one. Chart 3512 (1:80,000) and chartbook 3312 (1:40,000) show a stream connecting this cove with Quarry Lake. Three rocks in this cove are shown in chartbook 3312.

Cockburn Bay. Use chart 3512. Cockburn Bay is completely plugged by drying rocks, and is accessible only by small craft at or near high water.

Hidden Basin. Use chart book 3312; chart 3512. Hidden Basin is blocked by drying shoals and rocks, and currents run strongly through the restricted entrance. At a scale of 1:40,000, chartbook 3312 shows Hidden Basin better than chart 3512 (1:80,000). Entrance to Hidden Basin should be made—carefully—at high water slack. Secure anchorage is available once inside the entrance.

Blind Bay. Use chart book 3312; chart 3514 or 3512. Blind Bay has numerous anchorages, including one of the most popular in the area, Ballet Bay. Depending on the weather and your mood, the shores of Nelson Island, and especially Hardy Island, should be checked out for good spots to put the hook down. Chart 3512 (1:80,000) shows Blind Bay fairly well, but chart 3514 (1:50,000) is better. Chartbook 3312 (1:40,000) is better yet, as is strip chart 3311 sheet 4, (1:40,000). Nearly all anchorages will require a stern-tie to shore. Use your chart and depth sounder, watch for rocks, and go slowly. Our notes say, "Use your eyes."

The area behind Fox Island has a number of good possibilities. One of them is a narrow, almost landlocked cove indenting Hardy Island.

Near the opposite end of Hardy Island, we anchored one night behind a little thumb of land just where Telescope Passage opens up. The water was deep until close to shore and the bottom looked rocky, but the Bruce anchor bit on the first try. A stern-tie held us in place.

Ballet Bay. Use chart book 3312; charts 3514, 3512. Ballet Bay, on Nelson Island, is the most popular anchorage in Blind Bay. It is well protected, very pretty, and definitely worth a stay. While you can enter Ballet Bay from the north, many rocks obstruct the path and close attention is called for. The easier entry is from the west, between Nelson Island and Clio Island. (Clio Island is marked "Aquaculture" in chartbook 3312.) If you enter from the west, the rock shown at the point before you turn into Ballet Bay is truly there, and farther offshore than you might expect. Give it a wide berth. While many rocks in the area around Ballet Bay are marked with sticks or small floats, don't count on all of them being marked. Not all the rocks are charted, either. Go slowly and pay attention. The center of Ballet Bay is good-holding mud, but the bottom grows rockier toward shore. A trail connects Ballet Bay and Hidden Basin.

Telescope Passage. Use chart book 3312; charts 3514, 3512. Telescope Passage connects Blind Bay with Jervis Inlet, but is partly blocked by underwater rocks that extend from the 70-metre island at the north entrance. Strongly favor the Nelson Island side until past the 70-metre island. Then trend toward the middle of the passage to avoid charted and uncharted rocks along the Nelson Island side. When approaching Telescope Passage from Jervis Inlet, you might be confused (we were) by the presence of a tiny islet almost 100 feet high, just outside the entrance. Check the chart closely: the islet is shown as the smallest oval imaginable, with (26), for 26 metres high, directly beside it.

See area map page 140

JERVIS INLET

Use chart 3514; chartbook 3312. Jervis Inlet extends 46 miles into the British Columbia coast range, and is the route to the fabled Princess Louisa Inlet. Jervis Inlet ranges 1–1.5 miles in width, and often is more than 600 feet deep. Steep-to shores, with mountains rising directly above, make for few good anchorages. Currents in Jervis Inlet are light, and often affected by winds. Watch for drift. Heading up-inlet, Egmont and Bathgate are the last fuel stops.

Once beyond Foley Head and Egmont Point, you'll find only indifferent anchorages at Vancouver Bay, Deserted Bay, and Killam Bay. The 30 miles of Princess Royal Reach, Prince of Wales Reach and Queen's Reach do not have useable anchorages. Unlike most other of the deep fjords that penetrate from the sea, however, Jervis Inlet has a spectacular prize at the end: Princess Louisa Inlet.

Thunder Bay. Use chart book 3312; charts 3514, 3512. Thunder Bay, immediately inside the north entrance to Jervis Inlet, has anchorage along its western shore.

Saltery Bay. Use chart book 3312; charts 3514, 3512. Saltery Bay has a government float, a boat launch, and picnic sites. Saltery Bay is the ferry landing for road travel along the Sunshine Coast.

Saltery Bay Govt. Wharf, adjacent to the ferry landing. Visitor moorage is available on the 435 feet of dock space. Garbage pickup. Commercial vessels have priority.

Saltery Bay Provincial Park. Open all year, anchor only, or moor at the government wharf nearby. The park has a launch ramp, and picnic facilities above the sandy beach. Scuba divers can look for the underwater statue of the mermaid.

St. Vincent Bay. Use chart book 3312; charts 3514, 3512. Much oyster culture activity here, but Sykes Island and Junction Island offer good possibilities.

Hotham Sound. Use chart book 3312; charts 3514, 3512. Hotham Sound is a beautiful, 6-mile-long body of water, surrounded by high, rugged mountains. The sound is sheltered from most strong winds, and in the summertime the water is warm for swimming. Friel Lake Falls tumble 1400 feet down sheer mountainside near the Harmony Islands. Unfortunately, good anchorages in Hotham Sound are few indeed.

Wolferstan *(Cruising Guide to British Columbia Vol. 3, Sunshine Coast)* devotes an entire chapter, with superb aerial photos, to Hotham Sound, but for the most part even his advice comes down to finding little niches along the shoreline where you can get the hook down and run a line to shore. In general, if you find a creek mouth you can find anchoring depths. Baker Bay, at the head of Hotham Sound, can be anchored in.

Spectacular scenery surrounds Hotham Sound. This mountain is on the west side.

Harmony Islands Marine Park. Use chart book 3312; charts 3514, 3512. The Harmony Islands in Hotham Sound are a popular spot. The best anchorage is in Kipling Cove, among the three northernmost islands. The bottom is rocky, so be sure you have the right ground tackle and that it's well set. During high season you'll probably run a stern-tie to shore.

We have heard that flies can be aggressive. Our visit was in late June, and we were troubled by only a few flies in the evening—but they were indeed determined.

Malibu Rapids. Use chart 3512; chart book 3312. Malibu Rapids mark the entrance to Princess Louisa Inlet. The rapids are narrow and dogleg-shaped, and boats at one end cannot see the

Kipling Cove in the Harmony Islands was empty in mid-June, so we had room to swing. In crowded summer months, stern-ties will be needed.

See area map page 140

Dinghy Painters, Groundings, and Other Mistakes I've Made

There is at least one boating lesson each of us has to learn the hard way, and for most of us once is more than enough to drive the lesson home. DON'T BACK OVER THE DINGHY PAINTER!

One careless little slip, followed, usually, by an hour or two of duck diving in frigid waters, and we'll *never* do that again. I have wound various things in our prop since we backed over the painter many years ago, but *never again the dinghy painter.*

Once, for instance, I sucked an old piece of canvas into the prop while leaving Meydenbauer Bay Yacht Club's guest dock. *Nor'westing's* 46-inch prop, turning near the bottom of her 7½-foot draft, sucked up part of Meydenbauer Bay that hadn't been disturbed for years. I got part of it out, and we continued on to Shilshole Bay to help with a LifeSling demonstration. Skin divers were there, and one of them (Kathy Fryer, if I remember rightly) sawed away the remaining canvas.

Going aground is another thing. I became locally famous when I ground to a stop in Enterprise Channel off Victoria, and provided entertainment for hundreds of golfers enjoying a pleasant morning on the links a few yards away.

Unless you're very lucky, you'll have to wait for the tide to float you off, which it probably will, eventually. I've tried a few cover tricks, such as scrubbing the bottom while trying to look like I always careen the boat here, or, as I did one day while aground on the bar off the entrance to Hammersley Inlet, digging a few geoducks.

Although I'm *very* careful not to back over the dinghy painter, there are enough other goofs out there to make conversation around yacht club bars forever—and I've done most of them.

—*Tom Kincaid*

boats at the other end. It is courteous—and wise—to warn other vessels via VHF radio that you are about to enter the rapids, and the direction you are traveling. Most boats use channel 16 because it is the one VHF channel each boat is supposed to monitor. The transmission can be brief: "Securite, Securite. This is the 26-foot motor vessel *Surprise,* entering Malibu Rapids eastbound." With currents running to 9 knots creating large overfalls in the narrow entrance, passage through Malibu Rapids should be taken only at slack water. High water slack occurs about 24 minutes after high water slack at Point Atkinson, and low water slack occurs about 36 minutes after low water slack at Point Atkinson. High water slack is preferred because it widens the available channel slightly. High slack or low, before entering or leaving Malibu Rapids, local knowledge says to wait until the surf created by the overfall subsides entirely.

Princess Louisa Inlet. Use chart 3512; chart book 3312. Princess Louisa Inlet, 4 miles long, is the "holy grail" for cruising people from all over the world. Entered through Malibu Rapids, Princess Louisa Inlet is surrounded by mile-high mountains that drop almost vertically into the deep water (1,000 feet deep) below. Yachtsmen have said entering Princess Louisa Inlet is like entering a great cathedral. The author Earle Stanley Gardner has written of Princess Louisa Inlet, "It is more than beautiful. It is sacred." A 4-knot speed limit is suggested so as not to disturb the quiet.

The Young Life Christian summer camp for teenagers is on the north shore, just inside the entrance. The kids are welcoming and polite. If you tie up at the float they'll show you around. Farther into the inlet, several mooring buoys have been installed behind Macdonald Island. In many places, mooring rings for stern ties have been driven into the shoreside rocks.

At the head of the inlet, at the Princess Louisa Provincial Marine Park, a 895-foot-long dock will hold a large number of boats. If you wish to anchor out, you can anchor directly below Chatterbox Falls, which drops in a series of cascades from the mountains at the head of the inlet. The inlet is deep until quite close to the stream that runs from the falls. Take your boat as close as you dare and put the anchor down in 10 feet of water. Then back down to set the hook. The current will hold your boat facing the falls. It's elegant.

The dock is available at no charge and stays are limited to 72 hours. Since most people don't stay longer than a day or two, there's ample turnover. A boat at anchor need only to wait for the twice-daily departure of boats from the dock. Space then can be found before the next fleet of boats arrives from Malibu Rapids. Water is available, but no electricity.

Bailey and Cummings *(Gunkholing in Desolation Sound and Princess Louisa)* mention that life on this dock is more sociable and polite than often found, and our experience confirms their opinion. For those so inclined, a short walk to the pools near the base of Chatterbox Falls will yield a bracing bath/shower. A shampoo followed by a power rinse from the spray will make you tingle.

Trapper's Cabin is about a two-hour demanding hike from the dock area. The trail is poorly maintained and we have not made the hike. Cummings and Bailey describe it in excellent if unconventional detail in *Gunkholing.* They also give good directions.

⑨ **Princess Louisa Society.** The Princess Louisa Society was formed to buy and preserve the area around Chatterbox Falls for perpetuity. The Society gave the property to BC Parks, but maintains an active role in the care of the facilities. Memberships are affordable and encouraged.

Malaspina Strait to Sarah Point

Grief Point • Westview • Lund • Copeland Islands

Charts	
3512	Strait of Georgia, Central Portion (1:80,000)
3513	Strait of Georgia, Northern Portion (1:80,000)
3538	Desolation Sound and Sutil Channel (1:80,000)

Malaspina Strait. Use chart 3512; 3513; strip chart 3311. Malaspina Strait separates Texada Island from the mainland, and is about 36 miles long. While it looks protected from the open water in the gulf, storms can create high seas in the strait. In settled weather, Malaspina Strait poses no threat.

Grief Point. Use chart 3513; strip chart 3311. Grief Point marks the northern end of Malaspina Strait on the mainland side. When the wind is getting up, the seas off Grief Point can be very rough.

① **Beach Gardens Resort & Marina,** 7074 Westminster Ave., Powell River, B.C. V8A 1C5, (604)485-7734, fax (604)485-2343. Monitors VHF channels 16 & 68. Open all year, gasoline and diesel at the fuel dock, guest moorage available, 15, 20 & 30 amp power, washrooms, showers, laundry. This is an excellent, protected marina, just south of Grief Point, served by a busy and popular resort. Rooms and cottages are available. The indoor pool, sauna, showers, and fitness center are available at nominal charge. They have cold beer and wine, live bait, fishing licenses, and dive air on site. A golf course is nearby. The restaurant is very good; you'll probably need reservations for supper.

Reference only — not for navigation

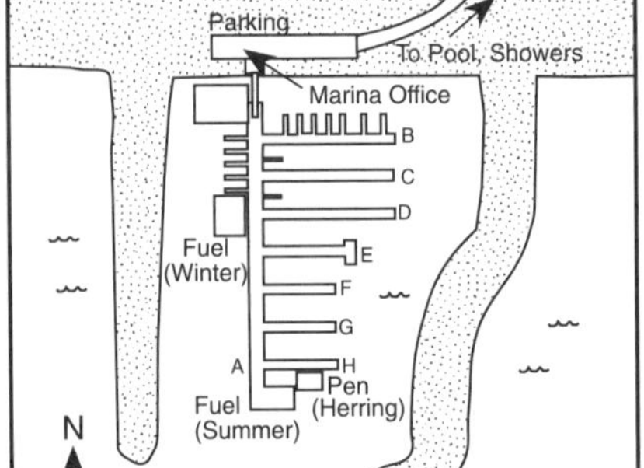

Beach Gardens Resort and Marina

Westview. Use charts3536, 3513; strip chart 3311. The public wharf at Westview is the pleasure boat moorage for the town of Powell River. The marina, protected by a rock breakwater, is divided into north and south sections. The north section is primarily permanent moorage; the south section is reserved for transient boats. Fuel, water and power are available, and nearby stores offer some supplies. Major shopping centers are a taxi ride (or courtesy bus in season) from the marina.

If the marina appears full when you pull in, don't give up hope. The dock manager usually can fit one more boat in—and another, and another. The fuel dock is located at the entrance to the south moorage. Marine and fishing supplies are available at the head of the dock, as are ice, a garbage drop, and waste oil disposal. Eateries, including good pizza, are on the main commercial streets, a short walk away. If you prefer to walk to find groceries, wear your walking shoes and bring your folding cart. The supermarket is located in a shopping center some distance away, up a steep hill, and it's a hike. The liquor store and other shops are in the same shopping center.

The town of Powell River is a couple of miles up the road from Westview. It's a pleasant walk. The small historical museum along the main road is definitely worth a visit.

The Beach Gardens Resort south of Grief Point has protected moorage, fuel dock, hotel facilities.

② **Westview Chevron,** 4391 Marine Ave., Powell River, B.C. V8A 2J9, (604)485-2867. Gasoline, diesel, kerosene and ice, at the entrance to the south section of the marina.

Savary Island. Use chart 3538; 3513; strip chart 3311. Savary Island is a 4-mile-long sandy island that lies approximately east and west, and is served by water taxi from Lund. A small public dock for short stays only is on the north shore. Anchorage is good, sand bottom, within easy dinghy distance of the shore. Savary Island has no real protected harbor. Contributing Editor Tom Kincaid has anchored overnight off the public dock, but by morning the wind had switched to the north, putting him on a lee shore. Nearby **Hernando Island** is

Reference only — not for navigation

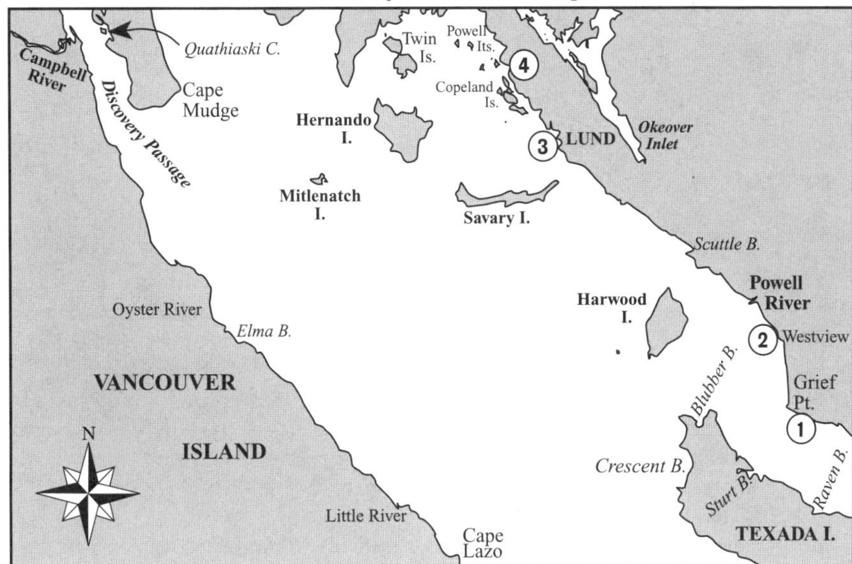

surrounded by rocky shallows, and is seldom visited by cruising boats.

Mitlenatch Island. Use chart 3538; 3513. Mitlenatch Island is located in the middle of the Strait of Georgia, roughly west of Hernando Island. It is a wildlife refuge, with a small, reasonably protected anchorage on its east side. There are trails ashore, and rangers ask people to stay on the trails to avoid disturbing nesting birds.

Lund. Use chart 3538; chartbook 3312; strip chart 3311. The town of Lund is the closest resupply port to the Desolation Sound cruising area. It is also the end of the road along the Sunshine Coast from Vancouver. The public marina at Lund is protected by a floating breakwater, and offers fuel, power and water. Nearby are the Lund Hotel, a store, a pub, and a complete marine supply and repair facility with marine ways. There is also a launch ramp, and a yard where trailers can be stored while their boats are off exploring Desolation Sound.

③ **Lund Harbour Authority Wharf,** open all year, 670 feet of dock space, breakwater-protected, launch ramp, 20 amp power, no garbage or oil disposal. Commercial vessels have priority.

③ **Lund Hotel,** General Delivery, Lund, B.C. V0N 2G0, (604)483-3187. Open all year, gasoline and diesel fuel, propane available, guest moorage on 200-foot dock, limited 15 amp power. This the last resupply point before Desolation Sound, so it can be crowded. The hotel has rooms, a restaurant and a pub. The general store carries groceries, beer and wine, bakery items, ice, some marine supplies, and kerosene. They have a gift shop and post office.

③ **Lund Marine & Diesel Ltd.,** Box 73, Lund, B.C. V0N 2G0, (604)483-9002; fax (604)483-4914. Marine ways for vessels to 75 feet or 80 tons, repairs on Detroit, Caterpillar, Volvo, Perkins engines, and Onan engines and generators. Marine hardware also available.

Copeland Islands. Use chart 3538; strip chart 3311. The Copeland Islands (locally known as the Ragged Islands) are a provincial park, with no facilities specifically for boaters. Anchorage is possible in several little areas among the islands, although most are exposed to wakes of boats passing through Thulin Passage.

④ **Ragged Islands Marine Ltd.,** P.O. Box 22, Lund, B.C. V0N 2G0, (604)483-8184. Open all year. Located on the Malaspina Peninsula, at the north end of the Copeland Islands, a little south of Sarah Point. Primarily a fuel dock with gasoline and diesel, but they do have limited guest moorage along 70 feet of dock space. Washrooms, no power. Clean, friendly, convenient.

Sarah Point. Use chart 3538; chartbook 3312; strip chart 3311. For boats running north through Thulin Passage along the mainland side, Sarah Point, at the tip of the Malaspina Peninsula, is the dramatic entrance to Desolation Sound. The high hills of the Malaspina Peninsula hide the Coast Mountain Range, but on a clear day, once Sarah Point is cleared the mountains come into magnificent view.

Lund is the end of the road, and a popular launch point for trailer boats. Lund has marine supplies, marine railway, hotel, shopping. Moorage is behind a floating breakwater, or along the breakwater itself.

Desolation Sound

Cortes Bay • Squirrel Cove • Von Donop Inlet • Gorge Harbour • Drew Harbour Surge Narrows • Octopus Islands • Hole in the Wall • Discovery Passage • Malaspina Inlet Prideaux Haven • Roscoe Bay • Refuge Cove • Teakerne Arm

Charts

3538	Desolation Sound and Sutil Channel (1:40,000)
3539	Discovery Passage (1:40,000) Seymour Narrows (1:20,000)
3540	Approaches to Campbell River (1:10,000)
3541	Approaches to Toba Inlet (1:40,000)
3542	Bute Inlet (1:40,000)
3537	Okisollo Channel (1:20,000); Whiterock Passage (1:10,000)
3555	Plans – Vicinity of Redonda Islands & Loughborough Inlet
3312	SMALL CRAFT CHART (chart book) Jervis Inlet & Desolation Sound

DESOLATION SOUND

Officially, Desolation Sound is that body of water north of Sarah Point and Mary Point, and south of West Redonda Island. When most people think about cruising these waters, however, they often consider Desolation Sound to include all the area north of Cape Mudge and Sarah Point, and south of Yuculta Rapids.

Since the area is close to the point where the tidal currents change, the water in Desolation Sound is not regularly exchanged with cold ocean water. During the summer, water temperatures of 70 to 80 degrees Fahrenheit are not unusual in some of the bays, making for excellent swimming.

Twin Islands. Use chart 3538; chart book 3312; chart 3513. Twin Islands, located off the southeast side of Cortes Island, are really a single island joined by a drying spit. Anchorage is possible close to the drying spit on either side, but a better anchorage is opposite the islands on Cortes Island.

CORTES ISLAND

① **Cortes Bay.** Use chart 3538; chart book 3312; chart 3513. Cortes Bay is well protected, but in many places the soft mud bottom doesn't hold well. Be sure to use chart 3538 when approaching. Several charted rocks and reefs near the entrance have claimed the inattentive. These include Central Rock, north of Twin Islands; several rocks around Three Islets; and a rock off the headland that lies midway between Mary Point and the entrance to Cortes Bay.

As you approach Cortes Bay, pay close attention to the beacon in the middle of the entrance. This beacon, with its red triangle dayboard, marks the south end of a nasty reef. Leave the beacon to starboard (Red, Right, Returning) as you enter. If you doubt the existence of this reef, one look at low tide will convince you. A government wharf, with room for several boats, is at the head of Cortes Bay. It is usually full during the summer. Rafting is required.

Seattle Yacht Club has an outstation along the south shore of Cortes Bay, at the location of a former marina. Royal Vancouver Yacht Club has a new outstation along the north shore. For anchoring, we have found the best holding bottom to be a strip east of the SYC outstation, a couple hundred yards offshore.

Wolf Bluff Castle: For an unusual and memorable dining experience, ask around to see if Wolf Bluff Castle still serves meals. The owner has built an authentic-appearing 14th-century European castle near Cortes Bay, complete with dungeon and torture chamber, and serves hearty breakfasts and suppers in the rugged dining hall. You'll need to lower your cholesterol levels afterward, but you won't get this kind of experience anywhere else.

"Bill the Baker" Rendall's cabin doesn't look like much, but his baked goods are superb.

Squirrel Cove. Use chart 3555 (recommended); chart book 3312; chart 3538. Squirrel Cove is made up of two bays. In the outer bay, a government float gives access to the Squirrel Cove General Store. The inner bay has better protection. During the summer the inner bay is usually full of anchored boats. A saltwater lagoon is at the head of the inner bay, with a connecting stream that acts like a river. The stream runs into the lagoon at high tide, and out of the lagoon at low tide. Contributing Editor Tom Kincaid's kids used to beat up the dinghy running these "rapids."

A colorful character named Bill Rendall runs a bake shop in a floating (high tide) cabin in the inner bay. We can recommend his bake goods. Allow time to chat with Bill while you're there. At low tide the cabin is beached. The walk from the ship's tender to temptation is through blue mud, and rocks covered with barnacles and oysters. Wear shoes or boots with sturdy soles.

② **Squirrel Cove Government Wharf.** Guest moorage available along 200 feet of dock. Close to the Squirrel Cove store.

Reference only — not for navigation

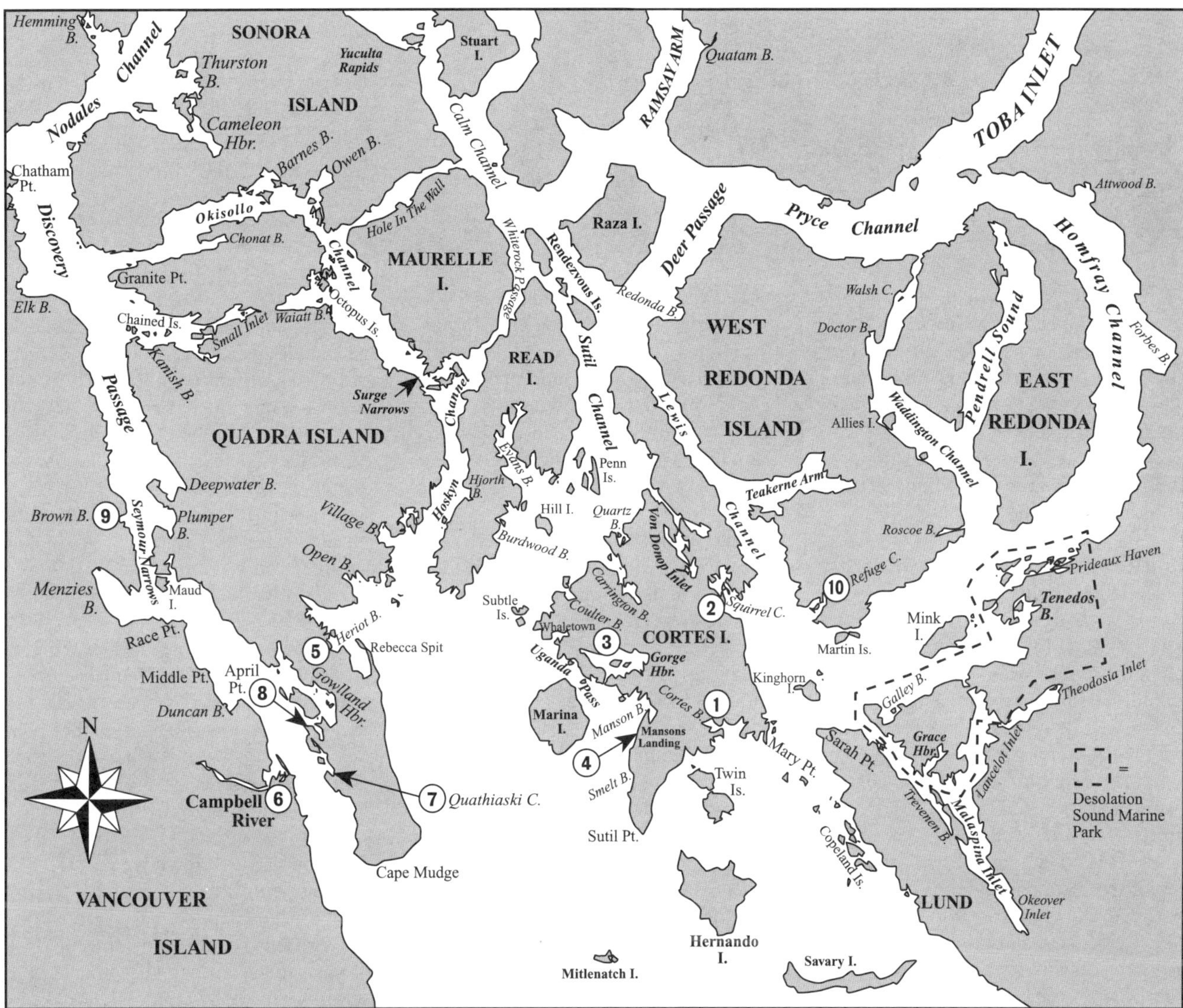

② **Squirrel Cove General Store,** Box 1, Squirrel Cove, B.C. V0P 1K0, (604)935-6327. Open all year, washrooms, showers, laundry. Gasoline is available, but it is upland; no fuel dock. Propane is available. This is a complete provisioning stop, with groceries, charts, books and videos, marine hardware, liquor and a post office. The lower level of the store is devoted to hardware, just about anything a person might need.

Von Donop Inlet. Use chart 3538; chart book 3312. Von Donop Inlet, on the northwest corner of Cortes Island, is entered through a narrow, 2-mile-long channel through the trees. In the narrowest part of the channel, about halfway in, you'll find a rock, often covered by kelp. When entering, we have found it better to keep that rock to port, even if tree branches try to brush the starboard side of the boat or rigging. Once inside, you'll find several coves that provide perfectly protected anchorage. The largest of these coves takes in the entire head of the inlet and has room for many boats. The bottom in this area is sticky mud. It is ideal for holding, but requires extra cleaning time when the anchor is brought aboard. A trail leads from the head of Von Donop Inlet to Squirrel Cove.

Von Donop/Háthayim Provincial Marine Park is a 3155 acre park, established in December, 1993. The park includes Von Donop Inlet, Robertson Lake, and Wiley Lake.

Quartz Bay. Use chart 3538; chart book 3312. Quartz Bay is unusually pretty, with good holding bottom. The eastern cove of the bay has several homes and two private docks along the shoreline. Near the head, you can anchor in 5-7 fathoms with swinging room, but you're in their front yards. The western cove has some aquaculture, one cabin on the shore, and anchoring depths near the south and west shores. You may have to run a stern-tie to shore. Just as you enter Quartz Bay you'll find a little nook on your starboard side. It is exposed to north winds, but it's a nice spot.

Carrington Bay. Use chart 3538; chart book 3312. Carrington Bay is very pretty, and well protected except from the north. The bottom is reported to be rocky, so be sure your anchor is properly set before turning in for the night. Carrington Lagoon, at the head of the bay, is interesting to explore. Drag the dinghy across the logs that choke the entrance to the lagoon. On a recent visit, a

See area map page 147

The Gorge Harbour Marina Resort has ample dock space, fuel, restaurant, store and large picnic grounds upland.

family that just had made the exploration described the lagoon as "untouched." A suggested anchorage is to the right, near the entrance to the lagoon, with a stern-tie to shore. We have seen other boats anchored in the little bight a short distance to the left of the lagoon entrance, and behind the tiny island just off the eastern shore of the bay.

Coulter Bay. Use chart 3538; chart book 3312. Coulter Bay is quite pretty, but as the chart indicates, most of the bay is too shallow for anchoring. You could anchor in the tiny nook behind Coulter Island, beside a little unnamed islet to the west. A couple of cabins are nearby, but they are screened from view and you won't feel as if you're in their kitchens.

Subtle Islands. Use chart 3538; chart book 3312. The two Subtle Islands are separated by a drying shoal. There is good anchorage off this shoal on the east side, particularly in settled weather. The little bay on the north side is very deep except at the head. It has a lovely (and exposed) view to the north. The islands are privately owned, and marked with "stay off" and "keep away" signs.

Hill Island. Hill Island is privately owned. According to *Sailing Directions,* a private lodge with a floating breakwater is located at Totem Bay. The island is not open to the public.

Whaletown. Use chart 3538; chart book 3312. Whaletown is the terminus of the ferry between Cortes Island and Quadra Island. A small public float, with garbage drop, is alongside the ferry dock. A store is at the dock. If you anchor north of the ferry dock watch for several marked and unmarked rocks, normally covered by kelp.

Uganda Pass. Use chart 3538; chart book 3312. Uganda Pass separates Cortes Island from Marina Island. The pass is narrow and winding, but well marked and easy to navigate. Red, Right, Returning assumes that you are returning from the south. Shark Spit is long and low, with superb sand. Judging from the people we have seen in the water, swimming is good. You can find anchorage south of the pass on either the Cortes Island or Marina Island side.

Gorge Harbour. Use chart 3538; chart book 3312. Gorge Harbour is a large bay with many good spots to put the hook down. The entry is through a narrow cleft in the rock cliff. Wolferstan, in his cruising guide to Desolation Sound, tells of Indian paintings on the rock wall to port as you enter. Current runs through the entrance. At maximum flow a slow boat proceeding against the current could have a difficult time. Inside there is good, protected anchorage in many parts of the bay. The Gorge Harbour Marina Resort, on the northwest shore, has many amenities, including a restaurant. Friends tell us the restaurant is quite good. Another marina used to be on the northeast shore of Gorge Harbour, but that is now private property. Chart 3538 shows a number of rocks behind islets along the north shore. Recently, a chartered 45-foot trawler, running at six knots, reportedly found one of those rocks, holing the hull and almost sinking. Caution advised.

Gorge Harbour Government Dock, located a short distance east of the Gorge Harbour Marina, 65 feet of dock, commercial vessels have priority.

③ Gorge Harbour Marina & Resort, P.O. Box 89, Whaletown, B.C. V0P 1Z0, (250)935-6433; fax (250)935-6402. Monitors VHF channel 73. Open all year, gasoline and diesel at the fuel dock, guest moorage available along 1800 feet of dock. Facilities include 15 & 30 amp power, washrooms, showers, laundry, well-stocked store with fresh vegetables, meats, dairy products, ice, video rentals, propane. The resort has an RV park, a campground, lodge accommodations, restaurant (open May-Sept.), float plane service, and a launch ramp. Glen and Verlie Carleton are the owners.

④ Mansons Landing. Use chart 3538; chart book 3312. The historic store at Mansons Landing has been closed, and the building moved. The 177-foot public dock is still there. Anchorage is good north of the public dock. The entire area is exposed to the south.

Mansons Landing Marine Park, 117 acres, open all year. The park has no dock of its own, but can be reached from the Mansons Landing Government Dock or you can anchor out. Hague Lake, with warm water and swimming beaches safe for small children, is about a 10-minute walk from the government dock.

Smelt Bay Provincial Park, 1 mile north of Sutil Point, on the west side of the peninsula. Good temporary anchor-

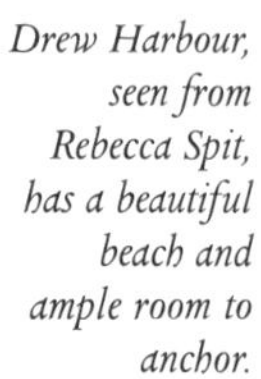

Drew Harbour, seen from Rebecca Spit, has a beautiful beach and ample room to anchor.

See area map page 147

age is available close to shore. The park has 23 campsites, picnic tables, and a white sand beach.

READ ISLAND, EAST SIDE

The east side of Read Island is deeply indented from the south by Evans Bay, where several little notches are worth exploring as anchorages. Most have drying flats at their heads. Bird Cove is probably the best protected, although Contributing Editor Tom Kincaid has spent a quiet night behind the little islets in the bay just to the north of Bird Cove. A small public float is near the entrance to Evans Bay, where there is a store and post office.

Burdwood Bay. Use chart 3538; chart book 3312. Burdwood Bay has a number of possible anchorages, particularly on the lee side of the little islands that extend from the south side of the bay, and in a notch in the north end. Burdwood Bay is not particularly pretty, but could be a good hideout in a storm.

HOSKYN CHANNEL

Hoskyn Channel runs between Read Island and Quadra Island, and connects at the north with Whiterock Passage and Surge Narrows. Although they are just south of Hoskyn Channel, we include Drew Harbour and Heriot Bay in this section.

Drew Harbour/Rebecca Spit Marine Park. Use chart 3538 or 3539; chart book 3312. Drew Harbour is large and well-protected, especially behind Rebecca Spit, where you'll find ample anchoring room in 4-6 fathom depths. Rebecca Spit Marine Park is very popular. The Drew Harbour side of Rebecca Spit has a lovely sand beach, and the exposed Sutil Channel side has a beach of remarkable small round boulders. Bill Wolferstan's cruising guide to Desolation Sound contains an excellent section that describes silvered tree snags on the spit, the result of subsidence during a 1946 earthquake. It also describes the mounded fortifications on the spit, thought to be defenses built 200-400 years ago by the local Salish Indians against Kwakiutl Indian attacks.

Heriot Bay. Use chart 3538 or 3539; chart book 3312. Heriot Bay is the location of the ferry to Cortes Island, also of a government dock, a grocery store, and the Heriot Bay Inn. During the summer high season the government dock usually is full and rafted several deep. The Heriot Bay Inn Marina lies between the ferry dock and the government dock. Its restaurant has an excellent reputation.

⑤ **Heriot Bay Government Wharf,** open all year, 670 feet of dock space, garbage disposal, telephone, launch ramp. Watch for ferry wash on the outer face.

⑤ **Heriot Bay Inn & Marina,** P.O. Box 100, Heriot Bay, B.C. V0P 1H0, (250) 285-3322; fax (250)285-2708. Monitors VHF channel 73. Open all year, gasoline, diesel, propane, ice. Guest moorage available on 1800 feet of dock, 30 & 50 amp power, washrooms, showers, laundry. Reservations recommended June through August. This is a popular destination. They have a hotel and cottages, restaurant and pub, and offer sea kayaking lessons and rentals. The store across the street has groceries, post office, and a liquor store.

Hjorth Bay. Use chart 3538 or 3539; chart book 3312. Hjorth Bay, on Hoskyn Channel along the west side of Read Island, is a good anchorage except in a strong southerly.

Surge Narrows Government Wharf, located at the much reduced community of Surge Narrows, just north of Surge Point on Read Island, across Hoskyn Channel from Beazley Passage. The dock has 60 feet of moorage. Use chart 3539.

Whiterock Passage. Use chart 3537; chart book 3312; chart 3539. The restricted, south portion of Whiterock Passage is navigable by most boats. This narrow dredged channel has a least depth of 5 feet at zero tide, with drying shoals on both sides of the channel. Use the large-scale inset (1:10,000) on Chart 3537. The inset shows the locations of two ranges that will keep you on course. Going either direction, one-half of your passage will require a crew with sharp eyes to sight astern to line up the range. While the current in Whiterock Passage does not exceed 2 knots, you must watch your heading to be sure it doesn't push you out of the channel onto the flats. Running Whiterock Passage at half tide is a good idea—it exposes the shoals on both sides but gives you a little extra depth.

A solitary cruiser enjoys a misty morning in the Octopus Islands.

SURGE NARROWS/ OKISOLLO CHANNEL

Surge Narrows and Beazley Pass. Use chart 3537; chart book 3312; chart 3539. Surge Narrows should be run at or near slack water. Spring floods set eastward to 12 knots, and ebbs set west to 10 knots. Current predictions are shown under Surge Narrows in the Canadian Tide and Current Tables, Vol. 6.

Although Beazley Pass, between Peck Island and Sturt Island, has the strongest currents in the Surge Narrows area, it is the preferred route between Hoskyn Channel and Okisollo Channel. Especially on an ebb current in Beazley Pass, watch for Tusko Rock, which dries 5 feet, on the east side of the pass at the north end.

According to *Sailing Directions,* the time of slack at Surge Narrows varies between 5 and 11 minutes. We have run Beazley Pass near slack and had no problems. *Sailing Directions* says that during flood streams, a wall of water 4 feet high

See area map page 147

Reference only — not for navigation

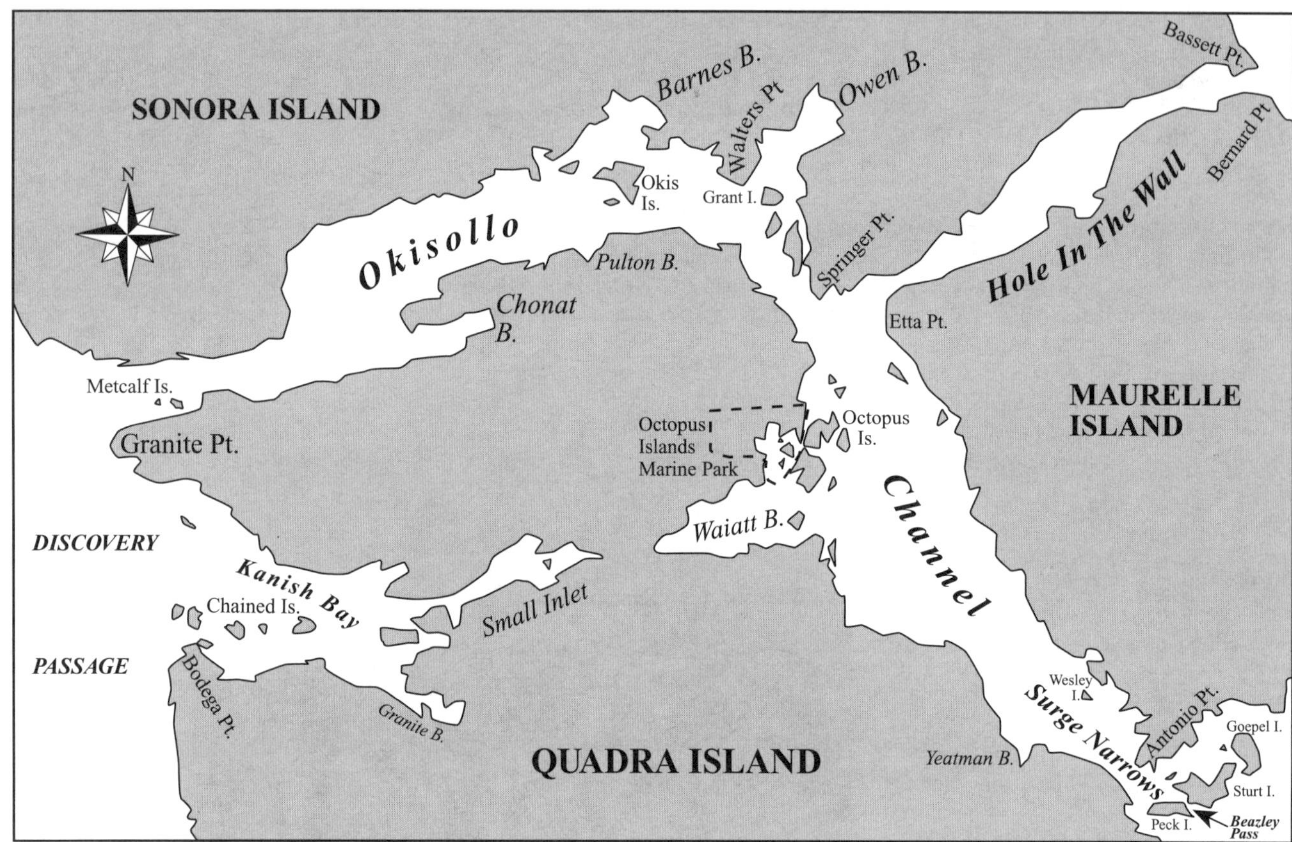

Okisollo Channel

will appear, but an article by Bill Kelly in a recent issue of *Pacific Yachting* quotes a researcher as saying the 4-foot wall of water does not exist. Either way, don't take chances, and use large-scale Chart 3537 (1:20,000). According to Contributing Editor Tom Kincaid, the passage north of the Settler's Group is useable, but notorious for rocks. Local knowledge is required.

Okisollo Channel. Use chart 3537; chart book 3312; chart 3539. Okisollo Channel runs along the west and north sides of Quadra Island, from Surge Narrows to Discovery Passage. Use small scale Chart 3539 (1:40,000) or large-scale Chart 3537 (1:20,000). In the lower part of the channel, the only dangers are Cyrus Rocks on the west side, and Barnsley Shoal, an isolated reef, on the east side. Hole in the Wall, which enters Okisollo Channel about mid-way, must be negotiated at or near slack. In the upper part of Okisollo Channel, the Upper Rapids and Lower Rapids are dangerous, and must be run at or near slack. Slack occurs 50 to 55 minutes before slack at Seymour Narrows.

Waiatt Bay. Use chart 3537; chart book 3312; chart 3539. Waiatt Bay is broad and protected, with convenient anchoring depths behind the Octopus Islands. The bay's entrance is choked with islets and rocks. *Sailing Directions* (written for large vessels) warns against entering. With the aid of large-scale Chart 3537 (1:20,000), however, a small boat can pick its way in along the south shore, or in the middle of the islets, or along the north shore. The chart shows the possibilities. A trail connects the head of Waiatt Bay with Small Inlet. Along the trail you'll come to an ice cold, crystal clear pool.

Octopus Islands Marine Park. Use chart 3537; chart book 3312; chart 3539. This is a beautiful and popular anchorage and exploration area, wonderfully protected. While you can enter from Waiatt Bay, the usual entry is by a narrow channel from the north. Anchor in any of several coves and run a stern-tie to shore.

A rock, clearly shown on chart 3537, obstructs part of the entrance to the first cove on the right, at the end of the channel as you enter from the north. This rock is easily seen as a white smear under the water. You'll be going slowly anyway; watch for it and you'll have no trouble.

Important: Despite the tidal rise and fall, the waters inside the Octopus Islands do not exchange well and are easily polluted. A letter in *Pacific Yachting* complained pointedly that by summer's end a lace-like fringe of toilet tissue could be found along the water's edge. It is our conviction that pollution is not an absolute, but a matter of degree. In the case of the Octopus Islands and other, similar waters, the degree of pollution can easily rise to unacceptable levels. The public response will be increased regulation or restriction. Both are unnecessary if we cruising boaters use courtesy and common sense. Proper management of solid waste (holding tanks are best) simply must be a voluntary requirement in the Octopus Islands. If your boat isn't properly equipped, don't go there.

Hole in the Wall. Use chart 3537; chart book 3312; chart 3539. Hole in the Wall connects Okisollo Channel with Calm Channel to the east. Boats accumulate on each side of the rapids at the western entrance to Hole in the Wall, waiting for slack water. In general, boats on the upstream side will catch the last of the fair current when the rapids calm down, leaving room for the boats on the other side to pick up the new fair current in the opposite direction. Slacks occur 50-55 minutes before Seymour Narrows, and last about 4 minutes. The flood current sets northeast. Maximum currents run to 12 knots on the flood and 10 knots on the ebb.

Upper Rapids. Use chart 3537; chart book 3312; chart 3539. These are the first rapids north of Hole in the Wall in Okisollo Channel, and are dangerous unless run at or near slack water. Slack occurs 55 minutes before Seymour Narrows. At full rush on a spring tide, the rapids, running at 9 knots, are frightening to watch. Almost until slack, a wall of white water can stretch nearly across the channel. When it's time to go through, trend a little east of mid-channel to avoid Bentley Rock. The chart makes the course clear.

Owen Bay. Use chart 3537; chart book 3312; chart 3539. Owen Bay is large and pretty. The recommended anchorage is in the second little notch on the west side of the bay. This notch is quite protected, and has room for about five boats if the spots are well chosen and shore-ties used. A government float is on the east side of the bay, and a trail leads from near the government float to Hole in the Wall.

Bill Wolferstan, in his cruising guide to Desolation Sound, says that Owen Bay has an ominous feeling. In person, he can tell a few ghost stories about it. We are happy to say that our experience in Owen Bay has been neither ominous nor ghostly.

Enter Owen Bay through a narrow channel between Walters Point and Grant Island. A reef, marked by kelp, extends from Walters Point nearly halfway across this channel. It will inspire you to hug the Grant Island side.

Caution: Don't fool around in the islands that separate Owen Bay from the Upper Rapids. The current is reported to run strongly through these islands, and it could suck you into the rapids. Wolferstan writes that in 1967 a dinghy was found floating below the rapids, upturned, the occupants lost.

While most of the waterways in the Desolation Sound area do not see large vessels, expect to meet commercial traffic in Discovery Passage. Here, a cruise ship heads south at slack water in Seymour Narrows.

Lower Rapids. Use chart 3537; chart book 3312; chart 3539. The Lower Rapids turn at virtually the same time as the Upper Rapids—55 minutes before Seymour Narrows. Currents run to 9 knots at springs, and you must steer a course to avoid Gypsy Shoal, which lies nearly in the middle. Go at slack water only. *Recommended:* Avoid the Lower Rapids altogether by going through Barnes Bay, north of the Okis Islands. At times other than slack you will still see considerable current, but you will avoid dangers.

These sailors are anchored in the little bight on the west side of Owen Bay.

Barnes Bay. Use chart 3537; chart book 3312; chart 3539. Barnes Bay and several small indents in this part of Okisollo Channel could be good anchorages, except for the large amount of log booming and aquaculture. There is possible anchorage in **Chonat Bay** and in the notch behind **Metcalf Island,** before Okisollo Channel enters Discovery Passage.

Granite Point. Use chart 3537; chart book 3312; chart 3539. If you are going between Discovery Passage and Okisollo Channel, you can safely steer inside Min Rock, north of Granite Point, and run close to Granite Point itself. You will be treated to the sight of some extraordinary rock on Granite Point.

DISCOVERY PASSAGE

Use chart 3539; 3540; chart book 3312. Discovery Passage is approximately 20 miles long, and separates Quadra Island and Sonora Island from Vancouver Island. It is the main route for commercial traffic north and south along the east side of Vancouver Island. Cape Mudge is the south entrance to Discovery Passaage. At the north end, Discovery Passage connects with Johnstone Strait at Chatham Point. An enormous amount of water flows through Discovery Passage, flooding south and ebbing north. Tidal rips are frequent. From south to north, the primary stops for pleasure craft are Campbell River, Quathiaski Cove, April Point, Gowlland Harbour, Seymour Narrows, Brown Bay, and Kanish Bay.

See area map page 147

This Indian cemetery is located a short distance north of the Discovery Harbour Marina.

Cape Mudge. Use chart 3539; chart book 3312. Cape Mudge, at the south end of Quadra Island, has been a graveyard for vessels of all sizes, particularly in the winter months. A strong southeaster blowing against a large, southflowing flood tide can set up high and dangerous seas. A college classmate of ours, a commercial fisherman, was lost off Cape Mudge in such conditions a few years ago. If a southeaster is blowing, *Sailing Directions* recommends entering at or after high water slack. Good advice.

On a flood tide, a backeddy often sets up at Cape Mudge, running north along the western edge of Wilby Shoals all the way to the Cape Mudge Lighthouse.

During the summer months many small craft will dot the area around Cape Mudge and Wilby Shoals. It's a world-famous hot spot for salmon fishing. Several resorts in the area cater to sport fishermen, and a large number of guides are available for hire in Campbell River.

Campbell River. Use chart 3539; 3540; chart book 3312. The city of Campbell River is working to become an important tourist destination, and for sport fishermen especially, it is succeeding. The city calls itself the "Salmon Capital of the World." While dozens of guideboats take sportsfishermen to the hot spots in Discovery Passage and off Cape Mudge, each year lunker-size salmon are caught from the marina breakwaters and the public fishing pier.

Campbell River has complete shopping, dining, and marine facilities, all close to the waterfront.

As you approach Campbell River from the south you will find three marinas, each protected by its own breakwater. The southernmost marina is a government wharf, with priority given to commercial fishing craft. Still, pleasure craft often can find room.

The second breakwater protects the Discovery Marina, which has a fuel dock and guest moorage. The ferry to Quathiaski Cove, on Quadra Island, lands adjacent to the Discovery Marina. Of the three marinas, this is closest to downtown Campbell River.

The third marina is the new Discovery Harbour Marina, with a fuel dock and considerable moorage. When calling these marinas by radio, be sure to call exactly the name you intend. If you mean to call the Discovery Harbour Marina but shorten your call to "Discovery," you'll get the Discovery Marina instead, and everybody will be confused.

Dining: We've had good meals at the Pier Street Cafe.

⑥ **Campbell River Government Wharf (South).** Open all year, ample dock space, close to marine supplies. Commercial vessels have priority.

⑥ **Campbell River Government Wharf (North).** Open all year, 4000 feet of dock space behind the same breakwater that protects the Discovery Harbour Marina. You'll find washrooms and showers, tidal grid, waste oil disposal, telephone, and a fuel dock adjacent.

⑥ **Discovery Marina/Sportfish Centre,** 975 Shoppers Row, Campbell River, B.C. V9W 2C5, (250)287-4911; fax (250) 287-7372. Monitors VHF channel 73. Open all year, guest moorage available, power, washrooms, showers, laundry. Located behind the middle of Campbell River's three breakwaters, with facilities for boats to 200 feet in length. A fuel dock is adjacent. The marina is just steps away from downtown Campbell River shopping. *(Marina map page 153)*

⑥ **Discovery Harbour Marina,** 1400 Weiwaikum Road, Campbell River, B.C. V9W 5W8, (250)287-2614. Monitors VHF channel 73. Open all year, washrooms, showers, garbage drop, ample guest moorage available, 30 amp power. This is the northernmost of Campbell River's three break-

See area map page 147

Reference only — not for navigation

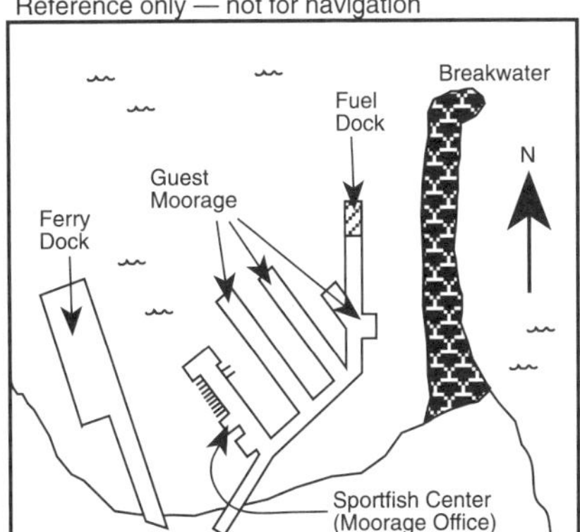

Discovery Marina

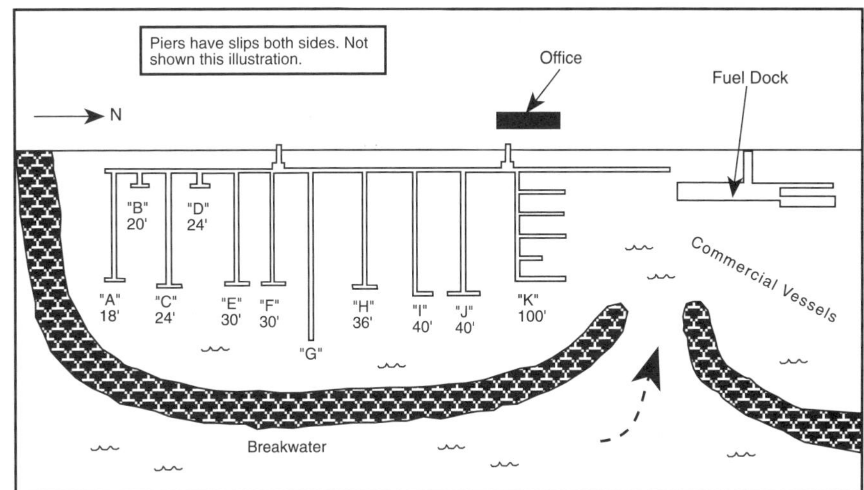

Discovery Harbour Marina

Reference only — not for navigation

water-protected marinas, and the newest. Excellent docks, friendly people, upland construction still underway. The marina can fill up at times; reservations are a good idea.

Major upland development is scheduled to begin in 1997. As planned, the extensive property behind the marina will hold condominiums, a large grocery store, a department store, a marine pub, and several other businesses. *(Marina map above)*

⑥ **Campbell River Chevron Marine,** P.O. Box 968, Campbell River, B.C. V9W 6Y4, (250)287-3319. Open all year, gasoline, diesel, stove oil, outboard premix, stove alcohol. Waste oil disposal available. Located in the Discovery Marina area (middle breakwater), near the ferry dock.

⑥ **Seaway Marine Sales,** Discovery Harbour Marina, P.O. Box 137, Campbell River, B.C. V9W 5A7, (250)287-3456. Fuel dock open all year, gasoline, diesel, washrooms, showers. Located behind the Discovery Harbour Marina breakwater. Also carries ice, small items. Stan Palmer is the owner.

Quathiaski Cove. Use chart 3539; 3540; chart book 3312. Quathiaski Cove is the Quadra Island landing for the ferry to Campbell River. A government dock lies to the right of the ferry landing, and may be rolly from ferry wash. A small shopping center is located a few blocks from the ferry landing. You can get fuel and repairs, including haulout, at Quathiaski Cove. Because of ferry traffic, the best anchorage is farther north, in the cove behind Grouse Island. Fingers of current from Discovery Passage work into Quathiaski Cove at some stages of the tide, so be sure the anchor is well set.

⑦ **Quathiaski Cove Government Wharf,** adjacent to the ferry landing. Dock has considerable mooring space. Waste oil disposal is available.

⑦ **Quathiaski Cove Petro Canada,** (250)285-3212. Gasoline and diesel, adjacent to the government wharf.

⑧ **April Point Lodge & Fishing Resort,** P.O. Box 1, Quathiaski Cove, B.C. V0P 1N0, (250)285-3621, 285-2222; fax (250)285-2016. Monitors VHF channel 73. Open all year, outboard premix is the only fuel available. Ample guest moorage, 20, 30 & 50 amp power, laundry, cable TV and telephone hookup. This high-quality destination fishing re-

See area map page 147

sort is located at the tip of April Point. They have everything for the most demanding guest, including excellent rooms, fishing guides, a renowned dining room, and scheduled air service by three different companies.

A red spar buoy marks a sand shoal near the entrance to the bay. Leave the buoy to starboard as you enter (Red, Right, Returning).

The marina, in the cove that extends south of the point, has 3500 feet of dock space, and is set up to handle the larger boats. You can find anchorage in this cove. A passage leads between the cove and adjacent Gowlland Harbour, but the passage is shallow and littered with rocks. If you lack local knowledge, the general advice is to stay out.

Gowlland Harbour. Use chart 3539; 3540; chart book 3312. Gowlland Harbour is a large, protected bay lying behind Gowlland Island, with considerable log booming activity along the harbor's shoreline. Before entering, study the chart so you can avoid Entrance Rock, which lies north of Gowlland Island.

You'll find good anchoring depths at the north end of the bay, but it's much prettier at the south end, especially behind Stag Island. Good anchoring also lies behind Wren Islet, Crow Islet, and the Mouse Islets, all of them a little to the north of Stag Island. These islets, which are protected as provincial park preserves, make excellent picnic spots.

Seymour Narrows. Use chart 3539; chart book 3312. The currents in Seymour Narrows run to 16 knots on the flood and 14 knots on the ebb, flooding south and ebbing north. *This is a passage to be transited at or near slack water.* From the south, you can wait for slack either in Menzies Bay, on the Vancouver Island side, or in the good-size bay behind Maud Island, on the Quadra Island side. South of Maud Island, the flood forms a backeddy along Quadra Island, sweeping northbound boats more easily toward Maud Island. Seymour Narrows is the principal route for north- and south-bound commercial traffic, including cruise ships. Give large vessels ample room to maneuver.

Before going through, we urge you to read the *Sailing Directions* section on Seymour Narrows. Especially on a flood, *Sailing Directions* counsels against the west side, because of rough water. From the north, Plumper Bay is a good waiting spot on the east side, as is Brown Bay on the west side. Brown Bay has a floating breakwater and a marina.

Both **Deepwater Bay** and **Plumper Bay** are too open and deep to be attractive as anchorages. There may be good anchorage in **Menzies Bay,** being careful to go around either end of a drying shoal which almost blocks the entrance. This area is used as a booming ground for the pulp mill in Campbell River.

In July 1996, the warship HMCS *Columbia* was sunk off Maud Island to create an artificial reef for diving.

⑨ **Brown's Bay Marina & RV Park,** P.O. Box 668, Campbell River, B.C. V9W 6J3, (250)286-3135. Monitors VHF channel 73. Open all year, gasoline and diesel, guest moorage available along 2000 feet of dock, 15, 30 & 50 amp power, washrooms, showers, laundry. This marina is located on Vancouver Island at the north end of Seymour Narrows. The new fuel dock has oil-changing facilities and waste oil disposal. The store carries groceries, ice, fishing gear and bait. The floating restaurant is fully licensed. Launch ramp. Boat rentals and guides are available.

Kanish Bay. Use chart 3539; chart book 3312. Kanish Bay has several good anchorages. You could sneak behind the **Chained Islands**, and with some thought and planning find a number of delightful spots, especially in settled weather. **Granite Bay** is well protected with a good bottom, but not very cozy feeling. The small bay between Granite Bay and Small Inlet offers protection from westerlies.

Small Inlet. A narrow but easily-run channel with a least depth of 8 feet leads from the northeast corner of Kanish Bay to Small Inlet. Small Inlet is beautiful, surrounded by steep, wooded mountains. Once through the entrance channel, a number of good anchorages can be found along the north shore. A couple of boats can fit behind a little nob of land near the southeast corner. The chart shows 3 rocks in this anchorage—actually, they're a reef with 3 high points. You can anchor in the cove at the head of Small Inlet, behind two small islands.

Otter Cove. Use chart 3539 or chartbook 3312. Otter Cove lies just in-

Big Anchors

Wolferstan says that the geography of Kanish Bay (and, we assume, Small Inlet) often allows them to escape strong westerly winds from Johnstone Strait and Discovery Passage. We can report that this isn't *always* the case.

On a recent visit we anchored behind the nob of land near the southeast corner of Small Inlet, and sailed wildly back and forth on the anchor in 35-40 knot winds. We paid out extra rode, and as the wind increased we paid it out again. The anchor rode required chafing gear at the bow roller. Gusts picked cells of spray off the flat surface of the water and carried them a hundred yards at a time. By morning the wind had died away. It takes only one such experience to convince a skipper that he wants a big, strong anchor—a *big,* strong anchor—and ample anchor rode.

–Robert Hale

See area map page 147

side Chatham Point. It's a useful little anchorage, with convenient depths and protection from seas rolling down Johnstone Strait. If you need a place to hide out until the wind or seas subside, it's a good spot. In 1996 Otter Cove and Chatham Point were preserved as Rock Bay Marine Park.

MALASPINA INLET

Use chart 3559; chart book 3312; chart 3538. Malaspina Inlet, Okeover Inlet, Lancelot Inlet, and Theodosia Inlet all are entered between Zephine Point and Myrmidon Point. Much of the Gifford Peninsula, which lies to the east of Malaspina Inlet, is Desolation Sound Marine Park. You'll find literally dozens of good anchorages throughout this area. You'll also find lots of rocks and reefs, most of which are covered by kelp during the summer and thus easily avoided. Aquaculture occupies a number of otherwise inviting anchorages. Small-scale Chart 3538 (1:40,000) gives a pretty good picture of the area, but large-scale Chart 3559 (1:12,000) really opens it up. Several pages in the Chart book 3312 are excellent as well.

Contributing Editor Tom Kincaid has anchored in a little bight behind Beulah Island and a couple of others just to the south, and behind the Cochrane Islands.

Grace Harbour. Grace Harbour has always been one of our favorites. The inner bay is almost completely landlocked, with anchorage for quite a few boats. Many of the anchorages are along the shore, so be prepared to tie the stern to shore. A rock, shown on the charts, is in the middle of this innermost bay. The anchor just skids across the rock before finding holding ground on the other side. On a crowded summer weekend, the empty spot in the middle is there for a reason.

Trevenen Bay. There appears to be good anchorage at the head of Trevenen Bay, but the bay is largely taken by aquaculture. The head of Trevenen Bay, incidentally, could be considered the real north end of the coast highway that continues through North and South America. At this point it is just a little dirt road, but it is an extension of the road past Lund.

Penrose Bay. You can find anchorage at the head of the bay. The Okeover Marina is on the west shore.

Lancelot Inlet. Isabel Bay in Lancelot Inlet is another of our favorites, with the best anchorage tucked in behind Madge Island. There is also good anchorage in Thors Cove. Contributing Editor Tom Kincaid once anchored right at the head of Lancelot Inlet, rowed ashore, and walked across the narrow isthmus that separates that inlet from Portage Cove on the Desolation Sound side. This little isthmus is private property, however, and should be entered only with prior permission of the owner.

Theodosia Inlet. Theodosia Inlet has a narrow, shallow entrance, but is navigable through kelp by most boats at all stages of the tide. Once inside, the bay opens up. Logging activity takes away from the remote feeling of the bay, but anchorage can be found in a number of gunkholes along the shoreline. Much of the shoreline is taken up with boomed logs.

Okeover Inlet. South of Penrose Bay a public float gives access to the road to Lund, with a natural launching ramp alongside. Oysters and other seafoods are grown in several places along Okeover Inlet, and are on private property where trespassing is forbidden.

Galley Bay. Use chart 3559; chart book 3312; chart 3538. Galley Bay is just east of Zephine Head. It is a good anchorage, particularly in the eastern end. At one time a "hippie" colony was established on the west shore. By close observation Contributing Editor Kincaid noted that among other idiosyncrasies, they practiced a clothing-optional lifestyle. He reports that some of the ladies would swim out to bargain for cigarettes. Alas, he says, they are now gone.

Mink Island. Use chart 3538; chart book 3312. Mink Island is private property, but you'll find excellent anchorage in the bay that indents the southeast shore, particularly if you work in behind the little island in the center of the bay. You'll probably run a stern-tie to shore.

Curme Islands. Use chart 3538; chart book 3312. There is possible fair weather anchorage among the Curme Islands, off Mink Island's eastern shore. Wolferstan describes the waterways as "challenging"; Bailey and Cummings, in their *Gunkholing* guidebook, describe the Curme Islands as being extremely tight, with shallow waterways, but with anchoring possibilities if the boat uses 4-way ties to hold position. For most people, dinghies and kayaks are probably the way to go.

Tenedos Bay. Use chart 3538; chart book 3312. Tenedos Bay (also called Deep Bay) is a favorite of ours, for a couple of reasons. First, it's a good, protected anchorage, with a landlocked basin behind the island off the northwest shore. This island is joined with the mainland by a drying shoal, shown on the charts. Second, it's a just a short dinghy ride to the mouth of the stream that runs from Unwin Lake, a popular freshwater swimming hole. A path leads beside the stream. Several pools, screened by vegetation, make good bathing places.

You'll find anchorages in a number of coves along the shore of Tenedos Bay. We like the little notch at the northernmost corner. Stern-ties to shore are the norm. The center of Tenedos Bay is too deep (50 to 100 fathoms) for convenient anchoring.

Caution: As you enter Tenedos Bay, a nasty rock lies submerged off the south side of Bold Head. Especially if you are headed to or from Refuge Cove, Mink Island, or around Bold Head to Prideaux Haven, this rock is located on your probable course. The rock lies farther offshore than you might expect. Give it an extra wide berth, just to be sure. Remember to study your charts before proceeding in these waters. A number of rocks are shown. All are easy to avoid if you are aware of them.

Otter Island. Use chart 3538; chart book 3312. A very narrow but navigable channel runs between Otter Island and the mainland. There is room for a small number boats to anchor, taking stern-ties to shore.

See area map page 147

Reference only — not for navigation

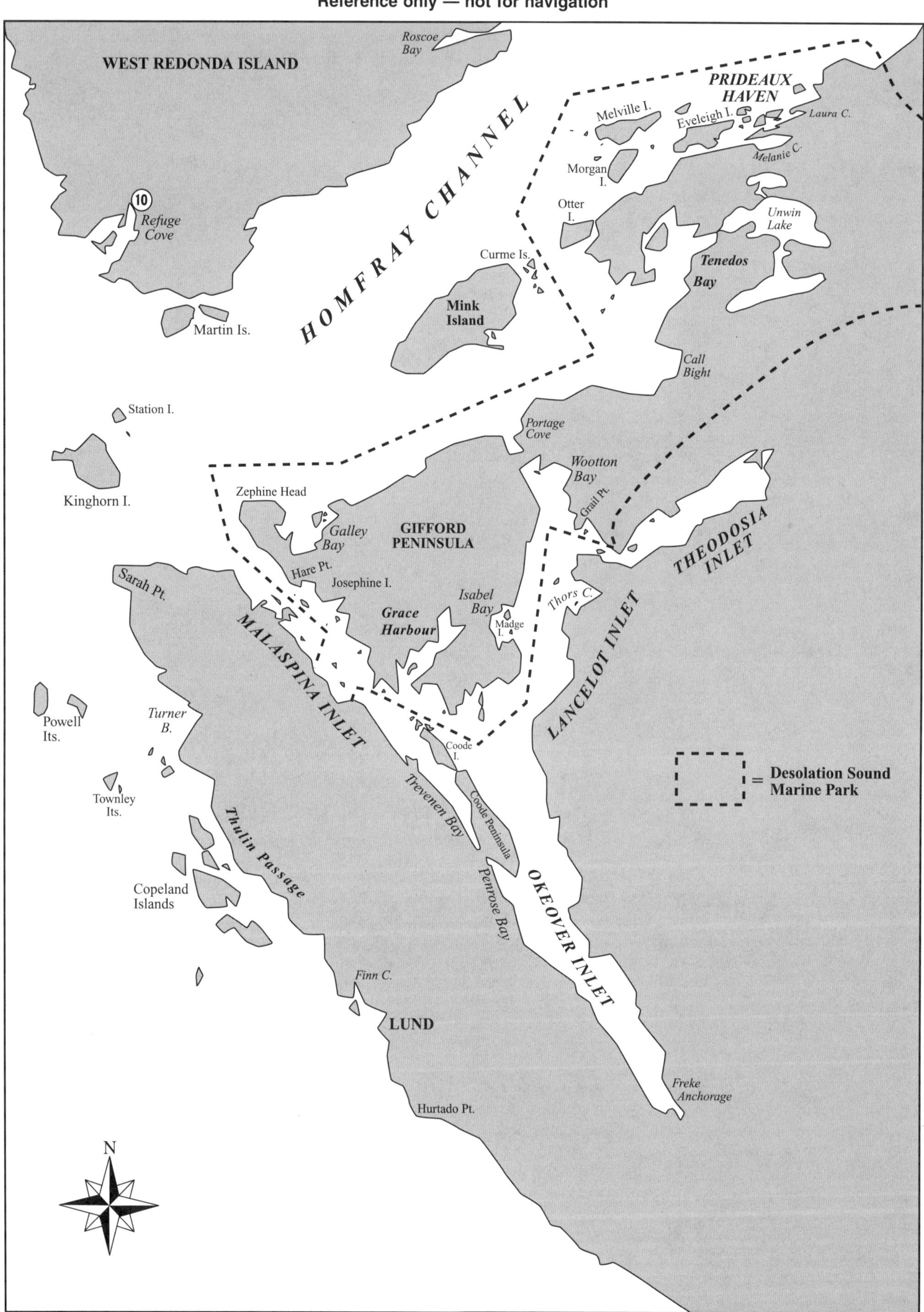

See area map page 147

PRIDEAUX HAVEN

Use chart 3555 (recommended); chart book 3312; chart 3538. The coves that make up the area generally known as Prideaux Haven are the most popular spots in Desolation Sound, with several anchorages—all of them requiring a stern-tie to increase the number of boats that can be accommodated. This area is just beautiful. It is described in great detail by M. Wylie Blanchet in her classic book *The Curve of Time,* and with different emphasis and stunning aerial photos by Bill Wolferstan in his *Cruising Guide to British Columbia, Vol. 2, Desolation Sound and the Discovery Islands.* Yet another perspective is found in Bailey and Cummings, *Gunkholing in Desolation Sound and Princess Louisa.*

You can go ashore and search for the site of the Flea Village, encountered in 1791 by a party of Capt. Vancouver's officers and men in the company of Archibald Menzies, the expedition's botanist. Wolferstan says the Flea Village site can be found, but doesn't say where. Beth Hill, in her book *Seven-Knot Summers,* says she knows the location—Copplestone Point. At the head of Melanie Cove you can find the remains of Mike's Place, and in Laura Cove the ruins of old Phil Lavine's cabin (both from *The Curve of Time).*

The entire clutch of islands and shallow waterways invites exploration by dinghy or kayak. During high season, the only thing missing is solitude. You'll have lots of company.

Important: Despite the fact that at 18.2 feet Prideaux Haven has the largest tidal range along this part of the coast, the exchange of water is poor, and the risk of pollution is great. As early as 1981, Bill Wolferstan, in his cruising guide to Desolation Sound, made mention (gently) of unsavory conditions in Prideaux Haven during July and August. It is our conviction that pollution is not an absolute, but a matter of degree. In the case of Prideaux Haven and other, similar waters, the degree of pollution can easily rise to unacceptable levels. The public response will be increased regulation or restriction. Both are unnecessary if we cruising boaters use courtesy and common sense. Proper management of solid waste (holding tanks are best) must be a voluntary requirement in Prideaux Haven. If your boat isn't properly equipped, don't go there.

Eveleigh Island. Use chart 3555 (recommended); chart book 3312; chart 3538. You'll find anchorage in Eveleigh Anchorage, the western cove behind Eveleigh Island. A drying reef connects Eveleigh Island with the mainland. Entry to the other Prideaux Haven anchorages is around the east end of Eveleigh Island. A reef almost, but not quite, closes this entrance. The entrance and its reef are shown clearly at a scale of 1:6000 on page 11 of Chart book 3312. Stay close to the Eveleigh Island side of the passage to pass the reef.

Prideaux Haven. Use chart 3555 (recommended); chart book 3312; chart 3538. Inside Eveleigh Island are the main Prideaux Haven anchorage and also Melanie Cove. Except in the very middle of Prideaux Haven and Melanie Cove, stern ties are the rule during the summer. *The garbage float that used to be anchored outside Melanie Cove no longer is there, a victim of budget cutbacks.*

Melanie Cove. Use chart 3555 (recommended); chart book 3312; chart 3538. Melanie Cove is perfectly protected, with ample room along both shores for boats to anchor and stern-tie. At the head of the cove, an overgrown apple orchard and the remains of Mike's cabin, described warmly in *The Curve of Time,* can be explored.

Laura Cove. Use chart 3555 (recommended); chart book 3312; chart 3538. Laura Cove has a shallow entrance that should be negotiated at half-tide or better. The remains of the cabin owned by Old Phil the Frenchman, mentioned in *The Curve of Time,* lie at the head of this bay. Anchorage is to the east of Copplestone Point, since the west end of the bay is a maze of rocks and reefs.

Roffey Island. Use chart 3555 (recommended); chart book 3312; chart 3538. If you can't find a place at Prideaux Haven, Melanie Cove or Laura Cove, try the little bay behind Roffey Island. There's room for one or more boats, and you're away from the "madding crowd."

Homfray Channel. Use charts 3538 and 3541; chart book 3312. Homfray Channel curves from the south end of West Redonda Island around East Redonda Island until it merges with Toba Inlet. The only bays of consequence are Forbes Bay and Atwood Bay, but both are too deep and exposed for convenient anchoring.

Roscoe Bay/Roscoe Bay Marine Park. Use chart 3538; chart book 3312. Roscoe Bay, on West Redonda Island where Waddington Channel meets Homfray Channel, is an excellent, protected and popular anchorage. This bay is divided into two in-line sections. The outer bay is just fine, with no obstructions.

A drying shoal, easily crossed by shallow draft boats at half-tide or better, leads to the inner bay. At high tide most sailboats can get in. This inner bay is very pretty, and except for the other boats enjoying the bay with you, is a good example of what cruising in these waters is all about. Dinghy ashore and take the short hike up to the nob that divides the two bays.

At the head of the inner bay a short stream connects with Black Lake. An old logging road leads to the lake. During summer months the water in Black Lake is warm and excellent for swimming or bathing. Trout fishing is said to be good. If you carry your dinghy up the road you can launch it along the lake's shoreline.

Elworthy Island. Use chart 3538; 3539; chart book 3312. A small bay offers good anchorage behind Elworthy Island, a mile north of Church Point, roughly across Waddington Channel from the entrance to Pendrell Sound. This island is called Alfred Island by Wolferstan, but chart 3538 shows it as Elworthy Island. No name is shown on chart 3541 or in chart book 3312. Enter the anchorage from either end, but watch for a drying rock near the north entrance.

Allies Island. Use chart 3541 or chart book 3312. Allies Island is connected to West Redonda Island by a drying reef. Anchorage is possible behind either end, with the north end preferred. A good spot is behind the small islet that lies between Allies Island and West Redonda Island.

Doctor Bay. Use chart 3541 or chart book 3312. Doctor Bay would be a good anchorage, but is taken up by aquaculture.

Walsh Cove Marine Park. Use chart

See area map page 147

3541 or chart book 3312. Walsh Cove Marine Park is a beautiful little spot, with room for a few boats to anchor on a rocky bottom. The cove is well protected from most winds. Enter from the south, since Gorges Island is connected to West Redonda Island by a rock-strewn reef. You'll find two sets of Indian pictographs at Butler Point.

Pendrell Sound. Use chart 3541 or chart book 3312. Pendrell Sound is the site of major oyster culture operations, providing seed oysters to growers all over the coast. It has been chosen for this activity because the summer water temperature dependably exceeds 68 degrees Fahrenheit. Indeed, because of the peculiar conditions warming the water, Pendrell Sound has been called the "warmest saltwater north of Mexico."

Strings of cultch material (often they are empty oyster shells) are suspended from floats in the bay until the oyster spat adheres to them, at which point they are shipped. Seed oyster growers ask for a 4-knot speed limit in the vicinity of their operations. Anchorage can be found at the head of the Sound, behind some small islets that are connected to East Redonda Island by a drying reef.

Another good anchorage is located on the western shore, about three-quarters of the way up the sound. This anchorage is tucked in behind a small islet, at the outfall from a saltwater lagoon. We tried this anchorage in deteriorating weather a few years ago, but found the best spots, close to the islet, taken.

The charts show the shore on the north edge of this cove as reefs, but we found a nice opening, perhaps 50 feet wide, between two fingers of reef. We were able to set the anchor in front of the opening and back in. A long stern-tie was run to rocks on shore. It took several changes in the stern-tie termination point to align the boat just right, but once done, the anchorage was snug and safe for the night—a night of wind, heavy rain, loud thunder, and flashes of lightning. We were rather proud of ourselves.

Toba Inlet. Use chart 3541 or chart book 3312. Toba Inlet extends 20 miles into the 8,000-foot-high coast mountain range until it ends in drying flats at the mouth of the Toba River. The water is very deep right up to the rock wall shores. Limited anchorage is possible in Brem Bay off the mouth of the Brem River, and at the head of the inlet.

LEWIS CHANNEL

Lewis Channel runs between West Redonda Island and Cortes Island, and connects at the north with Calm Channel.

Refuge Cove. Use chart 3555; chart book 3312; chart 3538. Refuge Cove, with a public marina, fuel dock, shops, and well-stocked store, is the most popular resupply port in the heart of Desolation Sound. Several homes, joined by boardwalks, surround the cove. Most of the moorage is public, although the store does have a small float for its customers. Anchorage is possible toward the head of the bay, but may be fouled by sunken logs and logging equipment. During high season traffic is exceptionally heavy. *Approach slowly,* and wait your turn for dock space or fuel. Turnover is rapid; you won't wait long. You may wait longer, though, for the laundromat. The machines seem to run without interruption, and it's not unusual to have several names on the waiting list.

Refuge Cove is a scheduled stop for float plane service. Many boats change crews here, flying new crew in and old crew out.

⑩ **Refuge Cove Government Wharf** serves the general store, gift shop, and hamburger stand at Refuge Cove. While commercial vessels may have priority, during the summer months it is taken entirely by pleasure craft.

⑩ **Refuge Cove General Store,** General Delivery, Refuge Cove, B.C. V0P 1P0. The fuel dock and general store are under one ownership; other shops are under different ownerships. For information purposes, we treat the complex as one.

Guest moorage is available along 2000 feet of dock space. The fuel dock has gasoline and diesel. Propane is available. Washrooms, showers, and laundry (waiting list not unusual) are available.

The store carries complete groceries, fresh produce, deli items including

The Refuge Cove Store, with its laundromat and nearby shops, is a major resupply point in Desolation Sound.

Boat traffic is heavy at Refuge Cove, especially around the fuel dock. Approach slowly and be patient.

See area map page 147

cheeses and meats, a complete liquor agency with interesting wine selections, some marine supplies, charts, books and magazines. The store has limited operating hours in the fall.

Other shops sell hamburgers, baked goods, and gifts. (On a recent visit, we avoided the fuel dock, but patronized the store for supplies, the hamburger stand for lunch, the baked goods shop for breakfast the next day, and the gift shop for friends back home.)

Teakerne Arm. Use chart 3538 or chart book 3312. Teakerne Arm is a deep inlet extending from Lewis Channel into West Redonda Island. Anchorage in Teakerne Arm is just inside the entrance on the south side, or in front of the waterfall from Cassel Lake at the head of the north arm, or in the south arm. Both arms are deep, except very close to shore. The area near the waterfall is a provincial park, and has a dinghy float. The waterfall is spectacular but quite short, so scrambling up to Cassel Lake for a swim is a popular pastime.

Much of the shallow water near shore is taken up with log booms, and often you must tie to the booms if you are to stay in Teakerne Arm.

Church House, at the north end of Calm Channel, is abandoned. The dock is in disrepair.

CALM CHANNEL

Use chart 3541 or chart book 3312. Calm Channel is appropriately named, often being wind-free when other areas nearby are breezy. It connects Lewis Channel and Sutil Channel in the south with Bute Inlet and the Yuculta Rapids in the north.

Redonda Bay. Use chart 3541 or chart book 3312. Redonda Bay has the ruins of an old wharf left over from logging days, but otherwise is not a good anchorage. The wharf is no longer usable. Several rocks in the bay are charted.

Rendezvous Islands. Use chart 3541 or chart book 3312. The Rendezvous Islands have a number of homes along their shores. There is possible anchorage in a bight between the southern and middle islands, but a private float and dolphins restrict the room available.

Bute Inlet. Use chart 3542 or chart book 3312. Bute Inlet is very deep. Except in small areas near the mouths of rivers and at the head of the inlet, it is not good for anchorage. Even in the places mentioned, the bottom drops away steeply, making a stern-tie to shore a good idea.

Nor'westing Winds and Tangaroa Winds, and How They Came to Be

Some 30 years ago, when "Ole" Hansen and I and our wives started *Nor'westing Magazine,* we ran a monthly feature about a cruise in the Puget Sound area. This required, of course, that we take a few days to go cruising, which we did after the magazine was "put to bed," and while the printer had it.

It was during these cruises, sometimes aboard Ole's 38-foot Atkins Ingrid *Tangaroa* and sometimes aboard my 30-foot Herreschoff ketch *Nor'westing,* that we developed our theorem of "Tangaroa Winds" versus "Nor'westing Winds." We came to count on one wind or the other, depending on which boat we were aboard.

The theorem's development began aboard *Tangaroa,* after a long haul south in headwinds to Little Skookum Inlet. We anchored in Wildcat Harbor, still in southerly winds. When the anchor chain was stopped off, the wind changed to the north, and remained from the north all the way home the next day.

Other cruises confirmed the existence of the "Tangaroa Wind," i.e. a wind that began forward of the bowsprit and blew straight back along the boat.

On the other hand, during an early cruise aboard *Nor'westing,* we left Friday Harbor to sail around Shaw Island. We had a pleasant southerly breeze on San Juan Channel, and being in no particularly hurry, we eased sheets and headed for Wasp Passage around the north end of Shaw Island.

As we entered Wasp Passage, the wind clocked around to the west, so we continued with eased sheets past Hankin Point. Amazingly, the wind continued to clock around as we entered Upright Channel. Now it was from the northeast, allowing us to continue under eased sheets. This new wind was still with us as we recrossed San Juan Channel and re-entered Friday Harbor, having circumnavigated Shaw Island with a fair wind all the way around.

Thus we found the "Nor'westing Wind"—a wind generated abaft the beam regardless of our course.

Having proven our theorem, we tended to depend on *Nor'westing* with its favorable wind for most of our cruises. Ole sold *Tangaroa* shortly afterward. *Tangaroa* is now cruising the Caribbean under her new owner, whether with her built-in headwind or not, we do not know.

—*Tom Kincaid*

Eastern Johnstone Strait

Yucultas • Big Bay • Cordero Channel • Nodales Channel • Blind Channel Greene Point Rapids • Whirlpool Rapids • Sunderland Channel • Johnstone Strait

Charts	
3539	Discovery Passage (1:40,000)
3543	Cordero Channel (1:40,000) Greene Point, Dent, & Yuculta Rapids (1:20,000)
3544	Johnstone Strait, Race Passage & Current Passage (1:25,000)
3545	Johnstone Strait, Port Neville to Robson Bight (1:40,000)
3555	Plans – Vicinity of Redonda Islands & Loughborough Inlet
3564	Plans – Johnstone Strait; Port Neville, Havannah Channel & Chatham Channel

NORTH OF DESOLATION SOUND

The southern tip of Stuart Island marks the northern boundary of Desolation Sound cruising waters. North of Desolation Sound you'll find colder water, harsher weather, fewer services, and a greater number of rocks, reefs, and tidal rapids. You should have good ground tackle and know how to use it. The farther north you go, the more remote conditions become, all the way to Alaska.

North of Desolation Sound you find fewer boats. A greater percentage of those boats are 32 feet in length and larger. Many stay out for four to eight weeks or more in the summer, and the larger boats allow more comfortable accommodations. On average the occupants are older, too.

Having just made the boats large and the occupants dottering, we remember a pair of 22-foot trailerable boats that roared into Sullivan Bay late one afternoon. Each boat held a couple in their 30s and a 12-year-old son. The two families had come from Tacoma in only *three days,* and were bound for a destination beyond Cape Caution. Early the next morning they were gone—a two-week vacation can race by quickly.

Much of the research for this book was done from *Surprise,* a very well-equipped Tollycraft 26 powerboat, about the smallest boat that we would rate as a mom-and-pop cruiser. For the two of us, long-married and used to each other's ways, the Tolly 26 has been completely adequate. Typically, however, when we were north of Desolation Sound we were one of the smallest boats—if not *the* smallest boat—wherever we anchored or docked. Those who are planning extensive cruises north of Desolation Sound should understand the nature of the experience, and look at their equipment accordingly.

Garbage Drops. While occasionally you will find a lack of garbage drops in Desolation Sound and south, garbage becomes a much greater problem until you reach Port McNeill. No longer will informal dumps suffice. Garbage now must be hauled from marinas and settlements to authorized dumps, usually on Vancouver Island. Since they must pay for hauling and disposal, most marinas charge a fee for garbage, if they accept garbage at all.

It's a good idea to use as little glass as possible, to wash and flatten cans, and pack paper flat. We've seen paper burned on the beach, but care must be taken to avoid the spread of fire. All traces of paper must be burned completely.

Fresh Water. Fresh water can be a problem even in Desolation Sound, and northward supplies are fewer. The resorts have access to water for drinking, cooking and cleaning, but few have enough for boat washing. Some stops, such as Blind Channel, have sweet spring water. Greenway Sound has lake water that it extensively filters. The Water Hole in Shawl Bay is highly regarded. Often you will find water with a brown cast from cedar bark tannin. We don't know of anybody who has had a bad experience from it.

Prices. For each of the facilities in these cruising grounds, the season is short and the costs are high. Nearly everything must be brought in by barge or air. Don't be upset when prices are higher than you see in the city. Remember too that during the season the marina personnel's workday starts early, ends late, and calls for a smile at all times. Sometimes it's easier to smile than other times.

THE INSIDE ROUTE

Most cruisers heading north choose the sheltered inside route over the possible mayhem of a long passage in Johnstone Strait. The inside route runs from the north end of Calm Channel (the south tip of Stuart Island), through Yuculta Rapids, Gillard Passage, Dent Rapids, Greene Point Rapids, and Whirlpool Rapids. It includes an approximately 14-mile open stretch in Johnstone Strait (which cannot be avoided) between Sunderland Channel and the safety of Havannah Channel, after which the currents of Chatham Channel must be negotiated. Careful planning is paramount. You need to know the times of slack water at each rapids, and you need to know how long it will take to get to each rapids.

Therefore, you *must* have complete and up-to-date charts on board, and a copy of the Canadian Tide and Current Tables, Vol. 6. Furthermore, you must be comfortable calculating the times of slack water at the various rapids, using the corrections shown in the Reference and Secondary Current Stations in the front part of the Tide and Current Tables. For anchoring and transiting shallow channels, use the corrections in the Reference and Secondary Ports pages to calculate the times and heights of tides.

Those who have not had experience with large tides and rapids may find this research and calculation daunting at first, but an evening spent reading the excellent instructions will clear matters considerably. For clarifications, ask a few old salts on the docks.

Since the waters north of Desolation Sound flood southward from the top of Vancouver Island and ebb northward, the northbound boat has a timing problem if it wishes to clear a number of rapids in

Reference only — not for navigation

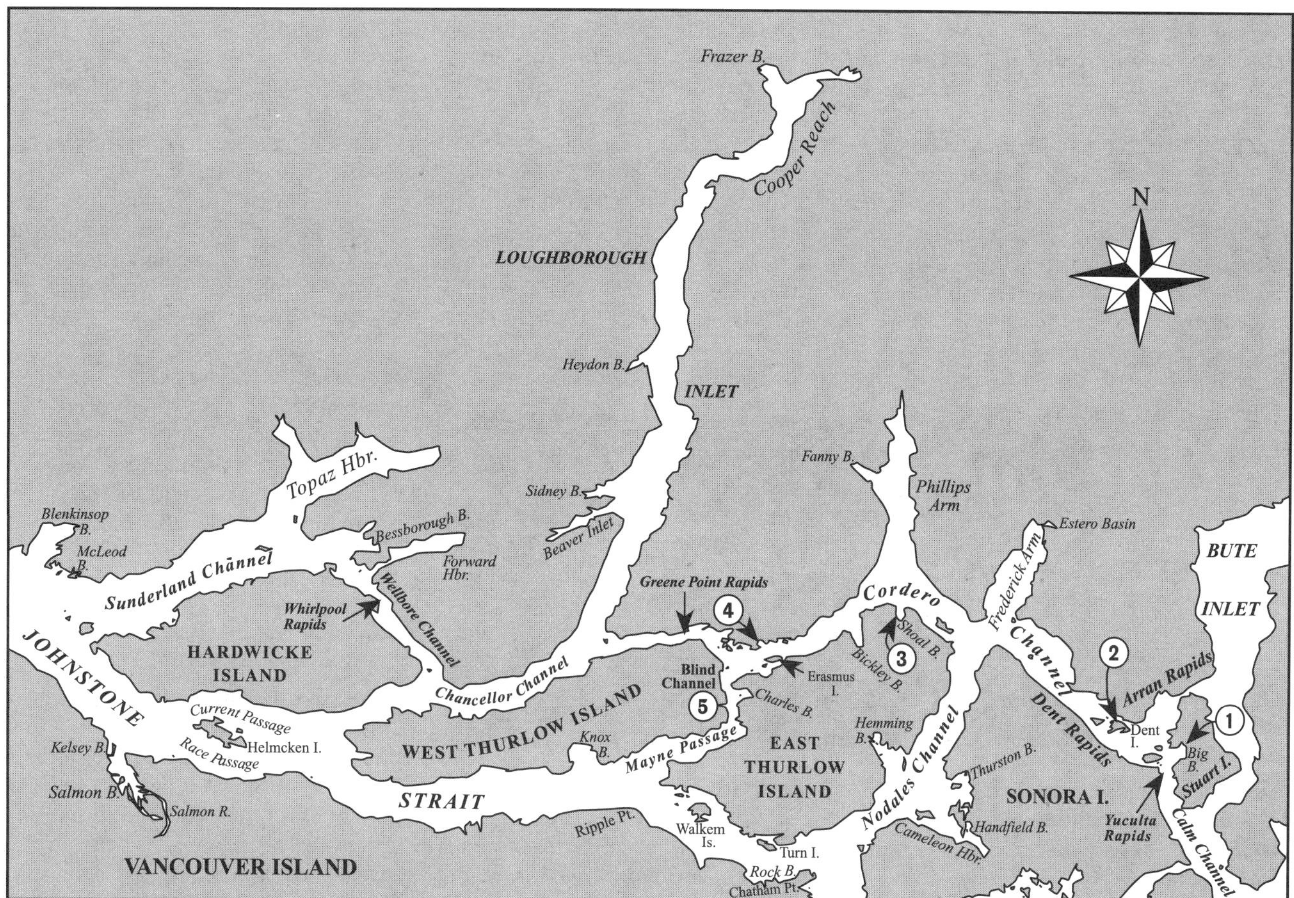

one run. Assuming a start with Yuculta Rapids, all the rapids to the north will have turned before slack water occurs at the Yucultas. The general plan is to approach Yuculta Rapids before the southbound flood current turns to the northbound ebb, and utilize two backeddies (described below) to help your way against the flood for the two or so miles to Gillard Passage and Dent Rapids that lie just beyond. Done right, you'll go through Dent Rapids against the very last of the then-weak flood current, and let the new ebb current flush you out Cordero Channel.

The ebb will already have been running at Greene Point Rapids, which turned earlier. Depending on your boat's speed, the ebb could be at full force when you arrive. Rather than go through in these conditions, many cruisers choose instead to overnight either at Cordero Lodge or Blind Channel Resort. Both have excellent restaurants. Shoal Bay and the Cordero Islands are other good places to wait for Greene Point Rapids to settle down.

The next day you can depart before high water slack and push through Greene Point Rapids in the dying flood current. Then you'll hurry to Wellbore Channel, to take Whirlpool Rapids early in the favorable ebb current. If this is done early in the morning, it is possible that the wind will not have got up for the stretch in Johnstone Strait. With luck it can be a pleasant run down Sunderland Channel and into Johnstone Strait, all the way to Havannah Channel. How this works depends on the speed of your boat, the actual conditions that exist, and the tightness of your schedule. *Caution:* A tight schedule is not justification for taking a chance with bad conditions. The dangers are real.

Southbound the options are greater. Take your first rapids against the last of the dying ebb, and let the new flood current flush you south. Each set of rapids in succession turns at a later time. Given the right conditions, even a slow boat can take all the rapids on one tide, with only a few hours' wait if the boat arrives at any given rapids when they are running too hard to risk transit.

We urge that you carry and use the guidebook *Cruising Beyond Desolation Sound,* by John Chappell. All cruising boats experienced in these waters use Chappell. We also urge that you carry and use the Canadian government book *Sailing Directions, British Columbia Coast (South Portion),* available through Canadian Hydrographic chart agents.

Yuculta Rapids. Use chart 3543; chart book 3312. The Yuculta (pronounced "Yew-cla-ta") Rapids run between Stuart Island and Sonora Island. Taken at slack they are benign; at full force on a spring tide, especially against an opposing wind, they can be extremely dangerous. Northbound, *Sailing Directions* recommends that slow and low-powered boats arrive at the rapids an hour before high slack, and use a back eddy along the Stuart Island shore until off Kellsey Point. Then cross to the Sonora Island shore to use a prevailing northerly current. This should position the boat to go through Gillard Passage and Dent Rapids

See area map page 161

satisfactorily. If you are late and unsure of Dent Rapids, wait in Big Bay for the next slack.

Big Bay. Use chart 3543; chart book 3312. Big Bay on Stuart Island is a major fishing resort center. It has both a government dock and a resort and marina. The public floats are 350 feet long, and lie behind a plank and piling breakwater to the south of the Big Bay Marina. A pub is near the head of the government dock. The Big Bay Marina offers moorage with power, fuel, supplies, a good restaurant, and scheduled float plane service in season.

A grandmother swings her granddaughter on the lawn at the Big Bay Marina Resort.

① **Big Bay Marina & Fishing Resort,** Stuart Island, B.C. V0P 1V0, (250)286-8107. Monitors VHF channel 73. Open May through September, gasoline and diesel at the fuel dock, washrooms, showers, laundry. This is a large, friendly, well-run marina with accommodations, a good restaurant, a lounge, and a well-stocked store, including liquor agency. It's a principal refueling and jumping-off point for waters north. They can handle boats to 130 feet in length, and have guides for salmon fishing in the Yucultas. Bruce and Kay Knierim and their family own and run the resort.

Gillard Passage. Use chart 3543; chart book 3312. Currents run to 13 knots on the flood and 10 knots on the ebb. Transit near slack water. Times of slack are shown in Tide and Current Tables, Vol. 6. Pass south of Jimmy Judd Island. Big Bay is a good place to wait if the current is too strong.

② **Dent Island Lodge,** Stuart Island, B.C. V0P 1V0, (604)286-8105. Monitors VHF channel 73. Guest moorage and power available, closed in the winter. The Dent Island Lodge is located behind Dent Island off the two small islands that choke the channel between Dent Island and the mainland. We are told the dining room is excellent. Martin and Katy Regan are the managers.

Dent Rapids. Use chart 3543; chart book 3312. Currents run to 9 knots on floods and 8 knots on ebbs. Time corrections are shown under Reference and Secondary Current Stations in Tide and Current Tables, Vol. 6. Per *Sailing Directions,* "In Devils Hole, violent eddies and whirlpools form between 2 hours after turn to flood and 1 hour before turn to ebb." People who have looked into Devil's Hole vow never to run the risk again. Favor the Sonora Island shore of Dent Rapids.

Tugboat Passage, between Dent Island and Little Dent Island, avoids the potential problems of Devils Hole, and the current is less. Use the large-scale inset on chart 3543, and favor the Little Dent Island side.

Arran Rapids. Use chart 3543; chart book 3312. Arran Rapids are between the north side of Stuart Island and the mainland, connecting Bute Inlet with Cordero Channel. Arran Rapids are unobstructed, but run to 9 knots, so should be taken close to slack water. We have hiked from Big Bay to Arran Rapids, and watched the water during a spring tide. The enormous upwellings, whirlpools and overfalls were sobering.

Frederick Arm. Use chart 3543; chart book 3312. Frederick Arm is deep, with almost no good places to anchor. You can anchor in several nooks along the eastern shoreline, or near the head, where the bottom shoals rapidly.

Estero Basin. Estero Basin, off the head of Frederick Arm, is uncharted. If the crowds are getting to you, this is where you can avoid them. The narrow passage into Estero Basin, called "The Gut," is passable only at high water slack. A dinghy with outboard motor would be a good way to go. We have not been in Estero Basin, but Wolferstan has. He writes convincingly about the strong currents in The Gut, and the eerie stillness of the 5-mile-long basin behind, with its uncharted rocks. Friends tell us that Estero Basin is absolutely beautiful, usually deserted, with small islands, sheer cliffs, and warm water that grows fresher the farther up you go. "Bring your lunch and shampoo," we're advised.

Almost overwhelmed by its backdrop, Big Bay is a favorite stopping point for northbound and southbound boats.

A young family aboard "Phoenix," 1914, enjoys an outing in Hemming Bay on Nodales Channel.

NODALES CHANNEL

Hemming Bay. Use chart 3543; chart book 3312. Hemming Bay is pretty, especially at the north end, near the head. Enter the bay leaving the Lee Islands well off your right hand to avoid Menace Rock, in the middle of the bay. Most of the Hemming Bay is deep, but you can find anchoring depths near the head.

Thurston Bay Marine Park. Use chart 3543; chart book 3312. Thurston Bay Marine Park includes Thurston Bay, Handfield Bay, and Cameleon Harbour. The park is large enough to hold many boats without feeling too crowded, and has good anchorages with exploring ashore. The land-locked inlet behind Wilson Point, on the south side of Thurston Bay, is best entered at half-tide or higher. Wolferstan calls this inlet Anchorage Lagoon. At the entrance, least depth on a zero tide is 2 feet or less. We tiptoed in near the bottom of a 2.9-foot low tide with the depth sounder showing 6 feet (*Surprise* draws 3 feet). Inside we found four boats at anchor in a pretty setting, with 9-10 feet of depth. This is a good place to know your vessel's draft and the tidal range during your stay.

Handfield Bay. Handfield Bay is entered from Binnington Bay, located to port as you enter Cameleon Harbour. Chart 3543 (1:40,000) makes it clear that you should enter Handfield Bay leaving Tully Island to port. Once inside, you'll find excellent protection and good anchoring depths. People have told us Handfield Bay is one of their favorite stops. Douglas Rock, in the entrance to Cameleon Harbour, may lie farther off Bruce Point than you expect.

Cameleon Harbour. Cameleon Harbour is one of the nicer anchorages in the area. It is a big, open bay with ample protected anchorage, depending on where you need the shelter. Be aware of Douglas Rock. which may lie farther off Bruce Point than you expect.

Phillips Arm. Use chart 3543; chart book 3312. Phillips Arm is deep, with little protection along the shores. **Fanny Bay** looks good on the chart, but has considerable log booming activity in it. A northwest wind can blow through a saddle in the mountains at the head of the bay. On a recent visit we found a stiff breeze in Fanny Bay, while outside in Phillips Arm, the air was calm. A friend, much experienced, tells us not to anchor in the area of Dyer Point. The bottom is foul with a tangle of sunken logs.

Shoal Bay. Use chart 3543, chart book 3312. Shoal Bay has a long government float, with good anchorage off the outboard end of the float. The water shallows dramatically at the head of the bay. Shoal Bay is protected from most winds blowing down Cordero Channnel, but is open to the wash from passing boats. You have a great view up Phillips Arm. This is a good place to wait for slack water at rapids north or south.

③ **Shoal Bay Lodge,** P.O. Box 818, Campbell River, B.C. V9W 6Y4, (250)286-6016, 286-2697; fax (250)286-2697. Open all year, washrooms, showers, laundry. Moor at the government wharf. They have a licensed pub, cafe, rooms to rent, ice, some gift items. An effort is being made to revive the lodge, and at press time the entire facility remains for sale. Tony and Gena Bennett, who have two beautiful children, are the managers.

Bickley Bay. Use chart 3543; chart book 3312. Bickley Bay on Cordero Channel has anchoring depths toward the head of the bay. Favor the east shore to avoid a shoal area. Friends who have cruised in the area extensively warn of poor holding ground, however, and won't go in anymore. Phil Richter at Blind Channel also warns of poor holding. Caution advised.

④ **Cordero Lodge,** General Delivery, Blind Channel, B.C. V0P 1B0, (604)286-8404. Monitors VHF channel 73. Open April through October. Guest moorage available, restrooms, no power on the dock, five guest rooms. Cordero Lodge is on log floats, behind Lorte Island, a short distance east of Greene Point Rapids. The lodge has rooms, a restaurant, and space at its dock for 8-10 medium-size boats, more if they raft out. The fully licensed restaurant serves excellent food, in the German style (May-Mid-Sept.). Call ahead on VHF channel 73. Reinhardt and Doris Kuppers and their daughter Kellie are the hosts.

Crawford Anchorage. Use chart 3543; chart book 3312. Crawford Anchorage, between Erasmus Island and East Thurlow Island, has been deemed chancy at best, with a rocky and poor holding bottom. Friends, however, report that they have anchored in Crawford Anchorage successfully, using a Bruce anchor and a stern-tie to Erasmus Island. We tried anchoring, with indifferent results. A large logging camp, with generators running around the clock, is now in the bay, making it even less appealing. Enter Crawford Anchorage from the west—rocks lie in the eastern entrance. Rocks also lie southeast of Mink Island.

Mayne Passage (Blind Channel). Mayne Passage connects Cordero Channel with Johnstone Strait. From Johnstone Strait the entrance can be hard to spot, hence the local name "Blind Channel." The current floods north and ebbs south. Currents reach 5

See area map page 161

Blind Channel Resort has good docks, excellent restaurant, and fresh baked treats in the morning.

knots at springs. Chart 3543 (1:40,000) shows rips in the northern part of Mayne Passage, and *Sailing Directions* warns of whirlpools and overfalls. We can attest that the waters do indeed get up in this area. Passages near slack make life smoother. The Blind Channel Resort, on the west shore of Mayne Passage, is excellent. On the east side of Mayne Passage, Charles Bay has convenient anchoring depths around Eclipse Islet, in the center of the bay. Just east of Eclipse Islet, however, the bay shoals to drying flats.

⑤ **Blind Channel Resort,** Blind Channel, B.C. V0P 1B0, (250)830-8620. Monitors VHF channel 73. E-mail: richter@oberon.ark.com. Or visit http://oberon.ark.com/~richter. Open all year, gasoline, diesel, kerosene, propane. Ample guest moorge on 2400 feet of dock, 15 & 20 amp power, washrooms, showers, laundry. This is a complete, well-run and very popular marina and resort, with accommodations, an outstanding restaurant, excellent store, fresh baked goods, post office, liquor agency, gift items, lots of hiking trails, and a sandy beach. They have their own spring for water and make ice from that water. Edgar and Annemarie Richter bought Blind Channel in the 1970s. Although their son Phil Richter is now general manager, Annemarie is an engaging hostess in the dining room.

Greene Point Rapids. Use chart 3543; chart book 3312. Currents run to 7 knots at springs in Greene Point Rapids. *Sailing Directions* warns of "considerable overfalls, whirlpools and eddies," and recommends transiting near slack. On small tides currents are much less. Slack water occurs about 1 hour and 30 minutes before slack water at Seymour Narrows. Current corrections are shown under Seymour Narrows in the Secondary Stations section in Tide and Current Tables, Vol. 6. When eastbound on flood tides, low-powered boats and boats with tows are cautioned against being set against Erasmus Island.

Loughborough Inlet. Use chart 3543; 3555. Loughborough (pronounced "Loch-brough") Inlet, off Chancellor Channel, is deep, with steep-to sides and few good anchorages. Although the inlet is about 18 miles in length, the best anchorage is just a short distance from the mouth on the western shore, in **Beaver Inlet**. Edith Cove in Beaver Inlet can be anchored in, but it shoals rapidly. Use a stern-tie to shore. It is reported that near the very head of Beaver Inlet the bottom is foul with sunken logging debris. We have had reports that Frazer Bay, at the head of Loughborough Inlet, can be anchored in if you are adventurous and know what you are doing. We have not tried it ourselves.

WELLBORE CHANNEL

Whirlpool Rapids. Use chart 3544. Whirlpool Rapids on Wellbore Channel has currents to 7 knots. The time of turn is based on Seymour Narrows, and the corrections are shown under Secondary Current Stations in the Tide and Current Tables, Vol. 6. The flood sets southeast and the ebb sets northwest. When the current is running, expect strong whirlpools, upwellings, and backeddies. The turbulence occurs south of Carterer Point on the flood, north of Carterer Point on the ebb. It is best to transit within a half-

(Continued on page 166)

How the

On July 22, 1994, we watched at Blind Channel as the fuel barge came in. Later, in the dead of night, we watched as another barge delivered supplies. We found the experience interesting and enlightening, and thought you might agree. Here is our report:

In late afternoon when the current was slack Imperial Oil Barge SN5 slowly approached the Blind Channel Resort fuel dock. The barge was massive, squat and black. On its deck we could see a number of 55-gallon oil drums, some large reels of wire rope, and a Ford truck. The barge was pushed by a tug with its wheelhouse high and forward, so the helmsman could see ahead. The crewmembers certainly knew what they were doing. They moved the huge barge to the dock in increments of inches. When the barge was secured, the hoses connected, and the pumps running, Ray Leroux, a bargeman/engineer, took time to talk with us.

Ray Leroux told us that he had been doing this kind of work for 27 years. He was about 50 years old, face weathered, medium height, strong and confident. Barge SN5 was 160 feet long, Ray said, 45 feet wide, and 11 feet deep. It could carry 1,400,000 litres of fuel. Of the total, diesel fuel took 824,000 litres. The remainder was divided among marine gasoline (a blend of regular and premium), regular gasoline, and Jet-A fuel. When they left Vancouver on July 16, fully loaded, the barge's freeboard was less than eight inches at the stern and two feet at the bow. They would be out a total of 12 days, make 26 stops, and range as far as Thompson Sound, gaining freeboard as they went.

The pusher tug was 60 feet long and 20 feet wide. It was powered by two 350-horsepower Gardner diesel engines. Underway, the typical speed was 5-5½ knots. Top speed was 6 knots. Tug and barge carried a crew of five—master, mate, two deckhand/cooks, one bargeman/engineer.

The barge had a house near the stern. The house held a small office, the pump room, the motor room, and the

See area map page 161

Coast is Supplied

Phil Richter watches as the fuel barge slowly approaches the dock.

The deck crew hustles to warp the barge to the dock. Note the tug helmsman steering from the top of the wheelhouse.

engine room. Two Caterpillar diesel engines made electricity that powered the motors. The motors ran the pumps, which delivered 20,000 litres of diesel fuel per hour, 22,000 litres of gasoline. Everything was isolated. Ray Leroux was very concerned about sparks.

The Ford truck on the deck was bound for a camp in Sechelt Inlet. They had left Vancouver with the truck, two semi-trailers, several reels of wire, and many drums of oil on deck. By the time they got to Blind Channel most of it was gone.

Ray hinted that it was time for him to get back to work, and we wanted to hike some of the trails at Blind Channel, so we parted. When we returned to the dock an hour or so later, the barge was still pumping. In the evening, after we had an excellent supper at the restaurant, the barge was at the dock, but not pumping. Ray Leroux had told us they were very cautious about weather and sea conditions. "When there's any question, we wait," he said. We presumed they were waiting for slack at the Greene Point Rapids, around 2300. Sometime in the darkness the barge left, having gained a few more inches of freeboard. We didn't hear a thing.

At 0226 we were wakened by bright lights shining in the cabin windows. The powered barge *Aurora Explorer* was arriving with freight, and we got out of bed to watch. The *Aurora Explorer* was like an oversize landing craft. It was about 90 feet long, had a superstructure three decks high located well aft, and a front gate that dropped open. Between the superstructure aft and the gate forward, the barge was filled with freight.

Phil Richter, who runs the Blind Channel Resort, was on the pier, watching the barge's approach. He gave directions as the barge eased up to the pier—again, inches at a time—and lowered its landing gate to the pier's timbers at Phil's feet. The barge used its engine to press the gate against the pier. No mooring lines were needed.

A compact hydraulic crane was mounted on the port side of the barge, forward, near the gate. When the crane operator pushed the control buttons the crane grew up and out. A deckhand looped a cable over the crane's hook and shackled the other end of the cable to a sling on a pallet of plywood. The the cable tightened. The pallet rose, slewed sideways a foot or so, and swung clear of the other cargo. Slowly revolving as it was raised high in the air, the pallet of plywood moved from the barge to the pier. Phil Richter caught the pallet and expertly guided the crane operator as the pallet was lowered to the pier decking. The support timbers creaked and groaned as the full weight of this first pallet came to rest on them.

Three men were on the barge deck, one more in the wheelhouse. Four men at least, running the boat around the clock. One after another, pallets moved from barge to Blind Channel Resort. Plywood. Lumber. Liquor. Four more pallets: food for the restaurant, merchandise for the store. When the pier had all it could bear the barge moved out to the fuel dock—again, in increments of inches. A pallet of roofing material was deposited, and several individual boxes. Phil Richter was there the entire time, directing operations.

At 0406 the *Aurora Explorer*'s bright work lights went out and the navigation lights came on. The barge left as quietly as it had arrived, back out into the channel. By then two teenage boys, one of them Phil Richter's son, had come down. Phil and the boys began moving food and merchandise up the dock to the store. We went back to bed.

At 0930, just up and sleepy-eyed, we went to the store to buy fresh-baked treats for breakfast. Phil Richter was behind the counter. He was alert and cheerful, and eager to help us.

—Robert Hale

See area map page 161

hour of slack, although on small tides boats seem to go through anytime.

Forward Harbour. Use chart 3544. The entrance to Forward Harbour is narrow but unobstructed, with good anchorage throughout. Most of the harbor is 10 to 15 fathoms deep, but a shallower area to port, just inside the entrance, is a good spot for pleasure craft. Farther into the harbor proper, Douglas Bay provides a very pretty anchorage, sheltered from the winds outside. The bottom drops off quickly, and you may find yourself anchored in 60 feet of water—a good reason to carry at least 300 feet of anchor rode. A trail leads from Douglas Bay to a white sand beach at Bessborough Bay.

Bessborough Bay. Use chart 3544. While you can find anchoring depths in the southeast corner of the bay, the entire bay is open to strong westerlies blowing up Sunderland Channel.

Topaze Harbour. Use chart 3544. Big and pretty enough, but little shelter for small boats.

Sunderland Channel. Use chart 3544. Sunderland Channel connects Wellbore Channel with Johnstone Strait. If the westerly is blowing and you find whitecaps in Sunderland Channel, local knowledge says that it will be worse in Johnstone Strait. In these conditions many boats wisely choose to wait it out in Forward Harbour.

All of the channels north of Yukulta Rapids—Nodales Channel, Mayne Passage, Chancellor Channel, and Sunderland Channel—lead to Johnstone Strait. Each provides some protection and a chance to observe conditions on Johnstone Strait before venturing out. A strong westerly wind opposed by an ebb current can make Johnstone Strait difficult for small boats.

JOHNSTONE STRAIT

(The following introduction to the Johnstone Strait area is adapted with permission from *Exploring the Inside Passage to Alaska—A Cruising Guide,* by Don Douglass and Réanne Hemingway-Douglass. Don is the author of *Exploring Vancouver Island's West Coast.* Réanne is the author of *Cape Horn: One Man's Dream, One Woman's Nightmare.* The Douglasses have over 100,000 miles of cruising experience from 60° North to 54° South.)

Johnstone Strait, named for Capt. Vancouver's shipboard master, extends 54 miles from Chatham Point to the west end of Hanson Island. The strait has a reputation for strong currents and rough seas. Many skippers report it to be the least enjoyed part of a trip to the great fishing, kayaking and exploring to be found at the north end of Vancouver Island.

In the spring, heavy river runoffs add to the already strong ebb current outflows in Johnstone Strait, and it doesn't take much more than a light northwesterly wind to create a nasty chop. Sometimes these strong ebb currents can completely overcome the surface flood current. When the seas are up, reduce speed. Continuous spray over the bow may seem like fun at first, but it strains the boat and crew.

Likewise, if large seas develop from astern, avoid surfing. You can easily lose control, veer sideways and broach. Under either condition, head sea or following sea, reduce speed, find protection, anchor and relax. Wait for the current to slack and the seas to calm down. A number of small coves and bights offer protection along Johnstone Strait, and you can get to them quickly if you have to.

To minimize the velocity of the current and reduce the presence of standing waves, avoid spring tides (new and full moon). Go during times of neap tides (first quarter and third quarter of moon). Many cruising boats avoid most of Johnstone Strait by taking the "inside route," described elsewhere.

If you plan to use Johnstone Strait, monitor the Comox weather channel and adjust your timing to take advantage of favorable currents and winds. Travel early in the morning when winds are minimal. Avoid mid-afternoon and periods when the forecast is for a strong wind that would oppose the current.

You'll see considerable current activity in Johnstone Strait, and much drift. On a recent passage we [Hale] saw entire trees floating, in addition to the usual logs, branches, and assorted chunks of wood.

Johnstone Strait is a spectacular passage. With careful preparation and a flexible schedule, you can minimize discomfort and use its powerful natural forces to your benefit.

Knox Bay. Use chart 3543. Knox Bay is located on the north side of Johnstone Strait, near the mouth of Mayne Passage. It would be a poor choice for an anchorage, but a good hideout to escape a strong westerly in the strait. The northwest corner of the bay is the best protected. Unfortunately it is deep, and devoted to log booming. We are concerned that sunken logs may foul the bottom. We would tie off a boomstick to wait out the weather. Shallower areas around the bay are increasingly exposed to westerly winds. Normally they are at stream mouths, and shoal abruptly.

Helmcken Island. Use chart 3544. Helmcken Island has an anchorage in **Billygoat Bay,** on its north side, that offers protection. The island has been clear-cut, but is growing back. Currents in this part of the strait run at 3 to 5 knots. When opposed by wind from the opposite direction, large seas can build rapidly. Billygoat Bay is a good place to hide out. Anchor in approximately 5 fathoms.

Kelsey Bay. Use chart 3544. Kelsey Bay has a breakwater made of five ship hulks—the Union Steamship *Cardena;* three WWII frigates: HMCS *Runnymede,* HMCS *Lasalle,* and HMCS *Longueil;* and one hulk whose name is not known. You can enter alongside this breakwater to a 150-foot-long government float. Quieter moorage can be found farther inside, at a second government wharf with 1160 feet of dock space. Kelsey Bay is about a mile by road from Sayward, where there are stores. An unused ferry dock is located just west of the moorage at Kelsey Bay.

Stay well off the river mouth. The water is quite shoal there.

The waters off Kelsey Bay can be brutal. The current runs strongly, and an opposing wind will build high, steep seas, with no distance between them. Calm conditions only, in our view.

Western Johnstone Strait

Port Neville • Havannah Channel • Chatham Channel • Minstrel Island • Clio Channel • Simoom Sound • Echo Bay • Kincome Inlet • Shawl Bay

Charts	
3544	Johnstone Strait, Race Passage & Current Passage (1:25,000)
3545	Johnstone Strait, Port Neville to Robson Bight (1:40,000)
3564	Plans – Johnstone Strait: Port Neville, Havannah Channel, Chatham Channel
3515	Knight Inlet (1:80,000); Simoom Sound (1:20,000)

Blenkinsop Bay. Use chart 3564; 3544. Blenkinsop Bay has reasonably protected anchorage along the west shore of Johnstone Strait, but swells from westerly winds work into the bay. The chart shows tidal rips off Blenkinsop Bay. The rips are there. **McLeod Bay** and an unnamed bay inside Tuna Point are also possible temporary anchorages if needed.

Port Neville. Use chart 3564; 3545. Port Neville is an excellent anchorage, with a 111-foot-long public float along the eastern shore. No other public facilities are in the vicinity, but Ole Hansen, at the farm/post office, has a soft spot in his heart for boaters. Call "Sea Scout" on VHF channel 06. If Ole is around, he'll probably give you a report on conditions on Johnstone Strait. Port Neville is heavily used by fishing boats in season, but there is plenty of room for everyone. Boomed logs are stored in several places toward the inner end of this 4-mile-long inlet.

Government dock at Port Neville.

HAVANNAH CHANNEL

Use chart 3545. Havannah Channel leads northward toward Knight Inlet and other channels to the north and west.

Port Harvey. Use chart 3545. Port Harvey is large, and open to westerlies from Johnstone Strait. You'll find good anchorage, however, mud bottom, at the head of the bay. Do not run the narrow canal that leads between Port Harvey and Cracroft Inlet. The channel dries and is studded with boulders.

Boughey Bay. Use chart 3545. There is anchorage toward the south end of Boughey (pronounced "boogie") Bay. John Chappell *(Cruising Beyond Desolation Sound)* tells of strong easterly winds that can spring up suddenly in the bay.

Bockett Islets. Use chart 3545. Contributing Editor Tom Kincaid has anchored for a few hours among the Bockett Islets awaiting a favorable current in Chatham Channel.

Burial Cove. Use chart 3545. Burial Cove is pretty, though open to most winds. It is well-protected from seas, however, and has a good bottom in 4 fathoms. A few houses are on the shore.

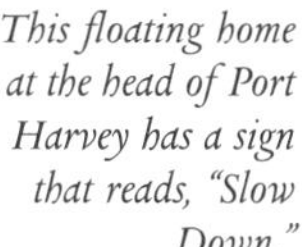

This floating home at the head of Port Harvey has a sign that reads, "Slow Down."

Matilpi. Use chart 3545. Matilpi is an abandoned Indian village. It is a beautiful spot, with a white shell beach, backed up by dense forest. Anchor behind the northern of the two islands, or between the islands. Protection is excellent.

Call Inlet. Use chart 3545. Call Inlet is approximately 10 miles long, and runs back through beautiful, steep-sided mountains. You can find anchoring depths in the Warren Islands, near the mouth of Call Inlet. They would be a pretty spot in which to wait for the current to change in Chatham Channel. A stern-tie to shore would be a good idea for overnight anchorage.

Chatham Channel. Use chart 3564; 3545. Chatham Channel is easier to run than would appear from the chart. The southern section is the narrowest, with the least room in the channel, and requires the greatest attention. The most pleasant approach is to wait for near-slack water, and go on through.

Slacks are based on Seymour Narrows predictions. Correction factors for the times of slack water will be found under Secondary Stations in the Tide and Current Tables, Vol. 6. Chart 3545 (1:40,000) shows the area, including the range locations. Chart 3564 (1:20,000), with its 1:10,000 insert of the southern

Reference only — not for navigation

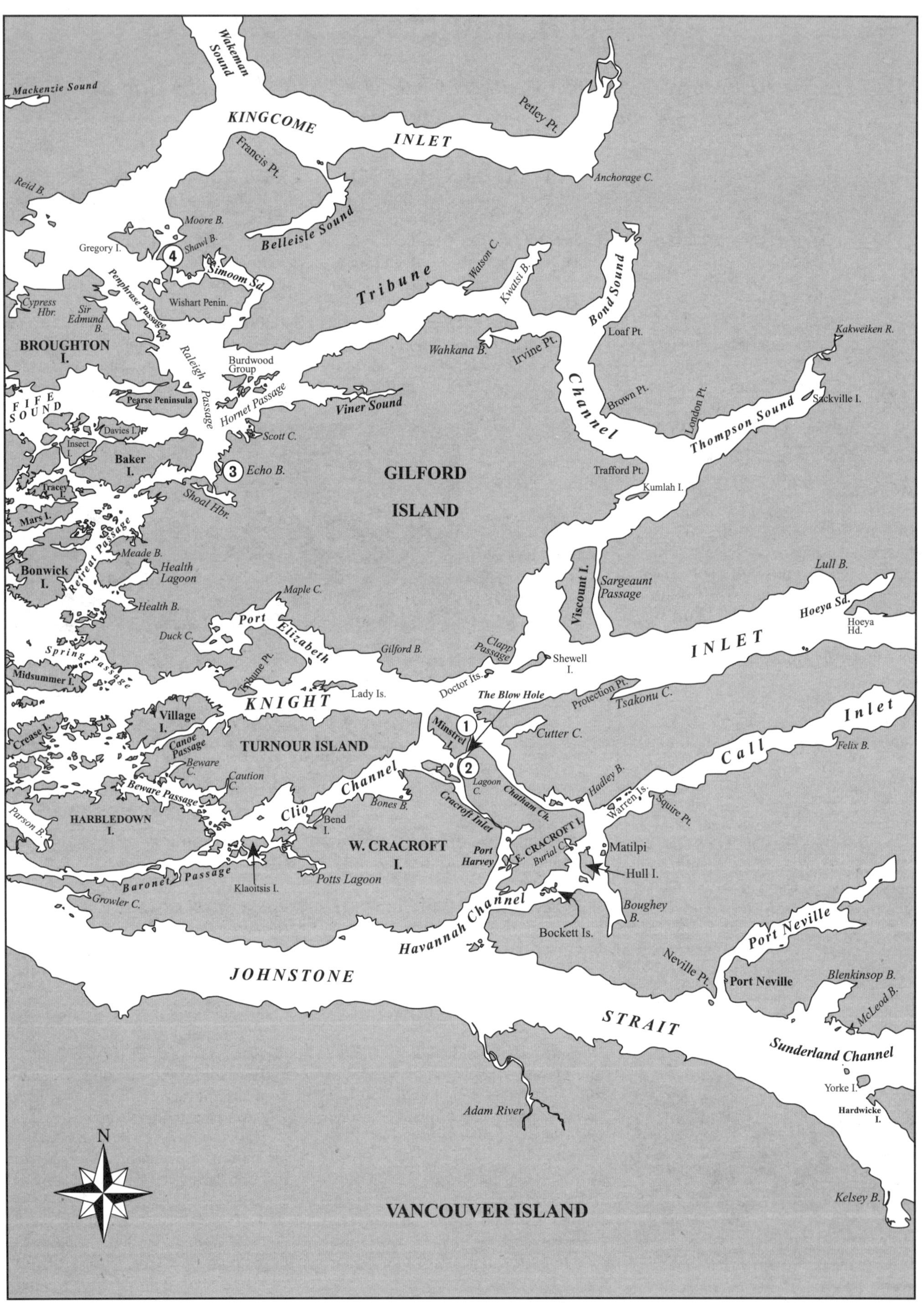

section, truly helps understanding. We highly recommend Chart 3564.

If you are running compass courses through the southern section, remember that the headings shown on the chart are True. The headings must be corrected to Magnetic, with any compass deviation factored in. We have found that the ranges are hard to locate from the far ends of the lower channel. A sharp-eyed crew should sight astern at the near range until it grows difficult to see. By then the range ahead should be visible. Maximum currents run to 5 knots at springs, with no significant swirls or overfalls. Chatham Channel thus can be taken at times other than slack water, but you should know what you are doing, and in the southern section *keep your boat lined up on a range.*

Lagoon Cove Marina is quiet, charming, and well-run. The setting is lovely.

Cutter Cove. Use chart 3564; 3545. Cutter Cove, located across the north end of Chatham Channel from Minstrel Island, is very pretty and an excellent anchorage, although exposed to westerly winds. Convenient depths, mud bottom, are available throughout the western half of the bay, which then shallows to drying flats at its head. Friends tell us that Cutter Cove is "alive with crab."

① **Minstrel Island Resort,** P.O. Box 69, Minstrel Island, B.C. V0P 1L0, (250)949-0215. Monitors VHF channels 73 & 06. Open all year, guest moorage available, gasoline & diesel at the fuel dock, 15 amp power, washrooms, showers, laundry, charts. While the Minstrel Island Resort has a rough-and-ready feel, it has long been a popular rendezvous point. Lodging is available, and the pub is popular. A cafe serves meals. During 1996 the liquor agency was discontinued, although the pub has off-sales of beer. The resort has trails to hike on, a picnic area, and a play area for the kids. Haulouts to 40 feet. They have scheduled float plane service from Seattle and Campbell River. Grant and Sylvia Douglas are the owners.

The Blow Hole. Use chart 3564; 3545. The Blow Hole is a short, shallow channel between Minstrel Island and East Cracroft Island. The channel gets its name from strong westerly winds that can blow through it at times. The channel, however, is easy to navigate. A reef does extend from East Cracroft Island on the south side of the channel, near the west end. Chart 3564 shows it clearly. Favor the north side and you'll have no problems.

Lagoon Cove. Use chart 3545. Lagoon Cove has good anchorage along the shorelines, although the middle of the bay is a little deep for most boats. Locals say the bottom on the west side of the bay is foul with logging cable, and recommend against anchoring there. The Lagoon Cove Marina is on the east side of the bay.

② **Lagoon Cove Marina,** c/o Minstrel Island P.O., Minstrel Island, B.C. V0P 1L0. Monitors VHF channel 73. Open all year, with caretakers in the winter. Lagoon Cove has gasoline, diesel, propane, kerosene, stove oil, washroom, shower. Dock power has been upgraded to 30 amps. The shower is a little primitive, and available only mornings and evenings, when the generator runs to heat the water. The small dock store carries fishing licenses, limited fishing tackle, ice, charts, a few essentials. Souvenirs are available. Bill and Jean Barber have made this one of the friendliest stops on the coast. They provide personal, attentive service, introductions, marshmallow roasts every evening, and a relaxed setting.

CLIO CHANNEL

Bones Bay. Use chart 3545. The entire bay is fairly open, although you may find temporary anchorage behind the islets along the south shore. Watch for rocks around the islets. A floating fishing lodge is moored behind these islets. They get going around 0400. Not the best place to anchor.

Bend Island. Use chart 3545. Bend Island is connected to West Cracroft Island by a drying ledge, but good anchorage exists in either end. Friends have anchored in the tiny nook just east of Bend Island, with a stern-tie to shore.

Potts Lagoon. Use chart 3545. Potts Lagoon, very pretty, gets progressively shallower as you near the drying flats at the head, but convenient anchoring depths can be found. The central portion is only 5 or 6 feet deep at zero tide, so check the tide book before stopping for the night. We have had reports of anchor dragging in the little bay that lies inside the 119 meter headland as you approach the entrance to Potts Lagoon. On a recent visit, we found 2 boats anchored in that bay, 5 boats in Potts Lagoon itself.

Klaoitsis Island. Use chart 3545. There is possible anchorage in the bay northwest of Klaoitsis Island, and in a notch on the south shore of Jamieson Island. Currents can run through these anchorages. For most boats, Potts Lagoon would be a better place to overnight.

Knight Inlet. Use chart 3545; 3515. Knight Inlet, some 70 miles in length, is the longest of the fjords that indent the British Columbia coast, extending from Midsummer Island to its head at the mouth of the Klinalini River. The inlet is about 2 miles wide, and along most of its length the shores rise steeply to 6,000-foot mountains. Since anchorage is "iffy" at best, the inlet's upper reaches are explored mainly by fast boats able to make the round trip in a single day. Boats with limited fuel capacity should top off at Lagoon Cove or Minstrel Island before

See area map page 168

making the trip.

In Knight Inlet, **Tsakonu Cove** is a pretty anchorage, protected from westerlies, but exposed to the east. We anchored near the head for a quiet lunch. Outside, a 20-knot inflow wind blew Knight Inlet into an uncomfortable chop. Logging activity has ceased and the hills are green again. Large driftwood logs on the shore suggest that outflow winds in Knight Inlet probably roar into Tsakonu Cove, accompanied by substantial seas.

Hoeya Sound is pretty, but deep and completely exposed to the westerly winds that are prevalent in the summer. **Glendale Cove,** an abandoned logging camp and cannery, offers minimal protection from strong northeast winds the often blow down the inlet. **Wahsjhilas Bay,** at the mouth of the Sim River, looks to be a possible anchorage, although we've never tried it, and anchorage is possible off the drying flats at the head of the inlet.

Port Elizabeth. Use chart 3545. Port Elizabeth is a great big bay bounded on the west by low hills that let westerlies in. Major logging activity is underway on the east side of the bay, near Maple Cove. You can find good anchorage near the western shore, west of the largest of the three islands. The two smaller islands are joined on the west by drying flats.

Sargeaunt Passage. Use chart 3515. Sargeaunt Passage connects Knight Inlet and Tribune Channel, and has anchorage at either end of the narrows. Post an anchor light, as the passage is transited at all hours by commercial fishing boats. The passage runs between steep-sided mountains, and is beautiful. The shoal in the middle of the passage extends from the east shore across much of the passage. Favor the west shore.

Thompson Sound. Use chart 3515. Thompson Sound has no good anchorages.

Bond Sound. Use chart 3515. Bond Sound has no good anchorages.

The inner basin of Kwatsi Bay on Tribune Channel is one of the most spectacular anchorages on the coast.

Kwatsi Bay. Use chart 3515. The inner cove of Kwatsi Bay, on Tribune Channel, is a stunning anchorage, one of the most impressive on the coast. The cove is surrounded by a high, sheer bowl of rock. Sunsets and sunrises are magnificent. Our log says, "Wow!" Kwatsi Bay is deep, though, 17 fathoms or more in much of the inner cove. We had a peaceful night in 10 fathoms with good holding off the two streams that empty into the western bight of the inner cove. The next morning, a patrol around the shoreline found several other 8-12 fathom possibilities. We suspect, however, that a 3-fathom spot near the north shore is an uncharted rock.

The outer cove of Laura Bay is pretty and sheltered, with room for several boats.

Watson Cove. Use chart 3515. Watch for a rock in the entrance, and favor the north shore while entering. Watson Cove is surrounded by beautiful rock and a dense forest, but would not be our first choice for overnight. A large fish farm is just outside the mouth, and a substantial float house is moored at the head of the cove. Extensive floats occupy the head adjacent to the float house. Anchorage is possible in 10 fathoms halfway down Watson Cove. We feel that Kwatsi Bay, a short distance away, is a much better choice.

Wahkana Bay. Use chart 3515. The inner cove of Wahkana Bay is attractive, but 20 fathoms deep except near shore. The east and south shores have several spots where you can anchor in 8-12 fathoms with swinging room, however. The head of the inner cove shoals rapidly. Watch out. Wind can blow through the saddle that reaches to Viner Sound.

Simoom Sound. Use chart 3515. Simoom Sound is a dogleg inlet, very scenic, but most of it too deep for convenient anchoring. The best anchorages are in O'Brien Bay, at the head of the Sound, and in McIntosh Bay and the bays adjacent to it, along the north shore. You'll be in 8-10+ fathoms in O'Brien Bay, and 3-6 fathoms in the McIntosh Bay area. We spent a quiet night in McIntosh Bay. In an emergency you could find anchorage off the northeast corner of Louisa Islet, and near the mouth of a creek on the Wishart Peninsula side.

Hayle Bay. Use chart 3515. After a visit to Hayle Bay our log reads, "Too deep, too exposed."

Laura Bay. Use chart 3515. Laura Bay is a very pretty spot, and a popular place to overnight. You'll find anchorage in two sections: one in the long neck that extends westward; the other in the cove between Trivett Island and Broughton Island. The westward-extending neck is marked by rocks at its mouth. Leave the rocks off your right hand on entering, favoring the southern shore.

See area map page 168

The cove behind Trivett Island is just lovely. A little islet is in the cove, but the chart incorrectly shows good water all around. A rock lies in the narrow passage to the east of the islet. Entering the cove, leave the islet to starboard.

A concrete breakwater marks the entrance to Echo Bay. Echo Bay Resort has full facilities and is popular.

Windsong Sea Village is snugged up against a beautiful rock wall. Small structure at the end of ramp is an art gallery.

Sir Edmund Bay. Use chart 3515. Sir Edmund Bay should be entered east of Nicholls Island to avoid a rock to the west of the island. This rock lies farther offshore than you might expect. Aquaculture pens are in the bay, but anchorage is possible in a cove at the northwest corner of the bay, and in another cove at the south corner. To use the northwest cove, go in just beyond the rocks that narrow the inlet, and find a suitable spot. The southern cove has anchorage behind a charted rock. On a recent visit, near the bottom of a 7-foot low tide, we failed to locate the rock. A friend who has anchored there says the cove is a good spot, however.

Viner Sound. Use chart 3515. Viner Sound is pretty, but narrow and shallow. An indent on the north side, a short distance down the narrow channel, will hold one boat near the opening. Just inside, the water shoals immediately. The long shoaling area shown on the chart at the head of Viner Sound is real. Watch your depth sounder as you explore.

Burdwood Group. Use chart 3515. The Burdwood Group is a beautiful little clutch of islands, a gunkholer's dream. The group is dotted with rocks and reefs, and Chart 3515 (1:80,000) shows little detail. With a sharp lookout, however, small boats can maneuver among the islands on slow bell. Anchorage is recommended in settled weather only. Given the opportunity, the cruising boat should consider it.

Scott Cove. Use chart 3515. Scott Cove is a busy logging camp. With so many quieter, excellent anchorages nearby, it's probable that you will skip this one.

Echo Bay. Use chart 3515. Echo Bay is one of the more popular stops on the coast, with moorage at two marinas, fuel, a hotel, cabins, an art gallery, the best store in the area, and a provincial park with float. The Echo Bay Resort has brought in a section of the old Lake Washington Floating Bridge to make a breakwater at the mouth of the bay. The signs requiring 100 yards offing should be disregarded. They just haven't been removed from the bridge section. Fishing is very good in this area. People have caught good-sized salmon and halibut while fishing from the Echo Bay Resort fuel dock.

Echo Bay Marine Park. The dock is limited to boats not more than 24 feet long, no rafting. The holding bottom is not good, so anchoring is not a good idea. The park has walk-in campsites and picnicking.

③ **Echo Bay Resort,** General Delivery, Simoom P.O., Simoom Sound, B.C. V0P 1S0, (250)949-2501; fax (250)949-4911. Monitors VHF channel 73, switch to 68. Open all year (limited days in the winter), gasoline, diesel, propane, 15 & 30 amp power, ice and water. Ample guest moorage, reservations recommended, washrooms, large, comfortable showers, laundry. This is a popular full-service marina, with lodging and a store. The store carries a good stock of groceries, including a walk-in cooler for dairy products and fresh produce. They carry charts and fishing licenses, and have a post office. Garbage is burned in an oil-fired incinerator, small charge made. Bob and Nancy Richter are the owners.

③ **Windsong Sea Village,** P.O. Box 1487, Port McNeill, B.C. V0N 2R0, (250)956-4005; fax (250)956-4080. Monitors VHF channel 73. Open May-September, guest moorage available. This is a small resort in Echo Bay, with two floating houses for rent, washrooms, showers, and a charming art gallery featuring local artists. Bottled spring water is available. James and Muffin O'Donnell are the owners.

Shoal Harbour. Use chart 3515. Shoal Harbour has good, protected anchorage, mud bottom. We would anchor just to the right, inside the entrance. Wherever you anchor, check the depth sounder before retiring—parts of the bay are indeed quite shoal.

See area map page 168

The easy life at Shawl Bay. Jo Didericksen, seated right, chats with visitors.

KINGCOME INLET

Kingcome Inlet winds 17 miles between high and beautiful mountains, terminating at the delta of the Kingcome River. The water is milky from glacier runoff. The surface water can be surprisingly fresh. At the head of the inlet, it is possible to leave the boat and take a powered dinghy up the river to Kingcome Village, occupied by the Tsawataineuk Native Band. Kingcome Inlet's great depths and sheer rock walls allow virtually no suitable anchorages in the upper portions.

Wakeman Sound. Use chart 3515. Wakeman Sound branches off Kingcome Inlet and extends about 7 miles north among mountains. While it has no good anchorages, the scenery is beautiful. On a good day it can rival Princess Louisa Inlet. Watch for drift in the water. Wakeman Sound is a center for logging activity.

Belleisle Sound. Use chart 3515. Belleisle Sound branches off Kingcome Inlet to the south. Entry is between two high green mountains, the kind that make you feel small. Belleisle Sound is generally too deep for easy anchoring, but a small area just inside the entrance is useable. The sound is beautiful and remote-feeling. Chappell and *Sailing Directions* warn that strong westerlies can blow through. On the day of our visit it was mirror-calm. The water was warm and people on another visiting boat took a swim, right out in the middle. Some years ago we spent the night in Belleisle Sound without difficulty, anchored and stern-tied to the little islet across from the entrance.

Moore Bay. Use chart 3515. Moore Bay is a short distance inside the entrance to Kingcome Inlet, on the east side. The bay is connected to Shawl Bay by a narrow canal that is reported to be navigable at half-tide or better. You can find anchorage behind Thief Island in the south part of Moore Bay (preferred), or near the outlet of the stream that runs from Mt. Plumridge at the north end. Two other nooks along the east shore might also serve, depending on the weather.

Reid Bay. Use chart 3515. Reid Bay, on the western shore, just inside the entrance to Kingcome Inlet, is open, deep, and uninteresting. It is no place to anchor. Just south of Reid Bay, however, an unnamed cove has possibilities. It is rather pretty and has good protection from westerlies. The chart indicates depths of approximately 6 fathoms throughout the bay, but our depth sounder showed 10-13 fathoms, except 5-6 fathoms close to the head. If you go into this cove, give a wide berth to the point at the south entrance. We saw one uncharted rock just off the point; Chappell says there are two.

④ **Shawl Bay.** Use chart 3515. Shawl Bay has a community of floating homes along its southern shore. The marina in Shawl Bay is a favorite of old-timers, many of whom whom return yearly to help out with maintenance and enjoy its extremely relaxed and informal atmosphere. For a time it was possible to buy a "I survived happy hour at Shawl Bay" T-shirt.

For many years the marina was operated by two sisters, Edna Brown and Jo Didericksen, helped out by Edna's son Gary. Gary died suddenly in 1994, and then, in March 1995, Edna died suddenly. The marina's future has been a matter of some speculation, but Jo is keeping it going.

In 1996 an engaging man named Dave Parker and his wife Corrie moved their float house into the marina, and Dave looked after maintenance. Corrie did a little baking. Friends tell us Corrie's offerings were delicious.

To reach the marina call "Atom" on VHF channel 73. Excellent water is available at the Water Hole, on a detached float a short distance from the marina. The channel between Shawl Bay and Moore Bay, to the north, is reported to be navigable at half-tide or better.

Rafting Dogs

Sooner or later, rafting dogs come in handy. As the photo shows, a rafting dog is a crude iron casting with a ring at one end and a point at the other. It is designed to be pounded into a log so a line can be passed through the ring. Rafting dogs (sometimes called log dogs) are just the thing for tying midway along a log boom, where nothing can be found to pass a line through.

If you use rafting dogs, be sure to pound them into the perimeter boomsticks (the logs that are chained to one another to hold the boom together). Do not put rafting dog into logs that are bound for the sawblade.

We found rafting dogs at Wood's Logging Supply in Sedro Woolley, Washington, telephone (360)855-0331.

—*Robert Hale*

Eastern Queen Charlotte Strait

Beware Passage • Mamalilaculla • Broughton Archipelago
Retreat Passage • Fife Sound

Charts	
3545	Johnstone Strait, Port Neville to Robson Bight (1:40,000)
3546	Broughton Strait (1:40,000) Port McNeill & Alert Bay (1:20,000)
3547	Queen Charlotte Strait, Eastern Portion (1:40,000)

Baronet Passage. Use chart 3545; 3546. Baronet Passage, very pretty, is partially obstructed by Walden Island, with the preferred passage in the deeper channel to the north of Walden Island. This is a popular channel for boats heading to and from Blackfish Sound. In this area the current floods west and ebbs east, the opposite of the situation in Johnstone Strait a mile to the south, and in Knight Inlet 4 miles to the north.

Beware Passage. Use chart 3545. If you read the place names from Chart 3545 (1:40,000), Beware Passage will scare you to death. The first fright is the name itself: Beware Passage. Then Care Rock, Caution Rock, Caution Cove, Beware Rock, Beware Cove, and Dead Point. Beware Passage is aptly named, but you can get through safely.

Sailing Directions recommends that lacking local knowledge, Beware Passage be transited at low water, when the rocks are visible. Assuming a passage from east to west, Chappell *(Cruising Beyond Desolation Sound)* mentions a route across the abandoned Turnour Island village of Karlukwees, somehow avoiding all rocks, and skirting the shore of Care Island, but he doesn't provide details. Chappell's second, and preferred, alternative, is to go through "Towboat Pass."

We offer the Towboat Pass route here, with refinements, courtesy of a couple from Nanaimo with nearly 20 summers' experience cruising these waters. It may be helpful to have Chart 3545 at hand, to identify place names as the instructions proceed. A sketch map illustrating the route is on page 174.

Towboat Pass Route, east to west: From the east, enter Beware Passage close by Nicholas Point on Turnour Island, and continue until Karlukwees is abeam to starboard. You'll recognize Karlukwees by its abandoned buildings, decaying pier, and white shell beach.

Karlukwees, with its abandoned buildings, deteriorating pier, and shell beach, is unmistakable.

When Karlukwees is abeam, turn to a course of 250 degrees Magnetic. This course will take you across Beware Passage to the Harbledown Island side, and south of a pair of small islands that lie just offshore from Harbledown Island.

Towboat Pass, marked 3 metres, runs between these small islands and Harbledown Island. The pass has kelp in it, but is reported to be safe at all tides. Go close to Harbledown Island, turn northward, and proceed through the pass. We went through at dead slow bell, one pair of eyes on the water, another pair on the depth sounder. Kelp and all, no problems.

Exit Towboat Pass on a course of approximately 292 degrees Magnetic. While underway, watch astern to starboard until you see three islands apparently spread across the water behind you. Turn to port, to run on a line that connects the middle island of these three islands with Dead Point, at the far end of Beware Passage. At the time of your turn, the middle island should be a little less than 0.5 mile away. Assuming good visibility, Dead Point, now off your bow, will be easily identifiable on a course around 270 degrees Magnetic. This course will put you a little close to a rock that lies off Harbledown Island, but you should clear it easily.

We drew the entire course on the chart before entering Beware Passage, marking all headings and agreeing on our plan. It went so smoothly that when we exited Beware Passage we wondered what all the fuss was about.

Caution Cove. Use chart 3545. Caution Cove is open to prevailing winds, but the bottom is good. Caution Rock, drying 4 feet, is in the center of the entrance. The rock is clearly shown on Chart 3545, as are the rocks just off the drying flats at the head of the cove.

Beware Cove. Use chart 3545. Beware Cove is a good anchorage, very pretty, with protection from westerlies but not southeasterlies. Easiest entry is to the west of Cook Island, leaving Cook Island off your right hand.

Dead Point. The unnamed cove just inside Dead Point offers protection from westerlies.

BLACKFISH ARCHIPELAGO

Use chart 3545; 3546. The name Blackfish Archipelago does not appear on the charts or in *Sailing Directions,* but generally refers to the myriad islands and their waterways adjacent to Blackfish Sound.

Goat Island. Use chart 3546. You'll find a good anchorage in the cove that lies between Goat Island and the southeast corner of Crease Island. Chart 3546 (1:40,000) shows it clearly. The view to the southeast is very pretty. Weed on the bottom might foul some anchors. This cove is excellent for crabbing. A study of the chart shows the safest entry is to the north of Goat Island, between Goat Island and Crease Island. That is the route we took, and it served well.

Mound Island. Use chart 3546. The Cove behind Mound Island is a good anchorage, paying mind to the rocks (shown on the chart) that line the shores.

Leone Island. Use chart 3546. A bay lies between Leone Island and Madrona Island. Contributing Editor Tom Kincaid

Reference only — not for navigation

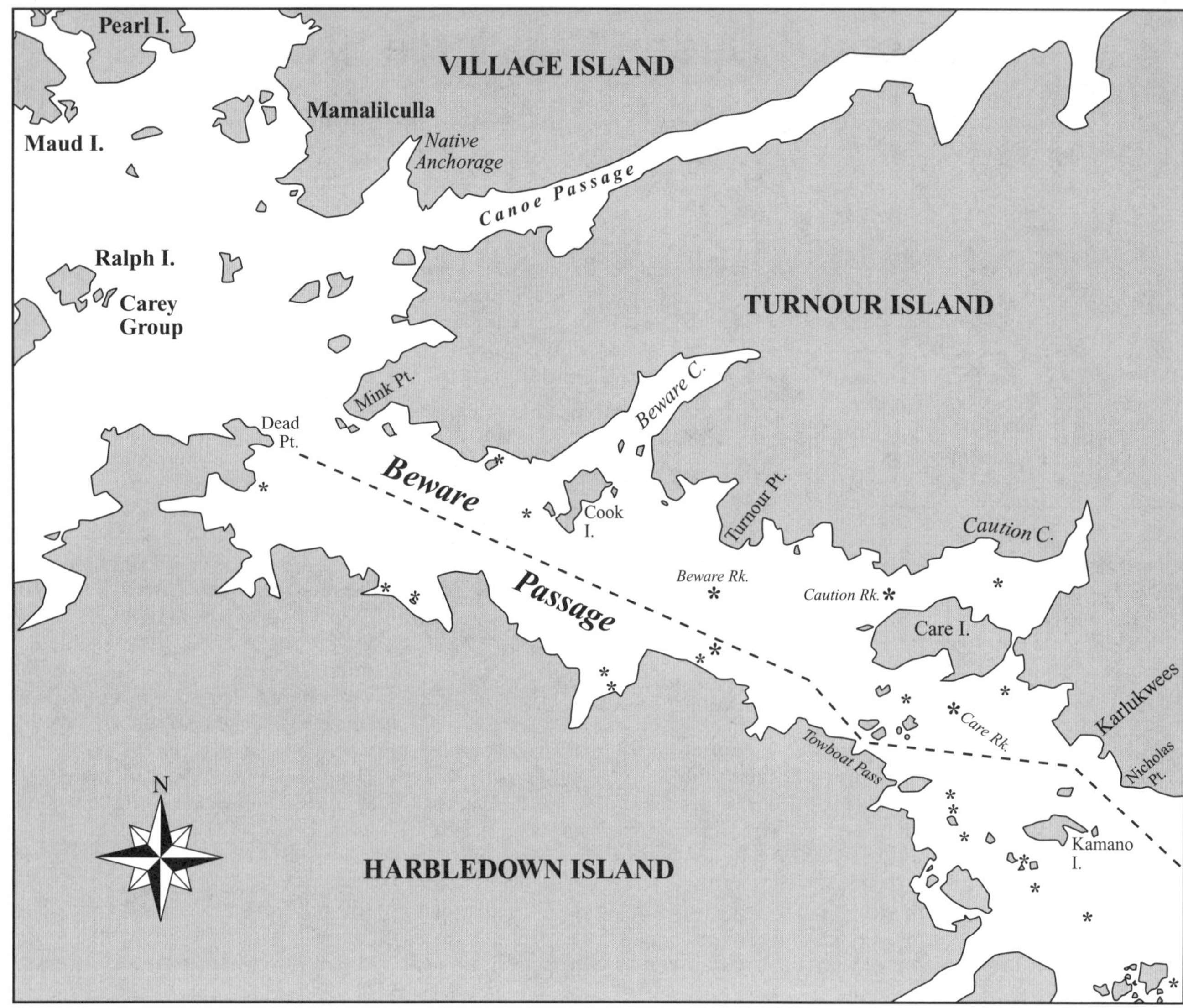

Beware Passage

has anchored there and recommends it. Other friends, with extensive experience in these waters, also recommend it. We, however, tried four different areas over two days to set our anchor, and failed each time. Twice the anchor failed to penetrate large, leafy kelp. Once it refused to set in thin sand and reedy weed. On the last time the anchor seemed to set, but it dragged with only moderate power (800 r.p.m.) in reverse.

Farewell Harbour. Use chart 3546. You'll find good anchorage in Farewell Harbour close to the Berry Island side.

① **Mamalilaculla.** Use chart 3545. In 1921, Mamalilaculla, on the western shore of Village Island, was the site of the "Christmas Potlatch," the last great potlatch on the coast. Potlatches had been banned since 1884, although the law had been largely ignored and unenforced. After the Christmas Potlatch, however, a number of participants were charged for violation. Their considerable ceremonial regalia was confiscated and distributed among museums and private collections. Today much of it has been recovered, and is on display at the U'Mista Cultural Centre in Alert Bay and the Kwagiulth Museum at Cape Mudge.

Mamalilaculla is the abandoned Indian village and later-day mission and hospital that M. Wylie Blanchet visited in *The Curve of Time.* In her description, Blanchet wove together the old Kwakiutl ways as they came up against the new white man's ways. Then she threw in the likelihood of Polynesian influences on the coast Indians.

With Blanchet as background, Mamalilaculla is a fascinating place to visit. The last of the totem poles have fallen to the ground and are rotting away. The mission houses and hospital are empty and haunting. Off the established trails, tall grass and stinging nettles make exploring difficult but not impossible.

Native Anchorage, near the southwest corner of Village Island, has a good bottom, but is exposed to westerly winds, and it's a bit of a walk to the village site. If you anchor in the little bay to the north of Mamalilaculla you will have better protection and a short, easy walk to the village. The old dock is in disrepair and dangerous. We doubt that you will be tempted to use it.

Canoe Passage. Use chart 3545. Canoe Passage runs roughly east-west between Turnour Island and Village Island. The waterway dries at low tide, but can be transited at higher stages of the tide, depending on a vessel's draft.

Continued page 176

Reference only — not for navigation

See area map page 175

Hanson Island. Use chart 3546. The rugged and beautiful north shore of Hanson Island is indented by a number of bays and coves that would be a gunkholer's paradise. The most popular anchorage is in Double Bay, also the location of the Double Bay Resort. Double Bay is apt to be crowded with commercial fishing boats during the commercial season. Enter only along the west side of the bay. The bay behind Sprout Islet, to the east of Double Bay, is also good for anchorage.

② **Double Bay Resort,** 371 McCarthy St., Campbell River, B.C. V9W 2R7, (250)949-2500; fax (250)286-1937. Monitors VHF channel 73. Open May through September only, guest moorage along a 700-foot dock, washrooms, showers. This is primarily a fishing resort whose guests fly in. Rooms are available. The cafe serves simple food (hamburgers, pie, etc.), not elaborate, but well prepared and hearty.

Growler Cove. Use chart 3546. Growler Cove, on the west end of West Cracroft Island, is an excellent anchorage, and popular with commercial fishermen who work Johnstone Strait and Queen Charlotte Strait. During the prime commercial fishing months of July and August, it is apt to be full of commercial boats, with little room for pleasure craft.

Broughton Archipelago. Use chart 3515; 3546. Much of the Broughton Archipelago is now a marine park. Some of the islands are private, however, so use discretion when going ashore. Our journal, written while at anchor in Waddington Bay after a day of exploring, reads: "A marvelous group of islands and passages, but few good anchorages. We navigated around Insect Island and through Indian Passage. Very pretty—many white shell beaches. Rocks marked by kelp. A different appearance from Kingcome Inlet or Simoom Sound. The trees are shorter and more windblown. The west wind is noticably colder than farther east. Fog lay at the mouth of Fife Sound; a few wisps blew up toward us. Great kayaking, gunkholing country."

This large group of islands west of Gilford Island does have anchorages, however, including Sunday Harbour, Monday Anchorage, and Joe Cove, all of which either we or Contributing Editor Tom Kincaid have used. The area is strewn with rocks, reefs, and little islands, which in total provide good protection, but also call for very careful navigation.

History rotting away at Mamalilaculla. The last great beams of the longhouse next to the abandoned house of later day settlement.

M. Wylie Blanchet *(The Curve of Time)* was blown out of Sunday Harbour, and we've had mixed reports about Monday Anchorage. Chappell isn't impressed with either one. Joe Cove is considered to be a good anchorage. Chart 3546 (1:40:000) should be studied carefully before going into these waters, and kept close to hand while there. Currents run strongly at times through the various passages.

Sunday Harbour. Use chart 3546; 3515. Sunday Harbour is formed by Crib Island and Angular Island, north of the mouth of Arrow Passage. The bay is very pretty, but exposed to westerly winds. The little cove in the northeast corner looks attractive until you try to enter and realize it is full of rocks. We would anchor in the middle of Sunday Harbour for a relaxing lunch on a quiet day.

Monday Anchorage. Use chart 3546; 3547; 3515. Monday Anchorage is formed by Tracey Island and Mars Island, north of Arrow Passage. It is large and fairly open. Chapell says you can anchor behind the two small islands off the north shore of the bay. We, however, anchored for lunch fairly deep into the first large cove on the south shore. The anchor bit easily in 7 fathoms, and we had good protection from the gentle westerly that was blowing.

Joe Cove. Use chart 3547. Joe Cove, perfectly protected and private feeling, indents the south side of Eden Island. The best anchorage is near the head. A little thumb of water extends southeast near the head of the cove, but access is partially blocked by several rocks. It is possible, however, to feel your way in.

RETREAT PASSAGE

False Cove. Use chart 3515. Although open to westerly winds, False Cove, on Gilford Island at the north end of Retreat Passage, has anchorage possibilities in two of the three coves at the head of the bay. The middle cove has 8 fathoms

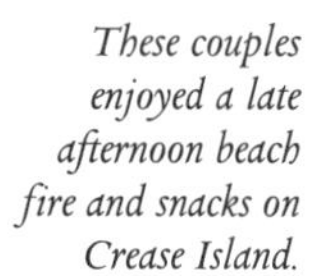

These couples enjoyed a late afternoon beach fire and snacks on Crease Island.

nearly to its head, then shoals quickly to 3-5 fathoms. The north cove shoals to 3-5 fathoms about halfway in. The south cove doesn't indent enough to serve. *Anchorage possibility:* South of False Cove, a thumb-like island protrudes northwest from Gilford Island. The cove that lies south of that island has about 5 fathoms at the entrance, shoaling gently toward the head. No name appears on the charts, but according to Chappell, it is known locally as **Bootleg Bay.**

Waddington Bay. Use chart 3546; 3515. Waddington Bay indents the northeast corner of Bonwick Island. The bay is well protected, pretty, and popular, with room for several boats. It has good holding ground in 3-5 fathoms. Lacking local knowledge, make your approach from the northeast. The approach is wide enough, but rocks bound it, and careful piloting is called for. Study the chart (chart 3546, 1:40:000), and know your position at all times. Waddington Bay shoals at the head, but the wind direction and your depth sounder will tell you where to put the hook down.

Grebe Cove. Use chart 3546; 3515. Grebe Cove indents the east side of Bonwick Island off Retreat Passage. The cove shallows to 7-8 fathoms about 200 yards from the head, and 5-7 fathoms near the head. A saddle in the hills at the head might let westerlies in, but the seas would have no fetch. On a recent visit, a couple in a 20-foot pocket cruiser called out to us, "Great anchorage! The otters will entertain you!"

Carrie Bay. Use chart 3546; 3515. Carrie Bay indents Bonwick Island across Retreat Passage from Health Bay. An aquaculture operation is at the mouth, but the head of the bay is quite pretty, and protected from westerly winds. The bottom shoals rapidly from depths of 7-8 fathoms in much of the bay to around 3 fathoms at the head.

Health Bay. Use chart 3546; 3515. The Health Bay Indian Reserve, with government dock, fronts on Retreat Passage. Health Bay itself is strewn with rocks. Anchorage is best fairly close to the head of the bay, short of the first of the rocks.

FIFE SOUND

Cullen Harbour. Use chart 3547. Cullen Harbour is on the south side of Broughton Island, at the entrance to Booker Lagoon. It is an excellent anchorage, with plenty of room for everyone. The bottom is mud, and depths range from 4 to 9 fathoms.

Booker Lagoon. Use chart 3547. The entrance to Booker Lagoon is from Cullen Harbour through Booker Passage, a tricky channel bounded by reefs on both sides. The channel has ample depths, though, and is about 50 feet wide. Aquaculture pens are in each of the four arms of Booker Lagoon, but anchorage can be found between them—the choice of arm depending on the wind.

Deep Harbour. Use chart 3515. The inner part of Deep Harbour is blocked by boomed logs, and the center of the bay is taken over by aquaculture pens, but there are little nooks around the edges with room enough for one boat to anchor.

Stern-Ties, and How to Carry Them

Stern-ties are desirable and often necessary when a boat anchors in the Northwest. In crowded anchorages, stern-ties keep boats from swinging into one another. Often they are essential if a boat is to remain safely at anchor between two rocks, rather than swing onto them.

We have seen stern-tie tackle of varying lengths and appropriateness, from sailboat spinnaker sheets tied together, to reels of rope cleverly mounted, ready for use.

While rope of any kind will serve in a pinch, we think the best choice is polypropylene. It's strong, it floats, and it's cheap. We also think it's better to have too much rope, not too little. A 600-foot reel of ½-inch polypropylene rope will meet almost any need, yet stow nicely on nearly any size boat. With 600 feet available, a stern-tie can be run around a tree and back to the boat. When it's time to depart the tie can be recovered without rowing ashore.

The trick is to mount the reel of rope so it can pay out and be recovered quickly, easily, and without tangling. The pictures here show some alternatives.

A carefully built, side-mounted reel.

This reel is mounted on its own stanchion.

This 32-foot Bayliner mounts its stern-tie rope on the stern rail.

Central Queen Charlotte Strait

Greenway Sound • Sullivan Bay • Grappler Sound • Mackenzie Sound
Drury Inlet • Sointula • Port McNeill • Port Hardy

Charts

3546	Broughton Strait (1:40,000); Port McNeill & Alert Bay (1:20,000)
3547	Queen Charlotte Strait, Eastern Portion (1:40,000); Stuart Narrows & Kenneth Passage (1:20,000)
3548	Queen Charlotte Strait, Central Portion (1:40,000); Blunden Harbour & Port Hardy (1:15,000)

SUTLEJ CHANNEL

Cypress Harbour. Use chart 3547; 3515. Cypress Harbour is one of the prettiest places in the area, with ample anchorage in Miller Bay or Berry Cove. Behind Roffey Point is a lovely anchorage with room for a few boats. Watch the depth sounder; the bay grows increasingly shoal until it becomes drying flats.

Greenway Sound. Use chart 3547. Greenway Sound features an outstanding resort marina, and along with Sullivan Bay and Echo Bay, is a favorite destination in the area. For those who prefer to anchor, the bay behind Broughton Point, at the east end of Carter Passage, is very pretty. You can also anchor in several little spots behind Cecil Island, near the mouth of Greenway Sound. Broughton Lagoon empties into this area.

Depending on conditions, you can find anchorage in any of a number of little nooks on both sides of Greenway Sound, and behind Simpson Island, near the head of the Sound. Leave Simpson Island to starboard as you enter. For exercise, Broughton Lakes Park, with access from the Greenway Sound Marine Resort, has received much work lately, and is a pleasant hike. Good fishing, beautiful views. An aluminum boat is kept at the lake, so you can go trout fishing.

① **Greenway Sound Marine Resort,** P.O. Box 759, Port McNeill, B.C. V0N 2R0, (250)949-2525, (800)800-2080, offseason: (360)466-4751. Monitors VHF channel 73, switch to 72. Open June 1 through September 15, ample guest moorage on 2200 feet of dock, 15 & 30 amp 110-volt power, 50 amp 208-volt power, spacious washrooms and showers, laundry. Greenway Sound is a wonderful and popular full-service destination resort. Reservations are advisable. They have an excellent restaurant (an elegant dinner at the restaurant is a tradition), as well as a beauty shop, snacks, ice, ice cream, a well-stocked store, and garbage drop.

The marina is located in the bay just east of Greenway Point, and cannot be seen from the mouth of Greenway Sound. As with most marinas in this country, the honor system prevails for payment, whether it's for moorage, dinner, ice, groceries, showers, or laundry. A tab is run, and visitors are scrupulously honest. The tab is settled before the boat departs.

Excellent fishing and crabbing are nearby, and a well-maintained trail leads to Broughton Lakes Park in the mountains. The resort has air service from several carriers, including its own *Greenway Sounder*, with service to Anacortes, Renton, and Tacoma, with Sea-Tac International connections. Boatsitting service is available for those who must fly home. The owners, Tom and Ann Taylor, are extremely knowledgeable and accommodating.

Air travel is commonplace up the coast. These guests have flown into Greenway Sound for supper.

Broughton Lagoon. Use chart 3547. A friend explored Broughton Lagoon recently, and our notes from his report are

See area map page 181

Chips fly as Pat Finnerty runs his portable sawmill at Sullivan Bay. Pat builds his own docks this way.

as follows: They entered the lagoon in their Whaler at low slack water, showing 15 feet of depth going in. Then it dropped off to depths of 300 feet. The lagoon was uncharted, and to all appearances, unvisited. They saw much wildlife, both in the water and on land. Coming out against the flood, they had the Whaler with its 40-horsepower outboard motor on a full plane and barely made headway against the incoming current—this on a neap tide. All went well, though, and our friend was excited about the experience.

Cartwright Bay. Use chart 3547. This bay is open to the wash from passing traffic in Sutlej Channel, but offers easy anchorage at its inner end.

② **Sullivan Bay Marine Resort,** Sullivan Bay Post Office, B.C. V0N 3H0, (250)949-2550. Monitors VHF channel 73. Use chart 3547. Open all year for fuel and post office, seasonally for guest moorage. Services include gasoline, diesel, propane, guest moorage, 15, 30, & 50 amp power, garbage drop, washrooms, showers, laundry.

Everybody likes Sullivan Bay, a fine and popular resort. It has ample moorage along 4000 feet of dock, a well-stocked store with post office and liquor agency, boat sitting service, and daily air service to Seattle and elsewhere. Floating homes provide summer residences for several families, including Pat Finnerty and Lynn Whitehead, the owners.

Pat Finnerty came to Sullivan Bay in 1969, and enjoys recalling the history of Sullivan Bay. The old buildings at the resort date back to the 1940s, although they were brought in from elsewhere after fire destroyed the previous buildings. The whimsical signs, the informal feeling, even the 1-hole golf course, make Sullivan Bay a relaxing place. Alley, the yellow resort cat, visits most boats as if they were his own, but remains a polite guest. We like Sullivan Bay.

Atkinson Island. Use chart 3547. There is anchorage in either end of the passage south of Atkinson Island.

Tracey Harbour. Use chart 3547. Tracey Harbour indents North Broughton Island from Wells Passage. It is pretty and protected. No anchorage is viable, however, until near the head of the bay. There, you can find anchorage on mud bottom in Napier Bay, or on rocky bottom in the bay behind Carter Point. You're apt to find log booms in Napier Bay, and the leftover buildings from what once was a busy logging operation.

Carter Passage. Use chart 3547. Since Carter Passage is blocked in the middle by a boulder-strewn drying shoal, it is actually two harbors, one off Wells Passage, one off Greenway Sound, with good anchorages in either end. The west entrance has tidal currents to 7 knots, and should be taken at or near high water slack. A reef extends from the south shore, so keep to the north of mid-channel. There are two pleasant anchorages in this west end.

The east entrance, off Greenway Sound, is somewhat easier, both as to tidal currents and obstructions. John Chappell's *Cruising Beyond Desolation Sound* describes the explorations needed

Reference only — not for navigation

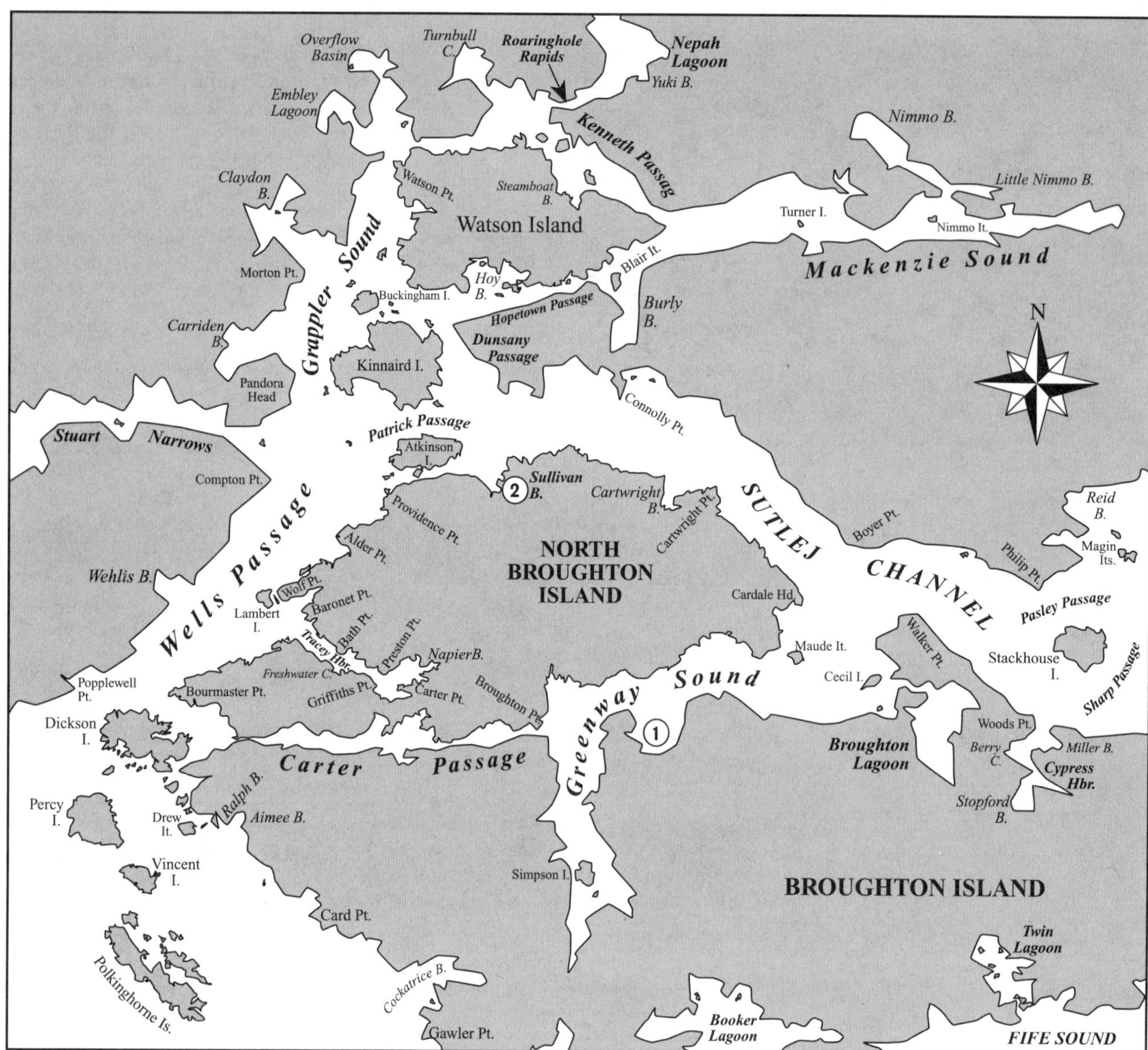

to safely transit the drying shoal between the two ends of Carter Passage.

Dickson Island. Use chart 3547. Dickson Island is located near the mouth of Wells Passage. The small anchorage on the east end of the island provides good protection from seas, but the low land lets westerly winds blow across the bay. Friends report that a large-diameter blue rope on shore offers a convenient loop to run the stern-tie through and back to the boat. Two other bays along the west side of Broughton Island are considered too exposed to westerly weather to be good anchorages.

Polkinghorne Islands. Use chart 3547. The Polkinghorne Islands are located outside the mouth of Wells Passage. A channel among the islands is fun, particularly on the nice day. The anchoring bottom we've found is not too secure, so an overnight stay is not recommended. [Kincaid]

GRAPPLER SOUND

Grappler Sound, north of Sutlej and Wells Passages, has several good anchorages.

Kinnaird Island. Use chart 3547. The bay in the northeast corner of the island is reported to be good in settled weather.

Hoy Bay. Use chart 3547. Some anchorage is possible in Hoy Bay, behind Hopetown Point, west of Hopetown Passage.

Carriden Bay. Use chart 3547. Carriden Bay is located just inside Pandora Head, at the entrance to Grappler Sound. It is a popular anchorage, with a good holding bottom and convenient depths throughout. As you look in, Pandora Head, a spectacular nob, rises on the left. If you're in, you see a beautiful vista of mountains out the mouth of the bay. This vista makes Carriden Bay exposed to east winds, however. It would be an uncomfortable anchorage in such winds.

Woods Bay. Use chart 3547. Woods Bay is exposed to westerly winds. Friends, however, report finding it to be a good spot in settled weather.

Embley Lagoon. Use chart 3547. Too

Reference only — not for navigation

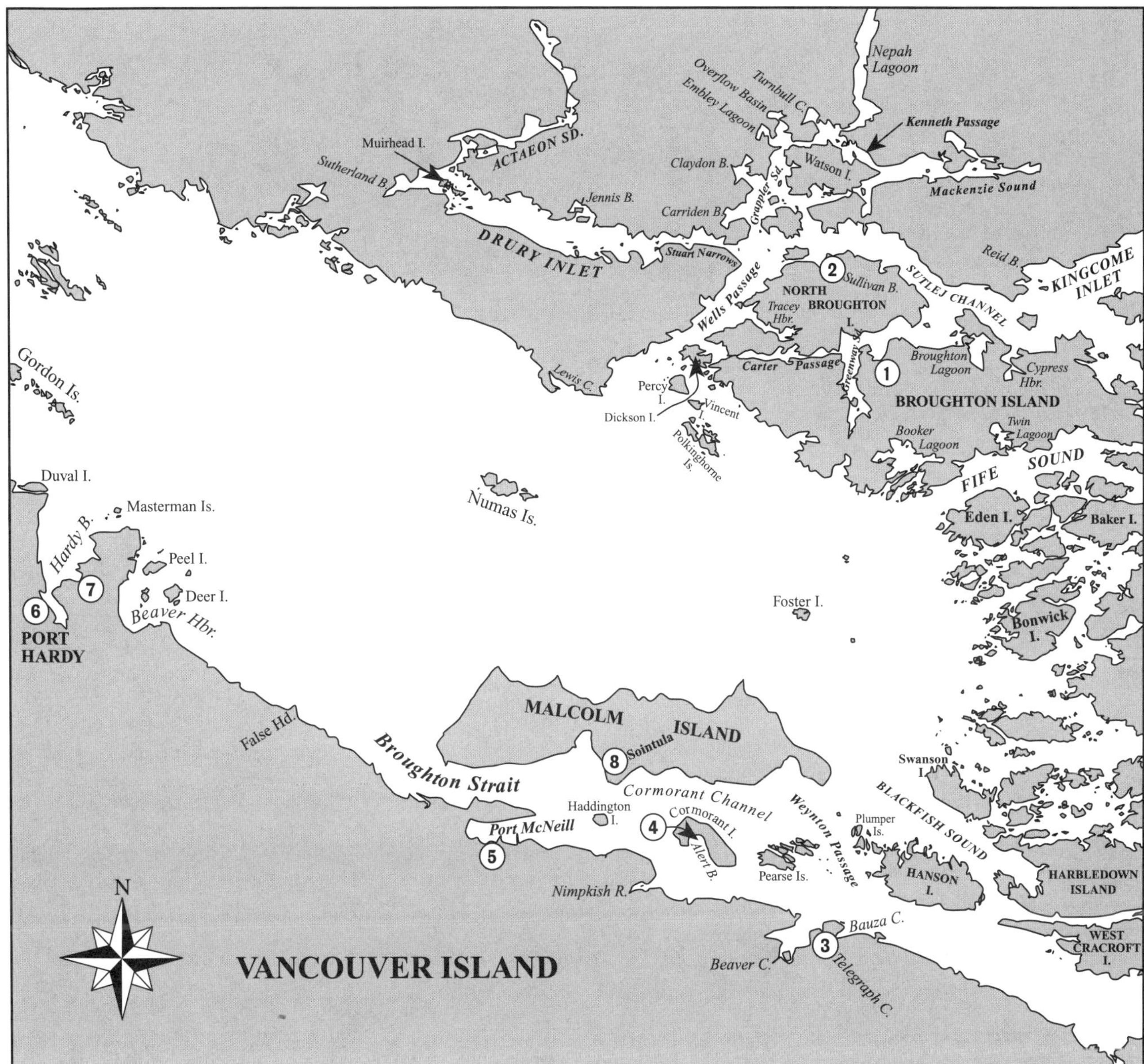

shallow for anything but dinghies, but it is an interesting exploration.

Overflow Basin. Use chart 3547. Dinghies only.

Claydon Bay. Use chart 3547. Entering or leaving, favor the Morton Point side. Foul ground, shown on the chart, extends from the opposite side of the entrance. In Claydon Bay you can pick the north or south arms, depending on which way the wind is blowing. Aggressive flies can be a problem, especially in the north arm. Crabbing is reported to be good.

Turnbull Cove. Use chart 3547. Turnbull Cove is a large and beautiful bay with lots of room and good anchoring in 30-50 feet anywhere you choose. Chappell warns that an easterly gale can turn the entire bay into a lee shore, however, so beware if such winds are forecast.

Nepah Lagoon. Use chart 3547. The adventuresome might want to try Roaringhole Rapids into Nepah Lagoon, but we've never done it. Passage, by dinghy with an outboard motor, should be attempted only at high water slack, which lasts 5 minutes and occurs 2 hours after the corresponding slack at Alert Bay. There is just 3 feet of water in this channel at low water. Nepah Lagoon doesn't appear to have any useable anchorages, except possibly a little notch about a mile from the rapids.

MACKENZIE SOUND

Kenneth Passage. Use chart 3547. Kenneth Passage is navigable at all stages of the tide, being careful of a covered rock off Jessie Point. Currents can be quite strong and whirlpools will sometimes appear. A slack water entry is advised, especially on spring tides. The best advice is to take a look and decide if conditions suit you and your boat.

Steamboat Bay. Use chart 3547. Steamboat Bay is shown on the small insert for Kenneth Passage on chart 3547. It is a good anchorage, with room for a few boats. The bay shoals to drying flats all around. Watch for the drying rocks along the east shore at the entrance.

See area map page 181

Burly Bay. Use chart 3547. Burly Bay is a good anchorage, mud bottom, but the muddy shoreline makes going ashore difficult. The little notch just to the west of Blair Island is better. Chappell *(Cruising Beyond Desolation Sound)* was not excited about Burly Bay, but our log reads, "Spectacular scenery, Ansel Adams photograph stuff, with rock wall on eastern shore falling straight into the sea." Guidebooks often are influenced by who visited, and what kind of day was had. Friends tell us of seeing grizzly bears on shore at Burly Bay.

Little Nimmo Bay. Use chart 3547. Little Nimmo Bay is a pretty anchorage, and the rock-strewn entrance is not as difficult as it appears on the chart. Anchorage is in 4 fathoms, mud bottom. Several small waterfalls tumble through the forest here. Grizzly bears are reported to be in the area. Make lots of noise if you go ashore. With care it is possible to go through to Nimmo Bay, which also has good anchorage.

Hopetown Passage. Use chart 3547. The eastern entrance into Hopetown Passage is blocked by a drying reef. Explore by dinghy first. If Hopetown Passage is attempted at all, it should be done cautiously, at high water slack in a shallow draft boat.

Stuart Narrows. Use chart 3547. Currents in Stuart Narrows run to a maximum of 7 knots, although on small tides they are reported to be much less. Times of slack are listed under Alert Bay, Secondary Current Stations, in the Tide and Current Tables, Vol. 6. The only hazard is Weld Rock. The current flows faster south of the rock, but passage can be made north of the rock as well. Leche Island should be passed to the north. A study of the chart shows a rock patch to the south.

Four boats from Fidalgo Yacht Club are rafted together in Turnbull Cove.

Drury Inlet. Use chart 3547. Drury Inlet is surrounded by low hills, much scarred by logging, that grow lower near the head of the inlet. It is much less visited than other waters in the area. The entrance, off Wells Passage, is clearly marked on the charts, as is Stuart Narrows, 1.5 miles inside the entrance. Anchorage is available in two arms of **Richmond Bay** (choose the one that protects from the prevailing wind); near Stuart Narrows; and in **Sutherland Bay,** at the head of Drury Inlet. Approach Sutherland Bay around the north side of the Muirhead Islands, after which the bay is open and quite protected from westerlies.

We anchored for the night in the southwestern cove of Richmond Bay, near Stuart Narrows, and found it superb. The cove was protected, tranquil, and private. Our notes read, "Best if enjoyed without other boats."

Helen Bay. Use chart 3547. Helen Bay lies just east of Stuart Narrows. It is reported to be a good anchorage, and halibut are said to be caught in the area.

The business end of Sullivan Bay. Fuel dock on the left, store with post office and spirits, then shower and laundry building.

Jennis Bay. Use chart 3547. Jennis Bay is the site of a small settlement, with anchorage very good just offshore and a little to the north of the settlement. Enter Jennis Bay around either end of Hooper Island. Keep to a mid-channel course to avoid rocks along the shores.

Davis Bay. Use chart 3547. Davis Bay looks inviting on the chart, but is not very pretty and is open to westerlies. Enter on the south side Davis Islet strongly favoring the Davis Islet shore.

Muirhead Islands. Use chart 3547. The Muirhead Islands, near the head of Drury Inlet, are rock-strewn but truly beautiful, and invite exporing in a small boat or kayak.

Actress Passage/Actaeon Sound. Use chart 3547. Actress Passage, connecting Drury Inlet with Actaeon Sound, is rock- and reef-strewn, narrow and twisting. It should be taken only at slack water. No time correction is given in the Tide and Current Tables, so you'll have to pick slack for yourself. A few years ago, a good friend, extremely experienced, got sucked into Actress Passage when it was really running, and almost swamped.

We have run Actress Passage near high water slack, when the current was quieter. Using chart 3547, we ran the channel between Dove Island and the mainland to the north, avoiding the charted rock, without problem. Regular traffic, however, uses the shorter channel east of Dove Island, splitting rocks marked with sticks at the entrance to Drury Inlet. Carefully run near slack water, both channels are safe.

Once into Actress Passage, the overriding navigation problem is the area between Skeen Point and Bond Peninsula.

At high water, we chose to wrap fairly close around Skene Point, but the depths shoaled alarmingly as we went around. We would not want to try it at low water. The better choice is to follow Chappell's suggestion of crossing from Skene Point to Bond Peninsula, and working your way past the charted hazards around the corner.

With slack water in our favor, we did not continue into Actaeon Sound but instead turned back. Earlier, however, we talked with a couple who had spent a day in Actaeon Sound. They told us that Actaeon Sound was uninteresting, and that a huge logging operation occupied the head of the sound. They overnighted in Skene Bay (uninteresting), and said the crabbing was bad.

Queen Charlotte Strait. Use chart 3547 & 3548. Queen Charlotte Strait is about 15 miles wide between the entrance to Wells Passage and either Port Hardy or Port McNeill. The prevailing winds are from the northwest in the summer and and the southeast in the winter. In the summer, morning is usually the best time to cross.

By late morning or early afternoon a sea breeze will begin, and by mid-afternoon it can increase to 30 knots with rough seas. The sea breeze usually quiets in early evening.

Tom Taylor, from Greenway Sound Marina Resort, has crossed the strait between Wells Passage and Port McNeill hundreds of times, and says that in good weather he can go (in a fast boat) as late as 1400. Any given day can go against the norm; the prudent skipper will treat Queen Charlotte Strait with great respect.

Robson Bight. Use chart 3546. Robson Bight is on the Vancouver Island side of Johnstone Strait, at the mouth of the Tsitika River. This is a gathering place for northern resident killer whales, usually during the summer months. Many of the whales will rub their stomachs on stones in the shallow water near the beach.

Robson Bight has been designated an ecological reserve to protect the whales, and boaters are required to stay at least a half-mile offshore. Other than volunteers, though, no enforcement is in place.

According to an article in the February, 1995 issue of *Pacific Yachting*, commercial fishing boats have been fishing for salmon within the reserve areas. Kayakers, seeing the commercial fish boats, will paddle through and camp on shore. Regardless, all vessels are asked to respect the reserve boundaries, and not approach or chase the whales.

Bauza Cove. Use chart 3546. Bauza Cove is an attractive but deep bay, with good protection from westerly swells. It is open to the wash of passing traffic in Johnstone Strait.

Telegraph Cove. Use chart 3546. Telegraph Cove, protected from westerly winds and swells, is picturesque, with a number of buildings on pilings, connected by boardwalk. In 1911 the Canadian Government established a telephone station at Telegraph Cove to connect the northern end of Vancouver Island with Campbell River. In World War II a telegraph station was installed and Telegraph Cove became a communications relay station. Today, Telegraph Cove is where trailerable boats are launched to fish in Blackfish Sound or explore the waters in this area. The Stubbs Island Charters operation is based in Telegraph Cove. They can take you down to Robson Bight to see the whales.

③ **Telegraph Cove Resorts,** Telegraph Cove, B.C. V0N 3J0, (250)928-3131. Open all year except Tuesdays through Thursdays only during the winter, gasoline, launch ramp, *moorage for resort guests only.*

Beaver Cove. Use chart 3546. There is fairly deep anchorage along the shores of Beaver Cove, the site of an old sawmill. Logs may be boomed in the bay, and the bottom of the bay is almost certain to be fouled with sunken logs and debris.

Alert Bay. Use chart 3546. The Indian culture and roots are very much in evidence at Alert Bay on Cormorant Island—one can learn more about it here, in less time, than anywhere on this part of the coast. Chappell *(Cruising Beyond Desolation Sound)* devotes considerable space to Alert Bay's history, so we won't repeat it here.

Be sure to stop at the Visitors' Centre, on the water side of the road, mid-town. There you will get get information about the several attractions in Alert Bay—the world's tallest totem pole; the U'Mista Cultural Centre; the "Gator Gardens," where you can see cedar trees stripped of bark; the Nimpkish (pronounced somewhere between "Namgis" and "Numgis") burial grounds; and much more.

You can land at a small public float with room for several boats, or in the breakwater-protected basin deeper in the bay. The landing for the ferry to Port McNeill is adjacent to this basin. The small public float, mentioned above, is exposed to all winds, and the current can run swiftly. On a recent visit, though, we used this float and found it completely satisfactory—it all depends on conditions.

These totem poles are a few of the many examples of native culture at Alert Bay.

The town has three grocery stores, three pubs, fuel, a shipyard, welding, hydraulics, and the other services you would expect in a fishing port. The protected basin is home to the fishing fleet. If the fleet is out you'll have room. If it's in, you'll have to raft off a fishing boat. Judge the situation as you find it and do what's right at the time.

Study Chart 3546 before going to Alert Bay. Note the 3-knot currents shown throughout the area, and be aware of the rough water that can make up when wind opposes current. Note also the various shallows and other dan-

See area map page 181

The Port McNeill Boat Harbour has ample moorage, but call on the radio before you come in. The office will assign a slip and usually send someone to help you land.

gers, and plot your courses to stay well clear.

④ **Save-On Fuels,** P.O. Box 570, Alert Bay, B.C. V0N 1A0, (250)974-2161. Gasoline, diesel and lubricants, only fuel in Alert Bay. Close to all services.

Mitchell Bay. Use chart 3546. Mitchell Bay, near the east end of Malcom Island, is a good summertime anchorage, protected from all but south winds.

⑧ **Sointula.** Use chart 3546. Perhaps because our recent visit was so pleasant, Sointula, on Malcolm Island, is a favorite of ours. The extensive public docks are behind a breakwater at the head of Rough Bay, 1.5 miles beyond the landing for the ferry to Port McNeill. The public moorage can be crowded when the fishing fleet is in port. A shipyard, capable of major work, is located near the boat basin. There is also a small public float in front of the town.

Sointula (meaning "place of harmony" in Finnish) was settled by Finnish immigrants who engaged in logging, fishing, and farming. At the head of the basin the Sointula Co-op runs a well-stocked hardware store, including a good selection of marine hardware. The co-op also runs an equally well-stocked (but much larger) grocery store in the village of Sointula. If you need food, you can get it in Sointula.

Probably from the Finnish influence, the architecture in Sointula is a delight, especially when compared to the makeshift and often neglected structures one sometimes finds along the coast. The people are friendly, too. While walking from the boat basin to the village, don't be surprised if you're offered a ride.

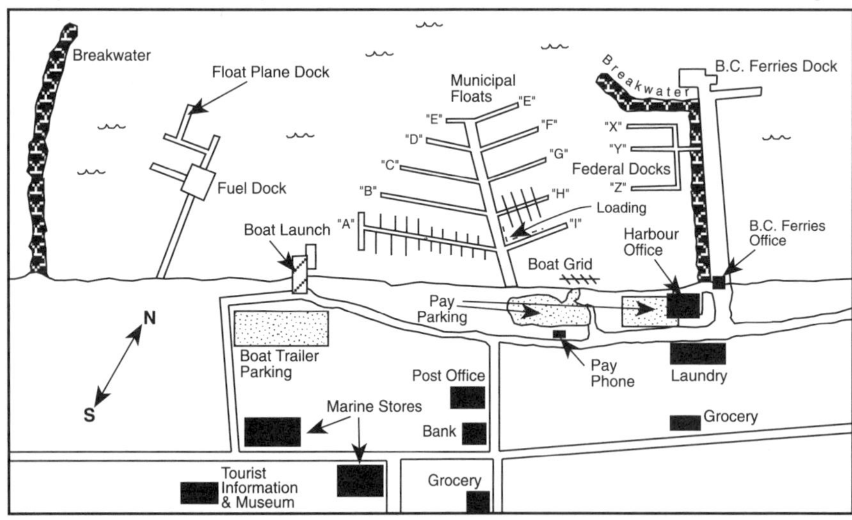

Port McNeill

Port McNeill. Use chart 3546. Port McNeill is a modern small city on the Vancouver Island highway, complete with banks, stores, hotels, restaurants, and communication by highway or airplane to the rest of Vancouver Island. With nearly all services located within easy walking distance of the boat harbor, Port McNeill has become a major resupply point for visiting boats.

The modern marina has ample space except during rush seasons. A laundromat is a short distance away. Two supermarkets are close to the marina, and free delivery is available. Fishing tackle, a post office, a large liquor store, drug stores, doctors, marine supplies and more are within a few minutes walk. Regular float plane service connects down-island and to Seattle. The Port Hardy International Airport is nearby. A fuel float is alongside the marina, as is a launch ramp. Anchorage is possible throughout the bay.

Dining: The Country Cookhouse is excellent.

⑤ **Port McNeill Boat Harbour,** P.O. Box 1389, Port McNeill, B.C. V0N 2R0, (250)956-3881. Monitors VHF channel

73. Call ahead on the VHF for slip assignment. Open all year, guest moorage available, 15, 20 & 30 amp power, washrooms, garbage drop, tidal grid, launch ramp. This is a good, comfortable marina, with room for all sizes of boats, and friendly management. No showers at the marina, however. Showers are available at the Dalewood Inn, about a block away. They hold back a couple of rooms for boaters, and provide soap and towels. At $5 the charge is noticable, but if you want a shower, they have it.

⑤ **Shell Marina,** P.O. Box 488, Port McNeill, B.C. V0N 2R0, (250)956-3336. Monitors VHF channel 73. Open all year, gasoline, diesel, stove oil, aviation fuel, propane. Located adjacent to the Port McNeill Boat Harbour.

Beaver Harbour. Use chart 3548. The islands in Beaver Harbour are quite picturesque, and offer anchoring possibilities. The west side of the Cattle Islands is protected. You'll anchor on a mud bottom in 5-7 fathoms. Patrician Cove has been recommended to us. Several white shell beaches are located throughout the islands.

Port Hardy. Use chart 3548. Port Hardy is the northernmost small city on Vancouver Island, and it's a nice town. A public float is attached to a large wharf in front of the city. For easy access to shopping, this is the place to be. We were told the Green Apple is good for Chinese food, and we had good supper of baby back ribs at the North Shore Hotel.

Port Hardy has a lovely park at shoreside, with a pleasant walkway past waterfront homes. The town is clean, prosperous-appearing, and friendly. The library houses a museum and artifacts section.

A mile or so farther into Hardy Bay you'll find the Quarterdeck Marina, which caters to pleasure craft and sport fishermen. A large public moorage, which caters to the commercial fleet, is adjacent. From this inner bay to downtown is a bit of walk, but it's not bad.

Port Hardy has all city amenities, including hospital and airport, with scheduled flights to and from Vancouver. Nearby Bear Cove is the terminus for the ferry that runs to Prince Rupert every other day during the summer.

⑥ **Fisherman's Wharf Small Craft Harbour,** 6655 Hardy Bay Rd., Port Hardy, B.C. V0N 2P0, (250)949-6332.

At Port McNeill, these children are playing on old logging equipment at a park near the marina.

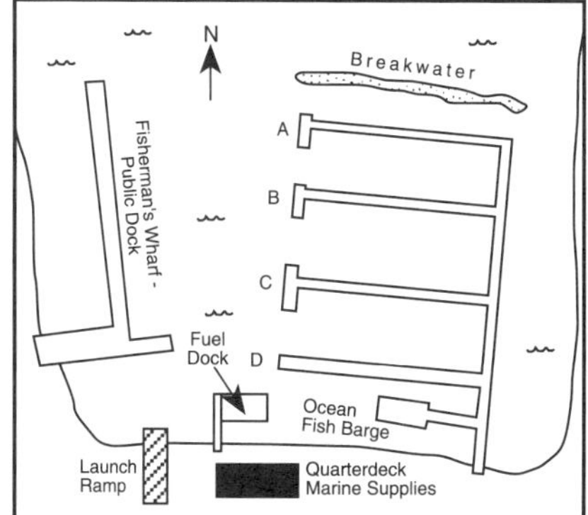

Quarterdeck Marina

Monitors VHF channel 73. Has 20 & 30 amp power. This basin is primarily for commercial fishing vessels, but usually has some room in the summer when the fleet is out. They have a launch ramp, a tidal grid, waste oil disposal and a garbage drop.

⑥ **Quarterdeck Marina & RV Park,** 6555 Hardy Bay Rd., PO Box 910, Port Hardy, B.C. V0N 2P0, (250)949-6551; fax (250) 949-7777. Monitors VHF channel 73. Open all year, gasoline, diesel, propane, guest moorage, 15 & 30 amp power, washrooms, showers, laundry. This is a busy marina with a well-stocked marine supplies and fishing tackle store, fuel dock, pub, haulout yard adjacent, and an RV park for those who come to fish for weeks at a time. The docks have been in poor condition for some years, but new owners (1996) plan a complete remodel. They have begun by installing some new docks, with power and lights.

⓪ **Port Hardy Esso Marine Station** P.O. Box 308, Port Hardy, B.C. V0N 2P0, (250)949-2710. Open all year, gasoline, diesel, stove oil, kerosene, naptha, waste oil disposal. Look for the sign, just inside the first marker as you enter Port Hardy. They carry charts, fishing supplies and bait, ice cream and snacks.

⑦ **Petro Canada Bear Cove,** P.O. Box 112, Port Hardy, B.C. V0N 2P0, (250)949-9988. Monitors VHF channel 09. Open all year, gasoline, diesel, kerosene, propane, CNG. Has washrooms and showers. They carry fishing tackle, bait, and ice, have waste oil disposal, and can arrange for towing and repairs. Possible guest moorage for 1997.

The West Coast of Vancouver Island

The boat. Large or small, a boat for the West Coast should be seaworthy, strong, and well-equipped. The seas encountered on the coastal passages will be a test, especially at Cape Scott, Brooks Peninsula, Tatchu Point, Estavan Point, the entrance to Ucluelet, Cape Beale, and the Strait of Juan de Fuca.

The wind accelerates as it is funneled at the capes and points, and the ocean's currents grow confused. Between wind and current, the seas grow noticably higher and steeper. Even on moderate days, a boat can be suddenly surrounded by whitecaps. Especially at Cape Scott and off Brooks Peninsula, pyramid-shaped waves seem to appear, break (or crumble into foam), and sweep past.

Often these "rogue" waves come from a direction different from the prevailing seas. Assuming a summertime westerly wind and a course in following seas down Vancouver Island, these waves can grab the broad sterns of many powerboats and make broaching a hazard. A double-ender, especially a double-ended sailboat with a large rudder, will not be affected as much. In fact, sailing in these seas with a 25-knot breeze from astern could be high points of the trip. But a planing-hull powerboat skipper will find himself paying close attention indeed to the waves and their effect on his boat. If he has not yet developed throttle and steering techniques for such conditions, he will do so quickly.

It is at times such as these that the skipper and crew know they are in serious water, and that their boat and equipment must be dependable. It is no place for old rigging, uncertain engines, sticky steering, intermittent electrical power, broken antennas, small anchors, unswung compasses, or clogged pumps. For a lifelong city-dweller, the West Coast is a wilderness, a wilderness with open seas and rocks a mile offshore. It pays to be prepared.

We think radar is all but essential. The local boats, even the little ones, have radar. GPS or loran are essential. Even on clear days in mild conditions, GPS or loran can identify turning points and confirm visual navigation. They take much anxiety out of navigating among ugly black rocks. In thick weather or fog, radar and GPS or loran will raise the comfort level aboard dramatically. And if you have to tell the Coast Guard where you are, GPS or loran will provide latitude and longitude coordinates within 100 yards or so.

Weather. The West Coast winter is stormy, and not a place for pleasure craft. Beginning in early spring, the weather begins to improve, and by June or July, the typical pattern of calm early mornings followed by rising westerly winds, establishes itself. In the evening the winds subside. Even in summer, storms of considerable force can hit the West Coast. The wise skipper monitors the weather broadcasts, and watches both barometer and sky.

Fog can be a problem, especially in August and September. We've heard the month of August referred to as "Foggust." The typical fog settles in early in the morning, and burns off in late morning or early afternoon—just as the westerly fills in. If an outside passage is planned but the morning is blanketed in fog, the skipper will appreciate having radar and GPS or loran. He will also be glad he did his chart navigation the day before, with waypoint coordinates plotted and loaded, distances measured, and compass courses established.

Plan for a little rain and cool temperatures. During the course of two to four weeks or more, most visitors will have a taste of everything.

The Coast Guard broadcasts continuous weather information from several locations along the West Coast. The reports are limited in scope to weather that affects the West Coast only. They begin with a summary of meteorological data, such as the location, description, and movement of ridges of high pressure or cells of low pressure, followed by a 24-hour forecast and an outlook for the following 24 hours. Then come wind and sea state reports from lighthouses and weather-monitoring stations. In surprisingly short time, the attentive visitor learns how to interpret the weather broadcasts and decide whether the time is right for an outside passage.

Fuel. While the West Coast is a wilderness, it is a wilderness with fuel. Gasoline and diesel are available all along the coast, within workable ranges for virtually any boat capable of safely being out there. The fuel stations exist to serve the large fishing fleet and the pockets of permanent residents, especially Indian communities. The fish boats use diesel; the outboard and IO-powered boats use gasoline. Fuel will be found at Winter Harbour, Coal Harbour, Walters Cove, Critter Cove (gasoline only), Zeballos, Esperanza, Tahsis, Ahousat, Tofino, Ucluelet, Bamfield, Port Alberni, Sooke, and Victoria.

Ice. Block ice can be a problem, especially at the many communities not served by road. The fish processing plants, however, have flaked ice for the fish boats, which take it on by the ton. A polite inquiry usually will yield enough ice for the icebox or cooler—sometimes for a charge, often not. Fish ice is "salt ice," and not recommended for consumption.

Water. Always check with locals before filling the water tank. Esperanza has excellent water.

Fresh vegetables. Scarce, uneven quality. They come in by barge or supply boat. Best to plan ahead and stock accordingly.

Government docks. Every community has a government dock, identified by its red railings, with moorage fees collected by a local resident. At a number of the docks the local resident isn't around, or doesn't bother to come collecting. Accept the no-charge tie-ups where you find them, pay gladly where the charge is collected.

Reference books and guidebooks. The Canadian Tide and Current Tables, Vol. 6 (blue cover) gives tides and currents south to the mouth of the Strait of Juan De Fuca. Vol. 5 (green cover) covers the Strait of Juan de Fuca and inland waters of Georgia Strait and Puget Sound. *Sailing Directions, B.C. Coast, South Portion,* is the official government publication, and should be considered essential. Note that *Sailing Directions* is intended for large vessels. A cove listed as good for anchoring may be too deep or exposed for small craft, but a passage listed as tortuous may be easily run by small craft.

Two good guidebooks exist, and we would buy both. The first is Don Watmough's *Cruising Guide to the West Coast of Vancouver Island.* It was first published in 1984, as part of the *Pacific Yachting* series on British Columbia cruising, and republished (unrevised) in 1993 by Evergreen Pacific Publishing Co. Although the unrevised 1993 edition contains now-outdated 1984 information, the rocks are unmoved since 1984, and the excellent aerial photos by George McNutt will help with navigation. The book was written before most boats had GPS, loran, and radar. Its dependence on traditional coastal navigation skills is instructive.

The second guidebook is Don Douglass's almost encyclopedic *Exploring Vancouver Island's West Coast,* published in 1994. The book is clear, easy to understand, and describes a large percentage of bays and coves along the West Coast. Not every bay described is a desireable anchorage, but Douglass tells the reader what to expect if he is forced to enter. Douglass's book was aboard during our own circumnavigation of Vancouver Island in 1995, and we would not make the trip without it. It is a major addition to the literature.

Charts. The Canadian Hydrographic Service has more than 30 charts that cover the coast between Port Hardy and Trial Island. Despite their cost, buy them all. Let the few that you don't use be insurance that you will have the chart you need, regardless of where you are. The charts are of excellent quality, and easy to read. The West Coast is no place for approximate navigation. If a $20 chart can take even a moment's anxiety out of a passage, the $20 is well spent.

Coast Guard. The Canadian Coast Guard stationed along the West Coast is simply incredible. They watch like mother hens over the fleets of fish boats, pleasure boats and work boats, ready to deploy helicopters and rescue craft instantly. They know what the weather is doing and where the traffic is. They know where help can be found. A call to the Coast Guard brings action.

Local communities often can get help out even faster than the Coast Guard. In the area off Kyuquot Sound, for example, we were told that a call to Walters Cove on VHF channels 06 or 14 would bring help a-running. Be sure to call the Coast Guard on channel 16, too.

Living on the West Coast: A crew socializes and attends to maintenance on a fish boat; a workboat and outboard-powered skiff are nearby; fishing equipment and another skiff are on the float; homes are connected by trail and boardwalk. Scene from Walters Cove.

Insurance. The insurance policies for most inshore boats do not cover the West Coast of Vancouver Island. Read your policy and check with your agent about extending the coverage for the period of your trip.

Oregon's Secret. Many of the boats cruising the West Coast come from Oregon. For years it's been their playground, their little secret. The reason is obvious. After the trip along the Washington coast, their first stop is the West Coast of Vancouver Island. In good weather it's a long but easy run. Boats from the population centers of Puget Sound or Vancouver/Victoria, however, must fight the Strait of Juan de Fuca or go around the top of Vancouver Island. Often, it is easier for them to enjoy the cruising in the protected waters inside Vancouver Island.

Strait of Juan de Fuca. For boats coming from Puget Sound or Vancouver/Victoria, the Strait of Juan de Fuca can be a difficult body of water. The typical summer weather pattern calls for calm conditions in the early morning, with a thermal wind building by afternoon, often to 30 knots or more. When wind and tidal current oppose, large, steep seas result.

On the American side, boats can leave Port Townsend at first light and get to Sequim Bay, Port Angeles, Clallam Bay, or Neah Bay before the wind builds. From Neah Bay, an early morning departure can fetch Barkley Sound while conditions are still calm.

On the Canadian side, boats can depart Victoria or Sooke at first light, and reach Port San Juan or even Barkley Sound, conditions and boat speed permitting.

These thoughts are for "typical" conditions. Variations often change "typical" conditions. We have seen the strait windy all day and calm all day. Listen to the weather broadcasts, watch the barometer and the sky, and be cautious.

Hardy Bay to Quatsino Sound

Goletas Channel • Nahwitti Bar • Cape Scott • Sea Otter Cove

Charts	
3549	Queen Charlotte Strait, Western Portion (1:40,000)
3598	Cape Scott to Cape Calvert (1:74,500)
3624	Cape Cook to Cape Scott (1:90,000)
3679	Quatsino Sound (1:50,000)
3681	Plans – Quatsino Sound
3686	Approaches to Winter Harbour (1:15,000)

Goletas Channel. Use chart 3549. Goletas Channel stretches west-northwest 23 miles between Duval Point (entrance to Hardy Bay) and the western tip of Hope Island. At the west entrance of Goletas Channel the notorious Nahwitti Bar blocks westerly swells from entering. Goletas Channel's shorelines are steep-to, so winds can funnel and grow stronger, but in customary summer conditions the channel, while it can get choppy, is not known for dangerous seas. Bull Harbour, the usual waiting point for slack water on Nahwitti Bar, indents Hope Island at the west entrance to Goletas Channel.

God's Pocket. Use chart 3549. God's Pocket, a favored layover, is in Christie Passage on the west side of Hurst Island, just off Goletas Channel. Boats bound around Vancouver Island probably will not see God's Pocket, unless to escape a chop in Goletas Channel. But boats planning a direct crossing of Queen Charlotte Sound to the Queen Charlotte Islands, or boats bound past Cape Caution, find God's Pocket to be a good jumping-off spot. God's Pocket is a local name, and not shown on the chart. The harbor is marked on the chart with a marina symbol and the notation, "2 buoys."

God's Pocket Resort, P.O. Box 130, Port Hardy, B.C. V0N 2P0, (250)949-9221. Room for a few boats at the dock, or tie to 2 public mooring buoys. No power or water to the docks. Washrooms and showers. Breakfast, lunch and dinner are available for their diving guests; others can be accommodated on an as-available basis, with reservations. This is primarily a diving resort. Harry Kerr and Molly Milroy are the owners. Nice people.

Waiting for slack water on the bar. Bull Harbour, indenting Hope Island, is a popular place to wait for Nahwitti Bar to calm down.

Bull Harbour. Use chart 3549. Bull Harbour is a lovely bay almost landlocked in Hope Island. It is the place to wait for slack water on Nahwitti Bar. Enter Bull Harbour around the east side of Norman Island, which blocks the southern entrance. Parts of Bull Harbour grow quite shoal on a low tide. Check the depth sounder and tide tables before anchoring for the night. The bottom is mud and holding is excellent. *Sailing Directions* says the southern portion of the harbor is reported to be foul with old chain and cable. During the fishing season commercial fish boats often crowd the harbor. A public float, not connected to shore, is in the southern part of the harbor. A public dock is on the east shore, north of Norman Island. If time allows, go ashore and cross the narrow neck of land at the north end of the harbor and watch the seas come into Roller

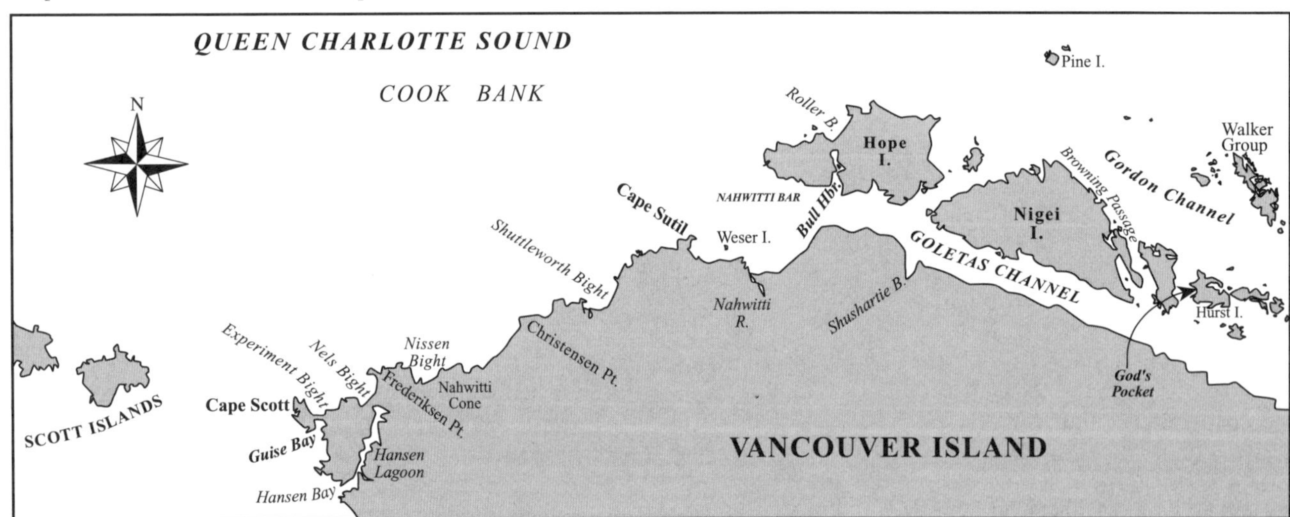

Reference only — not for navigation

Bay. Westerly winds can enter Bull Harbour, as can southeast gales. Be sure the anchor is well set, with adequate scope. In crowded conditions, achieving adequate scope can be a problem.

Nahwitti Bar. Use chart 3549. Nahwitti Bar should be attempted only at or near slack. Slack water and current predictions are shown in Tide and Current Tables, Vol. 6. Maximum tidal currents over the bar reach 5.5 knots. From seaward, the bar shoals gradually to a least depth of approximately 35 feet. When ocean swells from deep water hit the bar, their energy changes them from long and smooth to high and steep. We would be cautious about crossing against a strong westerly wind, even at slack water. If a strong ebb current opposes westerly winds, dangerous, and heavy breaking seas will develop.

It is often said that the ideal time to cross Nahwitti bar is at high slack water. At high slack a typical westerly wind blowing with the flood current will tend to keep seas down and permit a crossing a few minutes before the slack. The subsequent ebb current flows as fast as 3 knots along the coast all the way to Cape Scott. Slower boats will appreciate the free ride.

A crossing at high slack is not without its disadvantages, however. The ebb that follows high slack will be in opposition to the prevailing westerly wind. In a fresh westerly, a high, steep chop could develop along the run to Cape Scott. If our choices were between an early morning crossing at low water slack but calm conditions, or an afternoon crossing at high water slack but windy conditions, we would choose morning. Granted, a crossing at low slack water puts a boat into a building flood current. But in smooth water a faster boat will reach Cape Scott in about an hour, and a 6-knot boat will reach the cape in about three hours. Three hours would put the slower boat at the cape about mid-tide. The rips off Cape Scott may be too boisterous by then, so the slower boat may choose to wait for slack water again before rounding the cape.

Thus the wise skipper considers all factors before crossing Nahwitti Bar: current, weather, time of day, and the speed and seakeeping qualities of his vessel. At least 30 minutes should be allowed to get through the swells on the bar. Even fast boats usually must go slowly. At slack water in windless conditions, we found impressive swells extending out to Whistle Buoy MA, a total distance of approximately 2.5 miles, before they began to diminish.

Don Douglass, in his book *Exploring Vancouver Island's West Coast,* describes a quieter inner route, which he drew from June Cameron's *Pacific Yachting* article of September 1992. This route passes behind Tatnall Reefs and uses the reefs and kelp growing on them to reduce seas and current. While we have not yet taken this route, we will describe it here. A study of chart 3549 will make the route clear.

From Bull Harbour, cross Goletas Channel just east of Nahwitti Bar for a distance of a little more than 2 miles, on a course made good of 196° Magnetic. Crab if necessary to counter the effects of current and make good the course. Then turn west and run a course to pass between Weser Island and Vancouver Island, working into the bight that lies behind Cape Sutil. Fish boats reportedly hole up in this bight while waiting for westerlies outside to subside. Minimum depths for this route are reported to be 3 fathoms.

Douglass spent a day researching this route in 1994, and reports more extensively on it as part of a supplement (no charge) to his book. Those who purchased Douglass's book before the supplement was published should contact their bookseller or the publisher.

Reference only — not for navigation

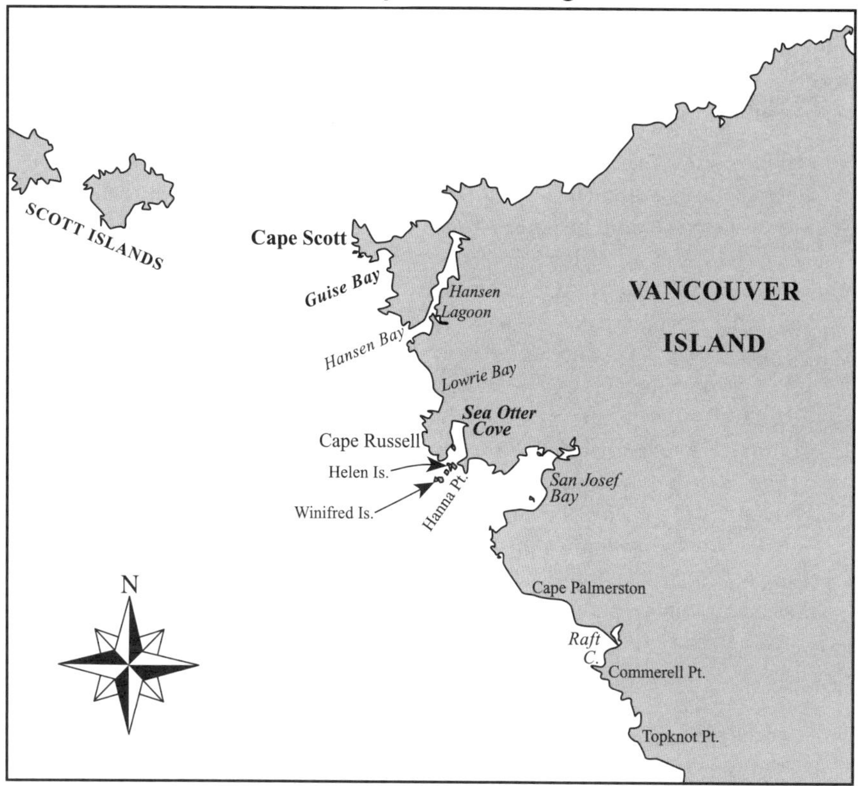

Cape Sutil to Cape Scott. Use chart 3598. *Sailing Directions* says the distance from Cape Sutil to Cape Scott is 15 miles, but this understates the actual running distance after crossing Nahwitti Bar. A more realistic distance would be measured from Whistle Buoy MA, and would be approximately 16.5 miles. Although the run across the bottom of Queen Charlotte Sound is exposed to westerlies, early morning conditions often are quiet, save for the relentless Pacific swell. Rocks extend as much as a mile offshore all along the way. A good offing is called for.

According to *Sailing Directions,* temporary anchorage can be found in Shuttleworth Bight, Nissen Bight, Fisherman Bay (SW corner of Nissen Bight), Nels Bight, and Experiment Bight. Study the chart before entering, and watch the weather.

Cape Scott. Use chart 3598; 3524. Cape Scott is the westernmost point of Vancouver Island. Dangerous rocks extend 0.5 mile offshore, northward and westward. The cape itself is a low piece of land connected by a narrow neck with

See area maps pages 188 and 189

Cape Scott

For 25 years, Cape Scott, the remote far north tip of Vancouver Island, had been a dream of mine. Cape Scott is exposed to weather and current, and to seas that could have begun thousands of miles away. It is the most significant landmark in a circumnavigation of Vancouver Island—one of the events that marks a *compleat* Northwest boatman. A rounding of Cape Scott implies that such a circumnavigation will become a reality.

Cape Scott can be rough. At their worst, Cape Scott's seas have capsized and sunk substantial vessels. Even quiet days can be uncomfortable, the result of swells that sweep in from the Pacific to meet colliding currents. Rocks lie offshore. If you find yourself in trouble off Cape Scott, you *are* in trouble.

Mrs. Hale, ever stalwart before, refused to face Cape Scott. So long-time friend Tom Hukle came aboard for the voyage around the north face of Vancouver Island and down the West Coast. Tom is a former sailboat skipper of the year at Seattle Yacht Club, an excellent seaman, knowledgable navigator, and superb shipmate (but lousy cook).

On a breakfast of buns from the bakery and hot coffee, Tom and I departed Port Hardy at first light and ran out Goletas Channel, the early morning sun behind us. *Surprise,* a well-equipped Tollycraft 26 repowered with a "big-block" 454 V-8 Crusader engine, cruises at an easy 15 knots. We made all 15 knots in the flat water of a windless Goletas Channel, and reached Bull Harbour an hour and 15 minutes before the predicted turn at Nahwitti Bar. With time to kill, we inspected and took pictures at Bull Harbour. A few minutes before the turn, we followed two fish boats into the up-and-down rollers of the bar.

We rolled across at slow speed, steering a course for Whistle Buoy MA, 2½ miles away. A short distance beyond the buoy the the bottom grew deeper and the seas flattened. We powered back up to 15 knots for the run to Cape Scott, confirming major landmarks as we progressed: Cape Sutil, Northwest Nipple, Christensen Point, Nahwitti Cone, Frederickson Point. At last Cape Scott lay ahead, with the uninviting Scott Islands offshore. Cape Scott was uninviting, as well. Rocks extended from the land. Seas broke heavily on the shore. A low salt mist hung over all.

Out where we were, in only 10-15 knots of wind, the seas began to lump up. They were not towering, but for a small boat their closeness and steepness made even modest height significant. It had to be the currents. At first *Surprise* shouldered into the seas well, but after a brief time Tom Hukle, who was on the helm, said, "I'd like to slow down."

Tom and I agreed that if this is what Cape Scott was like in good conditions, it could be unrelenting hell in foul. Speed reduced, we bucked along. Charts slid onto the cabin sole, and a few books rearranged themselves. The wipers cleared spray from the windshield.

At last, at 1015 on 28 June 1995, in erratic writing clearly affected by the motion of the boat, I made the log entry I had waited 25 years to make: "Cape Scott abeam to port 1.5 miles. Light wind. Confused 4-6' seas. We're going home. A major moment."

A major moment indeed. Tom turned chatty, but I stared out the side window at Cape Scott, watching it move past as we began our voyage down the West Coast of Vancouver Island. "Give me a few minutes," I said to Tom. "I know it's corny, but I've waited a long time for this. I want to savor it."

—Robert Hale

the main body of Vancouver Island. The Cape Scott Light, on a square tower 13 feet high, is on higher ground about 0.25 mile inland from Cape Scott.

Currents flowing on both sides of the cape meet at Cape Scott. Especially when opposed by wind, the currents can produce heavy seas and overfalls, dangerous to small craft. It is reported that even in calm conditions, seas can emerge seemingly from nowhere, the collision of currents. Our own rounding of Cape Scott was a little before half tide on a flood, with only 10-12 knots of wind. The size and nature of the seas, while not dangerous, definitely were out of proportion to the wind. With its seas, rocks, and shortage of convenient hidey-holes, Cape Scott is not a place to treat lightly. A vessel in trouble at Cape Scott could be in serious trouble, and quickly.

It is with good reason that guidebooks (including this one) and magazine articles emphasize the dangers and cautions at Cape Scott. One rounding, even in good conditions, confirms the fact that the waters can be treacherous. Yet in settled summer conditions, a well-managed seaworthy vessel, with a good weather eye, can make a safe and satisfying rounding. The standard advice is to round Cape Scott at slack. Other factors may persuade a skipper round at times other than slack.

In our own case, when we sensed that the 10-12-knot westerly was freshening, we decided to get around while we could, even though we were at least two hours past slack. Once around the cape we had wind and current from the same direction (astern), and an easier ride to Quatsino Sound. Each situation, each boat, is different. What worked yesterday may not work today. A careful skipper, fully aware that the safety of his vessel and crew truly are at risk at Cape Scott, must judge conditions and make the right choices.

In 1996 the Cape Scott Marine Park was extended to include nearly all the coastline between Cape Scott and Nahwitti Bar.

Cape Scott to Quatsino Sound. Use chart 3624. The run from Cape Scott to the entrance of Quatsino Sound is approximately 28.5 miles, depending on the courses chosen. This is where the depth sounder becomes an important navigation tool. To stay clear of off-lying rocks and reefs, the general advice is to follow the 20-fathom curve all the way down the coast. Douglass says he prefers the 30 fathom curve for an extra margin of safety. We are inclined toward Douglass's 30-fathom standard. In moderate conditions with excellent visibility we felt comfortable in 25-30 fathoms. Had conditions deteriorated, we would have moved out.

With the summer westerly in place, the run between Cape Scott and Quatsino Sound is a downhill sleighride. Powerboaters, especially those with planing hulls, will have to saw away at the helm and play with the throttle to stay in harmony with the relentless procession of rollers. They will arrive tired. Planing hull powerboats are not happy in powerful following seas. The sailboaters will have all the fun, especially if the boat and crew can handle a spinnaker. They too will arrive tired, but exhilerated.

Given the conditions, many boats make a direct passage between Cape Scott and Quatsino Sound, and leave the bays that lie between for another day. Sailboats, after a long passage at 6 knots, will be apt to put into one of those bays, particularly Sea Otter Cove. Boats heading *toward* Cape Scott might also be more apt to investigate the shoreline, choosing to spend the night in Sea Otter Cove, ready for an early departure and a rounding of Cape Scott before the westerly fills in.

Guise Bay. Use chart 3624. Guise Bay lies just south of Cape Scott. *Sailing Directions* says the entrance to Guise Bay is encumbered with rocks, and local knowledge is called for. The chart suggests that entrance is possible, but Douglass says that the rocks are often covered with foam and a strong heart is called for. We didn't even attempt it.

Hansen Bay. Use chart 3624. Hansen Bay was the location of a Danish settlement around 1900. Supply vessels could anchor in good weather only. The settlement failed. *Sailing Directions* says Hansen Bay "affords no shelter," although commercial fish boats do hole up there.

Sea Otter Cove. Use chart 3624. Sea Otter Cove, south of Cape Scott, is described in *Sailing Directions* as "indifferent shelter." Nevertheless, Sea Otter Cove is a favorite of fish boats, and well-known to yachtsmen. Enter from the south, between Hanna Point and the Helen Islands. Watmough shows swells breaking almost across the entrance, but careful attention to the chart will bring you in. The channel is narrow and shallow. Contributing Editor Tom Kincaid says he stopped watching the depth sounder because it scared him so. Once inside, 8 mooring buoys have been placed with strong anchors (see sidebar). We recommend tying to one of these buoys. We heard of a fish boat that anchored in Sea Otter Cove and found itself perched on a rock when the tide went out.

San Josef Bay. Use Chart 3624. San Josef Bay is protected from northerly winds, but open to westerly and southerly winds. Anchor in settled weather.

Sea Otter Cove

For boats rounding Cape Scott heading down the West Coast , the first fully protected harbor is Sea Otter Cove. Kayakers and rowers sometimes stop in Hansens Lagoon, where they can more easily pull their boats up on the beach. But for boats than need to anchor or take a mooring buoy, Sea Otter Cove is a welcome retreat, safe from whatever might be going on out on the ocean.

The entrance to Sea Otter Cove is protected by a group of small islands, each one of which is surrounded by a reef. Entry, using care, can be made on either side of these islands. If you choose the southernmost route, a single red light kept to starboard (Red, Right, Returning) provides a reference point for the very narrow channel between the reefs. The northernmost entry is broader and deeper, but more exposed to the ocean swells until you're well into the bay.

Once inside, you'll note that the entire bay is quite shallow, often less than a fathom. Be very careful during extreme low tides. You'll also note a row of government mooring buoys stretched part-way across the bay, and another row farther into the bay. Depending on how the fishing is going, Canadian trollers often are tied to the buoys.

My business partner Ole Hansen and I once entered Sea Otter Cove from a fairly rough sea, and took a buoy in the first string. A Canadian troller was on another buoy in our string, and a third troller occupied a buoy in the second string.

Now, you need to understand that Ole Hansen is a very careful seaman, the best I've ever met. Ole has a horror of tying to anyone's buoy if he doesn't know from first-hand knowledge how it's held to the bottom. Never mind that the buoys were put in by the Canadian government to hold fishing boats; never mind that the buoys were big and rugged looking—how were they attached to the bottom?

Ole had his skin diving gear with him, and promptly suited up for a personal inspection of our buoy's anchor. He was down for quite a while, but when he surfaced and peeled back his mask, he said, "If we blow out of here tonight, Vancouver Island is going with us!"

Whoever installed those mooring buoys had begun by using a long length of ship's anchor chain. Each end of the chain was wrapped around a little rocky island, then shackled to a convenient link in the chain. Thus secured, the chain snaked its way across the bottom of the bay, and the mooring pennants were shackled to it. As Ole said, the only way we could drag out of Sea Otter Cove was to take a significant part of Vancouver Island with us. We slept peacefully that night.

—*Tom Kincaid*

Quatsino Sound

Winter Harbour • Koskimo Bay • Pamphlet Cove • Quatsino Narrows • Coal Harbour

Charts	
3624	Cape Cook to Cape Scott (1:90,000)
3679	Quatsino Sound (1:50,000)
3681	Plans – Quatsino Sound
3686	Approaches to Winter Harbour (1:15,000)

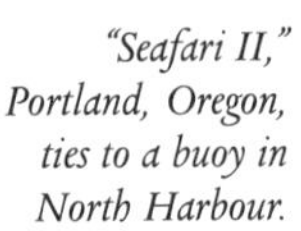

"Seafari II," Portland, Oregon, ties to a buoy in North Harbour.

Quatsino Sound is the northernmost of the five sounds that indent the West Coast. With the exception of Forward Harbour and Winter Harbour on the north side near the entrance, Quatsino Sound probably is the sound least explored by cruising yachts.

Quatsino Sound is, however, the first quiet anchorage after the 50-mile run from Bull Harbour, and a welcome sight it is after hours of rolling seas and anxiety at Cape Scott. The entrance is straightforward. Using large-scale chart 3686, identify South Danger Rock and Robson Rock (both of them well away from land), stay close to Kains Island, and proceed into Forward Harbour. North Harbour and Browning Inlet both are good anchorages, or you can continue to Winter Harbour.

VHF: We are told the fishermen work on channels 73, 84, and 86.

The Winter Harbour waterfront is set up for fish packing. Government wharf is at far end.

① **Winter Harbour.** Use chart 3686; 3624. Winter Harbour is a commercial fishing outpost. B.C. Packers owns the first major set of docks as you enter. Their fuel dock has gasoline and diesel and is open to the public. The Winter Harbour Authority public dock is a short distance beyond, and has moorage for a number of boats. A float house at the public dock contains showers and laundry machines. These facilities are reserved for the commercial fishermen, but we are told that if polite inquiries are made with the wharfinger, pleasure craft folk might gain their use. No guarantees. A pay phone is at the head of the pier.

The high structure at the end of the pier makes flaked ice for the fish boats. The attendant graciously offered all we needed, which in our case was a small amount for our ice chest. The store had no block ice. The gift of flaked ice, although small, was welcome and appreciated.

Winter Harbour has a well stocked general store. Up to the first of July the winter hours are Tues.-Fri. 1500-1800; Sat. 1500-1700. In the summer season the hours expand to 1000-2000. The store has what you need: meat, produce, canned goods, packaged foods and fixings, liquor, clothing, sport and commercial fishing equipment, charts.

We were told that good anchorage is available at the head of Winter Harbour, but did not inspect it ourselves. Given the excellent anchorage in North Harbour, we suspect the head of Winter Harbour is not much visited.

North Harbour. Use chart 3686; 3624. North Harbour, north of Matthews Island in Forward Inlet, is an excellent anchorage, popular with boats planning a morning departure from Quatsino Sound. Three mooring buoys are located close to Matthews Island, with good anchoring depths beyond. North Harbour is sheltered and quiet, yet close to the mouth of Quatsino Sound.

Browning Inlet. Use chart 3686; 3624. Browning Inlet is narrow and sheltered, with good holding in 3-5 fathoms. Crabbing is reported to be good.

Koskimo Bay. Use chart 3679. Koskimo Bay has a couple of anchorages, one behind Mabbot Island and one at Mahatta Creek. The Koskimo Islands are at the east end of Koskimo Bay.

Mabbott Island. Use chart 3679. The little area behind Mabbott Island would be a cozy spot to drop the hook if the large fish farm weren't there and a float house didn't take part of the anchorage. If you must anchor behind Mabbott Island it can be done. Given the choice, we would move on—and did.

Mahatta Creek. Use chart 3679. In Koskimo Bay, this is the place to be. Work your way east of the mouth of the creek, anchor in 5-7 fathoms. Put the dinghy out. At high tide explore the creek. Nice.

Koskimo Islands. Use chart 3679. Explore by dinghy. The narrow passage between the largest of the islands and Vancouver Island can be run (carefully), but with safe water just outside the islands, we see no need to.

Koprino Harbour. Use chart 3579.

Reference only — not for navigation

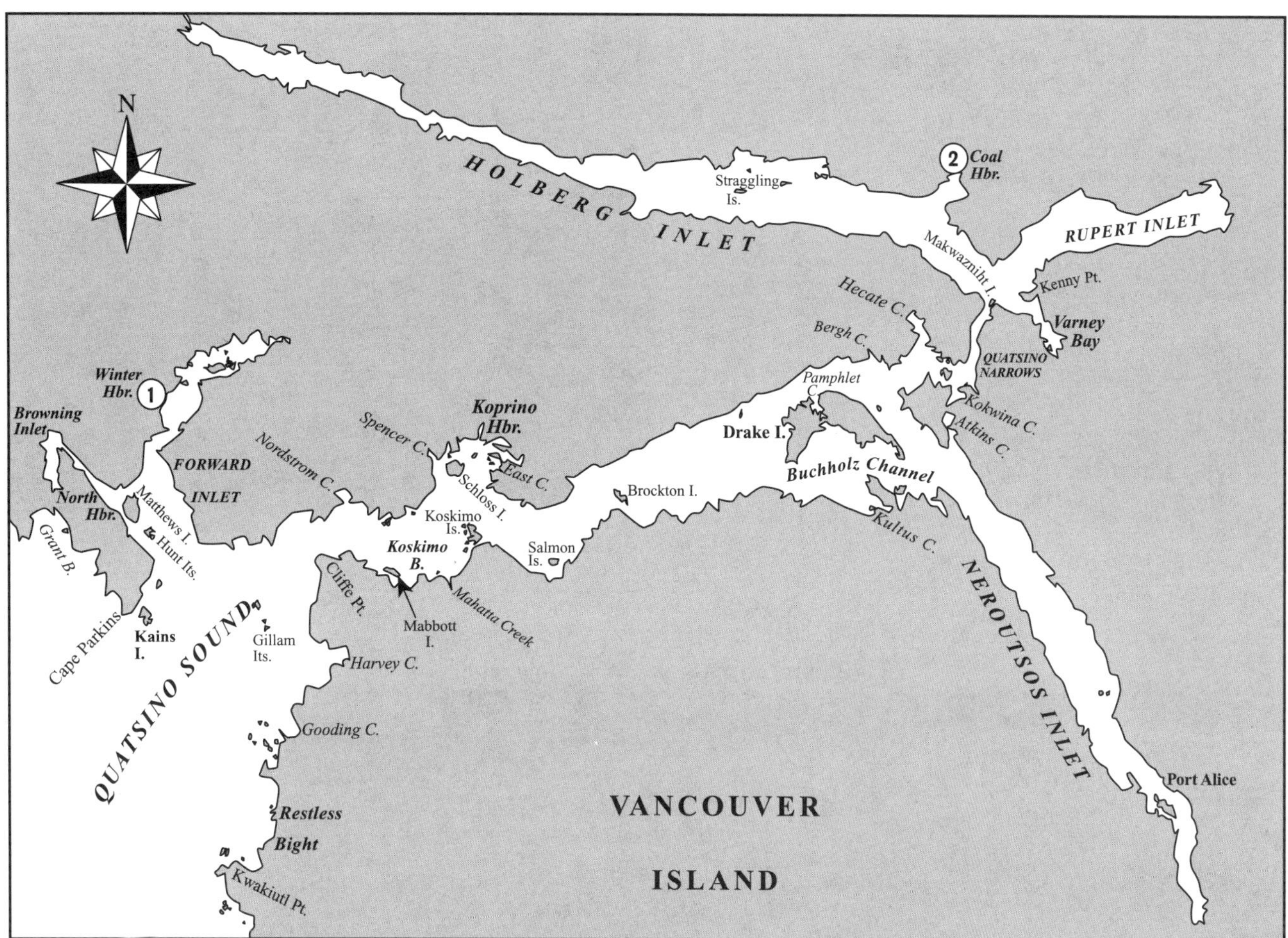

Most of Koprino Harbour is too deep for pleasure craft, but the area of East Cove, near the northeast corner of Koprino Harbour, is excellent. In 1996 a new marine park was created in Koprino Harbour.

East Cove. Use chart 3679. If East Cove were in Desolation Sound instead of Koprino Harbour, it would be filled with 25 boats every night. East Cove is tranquil, snug and tree-lined, with good dinghy access to shore—cruising as it should be. You'll probably run a stern-tie to shore. If East Cove is occupied, anchorage almost as delightful can be had just to the north, behind a group of little islets. The largest of these islets is identified on the chart as Linthlop Islet.

Pamphlet Cove. Use chart 3679. Pamphlet Cove, part of a provincial recreation reserve, is located on the north side of Drake Island, about 3.5 miles west of Quatsino Narrows. Pamphlet Cove is scenic and protected, an ideal anchorage. A tidal grid and remains of old docks are along the shore. You can go ashore and enjoy the reserve. Watmough reports a trail leading from Pamphlet Cove to the south side of Drake Island.

Neroutsos Inlet. Use chart 3679; 3681. "The wind blows hard every afternoon in Neroutsos Inlet," one knowledgable local told us. Neroutsos Inlet is long and straight-sided, with little diversion along the way. An important pulp mill is at Port Alice, near the south end.

Quatsino Narrows. Use chart 3681 *(strongly recommended)* or chart 3679. Quatsino Narrows connects with Rupert Inlet and Holberg Inlet, and the village of Coal Harbour. With tidal streams near Makwazniht Island running to 9 knots on the flood and 8 knots on the ebb, it is best to take the narrows near slack. Predictions for Quatsino Narrows are shown in Tide and Current Tables, Vol. 6. You'll find considerable turbulence near Makwazniht Island. A range on the eastern shore of the narrows will help you stay on course through the turbulence. Turbulence, though less than that found near Makwazniht Island, is present near the south entrance to Quatsino Narrows. At slack water watch for tugs with log boom tows.

Varney Bay. Use chart 3679. We did not visit Varney Bay, east of the north entrance to Quatsino Narrows. Douglass and Watmough, however, both recommend Varney Bay as scenic, tranquil and protected. Watmough calls Varney Bay a "delight." Anchor behind Kenny Point. Watch for rocks and deadheads as you enter.

Rupert Inlet. Use chart 3679. Rupert Inlet is the site of the giant Utah Mines open pit copper mine. Not much reason for the cruising yachtsman to go there.

② Coal Harbour. Use chart 3679; 3681. Coal Harbour has a small village with store, haulout, and fuel, and is only 8 miles by road from all the facilities of Port Hardy. The fuel dock is operated by Anchor Petroleum Distributors for the benefit of their own fishing fleet stationed at the same location. They are friendly, helpful people and welcome pleasure craft (not that many visit), and their pump can deliver fuel at a great rate. But they do not have the customary attendants waiting to serve you as you arrive. "Be patient with us," they ask. You can call ahead on VHF channel 10. Call "Coal Harbour."

Coal Harbour served as the last whaling station on the West Coast, the station ceasing operations in 1967. A whale's jawbone, several times a person's height, stands on display.

Holberg Inlet. Use chart 3679. Holberg Inlet is 18 miles long, narrow and deep, a classic fjord. It has few places to anchor, and not much for the cruising yachtsman. With its 36-mile round trip and no facilities or attractions, it is seldom traveled by cruising yachts.

These three fish boats tied to a buoy in North Harbour early in the evening, prepared supper, and snugged down for the night.

Reference only — not for navigation

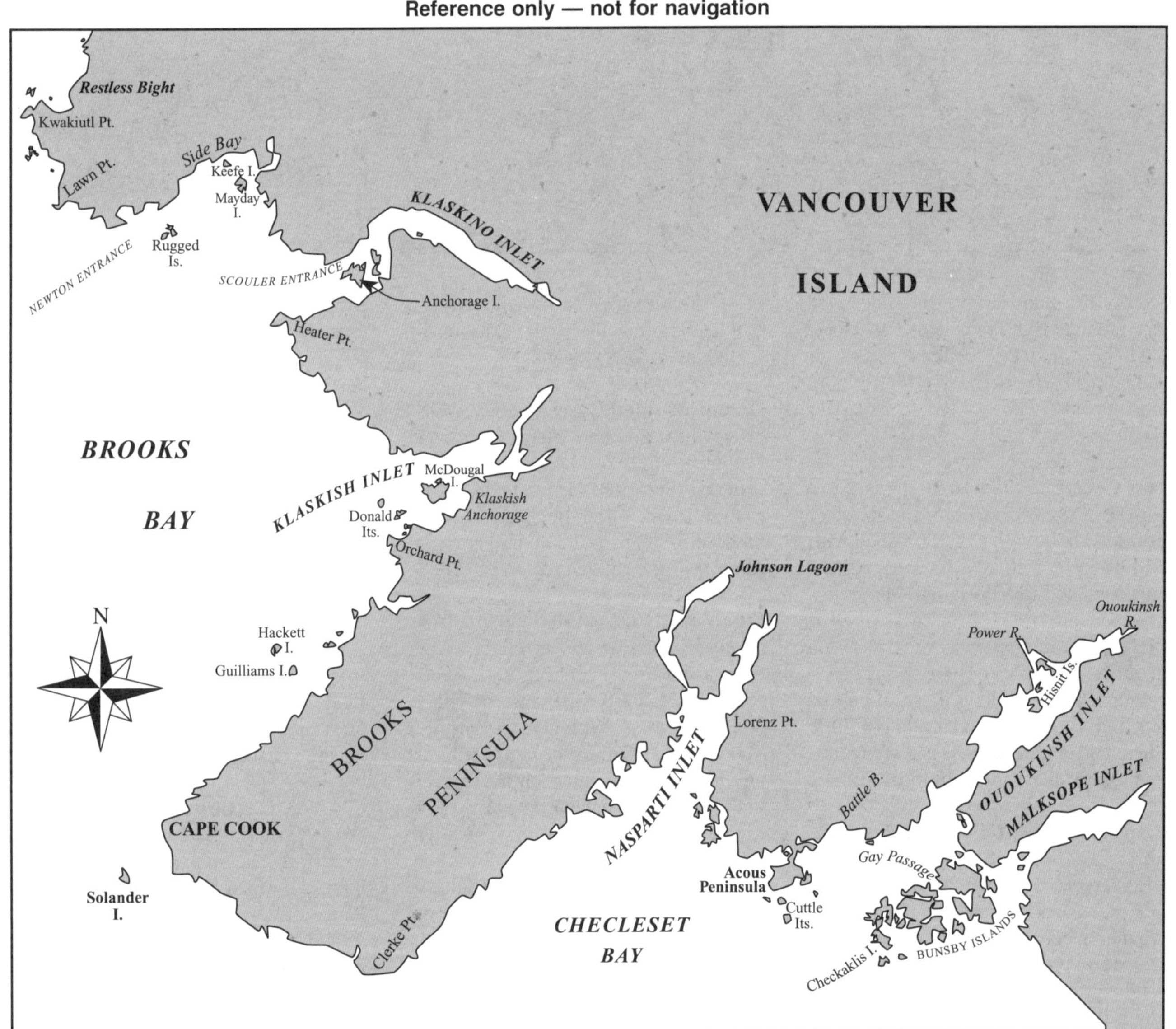

See area map page 194

Quatsino Sound to Kyuquot Sound

Cape Cook • Brooks Peninsula

Charts	
3623	Kyuquot Sound to Cape Cook (1:80,000)
3624	Cape Cook to Cape Scott (1:90,000)
3679	Quatsino Sound (1:50,000)
3680	Brooks Bay (1:38,300)
3651	Scouler Entrance and Kyuquot
3683	Checleset Bay (1:36,500)

Brooks Bay. Use chart 3624; 3679; 3680; 3651. It is approximately 19 miles from a departure point south of Kains Island, at the entrance to Quatsino Sound, to a point about 2 miles due west of Solander Island. From Solander Island to Walters Cove it is another 22-25 miles, depending on the course chosen—a total of at least 40 miles in the open sea. Those heading around Brooks Peninsula during a "window" of moderate conditions can be excused for foregoing exploration of Brooks Bay. Especially so because Brooks Bay is dotted with unmarked (but charted) rocks and reefs, and Brooks Peninsula looks so hostile.

As a result, boats exploring Klatskino Inlet and Klaskish Inlet on the north side of Brooks Bay should not be bothered by overcrowding. We have not explored Brooks Bay, for the reasons outlined above. Douglass and Watmough have explored Brooks Bay, however, and describe it fully in their guidebooks. We recommend them.

Brooks Peninsula. Brooks Peninsula, and the waters off Cape Cook, are, together with Cape Scott, the most hostile on the West Coast. The peninsula itself is a mountainous, rectangular promontory that extends 6 miles out from Vancouver Island, like a growth on the side of an otherwise handsome face. Rocks and reefs guard much of the Brooks Peninsula shoreline. Tangles of driftwood make beaches impassable. Cliffs rise from the beaches. At the tops of the cliffs, wilderness.

Cap on the Cape: When a cloud forms on top of Brooks Peninsula over Cape Cook, it often means that strong northwesterly winds will follow.

Cape Cook. Use chart 3680. Cape Cook is the northwestern tip of Brooks Peninsula. Rocks and shoals extend offshore from Cape Cook nearly to Solander Island. Thus the safe route past Cape Cook is well offshore from Solander Island.

Solander Island. Use chart 3680. Cape Cook (Solander Island) is an exceedingly difficult patch of water. When conflicting currents meet accelerating winds, conditions become dangerous. The marine weather broadcasts often talk of "local winds off the headlands" of 35 knots. The headland they have in mind is Cape Cook. While no headland on the West Coast should be taken lightly, Cape Cook (and Cape Scott) should be given the greatest respect. Listen to the weather broadcasts. If the weather sounds questionable, wait. When your opportunity comes, seize it.

Solander Island is an ugly treeless black rock 300 feet high, with a light on it. In 10-12 knots of morning westerly breeze we found the Pacific swells shortened and steepened, mixed with pyramid-shaped seas that ran at an angle 30 degrees different from the swells. Local advice was to keep 1.5-2 miles off Solander Island and Brooks Peninsula. We found this advice easy to follow.

We had to pay close attention to keep our broad-sterned cruiser square with the following seas, particularly when a cross-sea would grab the stern and try to twist us into a broach. Later, in Walters Cove, we spoke with a couple in their 70s, who had followed us in a slower but perhaps better boat for the conditions. They appeared relaxed and reported a "pleasant run."

Clerke Point. Clerke Point marks the southeast corner of Brooks Peninsula. Shoals extend at least 0.5 mile offshore, but a course following the 20-fathom curve will leave ample room for safety. We found that the pyramid-shaped seas we had battled at Solander Island had disappeared completely by the time Clerke Point was reached.

Once past Brooks Peninsula the weather warms and conditions improve. The remaining capes can throw some ugly stuff at you, but the hostility of Cape Scott and Brooks Peninsula are behind.

Checleset Bay. Use chart 3683. Checleset Bay has a number of delightful anchorages, including the **Bunsby Islands**, with its remarkable population of sea otters. We did not explore Checleset Bay. Douglass and Watmough have, however, and we recommend them.

Bunsby Islands

People cruising the west coast really should make a stop in the Bunsby Islands, just offshore from Malksope Inlet. Several delightful, fully protected anchorages are available, but more importantly, the Bunsby Islands are home to a large number of sea otters that were re-introduced to the area several years ago.

We enjoyed one of these otters, called Hollywood, because he's a real ham. If we dropped a spoon over the side he'd dive for it, bring it back, "hand" it to us, and then clap his "hands" with delight.

Hollywood climbed into our dinghy, tied astern, stood on his hind flippers, and clapped loudly. Then he'd dive in and put on a water ballet for us, surfacing from time to time to lead the applause for his act. We knew if we threw him something to eat, he'd perform for us until bedtime.

—Tom Kincaid

Reference only — not for navigation

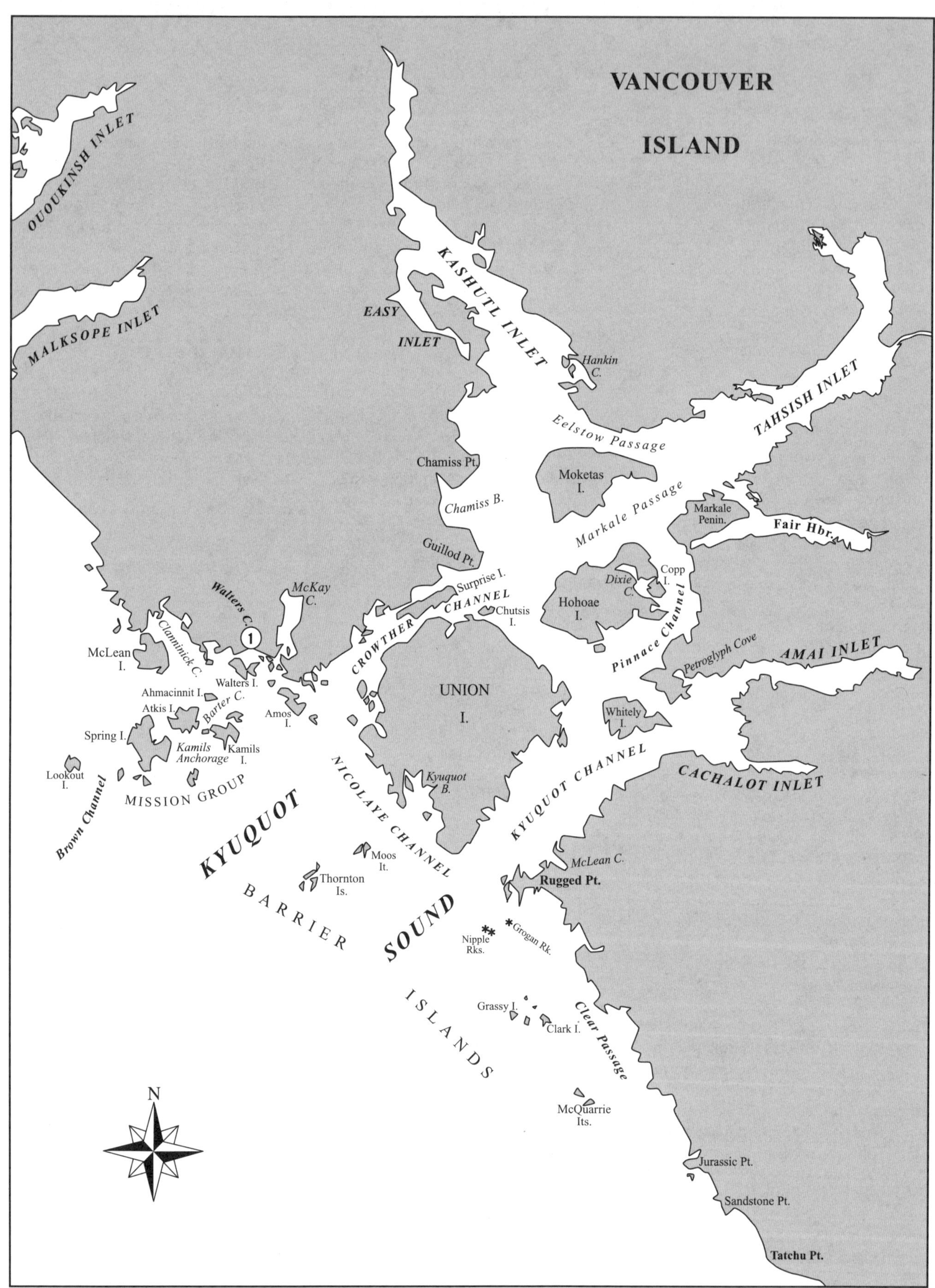

Kyuquot Sound

Walters Cove • Dixie Cove • Rugged Point

Charts	
3651	Scouler Entrance and Kyuquot Sound
3682	Kyuquot Sound (1:36,700)
3683	Checleset Bay (1:36,500)

The Walters Cove dock has long floats on each side, with room for several boats

With the exception of the outer islands and Rugged Point, Kyuquot (pronounced "Ki-yú-kit") Sound is protected and pretty, surrounded by high mountains, with easy waters. On the inside, only Dixie Cove and Don Douglass's "Petroglyph Cove" are excellent anchorages, but several others are attractive. The settlement of Walters Cove is a favorite.

From the south, enter Kyuquot Sound past Whistle Buoy M38. Leave the buoy to starboard, and proceed through Kyuquot Channel. Most visiting pleasure craft, however, will approach from the north, and stop at Walters Cove before entering Kyuquot Sound proper.

① **Walters Cove.** Use chart 3651; 3682; 3683. We are completely taken by the little settlement of Walters Cove. It has almost everything you might need after a week or two of working your way along the coast: fuel, ice, charts, a store, cafes, relaxed and friendly people, happy kids, lazy dogs, and Miss Charlie, a 34-year-old who's in love with Esko Kayra.

One thing Walters Cove does not have is liquor. Walters Cove is dry, by vote of the Kyuquot Native community, and there's not a drop to be bought. Nor is liquor in evidence, even on the dock.

The safest approach to Walters Cove in all weathers (and the approach we took) is from Whistle Buoy MC, at the entrance to Brown Channel. Use chart 3683. Go through Brown Channel and turn to starboard on a course to pass Gayward Rock to starboard. At Gayward Rock go to large-scale chart 3651 to work your way past the east side of Walters Island and into Walters Cove.

Without chart 3651, entry to Walters Cove would be a tricky matter. Although the channel past the east side of Walters Island is marked by buoys and a daybeacon, the channel is easy to misread, and the unwary skipper could find himself on a rock. With chart 3651, however, the channel is apparent, and following the rule of Red, Right, Returning, entry is safe. The one daybeacon along the way marks the narrow passage that leads directly into Walters Cove. Remember that beacons are attached to the earth: rock extends into the passage from the beacon. Don't cut it close. Use a mid-channel course favoring the north side between the beacon and the 51 meter island opposite. The chart makes the route clear.

Visitors relax with locals on the dock at Walters Cove.

Several locals insisted, "Don't anchor in Walters Cove!" The bottom, they said, is foul with debris. Furthermore, the water line serving the white community runs across the bay where a boat would be apt to anchor. Instead of anchoring, tie up at the government dock to the left as you enter.

Long floats are on each side of the the government pier. Both floats are available. The general store and post office, owned by Susan (Kayra) Bostrom and managed by her sister Lucy, is at the head of the pier. Summer hours are 1930-2130 every evening; 1300-1700 Mon., Wed., Fri.; 1500-1700 Sat. & Sun. Winter hours are 1300-1730 Mon., Wed., Fri.; 1500-1730 Sat. The fuel dock is owned by the fish packing plant and is next to the government dock. It's open daily 1300-1730 in the winter; all day in the summer.

The Kyuquot Band Native commu-

See area map page 196

nity of 250-300 is across the bay, served by its own government dock. A shop, with Native arts and crafts, is located there, but during our visit, early in the season, the stock was low and we know little about it. The shop would be worth checking out.

All transport is by boat in Walters Cove, and from an early age the Kyuquot children (and Indian children all along the coast) are accomplished boatmen. Their outboard-powered craft have two directions: forward and reverse; and two throttle settings: full-power—and off.

Walters Cove has been a popular gathering place for many years. Years ago it was home to five fish camps in the summer. When people were stuck in port waiting for the weather to break, the talk flowed. Long ago Walters Cove got its local name of Bull---t Bay, *BS* Bay in polite company. The cafe at the head of the fuel dock is called the BS Cafe. Sam Kayra's bed and breakfast is named the BS B&B.

In 1995 Sam Kayra opened a new eatery, which she calls Miss Charlie's. It's in the old Fishermen's Co-op building (1934), a few steps from the store. Miss Charlie's is bright and airy, and the food (we had fish & chips) is good. We happened to be there on opening night. The whole community turned out to get Miss Charlie's off to a good start. Sam, an attractive, charming woman in her 30s, was a little frazzled. Even so, Miss Charlie's got launched good and proper.

Next morning we had breakfast at the BS Cafe. Breakfast was what the cook decided to serve, and it was hearty fare: eggs, hash browns, toast, sausage, juice, and lots of coffee. The BS cafe is owned by the fish processing plant. Its first mission is to feed its fishermen. They serve good food and lots of it.

Across the bay a cafe was getting underway on the Kyuquot Indian Reserve. We had lunch there shortly after arriving at Walters Cove. You have to take the dinghy over and tie it up on the rocks, then climb up the rocks to the cafe. We had a big hamburger, with lots of french fries. Wherever you go on the West Coast, expect large portions of french fries.

In Walters Cove we were struck by the apparent willingness of the Indian and white cultures not only to tolerate each other but to work together and get along. For visitors such as ourselves, it made the experience at Walters Cove much more enjoyable. At Walters Cove the Indian children and the white children played together. And all of them played with Miss Charlie.

Miss Charlie, you might have heard from elsewhere, is a seal. Miss Charlie is age 34 now, the adopted pet of the Kayra family. Miss Charlie's mother was killed before Miss Charlie was born, and Miss Charlie was brought into the world by Caesarean section. The Kayra family adopted Miss Charlie. The man at the Stanley Park aquarium suggested that she be bottle-fed a mixture of 60 percent cod liver oil and 40 percent milk, but he held little hope of survival. Miss Charlie proved the man at the aquarium wrong. She thrived on the diet, and grew. She had the run of the house, and played in the bathtub.

After a while, in a wrenching but necessary move, the Kayra family returned Miss Charlie to the wild. Miss Charlie came back, lumbering up the path from the dock, and climbed the stairs to the house. She has been a pet at BS Bay ever since. She lounges on the docks, swims with the children, and serves as mascot for the community. For sustenance she hangs out at the fish packing plant. When a boat lands, Miss Charlie gets a salmon. If the salmon isn't volunteered, she climbs onto the boat and steals it.

Although a pet, Miss Charlie had her urges, especially in springtime. Early on, she decided that Esko Kayra, the father of the Kayra family, was the apple (or herring, or salmon) of her eye, and for a number of years Miss Charlie made Esko uncomfortable with her longings. While we felt it indelicate to ask Esko if Miss Charlie, at (then) age 32, was as forward as ever, we sense that age has taken its toll and Miss Charlie is more relaxed now.

Barter Cove. Use chart 3682. Barter Cove, in the barrier islands outside Walters Cove, is more wild feeling than the protected anchorages inside Kyuquot Sound. Leave Ahmacinnit Island and the tiny islet east of Ahmacinnit Island to starboard, and feel your way in.

Walters Cove

It had been blowing half a gale out of the southeast all day as *Nor'westing* punched her way south through visibility that was frequently only a few hundred yards. We were wet, tired, and trying to find the sea buoy off Kyuquot Inlet—our destination for the day was Walters Cove.

There is an inshore route through miles of rocks and reefs along this coast, but without good visibility we were afraid to get too close, which means we had to stay about five miles offshore to be clear of the hundreds of rocks and reefs, and yet stay as close as we could so as not to miss that sea buoy.

Eventually the buoy showed up through the murk, enabling us to follow a buoyed route into Walters Cove. As we entered the shallow, narrow entrance to the cove, what appeared to be a huge ship was approaching that entrance from the south. We assumed the ship was headed up Crowther Channel into the main part of Kyuquot Sound, so paid it no mind until we arrived inside the cove and anchored off the government float.

Alongside the government pier was a rickety looking cedar log float that gave access to the town's general store and fuel depot. As we watched in amazement that huge ship (which wasn't really that huge as ships go, perhaps 150 feet) poked its nose through the same entrance we'd just negotiated with our four foor draft, and tied his first few feet to that rickety float, and started discharging fuel.

We got to talk to the crew later that day, because they had to wait for another high tide in order to get back out of Walters Cove. This tanker, because that's what it was, services all the fuel docks and logging camps up and down the coast, from Vancouver to Prince Rupert. It was equipped with Cort nozzles, twin screw, and had a bow thruster, but even so it has to work its way into some of the darndest places you've ever seen.

I've seen that ship many times since then, have had the crew aboard for coffee or a beer, and been given a tour of their ship, but I'll never forget that murky, windy day when a "big" ship followed us into Walters Cove.

—*Tom Kincaid*

Kamils Anchorage. Use chart 3682. This anchorage is more exposed than Barter Cove. Enter, very carefully, through Favourite Entrance.

Amos Island. Use chart 3651; 3682. From Walters Cove, the easiest entrance to Kyuquot Sound is around the east side of Amos Island into Crowther Channel. Use chart 3651 to identify the channel between Walters Cove and Nicolaye Channel, then chart 3682 to find the route past Amos Island. The passage east of Amos Island is deep but narrow, and bounded by rocks. The first time through can be unsettling, but after you've done it once it's easy.

Surprise Island. Use chart 3682. Surprise Island, steep, round, and logged off to stumps, is located in Crowther Channel. On the south side of Surprise Island Crowther Channel is deep and open, but on the north side a narrow passage is interesting. At zero tide least depths in this passage are 15-20 feet. A ledge of rock, shown on the chart, extends from the north shore. Favor the Surprise Island side all the way through. Since our vessel is named *Surprise* we felt we had to run this passage. We enjoyed it and we'd do it again.

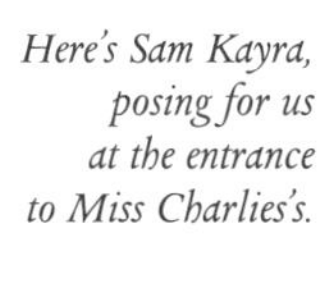

Here's Sam Kayra, posing for us at the entrance to Miss Charlies's.

Hankin Cove. Use chart 3682. Hankin Cove is located near the mouth of Kashutl Inlet, on the east side. It is a beautiful little cove with good holding, completely protected, but the hillsides are marred by evidence of past logging.

Dixie Cove. Use chart 3682. Dixie Cove indents the east side Hohoae Island, and is a *wonderful* anchorage. Enter south of Copp Island, through a narrow but deep passage to the first of two anchorages. This outer anchorage is approximately 5 fathoms deep, with good holding. Another narrow passage leads to the inner cove, completely secluded, with rock cliffs on one side. Depths here are approximately 3 fathoms. Highly recommended.

Petroglyph Cove. Use chart 3682. In his excellent book, *Exploring Vancouver Island's West Coast,* Don Douglass describes this previously-unnamed anchorage and calls it "Petroglyph Cove." Petroglyph Cove is located near the mouth of Amai Inlet, roughly due west of Amai Point. The cove's entrance is hidden until you're right on it. The entrance is narrow, and the channel shallows to a least depth of 2-3 fathoms, but has no dangers. Once inside you are protected. While in our opinion Petroglyph Cove is not as pretty as Dixie Cove, it is an excellent spot.

The fuel dock and fish packing plant at Walters Cove are close to the Govt. wharf.

Rugged Point Marine Park. Use chart 3682. Rugged Point marks the southern entrance to Kyuquot Sound. The beaches on the ocean side are spectacular, and deserve a visit. An old cabin offers shelter, and a trail leads through the park. Anchor along the inside beaches and dinghy ashore. The Pacific swell, though diminished, gets into the anchorage. While people have anchored overnight successfully, we think it is best for day use in fair weather.

Kyuquot Sound to Esperanza Inlet

Clear Passage • Rolling Roadstead • Queen Cove • Zeballos Nootka Mission • Tahsis Narrows

Charts	
3662	Nootka Sound to Esperanza Inlet (1:75,000)
3663	Esperanza Inlet (1:40,000)
3682	Kyuquot Sound (1:36,700)

Depending on the course chosen, it is approximately 13.5 miles between Rugged Point and the entrance to Gillam Channel, which leads into Esperanza Inlet. In good visibility, the route through Clear Passage is smooth and interesting. In poor visibility, we would head seaward from Rugged Point to entrance buoy M38, then turn southeastward toward Esperanza Inlet.

Clear Passage. Use chart 3682. Clear Passage takes you about 4 miles along the coast in waters protected by the Barrier Islands, past a steady display of rugged rocks and rock islets. The channel is free of dangers. To enter Clear Passage, leave Grogan Rock to port and Nipple Rock to starboard. You will have no trouble identifying Grogan Rock. It is an awful 23-foot black pinnacle, and it commands attention. Lay a course to take you north of McQuarrie Islets, and exit Clear Passage leaving McQuarrie Islets to starboard. The rocks and islets along Clear Passage have a similar appearance. It may help to plot a GPS or loran waypoint at the point where you intend to turn to exit past McQuarrie Islets.

Tatchu Point. Use chart 3682; 3662. Several local fishermen told us the waters from Jurassic Point past Tatchu Point could be an "ugly patch of water." We ran those waters in only a light breeze, but even in those conditions the seas had authority. In stronger conditions we could easily imagine the seas to be difficult.

ESPERANZA INLET

Esperanza Inlet is on the west side of Nootka Island, and ultimately connects with Nootka Sound. Esperanza Inlet is part of the "inside route" through this portion of the coast. This route is served by three communities—Zeballos, Tahsis, and Gold River—and by the Nootka Mission at Esperanza, with its fuel dock, hospitality, and excellent water. The waterways are beautiful, and contain several good stopping places. Esperanza Narrows connects Esperanza Inlet with Tahsis Inlet on the Nootka Sound side, and is not difficult to run. We like this inside route, and recommend it.

Rolling Roadstead. Use chart 3662. Rolling Roadstead offers acceptable anchorage in fair weather, but from the west the approach can be tricky. While we have not made this approach, Douglass, Watmough, and Kincaid have, and Douglass and Watmough describe the approach in their books. Kincaid writes about it in a series of articles published in *Nor'westing* magazine in 1975-76. All agree that careful navigation is called for, including the finding and identifying of the various rocks and reefs in the entrance. The hazards are easily identified, either by the breaking surf or kelp growing in the shallows. With the hazards accounted for, the entry is reported to be safe. All agree that it should be run in fair weather only, with good visibility. In 1996 Catala Island, which protects Rolling Roadstead, was preserved as a provincial marine park.

Gillam Channel. Use chart 3662. Gillam Channel, more than 0.5 mile wide and well-buoyed, is the safe entrance to Esperanza Inlet. Approaching from a course past Tatchu Point, you can raise entrance buoy MD, then turn into Gillam Channel. Since we were in clear weather, we took a course inside of buoy MD but slightly to seaward of buoy M42, which marks the west end of Blind Reef. When we were close to buoy M42, we turned northward to leave buoy M41 off our port side, and continued into Esperanza Inlet. The course was easy and anxiety-free.

Queen Cove. Use chart 3662. Queen Cove lies a short distance inside the entrance to Port Eliza, the first inlet to port as you enter Esperanza Inlet. Queen Cove is a safe and delightful spot to put the hook down and go exploring. The cove is well-protected, has excellent holding in 3-6 fathoms, and is large enough for several boats to swing. Concrete works on the west side of the cove have a Stonehenge appearance. A cabin with dock is at the north end. The Park River enters at the north end of Queen Cove, and makes a good dinghy exploration. Recommended.

Espinosa Inlet. Espinosa Inlet is deep and high-walled. No place to anchor.

The Government dock at Zeballos has room for a large number of boats, and is close to store, fuel and laundry.

Reference only — not for navigation

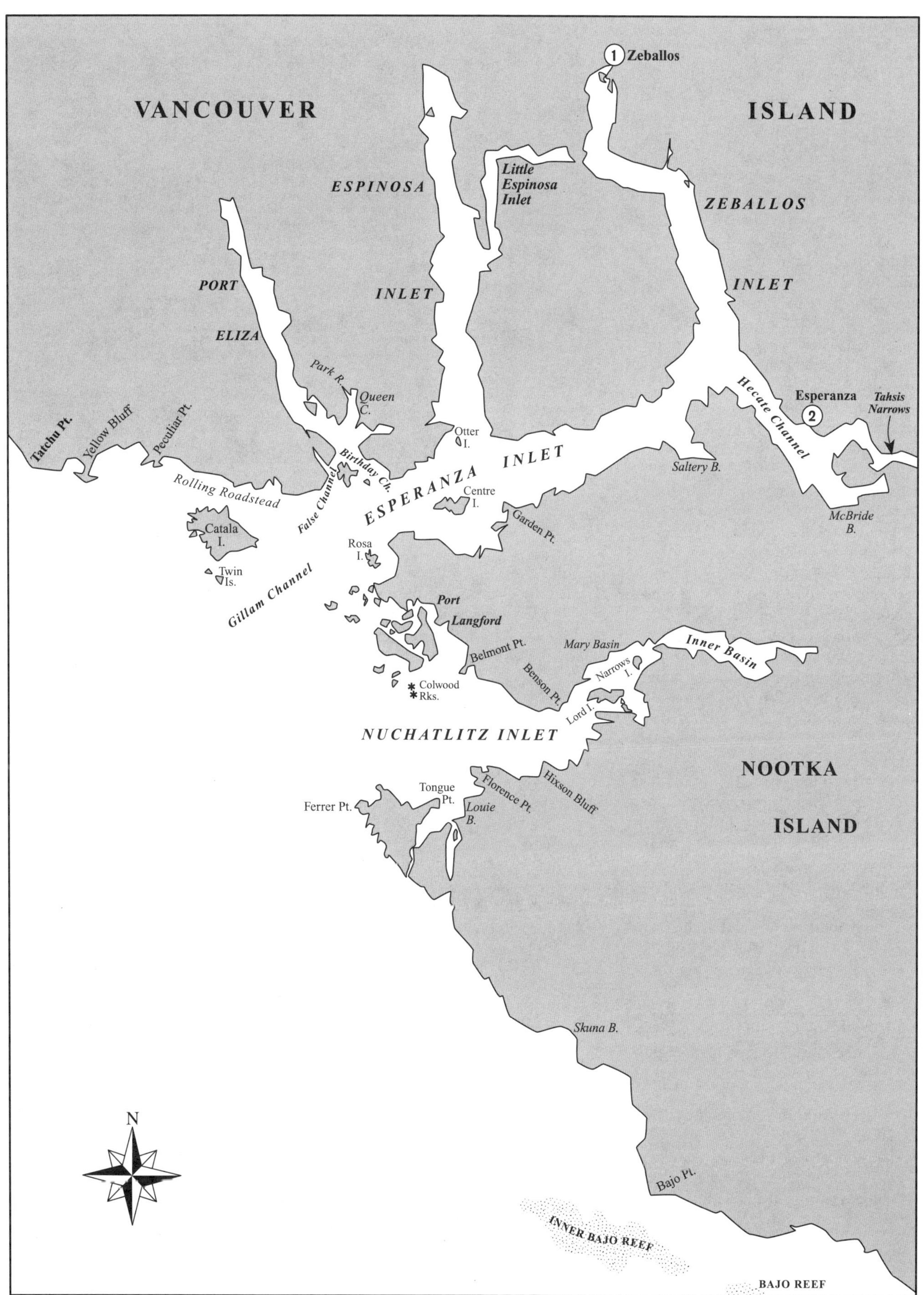

See area map page 201

Zeballos. Use chart 3663. To us, Zeballos (locally pronounced "Zabellos" —the "a" and the "e" change places) is the most interesting and unexpected town on the West Coast. While other settlements range from fishing camp (Winter Harbour) to bustling town (Tofino), Zeballos is singular. It is a mining town that looks like Cicily, Alaska (the fictional town made famous by the television show *Northern Exposure*), with wandering streets and false-fronted buildings. The town is built at the mouth of a river next to mountains that go *straight up*. More than once we could imagine Bad Bart swaggering onto the streets of Zeballos for a face-off with a brave but outgunned sheriff.

Zeballos can provide most of what a cruising boat needs—food, fuel, water, liquor, ice (flake ice for fish), frontier food in the old hotel's pub, good showers for $2 at the Zeballos Mini-Motel, laundro-mat, museum, and post office.

The mountains around Zeballos are highly mineralized, and much gold has been taken out of them. Over dinner at the hotel we talked with a wildcat prospector whose eyes burned bright as he told of pockets of gold still waiting to be taken—*he knew where they were*. We met Nick Nekolov, who spoke English with a thick Bulgarian accent and operated a portable sawmill. The sawmill was next to Nick's trailer, directly across the street from the hotel. Nick posed for us while we took his photograph.

Tie up at the government dock. The general store, dumpster, and waste oil drop are nearby. The fuel dock, a short distance away, has everything petroleum you might need. The day before we arrived someone caught a 21-pound spring salmon from the end of the float next to the fuel dock. Kids were on the float while we were there, trying their luck.

Zeballos is a good place to spend the night. The inlet leading to the town is long and beautiful. There's no point going both ways in one day.

① **Weston Enterprises Ltd.,** Box 100, Zeballos, B.C. V0P 2A0, (250)761-4201. Monitors VHF channel 68. Open all year. Gasoline, diesel, and propane are available. Fish ice available in season. Owners: Tom and Alice Weston.

② **Esperanza,** Box 398, Tahsis, B.C. V0P 1X0. Use chart 3663. Monitors VHF channel 06. Fuel dock with gasoline, diesel, kerosene, stove oil, naptha, lube oil. Showers and laundry are available. Excellent water. A small store on the pier has a few items. The telephone is expensive, but available for emergencies.

Zeballos. Nick Nekolov built a portable sawmill, and proudly shows off some of his work.

Located on the north side of Hecate Channel, Esperanza is the home of the Nootka Mission, whose history goes back to 1937, when the Shantyman Mission began a hospital at Esperanza. This was in the tradition of the Shantyman Mission, which was founded in northern Ontario in 1907 to serve shanty dwellers in outlying areas. The Esperanza hospital no longer operates, and the property is now a Shantyman Mission camp for children and teenagers, immaculately kept and welcoming of all visitors. The fuel dock is an important source of revenue. Meals of wholesome camp food are sometimes available in the dining hall, donation encouraged. The coffee pot is always on. We had some delicious homemade cookies with our coffee. The recipe for the cookies is contained in the *Esperanza Cookbook*, available at the store.

Overnight boats can tie to "Hospital Wharf," in the cove just west of the fuel dock.

Tahsis Narrows. Use chart 3663. Tahsis Narrows connects the Esperanza Inlet side of Nootka Island with the Nootka Sound side. From the chart, one would think tidal currents rage through the narrows 4 times a day, but they do not. The narrows are deep and free of dangers, with little tidal current activity. Passage can be made at any time.

The fuel dock at Esperanza is at the bottom of the ramp. Small store on dock, camp buildings on shore. Delightful place to stop.

Nootka Sound

Tahsis • Princesa Channel • Critter Cove • Santa Gertrudis Cove Ewin Inlet • Friendly Cove

Charts	
3663	Esperanza Inlet (1:40,000)
3662	Nootka Sound to Esperanza Inlet (1:75,000)
3664	Nootka Sound (1:40,000)
3665	Plans – Nootka Sound

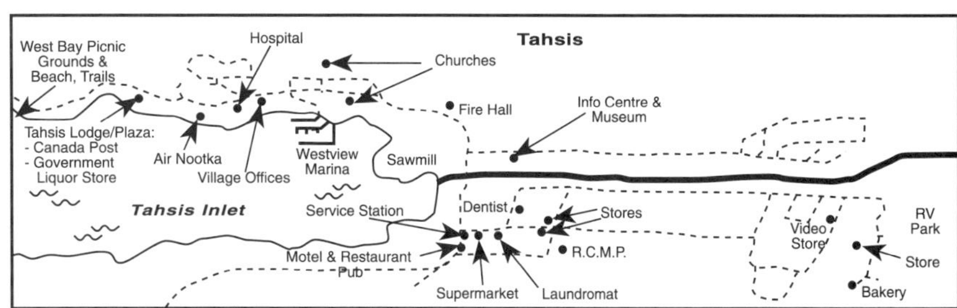

Tahsis and Westview Marina

Reference only — not for navigation

Tahsis Inlet. Use chart 3663; 3664. Tahsis Inlet is long and narrow, and bounded by mountains. The wind funnels and blows up-inlet or down, depending on conditions. We found a 2-foot chop that sent spray flying. The pulp mill town of Tahsis, at the head of the inlet, has full facilities, including post office and liquor. The town is located about a mile from the Westview marina. You'll have to walk or take a taxi. The major navigation danger in Tahsis Inlet is Tsowwin Narrows, created by the outfall from the Tsowwin River. A beacon marks the edge of the shoal. Pass between that beacon and another beacon on the west shore of the inlet. Remember that beacons are attached to the earth, and shoal water can extend into a channel from a beacon. Give each beacon a good berth. While we did not see much debris, Tahsis Inlet is reported to have considerable drift and deadheads. Keep a close watch on the water ahead.

① **Westview Marina,** P.O. Box 481, Tahsis, B.C., V0P 1X0, (250)934 7622. Monitors VHF channels 06 & 73. The fuel dock has gasoline and diesel, washrooms, showers and laundry, and a small store. Moorage is served by 15 & 30 amp power. Propane is available in town. This marina, at the head of Tahsis Inlet, is set up to serve the summer flotilla of small sportfishing boats. The docks have been expanded and the welcome mat is out for cruising boats. Call ahead for availability. Some friends stopped at Westview in 1996, and were treated very well. The marina is neat and attractive, the people helpful, and the fuel dock easy to approach.

Princesa Channel. Use chart 3665 (highly recommended); 3662. Princesa Channel runs between Bodega Island and Strange Island, and connects Tahsis and Kendrick Inlets. A route through Princesa Channel gets a boat out of the Tahsis Inlet chop and cuts some distance off a passage for southbound boats making for Friendly Cove. Unfortunately, the Tahsis Inlet entrance to Princesa Channel is narrow and bounded by an underwater rock. A northbound (flood) current can set the unwary onto this rock. With caution, a safe transit can be made. Be sure to use large-scale chart 3665.

From Tahsis Inlet to Kendrick Inlet (east to west) the problem is the flood tide. The flood current sets northward into Tahsis Inlet, and a boat entering Princesa Channel will find a definite northward set to its course. This northward set will tend to put the boat onto a submerged rock charted about 200 feet north of the Princesa Channel light, at the east entrance to Princesa Channel. Douglass believes the rock is closer to 100 feet from the light. One hundred feet or 200 feet, the rock is not far away. The goal is to wrap around the Princesa Channel light but avoid yet another charted rock south of the light, while not being set onto the rock 100-200 feet north of the light. Chart 3665 shows the rocks clearly. Study the chart and you will understand not only the challenge but the decisions required to meet the challenge.

We ran Princesa Channel in a stout flood current and had no problems. In our case, we ran south in Tahsis Inlet until the Princesa Channel light bore 235 degrees Magnetic, then turned toward the light. We kept the light on our

Reference only — not for navigation

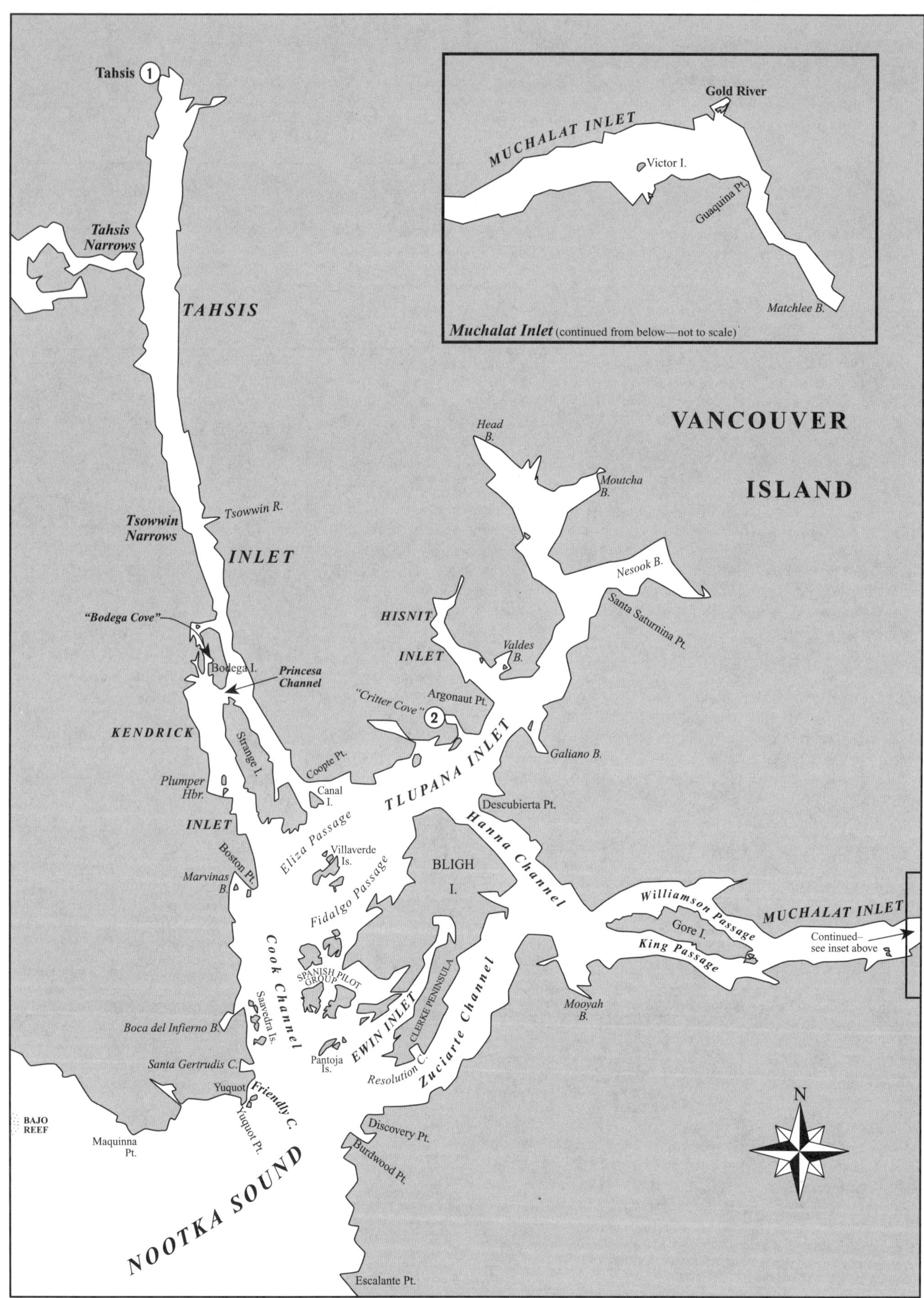

See area map page 204

nose (we had to crab to make good our course) until the light was close aboard, then laid off to starboard to give the light 50 feet of clearance, and entered the channel. The key was to be aware of the rock 100-200 feet north of the light and keep our course *south of that rock.* Once past the light we held a mid-channel course and waltzed on through.

Bodega Cove. Use chart 3664. Douglass calls this previously unnamed anchorage "Bodega Cove," and we see no reason to argue. Bodega Cove lies at the head of Kendrick Inlet, between Nootka Island and Bodega Island. The area has been logged, so the scenery is not that of primeval forest. Protection is excellent, however, and the shores accessible. Since a reef extends from the Nootka Island side of the entrance, favor the eastern, Bodega Island, side. As we approached we divided the entry channel in half, then split the eastern, Bodega Island, portion in half again (in other words, we were three-quarters of the way toward the eastern shore), and ran down that line. It was easy.

NOOTKA SOUND

Use chart 3664. Nootka Sound is where European influence in the Northwest began. It was at Friendly Cove in Nootka Sound that Captain James Cook first landed in 1788. In 1790 Captains Vancouver and Quadra negotiated the transfer of control of these waters and lands from Spain to England. At Friendly Cove Captain Meares built the *Northwest America*, 48 feet on deck, the first ship ever built on the West Coast, and launched it in 1788.

The long arms (Muchalat Inlet and Tlupana Inlet) that reach out from Nootka Sound have few anchorages, and they tend to be deep. The Port of Gold River is at the head of Muchalat Inlet. The town is 9 miles from the dock, and the waters are too deep for anchoring. Trailerable boats, most of them come for salmon fishing in Nootka Sound, are launched here.

Hisnit Inlet. Use chart 3664. Hisnit Inlet extends north from Tlupana Inlet, and anchorage is possible at the head. Two submerged rocks lie almost mid-channel a short distance into Hisnit Inlet. Do not be deceived (as we were) by the open and safe appearance of the inlet as you arrive or depart. We forgot about the rocks on leaving, and remembered them when they must have been very close. A sharp course change followed. Favor the south shore.

Anchorage at the head of the inlet is in 7-10 fathoms. It is open and not cozy feeling at all, but it is protected. Extensive clear cutting mars the hills. The shoreline is accessible.

Critter Cove. Use chart 3664, 3662. Critter Cove is the name given by Cameron and Dean Forbes to this previously unnamed spot about 1 mile south of Argonaut Point on Tlupana Inlet. The Forbes brothers have established a sportfishing resort in the cove and named it after Cameron Forbes' nickname of "Critter," when he played hockey. The resort is in the outer bay; the cozy inner cove is ideal for anchoring. A narrow channel with two charted rocks leads to the inner cove. We inspected the channel pretty carefully at a little less than half-tide, and believe the rocks to be underwater outcroppings from the south shore. A mid-channel course will clear them.

② **Critter Cove Marina,** P.O. Box 1118, Gold River, B.C. V0P 1G0, (604)886-7667. Gasoline only at the fuel dock, moorage, cabins, suites, restaurant, showers. Cameron and Dean Forbes, two of the nicest guys you'll ever meet, have quite a sportfishing camp here. If the docks are full (as they often are from June 23 through August), you can anchor in Critter Cove (see above) and take the dinghy over to the resort. The entire facility is on floats. The restaurant is small and rustic, but we found the food to be superb. Try a bowl of Critter Cove clam chowder. It's the curry and several other flavorings that make it unique. Most of the boats at Critter Cove are trailered into Gold River where they are launched.

Santa Gertrudis Cove. Use chart 3664. The western cove in Santa Gertrudis Cove is an excellent anchorage, cozy, good holding, protected. As you enter you will see an island in the northern cove. A submerged rock extends from that island a considerable distance toward the south shore, much farther than we expected. Be sure to identify this rock and give it room as you favor the south shore. The north cove of Santa Gertrudis Cove, around the island, is foul and tight.

Resolution Cove. Use chart 3664. Resolution Cove is near the south end of Clerke Peninsula, on Bligh Island. Cook put his ship *Resolution* into the cove to find and fit a new foremast. A flagpole and plaques commemorating Cook have been placed on a knoll above the cove. Anchor in 7-8 fathoms, either with a stern-tie to shore or enough room to swing. You'll probably make your visit a short one: this is not the best place for small craft.

Ewin Inlet. Use chart 3664. Ewin Inlet indents the south side of Bligh Island some 3 miles, with no anchorages until the head is reached. The cove to the west at the head of the inlet is quite protected and has depths of 5-7 fathoms. We rounded the little islet in the cove at low tide, about 100 feet off, and the depth sounder abruptly but briefly showed a depth of 15 feet. We suspect it found an uncharted rock. This is a nice cove, but the run up Ewin Inlet seems a little long. In 1996 Bligh Island was made into a provincial marine park.

Friendly Cove. Use chart 3664. Friendly Cove is big and shallow and fairly protected, with good anchoring on a sand bottom. Nearly all the land ashore belongs to the Mowachat Band, and a small fee must be paid to the caretakers both for landing or using the log float that extends into the bay. Ray and Terry Williams, the caretakers, will tell you where you may and may not go, since much of the land is sacred to the band. The spired Catholic church has two stained glass windows, a gift from the government of Spain, that depict the transfer of authority over the area from Spain to England in 1790.

You can walk from the Friendly Cove beach to the Nootka Light Station on San Rafael Island, but a call ahead on VHF channel 16 or 82 may result in an invitation to use the float that serves the light station. If you tie to the float, you will have to apply yourself to the stout rope that attaches the float to land, and pull float, boat and you up to the stairs that lead to the top. At the top you'll meet Ed Kidder, who has been at the Nootka Light Station for more than 25 years. Ed, in his early 50s, is friendly, informed, and easy company. He usually has time to show visitors around.

See area map page 204

By all means climb up the tower to see the light itself. Thanks to the miracle of the Fresnel lens, the light uses only a 500-watt projector bulb to cast a beam that can be seen for 16 miles. Nootka is a repeater station for Tofino Coast Guard radio, and has considerable radio equipment. Every 4 hours, from early morning until nightfall, the Nootka station reports weather conditions for the marine weather broadcast, including estimated wind strength and sea conditions offshore. The light station also is responsible for 5 aviation weather reports each day.

The Nootka Light Station and light keepers such as Ed Kidder are powerful arguments for retaining manned light stations along the coast. We urge anybody who would want to replace these resources with automatic equipment to skipper a small boat down this wild and hostile coast, relying on the light stations for accurate weather information. It is not enough to be a passenger or observer on such a voyage. The critic must *skipper* the small boat, and be responsible for the safety of the vessel and the people on board. *Then* he will understand why manned lighthouses are important.

The Nootka Light Station from seaward. Fully staffed, two families live here, and man the station 'round-the-clock.

Nootka Light

The Nootka light, 101 feet high, is perhaps the most visited light station on the West Coast. The light station is built on the summit of San Rafael Island, and casts a beam that can be seen for 16 miles. The fog horn sounds twice every minute. Ed Kidder, the lightkeeper, has saved many lives during his quarter-century of service at Nootka. The most recent was in October 1994, when Ed rescued a priest whose boat had hit a rock.

Ed Kidder has been the lightkeeper at the Nootka Light Station for a quarter of a century.

It's a bit of a climb from the mooring float to the light station, but worth every step. Supplies are brought up the railway.

Nootka Sound to Hot Springs Cove

Estevan Point • Hesquiat Harbour • Hot Springs Cove

Charts	
3662	Nootka Sound to Esperanza Inlet (1:75,000)
3674	Clayoquot Sound, Millar Channel to Estevan Point (1:40,000)
	Hayden Passage (1:20,000)
	Hot Springs Cove (1:20,000)
	Marktosis (1:10,000)
3603	Ucluelet Inlet to Nootka Sound (1:150,000)

Hot Springs Cove. A new plank for the boardwalk is being completed.

Hot Springs Cove is adjacent to Sydney Inlet, the northern entrance to the waters of Clayoquot Sound. Depending on the points of departure and arrival and the exact course chosen, the distance from Nootka Sound around Estevan Point, past Hesquiat Peninsula, and east to Hot Springs Cove, is approximately 30-31 miles. Hesquiat Bay can be a good spot to hole up if the westerly wind makes progress difficult after rounding Hesquiat Peninsula. In good weather, however, most cruising boats will proceed with single-minded determination to the delights of Hot Springs Cove.

A hot soak is just the thing after a week or more on the West Coast.

These bathers came from Tofino by high-speed tour boat.

Estevan Point. Use chart 3662; 3603 (1:150,000); 3674. Estevan Point is the southwest corner of Hesquiat Peninsula, another of the headlands where winds and seas build and become confused. While Estevan Point can be ugly in a storm, in more settled conditions it does not present the degree of challenge found at Cape Cook or Cape Scott. In fog, the problem with Estevan Point is its low, flat terrain, which makes its shoreline a poor target for radar. The presence of rocks more than a mile offshore makes Estevan Point unforgiving for the navigator who is off-course. We recommend GPS or loran.

From Nootka Sound, a rounding of Estevan Point first must clear Escalante Rocks and Perez Rocks, both on the west side of Hesquiat Peninsula. Unfortunately for the navigator, no one chart shows all of Estevan Point from Nootka Sound to Hesquiat Bay in large scale. You will be forced to plot your course on small scale chart 3603, which doesn't give much close-in detail. Once at Estavan Point, you can use the new chart 3674 to continue to Hot Springs Cove.

Especially with the lack of a single good large scale chart for the west side of Hesquiat Peninsula, the general advice, heard from several experienced Estevan Point navigators, is to give Estevan Point

Reference only — not for navigation

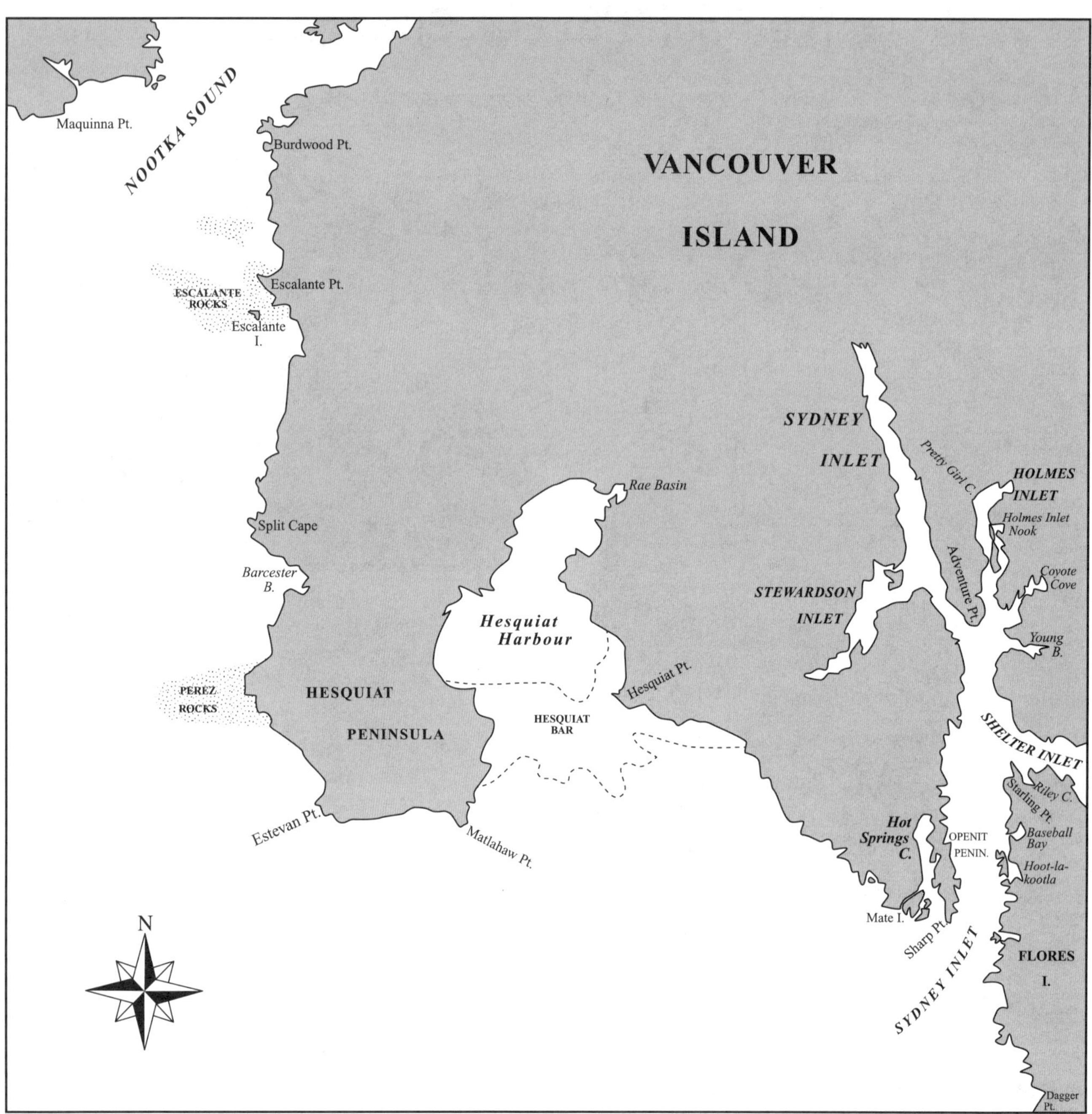

"lots of room." Our course was approximately 1.5 miles off Perez Rocks; our logbook entry says that we would have been happier 3 miles off. The wind was calm, visibility excellent, and the seas quiet. Skeptics take note.

Hesquiat Harbour. Use chart 3674. Hesquiat Harbour is protected from westerly winds, and Hesquiat Bar, with 4 fathoms over it, knocks down the Pacific swell. Beware the bar in a southeasterly; storm seas can break over it. Rae Basin is a cozy nook in the northeast corner of Hesquiat Harbour.

Hot Springs Cove. Use chart 3674. Hot Springs Cove is one of the reasons cruising boats do the West Coast. The challenge of getting to Hot Springs is sufficient to make the reward—a soothing bath in comforting water (no soap, please)—worth the entire trip. In earlier times most visitors came the hard way, up from Barkley Sound or down the West Coast from Cape Scott. Now the springs are visited several times a day by tour boats and even float planes, carrying visitors who have arrived without distress at Tofino, and up they go to Hot Springs. An hour by high-speed boat and they are there.

We, however, got to Hot Springs the old-fashioned way. We came around Cape Scott, and for us Hot Springs was a magnet. Hot Springs Cove is easy to enter. A study of chart 3674 shows that the mouth of the cove is open and the channel free of dangers. The marine park dock is approximately 1.7 miles farther into the cove from the springs themselves. Several mooring buoys lie a short distance from the park dock. You can anchor out in 25 feet of water, tie to a buoy, or lie along the dock. A charge is made if you use the government dock.

From the park, a 2-mile walk along a well-maintained boardwalk and path

See area map page 208

leads to the springs. Visiting craft have a tradition of bringing a 2x6 plank about 4 feet long to add to the boardwalk. On the plank is carved the name of the boat and the year of the visit, plus other information (crew list, etc.) as deemed appropriate. Many of the boards show remarkable artistic talent. A hike along the boardwalk is a hike down memory lane, a revisiting of earlier calls by boats one often knows.

This hike to Hot Springs, through rain forest, is easy and beautiful. Toilets are available at the end. The modest will find a pleasant changing room in which clothes may be doffed and a bathing suit put on. Traditionalists will choose to enjoy the hot springs in the old way, without encumberance of bathing suit. That's a little awkward when 25 visitors have arrived by airplane or tour boat, all with bathing suits, and you, who have *earned* the right to a *traditional* hot springs soak (as opposed to merely paying the fare), suddenly feel uncomfortable.

The kids from the village across the cove play at Hot Springs, in part (as Kincaid suggests) to further their study of anatomy, and in part to show off for the *touristas*. The braver young lads dive off the rocks into the surf. It's not Acapulco, but it's not bad. Watch your belongings. We lost a towel.

Dave Letson is the wharfinger at the park dock. Dave ties his Bill Garden-designed sailboat *Die Flyn* to the float, exchanges information with all who care to chat, and collects the fees. Dave used to run the bed & breakfast moored at Hot Springs Cove marine park, but at 0300 on June 28, 1995 the structure burned to the water.

Hot Springs has campsites, often used by kayakers. During our visit, a kayak-borne fisherman brought several catches to the dock and gave them away. They included rock fish, sea bass, and coho salmon. He went out to the rocks just outside the cove, made a pass, and came back with his catch. Each time his line went in the water it came up heavy.

Next year, Acapulco! A Native boy dives from the cliff into the surf at Hot Springs.

Here's a tasty supper: a Coho salmon, proudly displayed by two engaging young ladies. At the park dock, Hot Springs Cove.

Clayoquot Sound

Sydney Inlet • Young Bay • Bottleneck Bay • Bacchante Bay • Sulphur Passage
Ahousat • Calmus Passage • Heynen Channel • Lemmens Inlet • Tofino

Charts	
3673	Clayoquot Sound, Tofino Inlet to Millar Channel (1:40,000)
3674	Clayoquot Sound, Millar Channel to Estevan Point (1:40,000)
	Hayden Passage (1:20,000)
	Hot Springs Cove (1:20,000)
	Marktosis (1:10,000)
3685	Tofino (1:20,000)

Clayoquot Sound is a series of inlets and passages that circle islands and indent Vancouver Island for approximately 20 miles along the coast. A boat could spend considerable time poking around in Clayoquot Sound without being exposed to ocean swells. The only town is Tofino.

Sydney Inlet. Use chart 3674. Sydney Inlet is the northern entrance to Clayoquot Sound. It lies adjacent to Hot Springs Cove, and leads, the fairway unencumbered by dangers, approximately 11 miles back into mountains. Sydney Inlet has several good anchorages. Rounding Sharp Point after leaving Hot Springs Cove, beware of two charted but unmarked offlying rocks. The first is fairly close to Sharp Point and easy to avoid. The second lies about 0.2 miles off. Most boats will choose to pass between the two rocks. Be sure you know where you are.

Hoot-la-Kootla. Use chart 3674. We're using Douglass's name for this otherwise unnamed cove, which lies on the west side of Flores Island, approximately 1.4 miles from Sharp Point. The cove is protected by a 190-foot island offshore. You'll see a beautiful white beach as you enter. Although the water is a little shallow near the beach, it's the prettiest spot in the cove. You could also anchor at the north end of the cove, behind the island. Do not attempt to enter the cove at the north end. It is foul.

Baseball Bay. Use chart 3674. Once again we'll use Douglass's name for a bay with no name on the chart. Baseball Bay is located about 0.25 mile north of the 190-foot island in Sydney Inlet. The entrance is shallow, and a charted rock lies in the entrance, just south of mid-channel. We divided the channel north of the rock in half, and entered "mid-channel." Least depth on our sounder was 12.5 feet near the bottom of a 3.6-foot low tide at Tofino.

Norma Bailey's marvelous store (no longer a store) is moored in Baseball Bay. Norma quit the store and moved to town, and she gave the float, its quaint building, and even some of the store stock inside to the Clayoquot Biosphere Project. During our visit we met John Rupp and Joanne Hammer-Rupp, a husband and wife Biosphere research team. John Rupp told us he was curator of fishes at the Pt. Defiance Zoo and Aquarium, in Tacoma. He and Joanne were gathering data about the numbers, identities, distribution and behavior of basking sharks in Clayoquot Sound. The couple was living in the old store, and obviously treating it very well.

You can anchor in Baseball Bay, or, if it's okay with the Biosphere people, tie to their float.

This is Norma Bailey's quaint and inviting store, now used by the Clayoquot Biosphere Project.

Riley Cove. Use chart 3674. Riley Cove lies just east of Starling Point, on the northwest tip of Flores Island. It would not be our first choice for an anchorage. The cove is open and uninteresting, and a little deep for anchoring until close to the head. At the the head, Riley Cove is divided into two smaller coves, the cove to the west having a sandy beach. A rock, not shown on the chart, lies just off the point that separates the two coves. A shoal extends from the east shore near the entrance of Riley Cove. Favor the west shore.

Young Bay. Use chart 3674. Young Bay, on the east side of Sydney Inlet, is a lovely place to anchor, although a little deep unless you get close to shore. The middle is 8-10 fathoms deep, but along the shore it's easy to find 6-7 fathom depths. You may want to run a stern-tie to a tree. On the south shore a stream connects with Cecilia Lake, ½ mile away. Dave Letson, the wharfinger at Hot Springs Cove, told us a trail leads to the lake, and that trout fishing there is good.

Enter Young Bay right down the middle, to avoid shoals that extend from either side. Once inside you will see a small islet with trees on it. Pass to the south side of that islet.

Bottleneck Bay (Coyote Cove). Use chart 3674. This is an otherwise unnamed lagoon that Watmough fell in love with. We think he had a particularly satisfying time there. Bottleneck Bay is located just north of Young Bay, east of Adventure Point. The entrance is narrow but deep, and inside the wonderful treed hills make the feeling of seclusion complete. Easy anchoring in 5 fathoms.

Holmes Inlet Nook. Use chart 3674. This is the little nook that lies behind the

Reference only — not for navigation

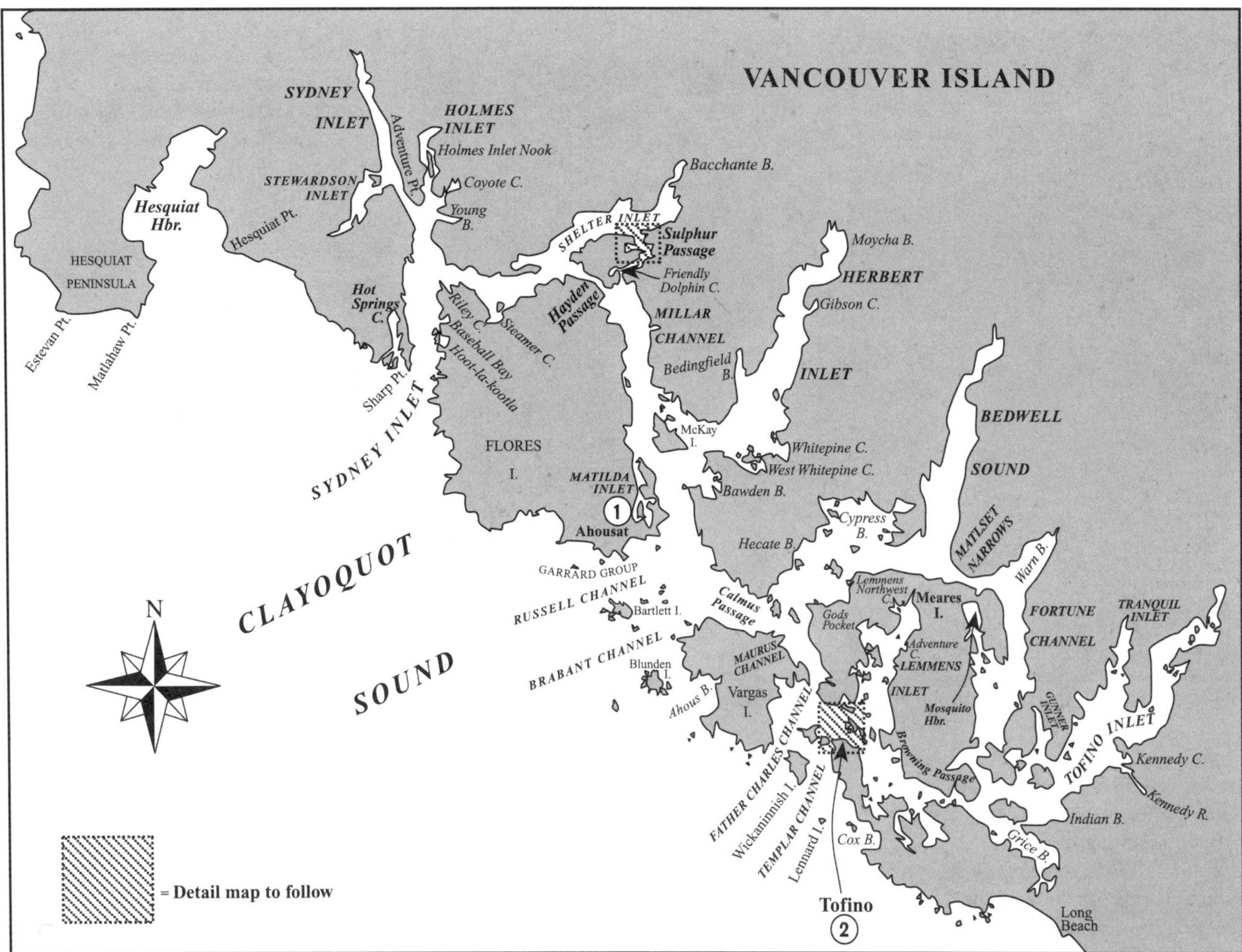

215-foot island in Holmes Inlet. Like Watmough's Coyote Cove, the nook is completely private and surrounded by lush forest, only it is much smaller and very cozy. We'd predict that romance would be almost assured for any couple lucky enough to anchor for the night. A stern-tie would be comforting, but the shore is rock right up to the tree line. At low tide it would be difficult to secure the tie.

To enter, go behind the 225-foot island, past the oyster farm (wave to the farmer), and through the narrow channel to the nook. Watmough says the extremely narrow channel north of the nook can be run at high water. Dave Letson, the wharfinger at Hot Springs Cove, told us he's run that channel in his 33-foot sailboat at nearly all stages of the tide. We didn't try. It was near low tide, and the lowest point of our boat is not a lead keel but the spinning blades of a bronze propeller. Granted we are cautious, but we have gone many miles without bending a propeller blade.

Shelter Inlet. Use chart 3674. Shelter Inlet, surrounded by high, beautiful mountains, lies east-west, and connects with Hayden Passage and Sulphur Passage, the quiet inside route through Clayoquot Sound. Shelter Inlet has only two good anchorages, Steamer Cove and Bacchante Bay. Of the two, Bacchante Bay is the more interesting

Steamer Cove. Use chart 3674. Steamer Cove is on the north side of Flores Island, behind George Island. The small cove at the southwest corner of Steamer Cove is well protected and has easy anchoring depths. Unfortunately, the hillsides around the anchorage have been logged clean right down to the water, so the outlook is uninteresting. If you're looking for shelter in a storm, the outlook would be irrelevant. Steamer Cove would serve excellently.

Bacchante Bay. Use chart 3674. Bacchante Bay, at the east end of Shelter Inlet, is a lovely spot, with high mountains to the west and an inviting grassy meadow at the head. The shallow entrance is narrow, and hidden until you are close.

We entered Bacchante Bay slowly, favoring the west shore, looking for a rock shown clearly on then-current chart 3648. We did not find the rock. In 1996, chart 3648 was replaced by a new chart, 3674. The new chart 3674 does not show the rock, but it does show another rock more distinctly on the opposite shore. We saw *that* rock. *Lesson:* Sometimes, even the rocks move. It pays to buy new charts when they come out.

Bacchante Bay has ample room for several boats to anchor in 7-8 fathoms. Holding is excellent. If you run to the head of the bay, watch for abrupt shoaling off the meadow.

Hayden Passage. Use chart 3674, including inset. Hayden Passage is on the west side of Obstruction Island, and connects Shelter Inlet with Millar Channel. Tidal current predictions are shown with

Reference only — not for navigation

Surprise's route through Sulphur Passage

Hayden Passage as a secondary station in the Tide and Current Tables, Vol. 6. Some confusion about tidal currents used to exist among the charts, the Tide and Current Tables, and *Sailing Directions*. The earlier chart 3648 showed the flood current setting *northwest*. But the Tide and Current Tables show the flood setting *southeast*. *Sailing Directions* says the flood sets southeast. The confusion has been resolved with the new chart, 3674. It shows the flood setting southeast, in line with the current tables and *Sailing Directions*. Hayden Passage's beacons are daymarked for a southeast-setting flood as well: the daymarks on the west shore beacons are black, and the daymarks on the beacons in the channel are red. Pass *west* of the red daymarked beacons (Red, Right, Returning).

Nevertheless, because the flood currents meet at Hayden Passage, you may find that the currents don't behave as predicted. The cautious passage would be at slack water. If transiting at other than slack, maintain a constant watch for current set, and crab as needed to stay in the channel.

Sulphur Passage. Use chart 3674. Sulphur Passage connects Shelter Inlet and Millar Channel on the east side of Obstruction Island, and is far more tortuous than Hayden Passage. The northern portion of Sulphur Passage is the tricky part. There, the channels twist and turn, and are bounded by submerged rocks. Douglass ran Sulphur Passage along the east side of the 38 meter island in the northern portion, and reported it to be a period of "high anxiety."

With Douglass's experience in mind, we ran a dogleg course from north to south on the *west* side of the 38-meter island. We found it to be straightforward—albeit with careful planning and close cooperation between navigator and helmsman. For reference, we describe our course here, and show it in the accompanying sketch map. (Following this course on chart 3674 will help understanding. The directions North, South, East and West in this description are True, not Magnetic.)

Our course left Belcher Point close to port and continued to the south corner of the charted fish farm. Then we crossed to a point of land northeast of a 290-foot hill on the west shore. (This hill was shown on the earlier chart 3648, but is not shown on the new chart 3674. The sketch map makes clear the course followed, however.) We turned south again and favored the west shore until we were past the 38-meter island and the tiny islet that lies south of it. Then we turned east, pointing the bow at the mouth of a creek that enters on the eastern shore. Once in the middle and approximately due south of the 38-meter island's western tip, we turned south once more and motored through. While other courses probably would have been safe, this course had the advantage of using easily-identified landmarks (the fish farm, the point under the high hill, the stream outlet, the tip of an islet) either as turning points or as points to aim at.

Friendly Dolphin Cove. Use chart 3674. Friendly Dolphin is Douglass's name for the cove that indents Obstruction Island, just inside the south entrance to Sulphur Passage. The cove is pretty, private, and appealing. Anchor near the head in 7-8 fathoms, probably with a stern-tie ashore to control swinging. Dave Letson, the wharfinger at Hot Springs Cove, told us he thought this cove was "too deep and too buggy." We didn't see any bugs, but we weren't there in the early evening, either.

Matilda Inlet. Use chart 3674. Matilda Inlet indents the southeast corner of Flores Island, and is bounded on the east by McNeil Peninsula. Anchorage is possible near the head of Matilda Inlet. From the anchorage a warm springs in Gibson Marine Park can be visited (best at high tide; at low tide it's a muddy

"Eden," Portland, Oregon, takes a break at Ahousat. From here, with full tanks and a good weather forecast, "Eden" departed for the run down the Washington coast and home.

hike) or a trek made to the beach. We did not visit the anchorage or the park, but Watmough did, and describes the area in fond detail. Recently, some friends made their way to the warm springs across the tidelands at low water, hence the advice above about visiting at high water. The Indian community of Marktosis is on McNeil Peninsula. Across the inlet and a short distance north are the store and fuel dock of Ahousat.

① **Ahousat.** Use chart 3674. Ahousat, with its general store, fuel dock, cafe, and marine ways, is on the west shore of Matilda Inlet, at the southeast corner of Flores Island. Hugh Clarke is the owner. The store is a rough-and-ready place, but it has what you need: groceries, miscellaneous hardware, and marine supplies. No charts or liquor. Hugh's sister has opened a cafe next door. The cafe wasn't quite in operation during our visit, so we can't report on the fare. We did note the humorous sign, seen in several places along the West Coast: "This isn't Burger King. You get it my way or you don't get the son-of-a-bitch at all."

West Whitepine Cove. Use chart 3674. Although unnamed, this delightful anchorage is called West Whitepine Cove by both Watmough and Douglass, and we shall do the same. West Whitepine Cove lies west of Whitepine Cove, near the mouth of Herbert Inlet. Entry is along the south side of the 67-meter island. We entered slowly, strongly favoring this island. Rocks were visible underwater and easily skirted. Once inside, the cove is lovely and protected. Bears are reported to frequent the south shore. We saw only one, briefly, some distance away.

A charted rock is in the cove, off the tip of the little peninsula that extends southwest from the 94-meter island. Although we anchored in the cove overnight, we did not see the rock, so before leaving in the morning we went to find it. We approached the approximate location slowly, but a cats paw of breeze ruffled the water, obscuring vision. As the cats paw passed we saw the rock, close to the surface and menacing. We put the helm over and the boat swung away. As we swung, the calm water behind the retreating cats paw revealed more of the submerged rock, growing closer. *It was as if the rock were swimming toward us.* Find the rock on the chart. When anchoring, stay away from it.

Gibson Cove. Use chart 3674. Gibson Cove indents the west side of Herbert Inlet, about 5 miles north of Whitepine Cove. Since Gibson Cove is not on the way to anyplace else, we suspect it sees few visitors. Those who do visit are in for a treat. The run up Herbert Inlet is even more spectacular than many other inlets along the coast. High, interesting mountains and rock walls line the shores. Deep alpine river valleys lead away into the mountains. Snowcapped peaks can be seen in the distance.

Gibson Cove is beautiful and protected, but a little deep for anchoring. We did find 6-7 fathom depths close to the south shore, and tested the anchor on 3:1 scope in 8 fathoms. The Bruce bit solidly, but if we had stayed we would have run a stern-tie to shore.

Calmus Passage to Heynen Channel. Use chart 3673; 3685. The route from Millar Channel to Heynen Channel via Calmus Passage and Maurus Channel is the beginning of shallower water. The channels are well marked by buoys and beacons. The depth sounder becomes an important navigation tool, and the navigator must stay alert and know the vessel's position at all times. In tight navigation among rocks, it's easy to stay alert. But in these wider, more open-feeling areas, concentration is more difficult. It's no trick at all to go aground in these waters. Large-scale chart 3685 is extremely helpful.

Lemmens Inlet. Use chart 3673; 3685. Lemmens Inlet indents Meares Island, just a few miles from the town of Tofino. Be sure to use large-scale chart 3685 while navigating around Tofino and into Lemmens Inlet. The entry channel to the inlet is amply deep, but bounded by drying flats. Once inside, you have your choice of one superb anchorage (Adventure Cove), and two other possible anchorages.

Adventure Cove. Use chart 3673. Adventure Cove, where Capt. Robert Gray built the small schooner *Adventure* in 1792, is a delightful anchorage, filled with history. The beach is easy to land on, and while walking in the woods one can almost feel the presence of Gray's Fort Defiance and the shipbuilding activity. Strips of survey tape mark remnants of the fort. Though now overgrown with large trees, we distinctly felt that in the past *something went on here.* Watmough and Douglass describe the history well. Anchor in 2-3 fathoms. A floathouse is in the north part of the cove.

Lemmens Northwest Cove. Use chart 3673. Lemmens Northwest Cove is Douglass's name for this anchorage in the northwest corner of Lemmens Inlet. It is identified on the chart by the 38-meter island and the fish pens in the mouth. Some drying rocks obstruct the entrance. Locate them and then run in midway between the rocks and the 38-meter island. Once inside, you'll find find good anchoring depths and adequate protection. We were not charmed by the cove, however. We found it somewhat open and uninteresting.

The 4th Street Dock is probably the best place to moor in Tofino.

Gods Pocket. Use chart 3673. Gods Pocket is the cove that lies northwest of Lagoon Island, on the west side of Lemmens Inlet. Protection is good, with anchorage in 4-5 fathoms. Two very nice float homes occupy the cove, however. You'll be anchoring in their front yards.

See area map page 211

Reference only — not for navigation

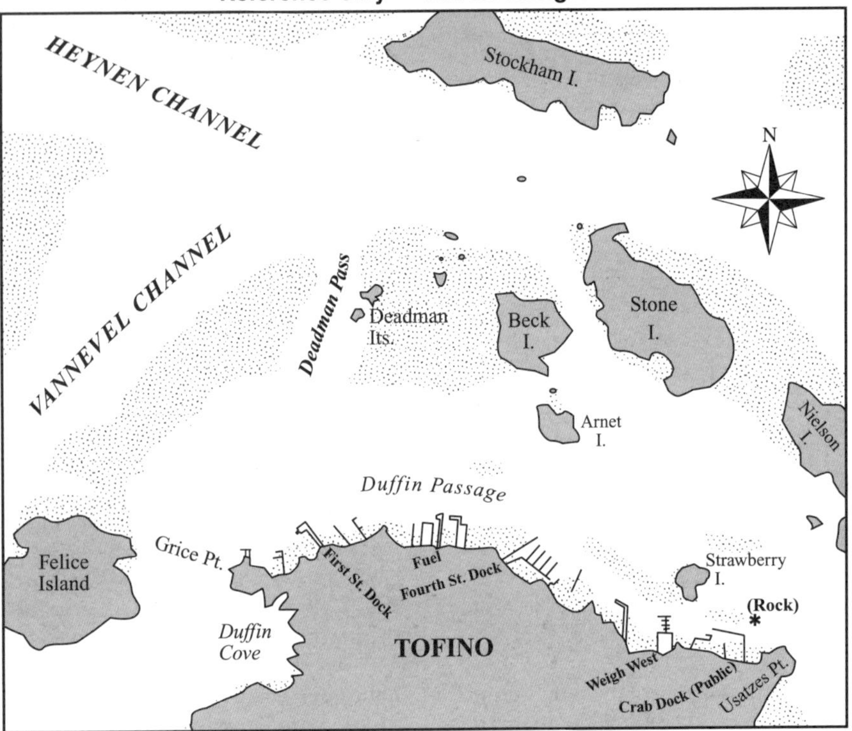

Tofino. Use chart 3685 (larger scale, preferred);3673. If you come from up-island, Tofino will be your first major town since Port McNeill or Port Hardy. During the summer season Tofino's bustle and busy-ness may surprise you. We found that pedestrians hurried past but didn't look us in the eye. The dogs were nervous. It's quite a contrast to the pace up-island, where strangers say hello to each other and the dogs, when they move at all, do so only to accept a morsel of food or a friendly scratch behind the ears. After growing accustomed to the charms of life up-island, Tofino, with its commerce, fast traffic and and loud engines, can cause culture shock. "Will that be all?" says the sales clerk. "Have a nice day. Next!" Welcome to the city.

As long as you're in the city you might as well spend some money. You can choose from several good restaurants, the kind that serve meals without french fries. Gift shops—at last!—are available for mementos and presents. The Co-op store, close to the waterfront, is a complete supermarket. It also carries clothes. Showers are available at the Paddler's Inn. The laundromat has enough machines to do all the ship's laundry in one cycle.

From seaward, enter Tofino via Templar Channel. While chart 3673 gives a good overall view, for the close navigation needed we strongly recommend large-scale chart 3685. Note how the buoyed fairway twists and turns to avoid shallows. Be sure to identify each buoy as you proceed, and leave the buoys off the proper hand.

A drying rock, shown here, blocks the eastern end of the Tofino waterfront. Don't go beyond the last government dock.

From the north, enter Tofino via Deadman Pass. Deadman Pass is narrow and bounded on both sides by drying flats. Be sure to use large-scale chart 3685. Note that while *you* may be returning to Tofino, the buoyage system is not. As you head south in Deadman Pass you will leave the red buoys off your *left* hand.

Stay close to the docks once at Tofino. A serious drying reef lies a short distance off. Currents can run strongly along the docks, so watch carefully as you land.

You can tie up at one of several docks. The public dock near Grice Point is closest to the Co-op and the liquor store, but it is busy day and night with water taxis and locals restocking their dwindling stores. Not for nothing is this dock called the Whiskey Dock. Moorage *may* be available at the Ocean West fuel dock moorage. It tends to be full during the busy season, but you can check. Whitey Bernard, who owns Ocean West, is a good guy.

The best moorage prospect is the 4th Street Dock, well-signed, and close enough to the commercial district. Although commercial fish boats have priority, with any luck you can find a spot. The 4th Street Dock has power, water, garbage dumpsters, waste oil drop and a washroom, but no showers. We spent the night at 4th Street Dock and would do it again.

Farther east, Weigh West may have space, but the docks usually are taken by their sport fishing guests. The easternmost public dock is called the Crab Dock. We found the Crab Dock to be a little funky for our tastes. Many of the boats looked rundown. Some may not have moved in quite a spell.

Do not proceed eastward past the Crab Dock. A major rock blocks the channel at that point.

② **Ocean West Ind. Ltd.,** Box 141, 380 Main Street, Tofino, B.C. V0R 2Z0, (250)725-3251, fax (250)725-2111. Open all year. Gasoline, diesel, lube oils, stove oil, propane, water, ice, divers' air, vacuum waste oil disposal. Moorage has electrical hookup, but moorage often is fully reserved in busy season. This is a modern, well-run facility, with a good chandlery that carries a wide range of equipment and supplies, including sport fishing gear, bait, some groceries, foul weather wear, and charts.

Barkley Sound

Amphitrite Point • Ucluelet • Broken Group • Effingham Bay • Turtle Bay Wouwer Island • Pinkerton Islands • Port Alberni • Robbers Passage Bamfield • Cape Beale • Nitinat Narrows

Charts	
3602	Approaches to Juan de Fuca Strait (1:150,000)
3603	Ucluelet Inlet to Nootka Sound (1:150,000)
3646	Plans – Barkley Sound
3647	Port San Juan and Nitinat Narrows
3668	Alberni Inlet (1;40,000)
	Robbers Passage (1:10,000)
3670	Broken Group (1:20,000)
3671	Barkley Sound (1:40,000)
3673	Clayoquot Sound, Tofino Inlet to Millar Channel (1:40,000)
3674	Clayoquot Sound, Millar Channel to Estevan Point (1:40,000)
	Hayden Passage (1:20,000)
	Hot Springs Cove (1:20,000)
	Marktosis (1:10,000)

The "Canadian Princess," with charter boats alongside, is a permanent fixture in the Ucluelet Small Craft Harbour.

Clayoquot Sound to Ucluelet. Use chart 3673; 3603; 3671. It is approximately 19 miles from Lennard Island, at the southern entrance to Clayoquot Sound, to Whistle Buoy Y42 offshore from Ucluelet Inlet. This 19 miles crosses the ocean face of the Pacific Rim National Park, but since you'll probably be about 3 miles out you won't see much of the park. *Sailing Directions* says to stay 2 miles off the coast; Watmough likes 3 miles. So do we. Plot a waypoint for Whistle Buoy Y42, go 3 miles offshore from Lennard Island, turn left, and make for the buoy. In fog, radar is a big help in avoiding all the fish boats that work these waters. Absent loran/GPS and radar, in fog we would go out to at least 30 fathoms and follow the 30-40 fathom curve to buoy Y42.

Amphitrite Point. *Use chart 3646.* We *italicize* this instruction. Amphitrite Point, at the end of the Ucluth Peninsula, can present a challenge. The essential navigation problem is to get around Amphitrite Point while staying well clear of Jenny Reef, shown on the chart, yet staying off the Amphitrite Point shoreline. The problem is made more difficult in fog, when the radar may lose buoy Y43 against the shoreline.

Carolina Passage is the entry suggested by *Sailing Directions,* except in heavy weather, when it can be too rough for safe navigation. The outer entrance to Carolina Channel is marked by Whistle Buoy Y42, the fairway entrance buoy. This buoy lies about 0.4 miles offshore. The channel leads past bell buoy Y43, which lies but 300 meters off the rocky shore. In reduced visibility, life can get interesting when you're trying to raise buoy Y43.

Douglass, following the recommendations of *Sailing Directions,* suggests that vessels approaching Carolina Passage first find Whistle Buoy Y42, then turn to a course of 030° Magnetic to raise buoy Y43. Douglass then refines the instructions in *Sailing Directions:* From buoy Y43, follow a course of 069° Magnetic for 1 mile, to clear Francis Island. Then turn to a course of 134° Magnetic to take you into Ucluelet Inlet.

We followed Douglass's instructions in good weather and excellent visibility, and they worked perfectly.

While we were doing so, we noticed that a steady stream of commercial fish boats chose to ignore Whistle Buoy Y42 and instead entered along the Amphitrite Point shoreline, leaving the 1.6-meter-deep shoal to starboard and buoy Y43 to port. We would like to try that route next time, especially if the weather is good and we can join a parade of fish boats to lead us in.

Fish boats line the dock at Ucluelet.

Ucluelet. Use chart 3646;3671. The channel leading into Ucluelet is well buoyed. Following the rule of Red, Right, Returning, you will have no problems. Spring Cove, to port a short distance inside the channel, is where many of the fish boats discharge their catches. The trollers lie outside Spring Cove

See area map page 217

while they bring their poles vertical.

Three fuel docks are located in the channel, all vying for business. The Ucluelet Small Craft Harbour is the principal marina. It lies west of the north tip of Lyche Island, and is the one we recommend. The floats have power and water. The *Canadian Princess,* a large white ship made into a floating hotel and restaurant, is moored in this marina permanently. The ship is part of a major sportfishing resort that has several charter boats. The boats depart early in the morning, filled with anxious fishermen, and return in the afternoon. At night the entertainment areas on the *Canadian Princess* are lively.

Another marina to consider is Island West Fishing Resort, on the west side of the inlet just before the turn to the small craft harbor. They have no designated guest dock, so call ahead by telephone or radio.

Showers are available at the West Coast Motel, adjacent to the marina. A good pizza spot and a couple of decent gift shops are in the area. In town, halfway up Ucluelet Inlet, Pioneer Boat Works has a marine railway for haulout, and facilities for repairs. Their chandlery, next to the ways, has a good selection of marine supplies, commercial and sportfishing tackle, and charts. Around the winding streets of Ucluelet you will find gift shops, art galleries, eateries, and other essential services. It's a pleasant hike out the road to the Coast Guard station at Amphitrite Point. We recommend it.

In Ucluelet Inlet, Lyche Island can be passed on either side. If passing on the west side (the town side), check chart 3646 and leave the buoys and beacons off the proper hands.

① **Ucluelet Small Craft Harbour,** Box 910, Hemlock St., Ucluelet, B.C. V0R 3A0, (250)726-4241.

④ **Island West Fishing Resort,** Box 32, Ucluelet, B.C. V0R 3A0, (250)726-7515; fax (250)726-4414. Monitors VHF channel 69. Call ahead. A busy fishing resort, often fully reserved a year ahead for August. They have 15 amp power, washrooms, showers, laundry, marine supplies, charts, ice, and deli takeout. Also a restaurant and pub.

Barkley Sound Use chart 3646; 3670; 3671. Barkley Sound is named after English Captain Charles William Barkley, who in 1787 sailed into the sound on his ship *Loudoun,* which he had renamed *Imperial Eagle* (Austrian registry) to avoid paying a license fee to the East India Company. With Capt. Barkley was his 17-year-old bride Frances. Barkley came to trade with the Indians for furs. Other than naming, he left no trace of his presence.

Barkley Sound is roughly square, measuring 15 miles across its mouth, and approximately 12 miles deep, not counting the 20-mile-long canal to Port Alberni. The sound is dotted with rocks and islands, and the waters are noted for their excellent fishing. A cruising boat could spend weeks in Barkley Sound, moving from one nook to another.

During the summer months fog often lies just offshore, and can sweep in to penetrate the sound in minutes, even with no wind evident. It is essential, therefore, that the navigator know the vessel's position at all times. GPS or loran will prove useful in foggy conditions, but be aware that their circles of accuracy (approximately 100 meters) are insufficient for close navigation through narrow passes bounded by barely-submerged rocks. Radar is a big help. Most boats cruising Barkley Sound, large and small, now have radar. Even with electronic help, the navigator simply must remain alert and aware.

If approaching from the south, such as from the Washington coast or the Strait of Juan de Fuca, you'll probably touch first at Bamfield, where customs can be cleared.

Effingham Bay, looking west at a Barkley Sound sunset.

If approaching from up-island, you probably will enter Barkley Sound from Ucluelet. If you pick a course to run across Sargison Bank from Ucluelet to the Broken Group, beware of a rock that lies approximately 0.7 miles east of Chrow Island. The rock is shown on the chart not with a rock symbol, but by a depth of 0.5 meters. It is easy to overlook while scanning the chart for dangers.

In Barkley Sound you will find superb exploring everywhere: the Stopper Islands, Pipestem Inlet, the Pinkerton Islands, Julia Passage, the Chain Group, the Deer Group, and the famous Broken Group. Settled summer weather makes it possible to anchor in any of hundreds of coves or nooks and explore by dinghy.

While off in the dinghy, we would carry charts in a plastic sleeve, pencil, dividers, a handheld VHF radio with spare battery pack, and a handheld GPS, just to be safe in the event of fog. If the dinghy were not equipped with a compass, we would carry a handheld compass. Everything but the charts could be placed in a small fabric bag. In even the smallest dinghy an out-of-the-way spot could be found to tie the bag.

Effingham Bay grows more sheltered near the head of the bay. Lots of room here.

Reference only — not for navigation

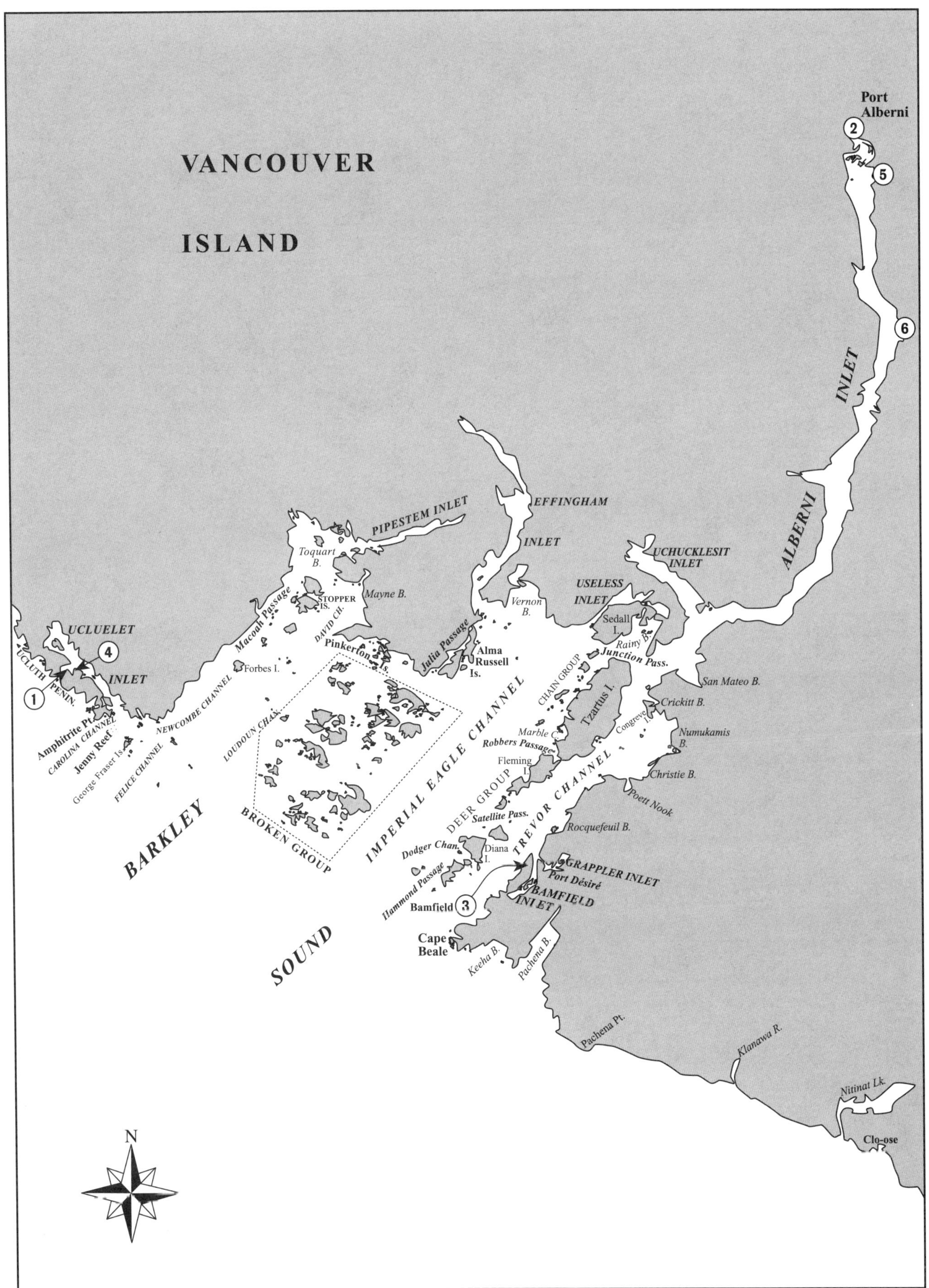

Reference only — not for navigation

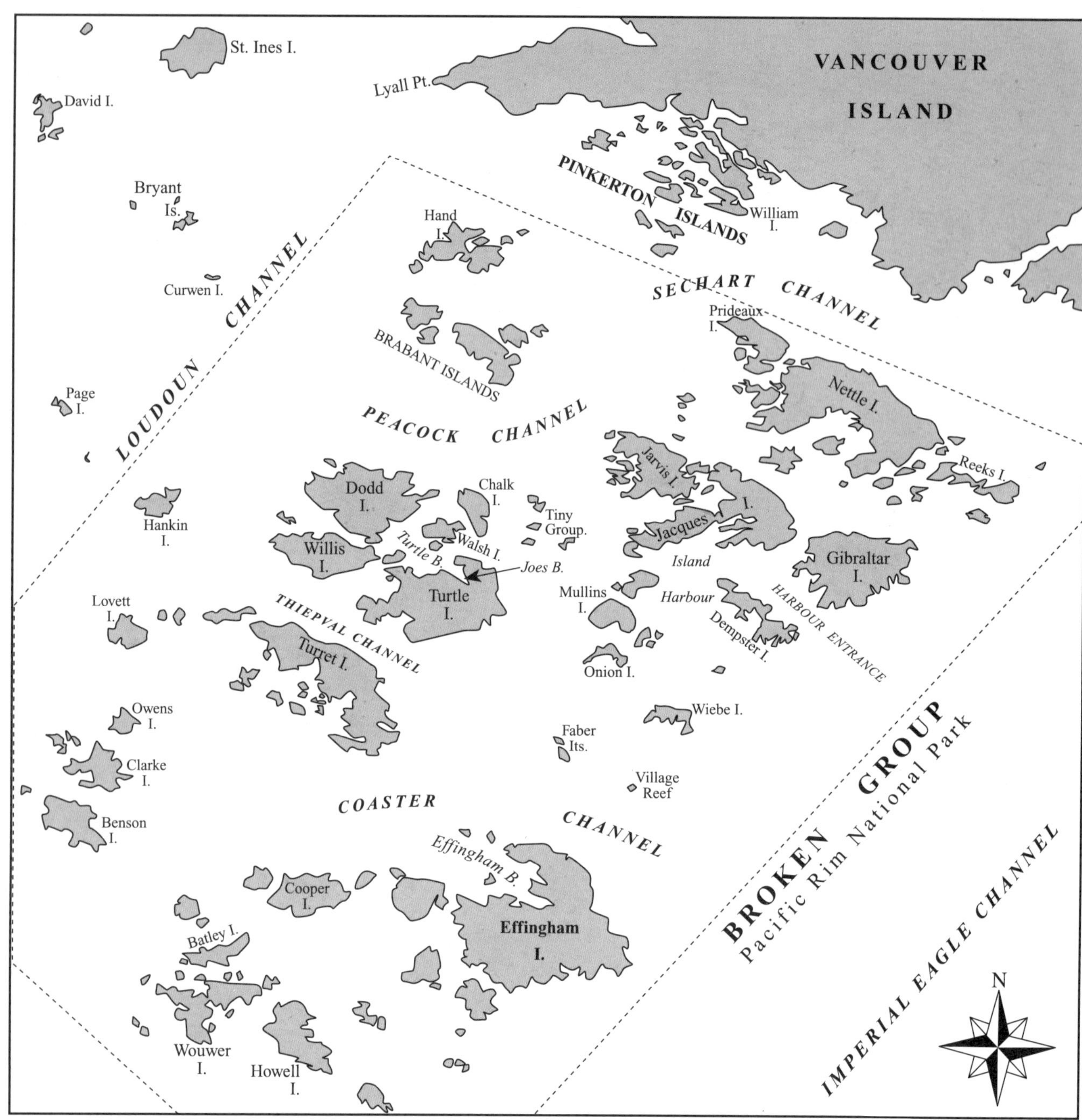

In all likelihood this navigation emergency kit would never see use. But if you were suddenly overtaken and disoriented by fog, the GPS could tell your position, the dividers and pencil could help you find the position on the chart, and the compass could point you in the right direction. The radio would make life less stressful for you and those back at the anchorage.

Broken Group. Use chart 3671; large scale chart 3670. The Broken Group islands extend from the wind-and-wave-lashed outer islands to peaceful islands deep inside Barkley Sound. The Broken Group is part of the Pacific Rim National Park, to be preserved in its natural state in perpetuity. For many Northwest boaters, a holiday spent in the Broken Group is the fulfillment of a lifelong dream.

Boats visiting the Broken Group for several days will find dozens of little nooks and bights to put the hook down, depending on weather and the mood on board. Both Watmough and Douglass describe a number of them in their books. The major anchorages are Effingham Bay, Turtle Bay, and Nettle Island. Of these, Effingham Bay probably is the most popular.

Effingham Bay. Use chart 3670. Effingham Bay is large, pretty, and protected. On the night of our visit we shared the bay with 10 other boats, yet the bay didn't feel crowded and everyone had room to swing. The chart shows the entrance. Anchor in 5-8 fathoms, good holding. Sunsets, seen out the mouth of the bay, can be spectacular.

Turtle Bay. Use chart 3670. Turtle Bay is a local name for the bay formed by

See area map page 217

Turtle Island, Willis Island, and Dodd Island. Joes Bay, the little nook where Salal Joe, the Hermit of Barkley Sound, made his home, is an appendage of Turtle Bay, indenting Turtle Island.

The best entrance to Turtle Bay is from the north off Peacock Channel, between Dodd Island and Chalk Island. A study of the chart shows the entrance channel bounded by rocks and drying rock outcroppings along the way. A careful entry, proceeding slowly and identifying the dangers, will bring you in safely. Those who have been in a few times know where the rocks are and understand that the rocks don't move. They roar right in.

Anchoring is in 4-5 fathoms on a mud bottom, good holding.

Nettle Island. Use chart 3670. Nettle Island has three good anchorages, one in the large bay that indents the southern shore, and the other two in the channel between Nettle Island and Reeks Island to the east. In Nettle Island's large bay, we prefer the eastern portion, off the park ranger's float cabin. The center of the bay is a little deep (8-10 fathoms, depending on state of tide), but you can find 3-5 fathom depths near the shore north of the ranger's cabin.

Watmough describes two other anchorages along the east side of Nettle Island, opposite Reeks Island. These nooks will hold a couple of boats each, and Watmough says they are delightful. The charted rocks are easy to identify and avoid.

Outer Islands. Use chart 3670. The outer islands of the Broken Group are marked by twisted trees, the result of relentless on-shore winds, especially in the winter. If your needs include the desire to navigate "out at the edge," the outer islands can satisfy that need. Here, you'll have your opportunity to run in wind and fog, with the Pacific Ocean swells beating against the rocks. The best anchorage is at Wouwer Island. We did not visit, but old friend Norm Culver has.

Wouwer Island. Use chart 3670. Wouwer Island is breathtaking, both in its scenery and gunkholing. At mid-tide or higher, most boats can make it through the slit between Batley Island and Wouwer Island. A bow watch only will scare you. Once through, and when you're breathing again, anchor in the middle of either of the next two little bays on Wouwer Island.

Nearly exposed to the ocean like this, the principles of anchoring are important. Use a heavy anchor and plenty of scope. Check throughout the entire 360° swing to be sure you have enough water at low tide.

From the deepest indent in Wouwer Island, a short trail (actually, a salal tunnel) leads to a beach that faces the Pacific Ocean. The beach is choked with drift logs tangled like a mass of Tinker Toys. At the south end of the island, the shorelines around the headlands offer teeming tidepools, carpets of mussels, roaring sea lions, and storm-torn trees with eagles perched in them.

Allow a few hours for this apparently short exploration, and carry a flashlight. The return trip is easy to get mixed up, and the salal tunnel is so black that once I almost spent a night in it. If it's dark as you return to your boat by dinghy, you may find the water literally aglow with the phosphorescence of scurrying fish. [Culver]

Pinkerton Islands. Use chart 3670. Far from the wildness of the outer islands, the Pinkerton Islands lie north of the Broken Group, next to Vancouver Island. The Pinkertons are small and protected, with narrow channels, and ideal for gunkholing. Watch for rocks. The easiest anchorage is in the cove northwest of Williams Island. Unless several boats want to share it, no stern-tie should be needed. A study of the chart will suggest a number of other possibilities, most of

Effingham Island

An ancient Indian village site is on the east shore of Effingham Island, reached by a short trail that leads from the bight in the southeast corner of Effingham Bay. There are perhaps a hundred such village sites in Barkley Sound; together they supported as many as 10,000 people.

A terrace at the village site is actually a 100-yard-long midden, 10 feet deep, where for centuries Indians ate shellfish beside their fires. Nurselogs have hemlocks growing out of them. On closer examination, the nurselogs are not round like trees, but squared, identifying them as longhouse beams.

Climbing around the big rocks and drift toward the ocean here isn't easy, but the seascape is worth it. Farther on, at lower tides, sea caves are accessible. One of the caves is 100 feet deep. Be careful to explore this area at low tide only. A rising tide can trap you.

—Norm Culver

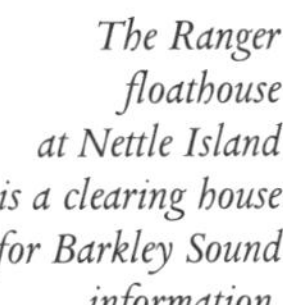

The Ranger floathouse at Nettle Island is a clearing house for Barkley Sound information.

See area map page 217

which will require a stern-tie to shore.

Alberni Inlet. Use chart 3668. Alberni Inlet begins between Chup Point and Mutine Point, where it meets with Trevor Channel and Junction Passage. The inlet continues some 21 miles into Vancouver Island to Port Alberni. Alberni Inlet is narrow and high-sided, with little to interest the cruiser along the way. Tidal current flows are less than 1 knot both directions, but the surface current can flow as fast as 3 knots when wind and current direction are the same. Boats without a reason to go to Port Alberni seldom make the trip, preferring instead to enjoy the manifold pleasures of Barkley Sound.

In the summer, an up-inlet thermal wind develops at 1300 ("You can set your clock by it," says a friend in Port Alberni), and will increase to 25-30 knots by mid-afternoon. The wind produces a short, uncomfortable chop. We would use Alberni Inlet in the morning.

Port Alberni. Use chart 3668. Port Alberni is a bustling pulp mill and sawmill town, with full services including a hospital. The first place visiting boats can find moorage is the breakwater protected public dock at China Creek, about 6 miles south of Port Alberni. China Creek Provincial Park, next to the marina, has picnic sites and a launch ramp. Close to downtown Port Alberni Fisherman's Harbour public dock has moorage. Haulout to 100 feet is available at Aberni Engineering and Shipyard. Three major fuel docks are located near Fisherman's Harbour, downtown. At the mouth of the Somass River the Clutesi Haven Marina has moorage. The Port Alberni Harbour Commission, which operates the China Creek and Clutesi Haven marinas, is developing another marina, with pleasure craft in mind, downtown. Development is in early stages, and completion is not expected for a couple years.

A good selection of marine supplies is available in Port Alberni.

In Port Alberni you can visit a nice little museum with changing West Coast history exhibits; take rides on an old steam logging train (summertime only); enjoy free logging shows sponsored by McMillan Bloedel (summertime only); and take tours of the pulp mill and sawmill.

⑥ **China Creek,** (250)723-9812. Monitors VHF channels 16 & 18A. Open all year. Gasoline & diesel, washrooms, showers, laundry, garbage drop. Has 2460 feet of moorage, 4-lane launch ramp.

⑤ **Fisherman's Harbour, Port Alberni,** 2750 Harbour Rd., Port Alberni, B.C. V9Y 7X2, (250)723-5312. Monitors VHF channels 18A & 68. Telephone customs clearance 24 hours (250)723-6612. Open all year, 2700 feet of moorage, power, water, washrooms, garbage drop. Fisherman's Harbour is adjacent to downtown Port Alberni, with all the services of downtown close by.

② **Clutesi Haven,** (250)724-6837. Monitors VHF channels 16, 18A & 68. Open all year, gasoline at the fuel dock, 2460 feet of moorage, power, water, garbage drop, 4-lane launch ramp. Clutesi Haven is located behind a breakwater near the mouth of the Somass River, and is best suited to boats 25 feet or less. Transient space is on a first-come, first-served basis. This marina is a popular launching spot for trailerable boats. Facilities, including hotels, pubs, and liquor store are within walking distance. Groceries are 1-2 miles away.

Poett Nook Marina, 2178 Cameron Dr., Port Alberni, B.C. V9Y 1B2, (250)724-8525. Gasoline at fuel dock, washrooms, showers. No power at the dock. This is a busy small-boat sportfishing resort, with 160 RV/camping sites and berths for 177 boats. Maximum length 26 feet. Most boats launch at Port Alberni or China Creek. Owners: Flo and Stan Salmon.

Robbers Passage. Use chart 3671; large-scale chart 3668. Robbers Passage leads between Fleming Island and Tzartus Island in the Deer Group, and is a likely route for boats bound between points near the head of Barkely Sound and Bamfield. The western entrance is bounded by drying rock. The S-shaped channel requires close attention, but with close attention it is safe. A study of large-scale chart 3668 will make the route clear. Inside the passage, the Port Alberni Yacht Club has its floating clubhouse and docks, and the welcome mat is out for visiting boats.

Across the bay from the yacht club an awful black whaling ship lies beached. It is a former Greenpeace vessel that once patrolled the seas to protest whaling. For several years it lay abandoned at Ucluelet, inhabited by squatters who burned interior woodwork to keep warm and generally made a mess of everything (according to what several people told us). The vessel was purchased at auction, and moved to Robbers Passage.

Port Alberni Yacht Club's Robbers Passage facility welcomes visitors.

Bamfield Inlet. Use chart 3671; large-scale chart 3646. Bamfield Inlet is open and easy to enter. The village of Bamfield is along the shores of the inlet. Several public docks are located on each side of the Bamfield Inlet. Commercial fish boats have priority, but space usually can be found for pleasure craft. At the head of the inlet, past Rance Island, is a quiet basin where you can anchor. *Sailboaters note:* a cable with 17 meters (55 feet) of clearance crosses the channel between Rance Island and Burlo Island.

Bamfield. Use chart 3671; large-scale chart 3646. Clear customs with Lorraine at the Bamfield General Store. While at the General Store, visiting boats can stock up with fresh fruits and vegetables, and a supply of spirits if so desired.

See area map page 217

The village of Bamfield covers both sides of the inlet. In Bamfield they call the inlet "Main Street." The west side, however, is not connected by road with the east side. A boardwalk runs along the homes and businesses of the west side, and folks get around by walking.

A small Red Cross Outpost Hospital is located on the west side. We dropped in one morning and talked with the nurse, who had been up all night treating patients. It is not unusual to have accident or altercation injuries late at night, she told us. Domestic violence is a problem. The hospital is set up to treat illness or injury, deliver babies, and dispense medication. It is operated by registered nurses, and a visiting physician calls on a regular schedule. They work closely with the Coast Guard for emergency helicopter transport when needed. A fee schedule accommodates non-Canadians who need medical attention.

The east side of Bamfield Inlet has roads that tie its businesses and homes together. They connect with the dirt road that leads to Port Alberni. The east side has the pub, the fuel docks, and, on Port Désiré, the launch ramp. The trail to Cape Beale begins on the east side of the inlet.

For marine supplies, see Hawkeye Industries, just north of Rance Island on the east side. Hawkeye has just about everything, including a fuel dock. Another fuel dock, the Bamfield Kingfisher Marina, is about 0.5 mile north of Hawkeye Industries, also on the east side.

The large building near the entrance on the east side of the inlet houses the Bamfield Marine Research Station. The station is owned by five universities in British Columbia and Alberta, and began operation in 1971. Visitors are welcomed, and tours are offered Saturdays and Sundays during the summer, no charge. This facility once was the eastern terminus of the transpacific cable that connected North America with Australia. Its first message was sent on November 1, 1902; its last message was sent in 1959.

Dining: If in need of an outstanding meal, make reservations at the Aguilar House Sport Fishing Resort, a short walk from the General Store, on the west side. You will not be disappointed.

③ **Bamfield Kingfisher Marina,** Box 38, Bamfield, B.C. V0R 1B0, (250)728-3228. Fuel dock, open all year, with gasoline, diesel, tackle, bait, ice, scuba air.

③ **Hawkeye Industries Fuel & Chandlery,** Bamfield, B.C. V0R 1B0, (250)728-3321. Open all year. Fuel dock has gasoline and diesel.

Grappler Inlet. Use chart 3671; large-scale chart 3646. Grappler Inlet joins near the mouth of Bamfield Inlet, and leads to Port Désiré, a protected anchorage with a launch ramp and a public dock. Although beautiful, Grappler Inlet is surrounded by homes. If it's solitude you seek, you will not have found it yet.

Cape Beale. Use charts 3602; 3671. Cape Beale, surrounded by offlying rocks, marks the eastern entrance to Barkley Sound. Trevor Channel exits at Cape Beale, and is the safest entry to Barkley Sound in thick weather or poor visibility. Seas can be difficult off Cape Beale when an outflowing current from Barkley Sound meets the longshore current outside. The collision of currents, combined with wind and shallow depths around the cape, can make for heavy going.

The usual advice is to plan to round Cape Beale in early morning, before the summertime westerly wind gets up. During our 1995 visit, however, the weather reports indicated calm conditions in the afternoon. We departed Barkley Sound and rounded Cape Beale at approximately 1330, and enjoyed absolutely flat conditions in clear weather all the way to Sooke. The experience affirms the importance of listening to the weather reports and making plans not only to fit typical conditions, but conditions as they exist on a given day.

Nitinat Narrows. Use chart 3647. Nitinat Narrows connects Nitinat Lake with the the Pacific Ocean. Entrance to the narrows is obstructed by rocks and a shallow bar. An onshore wind can cause breaking seas over the bar. A crossing of this bar and negotiation of the narrows to Nitinat Lake is considered a supreme Northwest navigation challenge by a small number of adventurers.

Each year during quiet weather a few boats do make it through. We admit that we are far too cautious to risk our boat or peace of mind on such an adventure, so we cannot report our experiences at Nitinat Narrows—there are none.

Douglass, however, has taken his Nordic 32 tug across the bar, through the narrows, and into Nitinat Lake. His guidebook *Exploring Vancouver Island's West Coast* describes the experience in detail, including the comment that his crew on that trip refused ever to try it again.

The Bamfield General Store has a wide stock of merchandise, including liquor and gifts.

The Northern B.C. Coast

Northern B.C. Coast, General. The northern limit of most cruisers' explorations seldom exceeds a line that runs from Wells Passage on the mainland to Port Hardy on Vancouver Island. North of this line, the hostile mouth of Queen Charlotte Strait and notorious Queen Charlotte Sound are a natural barrier. It takes time, a strong boat, and good navigation skills to proceed further up the coast. To be fair, a lifetime of cruising could be spent south of that line, with complete satisfaction.

But, to those with the time and inclination, the coast north of Wells Passage can be a treasure. The scenery is magnificent, the population small and self-sufficient, and the fishing exceptional. You can anchor in bays with no other boats, and the boats you do meet along the way often become instant friends. This is the part of the coast where you'll find the famous names: Nakwakto Rapids, Rivers Inlet, Fish Egg Inlet, Hakai, Bella Bella, Ocean Falls, Butedale, Fiordland, Ivory Island, Grenville Channel, Prince Rupert. It's a coast filled with history and opportunity. And if it's wilderness you seek, you can find it there.

Two fish boats at anchor on a misty morning in Rescue Bay.

Insurance. Most vessel insurance policies don't cover these waters without a special rider. Contact your insurance company to extend coverage.

The boat. You won't find many little boats cruising the northern coast. *Surprise,* our Tollycraft 26 powerboat, is definitely at the small end of the scale. It's common to see jerry cans filled with extra fuel or water lashed to the rails or in the cockpits. Radar and GPS or are affordable and should be considered standard equipment. (We found that loran's longitude calculations were off by about 1 minute in the Prince Rupert area. The error grew less as we moved south. Latitude was close enough for safe navigation.) This is remote country. The boat should be in top mechanical condition. Complete spares should be carried.

You'll commonly be anchoring in 10-15 fathoms, sometimes deeper, so you'll need ample anchor rode. For its trip in 1996, *Surprise* carried an additional 250 feet of rode tied to its usual 300 feet, a total of 550 feet. While we never got into the second 250 feet, we were happy to know we had a good reserve. Most anchorages along this coast are deep, with shallower water too close to shore to swing in comfort.

Bottoms often are rocky. Because of its ability to set and hold in nearly any bottom, including rock, Bruce has become the anchor most often seen. CQR plow anchors also are popular. You don't see as many Danforth type anchors. While Danforth type anchors are good in sand, they can have trouble setting in rock, and once wedged, are easily bent. Be sure to carry at least two anchors. We carry three. The primary and stern anchors are Bruce, and the backup is a Danforth that came with the boat. The intrepid explorer and author Don Douglass uses a CQR primary anchor and Danforth lunch hook, and author Hugo Anderson used a Bruce primary anchor on his several trips. Bill Kelly and Anne Vipond, who have cruised and written extensively on the coast, use a CQR primary anchor. Many commercial fishermen use Northill anchors, but Northills tend to be hard to store on cruising boats. Whatever the anchors chosen, be sure they are big, strong, and ready to deploy.

Fuel and water. Up to Klemtu, fuel is reasonably plentiful, both diesel and gasoline. Rivers Inlet has fuel at Duncanby Landing and Dawson's Landing, and you can get fuel at Bella Bella and Klemtu. Until recently, however, the 140-mile run between Klemtu and Prince Rupert was without fuel stops, and this kept many gasoline-powered boats from making that run. Our own *Surprise,* gasoline-powered, carries 140 U.S. gallons, and we reached Prince Rupert with 30 gallons to spare. We were blessed with good conditions, and we took no side expeditions. On the return trip we carried an extra 20 gallons in jerry cans. They allowed some side expeditions, but not as many, nor as extensive as we would have liked.

All that is changing, now that Hartley Bay has fuel facilities. Hartley Bay, located approximately half-way between Klemtu and Prince Rupert, has just installed a first-class set of tanks and plumbing for both diesel and gasoline, and it should be operational by the 1997 cruising season.

Butedale had fuel in 1996, though not until July. They barged in drums of gasoline and diesel (mostly gasoline), and dispensed it in jerry cans. It was expensive, but if you needed fuel, they had it. We expect Butedale to have fuel in 1997, although it would be wise to verify.

Water is generally available all along the way. Some if it may be tinged brown from cedar bark tannin, but people have been drinking cedar water for decades with no ill effects. Ocean Falls has sparkling clear water, all you can use. Bella Bella and Klemtu have recently installed multi-million dollar water treatment plants that deliver unlimited clear water. At Bella Bella the hose ran continuously, pouring water into the sea when it wasn't going into tanks.

Weather. Bring clothes for all conditions, from cold and rainy to hot and sunny. Expect wet weather at least part of the time. The residents of Ocean Falls call themselves "The Rainpeople" for good reason.

Plan for clouds down on the deck, fog, rain (both vertical and horizontal), and storms. Leave enough slack in your schedule to anchor through serious foul weather before moving on. Be sure the boat is well-provisioned, and equipped with generator or battery power to spend several days at anchor in one location.

Plan on a little sunshine, too, maybe a lot of sunshine. It can get *hot.* Bring bug spray, and equip the boat with screens on hatches, opening ports, and windows.

Cabin heat will make the trip much more enjoyable. Most boats use a Red Dot-style truck heater to warm the boat while powering, and a second heat source while at anchor. Depending on the boat, secondary heat can be electric baseboard (generator required), diesel furnace, diesel heater, oil galley stove, wood stove, or propane catalytic heater.

Sailboaters will need some sort of cockpit protection, from a companionway dodger to full cockpit enclosure. A way must be found to keep the cabin warm and dry, or you'll be miserable.

Marinas. There aren't many marinas on this coast. In Rivers Inlet, Duncanby Landing and Dawson's Landing have guest moorage, fuel and supplies. Shearwater, near Bella Bella, has moorage, a restaurant, and repairs. Ocean Falls has ample moorage. Hartley Bay has a small amount of moorage. Bella Bella and Klemtu have public docks, but they are busy and exposed to the wash of passing boat traffic, and would not be our first choice. The floats at Namu are rundown and unsafe-appearing.

Jerry cans extend the cruising range north of Cape Caution. With fuel now available at Hartley Bay, the jerry cans are less necessary.

If you're in a jam, you could get help at one of the sportfishing lodges along the coast, but their business is serving their fly-in guests, not visiting yachties.

Repairs. While it's best to carry complete spares and know how to fix whatever goes wrong, nobody can be ready for everything. Parts and mechanics can be flown in anyplace along the coast. The only full-service shipyard south of Prince Rupert is at Shearwater.

Charts and reference books. The Canadian Hydrographic Service has more than 65 charts that cover the coast from Wells Passage to Prince Rupert. Most boats will make the passage with fewer than 65 charts, but the number of charts on board a well-found boat likely will be closer to 65 than 35. Despite their cost ($20 Cdn.), buy every chart, both small-scale and large-scale, in the area you plan to cruise. Include a few extra charts for unplanned side trips, unless your schedule calls for a straight passage up the main route (Interstate 5, as one person called it). It takes a capital investment to cruise this coast safely and enjoyably. Several times on our 1996 cruise Mrs. Hale said—sincerely—"Thank you, Bob, for having the correct chart." That's the kind of appreciation every skipper needs from the crew.

A traveling peddler from an earlier era. The "Lillian D," with Barry Mark and Jane Stewart and their two small sons, travels the coast supplying it with everything from flashlight batteries to souvenir sweatshirts to microwave ovens. They take orders one trip, bring merchandise back on the next.

Tides and currents are shown in Canadian Tides and Currents, Vol. 6, (the blue book). North of Cape Caution you'll want *Sailing Directions, British Columbia Coast (North Portion).*

Most boats carry a copy of *Marine Atlas, Vol. 2.* The charts in the atlas are out of date, but the course lines are helpful. The book is a good quick reference.

The best guidebook is *Exploring the Inside Passage to Alaska,* by Don Douglass and Réanne Hemingway-Douglass. Other useful books include *Secrets of Cruising – North to Alaska,* by Hugo Anderson; and *How to Cruise to Alaska Without Rocking the Boat Too Much,* by Walt Woodward. Woodward's book is now out of print, but many copies are around. You probably can borrow one. Another interesting book is Iain Lawrence's *Far-Away Places,* an introspective and romantic description of 50 anchorages on the northwest coast.

We also recommend a subscription to *Pacific Yachting,* published in Vancouver, B.C. It is a well-done monthly magazine with special emphasis on boating on the B.C. coast.

Get them all, books and magazine. No single publication can capture the range of conditions, approaches, intricacies and history of this amazing coast.

Blunden Harbour to Slingsby Channel

Charts	
3547	Queen Charlotte Strait, Eastern Portion (1:40,000)
3548	Queen Charlotte Strait, Central Portion (1:40,000)
3549	Queen Charlotte Strait, Western Portion (1:40,000)
3550	Approaches to Seymour Inlet & Belize Inlet (1:40,000)
3552	Seymour Inlet & Belize Inlet (1:50,000)
3921	Fish Egg Inlet & Allison Harbour (1:20,000)
3934	Approaches to Smith Sound & Rivers Inlet (1:40,000)
3598	Cape Scott to Cape Calvert (1:74,500)

Wells Passage to Blunden Harbour. Use charts 3547 and 3548. The entrance to Blunden Harbour is approximately 11 miles northwest from the mouth of Wells Passage. Use chart 3547 to identify rocks that lie northwest of Wells Passage. Chart 3548 has an excellent 1:15,000 insert that shows the entry to Blunden Harbour.

Blunden Harbour. Use chart 3548. Blunden Harbour is a lovely, well-protected bay, with excellent holding ground and the remains of an abandoned Indian village on its north shore. As you approach the entrance, it is very important to identify **Siwiti Rock**, which we leave to starboard while entering. Study the Blunden Harbour inset on chart 3548. Note the several rocks that lie along both sides of the passage into Blunden Harbour. These rocks make a somewhat serpentine route necessary as you go in.

Once inside, anchor anywhere in the large basin, or between Moore Rock and Byrnes Island. We feel that Moore Rock lies closer to Byrnes Island than the chart suggests. At least that's the way it looks on the water. Along the north shore of Blunden Harbour the abandoned Indian village with its extensive midden makes an fascinating exploration. The beach is littered with relics, but they may not be removed.

We have not explored **Bradley Lagoon** at the northeast corner of Blunden Harbour, but those who have say it's interesting. Take the dinghy through the rapids at high water slack.

Skull Cove is a scenic little anchorage.

Southgate Group. Use charts 3548, 3550, 3921. The Southgate Group is a cluster of islands that lie at the corner of the route between Blunden Harbour and Allison Harbour. A passage between Southgate Island and Knight Island makes for a scenic, sheltered shortcut. Basins on either side of the narrows appear to be just right for anchoring. Chart 3921 shows the passage in large detail.

Allison Harbour. Use chart 3921 (preferred), 3550. Allison Harbour is long and nicely protected, but not as pretty as some other anchorages. You're apt to encounter log booms tied to the shore. We're told that crabbing is good in Allison Harbour. The best holding ground is toward the head, in 3-4 fathoms. Favor the western shore as you enter and leave, to avoid a rock that lies almost mid-channel, about halfway in.

Skull Cove. Use chart 3921 (preferred), 3550. Skull Cove is on Bramham Island, roughly opposite Murray Labyrinth, and is one of the prettier anchorages you will find. If approaching from the south, we would pass behind Southgate Island and follow the eastern mainland shore almost to City Point. Then we would turn northwest, leaving Town Rock to port, and go through the passage between the Deloraine Islands and Murray Labyrinth, thus avoiding all the rocks and reefs that lie offshore. If approaching from the north, we would follow the Bramham Island shore.

Enter Skull Cove on the east side of the unnamed island, and take anchorage in the cove immediately to port, 3-4 fathoms. The view on the west side of the island is superb.

Miles Inlet. Use chart 3550. Miles Inlet indents the west shore of Bramham Island, and is just beautiful. The narrow passage is lined with many silver snags. None of the trees is very tall. Winter storms here must be awful. Once inside, anchor with excellent protection in the T intersection. The two arms of the T shoal rapidly. Explore by dinghy at high tide.

The entrance to Miles Inlet is narrow, but using McEwan Rock as a reference the entrance is easy to locate. Be sure you know exactly where you are at all times.

These log beams are all that remain from an earlier structure. East shore, Blunden Harbour.

Reference only — not for navigation

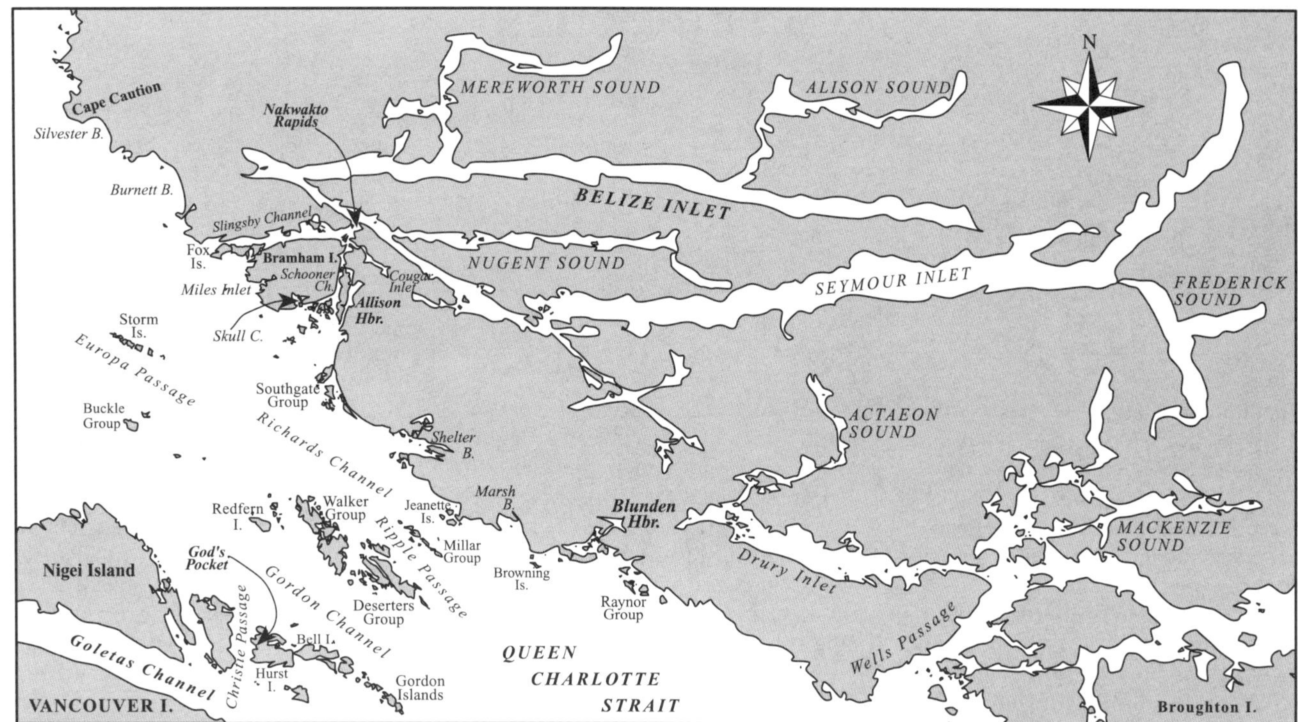

Off-lying rocks bound each side of the entrance, and you want to go directly down the middle.

Schooner Channel. Use chart 3921 (preferred), or chart 3550. Schooner Channel, along the east side of Bramham Island, is narrow, and requires constant attention to avoid rocks and reefs. With constant attention, however, the channel need not be difficult to run. Watch tidal currents closely. The flood can run to 5 knots, and the ebb to 6 knots. Schooner Channel currents are shown in Tide and Current Tables, Vol. 6 as a secondary station, based on Nakwakto Rapids.

An unnamed bay opposite Goose Point at the north end of Schooner Channel is mentioned in *Sailing Directions* as a good anchorage for small craft.

Slingsby Channel. Use chart 3550. Slingsby Channel runs between the mainland and the north side of Branham Island. Currents in Outer Narrows, between the Fox Islands and Vigilance Point, are shown as a secondary station based on Nakwakto Rapids in Tide and Current Tables, Vol. 6. Currents can run to 7 knots on the flood and 9 knots on the ebb. *Sailing Directions* warns that a westerly wind opposing an ebb current can set up dangerous seas at the entrance to Outer Narrows.

We have entered Slingsby Channel via a narrow, scenic channel that runs between the Fox Islands and Bramham Island. *Sailing Directions* mentions the channel but does not encourage it. We found the channel easy to run, however, and deeper than the chart shows.

Turret Rock (Tremble Island) looks tranquil enough when Nakwakto Rapids is slack.

Treadwell Bay. Use chart 3921 (preferred) or chart 3550. Treadwell Bay lies at the east end of Slingsby Channel, and is a good, protected anchorage. It is often used by boats awaiting slack water at Nakwakto Rapids. A small resort is located at the northwest corner of the bay. Favor the east shore as you enter, to avoid rocks off the Anchor Islands. The rocks are shown clearly on the charts. Inside, beware of rocks, shown on the chart, off the south shore of the bay.

Nakwakto Rapids. Use chart 3921 (preferred), or chart 3550. Nakwakto Rapids are among the world's fastest. Especially at springs, they must be transited at slack water only. At neap tides the window of safety opens much wider. Turret Rock sits in the middle of the narrows, with the favored passage on the west side. Turret Rock is known locally as Tremble Island because, we are told, it actually trembles during the full rush of a maximum tidal current. Brave mariners have nailed boards with their boat names on Tremble Island's trees.

Behind Nakwakto Rapids lie the extensive waterways of Seymour Inlet, Belize Sound, Nugent Sound and Alison Sound, which until recently have been almost unvisited by pleasure craft. Chart 3552, published in 1993, has opened these waters for the first time.

Smith Sound

Charts	
3934	Approaches to Smith Sound & Rivers Inlet (1:40,000)
3931	Smith Inlet, Boswell Inlet & Draney Inlet (1:40,000)
3932	Rivers Inlet (1:40,000)

Smith Sound doesn't see many pleasure boats, but it's reputed to be full of fish. We visited Smith Sound during an opening for commercial salmon fishing, and the boats turned out in force. Picking our way among the nets called for close attention, but all went well.

Smith Sound has no resorts or settlements, so you're on your own. Several bays are good for anchoring, although only one, Millbrook Cove, really appealed to us.

Smith Inlet, Boswell Inlet, and Draney Inlet all beg for exploration, now that chart 3931, published in 1992, opens them to cruising.

From the south, enter Smith Sound through Alexandra Passage, passing between North Iron Rock and Egg Rocks. We considered a course between North Iron Rock and South Iron Rock, but Jim Capadouca, a Greek fisherman from Vancouver with more than 70 years' experience on this coast, made it clear that the course between North Iron Rock and Egg Rocks was the one to take.

From the west, enter Smith Sound through Radar Passage. From the north, enter through Irving Passage. If you have GPS or loran, we suggest that you plot waypoints to keep you clear of rocks. This would be especially true in reduced visibility.

We entered Smith Sound from the north, through Irving Passage. A westerly was blowing, and we found ourselves in 6-foot beam seas from Paddle Rock to False Egg Island, and on our quarter after we turned into Irving Passage. Low clouds hung overhead, then dropped to the deck. With few visual reference points and an awkward sea, course-holding was difficult. Radar and waypoints brought us in. My notes, written later, say, "Bless the electronics!"

Table Island. Use chart 3934. Table Island lies in the mouth of Smith Sound, and the casual visitor would not think of it as an anchorage. But Jim Capadouca, the Greek fisherman from Vancouver, said that fish boats anchor along the east side, between Table Island and Ann Island, and have no problems. We have not tried this anchorage, but we did see several fish boats anchored there. A boat waiting to make a southerly dash around Cape Caution could find this anchorage useful, as could a boat seeking shelter from a westerly in Queen Charlotte Sound.

Millbrook Cove. Use chart 3934. Millbrook Cove is the outermost anchorage on the north side of Smith Sound. To us it is the favored anchorage in the sound. The cove is completely landlocked, with 4-6 fathom depths, good holding ground, and ample room for a large number of boats.

Getting in, however, will get your attention, at least the first time. After you've done it once, no problem. Begin by finding the red spar buoy E6 marking Millbrook Rocks. The buoy has a small radar reflector on top. Leave buoy E6 to starboard (Red, Right, Returning), and aim the boat toward the 30 meter island. Keep a sharp lookout for rocks on either side, especially the west side, as shown on the chart. The 30 meter island can be passed on either side, although the east side is a little deeper.

Once inside, watch for a drying rock a short distance off the northeast corner of the island. Watching your depths, anchor anywhere you like. If the fishing fleet is not in attendance, you could tie to the net-drying float moored in the bay.

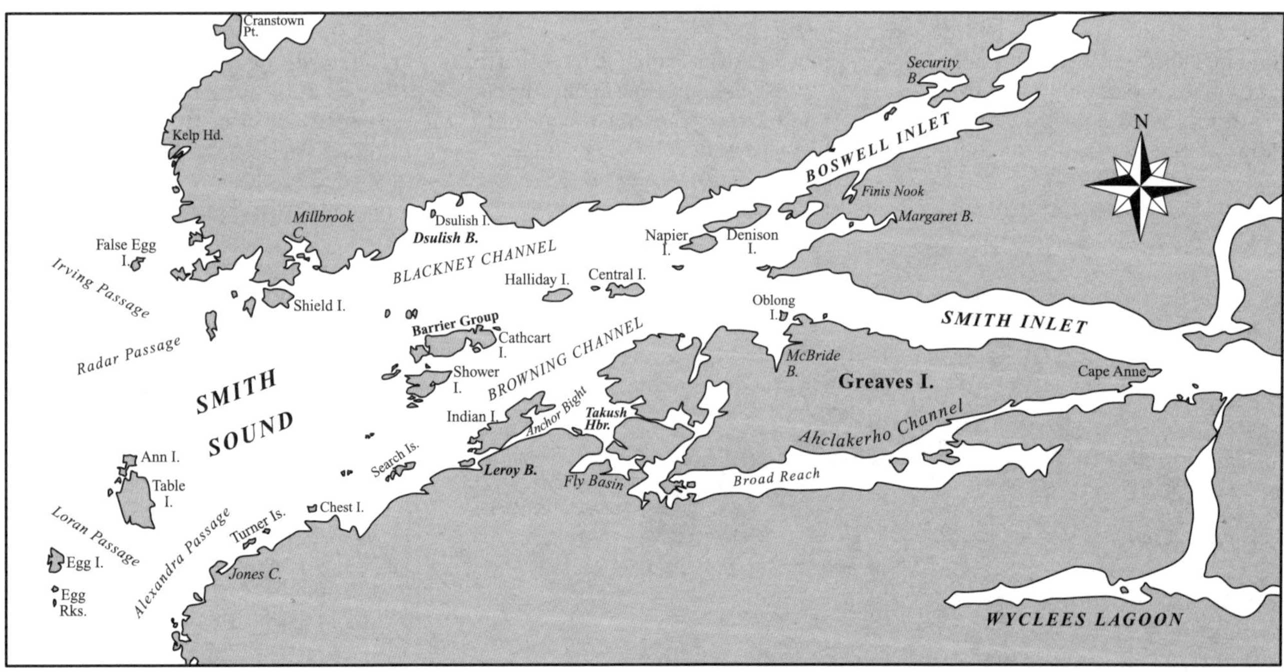

Reference only — not for navigation

Dsulish Bay. Use chart 3934. Dsulish Bay is on the north shore of Smith Sound, and has beautiful white sand beaches. A trail is reported to lead to Goose Bay to the north. The best anchorage in Dsulish Bay is behind the 46-meter island deep inside the bay. The anchorage is a little open but certainly workable. We also saw fish boats anchored along the west side of Dsulish Bay. In the right conditions it would be a good lunch stop, though we're not so sure about overnight.

Margaret Bay. Use chart 3931. Margaret Bay is located at the head of Smith Sound, on the point of land that separates Boswell Inlet and Smith Inlet. Chambers Island, rather small, is in the middle of the bay, about halfway in. West of Chambers Island depths are too great for anchoring. East of the island they shallow to 8-9 fathoms. The head shoals sharply, and old pilings take up much of the room at the head. Protection is excellent. A net drying float is moored just east of Chambers Island. Assuming it is still there and not in use, we would tie to that float.

McBride Bay. McBride Bay is on the north side of Greaves Island, at the east end of Browning Channel. It is very deep until near the head, where 5-7 fathom anchoring depths can be found. Protection is excellent, but swinging room is a little limited.

Jones Cove. Use chart 3934. Jones Cove is located on the south shore of Smith Sound, near the mouth. The cove is cozy and well protected, and often used by commercial fishing boats. A single piling is in the mouth of the cove, and fish boats tie to it rather than anchor. Anchor in 3 fathoms, with limited swinging room. Depending on the rise and fall of the tide and the presence of other boats, you may choose to run a stern line to shore.

Rivers Inlet and Fish Egg Inlet

Wadhams. Canneries such as this once dotted Rivers Inlet. Now they are empty and slowly falling apart.

Charts	
3932	Rivers Inlet (1:40,000)
3934	Approaches to Smith Sound & Rivers Inlet (1:40,000)
3727	Cape Caution to Goose Island (1:73,584)
3921	Fish Egg Inlet & Allison Harbour (1:20,000)
3784	Kwakshua Channel to Spider Island (1:36,800)
3785	Namu Harbour to Dryad Point (1:40,533)

RIVERS INLET

Use charts 3934 and 3932. Rivers Inlet is a famed salmon fishing area, and at one time was home for 17 salmon canneries. All the canneries are closed now, and most are sinking into ruin. Absent its commerce of former years, Rivers Inlet is prime cruising ground. The scenery is beautiful, the anchorages excellent. And the area is served by two well-stocked marinas, Duncanby Landing and Dawson's Landing.

Home Bay. Use chart 3934. Home Bay, on the south shore, a short distance inside the mouth of Rivers Inlet, is a pretty spot, but taken up almost entirely by the Big Spring fishing resort. The traffic of guided sportfishing boats makes Home Bay unsuitable for anchoring.

Just west of Home Bay is another nook, which Don Douglass calls **"West Home Bay"** in his book *Exploring the Inside Passage to Alaska.* This bay has no traffic, and offers anchorage behind the first of two islets inside the bay. Contrary to Douglass's illustration, however, after arriving at low tide and seeing the rocks that foul the western side of that first islet, we would pass the islet only to the east.

① **Duncanby Landing Store & Marine,** Rivers Inlet, B.C. V0N 1M0, (600)700-3558. Monitors VHF channel 06. Open all year, 7 days a week. Gasoline and diesel, propane, water, groceries, cube ice, fishing tackle and licenses, souvenirs, liquor. Ample guest moorage, showers, laundry. Ken Gillis bought Duncanby Landing in 1993, and has upgraded it considerably. Duncanby had been a commercial fishing camp since the 1930s, and in later years discouraged pleasure craft from calling. Ken and his wife Judy Chapman now welcome pleasure craft, and are most helpful. The facility is old and full of charm. The showers are free.

Goose Bay. Use chart 3934. Goose Bay, beyond Duncanby Landing, is empty now. The Goose Bay cannery is abandoned, after an effort to develop a sport fishing operation there was discontinued. The cannery buildings are interesting, though, and very photogenic.

Taylor Bay. Use chart 3934 or 3932. Taylor Bay indents the east shore of Walbran Island, and is a tranquil, lovely anchorage. Anchor all the way in, or try

Reference only — not for navigation

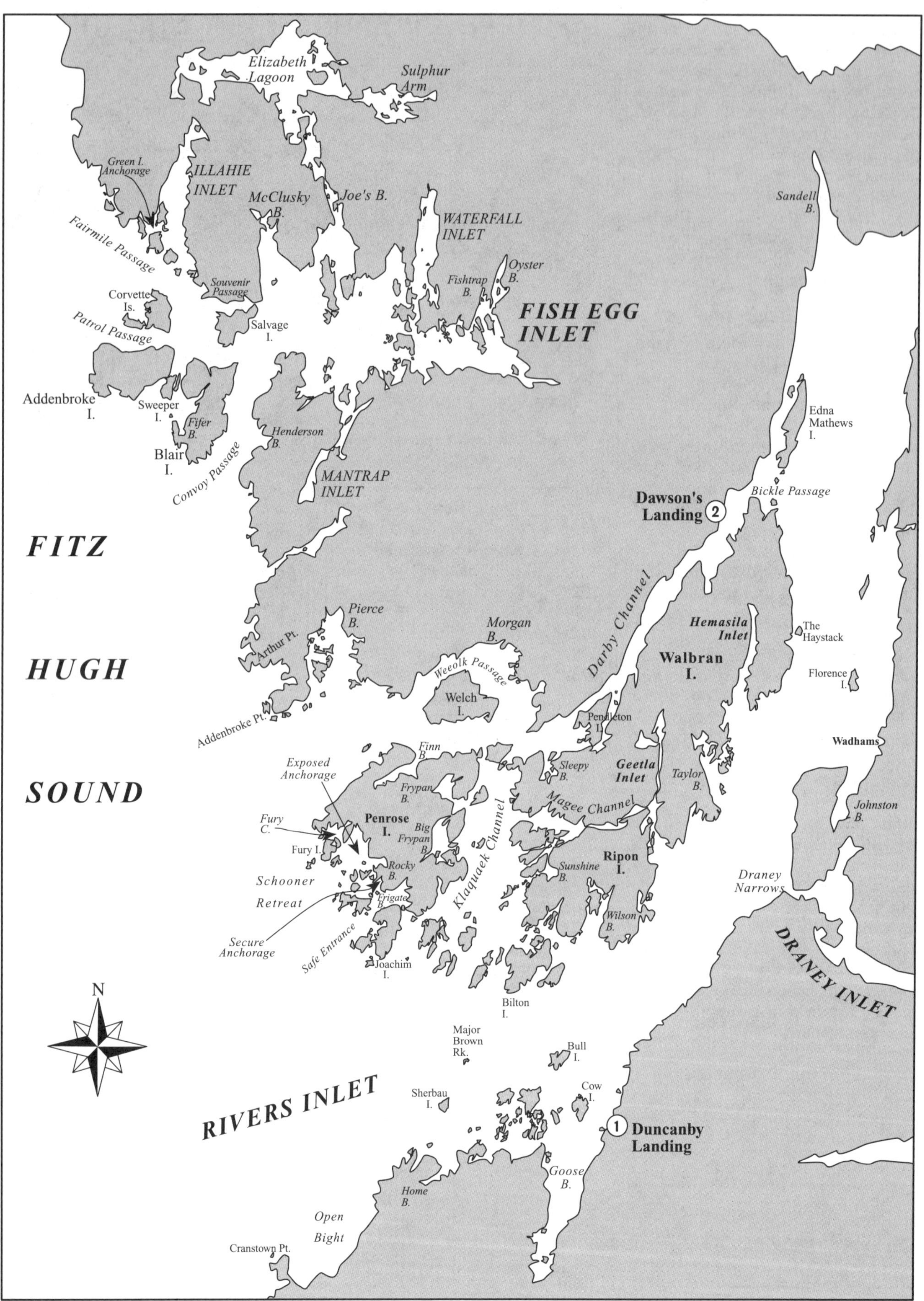

Dawson's Landing, Rivers Inlet. The store is wonderfully stocked. Room for a few boats to tie up.

the nook behind the north end of the inner island, between the inner island and Walbran Island.

Johnston Bay. Use chart 3932. Johnston Bay is on the east shore of Rivers Inlet just south of Wadhams, an abandoned cannery. The bay is is quiet and beautiful, but deep until very near the head, where an old and deteriorating float offers moorage. We have heard that development is coming to Johnston Bay, and the float will be removed.

② **Dawson's Landing General Store Ltd.,** Rivers Inlet, B.C. V0N 1M0, (604)949-2111. Open all year, gasoline and diesel fuel. Guest moorage, hardware, groceries, block ice, fishing and hunting gear and licenses, liquor, showers, laundry, post office, some accommodations. They have scheduled air service from Pacific Coastal Airlines. Dawson's Landing is owned by Rob and Nola Bachen, and it has been in the family since 1954. The accumulation and stock of tools and hardware, not to mention other store items, is impressive. The facility goes back a long way; it's a capturing of coastal history, right before your eyes. Rob and Nola are friendly and helpful.

Darby Channel. Use chart 3934. Darby Channel bounds the west side of Walbran Island, and is easily run. Southbound boats should favor the west shore of the channel to avoid being lured into foul ground behind Pendleton Island. The rock off the southwest corner of Pendleton Island is clearly marked by a beacon, and easily avoided.

Frypan Bay. Use chart 3934. Frypan Bay is at the northeast corner of Penrose Island, and was suggested to us by Rob Bachen at Dawson's Landing. We found the bay to be spacious and well protected, although lacking in scenic quality. Anchoring depths along the south shore are 4-7 fathoms, and in the middle are 8-14 fathoms.

Finn Bay. Use chart 3934. Finn Bay, on the north side of Penrose Island, is well protected, but a sport fishing camp is at the head of the bay, logging activity is on one side, and commercial fishing equipment is on the other.

Fury Island. Use chart 3934. The cove behind Fury Island, on the west side of Penrose Island, is a beautiful and popular anchorage with a perfect white sand beach, although open to southwest winds. Fury Cove, as it is commonly called, is entered by leaving Cleve Island to port, then turning to port to raise the narrow entrance. Cleve Island is mentioned in *Sailing Directions,* but shown on the chart only as a 61 meter island—no name. In a strong southwesterly, we would expect large swells in the vicinity of Cleve Island. *Breaker Pass:* Breaker Pass separates Fury Island from Cleve Island. Although we left Fury Cove in calm weather via Breaker Pass without difficulty (just to say we'd done it), we suspect it wouldn't take much of a southwesterly to make Breaker Pass live up to its name.

See area map page 228

FISH EGG INLET

Use chart 3921 for all the Fish Egg Inlet entries. Fish Egg Inlet indents the east side of Fitz Hugh Sound, behind Addenbroke Island. This is beautiful cruising country, and is rapidly becoming one of the most popular spots on the coast. Those who say you'll be all alone are wrong. The gunkholing possibilities are vast, but here are notes on some of the better-known anchorages.

Green Island Anchorage. Green Island Anchorage, just off Fitz Hugh Sound at the mouth of Illahie Inlet, is about as cozy and pleasing as an anchorage needs to be. Excellent holding in 6-7 fathoms. From seaward, wrap around the 70-meter island and follow the shoreline in. This would be a good spot to rest up after a crossing of Queen Charlotte Sound.

Illahie Inlet. The head of Illahie Inlet would be a delightful anchorage in 5-7 fathoms, mud bottom, good protection, except that logging has scarred the surrounding hillsides terribly. An eagle's nest is in a tree just north of the narrows.

Joe's Bay. Joe's Bay has suddenly become quite popular. When we visited in early July, five other boats were already anchored. It was as if we were back in Desolation Sound. Joe's Bay is worth the crowds, though. It's tranquil, tree-lined and snug. Anchoring is straightforward in the southern basin, but rocks and reefs make the northern portion somewhat trickier. A stern-tie to shore might be called for, to keep the boat from swinging onto a rock. Once anchored, the tidal rapids leading to Elizabeth Lagoon and Sulphur Arm are a big attraction. Bottom fishing is good along the walls outside.

Waterfall Inlet. Pretty spot, but we couldn't find any comfortable anchorages. We felt that the west entry, leaving the 99-meter island to starboard, was safest. Go slowly and watch for rock ledges that extend from each side of the narrow pass.

Fish Trap Bay. Awfully tight.

Oyster Bay. Oyster Bay, next to Fish Trap Bay at the head of Fish Egg Inlet, is a very nice anchorage, with a remote, end-of-the-line feel to it. We had a late and relaxed lunch there, anchored in 3 fathoms near the head of the bay. Recommended.

Mantrap Inlet. Once you're inside, Mantrap Inlet offers good anchorage. The entrance, however, is narrow, made more narrow by an uncharted ledge of rock that extends from the west shore. We would go in at half-tide or higher, dead slow, with lookouts. Our Tolly 26 had no problems, but a 40-footer would want to be very careful.

Duncanby Landing. Ken Gillis takes a minute to scratch his dog Jessie.

Even Electronics Can Fail

First you must understand the boat, a 1976 Glasply 28. The owner is a senior pilot with a major airline. He's smart, he understands equipment and maintenance, and he doesn't cut corners to save a nickel. Although the Glasply was 20 years old when this happened, it looked as if it were brand-new. Everything was shiny, and everything worked.

Except . . . except the electronics. The problem was connected with the trim tabs. On this trip, when the trim tabs were adjusted all the electronics stopped working. Never happened before. Not sure why. No depth sounder, no GPS, no autopilot, no radio . . . no electronics. Hmmm.

Now to *Surprise,* the *Waggoner* boat. *Surprise* has an electronic compass at the lower station, the only way to get the compass away from the magnets in the radar display. For two years the electronic compass worked beautifully, showing the boat direction exactly to the degree.

Then, while proceeding northwest in the Gulf Islands, we saw that the electronic compass showed a course of 380°. There being only 360° in a circle, we figured something was amiss. A call to the compass manufacturer confirmed that indeed something was amiss (a course of 380° needs confirmation?). The compass goes back to the manufacturer for repairs.

Lesson: Despite our belief that modern electronics are bullet proof, they can fail. We don't know what backups the Glasply 28 carried. On *Surprise,* we used a hand bearing compass to show our direction. Later, we realized that the autopilot compass was a workable substitute. These two experiences, however, have reaffirmed our policy of carrying non-techie old fashioned backup methods of doing whatever it is we trust our electronics to do for us.

I sure hope I don't have to use them again, though. The new electronics are fabulous—when they work.

—*Robert Hale*

Fitz Hugh Sound to Finlayson Channel

Hakai • Namu • Ocean Falls • Bella Bella • Fiordland • Finlayson Channel

Charts

3710	PLANS – Vicinity of Laredo Sound
3711	PLANS – Vicinity of Princess Royal Island
3720	Idol Point to Ocean Falls (1:41,100)
3727	Cape Caution to Goose Island (1:73,584)
3728	Milbanke Sound and Approaches (1:76,600)
3781	Dean Channel, Cousins Inlet to Elcho Harbour (1:36,507)
3784	Kwakshua Channel to Spider Island (1:36,800)
3785	Namu Harbour to Dryad Point (1:40,533)
3934	Approaches to Smith Sound and Rivers Inlet (1:40,000)
3962	Mathieson Channel, Northern Portion (1:40,000)

FITZ HUGH SOUND

FITZ HUGH SOUND BEGINS at Cape Calvert, and continues north to Fisher Channel. Boats crossing Queen Charlotte Sound from the south will find the ocean swells vanishing once Cape Calvert is behind them, although a southwesterly can still make things nasty, especially in a southflowing ebb current. Even in settled conditions, expect to find rougher water where Hakai Passage joins Fitz Hugh Sound.

Chart 3727 shows Fitz Hugh Sound in its entirety, but the chart's small scale of 1:73,584 does not allow much detail. The larger-scale charts 3727, 3784 and 3785 make navigation easier. Most northbound boats will stop either in Safety Cove or Pruth Bay. Now that chart 3921 opens Fish Egg Inlet, Green Island Anchorage would be another choice for passing traffic, and a pretty one, too.

Safety Cove. Use chart 3934 (preferred) or 3727. Safety Cove is a steep-walled, uninteresting bay that indents Calvert Island approximately 7 miles north of Cape Calvert. The bottom shoals sharply a fair distance from the head of the bay, and *Sailing Directions* recommends anchoring immediately when the depth reaches 17 fathoms. If you press in to find shallower water, watch your swing or you could find yourself aground on the shelf at low tide. Despite its name and regular use, Safety Cove would not be our first choice unless necessary.

Pruth Bay. Use chart 3784 (preferred) or 3727. Pruth Bay is at the head of **Kwakshua Channel**, some 7 miles north of Safety Cove. Pruth Bay has long been a favorite stopover point. It offers ample room, excellent protection, 7-8 fathom anchoring depths, a flat bottom and good holding. This entire area is part of the Hakai Recreation Area, a huge provincial park. A float house ranger station is moored on the north side of the bay. During the summer it houses two rangers and their wives, and we found them to be friendly and helpful.

The Hakai Beach Resort, a *very* deluxe fly-in fishing camp, occupies the head of Pruth Bay. For a couple of years the resort management aggressively turned away pleasure boaters, but in 1996 new owners changed that policy completely. A portion of the dock is now reserved for dinghies. Depending on availability, the dining room will be open to visitors. If a guide and boat are idle, short-term fishing charters can be arranged.

A trail (now a dirt road) leads from the resort across a narrow neck of land to a spectacular fine-sand ocean beach on the west side of Calvert Island. It's a perfect spot to play in the sand, build a beach fire, or admire the wonderful rock walls surrounding the beach.

Hakai Passage. Use chart 3784 (preferred) or 3727. Hakai Passage is one of the great fishing spots, yielding 50 and 60 pound salmon, and large bottom fish. Since it opens to the Pacific Ocean, the pass can get rough.

Kwakume Inlet. Use chart 3784. Our notes say, "This is the place." Kwakume Inlet is a beautiful and roomy anchorage, and if you can get into the inner basin it's unusually secluded and snug feeling. The short fairway into the inner basin is narrow and bounded by rocks, especially on the south side. Favor the north side of the passage. Half-tide or higher this little pass, dead slow bell, with alert lookouts.

The outer anchorage will hold the whole yacht club. Anchor north of the islet in the south cove, or east of the islet near the head of the main basin.

Study the chart closely before entering Kwakume Inlet. A rock is shown next to the 6 fathom mark outside the entrance, and you'll want to steer a course to avoid it. To enter, pass *between* the larger islet in the entrance and the little dot islet south of it. Once inside, two rocks are shown a short distance along the north shore, one of them drying at 5 feet. Near the head of the main basin, south of its islet, another rock is shown, this one drying at 6 feet. The markings for these rocks are inconspicuous on the chart, and would be easy to overlook without careful attention.

A beautiful, quiet morning in Kwakume Inlet, Fitz Hugh Sound. We were in the Inner Basin. The entrance channel is more narrow than the photo suggests.

Reference only — not for navigation

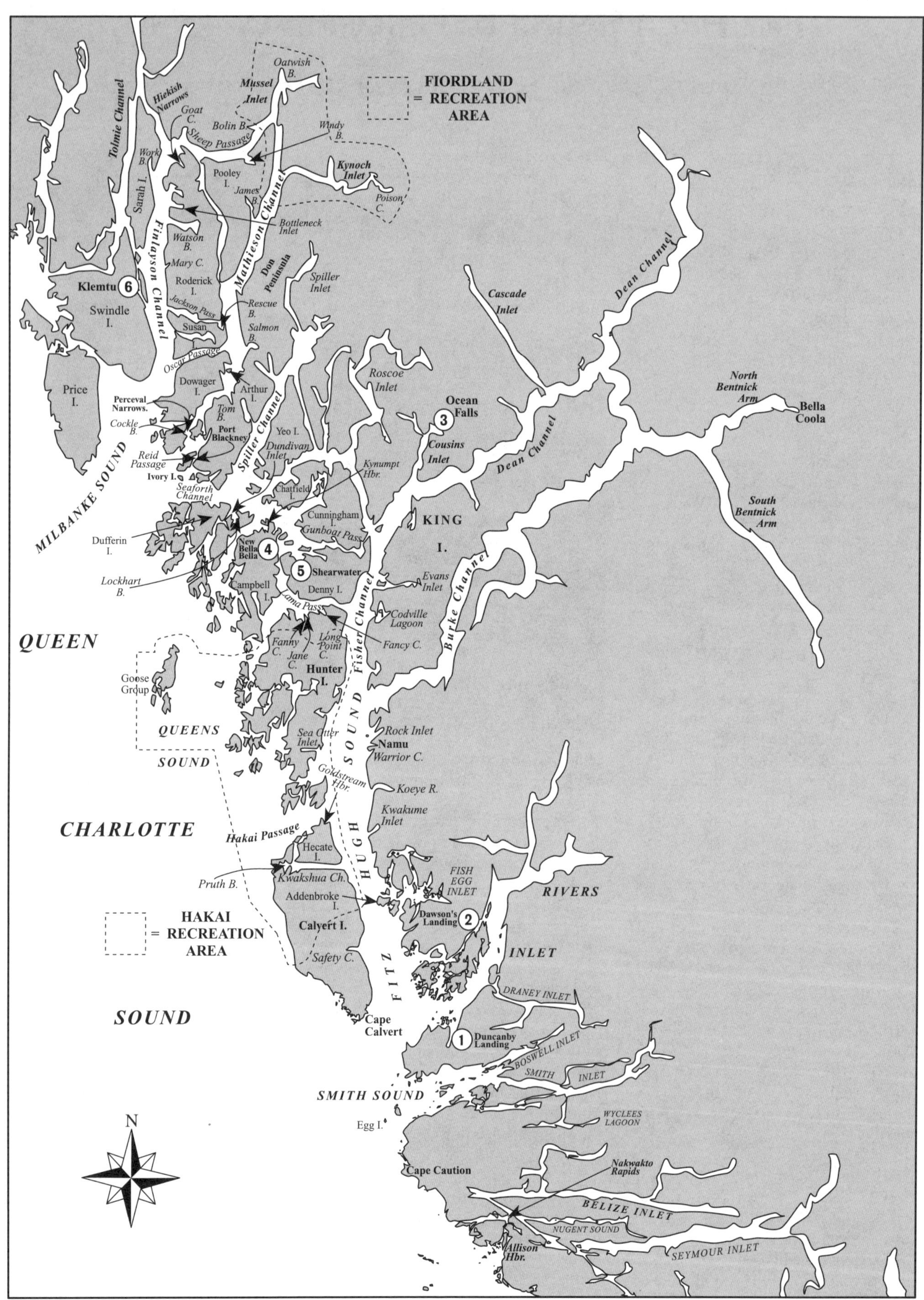

See area map page 232

Having a high tide when we arrived in early evening and another high tide the next morning, we felt our way into inner basin for the night. We were treated to glass-smooth water and the most plaintive loon's call we have ever heard. Next morning we were stopped cold by a wolf's cry—a long lonesome troubled howl, repeated just once.

Goldstream Harbour. Use chart 3784. Goldstream Harbour is a perfect little anchorage at the north end of Hecate Island. Enter from the east. Favor Hat Island, which extends from the south shore, about 0.2 miles inside. Don't favor Hat Island too closely, though; rocks extend out from it. Once past Hat Island, pass Dinner Rock, leaving it to starboard. Dinner Rock lies about 300 feet off the northwest corner of Hat Island. Inside, the middle of Goldstream Harbour is about 10 fathoms deep. Rocks extend out from the shore, so you'll pick your anchoring spot carefully to swing safely. We had lunch in Goldstream Harbour, and cleaned a small rockfish we had caught earlier that day. We didn't want to leave, but we had to move on. Nice spot.

Koeye River. Use chart 3784. Koeye River is not a good spot for overnight anchoring, but a dinghy trip up the river is reported to be interesting. A charted rock lies north of Koeye Point. Enter north of that rock and wrap around into the cove behind the point. A logging show is on the south shore, and some substantial construction is going on near the point.

Sea Otter Inlet. Use chart 3784. Sea Otter Inlet, Hunter Island, has two arms that form a T at the entrance. Crab Cove, the northern arm, was recommended to us by Andy Macdonald, the park ranger at Pruth Bay. Anchor near the head in 5-6 fathoms. The south arm is prettier than Crab Cove, and more private feeling. Anchor near the head in 6-7 fathoms.

Warrior Cove. Use chart 3784. Warrior Cove is on the east side of Fitz Hugh Sound, approximately 1.5 miles south of Namu. With a typical westerly wind a following sea will chase you into the cove, but the seas subside when you pass the 270-foot island. Inside the inner cove the water is calm. The inner cove is pretty and protected. Scout around for just the right spot, and put the hook down in 3-4 fathoms, good holding.

Ocean Falls. A substantial pulp mill city, now a ghost town.

Namu. Use chart 3785. What's going on at Namu? The B.C. ferry calls, but as of summer 1996 the café and store were closed, the floats on the south side of the main pier were overgrown with trees and weeds and in need of repair, and of course, no fuel. Rumors of new owners are heard, but nothing comes of them. This once-great cannery and supply point is falling into ruin.

Rock Inlet. Rock Inlet extends northeast from Whirlwind Bay (Namu), and it's a good, protected spot. Entering or departing, be sure to identify Verdant Island, near the mouth, and pass east of it. Keep a mid-channel course, and watch for rocks. The chart shows the way. Inside, anchor in 4-7 fathoms. We put the hook down in two spots, and found the holding only fair to good (maybe).

FISHER CHANNEL

The north end of Fitz Hugh Sound divides into Burke Channel and Fisher Channel. Burke Channel leads eastward to Bella Coola, which is connected by road to Williams Lake and all the highways inland. Bella Coola has facilities and is mentioned often by the few residents on this part of the coast, but is seldom visited by pleasure craft.

Fisher Channel is a continuation of the Inside Passage route, although the Inside Passage soon leads west and north, via Lama Passage or Gunboat Passage, to Bella Bella, and Shearwater. Instead of turning west to Bella Bella and Shearwater, if you remain on Fisher Channel you will reach Cousins Inlet and the city of Ocean Falls, the most complete and interesting ghost town on the coast.

③ **Ocean Falls.** Use chart 3781 with large scale inset, or chart 3720. Harbour Manager: Herb Carpenter, General Delivery, Ocean Falls, B.C. V0T 1P0, (250)289-3859. Monitors VHF channels 06 & 09. Open all year, government dock with water and 20 amp power. Although a ghost town (see sidebar), Ocean Falls and its neighboring community of Martin Valley have a population of approximately 160, a lodge with showers and laundry, two eating spots, a post office, a part-time medical clinic, some groceries and fishing tackle, haulout to 20 tons, ice, garbage drop, port-a-potty dump, and excellent docks.

The docks have free power and all the clear, sweet water you need for your tanks and boat washing. Moorage is collected every evening around 1900. A

The Ocean Falls docks are in excellent condition. Ample water is available for tanks and boat washing.

See area map page 232

The dam at Ocean Falls supplies power for Shearwater and New Bella Bella.

Ocean Falls

Ocean Falls, at the head of Cousins Inlet, is a ghost town, lost on the B.C. coast. When you round Coolidge Point in Cousins Inlet you see the "falls," the spillway from the dam. Below the dam are extensive docks, and on top of the docks a huge mill. To the left of the mill are tall, modern buildings. It is only after you land and walk uptown that you realize the buildings are empty, and the north coast wind is whistling through their open windows.

Until it closed in 1973, the Crown Zellerbach mill was the second largest on the coast, and Ocean Falls was a busy community of more than 5,000. We are told that championship swimmers came from its Olympic-size swimming pool. The pool is filled in now. Machinery sits on the dirt. When Crown Zellerbach gave up the mill, the province, unwilling to lose the jobs, tried to run it. In 1980 it too gave up. The mill's machinery was removed, and in 1986 bulldozers came to level the town. The town's residents stood in front of the bulldozers and backed them down, though not until after many of the houses and other buildings had been destroyed.

Downtown, fortunately, was largely spared. The Ocean Falls Hotel, tall and imposing, is empty. Its doors are chained shut and signs warn off trespassers. A dormitory where mill workers lived looks almost ready to accept a new crop of college students. Its doors too are chained shut. A 2-story garden-court apartment complex, 1970s style, is overgrown with weeds. The windows are broken and the plumbing fixtures torn out. We watched as a lonesome wind fluttered the few ragged and water-stained curtains that remained. We thought, a story longs to be written. A film waits to be made.

The best-maintained building is the Courthouse, occupied by the government. It houses the post office, the clinic, and the office of Gunter H. Hogrefe, the Chairman and Administrator of the Ocean Falls Improvement District. We found Gunter Hogrefe dressed neatly in slacks, necktie and sport jacket, surrounded by papers in his office. He worked in the mill for 30 years, starting in a rotten job called "the salt mine," and finishing as project coordinator. He told us he was one of the small band that de-

Gunter Hogrefe, Administrator for the Ocean Falls Improvement District, in his Courthouse Building office.

rustic lunch stop called The Shack, with excellent offerings, has been operating on the docks for several years, although family health concerns make its continued presence uncertain. A café is in Ocean Falls, but was not open the days we were there. The dam, which dominates the head of the inlet, supplies power for Ocean Falls, Shearwater and Bella Bella.

Most of the area's residents live in the 85-house community of Martin Valley, about a mile's walk down the road toward the mouth of Cousins Inlet. It's an easy, scenic walk, past plantings gone wild from what must have been homes years ago. The concrete ramp leading into the inlet at Martin Valley is for float planes. Martin Valley has a general store open 9-4 Tuesday through Saturday, and a second store open Monday, Wednesday, Friday and Saturday. The houses in Martin Valley were taken over by the province when Ocean Falls was abandoned. One at a time they have been sold to people who enjoyed the solitude of the area. With the now-regular calls by the ferry and its tourists, a small crafts industry has begun.

You can walk up the road to the dam behind Ocean Falls and back along Link Lake. Trout fishing is said to be excellent. The pulp and paper mill is fenced, gated and locked. Crabbing is good at the docks, and reported to be excellent off the mill. Halibut and salmon can be caught in the inlet. We think Ocean Falls is a "don't miss" stopping point.

Codville Lagoon. Use chart 3785. Codville Lagoon, a provincial park on the east side of Fisher Channel, is a popular anchorage, protected and pretty, with ample room for several boats. From out in the channel the narrow entrance is hard to locate, but Codville Hill, with its moonscape of barren, rock slopes and three peaks, is a good landmark. Favor

See area map page 232

fied the bulldozers in 1986.

Now he is looking for new business to revitalize Ocean Falls. A company tried to sell bottled water from the pure offerings of Link Lake, behind the dam. Stock was sold, and publicity sent out. The venture failed. Hogrefe points out that Ocean Falls has a perfect deep water harbor, and an infrastructure ready to go to work. Applicants welcome.

We also happened upon another citizen, Norman Brown ("Nearly Normal Norman, they call me"), the proud President of the Ocean Falls Historical Society Museum. The museum consists of what once was the company's large and comfortable guest house.

Vandalism, frozen and burst water pipes, and a leaky roof reduced the guest house to unlivability, and Norman is the one-man construction gang working on the slow restoration. The roof has been replaced, the water pipes repaired, electricity restored, and several of the rooms brought somewhat back. In the kitchen Norman showed where vinyl floor covering had been removed to reveal a wonderful late 1920s floor. In other rooms the removal of wall coverings brought forth elegant paneling. Norman showed us toilets that flushed—a major achievement. Then he took me (Mrs. Hale said she'd wait) into the attic to see the bats.

Norman Brown, President of the Ocean Falls Historical Society Museum. Some restoration work still needed.

Up the stairs we climbed, and through a door into the attic. The space was clean but musty-smelling. Small piles of loose material lay here and there—bat guano, excellent fertilizer.

The light was dim in the attic, and I couldn't see any bats. Norman walked to a corner, reached into the shadows, and produced two handsful of small furry creatures with doglike faces and skin-covered wings. He offered them to me, but I was not used to such animals and thought my strong grip might harm them. So he set them free. They flew sqeaking around the attic, and settled back in their corner. I urged Mrs. Hale to come see the bats, but she said no.

A short distance from the guest house/museum, a failing boardwalk fronts on what once were pleasant homes with a view of the inlet. The boardwalk is rotting and sagging and the houses are empty. Ocean Falls searches for industry and Nearly Normal Norman Brown makes slow progress on the guest house. Meanwhile, around the edges, Nature reclaims the land.

—*Robert Hale*

the south side of the entrance to avoid a rock off the north shore. Anchor in 6-8 fathoms along the east shore, opposite Codville Island. An unimproved trail runs from the head of the anchorage to Sagar Lake. Andy Macdonald, the park ranger, told us the trail is rough and difficult, but the lake is beautiful.

Long Point Cove. Use chart 3785. Long Point Cove is located on the west side of Fisher Channel, approximately 1 mile south of Lama Passage. Although *Sailing Directions* mentions Long Point Cove as a good anchorage for small craft, it isn't as scenic or interesting as other anchorages in the area. On entering, favor the west shore to avoid a 3-foot drying rock some 250-300 yards north of Long Point. The rock is shown on the chart.

Lama Passage. Use chart 3785. Lama Passage leads westward and northward from Fisher Channel to New Bella Bella. Cruise ships and B.C. ferries use this passage regularly. Keep a sharp lookout ahead and astern.

Fancy Cove. Use chart 3785. Fancy Cove lies on the south shore of Lama Passage, and is a delightful little anchorage. Don Douglass writes about the cove in his *Exploring the Inside Passage to Alaska*, and he deserves thanks from the entire cruising community for telling about it. Anchor in 2-4 fathoms wherever it looks good.

Fannie Cove. Use chart 3785. Fannie Cove, on the south shore of Lama Passage in Cooper Inlet, is a beautiful little spot, with an obvious anchoring nook on its eastern shore just inside the entrance. Unfortunately, the holding ground is only fair. We tried twice to get a good set in the little nook and once farther out, but each time we dragged without much effort. We would overnight in settled weather only. Study the chart before entering. Leave Gus Island and the little dot islet west of Gus Island to port as you approach.

Jane Cove. Use chart 3785. Jane Cove, on the south shore of Lama Passage in Cooper Inlet, offers shelter, but lacks scenic quality. Study the chart carefully before entering, to avoid shoals and rocks. We prefer Fannie Cove, despite its marginal holding, or Fancy Cove, which is spectacular by comparison.

Bella Bella. Use chart 3785. Bella Bella lies on the northeastern shore of Lama Passage, and is largely abandoned. A dock is located there, but if you're looking for a dock we suggest Shearwater instead.

④ **New Bella Bella.** Use chart 3785. New Bella Bella (Waglisla) is a major Indian village, with gasoline and diesel fuel, good water, garbage drop, a well-stocked band store with pay phone, liquor store, bank (limited hours), and hospital. This is the first fuel north of Rivers Inlet, and the fuel dock is busy. We found the attendants to be courteous. The recently-installed water treatment plant provides a steady stream of clear water at the fuel dock. The band store at the head of the dock has a good stock of meats, produce, frozen foods and baked goods. Selection is best shortly after the ferry brings stock. The help is friendly. A stairway (you may have to have it pointed out to you) leads to the lower level, where you'll find soft goods and souvenirs. The liquor store shares the lower level of the band store building, in the back. A water taxi runs between Shearwater and New Bella Bella.

See area map page 232

The concrete docks at Shearwater are wide and stable. Complete facilities make this a popular stop.

Kliktsoatli Harbour. Use chart 3785. Kliktsoatli Harbour is 2 miles east of New Bella Bella, and is the location of Shearwater. Those preferring to anchor out can find good anchoring and mooring buoys on the eastern shore, as shown on the 1:12,000 inset on chart 3785.

⑤ **Shearwater Marine Resort,** Bella Bella, B.C. V0T 1B0, (250)957-2305, (250)957-2366 (after hours); fax (250)957-2422; http://shearwater.ca. Monitors VHF channel 06. Use chart 3785. Open all year, guest moorage, limited 15 & 30 amp power, propane, showers, laundry, ice, restaurant, pub, telephones, haulout, garbage drop, recycling, store, boating supplies, charts, lodging, post office. Shearwater, 2 miles east of New Bella Bella in Kliktsoatli Harbour, is the most complete marine facility between Port Hardy and Prince Rupert. The docks are wide and comfortable, although electrical power extends only to the head of the dock. They can haul out boats to 70-80 feet, and repair almost anything, including electronics. A new restaurant and pub opened in 1996. The store carries licenses, charts, ice, boating supplies and limited groceries. An air field is a short distance away. A water taxi makes regular runs to New Bella Bella and return. The marina is on the site of a military seaplane base during WWII, and the large hangar now serves as the shop.

Gunboat Passage. Use chart 3720, with its 1:12,100 inset of Gunboat Passage. Gunboat Passage connects Seaforth Channel with Fisher Channel, and provides a scenic route for a run between Bella Bella/Shearwater and Ocean Falls. The passage is littered with reefs and rocks, but well marked with aids to navigation. The only tricky spot is the narrow fairway between Denny Point and Maria Island. We went through dead slow, with one eye on the depth sounder. When the bottom started coming up we altered our course northward slightly and the depths increased. Gosse Bay, west of Maria Island, is reported to be a good anchorage.

Kynumpt Harbour. Use chart 3720. Kynumpt Harbour indents the north tip of Campbell Island, at the eastern end of Seaforth Channel. *Sailing Directions* says the local name is Strom Bay. The entrance is open and easy, but study the chart carefully to identify and avoid rocks on the western and southern shores. The northernmost indent on the eastern shore is reported to be a good anchorage, as is Strom Cove, the arm that extends to the southeast. We poked around Strom Cove to find a good lunch stop, but saw mostly 9-13 fathoms on the sounder. At those depths, even a 3:1 scope would swing us too close to rocks near shore, so we anchored in the outer bay, 7 fathoms, west of Spratt Point. The Greenpeace vessel *Moby Dick* shared the bay with us.

Seaforth Channel. Use charts 3720 & 3728. Seaforth Channel connects the New Bella Bella/Shearwater area with Milbanke Sound to the west, and is part of the Inside Passage route. Ivory Island is at the western entrance.

Dundivan Inlet. Use chart 3720. Dundivan Inlet indents Dufferin Island near the eastern entrance to Seaforth Channel. It's a pretty spot, with several islets to break up the scenery, but the water is deep except near hazards. Of the two arms that make up Lockhart Bay near the head, the western is the more attractive anchorage. For overnight we would run a stern-tie to a tree. The eastern arm was deep (10 fathoms) until very near the head, and would require a shore-tie. Dundivan Inlet would not be a first choice unless weather was ugly and we were looking for a place to hole up.

Reid Passage/Port Blackney. Use chart 3710. In most cases, pleasure craft bound north or south will choose to avoid Milbanke Sound, and use the Reid Passage route east of Ivory Island. Chart 3710 makes the navigation straightforward. At the south end, be sure to identify all the rocks, islets, and buoy E50. In the middle of Reid Passage, pass to the east of Carne Rock. Port Blackney, at the north end of Reid Passage, has two anchorages, Boat Inlet and Oliver Cove.

Boat Inlet. Use chart 3710. Boat Inlet, at the southwest corner of Port Blackney, is reported to be a good anchorage, but guarded by shallow water in the entrance. Wait for half-tide or higher, depending on your vessel's draft.

Oliver Cove. Use chart 3710. Oliver Cove provincial park, on the east side of Port Blackney, is a safe and pretty anchorage. Enter carefully to avoid a charted rock in the middle of the fairway, and put the hook down in 6 fathoms.

Perceval Narrows. Use chart 3710. The Inside Passage route leads across Mathieson Channel between Port Blackney and Perceval Narrows. Chart 3710 shows all the rocks and islets clearly. Tidal current predictions are found as a secondary station under Prince Rupert in Tide and Current Tables, Vol. 6. From south to north, lay a course that gives Cod Reefs a good offing to port as you leave Port Blackney. Then turn to approximately 270° magnetic and cross Mathieson Channel toward Martha Island, leaving Lizzie Rocks to starboard. We found noticeable turbulence in Mathieson Channel off Lizzie Rocks on an ebb tide. If you're southbound, once clear of Perceval Narrows, steer a course of approximately 90° magnetic to give Walter Island and Cod Reefs a good offing.

See area map page 232

Cockle Bay. Use chart 3710 or 3728. Cockle Bay, a short distance north of Perceval Narrows, has a beautiful beach and good protection from westerlies. You can find 5-6 fathom depths along the south shore, and 10-15 fathoms in the middle, as shown on the chart.

Tom Bay. Use chart 3728. Tom Bay is on the east side of Mathieson Channel at latitude 52 24.2N. It's a good anchorage, though scarred by recent logging activity. As with most bays on this coast Tom Bay shoals at the head. Anchor in 10-12 fathoms wherever it suits you.

Arthur Island. Use chart 3734. The coves north of Arthur Island, approximately 1.5 miles south of Oscar Passage on the west side of Mathieson Channel, are mentioned in *Sailing Directions* as a small boat anchorage, but we're not convinced. Neither cove is very scenic, and driftwood clogs the eastern cove. We would choose Rescue Bay, Salmon Bay or Tom Bay instead.

Salmon Bay. Use chart 3734. Salmon Bay is on the east side of Mathieson Channel, opposite the mouth of Oscar Passage. It is *deep* until the very head, where the bottom comes up to 8-10 fathoms. The bay is cozy, and we heard a loon—always a refreshing sound.

Oscar Passage. Use chart 3734. Oscar Passage is a wide open and easily run route between Mathieson Channel and Finlayson Channel, the Inside Passage route. It's excellent for larger vessels, but small boats will find Jackson Passage, a short distance to the north, more scenic.

Rescue Bay. Use large scale chart 3711 (much preferred) or chart 3734. Rescue Bay is the most popular anchorage in this area. It is well protected, with good holding, and has room for many boats. Study chart 3711 carefully before entering, and steer a determined mid-channel course between the two islands and their reefs that mark the entrance. We noted that departing fish boats not only steered such a course on their way out, but got well clear of both islands before turning. Once inside Rescue Bay, scout around with the depth sounder and pick your spot carefully. We saw one boat on the western side find the bottom at low tide, after being too eager to get the anchor down. Note the rock that dries 3 feet in the southeast corner of the bay.

Jackson Passage. Use chart 3734 (with inset) and chart 3711. Jackson Passage is the scenic route between Mathieson Channel and Finlayson Channel. Jackson Passage is easily navigated, except for a tight spot at Jackson Narrows at the eastern end. The fairway through Jackson Narrows is quite narrow, but kelp marks the rocks. Strongly favor the *south shore* all the way through the narrows, and keep a sharp lookout. A transit near high water slack would be the least anxious.

James Bay. Use chart 3962. James Bay, on the west side of Mathieson Channel, is open to southerly winds, but gets you out of the chop in the channel. It is a pretty spot, but the bottom shoals *abruptly* in the northwest corner. Anchor in 13 fathoms, where the little anchor symbol is on the chart.

FIORDLAND

Use chart 3962. The Fiordland Recreation Area was established in 1987, and is some of the most beautiful country on the coast. The mountains are sheer and beautiful and the wildlife abundant, but the anchorages are just about nonexistent. Fortunately, good anchorage can be found in Windy Bay, only a short distance away.

Fiordland begins just east of Bolin Bay at the north end of Sheep Passage, and includes Mussel Inlet and Kynoch Inlet. We include Bolin Bay in this section because it is so beautiful, and Windy Bay because it is the best anchorage near Fiordland.

Windy Bay. Windy Bay is on the south shore of Sheep Passage, near the eastern end. The chart shows anchorage in the middle, but you can find more protected anchorage in what we call Cookie Cove, just east of the little island at the northeast corner of the bay. Put the hook down in 10 fathoms. Excellent holding.

Bolin Bay. Bolin Bay is set in a bowl of sheer rock mountains, with a beautiful drying flat at the head and a magnificent rock slide on the south shore. We did not anchor, but we did find a few spots with depths of 6-10 fathoms near the head of the bay. With care you might get a safe amount of scope out and stay off the flats. Windy Bay is a better choice.

Oatwish Bay. Oatwish Bay is at the north end of Mussel Inlet, and is shown in "Continuation A" on chart 3962. The bay is too deep for anchoring, but amazing Lizette Falls will have you reaching for the camera. We enjoyed lunch, drifting around at the base of the falls.

Poison Cove. The run across the top of Mussel Inlet to Poison Cove left us awestruck. Our notes on Poison Cove say, "Poison Cove dwarfed us. I run out of superlatives."

Kynoch Inlet. Kynoch Inlet, 8.5 miles long, leads off Mathieson Channel. With its rock walls and waterfalls it is stunning. If you go ashore watch out for grizzly bear. We are sorry we cannot speak from any more experience with Kynoch Inlet, however. When we visited, the hour was growing late and the barometer was falling rapidly. The cloud line was at 200 feet. Mist was gathering. We made for a safe anchorage.

Cookie Cove, Windy Bay

I had slept poorly the night before, and was struggling to stay awake when we anchored behind the little island at the entrance to Windy Bay. I needed a nap. The sky was cloudy, and we hoped that an hour's wait would yield clearing conditions and a more congenial skipper. Bears were reported to be on the shore. We didn't need another one in the helm seat.

The propane cabin heater was started and I crawled into the bunk. Mrs. Hale says it wasn't long before she heard me snoring. She, however, had slept well and was full of energy. So she fired up the oven and made two batches of oatmeal-raisin cookies. When I woke, the cookies were cooling and the cabin smelled like heaven.

The anchorage is not officially named. Since Snoring Bay already exists in the San Juan Islands, we decided to call this anchorage Cookie Cove. For us, Cookie Cove it always will be.

—Robert Hale

Finlayson Channel to Prince Rupert

Klemtu • Butedale • Hartley Bay • Grenville Channel • Prince Rupert

Charts

3711	Plans – Vicinity of Princess Royal Island
3734	Jorkins Point to Sarah Island (1:36,000)
3738	Sarah Island to Swanson Bay (1:1:35,800)
3739	Swanson Bay to Work Island (1:35,600)
3740	Work Island to Point Cumming (1:35,500)
3742	Otter Passage to McKay Reach (1:70,900)
3772	Grenville Channel, Sainty Point to Baker Inlet (1:32,200)
3773	Grenville Channel, Baker Inlet to Ogden Channel (1:36,500)
3927	Bonilla Island to Edye Passage (1:77,800)
3957	Approaches to Prince Rupert Harbour (1:40,000)
3958	Prince Rupert Harbour (1:20,000)

⑥ **Klemtu.** Use chart 3734 and large scale chart 3711. Klemtu is a major Indian village, located behind Cone Island on the west side of Finlayson Channel, at latitude 52 35.6N. The fuel dock, open Monday-Saturday, and the band store are at the north end of town. You'll find gasoline, diesel, propane, and stove oil, and ample clear water from a new water treatment system. The fuel dock faces the channel, and wash from passing boat traffic is apt to bounce you around. Be sure you are well-tied and well-fendered. The attendant is in the office shack on the pier, across from the upper end of the ramp.

Klemtu is the last fuel stop until Hartley Bay, approximately 65 miles north. (In season, Butedale plans to have gasoline and diesel, dispensed from drums into jerry cans.) Until 1997, when Hartley Bay's fuel system became operational, it was necessary to carry fuel for the entire 140 mile run between Klemtu and Prince Rupert.

The band store at the head of the fuel dock pier at Klemtu carries a wide selection of groceries and other essentials (no liquor), but the stock gets thin a few days after the ferry has delivered it. Ice is planned for 1997, as are showers and laundry. A pay telephone is just outside the store. The post office is some distance away in the village proper. The store manager offered to carry our outgoing mail over for us, and we accepted. The village has a public dock, but it is exposed to wash from passing boats. We would look for a quieter anchorage.

Mary Cove. Use chart 3734. Mary Cove is on the east side of Finlayson Channel, across from Klemtu. It is a pleasant little cove, but might be open to SW winds. Anchor in 8-9 fathoms inside. A salmon steam empties into Mary Cove. We saw a nice-size salmon jump. Just outside, a gillnetter had his net stretched halfway across the mouth of the cove.

Bottleneck Inlet. Use chart 3734. Bottleneck Inlet, at latitude 52 42.8N on the east side of Finlayson Arm, is an outstanding anchorage. It is protected and beautiful, and big enough for several boats. The north side of the inlet has superb rock walls. The entrance is narrow, but a mid-channel course will do nicely. Anchor in 4-6 fathoms.

Goat Cove. Use chart 3738. Goat Cove indents the east shore near the north end of Finlayson Channel. An inner basin is reached by running through a narrow neck. Inside, *Sailing Directions* says good anchorage can be had in 17 fathoms, which is pretty deep. Douglass likes this inner basin, too, and would anchor near the head of the basin in 6 fathoms. We, however, don't like it at all. We went in during a gathering storm, and wind gusts found their way to us with nothing to stop them. The bottom shoaled too quickly for us to anchor in 6 fathoms and pay out scope to stand up to the wind. "Oversold!" we said, and left.

Work Bay. Use chart 3738. Work Bay is located on the west side of Finlayson Channel, near the north end. The bay appears to be open to southerly winds, but we anchored there in the southerly storm that chased us out of Goat Cove, and found no wind and only remnants of a few rollers from Finlayson Channel. In our opinion Work Bay has room for just one boat at anchor unless all stern-tie to trees. The bay is 7-8 fathoms deep. With only a 3:1 scope (150 feet) of anchor rode out, you must be in the center or you will swing onto shore or onto the drying shelf at the head of the bay. Work Bay is pretty and snug-feeling. We like it.

Hiekish Narrows. Use chart 3738 (large scale inset). Hiekish Narrows connects with Sheep Passage and Finlayson Channel at the south end, and Graham Reach, the continuation of the Inside Passage, at the north end. Current predictions are given under Hiekish Narrows in the Tide and Current Tables, Vol. 6. Maximum currents run to 4.5 knots on the flood, 4 knots on the ebb. The flood sets north. The water behind

Butedale's buildings have seen better days, but new operators are bringing this great old facility back.

Reference only — not for navigation

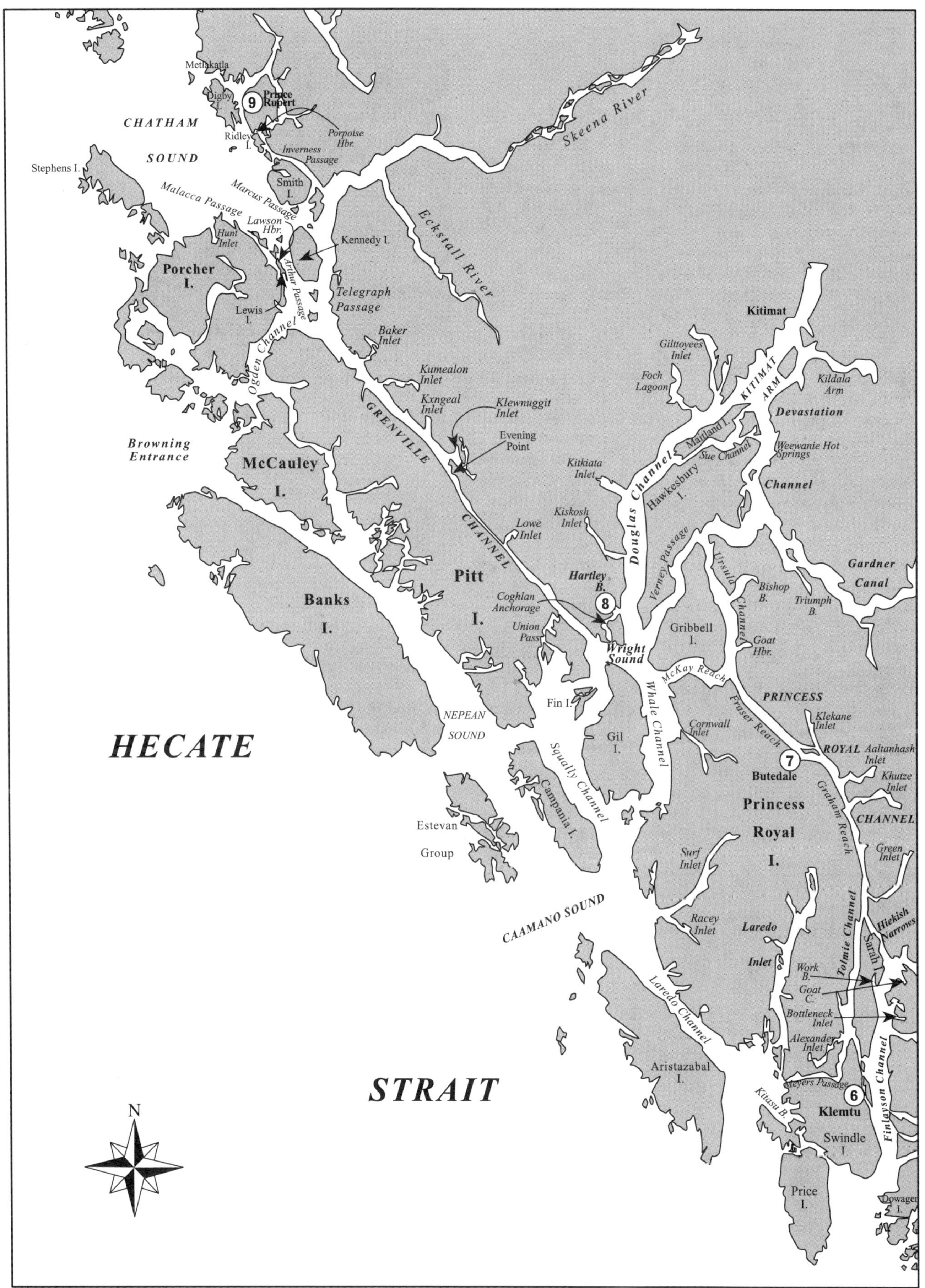

See area map page 239

Hewitt Island appears to be a possible anchorage, but the current runs strongly through it. We would choose it only for a short stop or a last resort. We found an incredible accumulation of drift at the south end of the narrows—trees, logs, rubbish, kelp and weed—a real mess.

Fraser Reach and Graham Reach. Use charts 3738, 3740 and 3742. Fraser Reach and Graham Reach are wide, straight and deep, and marked all along the way with beautiful waterfalls. Cruise ships make this their highway. The principal stopping point for pleasure craft is Butedale.

Hartley Bay's new fuel tanks. Completion scheduled for spring 1997.

⑦ **Butedale.** Use chart 3739. The ghost town of Butedale, at the south end of Fraser Reach, is an abandoned cannery that is struggling back to life once again. A group called the Butedale Founders, from Oregon, have leased the property. They have restored some of the houses to make them livable, created a rough-and-ready camping style dormitory, and brought fuel in (drums, dispensed into jerry cans). For current information on fuel, call (503)397-5392.

The access float is low, and we advise good fendering in case a B.C. ferry or a cruise ship goes by, which it will. You can anchor out in the bay, and take the dinghy to the float. Guided tours are available, but you must sign a release of liability. Butedale Lake is reported to produce large trout and dolly varden. The long warehouse building has timber in it that would make a builder's mouth water. In the power house the generators turn over lazily, awaiting reconnection to the rest of the property. Something about Butedale makes you walk softly and talk quietly. It's as if you don't want to disturb the memories.

Wright Sound. Use chart 3742. Wright Sound lies at the junction of Grenville Channel, Douglas Channel, Verney Passage, and McKay Reach. With all the currents present in this body of water, it doesn't take much wind to make it dowright ugly. A local told us that in an outflow wind from Douglas Channel, it is better to lay a course off Juan Point, at the north end of Gil Island. We tried this route in an outflow wind, and found it much smoother than our previous crossing, in which we tried a direct (and wet) route between Point Cumming and Cape Farewell.

Coghlan Anchorage. Use chart 3742 and large scale chart 3711. Coghlan Anchorage lies behind Promise Island, and is connected by Stewart Narrows with Hartley Bay. The anchorage is open to the south, but still decently protected. The mooring buoys in Stewart Narrows are private. We anchored briefly in 6-7 fathoms near a mooring buoy just north of Brodie Point, and found the protection and holding ground excellent, if not very scenic. Anchorage also is possible on the shore opposite Brodie Point, off Otter Shoal.

⑧ **Hartley Bay.** Band office 445 Hayimiisaaxa Way, Hartley Bay, B.C. V0V 1A0, (250)841-2500. Use chart 3742 and large scale chart 3711. Hartley Bay, near the south end of Douglas Channel, is a friendly and modern-looking Indian village, population 140-160, with a government dock behind a rock breakwater. The village has a store, but the hours are erratic and the stock uncertain. No liquor. No pay phone. A medical clinic has two nurses and a visiting doctor. When you land at Hartley Bay you are apt to be visited by a local artist named Eugene. Some of his art is pretty good, and he is an excellent salesman.

The big news at Hartley Bay is fuel. In 1996 storage tanks for gasoline and diesel fuel were installed at the head of the dock. Plumbing for delivery to the fuel float is expected to be completed by May 1997. Absent hoses on the float, gasoline can be dispensed into jerry cans (provide your own jerry cans), and diesel pumped from a 480-liter portable tank. Ed Robinson is in charge of the fuel dock. His usual hours are 9-5, longer in the spring and summer. In an emergency he's available 24 hours a day. Call Ed on VHF channel 06 or CB channel 14.

Txalgiu, or Talsh-giu

The actual name of the Hartley Bay village is Txalgiu, pronounced "Talsh-giu," a guttural expression with a soft L and a hard G. I worked with Kevin Reece, a pleasant and patient young man, trying to wrap my throat and tongue around the name of his village. "Talsh-giu," he said. "Talsh-giu," I replied, but mine didn't sound like his. "Talsh-giu," he said again, and my "Talsh-giu" sounded closer. Again. And again. And again several more times. Finally Kevin said, "That's pretty good!" "Talsh-giu, Talsh-giu, Talsh-giu," I repeated, gaining and losing ground as I went. Now, writing about it, I have no idea how Txalgiu sounds.

—*Robert Hale*

See area map page 239

Grenville Channel. Use charts 3742, 3772 & 3773. Though sometimes called "The Ditch," Grenville Channel is a straight, beautiful and unobstructed channel 45 miles long, running between Wright Sound in the south, and Arthur Passage in the north. Tidal currents flow in and out of each end. Flood currents meet in the area of Evening Point, about 25 miles from the south entrance. Ebb currents divide about 1.5 miles north of Evening Point. The waters often are turbulent in these areas, and drift tends to accumulate there. Tidal currents run to a maximum of 2 knots. The tide and current tables show no current predictions for Grenville Channel, but corrections for high and low tides are shown for Lowe Inlet as a secondary port under Bella Bella in the Tide and Current Tables, Vol. 6 (Index No. 9195).

Considerable time and fuel can be saved by timing a passage to carry the flood current into Grenville Channel and the ebb current out. Often pleasure craft will ride an afternoon or early evening flood part way in. They overnight in one of Grenville Channel's excellent anchorages, and ride a morning ebb out.

Be sure to give Morning Reef, north of Evening Point, a wide berth.

Lowe Inlet. Use chart 3772. Lowe Inlet, a provincial park, is 14.5 miles from the southern entrance to Grenville Channel, and long has been a favorite spot to overnight. You can anchor either in the outer basin or in Nettle Basin, the cozier inner cove. Walt Woodward, in his book *How to Cruise to Alaska Without Rocking the Boat Too Much*, recommends anchoring directly in front of Verney Falls where they enter Nettle Basin. Current from the falls holds the boat in place, and you are treated to a wonderful view of the falls. Holding ground is reported to be only fair, so be sure the anchor is well set and you have ample scope for high tide.

Don Douglass, in his book *Exploring the Inside Passage to Alaska*, likes the Verney Falls anchorage, but also suggests an anchorage along the south shore of Nettle Basin, off the shelf formed by a creek that empties into that area. We tried to put the hook down in 10 fathoms off that shore, but found that we would swing too close to the shelf. After two tries in wind squalls and heavy rain showers, we moved out to the middle and anchored in 17 fathoms with 300 feet of rode out. Shortly after we were settled, another boat came in, tried to anchor as we earlier tried, then moved out to the middle as we had. The holding ground was excellent. We had trouble tripping the anchor the next morning.

Lowe Inlet is beautiful. Our notes read, "If you're looking for a scenic spot, this is it."

Klewnuggit Inlet. Use chart 3772. At approximately 20 fathoms, Klewnuggit Inlet is too deep for most boats to anchor. We talked with some folks, however, who found crabbing to be excellent near the head of Klewnuggit Inlet.

East Inlet. Use chart 3772. East Inlet is adjacent to Klewnuggit Inlet. The inner cove of East Inlet is a superb anchorage, surrounded by high mountains and protected from seas. In a storm, however, winds might swirl through. If possible, anchor near the head of the inner basin in 8-9 fathoms. You can also find anchorage in the little cove on the south shore, just inside the entrance to the inner basin. We call this nook Fiddler's Cove, after the GB32 *Fiddler*, which spent a stormy night there.

Kxngeal Inlet. Use chart 3772. Kxngeal Inlet, on the north side of Grenville Channel approximately 4 miles northwest of Klewnuggit Inlet, is a beautiful bowl in the mountains. Favor either shore as you enter to avoid a nasty rock that dries 16 feet in the entrance. The inlet is at least 17 fathoms deep until it shelves at the head, and when it shelves, it shelves *right now.* Trees are at the head of the inlet, with logged areas on each side. The shelf is on a line with the points where the trees begin. Anchor in 15 fathoms.

Baker Inlet. Use chart 3772. Baker Inlet is entered through Watts Narrows, which was running too hard for our tastes, so we didn't go in. We feel somewhat cheated, because Baker Inlet is recommended by all who have overnighted there. According to the chart, high and low slacks at Watts Narrrows occur at approximately the same time as high and low slacks at Prince Rupert.

Kumealon Island/Kumealon Inlet. Use chart 3773. The cove behind Kumealon Island and Kumealon Inlet both are good anchorages. Behind Kumealon Island, anchor in 5-7 fathoms near the head.

Kumealon Inlet is well protected and has beautiful scenery, despite logging activity on the north shore of the outer bay. We would anchor in the inner basin. Dave Ellsworth *(Deyata)* reports that they had an excellent overnight in the inner basin, and that two uncharted rocks lie close to shore near the southeast corner.

THE RUN FROM THE NORTH END of Grenville Channel to Prince Rupert requires three and preferably four separate charts. Chart 3773 shows the northern entrance to Grenville Channel. Chart 3927 covers the run from Grenville Channel, north through Arthur Passage, and continuing through the passage west of Genn Island. Chart 3957 takes you across Chatham Sound from Genn Island to Prince Rupert, though in small scale. Large scale chart 3858 makes the approach to Prince Rupert much less confusing.

Lawson Harbour/Kelp Passage. Use chart 3927. Lawson Harbour indents the top of Lewis Island, and Kelp Passage lies on the east side of Lewis Island, across Arthur Passage from Kennedy Island. Neither would be our first choice for scenery, but if an anchorage is needed, they will serve. A reef extends from the western shore inside Lawson Harbour. Anchor near the south end of the reef in 6-7 fathoms.

In Kelp Passage, anchor in the area marked 4_5 fathoms, mud bottom.

Assuming a northbound route, on chart 3927 run from a waypoint west of Watson Rock, at the northern entrance to Grenville Channel, north to a waypoint off the flashing light on the southwest shore of Kennedy Island. Then turn westward slightly to run past the southwest corner of Hanmer Island, and leave bell buoy D9, marking Cecil Patch, to port. Continue to a waypoint in the passage west of Genn Island.

At Genn Island, change to chart 3957. Run to a waypoint east of the Holland Rock light. Then run to a waypoint west of Barrett Rock, at the entrance to Prince Rupert Harbour. As you approach Holland Rock it would be a good idea to change to large scale chart 3958. The entire area is well-buoyed, but it is easy to get the buoys confused. We would plot all courses and their reciprocals carefully and double-check our work. So too with waypoint coordinates.

See area map page 239

Do not trust loran in this area. We found that our loran would take us approximately 0.5 mile east of our desired destination. Our GPS, by contrast, was much more accurate. When we reached Prince Rupert and asked around, we were told that loran was not reliable in this area. Loran's latitude is good, but longitude is off. The effect extends some distance southward.

Prince Rupert. Use chart 3958 (preferred) or chart 3957. From Barrett Rock at the entrance to Prince Rupert Harbour, it is another 5.5 miles of slow speed travel to town. Three marinas serve Prince Rupert: Fairview at the south end, Prince Rupert Rowing and Yacht Club in the middle, and Rushbrook at the north end.

Fairview is primarily a commercial boat moorage, although some pleasure boats do tie up there. Rushbrook has better facilities for pleasure boats, but during the commercial fishing months many commercial boats occupy the slips.

Most pleasure boats go directly to the Prince Rupert Rowing and Yacht Club, located at Cow Bay.

Prince Rupert ("Rainy Rupert"), population 17,000, is a bustling, growing city. With a large fishing fleet to support, Prince Rupert has just about anything you need for your boat. What isn't there can be flown in. Fuel is available from four fuel docks, and waste oil disposal is available.

A shopping mall is a pleasant walk uptown, or you can take a cab. Groceries are available at three supermarkets. The liquor store is between the yacht club and the mall. The small natural history museum is excellent. Several restaurants are in the town, some of them pretty good (although at one recommended restaurant we had the very worst meal we can remember—the cook had a *really* bad night).

Room for many boats at the Prince Rupert Rowing and Yacht Club docks.

⑨ **Petro Canada, Fairview,** (250)624-6666. Open every day, extended hours in summer. Gasoline, diesel, stove oil. Washrooms, showers. Garbage drop. Small convenience store.

⑨ **Prince Rupert Chevron,** (250)624-3316. Open every day, extended hours in summer. Gasoline, diesel, stove oil, kerosene. Washrooms, showers, laundry. Block, cube, and salt ice. Dry ice. Holding tank pumpout. Small convenience store on pier. Garbage disposal, waste oil disposal. Located in Cow Bay, next to the Yacht Club.

⑨ **Petro Canada, Cow Bay,** (250) 624-4106. Open every day, extended hours in summer. Gasoline, diesel, stove oil. Garbage disposal.

⑨ **Esso Marine Station,** (250)624-5000. Open every day 0800-1800, except 0800-2200 in summer. Gasoline, diesel & stove oil. Showers and laundry. Closest fuel to Rushbrook.

⑨ **Fairview Small Craft Harbour,** (250)627-3127. This is the first set of docks as you approach Prince Rupert. Commercial vessels primarily, but sometimes room for a few pleasure boats. Electricity, water, garbage.

⑨ **Prince Rupert Rowing and Yacht Club,** P.O. Box 981, Prince Rupert, B.C. V8J 4B7, (250)624-4317. Monitors VHF channel 72. Open all year, 15 & 30 amp power, washrooms and shower, block ice, garbage drop. This is the preferred pleasure craft moorage in Prince Rupert. Donna and her husband Rick will fit you in. As you approach, call Donna on channel 72 so she can figure out where to put you. You won't find a harder working or more helpful person on the coast. She's apt to be busy, so be patient if you must. No laundry, but Donna can arrange to have your clothes washed and folded. Pay phone at the head of the dock. Close to good dining, or take a cab uptown. Open to all, no yacht club recripocals needed.

⑨ **Rushbrook Floats Small Craft Harbour,** (250)624-9400. Open all year, water, 15 amp power. Mostly commercial vessels in the summer, but room for pleasure craft too. Located about a mile north of town. Rushbrook has the only launch ramp in Prince Rupert.

TIME • SPEED • DISTANCE

KNOTS

MINUTES	1	2	3	4	5	6	7	8	9	10	11	12	13	14	15
	DISTANCE TRAVELED IN NAUTICAL MILES														
1	0.0	0.0	0.0	0.1	0.1	0.1	0.1	0.1	0.2	0.2	0.2	0.2	0.2	0.2	0.2
2	0.0	0.1	0.1	0.1	0.2	0.2	0.2	0.3	0.3	0.3	0.4	0.4	0.4	0.5	0.5
3	0.0	0.1	0.2	0.2	0.2	0.3	0.4	0.4	0.4	0.5	0.6	0.6	0.6	0.7	0.8
4	0.1	0.1	0.2	0.3	0.3	0.4	0.5	0.5	0.6	0.7	0.7	0.8	0.9	0.9	1.0
5	0.1	0.2	0.2	0.3	0.4	0.5	0.6	0.7	0.8	0.8	0.9	1.0	1.1	1.2	1.2
6	0.1	0.2	0.3	0.4	0.5	0.6	0.7	0.8	0.9	1.0	1.1	1.2	1.3	1.4	1.5
7	0.1	0.2	0.4	0.5	0.6	0.7	0.8	0.9	1.0	1.2	1.3	1.4	1.5	1.6	1.8
8	0.1	0.3	0.4	0.5	0.7	0.8	0.9	1.1	1.2	1.3	1.5	1.6	1.7	1.9	2.0
9	0.2	0.3	0.4	0.6	0.8	0.9	1.0	1.2	1.4	1.5	1.6	1.8	2.0	2.1	2.2
10	0.2	0.3	0.5	0.7	0.8	1.0	1.2	1.3	1.5	1.7	1.8	2.0	2.2	2.3	2.5
11	0.2	0.4	0.6	0.7	0.9	1.1	1.3	1.5	1.6	1.8	2.0	2.2	2.4	2.6	2.8
12	0.2	0.4	0.6	0.8	1.0	1.2	1.4	1.6	1.8	2.0	2.2	2.4	2.6	2.8	3.0
13	0.2	0.4	0.6	0.9	1.1	1.3	1.5	1.7	2.0	2.2	2.4	2.6	2.8	3.0	3.2
14	0.2	0.5	0.7	0.9	1.2	1.4	1.6	1.9	2.1	2.3	2.6	2.8	3.0	3.3	3.5
15	0.2	0.5	0.8	1.0	1.2	1.5	1.8	2.0	2.2	2.5	2.8	3.0	3.2	3.5	3.8
16	0.3	0.5	0.8	1.1	1.3	1.6	1.9	2.1	2.4	2.7	2.9	3.2	3.5	3.7	4.0
17	0.3	0.6	0.8	1.1	1.4	1.7	2.0	2.3	2.6	2.8	3.1	3.4	3.7	4.0	4.2
18	0.3	0.6	0.9	1.2	1.5	1.8	2.1	2.4	2.7	3.0	3.3	3.6	3.9	4.2	4.5
19	0.3	0.6	1.0	1.3	1.6	1.9	2.2	2.5	2.8	3.2	3.5	3.8	4.1	4.4	4.8
20	0.3	0.7	1.0	1.3	1.7	2.0	2.3	2.7	3.0	3.3	3.7	4.0	4.3	4.7	5.0
21	0.4	0.7	1.0	1.4	1.8	2.1	2.4	2.8	3.2	3.5	3.8	4.2	4.6	4.9	5.2
22	0.4	0.7	1.1	1.5	1.8	2.2	2.6	2.9	3.3	3.7	4.0	4.4	4.8	5.1	5.5
23	0.4	0.8	1.2	1.5	1.9	2.3	2.7	3.1	3.4	3.8	4.2	4.6	5.0	5.4	5.8
24	0.4	0.8	1.2	1.6	2.0	2.4	2.8	3.2	3.6	4.0	4.4	4.8	5.2	5.6	6.0
25	0.4	0.8	1.2	1.7	2.1	2.5	2.9	3.3	3.8	4.2	4.6	5.0	5.4	5.8	6.2
26	0.4	0.9	1.3	1.7	2.2	2.6	3.0	3.5	3.9	4.3	4.8	5.2	5.6	6.1	6.5
27	0.4	0.9	1.4	1.8	2.2	2.7	3.2	3.6	4.0	4.5	5.0	5.4	5.8	6.3	6.8
28	0.5	0.9	1.4	1.9	2.3	2.8	3.3	3.7	4.2	4.7	5.1	5.6	6.1	6.5	7.0
29	0.5	1.0	1.4	1.9	2.4	2.9	3.4	3.9	4.4	4.8	5.3	5.8	6.3	6.8	7.2
30	0.5	1.0	1.5	2.0	2.5	3.0	3.5	4.0	4.5	5.0	5.5	6.0	6.5	7.0	7.5
31	0.5	1.0	1.6	2.1	2.6	3.1	3.6	4.1	4.6	5.2	5.7	6.2	6.7	7.2	7.8
32	0.5	1.1	1.6	2.1	2.7	3.2	3.7	4.2	4.8	5.3	5.9	6.4	6.9	7.5	8.0
33	0.6	1.1	1.6	2.2	2.8	3.3	3.8	4.4	5.0	5.5	6.0	6.6	7.2	7.7	8.2
34	0.6	1.1	1.7	2.3	2.8	3.4	4.0	4.5	5.1	5.7	6.2	6.8	7.4	7.9	8.5
35	0.6	1.2	1.8	2.3	2.9	3.5	4.1	4.7	5.2	5.8	6.4	7.0	7.6	8.2	8.8
36	0.6	1.2	1.8	2.4	3.0	3.6	4.2	4.8	5.4	6.0	6.6	7.2	7.8	8.4	9.0
37	0.6	1.2	1.8	2.5	3.1	3.7	4.3	4.9	5.6	6.2	6.8	7.4	8.0	8.6	9.2
38	0.6	1.3	1.9	2.5	3.2	3.8	4.4	5.1	5.7	6.3	7.0	7.6	8.2	8.9	9.5
39	0.6	1.3	2.0	2.6	3.2	3.9	4.6	5.2	5.8	6.5	7.2	7.8	8.4	9.1	9.8
40	0.7	1.3	2.0	2.7	3.3	4.0	4.7	5.3	6.0	6.7	7.3	8.0	8.7	9.3	10.0
41	0.7	1.4	2.0	2.7	3.4	4.1	4.8	5.5	6.2	6.8	7.5	8.2	8.9	9.6	10.2
42	0.7	1.4	2.1	2.8	3.5	4.2	4.9	5.6	6.3	7.0	7.7	8.4	9.1	9.8	10.5
43	0.7	1.4	2.2	2.9	3.6	4.3	5.0	5.7	6.4	7.2	7.9	8.6	9.3	10.0	10.8
44	0.7	1.5	2.2	2.9	3.7	4.4	5.1	5.9	6.6	7.3	8.1	8.8	9.5	10.3	11.0
45	0.8	1.5	2.2	3.0	3.8	4.5	5.2	6.0	6.8	7.5	8.2	9.0	9.8	10.5	11.2
46	0.8	1.5	2.3	3.1	3.8	4.6	5.4	6.1	6.9	7.7	8.4	9.2	10.0	10.7	11.5
47	0.8	1.6	2.4	3.1	3.9	4.7	5.5	6.3	7.0	7.8	8.6	9.4	10.2	11.0	11.8
48	0.8	1.6	2.4	3.2	4.0	4.8	5.6	6.4	7.2	8.0	8.8	9.6	10.4	11.2	12.0
49	0.8	1.6	2.4	3.3	4.1	4.9	5.7	6.5	7.4	8.2	9.0	9.8	10.6	11.4	12.2
50	0.8	1.7	2.5	3.3	4.2	5.0	5.8	6.7	7.5	8.3	9.2	10.0	10.8	11.7	12.5
51	0.8	1.7	2.6	3.4	4.2	5.1	6.0	6.8	7.6	8.5	9.4	10.2	11.0	11.9	12.8
52	0.9	1.7	2.6	3.5	4.3	5.2	6.1	6.9	7.8	8.7	9.5	10.4	11.3	12.1	13.0
53	0.9	1.8	2.6	3.5	4.4	5.3	6.2	7.1	8.0	8.8	9.7	10.6	11.5	12.4	13.2
54	0.9	1.8	2.7	3.6	4.5	5.4	6.3	7.2	8.1	9.0	9.9	10.8	11.7	12.6	13.5
55	0.9	1.8	2.8	3.7	4.6	5.5	6.4	7.3	8.2	9.2	10.1	11.0	11.9	12.8	13.8
56	0.9	1.9	2.8	3.7	4.7	5.6	6.5	7.5	8.4	9.3	10.3	11.2	12.1	13.1	14.0
57	1.0	1.0	2.8	3.8	4.8	5.7	6.6	7.6	8.6	9.5	10.4	11.4	12.4	13.3	14.2
58	1.0	1.9	2.9	3.9	4.8	5.8	6.8	7.7	8.7	9.7	10.6	11.6	12.6	13.5	14.5
59	1.0	2.0	3.0	3.9	4.9	5.9	6.9	7.9	8.8	9.8	10.8	11.8	12.8	13.8	14.8
60	1.0	2.0	3.0	4.0	5.0	6.0	7.0	8.0	9.0	10.0	11.0	12.0	13.0	14.0	15.0

U.S. Marina and Fuel Dock Numbers

15th Street Dock	Tacoma	(206) 591-5014
Alderbrook Inn Resort	Hood Canal	(360) 898-2200
Arabella's Marina	Gig Harbor	(206) 851-1793
Ballard Mill Marina	Seattle	(206) 789-4777
Ballard Oil Inc. (fuel dock)	Seattle	(206) 783-0241
Bartwood Lodge	Orcas Is.	(360) 376-2242
Bay Marine	Suquamish	(360) 598-4900
Big Salmon Resort (marina & fuel dock)	Neah Bay	(360) 645-2374
Blaine Harbor		(360) 332-8037
Blaine Marina (fuel dock)		(360) 332-8425
Blakely Island General Store & Marina (marina & fuel dock)		(360) 375-6121
Boston Harbor Marina (marina & fuel dock)	Olympia	(360) 357-5670
Breakwater Marina (marina & fuel dock)	Tacoma	(206) 752-6663
British Camp Historical Park	San Juan Is.	(360) 586-2165
Camano Island State Park		(360) 387-3031
Cap Sante Boat Haven	Anacortes	(360) 293-0694
Cap Sante Marine (fuel dock & chandlery)	Anacortes	(360) 293-3145
Captain Coupe Park	Whidbey Is.	(360) 678-4461
Carillon Point	Kirkland	(206) 822-1700
Chandler's Cove	Seattle	(206) 628-0838
Chinook Landing Marina	Tacoma	(206) 627-7676
City of Des Moines Marina (marina & fuel dock)		(206) 824-5700
Coho Resort	Sekiu	(360) 963-2333
Covich-Williams Co. (fuel dock)	Seattle	(206) 784-0171
Curley's Resort	Sekiu	(360) 963-2281
Dash Point State Park	Tacoma	(206) 593-2206
Davidson's Marina (fuel dock)	Seattle	(206) 486-7141
Deception Pass Marina		(360) 675-5411
Deer Harbor Marina (marina & fuel dock)	Orcas Is.	(360) 376-3037
Delta Western Fuel Dock	Seattle	(206) 282-1567
Dockton Park	Maury Is.	(206) 296-4287
Eagle Harbor Marina	Winslow	(206) 842-4003
Elliott Bay Marina	Seattle	(206) 285-4817
Ewing Street Moorings	Seattle	(206) 283-1075
Fair Harbor Marina (marina & fuel dock)	Grapeview	(360) 426-4028
Farwest Resort (marina & fuel dock)	Neah Bay	(360) 645-2270
Fish'n' Hole, The (fuel dock)	Port Townsend	(360) 385-7031
Fort Ebey State Park	Whidbey Is.	(360) 385-4730
Fort Worden Marine State Park	Port Townsend	(360) 385-4730
Frye Cove County Park	Olympia	(360) 786-5595
Gene Coulon Memorial Beach Park	Renton	(206) 235-2560
H.C. Henry Marina	Seattle	(206) 624-6534
Harbor Island Marina (marina & fuel dock)	Seattle	(206) 467-9400
Harbor Marine Fuel (fuel dock)	Bellingham	(360) 734-1710
Harbor Village Marina	Seattle	(206) 485-7557
Harbour Marina	Winslow	(206) 842-6502
Hawley's Hilton Harbor (fuel dock)	Bellingham	(360) 733-1110
Hood Canal Marina (marina & fuel dock)	Hood Canal	(360) 898-2252
Hoodsport Marina & Cafe	Hood Canal	(360) 877-9657
Illahee Marine State Park	Bremerton	(360) 478-6460
Island Petroleum Service (fuel dock)	Orcas Is.	(360) 376-3883
Islander Lopez Marina Resort	Lopez Is.	(360) 468-2233
Islands Marine Center	Lopez Is.	(360) 468-3377
Jarrell's Cove Marina (marina & fuel dock)		(800) 362-8823
Jarrell's Cove Marine State Park		(360) 426-9266
Jerisich Park	Gig Harbor	(206) 851-8136
Jetty Island	Everett	(206) 259-6001
John Wayne Marina (marina & fuel dock)	Sequim	(360) 417-3440
Joseph Whidbey State Park	Whidbey Is.	(360) 678-4636
Kitsap Memorial State Park	Hood Canal	(360) 779-3205
Kopachuck Marine State Park	Carr Inlet	(206) 265-3606
LaConner Landing Marine Service (fuel dock)		(360) 466-4478
LaConner Marina		(360) 466-3118
Lakebay Marina (marina & fuel dock)	Grapeview	(206) 884-3350
Lakewood Moorage	Seattle	(206) 722-3887
Langley Marina (fuel dock)		(360) 221-1771
Langley Small Boat Harbor		(360) 221-4246
Larrabee State Park	S. of B'ham.	(360) 676-2093
Leschi Yacht Basin (fuel dock)	Seattle	(206) 328-4456
Lighthouse Marine County Park	Pt. Roberts	(360) 733-2900
Little Portion Store	Shaw Is.	(360) 468-2288
Lonesome Cove Resort	San Juan Is.	(360) 378-4477
Longbranch Improvement Club Marina	Longbranch	(206) 884-5137
Luther Burbank Park	Mercer Is.	(206) 296-2976
Marina Mart	Seattle	(206) 682-7733
Marina Park	Kirkland	(206) 828-1218
Marine Servicecenter (fuel dock)	Anacortes	(360) 293-8200
McMicken Island Marine State Park	Case Inlet	(360) 426-9226
Mercer Marine (fuel dock)	Bellevue	(206) 641-2090
Morrison's North Star Marina (fuel dock)	Seattle	(206) 284-6600
Murphy's Landing Marina	Gig Harbor	(206) 851-3093
Mutiny Bay Resort	Whidbey Is.	(360) 331-4500
Narrows Marina (fuel dock)	Tacoma	(206) 564-4222
Oak Harbor Marina (marina & fuel dock)		(360) 679-2628
Old Fort Townsend Marine State Park	Port Townsend	(360) 385-3595
Ole & Charlie's	Tacoma	(206) 272-1173
Olson's Resort (marina & fuel dock)	Sekiu	(360) 963-2311
Peninsula Yacht Basin	Gig Harbor	(206) 858-2250
Penrose Point State Marine Park	Carr Inlet	(206) 884-2514
Percival Landing Park	Olympia	(360) 753-8379
Pleasant Harbor Marina (marina & fuel dock)	Hood Canal	(360) 796-4611
Pleasant Harbor Marine State Park	Hood Canal	(360) 796-4415
Point Defiance Boathouse Marina (marina & fuel dock)	Tacoma	(206) 591-5325
Point Hudson Resort	Port Townsend	(360) 385-2828
Point Roberts Marina (marina & fuel dock)		(360) 945-2255
Port Angeles Boat Haven (marina & fuel dock)		(360) 457-4505
Port Angeles City Pier		(360) 457-0411
Port Hadlock Bay Marina	Port Hadlock	(360) 385-6368
Port Ludlow Marina (marina & fuel dock)		(360) 437-0513
Port of Allyn & Allyn Dock		(360) 275-2192
Port of Brownsville (marina & fuel dock)		(360) 692-5498
Port of Coupeville (marina & fuel dock)		(360) 678-5020
Port of Edmonds (marina & fuel dock)		(206) 774-0549
Port of Everett Marina (marina & fuel dock)		(206) 259-6001
Port of Friday Harbor		(360) 378-2688
Port of Friday Harbor Dock (fuel dock)		(360) 378-3114
Port of Kingston (marina & fuel dock)		(360) 297-3545
Port of Manchester		(360) 871-2510
Port of Olympia-East Bay Marina		(360) 786-1400
Port of Port Townsend		(360) 385-2355
Port of Shelton		(360) 426-1151
Port Orchard Marina		(360) 876-5535
Port Washington Marina	Bremerton	(360) 479-3037
Potlatch Marine State Park	Hood Canal	(360) 877-5361
Poulsbo Marina-Port of Poulsbo (marina & fuel dock)		(360) 779-3505
Quilcene Boathaven (marina & fuel dock)	Hood Canal	(360) 765-3131
Richardson Fuel (fuel dock)	Lopez Is.	(360) 468-2275
Roche Harbor Resort & Boatel (marina & fuel dock)	San Juan Is.	(360) 378-2155
Rosario Resort (marina & fuel dock)	Orcas Is.	(800) 562-8820
Saltwater Marine State Park	Des Moines	(206) 764-4128
San Juan County Park	San Juan Is.	(360) 378-2992
Scenic Beach State Park	Hood Canal	(360) 830-5079
Seabeck Marina (marina & fuel dock)	Hood Canal	(360) 830-5179
Seacrest Boathouse	Seattle	(206) 932-1050
Semiahmoo Marina (marina & fuel dock)	Pt. Roberts	(360) 371-5700
Shilshole Bay Marina	Seattle	(206) 728-3385
Shilshole Texaco Marine (fuel dock)	Seattle	(206) 783-7555
Silverdale Marina		(360) 698-4918
Skyline Marina (marina & fuel dock)	Flounder Bay	(360) 293-5134
Smuggler's Villa Resort	Orcas Is.	(360) 376-2297
Snow Creek Resort	Neah Bay	(360) 645-2284
Snug Harbor Resort (marina & fuel dock)	San Juan Is.	(360) 378-4762
South Whidbey State Park	Whidbey Is.	(360) 321-4559
Spencer Spit Marine State Park	Lopez Is.	(360) 468-2251
Squalicum Harbor	Bellingham	(360) 676-2542
Steilacoom Marina		(206) 582-2600
Sucia Island Marine State Park		(360) 753-5755
Summertide Resort & Marina	Hood Canal	(206) 925-9277 (360) 275-9313
Sunrise Motel & Resort	Hood Canal	(360) 877-5301
Thunderbird Boat House & Gifts (marina & fuel dock)	Pt. Angeles	(360) 457-4274
Totem Marina	Tacoma	(206) 272-4404
Tulalip Marina (marina & fuel dock)	Marysville	(360) 651-4999
Twanoh Marine State Park	Hood Canal	(360) 275-2222
Van Riper's Resort	Sekiu	(360) 963-2334
West Bay Marine (marina & fuel dock)	Olympia	(360) 943-2022
West Beach Resort (marina & fuel dock)	Orcas Is.	(360) 376-2240
West Sound Marina (marina & fuel dock)	Orcas Is.	(360) 376-2314
Wilcox's Yarrow Bay Marina (fuel dock)	Kirkland	(206) 822-6066
Winslow Wharf Marina		(206) 842-4202
Wyman's Marina (marina & fuel dock)	Anacortes	(360) 293-2410
Yacht Care (fuel dock)	Seattle	(206) 285-2600
Zittel's Marina Inc. (marina & fuel dock)	Olympia	(360) 459-1950

B.C. Marina and Fuel Dock Numbers

Active Pass Auto & Marine (fuel dock)	Mayne Is.	(250) 539-5411
Ahousat General Store (fuel dock)		(250) 670-9575
Alert Bay Gov't. Wharf		(250) 974-5727
Anchor Petroleum (fuel dock)	Coal Harbour	(604) 949-6358
Anchorage Marina	Nanaimo	(250) 754-5585
Angler's Anchorage Marina (marina & fuel dock)	Brentwood Bay	(250) 652-3531
April Point Lodge & Fishing Resort (outboard fuel, too)	Quadra Is.	(250) 285-3621
Barbary Coast Yacht Basin	Vancouver	(604) 669-0088
Bathgate General Store & Marina (marina & fuel dock)	Egmont	(604) 883-2222
Bayshore West Marina	Vancouver	(604) 689-5331
Beach Garden Resort & Marina (marina & fuel dock)	Powell River	(604) 485-7734
Beachcomber Marina (fuel dock with limited moorage)	Nanoose Bay	(250) 468-7222
Bedwell Harbour Resort (marina & fuel dock)	S. Pender Is.	(250) 629-3212
Big Bay Marina & Fishing Resort (marina & fuel dock)		(250) 286-8107
Black Fin Marina & Pub (marina & fuel dock)	Comox	(250) 339-4664
Blind Channel Resort (marina & fuel dock)		(250) 830-8620
Bluenose Marina	Cowichan Bay	(250) 748-2222
Bowen Island Marina	Howe Sound	(604) 947-9710
Brechin Point Marina (fuel dock)	Nanaimo	(250) 753-6122
Brentwood Inn Resort	Brentwood Bay	(250) 652-3151
Bridgepoint Marina	Richmond	(604) 273-8560
Broughton Strait RV Park		(250) 949-1164
Brown's Bay Marina (marina & fuel dock)		(250) 286-3135
Buccaneer Marina & Resort Ltd. (marina & fuel dock)	Secret Cove	(604) 885-7888
Burrard Bridge Civic Marina	Vancouver	(604) 733-5833
Campbell River Chevron Marine (fuel dock)		(250) 287-3319
Canoe Cove Marina Ltd.(marina & fuel dock)	Sidney	(250) 656-5566
Cape Mudge Boatworks (repairs & haulout)	Quadra Is.	(250) 285-2155
Captain's Cove Marina (marina & fuel dock)	Delta	(604) 946-1244
Catherwood Towing (fuel dock)	Vancouver area	(604) 462-9221
Chamberlain's	Sechelt	(604) 885-9358
Cheanuh Marina (marina & fuel dock)	Sooke	(250) 478-4880
Cherry Point Marina	Cobble Hill	(250) 748-0453
China Creek Marina	Pt. Alberni	(250) 723-9812
City of Victoria Causeway		(250) 363-3273
Clutesi Haven Marina	Port Alberni	(250) 724-6837
Coal Harbour Chevron (fuel barge)	Vancouver	(604) 681-7725
Coal Harbour Marina	Vancouver	(604) 681-2628
Coastal Shipyard & Marine Svcs.	Duncan	(250) 746-4705
Coho Marina	Pender Hrbr.	(250) 883-2248
Comox Bay Marina	Comox	(250) 339-2930
Comox Municipal Marina		(250) 339-2202
Comox Valley Harbour Authority		(250) 339-6047
Cordero Lodge	Blind Channel	(250) 286-8404
Crescent Beach Marina Ltd. (marina & fuel dock)		(604) 538-9666
Critter Cove Marina	Nootka Sound	(250) 283-7364
Crofton Gov't. Wharf		(250) 246-2456
Dawson's Landing (marina & fuel dock)	Rivers Inlet	(250) 949-2111
Deas Island Regional Park	Vancouver	(604) 432-6350
Deep Cove Marina	Saanich Inlet	(250) 656-0060
Delta Charters (haulout & charters)	Vancouver area	(604) 273-4211
Delta Vancouver Airport Hotel	Vancouver area	(604) 278 1241
Denman General Store (fuel al store)	Denman Is.	(250) 335-2293
Dinghy Dock Pub	Nanaimo	(250) 753-2373
Discovery Harbour Marina	Campbell River	(250) 287-2614
Discovery Marina/Sportfish Center (marina & fuel dock)	Campbell River	(250) 287-4911
Double Bay Resort	Hanson Is.	(250) 949-2500
Duncan Cove Resort	Pender Hrbr.	(250) 883-2424
Duncanby Landing (marina & fuel dock)	Rivers Inlet	(600) 700-3558
Eagle Marine Ltd. (fuel dock)	Ucluelet	(250) 726-4262
Echo Bay Resort (marina & fuel dock)		(250) 949-2501
Egmont Marina Resort (marina & fuel dock)		(604) 883-2298
Esperanza Marine Srv. (fuel dock)		(250) 859-9622
Esso Marine False Creek (fuel dock)	Vancouver	(604) 733-6731
Esso Marine Prince Rupert		(250) 624-5000
False Creek Yacht Club	Vancouver	(604) 682-3292
Fisherman's Cove Esso (fuel dock)	Vancouver	(604) 921-7333
Fisherman's Resort & Marina	Pender Hrbr.	(604) 883-2336
Fisherman's Wharf Small Craft Harbour	Port Hardy	(250) 949-6332
Fleming Beach Park	Victoria	(250) 386-6128
Ford's Cove Marina Ltd. (fuel dock)	Hornby Is.	(250) 335-2169
Forward Harbour Fishing Lodge		(250) 338-6689
French Creek Harbour (marina & fuel dock)	Parksville	(250) 248-5051
Freshwater Marina	Vancouver area	(604) 286-0701
Fulford Marina	Saltspring Is.	(250) 653-9600
Ganges Marina	Saltspring Is.	(250) 537-5242
Garden Bay Hotel & Marina	Pender Hrbr.	(604) 883-2674
Genoa Bay Marina	Duncan	(250) 746-7621
Gibsons Gov't. Wharf		(604) 886-8017
Gibsons Marina		(604) 886-8686
God's Pocket Resort		(250) 949-9221
Gold River Petro Canada (fuel dock)		(250) 283-5214
Goldstream Boathouse (marina & fuel dock)	Brentwood Bay	(250) 478-4407
Gorge Harbour Marina & Resort (marina & fuel dock)	Cortes Is.	(250) 935-6433
Greenway Sound Marine Resort	Broughton Is.	(250) 949-2525
Harbour Ferries Marina	Vancouver	(604) 687-9558
Hawkeye Industries Fuel & Chandlery	Bamfield	(250) 728-3321
Headwater Marina (repairs & haulout)	Pender Hrbr.	(604) 883-2406
Heriot Bay Inn & Marina (marina & fuel dock)	Quadra Is.	(250) 285-3322
Highwater Marina	Vancouver area	(604) 525-0612
Hyak Marine (fuel dock)	Gibsons	(604) 886-9011
Inn at the Water Resort	Cowichan Bay	(250) 748-6222
Inn of the Sea	Ladysmith	(250) 245-2211
Irvine's Landing Marina & Pub (marina & fuel dock)	Pender Hrbr.	(604) 883-2296
Island West Fishing Resort (marina & fuel dock)	Ucluelet	(250)726-7515
Ivy Green Marina Ltd.	Ladysmith	(250) 245-4521
John Henry's Marina Inc. (fuel dock)	Pender Hrbr.	(604) 883-2253
Kyoquot Sound Salmon (fuel dock)	Walters Cove	(250) 332-5219
Lasqueti Island Store & Marine (marina & fuel dock)		(250) 333-8846
Len's Shell & Grocery (fuel dock)	Fanny Bay	(250) 335-0920
Lion's Bay Marina Ltd. (marina & fuel dock)	Howe Sound	(604) 921-7510
Lowes Resort Motel	Pender Hrbr.	(604) 883-2456
Lund Hotel (marina & fuel dock)		(604) 483-3187
Lynnwood Marina	Vancouver area	(604) 985-1533
Madeira Marina Ltd.	Pender Hrbr.	(604) 883-2266
Manana Lodge & Marina (marina & fuel dock)	Ladysmith	(250) 245-2312
Maple Bay Resorts	Duncan	(250) 746-8482
Masthead Restaurant & Marina	Cowichan Bay	(250) 748-3714
Mill Bay Marina (marina & fuel dock)	Brentwood Bay	(250) 743-4112
Minstrel Island Resort (marina & fuel dock)		(250) 949-0215
Moby Dick Boatel	Nanaimo	(250) 753-7111
Montague Harbour Marina Ltd. (marina & fuel dock)	Galiano Is.	(250) 539-5733
Nanaimo Harbour City Marina		(250) 754-2732
Nanaimo Shipyard		(250) 753-1151
Nanaimo Yacht Club		(250) 754-7011
Newcastle Marina	Nanaimo	(250) 753-1431
Norseman Marine at Birds Eye Cove Marina (marina & fuel dock)	Duncan	(250) 748-7927
North Arm Marine (fuel dock)	Vancouver area	(604) 276-2161
North Saanich Marina (marina & fuel dock)	Sidney	(250) 656-5558
Oak Bay Marina (marina & fuel dock)	Victoria	(250) 598-3369
Ocean Falls Gov't. Dock		(250) 289-3859
Ocean West (fuel dock)	Tofino	(250) 725-3251
Ocean West Marine Fuels (fuel dock)	Victoria	(250) 388-7224
Oceanwood Counrty Inn	Mayne Is.	(250) 539-5074
Okeover Marina	Okeover Arm	(604) 483-2243
Otter Bay Marina	N. Pender Is.	(250) 629-3579
Pacific Lions Marina Ltd. (marina & fuel dock)	Sooke	(250) 642-3816
Pacific Playground (marina & fuel dock)	Oyster River	(250) 337-5600
Page's Resort & Marina (marina & fuel dock)	Gabriola Is.	(250) 247-8931
Pedder Bay Marina (marina & fuel dock)		(250) 478-1771
Pelican Bay Marina	Vancouver	(604) 682-7454
Pender Harbour Marine (repairs & haulout)		(604) 883-2367
Petro Canada Bear Cove (fuel dock)	Port Hardy	(250) 949-9988
Petro Canada Cow Bay (fuel dock)	Prince Rupert	(250) 624-4106
Petro Canada Fairvew (fuel dock)	Prince Rupert	(250) 624-6666
Petro Canada Steveston Barge (fuel barge)		(604) 277-7744
Pier 66 Marina Ltd. (fuel dock)	Cowichan Bay	(250) 748-8444
Pioneer Boat Works	Ucluelet	(250) 726-4382
Poise Cove Marina	Sechelt	(604) 885-2895
Port Browning Marina		(250) 629-3493
Port Hardy Esso Marine Station (fuel dock)		(250) 949-2710
Port McNeill Boat Harbour		(250) 956-3881
Port of Nanaimo (marina & fuel dock)		(250) 754-5053
Port Sidney Marina		(250) 655-3711
Prince Rupert Chevron (fuel dock)		(250) 624-3316
Princess Margaret Marine Park		(250) 387-4363
Quarterdeck Marina & RV Park (marina & fuel dock)	Port Hardy	(250) 949-6551
Quathiaski Cove Petro Canada (fuel dock)	Quadra Is.	(250) 285-3212
Ragged Island Marine (fuel dock)	N. of Lund	(604) 438-8184
Reed Point Marina (marina & fuel dock)	Vancouver area	(604) 931-2477
Richmond Chevron (fuel dock)		(604) 278 2101
Royal Reach Marina & Hotel	Sechelt	(604) 885-7844
Salmon Point Marina (marina & fuel dock)	Campbell River	(250) 923-6605
Salt Spring Marina		(250) 537-5810
Saturna Point Store (fuel dock)		(250) 539-5725
Save-On Fuels (fuel dock)	Alert Bay	(250) 974-2161
Schooner Cove Resort & Marina		(250) 468-5364
Seaway Marine Sales (fuel dock)	Campbell River	(250) 287-3456
Secret Cove Marina (marina & fuel dock)		(604) 885-3533

(Continued next page)

B.C. Marina and Fuel Dock Numbers (continued)

Sewell's Marina Ltd. (marina & fuel dock)	Howe Sound/Horseshoe Bay	(604) 921-3474
Shearwater Marina (marina & fuel dock)		(250) 957-2305
Shell Marina (fuel dock)	Port McNeill	(250) 956-3336
Shelter Island Marina Inc.	Vancouver area	(604) 270-6272
Ship to Shore Marine	Bowser	(250) 757-8750
Shoal Bay Lodge	E. Thurlow Is.	(250) 286-6016
Sidney (Beacon Ave) Gov't Wharf		(250) 656-1184
Silva Bay Boatel & Store	Gabriola Is.	(250) 247-9351
Silva Bay Resort & Marina	Gabriola Is.	(250) 247-8662
Silver Sands Resort	Bargain Bay	(604) 883-2630
Skyline Marina	Richmond	(604) 273-3977
Snaw-Naw-As Marina (marina & fuel dock)	Nanoose Harbour	(250) 390-2616
Sooke Harbour Marina		(250) 642-3236
Springwater Lodge Ltd.	Mayne Is.	(250) 539-5521
Squirrel Cove Store (fuel dock, too)		(250) 935-6327
Steveston Chevron (fuel dock)		(604) 277-4712
Steveston Esso Marine Station (fuel dock)		(604) 277-5211
Stones Marine Centre Inc.	Nanaimo	(250) 753-4232
Sullivan Bay Marine Resort (marina & fuel dock)	Broughton Is.	(250) 949-2550
Sunny Shores Resort & Marina (marina & fuel dock)	Sooke	(250) 642-5731
Sunset Marina (marina & fuel dock)	Howe Sound	(604) 921-7476
Sunshine Coast Resort Ltd.	Pender Hrbr.	(604) 883-9177
Telegraph Cove Marina (fuel dock to 26' & emergency moorage only)		(250) 928-3131
Telegraph Harbor Marina	Thetis Is.	(250) 246-9511
Thetis Island Marina		(250) 246-3464
Thunderbird Marina	W. Vancouver	(604) 921-7434
Tsehum Harbor Govt. Wharf	Sidney	(250) 363-6466
Ucluelet Chevron (fuel dock)		(250) 726-4472
Union Steamship Company Marina	Bowen Is.	(604) 947-0707
Van Isle Marina Co. Ltd. (marina & fuel dock)	Sidney	(250) 656-1138
Vancouver Marina (fuel dock)		(604) 278-9787
Victoria (Erie St) Govt. Wharf		(250) 363-3273
Victoria (Huron St) Govt. Wharf		(250) 363-3760
Victoria (Johnson St) Govt. Wharf		(250) 363-3760
Victoria (Ogden Pt) Govt. Wharf		(250) 363-3273
Victoria (Ships Pt) Govt. Wharf		(250) 363-3760
Victoria (Broughton St) Govt. Wharf		(250) 363-3760
Wampler Marine Services Ltd. (fuel dock)	Vancouver	(604) 681-3841
Westin Bayshore Yacht Charters	Vancouver	(604) 691-6936
Weston Ent. (Zeballos Fuel Dock)	Zeballos	(250) 761-4201
Westport Marina	Sidney	(250) 656-2832
Westview Chevron (fuel dock)	Powell River	(604) 485-2867
Westview Marina (marina & fuel dock)	Tahsis	(250) 934-7622
Windsong Sea Village	Echo Bay	(250) 956-4005
Zeballos Small Craft Harbour		(250) 761-4333

TOWING & MARINE SERVICES

U.S. Towing and Emergency Numbers

All Points Maritime (Vessel Assist) (VHF "Guardian")		(206) 628-0191
Block and Tackle Boatyard		(206) 878-4414
Marine Services & Assist	(360) 675-7900 or	(360) 679-0222
BOAT/US ***24 hour dispatch***		(800) 391-4869
Remedy Services (BOAT/US)	(800) 701-0306 or	(360) 385-0306
Shiveley Tugboat Co. (BOAT/US)		(206) 842-7595
Tim's Mobile Marine (BOAT/US)	(360) 376-2332 or	(360) 317-6002
Vessel Assist ***ALL LOCATIONS 24 hours***		(206) 453-1176 (800) 367-8222
Vessel Assist Anacortes		(360) 293-3000
Vessel Assist Everett		(206) 752-2697
Vessel Assist Lake Washington		(206) 669-5254
Vessel Assist Point Roberts		(360) 952-6287
Vessel Assist San Juans		(360) 378-4588
Vessel Assist Tacoma		(206) 272-2402
Wilson Marine (24 hour parts service, with air service from Kenmore Air)		(206) 284-3630 (800) 875-9111
U.S. Coast Guard Emergencies	***VHF Chan.16 or***	***(206) 217-6000***
U.S. Coast Guard District Office: Seattle		(206) 220-7000

U.S. Customs Clearance Numbers

The numbers below are for weekdays only.

Aberdeen	(360) 532-2030
Anacortes	(360) 293-2331
Bellingham	(360) 734-5463
Blaine	(360) 332-6318
Everett	(206) 259-0246
Friday Harbor/Roche Harbor	(360) 378-2080
Neah Bay/Port Angeles	(360) 457-4311
Port Townsend	(360) 385-3777
Seattle	(206) 553-4678
Tacoma/Olympia	(206) 593-6338

At all entry points nights, weekends, and holidays call: (800) 562-5943

Parks Information Numbers

Wash. State Parks Launch & Moorage Permit Program	(360) 902-8608
B. C. Parks General Information	(250) 387-5002

B.C. Towing and Emergency Numbers

Classic Yacht Services (towing)		(250) 361-7528
Vessel Assist Vancouver		(604) 469-9602

Canadian Coast Guard Numbers:

Search and Rescue: Vancouver	***VHF Chan. 16 or***	(800) 567-5111
Search and Rescue: Victoria	(800) 567-5111 or	(250) 363-2333
Search and Rescue: Other areas		(800) 567-5111
Canadian Coast Guard District Office: Victoria		(250) 480-2600
Search & Rescue ***Cellular Phones Only***		*311

B.C. Customs Clearance Numbers

All locations contact Canada Customs toll-free (888) 226-7277

CANPASS	(888) 226-7277
Communications Canada: Vancouver	(604) 666-5468
Communications Canada: Victoria	(250) 363-3803

Index

D

E

F

G

H

I

J

K

L

M

N

O

P

Q

R

S

Advertisers' Index

• NOTES •

A History *of* THE WAGGONER

(Adapted from Bowditch, American Practical Navigator, 1984 Ed., *pp. 8-9)*

About 1584 the Dutch pilot Lucas Janzoon Waghenaer published a volume of navigational principles, tables, charts, and sailing directions, which served as a guide for other such books for the next 200 years.

These "Waggoners," as they came to be known, met with great success, and in 1588 an English translation of the original book was made. During the next 30 years, 24 editions of the book were published in Dutch, German, Latin, and English. Other authors followed the profitable example set by Waghenaer. Soon, American, British, and French navigators had "Waggoners" for most of the waters they sailed.

The success of these books and the resulting competition led to their eventual demise. Each writer attempted to make his work more inclusive than any other; the result was a tremendous book difficult to handle. In 1795 the British Hydrographic Department was established, and charts and sailing directions were issued separately. Within a few years the Waggoners disappeared.

We hope you find this new Waggoner to be as useful as the Waggoners of old, but without their excess bulk or needless detail. Waggoner is an ancient name with a proud history. Use and enjoy!